PRINCE OF THE CITY

STARRING
TREAT WILLIAMS

EXECUTIVE PRODUCER
JAY PRESSON ALLEN

PRODUCED BY
BURTT HARRIS

SCREENPLAY BY
JAY PRESSON ALLEN AND SIDNEY LUMET

BASED ON THE BOOK BY
ROBERT DALEY

DIRECTED BY
SIDNEY LUMET

PRINCE OF THE CITY

THE TRUE STORY OF A COP
WHO KNEW TOO MUCH

ROBERT DALEY

BERKLEY BOOKS, NEW YORK

The Berkley book contains the complete
text of the original hardcover edition.
It has been completely reset in a type face
designed for easy reading, and was printed
from new film.

PRINCE OF THE CITY

A Berkley Book / published by arrangement with
Houghton Mifflin Company

PRINTING HISTORY
Houghton Mifflin edition published 1978
Berkley edition / October 1981

ISBN: 0-425-04450-5

A BERKLEY BOOK® TM 757,375
Berkley Books are published by Berkley Publishing Corporation,
200 Madison Avenue, New York, New York 10016.
PRINTED IN THE UNITED STATES OF AMERICA

But if thou wilt offer a holocaust, offer it to the Lord.

JUDGES 13:16

And Samson said to the lad who guided his steps: Suffer me to touch the pillars which support the whole house, and let me lean upon them and rest a little.

JUDGES 16:26

About the Author: Robert Daley was born in New York City in 1930. His work as Publicity Director of the New York Giants resulted in his first novel ONLY A GAME. He served as foreign correspondent of the New York Times in Paris and other locales in Europe and North Africa. During this time Daley wrote his second novel, THE WHOLE TRUTH. In 1971-72 Daley served as a New York City Deputy Police Commissioner. His bestselling novels TARGET BLUE and TO KILL A COP followed. Subsequently, he wrote PRINCE OF THE CITY: The True Story of a Cop Who Knew Too Much. Several of Daley's other books were inspired by his unusually adventurous personal experiences. THE CRUEL SPORT and CARS AT SPEED are about auto racing; STRONG WINE RED AS BLOOD, winetasting; THE SWORDS OF SPAIN is a photo essay on bullfighting; and TREASURE deals with diving for treasure in the Gulf of Mexico.

As well as being a successful novelist and journalist, Daley is an avid photographer whose works have been exhibited in The Baltimore Museum, The Art Institute of Chicago and other galleries. His photos, in addition to numerous articles and short stories, have appeared worldwide in such publications as *Esquire, Vogue, Life* and *Paris Match.* He lives in Connecticut with his wife and three daughters.

Author's Note: All of the events depicted in this book are a matter of factual record, and the people are real. No names have been changed. The dialogue has either been taken from concealed tape recordings made at the time the events took place or been carefully reconstructed through interviews with the participants.

Book One

1

THEY WERE NOT ordinary detectives, nor even ordinary narcotics detectives. They were SIU detectives— Special Investigating Unit, New York Police Department—and during the long wait in crowded arraignment courts they stood out, and this was by choice. Their appearance was special, their prisoners were special, and their evidence was special.

Other cops, waiting, were in uniform, or else, if detectives, they wore street clothes: usually lumber jackets, sweaters, corduroy pants, or jeans—the rough clothing of rough men. SIU detectives had adopted a kind of uniform of their own. In winter they affected full-length suede or leather coats, and a number of them, underneath, wore business suits and vests. In summer, SIU detectives tended to sport Italian knit shirts and forty-dollar tailored slacks and loafers. They were forever observing and approving of each other's attire. Also, their fingernails were usually manicured, and in some cases lacquered. They tended to smell of strong scents, and they gave the appearance most times of having just stepped up from a barber's chair—an expensive barber's chair—and in fact, this was often the case. It had become ritual for SIU detectives to spend an hour or two under hot towels, pampering themselves, immediately after breaking a case.

Their prisoners, caged in nearby holding pens, were as extraordinary as themselves. Other cops arrested common thugs, or in narcotics cases, street junkies. The thugs, caged, looked as feral as beasts. The junkies huddled in corners, snot and tears caked to their faces, sitting sometimes beside pools of vomit.

SIU detectives did not bother with junkies, and they came in contact with thugs only by accident—if they

3

happened, for instance, to witness a crime on the way home. Their prisoners usually were expensively dressed and often somewhat glamorous, being Frenchmen or Turks or South Americans, or high-ranking New York Mafiosi. These were the wholesalers, importers, and executives of the narcotics trade, and most of them, waiting caged with common criminals, were trying to puzzle out how the SIU detectives had ever got on to them.

As for evidence, other cops, as they waited, clutched a single gun or knife or crowbar—the weapon with which one or another caged defendant had stuck up an old lady or a store, or burglarized a house. Or, in narcotics cases, transparent evidence envelopes lay on the cops' laps. The envelopes could be seen to contain one or two, or four or five five-dollar bags of heavily cut heroin. Whereas SIU detectives held or sat beside brown paper bundles—or suitcases, or occasionally a steamer trunk—containing pure junk, uncut junk. Whatever the receptacle, it was filled to the brim with narcotics worth maybe a million dollars or more on the street.

Ordinary cops, waiting in court, were sometimes bloody and torn after violent arrests. SIU men always cleaned themselves up first. Court was, in a sense, their stage, and on it they were impeccable. Besides, they were so slick in the taking of prisoners that violence seldom was necessary.

Of course they were too close to the street to avoid it entirely, and certain of their exploits approached the status of legend among ordinary cops. Detective George Bermudez, driving along, one day witnessed the stabbing and robbing of one man by another. Leaping out of his car, he grappled with the assailant, who stabbed him in the heart. Bermudez not only did not die, he hung on to the assailant until help came.

Detective Eddie Codelia, having made an undercover buy in a Harlem tenement, was assaulted in the hallway by four men, who menaced him with guns and a hunting knife pressed to his face. Codelia fell to his knees weeping. He groveled. He begged for his life. He spilled money to the floor. The last thing to spill from his pockets was his gun, with which he shot all four men, killing two instantly.

SIU detectives disdained medals, and rarely put in for them. They were too good for medals; they didn't need them. But sometimes official recognition came anyway, and Codelia was awarded the Medal of Honor, the Police Department's highest decoration.

SIU detectives carried themselves with a kind of presence. They seldom mixed with other cops. In the police world they were as celebrated as film stars, and they were aware of this. In court, when the judge at last mounted the bench, whichever of them was senior would step forward and identify himself by full title: "Detective So-and-so, Special Investigating Unit, Narcotics Division."

He would then cut into the head of the line. Invariably, other cops and detectives would let him do it.

When major crimes, particularly homicides, occurred in the city, commanders often borrowed SIU detectives in hope of breaking the case quickly. Detective Robert Leuci, for instance, once brought in a wanted murderer named Johnny Loco singlehandedly at the end of only two days. But it was against the strange code of the SIU detectives to take credit for such arrests. Invariably the murderer was turned over to some squad detective, while the SIU detective went home. or back to the narcotics case from which he had been taken.

To other cops SIU detectives reeked of success. They had style; also, obviously, they had money, more money than cops were supposed to have. But for a long time no one in authority noticed this, or wondered where the money might be coming from.

Of course they were the object of envy.

Not because they had rank. They did not. Like all detectives, they were patrolmen who had been designated to serve as detective-investigators. They held authority over no one. The newest sergeant outranked the most senior first-grade detective, and the newest patrolman was, technically, his equal.

The envy existed because the SIU detective, though

perhaps still in his mid or late twenties, had reached the top of his profession; there was no other assignment as good as the one he had. The rules and procedures of the department, which weighted down every other cop, he ignored.

He was virtually unsupervised. SIU headquarters was on the third floor of the First Precinct station house, but some SIU detectives did not go near this office for months at a time, not even on pay day—they would send someone in to pick up their checks. Some of them, in effect, worked out of their houses or their cars.

They were rated on results only. All they had to do was keep making big cases, big seizures of heroin. That they worked hard was never questioned. They were men who would sit on wiretaps or surveillances for days, even weeks at a time, virtually without relief, and never put in for overtime. They were hunters. Theirs was the most elusive game of all, and the kill was always close—maybe tomorrow, maybe even today. They disdained overtime as much as medals or credit for arresting murderers.

But once a narcotics case was made, the major violators arrested, the heroin seized, once the ritual barbering had taken place, many would award themselves, unbeknownst to the Police Department, two weeks' vacation. Then, looking tanned, fit, and as expensively dressed as always, they would come back to work, begin a new case, a new hunt.

They had citywide jurisdiction. They chose their own targets and roamed New York at will. Someone once called them the Princes of the City, for they operated with the impunity, and sometimes with the arrogance, of Renaissance princes. They could enforce any law or not enforce it, arrest anyone or accord freedom. They were immune to arrest themselves. The Princes of the City—they liked this, and adopted it.

The Narcotics Division of the New York Police Department numbered, at the start of the sixties, less than two hundred detectives, all focused on street corner junkies and pushers. In October 1961 two such detectives, Sonny Grosso and Eddie Egan, stumbled upon a Mafia supply ring that imported heroin direct from France. A small squad of the best narcotics detectives then available was thrown together—never more than twenty men in all —and that was the start of the Special Investigating Unit.

Working in conjunction with federal narcotics agents, SIU detectives over the next several months put together their case, effected their arrests, and seized ninety-seven pounds of heroin—the largest street seizure ever up to that time—and in so doing they destroyed the Tuminaros as a major Mafia family. This famous case became a best-selling book in 1968 and an Academy Award-winning movie in 1971. Although the world knew it as *The French Connection,* inside SIU it was always spoken of as the Tuminaro case. Conceptually it became the case every detective sought to match. And on the operational level it made possible the extraordinary freedom of movement SIU detectives came to enjoy; it dominated SIU for the twelve years the unit lasted.

During the sixties, as public outcry swelled and as the Narcotics Division expanded, SIU expanded too, though it never exceeded ten percent of the division's complement. From 1967 to 1972, the period of this story, it stood at about sixty detectives.

One captain, one lieutenant, and five sergeants comprised its command structure—not nearly enough to exert supervisory pressure over so many detectives working alone or in small groups in obscure corners of the city. Several commanders over the years attempted to put in controls, all of which were bitterly resisted by the star detectives, and all of which failed.

The sixty detectives operated normally in four-man teams. One member of each team usually was acknowledged by the others as team leader. It was the team leader's job to pick the target of each investigation and to give out assignments each day.

The team leaders were the elite of the elite. Most were in some way unique. Detective Carl Aguiluz, born in Honduras in 1935, and a naturalized American citizen only from the age of twenty-two, was an exceptional wire man and bugger, the best in SIU. An electronic technician before he became a cop, he knew telephones.

He had never been a patrolman in uniform, for immediately after graduation from the Police Academy he had gone to work undercover for BOSSI, a super-secret police intelligence squad, and he had infiltrated a communist cell in the East Village. When that assignment ended, he went immediately into the Narcotics Division as an arresting officer, and in time was promoted into SIU.

Most SIU detectives could tap a phone at the box in an apartment house basement. But Aguiluz could find the pair of wires that he needed four or five blocks away from the suspect's house. He could read where telephone lines went, and find the binding post. He could bridge his tap onto a dead line so that even experts—the FBI or telephone security—couldn't find it. Planting bugs inside suspects' houses was another of his specialties. He was a good burglar, and he understood the principles of directional transmitters. He left no clues, and no bug he planted was ever discovered.

Also, he spoke Spanish. He was among the first SIU detectives to concentrate on major Hispanic importers, and he quickly developed the technique which, in a later case, led him to the most monumental seizure of all, an entire closet load of heroin and cocaine straight from France. One of his partners was Joe Novoa, who was of Spanish extraction and spoke Spanish with a Castilian accent. Novoa, however, was fair skinned—he looked Irish or even Scandinavian.

In the presence of prisoners, Aguiluz would address Novoa only in English. He would then curse the prisoners roundly in Spanish, and angrily leave the room.

Invariably, the prisoners, as soon as the door slammed, would turn toward each other and begin to discuss their predicament in Spanish, never suspecting that the fair-skinned Novoa, staring stupidly off in some other direction, was at the same time drinking in every word.

Thus it was Novoa who learned of the existence and location of the secret closet, and its secret contents. But it was Aguiluz's ploy, Aguiluz's case.

The next day a newspaper photo went up on the SIU office bulletin board: eight or ten grinning detectives, arms around each other, standing behind a table on which reposed a hundred kilos of narcotics. Over this photo was pasted a hand-lettered headline: CAN YOU TOP THIS?

Detective Joe Nunziata, born in 1932 and raised in Brooklyn, had scarcely ever seen a horse before entering the Police Department. Nonetheless, he became a mounted patrolman in midtown, and it was on horseback that he made his earliest reputation. He seemed to understand everything about horses just as, when he came into Narcotics, he immediately seemed to understand everything about the drug scene, too.

As a team leader, Nunziata was a detective of extraordinary vision. He had instincts, and he obeyed them. He knew how to pick targets, and as soon as he had fastened onto one, he immediately saw the entire case as it would eventually take shape. Most times he was able to puzzle out, once arrests had been made, where the narcotics must be concealed. He once tracked down eighty-eight pounds of heroin hidden in the bottom of wine bottles in the McAlpin Hotel.

Nunziata had an exceptionally open and engaging personality. Everyone liked him at once. Without trying, he tended to dominate every gathering he attended. At a party, before long, everyone in the room would crowd around Nunziata, for he exuded magnetism and charm. This same charm he used as needed when breaking cases. He could talk his way inside private places, and when he went looking for information, whether to the state parole board, or to one or another agency, the men he addressed were always anxious to give him whatever he wanted. Of all of the detectives in SIU, he was the one most admired by the others.

Detective Robert Leuci, as team leader, had more and better informants than anyone, for he was willing to spend as much time as was necessary to win a potential informant over. Once, when he learned that a certain dealer was about to enter his territory, he mobilized sixteen or seventeen junkies, furnished them with a description of the dealer, and stationed them at strategic places. Then he simply waited in the station house for the phone call that would tell him where his quarry had holed up.

Born in 1940, he was much younger than Aguiluz and Nunziata—also much younger than the other three members of the team that he led.

Though not as good a wireman as Aguiluz, he was adequate. Though not as magnetic as Nunziata, he was charming and perceptive, and when he went to people for information or help, they were anxious to accord it. He worked always against the biggest names in the narcotics trade, and he produced a great number of arrests, a great many seizures of substantial—as opposed to spectacular—bundles of narcotics. He had the best organized crime connections of any SIU detective, because his first cousin, John Lusterino, was a captain in the Colombo Mafia family.

In the street Leuci was known as a compassionate cop. He was the type of cop to whom vicious fugitives, fearing a savage beating from other cops, sometimes chose to surrender. They knew he would not hurt them.

All of the detectives mentioned so far are part of the fabric of this story, but its principal actor is Leuci—with Aguiluz and Nunziata as chief supporting players, and various prosecutors in the role of Greek chorus.

Leuci prided himself on being a tough cop—they all did—but in the end he proved far less tough than any of the others. Perhaps he had more conscience than they did, or perhaps he merely was more troubled by what all of them were doing. In any case, he was the one who stepped forward, and, in so doing, brought on the ruin of everyone else. It was almost biblical. Like Samson, he first did penance, and then he pulled the temple down.

2

IN MID-FEBRUARY of 1971 Detective Leuci was called before the Commission to Investigate Alleged Police Corruption—the so-called Knapp Commission.

He was a few days short of his thirty-first birthday. He had a wife of seven years, Gina; a son, Anthony, who was five; and a newborn daughter named Santina. He lived fifty miles east of the city in a Long Island town named Kings Park, in a tract house in a development of tract houses, and six of the nine houses on his street were owned by New York cops. Thousands more cops lived in that town, and in surrounding towns just like it, and their cars, like an invading army, advanced on the city every day.

Leuci, both on and off duty, was a cop among cops.

A few months earlier he had been routinely transferred out of SIU, and his team routinely dispersed. He was now a precinct detective investigating common crimes, and his past, he had resolved, was behind him.

But he had been summoned to the Knapp Commission offices, where he was made to wait for an hour in a starkly furnished waiting room. He could see into certain offices. People came and went carrying dossiers. The purpose of the Knapp Commission, of those people, of those dossiers, was to send cops to jail.

The Knapp Commission had nothing on Leuci, but he didn't know this. He was waiting to be interviewed by a man named Nicholas Scoppetta, whom he had never met. As he waited, he had become increasingly tense.

Scoppetta, a former assistant district attorney under Frank Hogan, appeared at last in the waiting room.

"Bob Leuci?"

"Yes."

Scoppetta, thirty-eight, had a flat nose and looked like a light heavyweight prizefighter.

"Come into my office."

Leuci, though afraid, flashed a boyish kind of smile.

Scoppetta had expected to meet a case-hardened detective. Instead he was surprised at how young Leuci looked, and by the disarming smile. Leuci's countenance, Scoppetta thought, was almost cherubic. Though thirty-one, he looked as innocent as a choir boy.

Scoppetta's office was as stark and temporary as the waiting room.

"Why don't we talk for a bit? Let's talk about what we, the Knapp Commission, are doing here."

Leuci's fear had gone over into a kind of ingratiating anxiety. "I'd like to get out of here, personally," he said lightly.

Scoppetta at the filing cabinet was replacing folders. "Don't I know you?" he asked over his shoulder. "Didn't we put some cases together in Manhattan?"

He was trying to put Leuci at ease, but failed.

"No," said Leuci.

Scoppetta had studied Leuci's personnel folder, but it told little. He decided to switch away from Leuci to other cops.

"Let me ask you some particular questions. What about Carl Aguiluz? What about Joe Nunziata?"

"Outstanding detectives."

Scoppetta glanced at him sharply. "There have been a lot of allegations of misconduct against them."

Leuci said, "There are allegations against federal narcotics agents too."

"That's true. We can talk about that later. But for now we ought to talk about cops."

"Obviously. We are easy, aren't we? Cops are easy."

This interview, Scoppetta saw, was going nowhere. But the intensity of Leuci's anxiety was interesting. What, the prosecutor wondered, was behind it?

Scoppetta was, at this time, an unknown but ambitious lawyer. He had grown up in an orphanage. Later he worked his way through college, and through law school, working during the last three years for the Society for Prevention of Cruelty to Children. When he went to work as an assistant D.A., he showed himself to be a dogged but successful prosecutor.

Twice he had left public service to join law firms at big salaries; each time he had returned to low-paying jobs like this one with the Knapp Commission. The career he sought—the prestige, the relatively good money—he was determined to find while also contributing to the public good. The Knapp Commission was, to Scoppetta, either a six-month interlude before returning to private practice, or his best chance yet at a successful public career.

He decided to invite Leuci home to dinner.

"How about coming over to my place," he said. "My family is away. We'll have dinner. Maybe you can give me some tips on how I ought to approach my investigation."

Their eyes met across the desk.

Scoppetta began to refill his briefcase. "We'll ride up there now," he said decisively.

In Scoppetta's West Side apartment, Leuci walked around studying the pictures on the walls. Most were blowups of Scoppetta's wife and children. They were of exceptional quality, and they had been taken by the prosecutor himself.

"Tell me," called Leuci to Scoppetta, who was in the kitchen, "what do I call you?"

Scoppetta's head appeared in the doorway. "Call me Nick."

"Nick, what is it? What is it you want to ask me? I didn't do it, whatever it is."

"You're not under investigation. What are you thinking about?" Leuci had been identified to him as a totally honest detective who might be able to cast some light on corruption in Narcotics.

"Apparently you got something on your mind," said Leuci. "I wish you would tell me about it, and let me deny it and leave."

Scoppetta's head again appeared in the kitchen doorway. He smiled. "No, it's nothing like that. How do you like your steak?"

"Why don't you spend some time doing something important?" asked Leuci, feeling somewhat reassured. "Like investigating lawyers. You were in the Manhattan D.A.'s office, right? I'm sure there is all sorts of corruption in that office."

"There is no corruption in that office. I never heard even a hint of it. But maybe you know something I don't."

Leuci snorted derisively. "You're kidding."

"This conversation is starting to bore me," said Scoppetta, and he strode back into the kitchen.

But Leuci followed him. "The conversation immediately becomes boring when we talk about corrupt lawyers and district attorneys. You want to talk about cops."

Scoppetta put steaks and salad onto the plates and carried them to the table. As soon as the two men sat down to eat, Scoppetta resumed talking about corruption in the Narcotics Division.

But Leuci interrupted.

"Why don't we talk about lawyers I know to be corrupt," he said. "Why don't we talk about district attorneys that are corrupt?"

"Well, if you know anything about lawyers and D.A.'s I'd love to hear it. We'll work on that. But you know the Knapp Commission is here to investigate cops."

Neither was eating.

"Is it common practice to sell narcotics in the Narcotics Division?"

The detective's anger appeared genuine, though how could the prosecutor be sure?

"Those are the kinds of asinine stupid things that people write in the *Village Voice* or the *New York Times*. We don't sell narcotics. Dope dealers sell narcotics. We're not dope dealers, we're policemen."

"It's hard to distinguish between the dope dealers and the policemen sometimes," retorted Scoppetta.

Leuci said, "Why don't we talk about corrupt lawyers? Why don't we talk about how we can approach that?"

Scoppetta began to cut through the steak on his plate. "Why don't we eat;" he said, "and forget all the bullshit?"

During dinner Scoppetta's questions became personal,

and there was no talk of corruption. The experienced prosecutor, probing for a weakness, asked about Leuci's schooling, about his wife and kids, about his feelings for life, love, and the police department. About the Italian heritage both men shared.

From the age of sixteen, Leuci had had no other ambition than to become a cop, he said. He had passed the Civil Service test at nineteen, and had gone into the Police Academy at twenty-one in the first class for which he was eligible. Five months later there he was, a cop in uniform patrolling the streets of the city, and even the borough—Queens—in which he had been born.

There was no wife or kids or tract house yet. He lived with his parents and with his younger brother and sister in a quiet house on a quiet residential street. His father, formerly a semi-pro pitcher known as Hooks Leuci, was foreman in a pipe factory. His mother worked in a sewing-maching plant. They were honest, hard-working people who had come up out of an Italian ghetto in Brooklyn, and the day their son graduated from the Police Academy was possibly the proudest of their lives. They saw him as a police captain one day.

There were Mafia elements all around them, even within their own family, but they avoided these people, and they tried to instill their contempt for them in their son. Hooks Leuci, whenever he was in the presence of his sister Rosa Lusterino, realized that his son was a policeman, whereas Rosa's son Johnny was usually in jail.

Detective Leuci was the first member of his family ever to finish high school, and it was a big family—there were nine aunts. By police standards he was highly educated, for at eighteen he had gone to Baker University in Kansas to play football. He was a chunky, five-foot-nine-inch fullback. In Kansas, surrounded by prairies and by middle-class Wasps, he was miserably homesick. He yearned for the streets of New York, and when freshman year ended he hurried home to wait to be old enough to become a New York cop.

Every squad to which he was assigned he had led in arrests, and so his rise was quick. In February 1966, after less than four years in uniform, he was promoted to detective third-grade, and he got second grade in August 1969. These were pay grades only; as a second-grade detective he was earning sergeant's wages.

By then he had moved up into SIU, and was one of the elite. His street nickname had been Babyface, and now Scoppetta asked him about it.

Part of his success as a cop had been due to his exceptionally innocent appearance, Leuci replied. He always looked far younger than his years. As a rookie patrolman he could pass as a teenager, and even as he neared thirty he still looked very young. Hoodlums and dope pushers often failed to take him seriously until it was too late.

After dinner Scoppetta and his guest moved to the living room, and the interview continued. Scoppetta was searching for tidbits of information. But Leuci continued to refuse to talk about corruption, or about SIU.

"You're a very disarming guy," Scoppetta said. "I heard a lot about Bob Leuci before I met him today. The tough detective I heard about was nothing like the one I met and that I'm talking to now. The Bob Leuci I heard about I never would have invited to my home."

Scoppetta was still probing, still choosing each word carefully, still watching closely for each reaction by Leuci.

"All cops are like me," responded Leuci. "I'm no different. I represent what we all are."

"There are cops that are criminals," Scoppetta said. "There are cops that are real criminals. They have destroyed you. They have destroyed this Police Department."

Scoppetta probed more deeply still. "I know there is more to you than people think. First of all, some people think that you are a totally honest guy. I don't think that's true."

Leuci stared him in the eye. "I go out there and do what I have to do. I do my job."

Earlier, Scoppetta had extinguished all illumination within the apartment except for one lamp burning on the end table beside Leuci. Its circle of light enclosed both men. They were as isolated as characters on a stage. Beyond was outer darkness—the dark apartment, the darker city. Scoppetta had not contrived the lamp, he merely noticed it, recognizing its importance to Leuci's mood. It shut out the world. It established the intimacy of a confessional. Leuci was about to confess something, Scoppetta was sure of it. Whatever Leuci might confess only his confessor, Scoppetta, would hear.

Scoppetta said, "There's a lot going on inside you. I don't know what it is exactly, but certainly you feel guilty about something. Do you want to talk about it?"

"If I did talk about it, I would destroy myself."

"Not necessarily. You ought to think about telling me what's bothering you. You ought to think about a new beginning. A new life."

Leuci grasped at this notion. "You mean there's a potential that I could start over again?"

"You could cooperate with us, wipe the slate clean. Will you think about it?"

After a moment, Leuci said, "I'll think about it."

It was nearly dawn when they walked to the door. "I want you to go home now," Scoppetta said, "and I want you to ask yourself some questions. How do you visualize yourself? What do you see reflected in the mirror in the morning? What does your wife think of you? What are your children going to think of you three or four years from now when they're old enough to decide for themselves what you are? That's what we'll talk about tomorrow."

The two men watched the dawn come, Scoppetta from his window overlooking Central Park, Leuci as he made the fifty-mile drive out onto Long Island. Leuci, driving, wondered what he had started to tell Scoppetta, and why. His own willingness to talk, which he did not understand, was frightening, because he did not know where it would take him.

Scoppetta, on the other hand, was elated, and planning tomorrow's day. Leuci perhaps represented a breakthrough, the Knapp Commission's first. After six months no significant corruption had yet been proven by the commission. Where other commission lawyers had failed, he perhaps would succeed. He sensed an enormous potential in Leuci. The Police Department files were full of allegations about serious corruption in the Narcotics Division, and Leuci seemed on the verge of talking about it.

3

THEY TALKED the next night away, and also the next.

Yes, Leuci admitted, there was massive corruption in the Detective Division. There was massive corruption in the Narcotics Bureau. He was nodding vigorously. There was also massive corruption at every stage of the criminal justice system, starting with assistant district attorneys who helped detectives prepare wiretap orders, and routinely told them to perjure themselves, to lawyers who met them in hallways wearing three- and four-hundred-dollar suits, and came over and whispered that this case didn't mean anything, here's $50, $100, $500, $15,000, let's forget it.

The two men stared at each other.

Scoppetta said softly, "What are you going to do about it?"

"I can't do anything about it," Leuci cried. "What are *you* going to do about it? You are the guy who has the power to do something about it."

Scoppetta was an extremely skillful interrogator.

"Let's talk about my family, and your family, and the comparison," he said. "We are the same blood." It was an abrupt switch in mood, and it worked.

"Yeah, we are the same blood," agreed Leuci after a pause.

What about Leuci's brother, his sister, Scoppetta asked.

It was as if there was a switch concealed somewhere inside Leuci that Scoppetta, without knowing it was there, had somehow tripped. The detective began to talk about his brother Richie, who was five years younger, and who almost from infancy had had to wear thick glasses. The boy's parents had regarded this as a deformity—no one in the family had ever had to wear glasses before—and Hooks Leuci and his wife had been consumed by shame. They went to doctors to be assured that Richie's deformity was not hereditary, not their fault, and because of their shame, they shamelessly coddled the child, seeming to prefer him to Bobby, who was strong and would grow up to become a policeman.

But their shame over Richie's eyesight was as nothing compared to their shame when they discovered only a few months ago that he was also a heroin addict. Leuci's voice became husky as he described his brother's suffering, and his parents'. Richie had lost all manhood. He wept, he groveled, he would not work or even keep himself clean. He lived from fix to fix, and constantly begged his brother, the narcotics detective, for heroin with which to feed his habit.

Worst of all, said Leuci, and tears started to his eyes, he himself was being blamed by his parents for Richie's habit, for the disgrace and misery that had come to the whole family. According to Hooks Leuci, it was cops like his son who had allowed it to happen, cops like his son who allowed dope pushers to do their business, to hang around and infect innocent children.

Now Leuci began to describe a backyard barbecue. He had invited a number of narcotics detectives and their wives to his house, and suddenly, unexpectedly, his father had appeared in the garden. He had been out for a ride, and decided to stop by and see his son. Accepting a drink, he began to speak to the detectives. At first he seemed pleased with them, commenting, "These are nice Italian boys." Then he began to notice how well-dressed they were, and how their pinky rings flashed in the sun; he listened to them talk about their trips to Miami and Las Vegas. His smile faded, he put his drink down, and he sought out his son, saying, "These guys are corrupt cops, and you're a corrupt cop."

Hooks Leuci had been a neighborhood hero, and of course a hero to his son. It had been Hooks Leuci's respect that Robert Leuci had always coveted most. Now Hooks strode to the door with Leuci calling after him, "Dad, you'll never understand. I couldn't begin to tell you what it's like, and what I have to do."

But his father went out, slamming the door behind him.

Scoppetta, listening, had been moved, partly by the story itself, and partly by Leuci's suffering as he told it. Tears had overflowed Leuci's eyes, and he had begun to weep. What did his parents expect of him? It wasn't his responsibility to watch Richie. They should have watched him themselves.

After a time, his tears dried, and he began to get angry. His parents understood nothing about the pressures on cops, and neither did Scoppetta, he said. What gushed forth next was, mostly, Leuci's shame. It was impossible to tell what exactly he was confessing to, or if in fact he was confessing to anything at all.

You people on the Knapp Commission, he said, are focusing on the Police Department. You tell cops that you are out to catch them taking meals, taking Christmas presents, giving drugs to junkies. It's absolutely incredible. Cops are looking at you and saying: You bastards. It's you guys, the assistant district attorneys, lawyers, judges who run the system, and the whole fucking thing from top to bottom is corrupt. We know how you become a judge. You pay $50,000 and you become a judge. We see stores open on Sunday on Fifth Avenue, but they can't be open in Little Italy. And then you wonder why cops stick together. The only people that know us, care for us, love us, are other cops. You people are just looking to hurt us. You want to lay on us the responsibility of fucking up the system.

Do you know what it's like to be a narcotics detective, Leuci continued. Do you have any conception? Do you know what it's like on a February night in South Brooklyn a block from the piers with two addict informants in the back of the car, both of them crying, begging you for a bag of heroin? Do you know what it's like going home fifty miles away, and getting a phone call five minutes after you're home saying, I blew the shot, please come back and give me another bag. And driving fifty miles back in, and watching him tie up, and walking out of the room. Then working with him the next morning and locking up some dope pusher that's just as sick as he is. It's an insanity. And going into the office and the lieutenant says you have to make five arrests this month. Do you know what it's like working six, seven days a week? You have to be one of the best, otherwise you go back to swinging a stick.

Scoppetta's every nerve was attuned to Leuci's mood. But his mind was racing, looking for the key word, each time Leuci paused, to keep him talking.

You're in Westbury, or West End Avenue, Leuci ranted on. We're in El Barrio, we're on 125th Street. You want us to keep everybody inside the barricades so you can stay outside. I'm on Pleasant Avenue and 116th Street at three o'clock in the morning, just me and my partner and Tony somebody that we have been following for three weeks, and he's going to offer me money, and me and my partner are going to decide whether we'll take it or not. You don't care about me. Some black revolutionary is going to whack me out if he gets a chance. Some newspaper is going to call me a thief whether I do it or don't do it. The only one who cares about me is my partner. It's me and him and this guy we caught. We're going to take him to jail and lock him up. We're going to take his money. Fuck him, fuck you, fuck them.

Scoppetta listened, waiting.

I see what kind of man you are, and I see what kind of man my partner is, and there's just no comparison, see? I'm going to side with him. He tells me it's okay Bobby, hey Bobby, it's you and me against the rest of the world. You guys are eating in the Copa six nights a week. We try to get forty dollars expense money, and the department won't even give us that.

Leuci swallowed painfully.

You're winning in the end any way. We're selling ourselves, our families. These people we take money from own us. Our family's future rests on the fact that some dope pusher is not going to give us up, or some killer, some total piece of shit, is not going to give us up.

To you, cops are detestable kinds of people. But the vast majority of cops are good, honest, law-abiding, family-loving, decent men. Some of them do criminal things once in a while, but they are the only people between you and the jungle.

The long monologue ended. It had been dramatic but unspecific. The only thing clear was that the young detective was in the grip of extremely powerful emotions which Scoppetta might somehow be able to harness.

He said calmly, "Why don't you do something about it? You have knowledge. You can provide evidence. You can make cases."

"I can make all kinds of cases. I can make cases against lawyers, too. I can make cases against district attorneys, I can make cases against people who pay cops. Why don't we do that?"

The Knapp Commission, Scoppetta said firmly, was obliged to concentrate on cops.

"Then fuck the Knapp Commission."

The following night Leuci was calmer, and the two men discussed in detail the type of investigation Leuci might be willing to undertake. First, said Leuci, Scoppetta should leave the Knapp Commission and set up a separate office.

Scoppetta nodded. It could perhaps be done. He saw himself accorded funding by the Justice Department and setting up a separate office, perhaps under the U.S. Attorney for the Southern District of New York State.

Leuci meant to work primarily against corrupt lawyers, he declared. He wanted to put in jail district attorneys and judges who regularly solicited bribes, and defense lawyers who regularly seduced cops. If the focus was to be strictly on the cops themselves, then he would not take part. Any corrupt cops whom he might, so to speak, stumble over would go to jail too. But they would be incidental to his investigation. And he would not work against cops who had been his friends and partners in SIU. He was willing to wear a recording device. He was willing to handle marked money. He was willing to play a role, to risk his life for however many months or years the investigation could be kept secret.

Scoppetta was jubilant. "Do you realize how important this investigation can be? We'll do it together. I'll be with you every step of the way. What kind of cases can we make?"

As Leuci began to outline possibilities, it became clear to Scoppetta that what he was sketching were real cases, cases involving police misconduct. Leuci then selected one specific case, and painted in most of the details.

An SIU team, he said, had conducted a long investigation into a Mafia drug ring, but had failed to come up with enough solid evidence to obtain an indictment. The team then decided to contact the subject of the investigation, and offer to drop the case—which would have been dropped anyway—in exchange for money. Legally this was certainly bribe soliciting, and probably it was extortion—the line between the two crimes is somewhat blurred.

Leuci, because of his superb Mafia contacts, was enlisted by the team to make contact with the subject. He did this, and when the drug dealer agreed to pay $10,000, the case was dropped and Leuci collected a commission, though he did not tell Scoppetta how much.

Scoppetta had listened grim-faced to his tale. "What else?" he demanded, when Leuci had finished.

He had been involved in two other similar situations, Leuci said. He did not elaborate. He was watching Scoppetta carefully. He was not worried about being prosecuted. If Scoppetta tried it, which was inconceivable in light of the investigation offered, Leuci could always recant in court.

Nonetheless, he had just admitted to crimes, an admission he did not have to make, and there were some later who found this amazing. His motive, it seems clear, was twofold. First, he was sorely troubled by his past. Guilt and shame afflicted him like a disease. He wore remorse like a heavy overcoat everywhere he went. In making confession, he had hoped to assuage this crushing burden. And indeed, he did feel lighter after speaking out. Second, he was attempting to establish his credentials with Scoppetta; he was saying that, because his own past was dark, the investigation would work—he would be able to get close to some very bad men.

"Three things," said Scoppetta grimly. "Is that all you've done all these years?"

"Nick, that's it," said Leuci.

Scoppetta studied him carefully, then pounded his fist into his hand. "We're going to do something important," he said enthusiastically. "What this investigation has going for it is a real detective."

4

THERE IS ample evidence that Leuci himself was deeply troubled by what he had decided to do. After talking each night away with Scoppetta, he floundered by day through the city, seeking advice from other cops incompetent to give it, one of them a sergeant noted for his incorruptibility, another a former partner who was quite the opposite, and in both cases he risked blowing his cover before it was ever assumed.

There were long, tormented conversations with his wife, most conducted by dawn light as the infant Santina, on Gina's lap, alternately gurgled and sucked at a bottle. The words spilled out of him—words that, to Gina, sounded dangerous.

She had come from Europe at twenty to visit a cousin, and had met Patrolman Leuci. "Talk to her, Dad," Leuci had said proudly the first time he brought her home. "She speaks beautiful Italian."

She still had her Italian passport.

"Gina," she heard her husband say now, "I think I may have found an important friend. Tonight I wanted to tell him everything. I wanted to get it all out. All the things I've been uptight about, sick about over the last several years."

"Who are you going to hurt?" she said. She began to mention detectives Leuci had worked with: what about his three former partners? What about Joe Nunziata, Carl Aguiluz? "Are you going to implicate them? Are you going to ruin their lives?"

"I'm not going to implicate any one close to us."

"Do you think they will allow you to do whatever you choose to do? Do you think they will say: Okay, Bob, whoever you want to tell us about. You decide. I don't

26

think they will allow you to do that."

After a moment she added, "I know you feel guilty. Stop feeling guilty. Other people are responsible, not you. They are guiltier than you are."

In a low voice he replied, "I want to end this life I have been living."

"Then quit the Police Department."

But he loved the Police Department. "And do what? Sell insurance? Work in a bank?"

Gina said, "I know you. It's going to kill you. They will force you to hurt friends, people who have done no harm to you, only good. When you were sick, they all came. They called me every day. I know what kind of man you are. I know what you can live with and what you can't live with. This will kill you. You tell me the feelings you have for informants, and now you are going to be an informant. How are you going to live with that? How am I going to live with you, as you live with that?"

Leuci said, "I am going to make the decision. You are going to decide to stay with me, or not to stay with me. But I am going to make the decision."

This conversation sent him rushing to Brooklyn to see Detective Frank Mandato, one of his ex-partners from SIU. Mandato lived in a new highrise building on Ocean Parkway. He lived on a detective's salary, but there was a doorman downstairs and from his balcony one looked out over New York harbor. Mandato let him in, and they stood in the kitchen while Mandato cooked up a pot of espresso coffee.

Mandato, then thirty-five, had black curly hair, black eyes, and a sculptured black beard. Behind his back, he was sometimes referred to by other detectives as Jesus Christ, or else as The Devil.

Leuci's other two partners had been Les Wolff and Dave Cody, but he felt closest to Mandato, and so it was to Mandato that he had come. He and Mandato had been partners for five years, and they were both Italians.

"I walk into a courtroom," Leuci told Mandato. He was pacing Mandato's living room, tiny cup in hand. He was obviously agitated. "I walk into a D.A.'s office. Guys don't call me Leuci. They smile and say, how's Babyface? It's not funny any more. Because to me Babyface represents the most vile kind of guy."

"What do they know?" Mandato asked soothingly. "Do they know anything about you?" He put his cup down on the coffee table.

Leuci went out through the French doors onto Mandato's balcony. The other detective followed. They stared out over the harbor.

"Remember, Frank," Leuci said, "how we would get together in a restaurant the night before we planned to hit some place? You and me and Les Wolff and Dave Cody. We would have these great spaghetti dinners, and I think we were all afraid. Because the next morning we were going to be kicking doors down. We needed each other. We would talk about the guy we were going to take, and someone would always say: Tony, or Marco, or whatever the guy's name was, I hope you're getting laid tonight, because it's going to be the last time for a long time."

Mandato was watching him carefully.

"Do you understand, Frank? Maybe there are guys doing that right now with you or me, or Wolff or Cody. And I don't want to live that fucking life now. I don't want you to be nobody's fucking target."

This was only part of what Leuci felt: the fear. His remorse was much harder to explain.

Mandato said, "Are you afraid that one of us will turn on you? Is that what it is? Les? Or me? Or Dave?"

"I'm not afraid of you guys turning on me. I'm afraid of me turning on me. I just can't take it any more."

Leuci's voice began to rise until he was yelling. "I don't want to be anybody's target. I don't want to be anybody's target."

Mandato said, "Come on inside. It's cold out here."

It was cold outside the old partnership, outside SIU.

Back in the living room, Mandato said quietly, "What are you going to do, Bob? Should I go perch myself on a ledge right now? Are you going to let me know before they come and drop the safe on me?"

Leuci gazed at his friend. In the last five years he had

spent more time with Mandato than with Gina, had shared more emotions with Mandato than with Gina, and it was possible even that he loved Mandato more than Gina.

"Frank, I'm not going to do anything. What the fuck can I do?"

These scenes show something of Leuci's suffering, something of his indecision, though they fall short of explaining his motivation satisfactorily.

In the end he went back to Scoppetta. It was Scoppetta who projected the strength he was looking for. It was Scoppetta who had sworn to uphold the same laws as himself—and who was doing it. It was Scoppetta who seemed to him to understand all that could not be spoken.

Leuci certainly did not think it out in any reasoned way. He went into the investigation with his eyes firmly closed. He was arrogant enough to believe he could control Scoppetta, could control any prosecutor, could protect himself, could protect his former partners, could protect all of SIU.

He seems to have imagined he could create a new Robert Leuci. "And then I met Scoppetta," he was to say later, "and we changed what I was."

Scoppetta, about to fly to Washington to request funds for the new office, needed some sort of dramatic evidence to bring with him.

By then Leuci had made up his mind. "What would you say," he asked, "if I told you that with a single phone call I can buy the location of every wiretap in the city?"

Scoppetta refused to believe him.

Leuci made the call—to Detective Bernie Geik in the Criminal Investigation Bureau—and later Leuci met with Geik on a midtown sidewalk while wearing a recording device. Scoppetta himself taped the conversation on a machine lying on his lap in a car parked half a block away.

Both horrified and elated by this awful tape, the prosecutor hurried to Washington for meetings at the assistant attorney general level. The funding he needed was accorded, backup agents were assigned him, and arrangements were made to swear him in as a special assistant U.S. attorney in charge of the Leuci investigation. There were later meetings in New York with Justice Department officials, and with Whitney North Seymour, U.S. attorney for the Southern District, and there was a long and rather poignant meeting at Whitman Knapp's club at which the Knapp Commission formally gave Leuci, its prize catch so far, over to federal authorities, and to Scoppetta.

And so the Leuci investigation was begun.

5

SCOPPETTA SET UP his office in the same building as the Knapp Commission, and he began to coordinate his plans with E.M. Shaw, aged thirty-four, seven years a prosecutor, head of the Anti-Corruption Unit in the office of U.S. Attorney Seymour.

Since Leuci could not afford to be spotted in or near any building housing the Knapp Commission or prosecutors, nor in the company of Scoppetta either, strategy meetings began to be held at night in Shaw's apartment in Brooklyn Heights. Shaw's wife Margaret would serve dinner. Afterward the two prosecutors and Leuci would sit around the living room, plotting. Usually Margaret sat cross-legged on the rug, listening with fascination.

Boston-reared and Harvard-educated, Shaw stood six feet five inches tall, and he had the absolute assurance that family lineage and family money sometimes confer. Shaw was a man who could look wealthy even when wearing paint-spattered blue jeans and a T-shirt.

Leuci, though basking in so much attention, was now having second thoughts about his ability to control the directions the investigation might take. He was worried. He wanted to climb up into the criminal justice system as high as district attorneys and judges, but without banging into someone lower down that he cared about. He was trying to figure out how this could be done. He knew he would have to use cops to work his way up higher. He knew he was going to have to implicate cops. But he wanted to be selective. He wanted to pick his targets himself.

Shaw was in a hurry. "Where do we start, and how?" he kept saying, and he kept proposing ideas. But many of these were unacceptable to Leuci.

One of his first plans was to call in the leaders of each of the city's five Mafia families. We tell them, Shaw said, that they may be prosecuted for tax evasion. Then Bob, here, reaches out to them through his organized crime connections. He lets it be known that he has access to the IRS files. Then he meets with them, and they bribe him to get these files. Then we arrest them for bribery of a police officer.

"I can't do that," Leuci protested. "That's a total frame."

Mafia guys were no different from accountants living in Scarsdale, he explained. Tell a man he's being audited by the IRS, and he panics. Sure a Mafia guy would pay Leuci money. So would the accountant in Scarsdale. So would Leuci's next door neighbor, or Shaw's.

And how would Leuci reach these organized crime people? he asked rhetorically. Through his cousin John Lusterino, right? And what would happen to Lusterino afterward? The whole story would be a fabrication, and when the fabrication came to light, Lusterino would be killed.

"What you can't do to organized crime guys," Leuci told Shaw earnestly, for he knew these people, and Shaw did not, "is embarrass them in a make-believe situation, fool them, emasculate them. If there is a real situation, and they come to me, that's another story. My cousin would be clear, even though he recommended me originally. Whenever he introduces me to somebody, he always says, 'Remember, this guy is a cop.' Being a cop is a sickness to Johnny. Anyone who wants to put people in jail, anyone who wants to take someone else's liberty away—there is something wrong there. My cousin always made that clear. All cops are rats. That's the bottom line."

Leuci continued: "But this income tax fabrication you're talking of—that's a total frame, and he would definitely be killed."

Shaw nodded, and the tax idea was dropped.

Leuci's car, a new 1971 Pontiac, was driven up to Boston to Bell and Howell. A false wall was built into the trunk with a tape recorder behind it. A telescopic microphone was planted in the ceiling of the car, one so sensitive it could pick up even whispers. The on-off switch was built into the buckle of the safety belt.

Leuci began to insist that he be transferred back into SIU, so that he could move freely about the city, so that he would stand constantly with lawyers, judges, D.A.'s in situations where big money existed and payoffs tended to occur.

But no one had ever been transferred back into SIU. Scoppetta would have to go directly to Police Commissioner Patrick Murphy, and this seemed a dangerous step.

In his public statements the new commissioner had proclaimed himself a foe of corruption. But Murphy, underneath it all, was still a cop. A single second-grade detective now threatened possibly to tear Murphy's department apart, and Murphy could not be expected to be handed this knowledge and then do nothing. He would have to tell someone, at least his first deputy, and total security would be over. It was too risky. If Leuci's cover was blown, the investigation was blown—all that time, work, money wasted. Furthermore, if Leuci got caught wearing a recording device while gathering evidence against corrupt people, he could get killed.

So Shaw returned to the idea of Lusterino. Lusterino was a captain in the Colombo family, Shaw noted. As such he represented a rich source of potential intelligence. Shaw asked if Leuci would be willing to make secret tape recordings with his cousin, provided certain conditions were met.

The recordings would be used for intelligence purposes only—for whatever insights they might provide into the Mafia. Shaw would personally listen to them himself. The tapes would be kept in his personal safe. Under no circumstances would they be made public, or used as the basis of a prosecution. There was no way that the tape or tapes could hurt Lusterino, who would never know they had been made.

"You want me to secretly tape my cousin," cried Leuci angrily. "I won't do it."

Scoppetta at such times had a way of putting his head

in his hands. Or else he would look down and rub his eyes. He was afraid Shaw would scare Leuci away. In private conversations Shaw and Scoppetta would agree to be patient with Leuci. Still, they had to get this investigation moving.

Shaw was interested only in the Mafia itself, he told Leuci. Not Lusterino at all: Lusterino was safe with him. But how did the Mafia work? How were new soldiers inducted? How was money moved from one place to another? How did the different families get in touch with one another?

When Scoppetta and Leuci had left Shaw's apartment, Scoppetta said, "He knows better than to push you on that. We'll talk to him some more about it."

Shaw kept pleading. The Lusterino tapes would provide law enforcement with invaluable knowledge.

Again Leuci refused. "My father would despise me. He has no great love for Johnny, but it's his nephew. It's his sister's son. Johnny's my cousin. Do you follow me?"

To Shaw, Lusterino was a forty-two-year-old mobster who had already served more than fifteen years in prison. But all he said was, "Of course I do. Please believe that we will never force you to do something that you can't live with."

6

IN MARCH 1971, with the Leuci investigation barely two weeks old, two FBI agents presented themselves at the Bureau of Criminal Investigation, where they were received by Detective Bernie Geik. They asked to research the files on Mikey Coco.

Mikey Coco had been, in his youth, a Mafia street enforcer. Now forty-eight, he moved in the hierarchy of organized crime. He operated a luncheonette at 100th Street and Central Park West, and was believed to own part of a Bronx travel agency. He was allegedly part of a group of organized crime figures who, using strong-arm methods, were taking over legitimate businesses on Long Island, including bars, restaurants, used car lots, and garbage companies. He was seen frequently at the Blue Lounge, Chez Joey, and Sleepy's Lagoon Clam House, all in the Bronx, all known mob hangouts, and all kept under almost permanent surveillance by law enforcement agencies. He was reputed to be attempting, through a front, to gain control of the Clam House.

His associates were almost exclusively Mafia figures believed to be involved in drugs: Joe Indelicata, Dom Trinchera, David Petillo, Anthony Novello, Sal Panico. Previously Coco had been closely involved with Frank Mari, a Mafia underboss and drug dealer now missing.

Coco himself was a major narcotics importer. He lived in the suburb of Dobbs Ferry with his common-law wife Phyllis, who had once been wanted for questioning in the shooting of Detective Vince Albano outside Chez Joey.

Coco's cousin, Oscar Ansourian, was believed to have shot Emmanuel Morris, and to have dumped the body on the lawn of Joseph "Bug" Bugliarelli in Dobbs Ferry three years before. Coco was believed to have been involved in this murder and in numerous others, including that of Frank Salzberg, who died of multiple stab wounds in the back in 1968. More recently a gang of young hoodlums had kidnapped Mafia figures and held them for ransom. Certain law enforcement figures believed Coco and several others had trailed this gang to Louisiana and killed four of them. Altogether, police intelligence files connected him with up to seven murders.

Coco was unusual among high-ranking Mafiosi in that he was not Italian. He was the son of Armenian immigrants, and his legal name was Murad Nersesian. He had been a teenage paratrooper during World War II and had seen bloody fighting in North Africa. He had won medals for killing Germans. When he came back from that war, never having learned a trade, knowing nothing, he went into the streets. He went back to the one trade he knew: he went back to war.

The war he came home to was not much different from the one he had left. The late forties were tumultuous for the New York underworld. Mafia families reached for power, and the streets were full of corpses with Italian names. Young thugs who had seen heavy fighting in Europe were lining up on the different sides, not only for or against the five major families, but also for or against various family segments. Mikey Coco had sided with Joey Gambino's people in the Bronx.

There was a group of these freelance shooters and they were called the paratroopers. Carmine Persico, Mikey Coco, Alphonse Indelicata, Sonny Pinto, Joey Accafelli. These were all ruthless young men, some of whom developed into cold-blooded killers, but they were also more intelligent than most street hoodlums. Their allegiance was to Joseph Gambino, and through him to Carlo Gambino. When Carlo Gambino came out on top as *capo di tutti capi,* the paratroopers became, as Mafia jargon had it, "made" men, and after that they had few worries. Money began to come to them from loan-sharking and gambling. Coco during the fifties was earning up to $1000 a week.

Being an Armenian, he always sensed that he was not

totally accepted. "I'm more of an Italian than all of the Italians," he would say. "I have more heart than all of them."

He had enjoyed a big reputation. He was brave and he was vicious.

"A tough guy is not someone who can pull the trigger," he said once. "A child can pull the trigger. A tough guy is someone who can go out and eat a good dinner afterwards." He pointed to Carmine Persico, who was almost a cripple, as a tough guy.

He himself was a tough guy also.

Before long Frank Mari, a major narcotics dealer who was having trouble collecting, took Coco in as partner. Once customers knew they were dealing with Mikey Coco, there was no longer any problem collecting.

Overnight, narcotics made him a wealthy man. Within two months he was earning $5000 a week—some weeks $10,000 or even $15,000—without doing much for it. He made certain arrangements. He went to Florida a lot to close deals. He never went near a package himself.

He had no great understanding of narcotics personally, no idea how drugs were processed, or even how they were used.

"Marijuana makes you stupid," he said once. "Why would I use marijuana? I'm stupid enough already. I should take marijuana to make me more stupid? What do these addicts do with it, anyway? I know they smoke it. But they also shoot it up, don't they?"

He was a big spender. At one time he drove a Rolls-Royce. He was capable of leaving a waitress a fifty-dollar tip. Since he was frequently under surveillance, friends called such behavior outrageous and remonstrated with him for bringing attention onto himself.

But attention was what he wanted. "What else am I living this kind of life for?" he asked. "I walk in here next week and she'll remember me. They will all remember me. I'll do my time in jail when they catch me. Meanwhile, I'm out here. I'm an important guy. If I can have one year on the street, I'll do five years in jail any time."

He had been sentenced at age sixteen to three years for

armed robbery, and in later cases he drew a three-year term for possession and sale of counterfeit money, and an eight-to-ten-year term for sale of heroin. Other arrests were for disorderly conduct, for possession of an illegal gun, for violation of the gambling laws, and for contempt of court. When subpoenaed to testify anywhere, he regularly refused to answer questions; at least once he was jailed a month for civil contempt.

Most of the foregoing information the two FBI agents found in Coco's file, while Detective Geik hovered nearby, paying close attention to their conversation. As soon as they were gone, Geik phoned his friend Leuci.

"They were trying to associate Coco with someone else," Geik reported, "someone who is also an organized crime guy, only they don't know his name. They were trying to identify this other guy. He is supposed to be short and stocky, in his early forties, with mixed gray hair." There was a pause. Then Geik said, "You know Coco. I'd like to sell this information to him. I'd like you to reach out for him for me. See if he is interested in it."

Leuci did know Coco, and after hanging up, he thought about Geik's proposal—and about Coco—for a long time.

To reach Coco, one dialed the number of Sleepy's Lagoon Clam House and left a message. Leuci did this, and in due time his own phone rang. He picked it up. Coco had numerous aliases, but on the phone, for unknown reasons, he always identified himself as Sidney.

"Bobby," he rasped, "this is Sidney." It was a voice like broken plates grating together in a sack.

They agreed to meet at night in the parking lot of the Baychester Diner in the Bronx. Leuci, as he drove his altered Pontiac toward this meeting, was as troubled as if he were on his way to entrap a fellow cop. He had known Coco so long that the man was almost a close friend. Leuci in no way romanticized Coco, yet he had from the beginning been fascinated both by the man himself, and by the glimpses he permitted into the Mafia world. In addition, Coco had always been nice to him, and concerned about him. Most of Leuci's other Mafia contacts were crude, vicious men, and some were psychopaths.

His earliest meeting with Coco had been set up by Lusterino, who had told him, "Mikey Coco wants to meet you. I don't know what about."

So he and Coco had sat together in a booth in a diner in Queens. Coco, Leuci noted, not only had the voice of a Mafia enforcer, he also looked like one. He was five feet ten, weighed 210 pounds, and was built square. His hair was black, his eyes were deep-set and black, and his flat nose had been broken many times. He had a dark pockmarked face. Both his arms were tattooed: two eagles, a tiger, a dagger, and the words "U.S. Army."

Of course Leuci knew of the tattoos, and of Coco's reputation as an enforcer, only from the files.

The drug dealer had been wearing a leather zipper jacket, but it was an expensive one. His shoes and trousers were expensive too. Leuci judged that Coco's outfit had cost about $500. Despite his burly build and pockmarked face, the mobster looked, to Leuci, very nice, and he had asked, "What did you want to see me about, Mike?"

It seemed that Coco and his partners had just been shaken down by two SIU detectives: pay or get arrested. They had paid. Now a third detective was demanding money too. "I'd tell him to fuck off," Coco said, "but I'll meet him if I can trust him. Everybody's got to earn. I like to see people earn, but I'm not going to meet some cop that turns out to be a rat, too. You come on a very high recommendation from your cousin. I want you to tell me if I can trust him. His name is Detective Bell."

Leuci had said carefully, "If you'd like, I'll meet him for you."

"No, I want him to look in my face one time. I want him to see my eyes once."

Leuci said, "Are you as bad as everyone says you are?"

Coco said, "A lot worse."

Reaching into his pocket, Coco had withdrawn a wad of bills, which he handed to Leuci.

But Leuci said, "Mike I don't want money from you. You're asking me if you can trust Dick Bell? You can trust him. Is that such a big deal? You don't feel good unless you give me money. Feel good. I like you. We'll be in touch with each other."

Coco laughed. "You're pretty good," he said.

After that first meeting, Leuci had begun to meet Coco from time to time. The mobster wanted to know what life was like in the police world, and in exchange he talked often about his own life and code.

Now, four years later, as Leuci in his car in the parking lot waited for Coco to appear, these memories and others crowded his head, and he attempted to give himself a pep talk. He was not betraying anybody here tonight. He was doing his job. Mikey Coco was a major Mafia drug dealer. Geik was a corrupt cop. Leuci was about to put together a case involving the sale of confidential police information by the corrupt cop Geik to the Mafia drug dealer Coco. It was the perfect kind of case, the kind he really wanted to make.

After tonight, Coco would go to jail. It would be an easy case. The reason it would be easy was because Coco trusted him.

As Leuci's fingers toyed indecisively with the switch built into his seat belt, a new Mercedes pulled into the parking lot. He watched Mikey Coco jump out, cross the lot, and slip into the seat beside him.

The drug dealer was glad to see him, and greeted him warmly. Freeing his hand from Coco's grip, Leuci reached down to the seat belt, and threw the switch. He then began to explain about Detective Bernie Geik, about the FBI investigation, about the man with the mixed gray hair whom they were trying to link to Coco but who was otherwise unidentified.

Coco said, "Forty years old with mixed gray hair. It could be anybody. This is a fucking puzzle. You brought me a fucking puzzle. Is this guy I'm supposed to have met in junk?"

"No, gambling."

Above their heads the concealed microphone plucked their words out of the air, and behind the dummy panel in the trunk the tape recorder preserved each one.

"Gambling is worse than junk. You have more people watching you for gambling than anything else." Coco took a roll of bills from his pocket. "Here's a thousand dollars. Give it to this Detective Geik. Tell him I'd like to get together with him. You take whatever you want from there."

Leuci nodded politely. He thought of the tape turning, and of the money in his fingers. Two solid pieces of evidence. The case was solid. Coco, already in prison for half his life, faced more of the same.

Business concluded, Coco began to talk about other subjects. Black revolutionaries, he had read in the paper, had begun shooting at cops from ambush. A gruff affection came into his voice. The article had made him worry about the safety of his friend Bobby.

"You cops spend all your time chasing guys like me around, looking to give us aggravation," Coco continued, "while some black son of a bitch is looking to come up and blow your brains out. Those are the guys you should be worried about. We'll never kill you." Suddenly he grinned, having found a solution to the problem. "Give me a year or two, and one day I'll poison the packages and kill a million of the bastards."

Very funny. Leuci was laughing. But a jury, he realized, probably a jury with one or more black jurors on it, would soon listen to this tape, and they were not going to laugh. Secret tapes, Leuci reflects, represented insights into a defendant to which juries normally were not entitled. He was guilty of betraying Coco more deeply even than he had imagined, of exposing to jurors even the man's casual prejudices.

"You know why I don't carry no gun?" said Coco amiably. "Because every nigger I know has got a gun. You got a gun, you get in trouble. I don't need no gun. I got a little hatchet that I keep under the seat of my car. Some son of a bitch bangs into my car, I jump out and beat him with the hatchet."

This time Leuci only smiled.

Coco, lounging against the car door, began to talk about stool pigeons, how much he loathed them. The drug business was plagued by them, he said. A stool pigeon was a rat, a cancer. The only solution was to eradicate every one you found, for there was no lower form of life.

It made Leuci squirm in his seat. He has learned to like me, Leuci thought, and to trust me, but tonight, as far as he is concerned, I have become a stool pigeon, indistinguishable from any other.

Leuci had fallen silent. The drug dealer, noting this, was immediately concerned. "You're not yourself tonight, Bobby. What's the matter? Don't you feel well? Is it your job? Would you rather be a steelworker? I can get you into the steelworkers' union. But you've got to be nuts to want to be a steelworker, and go up there and break your back."

When Leuci remained despondent, Coco said soothingly, "We need you where you are, Bobby. You know we need you. We trust you. These other cops are out to suck our blood. Not you. You got to stick around because you're the only one we can trust."

An hour later in Scoppetta's living room, Leuci threaded the tape onto the machine, and they sat listening to the gruff-voiced mobster.

"Here's a thousand dollars. Give it to this Detective Geik . . ."

That one line was enough, Leuci realized. Coco would go to prison because of a forty-year-old guy with mixed gray hair whom he couldn't even remember. He'd go to jail because of a thousand dollars, and by his own lights he wasn't trying to bribe anyone, he was just buying goodwill.

Scoppetta had stayed up late, reading a book of short stories, waiting for Leuci. Now, listening with considerable excitement, he kept saying, "This is a great case."

But Leuci said, "Tonight I felt like a snake that had crawled into this guy's bed, and I struck out at him. I have difficulty handling this thing."

Scoppetta turned off the machine. Watching Leuci closely, he said, "That's why you are so important, Bob. That's why you are about to make such a meaningful contribution to society. No ordinary undercover cop could get involved in this at the level you can. Do you realize what you have done here today? You have a cop in an extremely sensitive position selling confidential information to an organized crime guy. A guy who has killed a number of people."

But Leuci shook his head. "Going out and making cases against people I don't know," he said, "developing new situations—I have no trouble with that. But I don't know if I can handle much more like tonight. The conversation on that tape"—he gestured toward the machine—"was not between a cop and an organized crime guy. It was between two people who knew each other. Maybe I don't belong inside his world, but I was there with him tonight, and he was totally disarmed. He wasn't guarded in his conversation. He trusted me totally. He's going to pay for that."

Scoppetta said, "Coco's a killer. Think about the times he sat in the back seat of a car, and some unsuspecting guy was sitting in front of him, and they drove the guy some place. He did that to a number of guys. You know he did. He lives in a world that we've got to get rid of."

Later, as he slid into bed beside his sleeping wife, Scoppetta felt pleased with himself. He thought he had handled Leuci's misgivings carefully and well.

Leuci thought this also. When he got home he said to Gina, "Nick was very good tonight."

Nonetheless Leuci lay awake for a long time. To reinforce the case he would have to meet Geik and hand over the bribe. After that he would have to set up a meeting between Geik and Coco, putting them together on the same tape. Two bad characters would be put out of circulation, justice would be served. He foresaw no risk, because Geik and Coco both trusted him. In the interest of a higher good he would betray two men who trusted him. He lay in the dark feeling depressed.

7

AS ALWAYS, Scoppetta sat with a legal pad on his knee, alternately reading from and jotting down notes. Across the room, the tall, skinny Shaw lay on the sofa with his shoes off, his long legs hanging over the end, and he watched Leuci over steepled fingers.

"What about Captain Tange?" inquired Scoppetta.

Daniel Tange had commanded SIU during Leuci's years there; in fact it was he who had promoted Leuci into the elite unit in 1967. Then only thirty-six, Tange was one of the youngest captains in Police Department history, and one of the most brilliant as well. It was predicted that he would one day rise to chief of detectives at least, if not police commissioner.

Tange had been sent into Narcotics on temporary assignment at first. His job was to investigate allegations of misconduct against detectives. He took over office space and began summoning detectives. Word spread quickly through the division: this guy Tange is bad news.

Leuci's turn had come. Captain Tange was not smiling, and he did not invite the detective to take the empty chair beside his desk. He showed a letter that had come in signed by a man named Carti. According to Carti, Leuci had planted narcotics on Carti's cousin, arrested him, and taken money from him.

"It's all bullshit, captain," said Leuci. But he was scared. All detectives, guilty or innocent, were scared of investigations like this.

There were a number of similar allegations against Leuci, Tange said, and he had been studying them for several days. "They can't all be bullshit," he declared.

He was dressed in sports coat and slacks, with a buttondown collar and rep tie. He was college-educated, articulate, handsome. Being of Irish Catholic extraction, he fitted easily into the Police Department power structure, but he seemed to represent—as opposed to the boorish, cigar-smoking officers of the past—the best of the new young officers now rising to the top.

Allegations against active detectives were not unusual. Friends and relatives of men they had arrested often wrote scurrilous letters to the police commissioner or a district attorney. The defendants were fighting to stay out of jail after all. The vast majority of allegations were false, and, in the past, no detective had had much to worry about. The allegation would be bucked down to his own lieutenant, who would interview the complainant and usually try to arrest him. The street people knew this, and were loath to make allegations at all. Even if, after investigating an allegation, the lieutenant believed it to be true, still he would probably bury it, for the alternative was to arrest one of his own detectives, and this, in 1967, just was not done.

Captain Tange began mentioning to Leuci names of other allegations against him. Had he ever given narcotics to these people? But Leuci had denied every charge.

Beginning the next day Tange went out and himself interrogated certain of the complainants, after which he informed Leuci that every allegation lacked corroboration. Therefore he was closing them all out.

"But the next time," he threatened, "I'll have your head. You can tell every detective out there that if I catch anyone one inch off base, they are going to jail. I don't care how things were done before I came here, but they will be done differently from now on." Then he added, "I'm recommending that you be moved up into SIU."

Midway through 1967, Tange himself was appointed commander of SIU. For several days he walked in each morning wearing his freshly shaven face and his nice collegiate clothes, walked past all the detectives without so much as a nod, entered his office, and closed the door. Everyone was concerned. What would he do?

A message went up on the bulletin board: Office meeting for tomorrow morning at ten o'clock.

The detectives were waiting nervously when Tange strode to the front of the room and demanded order.

"Apparently this office is made up entirely of superstars," he began, once they were silent.

For the last several days he had been studying their case folders, he told them. Though they might be superstars, their case folders proved some of them incompetent and inefficient, and suggested that others were corrupt. Well, the incompetents were about to get bounced out of SIU; those who stayed had best understand his feelings about corruption. He hated it. He would arrest without a qualm any cop he caught.

The assembled detectives began sliding down in their seats, and when Tange had left the room they gathered, shaken, in small groups. Mostly these groups broke down along ethnic lines, for that was the way close friendships tended to form in SIU. Leuci talked it over with Nunziata and Mandato while Aguiluz, Codelia, and the other Hispanic detectives conversed volubly nearby in Spanish. Nunziata at this time was already the most magnetic and respected cop in SIU, but Aguiluz, his monumental seizure still two years in the future, was not yet even a team leader. Instead he worked on the fringe of Nunziata's team whenever a wireman or translator was needed.

Nunziata was extremely worried by Tange's tough speech, he told Leuci. He was convinced that Tange was straight—straight enough even to lock up another cop. Leuci was worried too, but he was also in some strange way elated. A man like Tange could change SIU into the efficient, incorruptible, elite unit it was supposed to be. He could turn them all back into knights on white chargers again.

Tange's first order was to clean the office up. He wanted the floors swept, the files organized. No longer aloof, he moved through the corridors with his sleeves rolled up and his tie down, giving orders. He talked to his detectives in small groups, giving them direction, promising money to make buys, money to pay informants. He promised new equipment too, especially radio equipment. He made them rewrite their wiretap and search warrant applications, and more of these began to be accorded than ever before.

A number of detectives were afraid of Tange. A number watched him shrewdly, waiting with a certain cynicism to see him show his true colors. And a number, Leuci for one, were delighted with the young captain, and with the sense of mission he had brought to their lives.

Next Tange tried to put in controls. He wanted at least one member of every team in the office every day, and he gave orders to this effect. But the detectives screamed loudly that the dope dealers were out there, not in here. They protested so much and resisted so hard that Tange rescinded his order after about two weeks.

One night, about two months after Tange had taken command, Sergeant Jack Hourigan passed the word to several detectives: Tange wanted to meet them, separately, in Jimmy's bar across the street. "The worm has turned in the apple," said Hourigan cryptically. "You have a new partner."

Leuci went to confer with Nunziata. "What's going on, Joe?"

Detective Nunziata, grinning broadly, was shaking his head back and forth. He had to meet Tange at 6:30, he said, thirty minutes before Leuci. "I think the guy is Italian, and he changed his name," Nunziata joked.

At seven o'clock Leuci sat opposite Captain Tange in a booth in Jimmy's bar.

"Would you like a drink?" inquired Captain Tange.

Tange, in civilian clothes, began by praising Leuci's work. There were only a few SIU teams who knew their jobs, he said. One of the best was Leuci's team. Leuci was an outstanding detective.

Leuci's drink was set down before him.

As for himself, Tange said, he would not remain a captain long. He was the youngest captain in the job. His future was unlimited. To Leuci the inference was clear. Every detective needed a rabbi to help his career along and Tange figured to be as good a rabbi as Leuci could hope for.

"But I've got a long way to go," Tange said. His hand toyed with his glass on the table. "And I just bought a house out in Northport. I went way over my head."

For Leuci a light dawned, and he understood at last what was coming. He had heard enough other cops, who had never taken money before, try to rationalize doing it. Tange described his house: it was on four acres overlooking Long Island Sound, he said, and had to be seen to be believed. "I thought I could afford it. But I can't."

"What are you trying to say, captain?" asked Leuci bluntly.

"You have a new partner, and it's me," said Tange. He was studying his glass. "I get an equal share of anything you do."

Now it was Leuci's turn to stare at the table top. He had never committed a dishonest act in his life, he said, and he didn't know what Tange might be referring to.

Tange only nodded. His voice grew hard and he sounded like a commander again. "If I find out that you have done anything and haven't paid me my share," he said, "I'll not only have your job, I'll have your head." The money was to go through Sergeant Hourigan, who would serve as bagman.

Tange served three years as SIU commander, and during that time had no difficulty meeting payments on his house in Northport. Meantime, with each major heroin seizure by SIU detectives his reputation soared within the department, and shortly before the Leuci investigation began he had been handed a new and choice assignment— command of the Twenty-eighth Precinct in Harlem, one of the most sensitive jobs in the department and one calling for deputy inspector rank. He was still only thirty-nine. His rise to the top had begun.

But now Scoppetta, studying old SIU rosters, had chanced to notice his name and, with Leuci sitting across the room, had asked, "What about Captain Tange?"

At first Leuci defended Tange as a fine and honest man, adding, "He'll be chief of detectives some day."

But Scoppetta rejected this remark. "If there was corruption in the unit," he said doggedly, "and if Tange was so bright, then he should have known about it."

Scoppetta studied Leuci. The detective was a good actor—the tapes with Geik and Coco proved it—but a bad liar, for his emotions were close to the surface, as now. In his shifting eyes, in the pinch of his mouth, Leuci's inner conflict showed.

It was a question of loyalty, Scoppetta judged. Loyalty to Tange and SIU versus loyalty to Scoppetta. Scoppetta had never yet betrayed Leuci. Had Tange?

After a moment, having made his decision, Leuci muttered, "He'll take money."

Though Scoppetta and Shaw immediately tried to interrogate Leuci, he refused to say how he knew this about Tange, or what his experiences with Tange had been. Instead, he demanded $500. He would hand $500 to Tange and would make a recording, he said. If Tange took the money, this would prove him a crook. There was no need to go back into the past.

But money to Scoppetta was money. He was afraid someone would judge his investigation too expensive and shut it off. Certainly he now wanted to nail Tange if possible—who else had nailed a police captain?—but he wanted to do it cheaply.

Also he wanted more information from Leuci, and he went on questioning him. What possible grounds did Leuci have for handing Tange money, he demanded? And when Leuci declined to reply, he added, "I mean, you can't just hand him five hundred dollars for no reason."

"Don't tell me what I can do and what I can't do," Leuci retorted. "I don't need a reason to give him money."

Scoppetta sighed, and the next day signed out the money and, in a disgruntled mood, handed it over to his undercover detective. This was no way to conduct an intelligent long-term investigation, he told himself. It would never work. But for the moment he had no choice. Leuci, he realized, had begun to try to take control of the investigation into his own hands—a drift that would have to be stopped at once.

* * *

That night Leuci drove up into Harlem. He had $500 in his pocket and an appointment with Captain Tange. It was raining. The streets were wet and glistening.

You could have led us, captain, Leuci brooded as he drove along, windshield wipers swishing. We were the best detectives in the city. You could have given us purpose, you could have won us the kind of honor and respect we had never had before. Instead of that, you set yourself up as a partner. You appointed Sergeant Hourigan as bagman. Hourigan was a lovely guy, but he was weak, and he was a drunk. He was a bad drinker, a dangerous drinker. Dealing with Hourigan was like dealing with dynamite.

A leader must be able to pick his subordinates, captain. And who did you pick? You picked Hourigan, a crony from your days as a motorcycle cop. What kind of a captain is that? Did you ever hear Hourigan's great line, captain? "The worm has turned in the apple." He not only told me, he told the clerical man, and the switchboard man. Once he walked into an office containing nine SIU detectives. Nine men stood up in unison and chanted, "The worm has turned in the apple." This was Hourigan's big secret—and yours—that he was telling to everybody.

Leuci parked outside the station house, and felt himself briefly. The money made a bulge in one pocket, and the transmitter made a bulge at his belt. He ducked through the rain into the station house, and went into Tange's office. Tange seemed glad to see him, for his handshake was firm, his greeting effusive.

The two old friends chatted about recent transfers and other department gossip. Leuci remarked that he hoped to get back into SIU soon. Then, claiming that he had something personal to discuss, he invited Tange for a ride in his car. One can't hand over money inside a station house.

The two men drove along in the rain. A captain in the Police Department is like a Mafia don, Leuci thought, as he tried to explain to himself what was about to happen. I will give him money on general principles, and he'll take it. I will give him money because he's the reason I'm in this mess. He's the reason I'm betraying cops. He could have saved all of us.

Not that he was trying to punish Tange for the past, Leuci assured himself. All Tange had to do was refuse the money. If he did, then Leuci would never tell anyone about Tange's past, about going into partnership with his men. If Tange refused the money tonight, then he was in the clear.

It was Leuci's game, and he had begun changing the rules because these new ones were the only ones he could live by. Because Scoppetta's were too strict. It was complicated, and, to anyone else, incomprehensible.

And if Tange took the money? If he took it, then his career was over at thirty-nine, and to some extent his life. But if he takes it, Leuci told himself, it will not be me ruining Tange's life, it will be Tange ruining his own life.

And so, taking one hand off the wheel, Leuci put it into his pocket and found the wad of money there. He brought it out.

"Listen, captain, I did something last week," he said. "I want to give you something," and he handed across the $500.

Tange took it. "I appreciate that," he said. "Do you want to play golf next week?"

In Shaw's apartment later that same evening, Leuci played the recording for the two prosecutors. "I don't hear the money being passed," Scoppetta said, listening hard. "I don't hear him receiving the money."

Leuci pushed the reverse button on the machine, stopped the tape, then started it forward again. "I tell him, 'I want to give you something,' and he answers, 'I appreciate that.' There, hear it?"

Scoppetta heard it, and it made him angry. "That's no good in court, and you know it," he snapped. "You never even mentioned money. When you hand somebody money, tell him, 'Here, here's the money'. Count it, dammit, say something to show you're giving over money."

"I'm the cop," asserted Leuci. "I'm the undercover

agent. If I say to him, here's the money, Tange will either go into shock, or he'll jump out of the car and call Internal Affairs. He'll do something crazy, because I've never spoken to him like that before. No one speaks to someone like that when giving money." Leuci snorted derisively. "Here's the money. Don't tell me how to pass money to someone."

Both had lost sight—Shaw too—of the essential fact revealed: how did Leuci know all this?

Scoppetta stomped angrily about the room.

Leuci had been searched by his backup agents before leaving to meet Tange, and then had been handed the $500. The two agents had never lost sight of him, except while he was inside the station house. After he had left Tange they had searched him again, and the $500 was gone. This was good evidential procedure. Still, if Tange ever came to trial, his defense lawyer could always suggest that Leuci had secreted the money inside the station house, or even thrown it away.

Scoppetta said, "That's $500 wasted. Maybe you don't want to make a case against Tange. Is that it? You'll have to meet him again. There's not enough here."

Leuci, furious, stared at the back of Scoppetta's head.

"We want him solid," said Scoppetta, turning to face the detective. "And from now on I want to hear money exchanged. If you're going to exchange money I want to hear it."

The two men glared at each other.

Shaw, reclining on the room sofa with his shoes off, said, "Calm down, Nick."

Scoppetta was very upset.

"He's a police captain, Bob," said Shaw. "In a one-on-one situation the jury would believe him, not you. You'll have to get a better recording."

8

IT WAS Leuci's job to set up another meeting with Coco, this time putting him together with Detective Bernie Geik.

To this meeting Leuci wore a one-watt Kel transmitter that was about the size of a Zippo lighter. Together with its small but powerful batteries, it was taped flat to his waist. The bands of tape had been wound as tightly as he could stand them around his middle, so that transmitter and batteries were pressed into his body. Afterwards the tape had been patted as smooth as careful fingers could make it. There were no rough edges. Anyone giving Leuci a casual search would feel what appeared to be just another roll of flesh.

The tiny microphone was taped to the middle of his chest; it could be mistaken for a button, or for medals or jewelry hanging from his neck by a chain. The microphone wire running up his belly and sternum was under tape, and two antenna wires, which ran up over his shoulders, were taped in place also. Leuci believed himself safe from discovery unless someone ordered him stripped, or unless he was carefully patted down by someone who knew what he was looking for.

His backup agents were two IRS men lent to Scoppetta for this purpose. Their job was to stay close enough to Leuci to record his transmissions, which carried only a block or two, and also to rush forward as bodyguards if needed. But they were men used to catching crooked accountants and tax cheats. They were not street people and they were incapable—as was about to be proven—of maintaining a difficult tail.

Tonight's meeting place was again the parking lot of the Baychester Diner. The difference was that this time, instead of climbing into Leuci's car, Coco invited Leuci and Geik, who had arrived together, into his Mercedes. He then accelerated in a squeal of rubber, made a violent U-turn, jumped the divider, and sped north out of the city—maneuvers the IRS backup team failed to follow.

Leuci, wearing his incriminating gear, was now alone in the night in a car with a corrupt cop and a Mafia enforcer. There was nothing he could do about it. He settled back in his seat and tried to calculate his options. Both these men faced jail terms because of him. If they were suspicious of him, what would they do about it? His biggest risk was that they would demand to search him, and he tried to figure where and how this would be done, and what his reactions should be.

Geik was armed. Coco was possibly armed.

Geik, chatting amiably in the back seat, did not seem suspicious. Coco was silent. He drove normally now, and as he gazed out over the wheel his pockmarked face revealed nothing.

Had he spotted the backup car back at the parking lot? If not, why all those violent turns? Did he associate the backup car with Leuci?

Geik was a detective, Leuci reflected. Geik knew about wires. If Geik patted him down, he would find it.

As he considered all this, Leuci became increasingly nervous, with the result that he began to sweat, and almost immediately he became conscious of a sharp burning pain near his navel, where his batteries and transmitter were taped. The excessive sweat pouring off him seemed to have set off a short circuit. The batteries and transmitter were burning him, but there was nothing he could do about this either, unless he wished to rip open his shirt and yank off that tape.

Coco drove steadily north. Leuci beside him sat perfectly still, his mind focused now on the pain at his waist.

In Yonkers, thirty minutes later, Coco pulled into the parking lot beside an Italian restaurant. The three men walked inside, took a table, and ordered dinner.

Excusing himself then, Leuci carefully stood up, and went carefully out through the tables and into the men's room. Once inside, he looked for a way to bolt the door, for he wanted to get his fingers under the tape, to get that transmitter away from his flesh.

Unfortunately there was no bolt, no way to lock the outer door at all. There was no door on the one toilet stall either. To get at the tape around his middle he would have to open his clothes, but Geik or Coco at any moment might walk in on him. He couldn't risk it. Standing at the urinal with his fly open, he reached upward and tried to dig his fingers under the tape. But the gum had melted. He tried to pluck the transmitter, which felt now red hot, away from his belly, but he failed. The tape would not come free. He could not get his fingers under it.

So he went back to the table. He had been gone a long time, and Coco, watching him approach, looked worried. "You don't look too good," said the mobster solicitously. A candle burned on their table. The flame sent strange shadows flickering across the flat nosed, pockmarked face, imparting to it the look of a friendly satyr. "Are you sure you're okay, Bobby?"

Leuci managed a smile. "Sure, Mike."

Reassured, the mobster began to eat. Leuci watched him devour a huge mound of fettucine swimming in clam sauce, followed by a plate of dripping cannelloni stuffed with veal and sausage. Salad was served. Then dessert.

At last the bill was paid, and they were crossing the parking lot toward Coco's Mercedes. Coco started the car and steered back toward the city. Leuci's pain seemed to have doubled in intensity. He was trying to hold himself very still, thinking that if he once began to squirm, he wouldn't be able to stop. Coco and Geik were talking about electronic surveillance. Geik was revealing all the department's secrets. Coco, driving slowly, was listening with fascination.

Leuci's pain had become terrific, and he was trying, as inconspicuously as possible, to slip his fingers through his shirt and under the tape. But the transmitter remained inviolable. Afraid Coco might notice, Leuci brought his fingers out of his shirt. But they soon went back in again, trying and failing to dig under the tape. Also he had began—only slightly for the moment—to squirm.

Presently Coco began to sniff the air. "There's a terrible stink in this car," he said. "Did someone step in some dog shit or something? Hey, this is an expensive car. Check your feet." He pulled over to the curb, and the overhead light came on. Three grown men examined the soles of three pairs of shoes.

"I don't know what it could be," Coco said, driving on, "but there's still a terrible stink in here."

Leuci, focused in on his pain, had at first smelled nothing. But the odor got through to him now and he recognized it. It was burning flesh, his own, and this realization made him squirm worse than before.

Half an hour later the neon sign of the Baychester Diner at last came into view. Coco drove into the lot and parked beside Leuci's car. By then sweat was pouring down Leuci's face, and the mobster, after turning off the ignition, noticed it. Reaching over, he felt Leuci's forehead. "I think you got a fever," Coco told him. "You're coming down with something."

"My God, your whole back is soaking wet," said Geik. He was leaning over the seat, his hand on Leuci's back.

"You better get home and get to bed," Coco said, his face showing great concern. Leuci didn't want advice; he wanted Coco to leave, and Geik to leave.

Coco at last drove off, but Geik still waited beside Leuci's car. He was waiting to be driven home. Leuci was scarcely aware of this.

"I have to go to the bathroom," he mumbled, and ran. He ran into the diner and through into the men's room, where he closed the door of the toilet stall, tore open his clothes and, with his trousers half way down his legs, tried to rip the tape from his body. But it was still stuck to him, and the pain had made his fingers blunt and inaccurate. At last it began to come free. He kept pulling at it, ripping it off his skin, until at last the Kel set and the batteries were revealed. The transmitter, he saw, had slipped out of its pouch and was stuck to his flesh. When he had peeled it carefully off himself, he saw it had burned away a patch of skin the size of a half dollar.

Now that he had the belt off, he didn't know what to do with it. He couldn't just leave it in the toilet stall—it would cause talk and this was a place Coco frequented. So he put it back on—gingerly. He patted the tape back down, tucked his shirt back into his trousers, and went outside to Geik.

In the parking lot he told Geik he was sick, and to grab a cab home. But Geik protested that he didn't really know where he was, didn't know how to get to his apartment from here. Punishing himself, Leuci drove the corrupt detective all the way home.

The night was not over. He still had to report to Scoppetta, who had been waiting up. "How did it go tonight?" he asked when Leuci walked into his apartment.

"Terrific," Leuci said, "There's no recording. Those IRS guys lost me."

Scoppetta became angry.

But Leuci was in such pain he barely noticed. Undoing his clothes, he once again removed the belt of tape, the transmitter, the batteries. He peered down at the circle of raw flesh where the skin had been burned away.

"We've got to find something else, some better gear. I just can't wear this belt," he said.

Scoppetta stared with sympathy and horror at the terrible burn.

Once the pain had abated somewhat, Leuci began begging for New York City cops as backup men. "If you don't get cops who know the street, this is going to happen all the time. We're going to lose many valuable recordings. We've got to get cops."

Leuci had brought this up before. But Scoppetta couldn't arrange backup cops without going to Police Commissioner Murphy.

Then go to him, Leuci insisted. Besides, only Murphy could transfer him back into SIU—where he would have the jurisdiction and freedom he needed to make big cases.

Big new cases, Scoppetta silently amended. Cases against people he didn't know, rather than against these ghosts who haunted his past.

"All right," Scoppetta said, "I'll talk to Murphy."

An hour later and fifty miles east, Leuci lay on his bed on clean cool sheets while Gina smoothed salve onto his wound. She was gentle and concerned, and spent a lot of time on it. Leuci told her how the transmitter had begun to burn him, how much he wanted to work with fellow cops, not IRS agents. He wanted this to be a police investigation, not an IRS investigation. He wanted other cops in it with him.

He wanted not to feel so guilty.

In the middle of the night he awoke and remembered tonight's terrible pain, and he wondered how much of it might have been self-induced. What he was doing, though good, nonetheless felt evil. Perhaps subconsciously he believed that he deserved such pain. And he began to fear that every time he put that belt on it would burn him again, because that's what he deserved and perhaps even desired.

9

A NUMBER of new detectives had been assigned to SIU in Leuci's absence, but many he had known were still there, some of whom regarded him with suspicion from the moment he sat down behind his new desk. For he had accomplished what no detective had ever accomplished. He had come back to SIU.

But other old-timers were friendly to him, and one even greeted him with a bear hug. He looked around him. His own former partners had been rotated out of course. Nunziata was gone too. But Aguiluz was still there, his team intact, and so were Eddie Codelia, Jack McClean, and other old friends.

All of these Leuci intended at all costs to avoid. Leuci knew he would be assigned partners. He was determined that they should be men he had never met before.

The next day these partners were introduced to him: Detectives Jim Sheridan and Bill Hubert. Both had been working in Narcotics in Harlem, had compiled good records there, and had just been promoted into SIU.

He met Sheridan first, a tall blond Irishman from Belfast, who spoke with the heaviest brogue he had ever heard. Leuci was determined to keep this relationship strictly professional. He didn't want to know about Sheridan's family. He didn't want to know about his problems. Because if he turned out to be a corrupt cop, he was going to jail.

But the Irishman greeted him with such an open, bubbling kind of personality that Leuci thought at once: I'm going to be in trouble with this guy. It's going to be impossible to keep him at arm's length.

Later he met Hubert, who seemed, in contrast to Sheridan, a blunt, tough cop. It was Hubert who suggested the Leuci join him and Sheridan for dinner that night. The three of them should get acquainted, and drink to the future successes of their new team.

But Leuci walked away, saying, "I have other things to do."

The first job for any detective beginning a new assignment was to contact the junkies, ex-convicts, and other street people he had known in the past. And to probe for information.

Leuci did this, and before long he learned of a man in the Bronx named Joseph Andretta who was supposed to be selling drugs. Andretta, though only a mid-rank dealer himself, was supposed to be buying from a man with access to vast quantities of heroin.

Hoping to be led to this connection, Leuci, Hubert, and Sheridan set up surveillance outside Andretta's house. Working in relays, they sat for hours in parked cars waiting for him to come out, and when he did they trailed him wherever he went. But days passed, and Andretta led them nowhere.

Sheridan and Hubert were stumped; they did not know what to do next. But to Leuci, this was a typical SIU case; it was just beginning to get interesting. The only way they were going to find Andretta's connection, Leuci told them, was to wiretap his phone. And they certainly didn't have enough evidence to get a legal wiretap order.

Sheridan agreed. "Let's get on his phone. Let's find out who he's calling, who he's doing business with."

But an illegal wiretap was a federal offense, and Hubert was reluctant. "Do we have to do that? If we get caught we'll get locked up."

Back in the station house they conferred with their supervisor, Sergeant Norman Cohen. It was decided they should check out Andretta's basement. They would find and look over his phone box, and would make their final decision then.

Driving up to the Bronx to Andretta's address, they picked the entrance door lock, then descended to the basement, where they pushed through dim corridors looking for the phone box. An easy phone to tap, Leuci told the others when they had found it. They would come back tonight and do it. Leuci also checked out the nearby storeroom, which was clogged with bicycles, baby carriages, and unused appliances, and when the others asked what he was looking for, he told them they would soon find out.

That night the three detectives crept down into Andretta's basement. A quick jerk on the telephone box cover revealed the wires inside. The pairs stood in rows. In some buildings the pairs were marked by the apartment they serviced. These weren't. Leuci would have to find Andretta's pair. Removing a hand set from his bag, he attached its two alligator clips to a random pair of terminals. He could now make an outgoing call, and he did so, dialing Andretta's number. As the dial spun back from the last digit, Andretta's phone began to ring upstairs.

In the cellar Leuci licked the tips of his fore and index fingers, and ran them up and down the pairs of terminals, waiting for the mild shock. His hand jumped back as he touched the pair on the bottom right side. "That's it," he told Sheridan and Hubert, and he yanked his hand set loose. Andretta, if he had picked up his phone at all, had just been disconnected.

With needle point pliers from his bag, Leuci loosened the two terminal bolts. Selecting a coil of telephone wire from his bag, he stripped one end and attached the terminals to the two screws. This wire he ran up through the hole in the top of the box, entwined it with the telephone company's wires, and shoved it through one telephone company leader after another until he had reached a point opposite the basement storeroom. Branching off here, he led his own wire into this dark, junk-cluttered place. Running his wire as far as a derelict stove, he attached it to the jacks on his Craig tape recorder, then slid the tape recorder into the oven, and closed the door on it. Walking back to the telephone box, he dialed Andretta's number again. But as soon as the phone began to ring, he pulled his hand set free.

Returning to the storeroom, he opened the oven door

and studied his self-starting tape recorder. The reel had turned one full time. The phone tap was made, the tape recorder was working perfectly. Leuci closed the oven door and pushed a refrigerator up in front of it.

As the three detectives left the building, Hubert said anxiously, "This is all very exciting, very new to me. It's terrific that we are going to be able to get this kind of inside information. But if we get caught, we're going to get locked up."

There was no way they could get caught, Leuci assured him. Hubert was now an SIU detective, was he not, and this was the way SIU detectives worked. He then explained the rest of his plan. His informant would order heroin from Andretta. Andretta would telephone his connection for the merchandise. Since they would be listening in on the conversation, they would know where and when Andretta would take delivery. They would tail him to this meeting and arrest both him and his connection. It would be easy.

The two less experienced detectives were awed by this plan, but Scoppetta, the night Leuci revealed it to him at his apartment, was furious. The prosecutor paced the rug. "That's an illegal wiretap," he fumed. "You're breaking the law. You can't do that."

"Nick," Leuci fired back. "I didn't do it. They did it and I went along. If I am going to be believable as an SIU detective, then I have to be allowed to go along with them. And in a case like this, every SIU detective I know would tap Andretta's phone. They wouldn't think twice about it. How do you think they made all those big cases? If you want to burn me, then just tell me I should blow the whistle on this illegal tap."

Scoppetta, shocked, stared at Leuci. After a moment he admitted the validity of Leuci's logic, but the law was the law. He did not have the power to give Leuci permission to break the law. He would talk to Shaw; he would talk to U.S. Attorney Seymour.

Scoppetta was greatly troubled by what he was learning about SIU. There were serious questions that Leuci must be asked, and Scoppetta would soon have to ask them.

A number of conferences took place the next day involving Scoppetta, Shaw, U.S. Attorney Seymour, and other prosecutors as well. A consensus was reached. To preserve Leuci's cover, and to gather evidence of illegal wiretapping, his team would be permitted to continue the tap on Andretta's phone.

The Andretta case went forward. The informant duly met with Andretta and ordered the heroin. The detectives, sitting in surveillance in a parked car, watched this meeting, then tailed Andretta back to his house. As Andretta entered his apartment upstairs, they were already in the basement pushing the refrigerator away from the stove to get at their tape recorder in the oven. Even as the oven door flopped open, the spools began to turn.

Andretta had telephoned someone named Joe at a poolroom. He and Joe had agreed to meet the following night on Boston Road in the Bronx. Joe would have with him an eighth of a tire.

Leuci snorted derisively as he heard this. "Tough code to break," he muttered.

As the three detectives walked out through the lobby of Andretta's building, Hubert said, "Is it going to be that easy? Are we going to go up to Boston Road, and wait for this guy to show up with an eighth of a kilo of heroin?"

"It's going to be that easy," Leuci said.

And it was. The following night the three detectives and their supervisor, Sergeant Norman Cohen, arrested three men: Andretta, Andretta's shotgun rider, and Joe, whose name was Joseph Marchese; and they seized an eighth of a kilo of heroin.

It was still a typical SIU case: imaginative, efficient, illegal. And it remained one to the end. Once in the station house, Marchese offered Sergeant Cohen "a couple of thousand" to secure his release.

Cohen, drawing Leuci aside, reported the bribe offer. Immediately the room went electric with tension. Everyone was whispering. Everyone was staring at everyone else. Sheridan and Hubert had overheard a word or two, and had guessed the rest.

Cohen, still whispering to Leuci, said, "I don't trust

Hubert. As a matter of fact, Leuci, I don't trust you. There are a lot of rumors about you."

"If you don't trust me," Leuci said, "forget about it. We'll lock the guy up. I don't give a shit."

Sheridan now drew Leuci aside. Leuci was team leader, he said. He and Hubert would agree to whatever he decided. "This Marchese has a lot of money," Sheridan added. "Did you notice his fucking shirt? That shirt cost more than my whole wardrobe."

Marchese came over to them. He owed money in this precinct, he said, and wanted badly to leave at once. It was worth $4000 to him.

"Sold," said Cohen.

There remained the problem of Hubert. "I don't want to do it," he said. "What are we going to do, arrest the two shit heads? And let the connection go?" He glanced from Cohen to Leuci to Sheridan, seeking support.

Stepping across to Hubert, Cohen snarled, "This guy is a businessman. He owns a taxicab company in Yonkers. We're letting the guy go. He owes people money and wants to get out of here before they come looking for him. That's the reason we're getting the four thousand, not because he's the connection."

Hubert stared at the floor.

"You don't belong in SIU," Cohen told him. "You belong back in the fucking field group, chasing niggers up in Harlem, that's where you belong." And he strode angrily away, leaving Hubert still staring at the floor.

I've got a good case here, Leuci thought, as he watched the disconsolate Hubert. I got Marchese. I got Cohen. I got Sheridan. And I'm going to have Hubert. "Bill, listen," Leuci said, "do you want to take the money or not? You tell me what you want to do. I'm not your father. Don't expect me to make decisions for you. You make your own decisions. Whatever you want, I'll do. If you want to lock the guy up, then we'll lock him up."

"I hate this fucking thing," Hubert said. "This is the nicest collar I ever fucking made. And so quick. I've kicked in a thousand doors. I never saw that much junk before. All I ever got before was little bags, four or five little bags at a time maximum. I work with you two days, and in twenty minutes I got a fucking Mafia guy. I got an eighth of a kilo of heroin."

Leuci watched him.

"I'll do whatever you do," mumbled Hubert miserably. "But I don't want to talk to that little fuck of a sergeant again, because I might punch him out. This prick will put me back in the fucking field group tomorrow unless I take the money. And after that back to uniform."

Thirty minutes later Marchese was on the street, and Leuci drove him to a bar and grill. Double-parking outside, Leuci waited with the motor running until Marchese came out carrying a paper bag. The drug dealer handed the bag in through the car window. Leuci felt that it was full of money.

"Will you drive me home?" Marchese asked pleasantly.

"Fuck you," said Leuci, and drove back to the station house.

Hubert was waiting for him on the sidewalk. Sheridan and Cohen had gone ahead to the restaurant where the money would be split up. Hubert got into the car beside Leuci.

Leuci, as he accelerated down the street, pushed the paper bag across the seat. "There should be four thousand dollars in there. Count it."

Hubert, counting, said, "This makes me sick, Bob."

Leuci did not look at him. "You mean to tell me you've never done this before?"

"Nothing like this. Never."

"How much money is in there?"

The answer was $3600. Marchese had beaten them out of $400.

"Take nine hundred for yourself," Leuci said. "And take a share for Sheridan. I'll give Cohen his."

The two detectives went into the restaurant, where they slid into the booth opposite Cohen and Sheridan. Reaching under the table, Leuci passed Cohen $900. Cohen, as he gripped the money, began chuckling happily. Hubert passed over Sheridan's share, but as he did so, he was trembling.

The next day, meeting with Scoppetta, Leuci handed over his $900 to be vouchered.

"That's a solid case," said Scoppetta, very pleased. "You've got the Mafia guy and the sergeant solid. You got the two detectives solid. All you need to do is get corroboration."

The prosecutor decided that Leuci should go back to all four men wired, and talk over the case. This would be all the corroboration needed. But when Scoppetta looked up he saw that Leuci's face was grim.

"I want to tell you right now," Leuci said, "that if you try to prosecute Hubert, I'm finished. Let's find out right now what kind of guys you are. I will not allow Hubert to be prosecuted."

Scoppetta studied him. Each of these crises of conscience, these pangs of guilt or remorse, called for a separate judgment by Scoppetta. Would he overrule the detective, or humor him, or what? "Did it happen the way you're telling me?" Scoppetta asked.

"Exactly that way."

"I don't believe you. If Hubert was totally honest, he wouldn't have taken the money."

This produced another emotional monologue by Leuci. "You don't have the faintest idea what it's like to be a cop, do you?" he cried. "After working years in a precinct, you finally get a chance to come into the Detective Bureau. You finally get a chance to work in Narcotics. You finally get into SIU. And then your whole career goes out the window because you run into some thieving little sergeant who is ready to bust you back to uniform. Do you understand the pressure that Bill Hubert was under? And then he looked to me for direction, and the direction I gave him was: Take the money. Now you want to prosecute this kid. If that's what you're going to do, I quit."

After a moment Scoppetta said, "Prove to me this kid is honest, and we won't prosecute him."

Leuci said, "I'll prove it to you, and after that you're going to get him transferred out of Narcotics. You're going to send him some place where he can do his fucking job."

Scoppetta shrugged. "Let's see what happens."

Corroborating tapes. Leuci wanted three that proved criminal guilt, and one that would be exculpatory.

So he met again with Marchese, who talked about handing over the bribe. Leuci's battery transmitter picked this up and it was recorded in the car of his backup team.

Again wearing a wire, he spoke with Cohen. Cohen was cagey, but enough went down on tape to corroborate the case.

Leuci's third meeting was with Sheridan. Sheridan was no problem. Sheridan was entirely open, trusting, ebullient, friendly. But Leuci didn't want to be friends with Sheridan. It was easy not to be friends with Cohen, but with Sheridan and Hubert it was another story.

Leuci phoned Hubert, and they met in Leuci's car. Leuci pushed down on the seat belt, activating the secret tape recorder. They began to talk about the money from Marchese. The unsuspecting Hubert said into the tape recorder that he hadn't been able to spend the $900. He wanted to give it back. It made him sick when he looked at it. He couldn't face his wife, his kids. He wanted no part of this shit. He just wanted to be a cop and do his job.

Leuci rushed back to Scoppetta with this tape, threaded it onto the machine, and started it forward. Scoppetta listened carefully until the tape ended, then said, "You led that whole conversation. The case against Hubert is a prosecutable case."

"I don't care if it's a prosecutable case," Leuci cried.

Recognizing the state Leuci was in, Scoppetta agreed to talk it over with Shaw.

By this time, Leuci in his undercover role was conducting several cases simultaneously. He was meeting with and making secret recordings with two other Mafia drug dealers, and with two suspect lawyers. He played golf with Captain Tange while his backup team trailed in a golf cart recording their conversation. In addition there were constant strategy meetings with Shaw and Scoppetta.

As a result Leuci often missed meetings with Sheridan and Hubert, who were not experienced enough to operate without him. They began to complain. They were cops, they wanted to make cases. Leuci gave them excuses. He had to meet a confidential informant. He had to go to the dentist. He had to meet a girl.

Eventually they ceased to believe him. They got angry. They gave him an ultimatum. Either he would show up for work tomorrow morning or they would report him.

But the next morning Scoppetta summoned Leuci to an urgent strategy conference.

Knowing Sheridan and Hubert would be furious, Leuci phoned SIU and left a message for them. His son had been hit by a car. He couldn't meet them.

When he reached home that night, Gina was in tears. "What are you doing?" she wept. "You're driving me crazy. I can't stand this any more. All day long I've been getting phone calls from this lovely Irish lady, and this lovely Irish man with a beautiful accent. They want to come out to the house. They want to know how badly hurt is my child."

Leuci was appalled.

"The phone has not stopped ringing," Gina sobbed. "They call me every hour. I sound nervous to them. They will drive out from the city. Sheridan said to tell you not to worry. You should take the week off. He'll cover for you. I talked to this Bill Hubert. He said he's your partner. You shouldn't worry. He'll cover for you."

Leuci was unable to speak.

"Horrible. Horrible," she said. "You're going to hurt these people."

When Leuci reported this to him, Scoppetta attempted to soothe the anguished detective. He had talked to Mike Shaw, he said. "Shaw thinks you are absolutely right. We decided that there may not be a prosecutable case against Hubert if he agrees to cooperate against the others."

A little later Leuci learned that Hubert was being transferred to Intelligence. Scoppetta and Shaw told him they had not instigated this. Leuci thanked them anyway, and rushed to tell Hubert.

"You ought to go to Intelligence," Leuci told him. "Work on big-time cases."

"I'd love to go to Intelligence." But Hubert's voice fell. "I'll never get there."

"Don't worry about it, Bill. You're going to get there."

When the transfer came through, Hubert phoned Leuci. "I don't know how the fuck you did it," he cried exultantly, "but I've just been transferred to Intelligence."

Some months later an enormous Mafia roundup was made by Hubert and several other Intelligence detectives. Attempting to buy his release, one of the Mafia figures handed over to Hubert and his partner $120,000 in cash. Hubert and his partner rearrested the subject on a bribery charge, and turned in and vouchered the $120,000.

Meanwhile, Leuci continued to suffer with Jim Sheridan, who stood constantly beside him, wanting to be friends. Leuci asked for a new partner, saying he wanted no part of Sheridan, a clod. But Sheridan was not a clod, Leuci well knew. He was a brave, tough guy. He invited Leuci to his home many times. Always Leuci refused. He showed Leuci pictures of his daughter, pictures of his wife. He talked about his years in the IRA. He had been in jail in Ireland as a revolutionary. He said that his ambition was to make enough money to get out of New York, "to leave this fucking miserable city and go back to Ireland."

Leuci kept trying to hold him off: He could not afford to become friendly with Jim Sheridan.

10

HIS THREE FORMER PARTNERS—Frank Mandato, Les Wolff, and Dave Cody—Leuci had scrupulously avoided for months, fearing to ensnarl them.

Once, early on, it almost happened. He had an appointment to meet Mikey Coco and was wired. He had just got into his car when the other door opened and Mandato jumped in beside him. All Mandato wanted was to ask Leuci to use his apparent influence to get Mandato back into SIU too.

"I can't talk to you, Frank," Leuci had protested, immediately turning the radio up loud. "I got to go up to the Bronx."

"I'll ride up with you," said Mandato, turning the volume down.

Behind them trailed the backup car, one IRS agent driving, the other adjusting the dials of the tape recorder that lay open on his lap, spools turning.

Leuci kept turning the radio up, Mandato kept turning it down. Leuci was trying to talk his ex-partner out of the car. Mandato wold not go. He didn't mind riding up to the Bronx, and he wanted Leuci to get him back into SIU.

In the Bronx Mandato moved to the back seat, and Mikey Coco slipped in beside Leuci. By then Leuci was in a panic, worried not only about what Mandato might say, but also about what Coco might say that Mandato might hear and not take action on. Dereliction of duty. A felony.

Leaning across Coco, Leuci turned the volume up as high as it would go.

In the back seat, as he grasped what must be happening, Mandato stiffened. Leuci saw this in the mirror. Beside him the gravel-voiced mobster merely spoke louder, his conversation overriding the music. But

Mandato in the back seat remained rigid, and spoke not one further word.

Leuci had stayed away from his former partners ever since.

But now a case they had made two years earlier brought them suddenly together again. The trial would begin the next day, and they were led into a small room in the Bronx County Courthouse by the assistant district attorney who would prosecute the case.

The D.A.'s name was Carl Bornstein. He ordered them to study their memo books, and to get their stories straight. This was an extremely important case, Bornstein told them, but there was a problem with it, a very serious problem about which he would interview them shortly. Bornstein was a young man with the smooth untroubled face they saw often on lawyers, and his attitude toward cops was familiar too, a combination of arrogance and contempt. Their case had become his case. He was the star now. He wished he didn't need them at all, but unfortunately he did need them. He needed their testimony. And he needed an explanation from them about this "problem."

Bornstein went out. The door slammed.

The four former partners looked at each other, and for a moment no one spoke.

Leuci had been hoping to be greeted with the warmth and intimacy of the past. From Cody, who was an older man and different from the other three partners, this was exactly the greeting he had got. But from Mandato and Wolff came a certain coldness, a certain reserve, and he looked into their faces and saw that they did not trust him. They seemed to be waiting for an explanation of some kind.

The tension became so pronounced that even Cody noticed it, and he began to glance from face to face trying to puzzle out what it was he sensed.

Mandato and Wolff were both thirty-six years old, five years older than Leuci, but Cody was forty-five. He was, in the police world, of a different generation. He had been in the navy in World War II, and often talked about "the war"—each time making the other three glance up sharply, wondering which war he was talking about. To them, Cody's war was ancient history.

Cody was a thin, almost emaciated man, and in contrast to most SIU detectives he wore out-of-date, baggy clothes. He slouched. He looked sickly, even undernourished, which perhaps he was. He had never married, didn't eat properly, and took many of his meals in bars. Since he had no wife or kids to go home to, he was the one whom the others often left behind to sit on surveillances half the night. They would leave him, saying, "Don't get hurt, Dave." They were always concerned about him, for he looked so frail. But in the macho police world, any expression of affection had to be tempered at once, and one of the other partners would always add quickly, "Because if you do get hurt, we'll be filling out forms for the next three days."

Mandato, with his sculptured black beard and expensive clothes, seemed more Jewish than Italian. He much resembled a young Jewish businessman. The son of a court stenographer, he had been among cops most of his life, and it was his father who had urged him toward the Police Department. Paper work bored him. So did early stages of any investigation, when he sometimes did not come to work for days at a time. But there was a certain brilliance about him. He was rich in ideas. Once Mandato borrowed a black detective as chauffeur, and hid himself in the trunk of a rented limousine in order to get inside a Harlem garage where narcotics were believed to be hidden in derelict cars.

The black detective parked inside the garage and went away. Mandato let himself out of the trunk and waited alone in the dark until the dealer, who was heavily armed, entered the garage and approached his stash. Mandato took him alone. No violence. No problem of any kind.

The stolid, hard-working member of Leuci's team had been Wolff, who often disapproved of Mandato and Mandato's ways, and said so. Both were muscular six-footers. Mandato was often taken for a Jew, and Wolff was in fact a Jew, but in dress and personality they were very different. Mandato dressed with considerable elegance. Wolff, though born and bred on the streets of New York, favored clothes with a western flair, much of it leather. He often wore boots, and sometimes looked like a cowboy.

For all of their differences, these four men had been, emotionally, extremely close. In police terms, they had been tremendously effective too—they put a great number of major narcotics dealers in jail. When, almost a year ago, their partnership had been dissolved for no very good reason by order of higher authority, all four had been filled with regret.

But now they were together again in a small room preparing to testify in an old case, and if there was suspicion of Leuci on the part of Wolff and Mandato, this was Leuci's own fault, and he knew it.

However, these tense opening moments passed. No one articulated them. Instead the four men began to discuss the old case that was about to come to trial; it was one of the best they had ever put together. It was an important case, but it was rich in laughs too, and as they discussed it their faces brightened, they began to chuckle, and the old warmth and intimacy began to reassert itself. They also knew what Bornstein's "problem" was, but they were not worried about this themselves.

The case was this. A man named Raymond Acervedo had owned a drugstore at 116th Street and Madison Avenue, out of which he sold principally quinine, the basic ingredient in narcotics mixing. He would sell quinine in thirty- or forty-pound sacks. Mandato, Wolff, Leuci, and Cody had begun an investigation of Acervedo, who, they learned, also owned a large drug discount store in the Bronx.

Presently the four detectives requested a legal wiretap on this discount store. When the wiretap was accorded, they set up their gear in a basement around the corner and, working in relays, they began monitoring Acervedo's calls. It was a good narcotics case. They felt professional. They were enjoying it.

But a call came in unrelated to narcotics. A rough,

Italian-sounding voice said, "Raymond, I'm going to come to your store tomorrow. I need your store only for a couple of days."

Acervedo had a quiet, almost faint voice, and he spoke in Hispanic cadences. He said he wasn't sure he understood.

"We need a place to unload a truckload of television sets."

The four detectives, eavesdropping in their basement plant, looked at each other in shock. The man was talking about hijacked TV sets, and they couldn't believe he would say such a thing right over the phone.

The Italian voice continued, "I don't know how many sets. Maybe three hundred television sets."

Acervedo's voice, showing panic, said, "I just opened this store. It's a drugstore. It's only open a couple of days."

The Italian voice said, "We'll be there tomorrow."

The four detectives stared at each other. A truckload of hijacked television sets was about to be unloaded into the middle of their investigation.

But they had no time to discuss this, for the tape spool began turning again, and they listened to Acervedo's plaintive telephone calls to friends. The Hispanic was nearly in tears. "These Mafia guys are going to come in and lay these television sets on me," they heard him say. "I don't know what to do with them. I got no room in the store. They are going to fill up all my aisles with television sets."

Silence. In the basement room the spool stopped turning. For a moment the four detectives were silent. Then the discussion began. Their narcotics case had just become a hijacking case. What should they do?

After checking out cameras with telescopic lenses, they talked their way into an apartment directly across the street from the drugstore.

The apartment was upstairs above a tailor shop, and it belonged to the tailor, an aged Jew whose language was Yiddish, not English. It was Leuci who convinced the tailor to hand over the keys to his house. Leuci never mentioned narcotics, nor Mafia, nor hijacked TV sets, for

these subjects might have terrified the tailor. Throwing in
Yiddish phrases, claiming to be a Jew himself, Leuci
invented a story about black revolutionaries who planned
a weapons drop here in this white neighborhood. The
tailor looked into the open, engaging countenance of
Babyface, and did his civic duty. He handed Leuci the
keys.

Once installed upstairs, the detectives began photo-
graphing everyone who entered or left the drugstore.
They planned, when the truckload of television sets
arrived, to film the entire scene. Simultaneously, one or
another of them would continue to monitor the tapped
telephone in the basement around the corner.

At four o'clock in the afternoon the truckload of
television sets arrived. What happened next was, to the
watching detectives, almost unbelievable.

The truck pulled up. Wolff and Mandato began taking
pictures. Three men got off the truck. Three others got out
of a car. Not one of them, the detectives judged, was
wearing less than a five-hundred-dollar suit. They began
unloading the truck, but they tired quickly. It was
amusing to watch. There were some kids in the street, and
they began hiring the kids to help them unload the truck.
They were moving all the television sets into the store.

When at last the truck was empty and the drugstore
full, they went across the street into the diner and ordered
coffee. While they were drinking it, a man in street clothes
came walking up the street. The detectives watched him
from the window. They made him as a cop at once, and
they watched with a kind of horrified fascination to see
what he would do.

Obviously he wanted to get a pack of cigarettes or
something from the drugstore. He tried the door, but it
was locked. It was the middle of the afternoon, and he
couldn't get into the store. He looked around and saw the
truck parked out front. He peered in through the
drugstore window. It was a drugstore, but he saw
television sets stacked up and down the aisles. Every place
he looked was television sets. There were television sets up
to the ceiling.

The plainclothes cop turned away from the window,

crossed the street to the diner where the six hoods were drinking coffee, and called in a ten-thirteen on himself: assist patrolman. About thirty seconds later one could hear the sirens. There were police cars coming from all over. The hoods must have been aghast, but their faces showed nothing. They simply paid their checks and vanished.

Within ten minutes there were fifty cops in the drugstore. The first arrivals broke the door down, went in, and found men in there from whom they demanded bills of lading for the TV sets. When these were not produced, the men were arrested—cops came out of the store dragging them in handcuffs.

After that more cars began to pull up. Not police cars, but Volkswagens, station wagons. Nearly every cop in the precinct pulled up in his own car, and they started lugging television sets out of the store. They were tying television sets onto the roofs of the Volkswagens, they were shoving television sets into the station wagons. Up and down the street television sets were being carried to their cars. There must have been fifteen private cars with cops in uniform behind the wheel. They were waiting in line to get the television sets.

Worse was to come. The detectives hurried around the corner to their wiretap plant, turned their tape machine to playback and listened horrified as one cop after another spoke into Acervedo's tapped telephone. They were spreading the word about the TV sets. A squad commander called his division commander: "Hey, I've got a television set for the office." There were twenty or more calls on the tape of cops phoning friends and relatives: "Get over here fast. I got a television set for you."

After turning off the machine, the detectives sat in stunned silence. All realized the implications. This tape was evidence, and would be presented in court whenever either the hijacking or narcotics case came to trial, at which time it figured to convict twenty-five or so cops of stealing television sets. Of course part of the tape could be erased, but what was left still would indicate that 300 television sets had been delivered to the discount drugstore, and that about half had subsequently been stolen by someone.

Their tape would be enough to start a big investigation. As evidence, it would convict cops. They had best get over to the station house immediately, and warn the commander. The commander would have to get those 150 sets back, and voucher them all. Most of all, he should keep the rest of his cops away from the remaining television sets and off the tapped phone.

But as the four detectives drove to the station house, they once again became concerned about their narcotics case. If they mentioned their wiretap in the station house, this information surely would get back to Acervedo.

"Let me handle it," said Mandato, and he strode into the station house.

But the commander was not there. In a few minutes, Mandato came out muttering angrily. "I had a conversation with the lieutenant on the desk," he reported to his partners. "A big Irish fucking jerk. I said to him, 'Get those TV sets back. The walls have ears in that place,' and he starts screaming at me. Where was I from? Who was I? I told him I was from Narcotics and that the walls have ears."

"This guy doesn't know that the walls have ears," said Wolff. "He's a desk officer. Let me handle it."

Wolff went into the station house. Presently he came out and got into the car. "He understands," said Wolff.

But apparently the lieutenant did not understand at all, for no sooner were they back at their plant and clustered around their tape recorder than the tapped phone was in use again. Another cop was in the store. After identifying himself, the cop said, "How much do you think a twenty-inch RCA is worth? What if I can get you one for a hundred dollars?"

Leuci cried angrily, "Didn't anybody in the station house tell these guys?"

Cody said, "Let's go back to the station house, and speak to that lieutenant again."

This time Cody entered the station house. He and the

lieutenant were the same age, and the lieutenant listened to him. When Cody came out he looked satisfied. "I drew him a picture," Cody said. "I told him to get those TV sets back. I told him the goddamn phone was tapped. I told him enough. Don't use the phone. We are watching the place, lieutenant. Keep your cops out of there and don't use the phone there."

A single patrolman was sent to stand guard at the drugstore. It was now early evening. Upstairs the tailor and his wife were at dinner, and so the detectives decided to discontinue surveillance from there—there was nothing further to see anyway, except a bored cop across the street in the doorway.

So they returned to their basement plant, and tried to decide what to do with their narcotics case against Acervedo, and with this new hijacking case that had just fallen full-blown into their laps. The hijacking case was very strong—they actually had photos of the conspirators unloading the truck into the drugstore, and they had the voice of one of them on tape.

Very carefully they erased from their tape all the voices of cops stealing TV sets. After that they continued to wait in the basement room. They were waiting for Acervedo.

Outside in the streets darkness fell. The hours began to pass. The four detectives munched sandwiches, and waited. It seemed logical to expect Acervedo. He had not been there all day. He would want to look over his store. He would want to see how the hijackers had stacked the TV sets. When he found the cop on guard, perhaps he would phone someone, speak a guarded warning of some kind. This would tie him further into the hijacking conspiracy. With leverage like that, maybe they could get him to talk about his narcotics connections.

Suddenly the detectives were listening to still another outgoing call on the tapped line. The cop on guard was phoning the station house. He wanted to speak to the clerical man, he told the switchboard operator.

The clerical man, from his voice, was an old-time cop. From the conversation that ensued, the eavesdropping detectives judged that he was this young cop's mentor.

The kid wanted advice from his mentor, because in the desk in the store he had just found $2000.

The advice the old-timer gave him was to put it in his pocket.

But the patrolman was a rookie still on probation, and he pointed this out to his mentor. He didn't want any trouble, he said.

"That money is your money," the old-timer interrupted harshly, and for the next few minutes he pressured the rookie to steal it. "Nobody will know you took it. Any of the people who work in the store could have taken it. There were narcotics cops in the place today, weren't there?"

"Yes," whispered the rookie. This was true. Mandato and Wolff at one point had walked across the street and watched in amazement as the television sets went past them.

The old-timer said, "The narcotics guys took the money. Those are the fucking guys who took it. Put it in your pocket. Is it in your pocket yet?"

"Okay, it's in my pocket, but—"

Rushing to the drugstore, Leuci and Mandato rapped on the glass door. The tapped phone was on the wall close to the door. They could see the cop through the glass. He was still talking to his mentor on the phone. He had his overcoat off. He was wearing his gun belt, peering out at them.

Leuci held his shield up against the glass.

The rookie cop hung up the phone, and opened the door.

Leuci and Mandato strode into the store. "I'm Sergeant Russo from Internal Affairs," Leuci said. "What do you have in your pocket?"

The rookie cop wet his pants immediately. Everything went. He stepped backwards out of the puddle. He grabbed at his hair. Weeping and blubbering, he begged them not to arrest him.

"The owner of this store has been paying cops for years," Leuci said. "We have his phone tapped. Every word you just said was recorded. You fucking moron."

The rookie cop, tears streaming down his face, begged them to give him a break.

It was Mandato who took pity first.

"Listen, kid," he said. "We're not from Internal Affairs, we're from Narcotics. But that phone is tapped and there is a district attorney who is going to listen to our tapes. How many times do we have to tell you fucking guys? Now take that money and put it back in the desk."

For the third time that day, the four detectives drove to the station house.

Behind the desk was the same lieutenant. "You know, lieutenant," Mandato said in an icy voice, "I told you this afternoon we were watching the place."

The lieutenant's tour of duty had ended hours earlier. He was still in the station house because he had packed a television set and was waiting for transportation to take it away.

"You don't have to tell me my business," he screamed. "Who do you think you're talking to?"

Mandato said, "I'll tell you something." He turned around so that his glance included every cop in the muster room. "I'm going to say it loud enough for all you guys to hear. If we had a pair of handcuffs big enough to put around this whole fucking station house, we'd take the whole bunch of you. You know we are watching that place, we're taking pictures, we've got a wiretap on the phone. I suppose you never heard of wiretaps? It never occurred to any of you that the phone was wired? Everyone of you jerkos used that phone. Now I want to know who was the clerical guy that this young kid was just talking to?"

No one spoke.

Leuci said, "You guys are a disgrace. You guys are so fucking bad. You should all go to jail."

The lieutenant began to apologize, but Leuci cut him off. "And get all those television sets back. How many did you voucher, a hundred twenty-five? It's on the tape how many sets there were."

The lieutenant said, "We'll never get them back."

"You better get them back. Someday somebody is

going to play that tape. They are going to hear about three hundred television sets."

The lieutenant said, "We'll try to get them all back."

Now it was two years later, and the four former partners sat in the small office discussing the case. Four of the six men in their photos had turned out to be major Mafia figures. One of the four had been matched by his voice to the tapped telephone. It was these four who were about to go on trial.

By now the four detectives had been, in effect, talking about old times an hour or more, and suspicion of Leuci had evaporated. Caution was gone. These were four very close friends who, until a year ago, had virtually lived together, had risked their lives together.

They recalled that, finally, only about 170 television sets had been vouchered. The missing sets had not been noticed; no investigation had ever been done. The whole case was really rather funny—though serious too, for they were about to put four Mafia hoods in jail.

Just then Assistant D.A. Bornstein reentered the office, and he began to talk to them about their wiretap, and about the tape-recorded conversations off Acervedo's phone that formed part of the evidence.

"There is something I want you to hear," Bornstein said. "You guys are experts on wiretaps, right?"

The four detectives, suddenly aware of what was coming, gazed attentively at Bornstein, trying to look innocent. Bornstein played the tape. They listened to the sound of an incoming call. There was a short conversation, after which both parties hung up.

There had been an underlying subsidiary sound on the tape also. They all heard it. Bornstein played this section several times, then said, "What the hell is that? There is something strange on the tape. Let me play it a little further."

They listened to another incoming call, under which was the sound of a slight hissing.

Leuci turned to Mandato. "What the hell do you think that is, Frank?"

Mandato said, "Defect in the machine."

Bornstein looked at him.

Dave Cody jumped to his feet and said, "I have to go to the bathroom."

As soon as Cody had slouched out of the room, Wolff said to Bornstein, "Dave was taking care of the machine that day. Once in a while he gets a little nervous, and he probably screwed up on this particular afternoon."

Bornstein said, "The defense attorney has listened to this tape, and he said that it sounded like an erasure to him. I have a problem with it. Because it sounds like an erasure to me, too."

"What the hell are we going to erase?" Leuci protested. "It doesn't make any sense that we would erase anything."

Bornstein pointed out that on the following day they would be asked to swear in court under oath that the tape had not been tampered with. "Are you all willing to do that?"

They said they were.

Later they talked it over, but only briefly. The erasure had to do with protecting the precinct cops only. Tomorrow they would deny the erasure under oath. This was perjury, but it was irrelevant to the case of the four hijackers. It was the type of perjury that detectives— especially SIU detectives—committed all the time in the interest of putting bad people in jail.

End of discussion. There was no way that Leuci could dissent from this group decision short of announcing that he was now bound by stricter rules than in the past.

And so they went out of the courthouse and across to a bar where they had some drinks, and all of the old warmth and comradeship was there for an hour or so. Then Leuci left them and went back downtown to report to Scoppetta and Shaw.

In Shaw's apartment he told them what had happened. He told them about the hijackers, about the stolen TV sets, about tomorrow's courtroom testimony. His hand on his chin, Scoppetta listened to Leuci's story. Sometimes he laughed. Sometimes he said, "I just don't believe it."

But it wasn't a funny story and he and Shaw were grim-faced before it ended. Because tomorrow Leuci would testify under oath.

"If you testify," Shaw said, "you're going to commit perjury. We can't allow you to do that."

The two prosecutors talked it over. They would have to begin an investigation into the stolen TV sets, that was clear, even though the case was two years old and might jeopardize Leuci's cover. Above all, Leuci must be kept off the stand tomorrow—and the other three detectives must be prevented from perjuring themselves also.

How were they to do this? At the close of the business day, they decided, they would drive to the Bronx to talk to District Attorney Burton Roberts. Roberts would have to be sworn to secrecy, of course. For maximum weight they ought to bring U.S. Attorney Seymour with them.

This was done. Their story, when they had told it, was followed by a stream of violent curses by Roberts. But after a time he calmed down, and it was he who worked out the only way possible to keep Leuci and the other three detectives off the stand.

"We're going to give these four hoodlums a misdemeanor plea," Roberts said disgustedly. "They've been after a plea for a long time. But we had them cold. Now we'll have to give it to them. That's it. We get a conviction on the books, and they walk."

The next morning the four detectives were waiting in a witness room when Bornstein entered and announced that the case was over. The people had decided to accept a misdemeanor plea.

Bornstein was not at ease. He seemed to look calculatingly at each face in turn. Apparently he had been told that a big investigation was going on, that one of these four men was involved in it, and so could not testify. Now he was asking himself: which one?

So the four detectives left the courthouse, and went out and had lunch together. In the restaurant Mandato never stopped watching Leuci. He sensed something that Wolff and Cody sensed also. During the meal, though all four men talked a good deal about the old days, the old warmth was not really there, and there were moments when the other men seemed to take a step back from Leuci, as if to say: We're not sure of you any more.

Lunch ended. Out on the sidewalk they all shook hands and called out, "Let's stay in touch."

Leuci drove away. The others watched him go. After a moment they too went off in separate directions.

11

AFTER DINNER in his Brooklyn Heights apartment, Shaw brought out a folder, and showed the photos of two enormously fat individuals whom he identified as bail bondsmen. Did Leuci recognize these men?

The detective responded cautiously that one seemed familiar. Actually, Leuci had recognized both photos. But he was watching Shaw carefully.

Shaw began to explain that these bondsmen, together with a third one, were reputed to be case fixers. They worked almost as a team, and they were part of what had become known to law enforcement as the Baxter Street Crew. Baxter Street ran behind the courthouse. It had one or two bars usually filled with cops waiting to testify, and above the bars were the offices of lawyers and bail bondsmen. Lawyers who worked out of Baxter Street were called the Baxter Street Bar. Many were ambulance chasers. Others, it was rumored, regularly bribed cops and other witnesses to change testimony. It was often said that the worst of the legal profession kept offices on Baxter Street.

According to Shaw, a South American drug dealer named Felix Martinez, who was in jail, had denounced these bail bondsmen. Martinez had been arrested by four SIU detectives, and his narcotics seized, and one of the bail bondsmen had come to him in prison. If Martinez would pay $110,000, his seized narcotics would come back from the police lab marked "no narcotics."

Martinez remained two days in jail while his wife scraped up $90,000 and turned it over to the bail bondsman. The following day Martinez was called into court and his case dismissed on the grounds that the physical evidence against him had proven to be not narcotics at all.

As soon as he was on the street again Martinez received a visit from the same bail bondsman who informed him that he still owed $20,000. Martinez protested that he had no more money, that his wife had borrowed from every relative, had scraped up every last cent.

The bail bondsman suggested that Martinez go back to pushing dope in order to come up with the missing money. Martinez had done so, and promptly been caught again by a different team of detectives. He was now back in jail awaiting trial.

Martinez's allegations against this bail bondsman were of little legal value, Shaw told Leuci, because they were the unsupported statements of a co-conspirator. Additional evidence would be necessary before law enforcement could move against this one bail bondsman, and it would be nice at the same time to move against all three.

Was there any way, Shaw asked Detective Leuci, was there even a one-in-a-million chance that Leuci could get inside this Baxter Street Crew, could expose and clean up the whole mess?

"Any chance at all?" inquired Shaw hopefully.

Leuci studied the two mug faces again. One, Nick DeStefano, was especially familiar, and he realized now that he had often seen him in the company of a detective named Nick Lamattina. It seemed to Leuci that Lamattina could be his entrée to DeStefano, and that DeStefano could be his entrée to the Baxter Street gang.

But he said nothing to Shaw or to Scoppetta, both of whom were watching him anxiously. Instead he promised to think about it, and to give his answer tomorrow.

The next morning Leuci sat at his desk at the SIU office and brooded about Detective Lamattina, who was not a SIU detective. In the past, any detective who had arrested a South American would sometimes find a note in his box saying: *Please call Nick Lamattina.* This had happened to Leuci only once. Subsequently he had met with Lamattina, who had said, "I know some people that are interested in this case. Do you want to sell the case?"

Leuci had considered Lamattina's blunt approach both stupid and insensitive. How did Lamattina know what kind of case it was, or how the arresting detective, Leuci, felt about it? Lamattina had never even sounded Leuci out. Just, "Do you want to sell the case?"

"I can sell my own cases," Leuci had answered with annoyance. "I don't need you to do that."

Now Leuci continued to brood about Lamattina, who was a friend of DeStefano, and about DeStefano, who was in tight with every corrupt lawyer and bail bondsman on Baxter Street. Studying a case folder at a nearby desk sat Carl Aguiluz, most of whose cases had involved South Americans. Had Carl ever had a note like that from Lamattina? Leuci wondered. Could Aguiluz tell him anything about either Lamattina or DeStefano?

Contrary to what outsiders seemed to think detectives never sat around recounting old scores, and in fact would recoil in suspicion from certain types of direct questioning even by partners. So Leuci, who had never worked a case with Aguiluz, knew of no specific past act of misconduct by the Honduras-born detective. He simply sensed that there had been some—no, many—such acts. It was an instinctive conviction based on small, scarcely perceived details, but it was so strong as to constitute knowledge— knowledge one could act on. If asked, Leuci would have been hard put to explain his conviction: it was based not so much on Aguiluz's nice clothes as on the way he talked, the way he walked. He moved with the assurance of a man with money in his pockets. Although there was a handful of honest detectives in SIU, Leuci was certain Aguiluz was not one of them.

"Carl, did you ever do anything with Lamattina?" The SIU euphemism, "anything."

Leuci was standing in front of Aguiluz's desk. He had decided to ask his question outright, and as he did so he was confident that Aguiluz would answer, for this was the type of question one detective could ask of another. It was a legitimate question. There was a reason for asking it.

Aguiluz glanced up sharply. Then thirty-six years old, he had been a cop for only seven years, but, because of his one astounding seizure, he had gained enormous fame. Before the seizure he had not even had a desk of his own, or else he had had to work at a desk in the hall. After it he was a star, and other detectives were eager to join his team. In SIU the detectives were always talking about "The Door." One day, all liked to boast, they would go through "The Door," and their lives and careers would be made. They would never have to worry again.

Aguiluz, almost alone among them, had actually been through "The Door."

For a moment Aguiluz studied Leuci, as if deciding how much to say. The two men were built somewhat alike—Aguiluz, who stood only five feet nine, weighed 190 pounds—and they even looked somewhat alike: black hair and eyes, dark skin. Leuci had a Sicilian cast to his face, whereas Aguiluz looked Central American, almost Indian, as if there were a faint admixture of Mayan or Aztec blood in his past.

"Stay away from Lamattina," Aguiluz advised Leuci now. "Him and Nick the Bondsman are unbelievable guys to deal with. Don't trust them. Do it any other way. Everybody that deals with them winds up getting allegations, because they are shaking people down after you have done your contract. They go back and ask for additional money."

Leuci was encouraged. He felt free to go after Detective Lamattina, a fellow cop.

"Thanks, Carl," Leuci said, and he meant it.

Aguiluz did not inquire why Leuci had wanted or needed information about Lamattina. In SIU a rigid code applied: no unnecessary questions were asked.

Without advising either Scoppetta or Shaw, Leuci phoned Lamattina and told him a concocted story, half of it true, half false: the drug dealer, Martinez, was cooperating with the prosecutors. A bail bondsman was involved. His information, Leuci said, came from a friend who was a corrupt agent working inside the federal attorney's office. Lamattina sounded eager, and agreed to meet him the following day.

So Leuci went back to Scoppetta and Shaw, and told them what he had done. The case was under way. Through Lamattina he would try to get close to the Baxter Street bondsmen.

"I told him there was a corrupt agent inside your office who wants to sell the case," Leuci added.

This amused Shaw. "That doesn't make us look good."

"I'm not worried about you guys looking good," said Leuci.

Scoppetta studied Leuci with a worried frown. He was always worried when Leuci made moves on his own, for this threatened Scoppetta's control of the investigation. In addition he had begun to worry about Leuci's safety, for the detective had been searched, or threatened with a search, several times already. Always, so far, he had managed to talk his way out of trouble.

Once he had gone to the Mafia hoodlums Louis Tolentino Sr. and Jr. He had arrested Junior the year before, and the case was now coming to trial. The Tolentinos were trying to bribe him through their lawyer. Suddenly Junior Tolentino had broken off the conversation with Leuci saying, "You're not wearing one of those things, are you? I'm going to search you."

This was in the street in the Bronx in front of the private garbage company the Tolentinos owned. As Junior's searching hand neared the microphone taped to the detective's chest, Leuci grabbed it saying, "That's not where you look. If you are searching a guy for a microphone, you grab him by the balls, because that's where he is going to hide it. He knows you are not going to pat him there."

So saying, Leuci guided Junior's hand toward his groin.

The drug dealer jerked his hand back, saying, "If you got it there you can keep it."

Scoppetta, listening to this dialogue on the tape later, had been profoundly sobered. How long could such luck last? And it had frightened Scoppetta when he looked across at Leuci and found the detective grinning with pride in himself. He was almost laughing. Now Leuci, wired for sound, wanted to walk in on the Baxter Street Crew, men who were considered extremely dangerous. Certainly they would, Scoppetta felt, want to search Leuci before talking to him.

Scoppetta had recently spoken with Bell and Howell.

New equipment was available, he told Leuci now. It was possible to fit a microphone into the heel of a shoe. There was a fake .45 caliber automatic with a transmitter in the handle where the bullet clip should be.

But Leuci objected. He preferred to leave his gun in his attaché case, he said, or in the trunk of his car. He preferred to walk about unarmed most of the time. He had no intention of carrying a .45, nor of sticking his foot in the mouth of somebody who was talking. He was happy with the transmitter he had been wearing. He had been able to talk his way out of every tight spot so far, had he not? What was there to worry about?

"That's what it's all about, Nick," said Leuci. "Anything that comes easy isn't going to be worthwhile."

The following day, Leuci met Lamattina as agreed at the information booth at the courthouse. It was noon, and crowds of people moved through the vast lobby.

Leuci's backup agent today was John Buckley, another IRS man. Buckley, newly assigned to Scoppetta, was a rumpled little man, only about five feet six inches tall, and over fifty years old. He had had a partial stroke, and was crippled in one arm, and his principal value was his inconspicuousness. Carrying his recording gear in an attaché case or gift-wrapped box, he could move in close. To any cop, bail bondsman, or lawyer who might notice him it would seem inconceivable that this little fellow could be The Man.

Lamattina and Leuci walked out into the street. It was lunch hour on a bright sunny day, and hundreds of people moved by them.

Up the street the two detectives entered a Chinese restaurant. It was empty. Leuci had expected crowded tables and considerable noise. When Buckley came in he would be conspicuous. The new investigation was not yet twenty minutes old, and Leuci had lost control of it.

A great fat man came into the restaurant and approached their table. Lamattina introduced him: Nick DeStefano.

Leuci and DeStefano shook hands. All three men then sat down, studied their menus, and ordered. When these details were taken care of Leuci repeated the tale he had already told Lamattina: that he had learned from a friend in the courthouse that the drug dealer was squealing. DeStefano himself was threatened.

DeStefano listened intently. Only when Leuci's narrative ended did he start to speak, but he was interrupted by the waiter setting dishes before them. Even before the waiter had gone, the fat man began to eat. He ate avidly, singlemindedly, and with considerable noise.

At the next table John Buckley was trying to consume four courses of Chinese food. The little man had his gift-wrapped box on the table. He wore grandma glasses, and every once in a while he would peer at Leuci.

Eventually DeStefano could eat no more. Turning to Lamattina, he said, "Maybe this guy can help us with the other thing."

The two men nodded at each other. Then Lamattina addressed Leuci.

"Look, there's something else we got going. It's very important."

He began to outline a narcotics case in which Leuci could earn immediately, if he would take part. If he would register a certain drug dealer as an informant and predate this registration by several months, he would be paid $6000. Two lawyers, the assistant district attorney, and the presiding judge in the case were also being bribed to see to it that the dealer went free.

"I'm going to tell you something that's even more important than these two cases we've discussed so far," said DeStefano. "Did you ever hear of a guy named Eddie Rosner?"

"Yeah," said Leuci, who had no idea who Rosner was. "I heard he's a fucking creep."

"Why did you say that? I know he has a bad reputation, but he's a good guy."

There was a case pending against Rosner for subornation of perjury, DeStefano explained. Subornation means to cause perjury to be committed. Rosner, a lawyer who often defended major dope dealers, would pay plenty to find out what was going on in his case, DeStefano added.

Leuci said he would talk to his friend in the courthouse.

"If I can help you and Rosner I'll be glad to do it."

In a state of considerable elation Leuci hurried away from the restaurant. It was an incredible beginning for any investigation, and he knew it. Everything anyone had ever thought about the Baxter Street Crew had been detailed in this first meeting. These people could get to judges, district attorneys, lawyers, cops.

Leuci did not realize then that the most important name dropped that night was Edmund Rosner. Rosner was the defense attorney who stuck in every prosecutor's craw. "Every era has a public enemy number one among lawyers," said an assistant U.S. attorney about this time, "and Rosner is ours."

Rosner was then thirty-five years old, and he was rich and successful. His specialty was taking heroin dealers that the government had cold—and then winning them acquittal. Rosner won case after case. He won many of them the same way—by bringing in alibi witnesses who swore that the defendant had actually been with them in some other place. Each time this happened the government screamed perjury, but no perjury could be proved. The defendant walked free. Rosner banked his big fee. And government lawyers huddled to see if they could not somehow prosecute Rosner for making a mockery of the law, of judicial procedure, and of themselves.

He was a large, somewhat overweight young man, with a slightly pockmarked face. His manner was arrogant. In court he strutted, he postured, he was loud—and he carried this performance to such lengths that his opponents conceived for him a physical distaste as well as a legal one. They called him obnoxious, a man (according to one assistant U.S. attorney) with a detestable face.

They saw him as standing constantly on the fringe of cases where witnesses appeared to have been bribed, where perjured testimony was apparently given. Other times witnesses had simply disappeared and at least one was believed by prosecutors to have been murdered to prevent his testifying.

Rosner was an affront to all they stood for.

The Hernandez case was, to them, typical. A federal

agent had made a direct undercover narcotics buy from Hernandez, a Cuban. Hernandez retained Rosner as his attorney. The case went to trial. It seemed open and shut, and at the end of a single day the government rested.

Rosner then called three defense witnesses. All three testified that Hernandez could not have committed any narcotics sale in New York that day for he had been with them in Florida planning a secret mission to Communist Cuba for the Central Intelligence Agency.

Shocked, the government attorneys requested a recess while they checked with the C.I.A. One of the three alibi witnesses was, in fact, a paid operative in the Miami area. All three of these alibi witnesses were lying, the prosecutors believed, but the case seemed ruined— Rosner was about to beat them once again, and they were enraged.

But Hernandez had got married around the time of the sale, and now one of the prosecutors, Dan Murdock, went down to the marriage license bureau, thumbed through hundreds of records and found that, on the day of the sale, Hernandez was not in Miami at all, but in New York getting a blood test to get married.

Murdock hurried into court and blew Hernandez's alibi to pieces. The dealer was promptly convicted. All three alibi witnesses were then put before a grand jury. All retained Rosner as counsel, and all refused to admit perjury or talk about Rosner.

Meanwhile, Hernandez was in jail, and he did not like it there. He retained Rosner to appeal his conviction for a fee estimated at $10,000. Time went by. Hernandez heard nothing about his appeal, and then he came to the conclusion that Rosner had never bothered to file it. Furious, Hernandez wrote a letter about Rosner to the presiding judge.

After interviewing Hernandez in jail, drug enforcement agents went to Miami, where they found witnesses willing to testify against not only Rosner but also against Nick DeStefano and Nick Russo, both of them New York bail bondsmen. According to this testimony, Rosner had sent DeStefano and Russo to Miami to bribe the Cubans to give the perjured testimony that was supposed to have acquitted Hernandez.

At last a case against Rosner. He was indicted for subornation of perjury, and Hernandez was released from jail on parole. The government appeared to have a strong case against Rosner, for not only would Hernandez testify against him, but so would Gilberto Pulido, one of the other Cubans.

But the trial was repeatedly adjourned at Rosner's request. Hernandez began to complain to the prosecutors that he feared for his life. He was terrified of Rosner, he said. Pulido was put into protective custody in time, but not Hernandez, who one day disappeared without a trace.

Immediately Rosner moved to go on trial at once, and now it was the government who was obliged to request one adjournment after another. Without Hernandez, a prosecutable case against Rosner simply did not exist—unless Leuci was about to develop a new one now.

When Shaw had heard Buckley's tape, he ran over to Leuci, and grabbed his hand. Leuci looked across at Scoppetta, then up into Shaw's intense face. The six-foot-five-inch Shaw said, "Bob, if nothing else happens except that we get evidence of what Eddie Rosner has been doing, we'll be happy." And he began to describe Rosner with some heat.

Scoppetta then switched the conversation. He wanted to know if Leuci had been searched.

"Lamattina didn't search me," Leuci said. He looked and sounded cocky. No one was suspicious and Scoppetta was foolish to worry.

However, when he lay in bed later, Leuci found himself brooding about the prosecutor's warnings, and he continued to brood about them, off and on, all the following day.

When night came he went to meet Lamattina. The meeting place was a bar in Brooklyn. Leuci stood out on the sidewalk waiting. At last the other detective came walking up. They greeted each other like old friends—which they were not—after which Lamattina gave a kind of embarrassed cough.

"DeStefano called some people," Lamattina said apologetically. "They said they didn't know if you could be trusted or not. I told him it was all bullshit, but he wants me to search you."

Leuci stared at him.

"I told Nick it was all bullshit," repeated Lamattina apologetically.

Leuci, thinking fast, supposed that once they were inside the bar, he would be invited into the men's room and told to open his shirt. This would take only a moment, and it would of course reveal any wires taped to his torso.

"Where is the sonuva bitch?" said Leuci.

"He's waiting inside."

They walked into the barroom. It was crowded. They walked down the bar. There were tables in the back. DeStefano sat at one of them. Looking like a fat, gloating Buddha, he watched the other two men approach. Behind his back were the doors to the rest rooms.

Leuci stopped in his tracks. He looked hard at Lamattina. "Go ahead and search me," he said coldly. "Search me right in front of him. I want to look at him, and when you don't find anything I'll knock him on his fucking ass."

"Don't get excited, don't get excited," pleaded Lamattina. "That will ruin the whole thing."

Leuci had one advantage and one only: body searches were an embarrassment on both sides.

"I'm supposed to search you without you knowing it," said Lamattina lamely.

Leuci gave him another icy glare. "How are you going to do that?"

"I know how to search somebody for a wire. Do you think I'm a jerk?"

At his table sat the fat bail bondsman, watching. On his face was an expression that could only be described as a smirk.

A few feet from the table Lamattina suddenly grabbed Leuci by the back of the head, as if with rough affection. He then—mimicking affection still—rubbed his hand across Leuci's shoulders and down his back, and then whacked him on the ass.

Still smirking, DeStefano looked at Lamattina and said, "Well?"

"The guy's not wired."

Leuci said, "If that's what you're worried about, let's skip it. I'll see you around." He started for the door.

But the other two men pulled him down into a chair. "I heard some stories," the fat man said. "People wonder about you. This whole situation you bring me seems too good to be true." His jowls moved. His head nodded up and down. "Too good to be true," he repeated.

Leuci shrugged, concealing his admiration for DeStefano's instincts. These instincts had been nurtured in dozens of shady deals. But DeStefano failed to heed them now.

"Okay," he said, and his voice changed cadence, "I've talked to Rosner. Here's what we want. We want the grand jury minutes of the rat who testified against him. And we want the thirty-five-hundred material."

"What the hell is thirty-five-hundred material?"

"That's witnesses' statements."

"I never heard of it."

"Well, that's what we want."

By law grand jury minutes were secret. So was thirty-five-hundred material.

"I don't know," said Leuci, "I'll ask my friend."

Lamattina glowed. He had brought DeStefano and Leuci together, and he was a part of it, and there was going to be money paid.

"Eddie wants to meet you," DeStefano said. He leaned forward, his great bulk pressing against the edge of the table, and in an instant he became no longer Rosner's partner, but Leuci's. "This is worth plenty to Rosner. It's important that you and I get together and lean on him. Eddie's got a lot of money. He'll pay a lot of money. You got the drift?"

Leuci returned late to Shaw's apartment, and made his report. Margaret was already in bed. Scoppetta sat there in a business suit. Shaw was wearing chino pants and a

T-shirt, and Leuci's report enraged both men. "This guy DeStefano is bad enough," said Shaw, "but Rosner is a cancer. It's unbelievable that a lawyer could behave that way. You've got to make this case, Bob."

But there had been no recording of tonight's conversations.

"Why weren't you wearing a wire tonight?" asked Scoppetta.

"Because I was searched tonight," Leuci retorted. "He could have found it easily enough. Look, I don't want you to tell me when I should or should not wear a wire. I can tell when I can wear one, and when I can't."

The next meeting took place in an Italian restaurant in Brooklyn. John Buckley sat at the table opposite with his attaché case on the floor. Leuci avoided looking at him, and never once did Lamattina or DeStefano even glance in his direction.

"I got another proposition for you," said DeStefano. He plucked a squid out of a dish, held it aloft on a fork, then plunged it as if for punctuation into his mouth.

That night five different corrupt situations were outlined—Leuci was asked to reach and pay off five different teams of detectives. DeStefano had commitments from defendants, all of them South American drug dealers, in all five cases, he said. More than $150,000 was involved. Principally DeStefano wanted testimony changed. But in other cases, just to be safe, he planned also to pay off the assistant D.A. prosecuting the case, or the judge presiding so as to get the case thrown out.

The fat bail bondsman thought of himself as serving the public good, he said. He was aiding South Americans who could hardly speak English. He would help such men. He would help them solve their problems.

The dinner meetings between Leuci, Lamattina, and DeStefano continued for most of a month. The three Italian-Americans gorged themselves on Italian delicacies, mostly pasta afloat in seafood. They mopped up sauces with bread, they swilled Italian wine. Night after night John Buckley took up position at the table opposite, or even at the adjoining table.

12

AT LAST to one of the Italian-American dinner meetings came Lawyer Edmund Rosner in person. Sitting down beside Detective Leuci in Ruggerio's restaurant in Brooklyn, he attempted to discern exactly how well connected Leuci might be—and once the lawyer became convinced that Leuci was very well connected indeed, he reiterated that he would pay good money for any secret material Leuci could get.

Rosner now relaxed, and as he sat at dinner with the other men he talked easily and fluently on a variety of subjects. Though not much older than Leuci himself, he was well dressed, well educated, obviously successful and prosperous. From time to time, when the conversation leaned in that direction, Rosner would berate the government, accusing prosecutors of abusing their privileges to execute the law. Rosner felt that he had every right to use any tactic available to him to defend his clients. He spoke aggressively, like a street fighter, but also with a good deal of charm. He even spoke of Hernandez, the missing witness in the case against himself.

"The government thinks I killed him," he said. "I didn't kill him. He's just hiding out."

As the conspirators consumed dish after dish of Italian specialties, and bottle after bottle of red wine, the conversation turned to Rosner's current big case, which involved one Alvin Bynham, whom the police believed to be the biggest black narcotics dealer in the country. This was a conspiracy case, and there were a number of high-ranking Mafia figures involved with Bynham. According to the indictment, the Mafia was the supplier, and Bynham the buyer, of vast quantities of heroin.

The case would soon come to trial, at which time the

government, Rosner had learned, would spring a secret witness on him. This witness's testimony would perhaps be devastating to Bynham. Rosner supposed it was a man by the name of Jack Stewart. Could Leuci find out who the secret witness was?

Probably, the detective replied. Then he added, "But you have to guarantee that he isn't going to get hurt."

Rosner got up from the table and walked some distance away. DeStefano glanced toward Rosner, and then at Leuci, and said, "Hey, there's no way we can guarantee you that."

Leuci muttered that he was not going to be responsible for getting someone killed.

The fat man's face grew dark. "The guy's an informant. He's a rat. He deserves to be dead."

Around midnight they came out of the restaurant onto the sidewalk. They were sated with food, good wine, and three hours of apparent conviviality. Negotiations were over. The deal was sealed. On the sidewalk there was handshaking, backslapping, and friendly laughter. When the other men had driven off into the night Leuci, trailed by Buckley, drove to Shaw's apartment.

Ripping the paper off his gift-wrapped box, Buckley set up the spools, and the men leaned forward, trying to separate the voices, trying to decipher the words, trying to hear Rosner offering the bribe to Leuci. There was Italian music in the background, people laughing, dishes clacking. The men were listening hard. "There—" Leuci said. "Hear it?"

But Shaw had heard nothing. The machine was stopped, and the same section played again—and then still again. Shaw listened and didn't hear it, and listened and didn't hear it. Six times Leuci played the incriminating words. "I hear it," Shaw shouted. "That time I heard it. That's his voice. That's him. It's there, it's there."

No money had changed hands. Legally this wasn't necessary. The offer alone was enough. There was evidence on this tape sufficient to convict Rosner of bribery.

Shaw moved about the room clapping his hands, grinning. "We got the son of a bitch." He slapped Leuci on the back. "You have done a fantastic service for your government tonight."

Perhaps a jury would not be impressed. It was best to reinforce the evidence, if possible.

So Leuci continued to meet with Rosner and DeStefano, usually at the same restaurant. At each meeting Rosner probed for secret information: witness identities, locations where witnesses were kept under guard, secret testimony against the dope dealers he represented. Also, he was trying to beat down Leuci's price for the secret documents in the government's case against himself. At one of these dinner parties Leuci handed over these documents. At others he was paid money—$2850 in all.

Also the detective was searched many times, by both sides. If it was expected that bribe money might change hands that night, then Leuci would be searched by one of the IRS agents, and the contents of his pockets noted, before he set out to meet Rosner. He would be searched again after leaving Rosner, and the extra money he now carried would be vouchered, and a memo made for later presentation in court.

Regularly Leuci was searched also by Lamattina, who was taking his orders from DeStefano. DeStefano continued to sense that there was something wrong with Leuci. At every meeting, the hair on the back of his neck would rise up. But he did not know what to do about it, other than to order Lamattina to pat Leuci down.

Leuci seemed able to guess in advance which nights he would be searched, and when Scoppetta or one of the IRS agents came forward with the equipment, he would hesitate a moment, then refuse it. It was as if he could measure from across the city the intensity of DeStefano's instincts. Later, in a barroom or restaurant, he would stand docilely while Lamattina quickly patted him down.

Lamattina was always surprised, at the conclusion of each search, to find that Leuci was unarmed.

"Where is your gun?" It was a cop's question. Lamattina asked it repeatedly. Cops came to feel naked without a gun's weight on their hips.

But Leuci's gun was in his attaché case locked in the trunk of his car. "If I'm working, I carry it. If I'm meeting guys for dinner, I don't. Besides, you have a gun. What do I need one for?"

This answer failed to satisfy Lamattina, or DeStefano either. It seemed further proof that Leuci was "strange."

Leuci decided to play on DeStefano's fear in an attempt to relax him.

"Let's not sit next to the jukebox tonight, because I am not getting any kind of recording."

"That's not funny," said DeStefano.

Leuci began to brag that he was indeed working for the government, and so was that barmaid across the room, whose transmitter was stuffed in her—

They all laughed, but DeStefano's laugh was dry.

To Shaw and Scoppetta, DeStefano's suspicions had become so intense they were almost visible. DeStefano was a sinister man. How soon before he ordered Leuci stripped, and found the transmitter?

Once he found it, what would he do next? Leuci wouldn't be able to defend himself because he didn't carry his gun. The two prosecutors had long since realized the awful responsibility they bore for whatever might happen to Leuci.

"Will you please carry your gun," Shaw begged. New York cops were obliged to wear their guns at all times, on or off duty. To be unarmed was a breach of regulations and it was also, in Leuci's case, extremely dangerous. "Carry it, please," said Scoppetta.

But Leuci continued to refuse, until Scoppetta began to believe that this refusal was part of the ambivalence Leuci felt toward his role. If he was found out by DeStefano—or any other subject—and if his duplicity was felt to be so heinous that the verdict was to kill him, then he chose in advance not to be able to defend himself.

DeStefano, never able to quiet his suspicions, kept calling people around the city, people he trusted: Do you hear anything about Leuci? Do you know anything about Leuci?

It was now October 1971. The Knapp Commission was

about to begin televised hearings. It was known that a number of cops, their identities still secret, would testify. Rumors began to circulate that one of these witnesses was Leuci. Once the rumor started, it began to acquire weight, for it sounded reasonable. Leuci was acting funny. He was avoiding friends from his past. He was seen in odd parts of the city at odd hours.

Leuci knew he was hot. In an attempt to negate the rumors, he began to make jokes about them. When the Knapp Commission hearings started, everyone was going to know who the rats were, he told people. The rats were going to come out from the woodwork. He himself was going to be the star rat, and he was planning to buy a new suit, and get his hair cut for his television appearance.

Scoppetta and Shaw had become extremely nervous. They wanted Leuci to drop out of sight until the Knapp Commission hearings were over and the heat had died down. They again insisted that he start carrying his gun. But Leuci, growing cockier, laughed at their fears. "We have this thing going now," he said. "Let's keep it going."

DeStefano, meanwhile, continued to place calls, continued to ask questions, and in this way he learned that a mystery witness would testify before the Knapp Commission, and would blow the lid off narcotics. The name of the mystery witness began with the letter B.

To DeStefano this information constituted solid proof. The mystery witness must be Leuci, and he should have paid attention sooner to the hairs crawling on the back of his neck. But it was perhaps not too late. He phoned Lamattina, and they set up a meeting with Leuci. Leuci should wear a suit, they told him. They would go to a nice restaurant and then maybe meet some ladies. They would meet on a street corner near Little Italy.

Leuci alerted his IRS backup team and also Shaw, taped his wires into place, and drove toward this meeting. He suspected nothing.

13

AFTER parking his car some distance off, Leuci approached the street corner on foot. DeStefano and Lamattina were already there. They looked agitated about something. They were circling each other. DeStefano's finger waved in the air. Lamattina's head was down, and he was shaking it back and forth.

As Leuci greeted them, he realized that for him this was a dangerous area of the city. It was a neighborhood full of brick-strewn alleys and empty loft buildings.

Immediately Lamattina put his hand on Leuci's back and began to rub in a circle, obviously searching for the wires. The dialogue that follows was recorded in the backup car, and is from the transcript.

Leuci said, "Are you guys all right? What's the matter?"

DeStefano said, "Bad. We're doing, we're doing bad."

"Bad? What's the matter?"

"Everything's wrong," said Lamattina. "Walk."

"What's wrong with you two guys?"

"Walk." Lamattina grabbed Leuci's arm, and turned him down Crosby Street.

"Walk," DeStefano said. "We've got to clip this guy."

"What's wrong with you two guys?"

Leuci shook loose from Lamattina. Recognizing DeStefano's panic, and his own peril, he began to glance around for his backup team. But he was being marched down Crosby Street against the traffic, and the backup car, unable to follow, had already lost visual contact.

To right and left passed warehouses, abandoned tenements, lofts. Leuci was not yet worried about being killed, only about being searched. They could drag him into one of these empty places, search him, and find the wire.

Scoppetta had been right. This was incredibly

dangerous. Why had he not listened? Why had he chosen to wear the wire today?

DeStefano said, "You know what we heard a little while ago?"

"What?"

"That you are a rat, and you are going to testify tomorrow."

"Yeah, right. Let me tell you something. I've been telling that to everybody in the office. I'm fucking them around. You got the same kind of fucking attitude as those guys in the office, understand. Leave me alone now. Wanna leave me alone?"

Leuci was trying to remain calm, but DeStefano's fear seemed contagious.

"Wait until after next week, if that's the way you feel about it," Leuci said. "This thing was a big fucking joke. These guys in this office are unbelievable. Forget it. Forget it."

DeStefano said, "Who you tell it to?"

"Everybody."

"Who's everybody?"

"I was in the office yesterday. There was seventeen guys in the office. Everybody says, hey tomorrow you gonna testify before the Knapp Commission, right? I said, yeah, that's right. Hey, hey, Nickie, you wanna do something? Just call up my office and talk to the trainee there. There were twenty people in there and I'm saying I'm gonna be the next guy to testify at the Knapp commission."

They had him by both arms. As they marched him along he realized that until now he hadn't seen the danger at all. How could he not have seen it?

Lamattina pushed him against a wall and searched him up and down, hands moving underneath the arms, around the chest. Before Lamattina's hands got inside his jacket, Leuci pushed him off. Lamattina said, "Where's your fucking gun, Bob?"

"You all may think it was a joke. I don't wear a gun."

"Where's your gun?"

"It's in my trunk, do you want to go get it?"

"No," Lamattina said.

"I never wear the fucking thing. I only wear it when I'm

working. All kidding aside, you really gonna give me a fucking attitude. I ain't kidding you, Nick."

They were holding him tight by both arms.

"I'm—I'm—really—no fucking joke. This bullshit, playing fucking games."

DeStefano stuck his finger in Leuci's face. "We're not fucking playing games here."

The two IRS agents, frantically trying to find Leuci, were moving further and further out of range. From time to time their receiver lost his voice entirely. There were gaps in the transmission of thirty-one seconds, eighteen seconds, twenty-four seconds. They were driving in circles, looking for him. The transmission gaps became longer: a minute and five seconds, four minutes fifty-seven seconds, seven minutes fifty-three seconds.

Leuci began to protest that, because he was due at any moment in court, he had to phone the SIU office, get someone to phone and get the case adjourned. This was the last time the case was on. If he didn't show up, the case would be thrown out, and he would get in trouble.

But Lamattina and DeStefano continued to walk him fast along the sidewalk and they were carefully looking over each tenement and loft they passed. It was broad daylight, and incredible, Leuci thought, that this could be happening to him. The streets were full of people but these two thugs were looking for a place to kill him and dump the body. But he was still a cop. They would have to kill a cop. They were not sure yet.

Leuci insisted that he had to phone about his court case. It was an argument which, to the bail bondsman DeStefano and to the detective Lamattina, had great weight. Besides, they needed a moment to talk to each other, and so Leuci was allowed to step into a grocery store to phone SIU. They stood close while he attempted to force a dime into the pay phone. At first he could not get the dime in. It was his intention to phone Shaw. There was no one at SIU he could turn to, or so he imagined, and Shaw was more likely to be in his office than Scoppetta. He would speak in code. He would tell Shaw that these two thugs were going to kill him. Shaw would save him.

But he misdialed, or else the phone was out of order.

He could not make it work. He tried again.

This time Shaw's secretary came on the line. "Mr. Shaw is out," she said curtly.

"It's Bob Leuci. This is very important."

"Who?"

"Detective Leuci. Sonny." Sonny was Leuci's code name.

"Mr. Shaw is out. How many times do I have to tell you? Don't you understand English?" She hung up.

Outside the grocery store, DeStefano and Lamattina again had Leuci by the arms, again marched him along. They had had a conference, and their indecision was over. That was the frightening thing. They knew what they were going to do, and where they would do it.

Leuci, talking fast, began embroidering on past stories, and inventing new ones. He realized he was groveling in front of Lamattina and DeStefano. Scared as he was, he was furious with himself for groveling, furious with himself for not having his gun. He wanted to blow his cover, tell them who he was, arrest both of them. Most of all, he wanted to live. He remembered something Mikey Coco had said to him one time, "Bobby, everybody cries before he dies."

In a moment he believed he would beg them to spare him. They were a couple of shits. Nonetheless, when they dragged him off the street into some alley, he would beg for his life. He glanced up at street signs, searching for something to save him. They had come into Little Italy now, and there on the corner of Elizabeth Street stood Alphonse Indelicata, the Mafia killer known as Sonny Red.

"Look," Leuci said. "Go talk to that guy. If he don't vouch for me a thousand percent, I'll go some place and you can pull the fucking trigger then."

"Don't go down asking for that," DeStefano said.

DeStefano and Lamattina eyed each other. Then, while Lamattina held Leuci tightly by the arm, DeStefano strode across the street and conversed with Sonny Red.

Sonny Red had been a contract hit man. In prison for first-degree murder, he had once hung suspended in handcuffs for two days rather than tell his guards the name of whoever had supplied him with sandwiches. There was testimony on record that he had once killed a man by driving an ice pick so hard through the victim's chest and into the floor that the body had to be pried up with tire irons.

Sonny Red and John Lusterino had been in prison together. Leuci had met him and done him a favor once. Did Sonny Red remember?

Leuci peered across the street. Sonny Red, his head down, stared at the sidewalk. DeStefano stood close to him, belly almost touching, talking urgently.

Leuci saw Sonny Red's head come up. The killer's eyes flicked toward him across the street. After a moment a grin came onto Sonny Red's face. That grin could mean anything. It's a nice kind of grin, Leuci told himself. At least a sign of recognition. Leuci saw Sonny Red nod to DeStefano, and then walk slowly away.

DeStefano waited for a break in the traffic, then waddled quickly across the street toward Leuci and Lamattina.

"I said to him, we think he's a rat, we think we should kill him," DeStefano reported. "He tells me, if you think he's a rat, then you should kill him, but if you kill him you better be sure he's a rat, because he's a friend of ours."

On Leuci's arm Detective Lamattina's grip softened.

The fat bail bondsman smiled warmly. "No hard feelings," he said.

They let Leuci go. He made it to a phone booth. The good guys wanted to kill me, he told himself. The bad guy saved my life.

He dialed Shaw's office a second time. The same secretary came on the line. He said, "You tell him that Sonny called and I'm going to be at his fucking house. Tell him I'm pissed, really really pissed. Tell him just like that."

"Mr. Leuci, Mr. Sonny—"

"Tell him. Tell him just like that."

Leuci got to his car. He drove across the Brooklyn Bridge, across the sparkling New York harbor. Outside Shaw's apartment he paced the promenade along Columbia Heights Street. He could see lower Manhattan, and most of the East River.

When he turned around he was looking at the third button of Mike Shaw's shirt.

"Mike, you are a fuck."

"I'm really sorry," Shaw said. "I'm really, really sorry."

"Those fucking guys nearly knocked me off. All you had to do was be there. Who did you go out to see, and how important was it? I nearly got killed."

Tears welled up in Shaw's eyes.

"Mike, you don't give a shit about me."

"Don't ever say that to me again," said Shaw. "I give you my word that this will never happen again. Whenever you need me, I'll be there. From now on. I'm so sorry. I'm so sorry."

A taxi pulled up, and out jumped Scoppetta. "Bob, are you okay?"

The three men went up to Shaw's apartment. "I want New York City cops with me from now on," Leuci said. "I was walking along the street with these two jerks, and those IRS agents didn't understand what the hell was going on. A cop would have seen it. A cop would have known what to do. I want New York City cops. These IRS agents are only worried about blowing the investigation. Cops would be worried about me. I want cops."

They were trying to calm him down. Shaw handed him a shot of liquor.

"DeStefano said to me that it was a good thing I showed up," Leuci babbled, "because they were on their way out to my house. My wife, my kids are out there alone. For all we know these sons of bitches have sent somebody out to my house already. I want New York City cops. I want this cop that lives across the street from me involved. I want some cops who know the streets."

The fear that he had controlled earlier he could control no longer. He burst into tears.

"I think it's over," Shaw said. "I think we ought to end it. You're too hot. It's too dangerous for you."

But Leuci immediately began to protest, "Let this Knapp Commission thing die down. The public hearings will be over, and I won't have been on them. Everything will be fine after that."

"You need a vacation," Shaw said. "We need one, too. I want you to take your wife and kids and go away for a couple of days."

"Where am I going to go?" Leuci said. "We never had a vacation. We wouldn't know where to go."

Shaw said he'd make arrangements. The cost would be on the government.

Scoppetta phoned Gina Leuci. In a soothing voice he assured her that everything was all right, but that her husband needed a rest. "We want you two to go away for a couple of days. We want you to make sure he goes. We want you to go at once."

This message terrified Gina. Close up the house and go. Take the kids and go. Immediately. Go.

Leuci left there and from the nearby Seventy-sixth Precinct telephoned SIU to check in with his boss, Sergeant Cohen—corrupt Sergeant Cohen whom he believed he despised.

He was not prepared for Sergeant Cohen's frantic voice. "We were afraid you'd been hurt," cried Cohen. "You didn't go to court. You didn't call in. Some cops saw you in the street with some rough-looking guys."

"I did have some problems with some fucking guys," Leuci admitted.

"Are you okay?" Cohen demanded. "Stay right there. Maybe those guys are still around. I'm going to bring help. Sheridan and I will be right there. Stay where you are. We're coming right away."

A few minutes later a car pulled up. Out jumped Cohen and Sheridan. When Leuci told them what had happened, that Lamattina and DeStefano had threatened to kill him because they thought he was going to testify at the Knapp Commission, Sheridan flew into a rage. He wanted to go after Lamattina and DeStefano. "I'll find those two sons of bitches and—"

"You're always kidding around like that," said Cohen to Leuci. "That's a serious thing. You've got the guys in the office upset. I know you are not going to testify. Jim knows you are not going to testify. But you shouldn't kid about it."

Driving home, Leuci thought about Sheridan and

Cohen, who were on their way to jail but didn't yet know it, and about how much he wanted to dislike both of them. But it was impossible to dislike them, especially Sheridan. Sheridan was so strong, and being with him made Leuci feel so strong. He was a big, physically strong man, an intimidating man, and it was an awful thing to betray him this way. And Cohen. How could he hate a man so willing to rush to his defense when needed?

By the time he got home, Gina had the kids dressed and the bags packed. She was ashen. It was then about six o'clock at night. She knew something was wrong.

They drove out to Montauk Point. Shaw had arranged for them to live in a kind of chalet on the beach overlooking the ocean. In front of the window was a sweep of sand dunes, and then the waves. Both found the scenery absolutely breathtaking. It wasn't summer anymore, and there was no one else on the beach. For hours they walked up and down the beach, and talked about their life, and about where Leuci's path would lead them. Once Gina said, "You got caught doing something, didn't you? That's why you are doing this thing."

Leuci shook his head. No, he hadn't been caught.

After a moment Gina said, "The most horrible thing that could happen is that I lose you. If I lose you like this, there is no honor in it for you." They stood on the beach gazing out to sea. "I know how you watch those inspectors' funerals on TV," Gina said, "and how carried away you get with it all. If those two men had killed you, there would be no inspector's funeral for you. You would have been described as a corrupt cop who was caught in a bad situation."

Leuci thought about it. "That's not true. They would have had an inspector's funeral for me."

"No. How could they have an inspector's funeral if you were killed by another cop? They wouldn't do anything. The politicians would be explaining you for three weeks."

Leuci thought about this. It was perhaps true. "What makes you think it's important for me to be buried in an inspector's funeral?" he asked Gina.

"I know you so well. You look forward to your death,

and this whole business of having that kind of funeral. But I don't look forward to it."

Once long ago he had told her that if he had to die young, he wanted to be killed in the line of duty. He didn't want to be killed in an automobile accident, or a plane crash, or fall off a goddamn sailboat and drown. If it was meant for him to die young, then he wanted to die among his friends. He had said that to her never thinking she would remember.

They talked about what they would do when this job was over. Leuci told her then something of what he felt, even though he still had not been able to explain it very well even to himself. But he wanted to feel clean again. He wanted his former innocence back. He wanted to feel about being a cop the way he had felt at twenty-one when he first came out onto the street wearing his blue uniform.

He told his wife that he was totally committed to this road he had taken, and by the end of the weekend Gina was very much in his corner. By then, romping on the beach with the children, Leuci was relaxed enough to laugh, to fool with the little ones, to do impromptu dances on the sand with his wife. Once Gina said, "The Bob Leuci I knew is gone. We haven't laughed and kidded with the children like that for months and months and months. I want you to see this whole thing through and be proud of yourself again. Then you can laugh again all the time the way you used to."

This was the first time Leuci realized how grim he—like his life itself—had become.

On television they watched the Knapp Commission hearings. The secret witness was indeed a corrupt cop whose name began with B: Patrolman Bill Phillips.

The hearings ended. The Leucis' days at Montauk Point ended also, and they drove home. It had been a super weekend for them both, and for their marriage, and it was also a super weekend for the investigation because the Knapp Commission hearings had taken place and Detective Bob Leuci had not appeared to testify. When he reported to the SIU offices the following morning, everyone was glad to see him again, and the heat was off.

14

FOR THE REST of the year Leuci went on working full time at SIU. He was still team leader. It was his job to select the targets his team would zero in on—a steady succession of targets—and now he selected a man named Peter Corso.

As with most SIU targets, the selection of Corso was accidental, almost arbitrary, but from the moment that selection was made, Corso became a man with problems. He had three highly skilled detectives after him. They intended to pin something on him, narcotics if possible; otherwise—anything. His chances of escaping were slim.

Some months previously a convict serving a long sentence on narcotics charges had asked for an interview with Leuci. The convict had wanted to trade information on his former colleagues. He wanted a reduced sentence, and he had mentioned Peter Corso. Corso, the convict said, regularly moved big packages. Leuci, who was not even in SIU at the time, had done nothing with this information. Leaving the convict to rot, he had merely filed away the name. Now, needing a target, he brought it out.

Where to find this Corso? A check of SIU records showed he had been in jail, but was out now. The state parole board said he had not reported for months. The parole board, supposedly, was looking for him. They provided Leuci with a recent picture, and with Corso's last known address, a brownstone house in Brooklyn.

The thing to do then was to begin surveillance on Corso's house, where his wife and children still lived. The team, Leuci decided, would watch the house for a full week, ten hours a day. It was Leuci's hope that, in the course of a week, Corso might return to visit his family.

Sitting in a parked car opposite Corso's house and some distance up the street, the three detectives—Leuci, Sheridan, and a new man named Stanley Glazer—began their watch. The hours began to pass, and then the days. They relayed each other. Sometimes two men sat in the parked car, sometimes only one.

It mattered little if the presence of the detectives was noted and caused talk in the neighborhood—the subject, after all, lived elsewhere. Still, basic precautions were taken. If a detective watched alone he sat on the passenger side of the car, as if waiting for the driver to return. Two detectives would sit one in the passenger seat and one in the back. Same thing.

Six days passed. Around noon on Sunday morning a car pulled up; and a man climbed out carrying what looked like a box of Italian pastries. He was well dressed, and he walked without hesitation straight into Mrs. Corso's brownstone.

The detectives on watch were immediately excited. Although stationed too far away to see the man's face, they were sure this was Corso. They waited outside for four hours. When Corso at last came out of the building, they tailed his car across the bridge into Manhattan. Once they pulled almost alongside—close enough to match his face to the picture they had. Peter Corso. There was a good resemblance. It was probably the same man.

They tailed him to a building on East Seventh Street. He got out of his car, locked it, and entered the building. Five minutes later Leuci sauntered into the lobby. His eye ran down the names on the mailboxes. He didn't expect to find the name Corso. He did expect something close. One name stood out—Peter Carbone. People living under aliases almost always chose something close.

One week had already gone into this surveillance. Now they decided to invest another in tailing the subject through the streets.

But during that week, nothing happened. They took Corso-Carbone to a few bars on the East Side, and to a particular bar near his house. They watched him smoke some pot. He was an older man—close to 60—but was behaving like a kind of hippie. Usually he was in the company of a very beautiful girl, and he seemed to be trying to pretend he was her age. The detectives recognized the pattern—Corso had been in jail for a long time and now, in the street again, he wanted to be part of the new scene. His behavior was ridiculous, but also sad.

The second week ended. Corso had talked to people in bars, but there had been no furtive meetings that might have been drug transactions. He had met no one who gave the appearance of being a big-time drug dealer.

After a conference with Sergeant Cohen, the decision was again made to put in an illegal wiretap. The reason was the same—it was the only quick, simple way to see if Corso was doing any narcotics business. Leuci, Sheridan, and Glazer went down into the basement of the building on Seventh Street. Leuci found and branched into Corso's wires, hid the self-starting tape recorder in a closet, and they went back up to the street.

Now the surveillance of Corso was considerably easier, for the tapped line informed them of his movements in advance. The man kept strange hours: he was out most nights till dawn, and then slept all day. The three men stalking him arranged their schedule around him.

Corso's beautiful girl friend, called Poopsy, had moved in with him. It was Poopsy's habit to get on the telephone and talk for hours. The detectives considered her a total moron, but they learned more information from her rambling conversations with girl friends than from calls Corso made. Corso was an old-time Italian hoodlum. On the phone he was guarded. Whereas Poopsy would tell everybody where they had gone the night before, whom they had seen, and where they planned to go next.

A good deal of telephone conversation concerned Corso's son-in-law, a man known as Jack. We saw Jack last night at the Copa. Jack looks terrific. We were with Jack last night—Jack seemed increasingly interesting, but the eavesdropping detectives couldn't identify him.

From these same phone conversations the detectives gathered that Corso had two daughters. They would occasionally phone their father. It was Frances who was married to Jack. The detectives were puzzled. They decided that the missing ingredient must be the son-in-law, Jack.

One day Frances made a collect call to her father's house. She identified herself as Frances Bless. The name rang a bell with Leuci, who had by now been a narcotics detective for most of eight years. He looked up Jack Bless in the SIU files, and cross-checked with the Federal Narcotics Bureau.

The first name was spelled Jacques. Jacques Bless was listed in both places as a major narcotics dealer and as a close associate of Spanish Raymond and Anthony Angeletti, major dealers from East Harlem. His French first name was an affectation. Bless was of Hispanic origin. He was alleged, in police circles, to have ordered and/or participated in a number of killings. He had been marked "extremely dangerous."

The case, now in its fourth week, was starting to come together, and the three detectives were extremely excited. However, they still had overheard no conversation involving narcotics nor had Corso made contact with Bless.

But one night the following cryptic telephone call came in:

"This is Johnny from Brooklyn. Hey, I ran into somebody. It sounds like something very nice. These people have a lot of money."

"We'll meet tonight," said Peter Corso.

An address was specified, but as old Peter Corso left his house that evening, Leuci decided not to tail him. "This looks really good, whatever it is," he said. "I don't want to take a chance on blowing it. Let's wait right here."

Some hours later Peter Corso returned. The three detectives gave him time to get upstairs, then hurried down into his cellar. Corso made just one telephone call—to his son-in-law, Bless. The three detectives listened as he made it.

"This is your father-in-law calling."

"If you got something to talk to me about," said Bless, "come up to my house. We'll talk about it."

Corso left his house, got into his car and, tailed by the three detectives, drove to an elegant apartment building on the Upper East Side. As the doorman took Corso upstairs in the elevator, Leuci checked the bells and found the name he was looking for: Jacques Bless.

In their own car, the detectives talked it over. They had identified Bless's address. They had Corso meeting Bless. There was apparently some kind of a deal going down.

The following day, crouched over their tape deck in Corso's basement, they listened to Corso talking to Bless, and heard Corso order "three shirts." As far as the detectives were concerned, this meant three kilos of heroin. They were as eager as rookies. What else could it be? Three ounces? Three-eighths of a kilo? No, it was three kilos. Jacques Bless was not going to get involved with anything less.

So they hurried to court, where they applied for and were accorded search warrants for Corso's house and Bless's house both. Before executing the warrants, they made a final check on the tape recorder in Corso's basement. There was only one brief conversation on the tape: Corso and Bless would meet in a few minutes at Jack's Barbershop on Sixty-ninth Street and Madison Avenue.

With the three kilos? Without? And what did "in a few minutes" mean?

The detectives had no notion of how old this conversation might be, and so they sped hurriedly uptown toward Jack's Barbershop. There, however, they found no one except barbers. No Corso. No Bless. Nobody waiting on the corner. And no heroin.

It was noon.

Back to Corso's apartment. Three o'clock passed. Four. Repeated checks were made on the tape in the basement, but no new calls were registered. The detectives sat hunched and despondent in their car. Dusk fell, and then it was night. There was no sign of Corso, and no conversation on the phone. At last two calls did come in. They were widely spaced. Both were from Jacques Bless to Corso's girl friend, Poopsy: Have you heard from Pete?

But no one had heard from Pete.

At midnight the detectives were still there, waiting. And they were ducking into the cellar with ever greater frequency. At last a call came in. "Are you sitting down, Poopsy?" asked a woman's voice. "I have some bad news."

Poopsy began screaming, "They have killed my Pete!"

"No, no, it's worse. He's been locked up. So has my Ralphie."

"No, no! Pete's on parole. I'll lose him forever."

The three detectives were first shocked, then terribly disappointed. Who had arrested Peter Corso? The cops? The feds?

They trooped disconsolately back to the SIU office, where their first job was to find out who had arrested Peter Corso. They phoned around. The answer turned out to be the Joint Task Force, and the arresting officer had been Detective Joe Nunziata.

The Joint Narcotics Task Force of detectives and federal agents was a small elite unit that had been conceived as a kind of super SIU. It fed arrested dope dealers into federal courts, where they were tried promptly under the strict, new federal laws. The Task Force was heavily funded, and one of the first SIU detectives assigned to it had been Joe Nunziata.

At one o'clock in the morning, Nunziata and Leuci sat opposite each other in a diner on West Street. Nunziata, who was then thirty-nine, wore a suit and a topcoat, and with his graying hair he looked like a prosperous business man. Both men had been working now all day, but Nunziata appeared fresh, whereas Leuci was bleary eyed. The two men ordered coffee.

Leuci was there to worm information, if he could, out of Nunziata. Leuci and his team had just lost Corso to Nunziata, plus what had turned out to be three kilos of pure heroin. But Bless was still at large. Leuci wanted to know if Nunziata was onto Bless too. The difficulty would be to find this out without having to give up Bless's name.

"We were on Corso," Leuci began. He stirred his coffee. "We were wondering how you happened to get on him?"

Nunziata, grinning expansively sat back and blandly

announced that Corso's heroin had come straight from Little Italy—"from The General and Sonny Meatballs."

Leuci, knowing it had come straight from Jacques Bless, nodded. "That's what we thought too."

At one time Nunziata, who was eight years older, had been Leuci's mentor and almost, in a Police Department sense, his father. The relationship between them was still very close—affection on Nunziata's side, admiration on Leuci's. But as they sipped their coffee in a cheap diner in the middle of the night, they went on sparring with each other.

They had first met eight years previously, when a mass of demonstrators had converged on a precinct station house being guarded by a single patrolman, Robert Leuci, aged twenty-three. One moment Leuci had stood between the mob and the station house door, and the next he was on his back in the doorway, and they were trampling him. One demonstrator had Leuci by the neck and was banging his head against the floor.

Just then about twenty cops on horseback came galloping down the street. The demonstrator pummeling Leuci let out a scream, went flying backwards into the wall of the station house, and remained pinned there by the butt of a police horse. The horse was halfway up the station house steps, and the cop in the saddle, Patrolman Joe Nunziata, looked down on Leuci with an enormous grin, saying, "Are you okay? Are you going to take this collar?"

"He's my collar," Leuci said. "I want him."

"Let me just take some of the wind out of him first," said Nunziata, and he pulled back on his horse. The demonstrator let out a muffled scream and collapsed to the ground. "I'll see you around," said Nunziata, grinning, and he galloped away.

Once both were in Narcotics they worked cases together, made arrests together, dined and drank together, and Leuci fell somewhat in awe of the older detective's style and skill. They were not partners. Nunziata had a steady partner, and Leuci's was Frank Mandato. Later, when Leuci moved up into SIU,

Nunziata, who was already there, asked him to join his team. But Leuci refused because he wanted to be a team leader himself. As the years passed, the two men had become even closer friends.

But rivals, too.

Leuci, now stirred his coffee. "Do you know who Corso's connection is, Joe?"

"Yes. Do you?"

"Yes."

Nunziata was grinning fondly at his former protégé. "Are you going to tell me who it is?"

"No. Are you going to tell me?"

"I don't think so," said Nunziata affectionately.

Leuci left the diner convinced that Nunziata knew nothing about Jacques Bless, that he had been investigating someone else and had dropped Corso almost by accident; and this is what he reported to Sergeant Cohen and to Sheridan and Glazer a few minutes later. Though they had lost Corso and three kilos of heroin, they might still make a case against Bless.

They still had their search warrant, but they couldn't decide whether to serve it now in the middle of the night or not. Sheridan wanted to ride uptown and kick Bless's door in. They would find whatever they might find. To this plan the others presently agreed.

An hour later all four men were parked across the street from Bless's apartment building. They could see the doorman in his uniform standing behind the glass doors. They were calmer now and were having second thoughts about kicking Bless's door in. It was unlikely that a man like Bless would keep any heroin in his house. If he had stayed untouchable until now, it was because he never handled narcotics himself.

So what was the best thing to do?

"I think," said Sergeant Cohen, "that Bless would be interested in buying our tapes of him talking to Corso."

This produced excited conversation inside the car. Bless didn't know the wiretap was illegal, all agreed. He would think the tapes put him in the middle of the conspiracy. They could threaten to turn the tapes over to

Nunziata and the Task Force unless he paid them. Cohen paused a moment, then added, "Now we are talking about big money."

Sitting in their parked car, watching the doorman through glass across the street, the detectives talked about money. It seemed to them that Bless might be willing to pay up to $50,000 to have the tapes destroyed.

That was the price decided upon: $50,000. The other three appointed Detective Leuci to sell the tapes to Bless on their behalf. Leuci was the most experienced and also the most devious among them, and surely he would be able to work out a way to contact Bless and to complete the sale.

And so, the long day ended. They put away their search warrant, turned from Bless's house, and went home to bed.

Leuci reported all this to Scoppetta and Shaw the next morning. The story excited them, and they ordered him to go through with the sale. There seemed, they said, a real opportunity here to nail Bless for bribery—which was important, because the man had proven immune to the narcotics laws. And to nail Leuci's three partners for bribe receiving, of course.

Fifty thousand dollars. The case was so important that five men—Scoppetta and Shaw on one side, and Cohen, Sheridan, and Glazer on the other—began to press Leuci every day: Have you managed to contact Bless yet? How soon will he come up with the money? But contacting Bless proved not so easy to do.

15

IT WAS NOW Christmas 1971. Ten months had passed since Leuci's first conversations with Scoppetta.

One night when Leuci appeared for dinner at Shaw's Brooklyn Heights apartment, a man he didn't know was already there, sitting on Shaw's sofa with his shoes off and his feet up. He introduced himself as Andrew Tartaglino.

The Leuci investigation was about to move onto a new and higher plane.

"I've heard all good things about you," Tartaglino said to Leuci. "The bad things that I've heard over the years I think I'm going to forget about. I like to hear these new good things."

Tartaglino was a small man. There was something careful and immaculate about him. He spoke softly, almost monotonously. Hardly anyone, meeting him for the first time, suspected the force that drove him, and he did not seem a man to fear. Most of the people he had put in jail had not feared him until it was too late. Certainly Leuci, who had never heard of him before, did not fear him now.

Tartaglino was Number Two man in the Federal Bureau of Narcotics and Dangerous Drugs. His specialty was integrity. He was often called the finest integrity agent the United States had ever produced. Those who hated Tartaglino, and they were many, accused him of being obsessed with corruption. When he found it he would crush it, and the people involved in it, too, according them no sympathy, no understanding, and no quarter.

Tartaglino, then forty-six years old, had graduated from Georgetown, had served as a U.S. Navy lieutenant, and had then become a narcotics agent. After four years

121

assigned to New York, he had spent five years in Italy and
France—he spoke Italian fluently—attempting to crush
the New York drug trade at its various sources. Returning
to the United States, he had moved quickly upward in
rank.

Four years previously he had heard Leuci's name for
the first time. An integrity unit under Tartaglino had been
sent into New York to root out corruption among federal
narcotics agents. The investigation was so sensitive that
only senior people were chosen to work under Tartaglino.

There was a direct relationship between the rise of the
drug traffic and failure to combat corruption, Tartaglino
believed: "I could map you a graph showing the direct
parallel between the rising heroin traffic in the nineteen-
sixties and the lack of effort to fight corruption. New
York City was the hub of it all."

In New York in 1967 Tartaglino began arresting men
he knew intimately, men whom he had gone through
treasury school with. It was said that, in a cold-blooded
business, Andrew Tartaglino was the most cold-blooded
of all.

Technically, Tartaglino was investigating corrupt
federal narcotics agents only, but one case led him directly
to Detective Frank Mandato, and from there to
Mandato's partner, Leuci. Tartaglino cut the case in half,
as was the policy at that time, and turned his
Leuci-Mandato material over to the Police Department,
where it was vaguely investigated, then dropped.

Leuci had been just a name to Tartaglino. He never met
him. But it was a name that recurred, and the name
Babyface recurred also. There may have been more than
one Babyface, but Tartaglino did not think so. Anyway,
prior to tonight's meeting he had refreshed his memory by
reading through the Leuci file. He was aware that Leuci,
in admitting to Scoppetta two or three acts of minor
misconduct, had vehemently denied participation in the
drug traffic itself; he said he had never bought or sold
drugs. But Tartaglino's intelligence file—and his memory
as well—indicated otherwise. Tartaglino had no proof.
He did have solid suspicions.

Tartaglino, sitting at dinner in Shaw's house, had chosen not to reveal to Scoppetta and Shaw that he believed Leuci to be a villain, because, in a world of trade-offs, the villain, now, could be extremely useful to him. Tartaglino was considering taking over the funding and staffing of the Leuci investigation, and directing it himself. The purpose of tonight's meeting was to get a feeling both for Leuci and for the new directions in which Tartaglino might point him.

A few days later Shaw handed Leuci a government travel voucher and told him to fly to Washington to see Tartaglino a second time. The experienced detective was immediately fearful. He had never been to Washington before. Why was he being summoned?

In Washington he was ushered into Tartaglino's office, and it impressed him tremendously. Tartaglino, who was on the phone with a senator, gestured Leuci toward an armchair. Leuci gazed about him wide-eyed. Machines standing against the wall provided direct link-ups to many of the major cities of the world. Tartaglino's desk and filing cabinets were in the next room—this room contained only a couch, armchairs, a sideboard, a television set. Leuci had never before known a man who occupied not an office, but a suite. This guy is not a nobody, he told himself. This guy is an important guy.

Tartaglino took his shoes off, sat on the couch with his feet up, and began to explain that he had agreed to commit men and funds to Leuci's investigation. He would bring in an agent from Saigon, he said, and another from Dallas. He would bring other good agents in from elsewhere. Leuci, henceforth, would not be alone. He would be surrounded by many of Tartaglino's best men. Tartaglino himself planned to spend a good deal of time in New York.

"We also have an undercover guy," Tartaglino said, watching Leuci carefully. "We would like to put him with you as soon as possible."

There was a heavy silence. They're going to push me out, Leuci thought, and bring in their own undercover guy.

Even before he could articulate this thought, Tartaglino said, "Don't think what you're thinking. You're the guy that knows this setup. We may bring in another undercover guy, if you agree, just to help you in a couple of situations. He's an Italian." The two Italian-Americans nodded at each other. "He's very bright. He's stationed in France right now, but we would like to bring him in, if you'll agree."

Tartaglino put his arm around Leuci. "Let me drive you back to the airport."

But the detective, unwilling to take up the time of such an important man, declined. He would take a cab. On the plane back to New York Leuci brooded. Tartaglino was bringing in agents. The investigation had moved out of New York. The federal government was running it now. Henceforth, Tartaglino had assured him, he would be flying to Washington frequently. It was still his investigation, though. It had merely gotten bigger. he felt extremely heady. He felt like James Bond.

When he got home he recounted the entire experience to Gina. He was filled with excitement, but Gina began shaking her head.

"This started off small," she said. "Now it is growing into something very big, very important. The more important this investigation gets—don't you realize—the more important you are going to be. The more important it will be, maybe, to hurt you."

"Who's going to hurt me? No one is going to hurt me. Why should anyone want to hurt me?"

Tartaglino wanted to know everything Leuci was doing, and he began to study each segment separately, and then he began to bring in his own agents, one from Tokyo, others from Europe. He moved in some female agents to take over surveillances. He provided the investigation with new cars, new wire transmitters and recorders, and two cover apartments, one in the Stanhope Hotel and the other in a private apartment house on Sutton Place. These were fancy luxury apartments; when they were not being used for conferences and debriefings, Tartaglino's agents slept there. Tartaglino himself came often to New York, and he summoned Leuci regularly to Washington.

To Shaw and Scoppetta he seemed the most creative law enforcement man they had ever known. They were dazzled by him and by his ideas.

"I believe in testing people," Tartaglino told them. "If you have allegations against a certain agent or police officers, you can test that man. You can create a set of circumstances that are not real.

"For instance, suppose an officer told you that he participated in a raid with three other officers; they kicked the door in, and there was a lot of money, and a lot of drugs, and they cut the money up—I think you can test those other three officers. You can cause those officers to go through the same type of raid again, to see how they would react. You can set up an apartment with heroin and counterfeit money. You can put one-way mirrors in there, and wire the room up, and cause them to raid it—you can cause that to happen. Now the raid in question may also serve to exonerate them. You know exactly how much money was put in there, the quantity and purity of the drugs, and you can watch to see what ends up vouchered with the property clerk. You know what was in the room. You know whether these officers are honest or not."

"As an investigative technique, this one has been very, very successful in the past. It has been the basis for many prosecutions."

The more Tartaglino studied Leuci's operations so far, the more he focused in on a Queens sergeant named Peter Perrazzo.

Leuci, during the past several months had made a number of recordings with Perrazzo, for whom he had once worked. Perrazzo had bragged about being able to fix the Brooklyn district attorney's office, and also the Queens district attorney's office. But he could not be indicted or prosecuted, because it was all talk—so far. Leuci had waited for the conversations to turn into action, for Perrazzo to take him somewhere. But this had not happened.

It was Tartaglino's idea now to have Leuci move

someone else in with Perrazzo. It was not that he was dissatisfied with Leuci's performance, he said. Rather he wanted another agent moved in as a kind of insurance policy. And he wanted Leuci insulated from Sergeant Perrazzo.

The agent Tartaglino had in mind was Sandy Bario, whom he flew in from France, and he arranged for Bario and Leuci to meet. He himself did not attend this meeting. Afterward, Leuci met with Tartaglino, Shaw, and Scoppetta, and listened to the plan Tartaglino had concocted.

First of all, Tartaglino said, Leuci would go to Perrazzo. "You will tell him you have information about a narcotics courier, Bario, who is going to be at a motel at the airport, who can be ripped off."

Realizing that Tartaglino must have used this same plan many times in the past, Leuci interrupted. "Why don't I rip this guy off myself?"

"You can't. You're doing business with his people."

Leuci nodded.

Tartaglino continued, "You don't want Bario locked up, for the same reason. Perrazzo should simply rip him off, but you want your share in the score."

"That doesn't sound so bad, so far," Leuci said. "Is he going to have drugs?"

"He's not going to have drugs. What he is going to have is a phony passport. And he's going to have a lot of money. Tell Perrazzo about the phony passport. Perrazzo should threaten to arrest Bario because of the phony passport, and Bario will pay to avoid arrest."

Tartaglino gave his gentle, quiet smile. "Bario's going to be wired. The room is going to be wired. Perrazzo is going to rip him off, we hope. We don't know. Whatever money Perrazzo takes you have to share in, because we want some of our money back, and in addition the money he gives you will serve as evidence in court."

So Leuci went to Perrazzo, and retold this story. Perrazzo, who was a middle-aged man with twenty-five years in the Police Deparmment, was delighted. He had some detectives he could trust, he said. He and these detectives would be able to take care of this courier. No problem.

The next day Perrazzo and two detectives broke in on Bario, threatened him with arrest, and stole $8000. Perrazzo, when he met Leuci later, was exultant. "Every time this guy comes to town he's going to give me a couple of thousand," Perrazzo reported as he handed Leuci money. "You'll get your share, Bobby. I won't forget you for introducing me to this guy. We got a nice association going. We spoke to each other in Italian."

Leuci went to see Tartaglino.

"We now have a solid case against Perrazzo," Tartaglino told him. "And Bario is in solid with Perrazzo. That is only step one. We have a long way to go."

Tartaglino was thinking it out. "What we have to do now is plan our next step," he said. "How are we going to use Agent Bario and Sergeant Perrazzo together?" Tartaglino was studying Leuci carefully.

"What I would like to do," Tartaglino said presently, "is send someone else in to Perrazzo. Another agent. But we'll make this one too big for a sergeant. We'll make him a don from Detroit. We're going to figure out a way that Sergeant Perrazzo can move this guy directly into the Queens district attorney's office."

Presently Tartaglino put together a grandiose scheme, and Scoppetta and Shaw, when they heard it, were as awed by Tartaglino as Leuci was.

To Leuci, Sergeant Perrazzo had once bragged of his friendship with a high-ranking assistant district attorney in Queens. Tartaglino said, "We'll set up a situation in which the sergeant brings this Mafia don from Detroit directly to this assistant D.A. We know now that Sergeant Perrazzo is a corrupt cop. Our intelligence data says that the D.A. is not what he should be. The Mafia don will have plenty of money. Let's see what happens."

Again Leuci was employed as first actor in the drama. Meeting with Sergeant Perrazzo, he explained about the don from Detroit. He warned Perrazzo to be careful of how he talked to this man. This was a man who had to be treated with respect. He had a lot of money, and wanted to set up something out at the airport.

The meeting between Mike Paccini, federal narcotics agent, alias the don from Detroit, and Sergeant Peter Perrazzo took place in Tartaglino's cover apartment in the Stanhope Hotel. Agent Paccini, a big burly man, looked tough but was a consummate actor, and he played his role with a kind of quiet sensitivity. Without ever raising his voice, he communicated the Mafioso power Sergeant Perrazzo was looking for, and he explained that he wished to set up regular payoffs by organized crime to law enforcement personnel so that certain goods could move freely in and out of Kennedy Airport. To do this it was necessary to fix the Queens district attorney's office. It was Perrazzo's job to arrange a meeting between Paccini and the assistant D.A. in charge.

Sergeant Perrazzo seemed extremely impressed by the expensively dressed, scented don from Detroit, and a number of meeetings between them followed. But Perrazzo was never able to bring the D.A. in person to any of these meetings. The D.A. was agreeable also. But, according to Perrazzo, he wanted Perrazzo to collect the money and bring it to him.

So that scheme of Tartaglino's fell through. Tartaglino was disappointed, Scoppetta was disappointed, Shaw was disappointed. Paccini and Leuci were disappointed also. "On to bigger and better things," said Tartaglino, and he began to concoct his most grandiose scheme yet.

16

FROM BOTH SIDES Leuci was being badgered about the Jacques Bless case. Had he made contact with Bless yet, asked Scoppetta. Would the $50,000 bribe go down or not, demanded Sergeant Cohen. The incriminating tapes were growing moss. What was Leuci waiting for?

Leuci was telling the same story to everyone. It had to happen naturally or it wouldn't work. Bless was shrewd and he was dangerous. If he was still untouched by the law, this was because he insulated himself from every transaction. Intermediaries went to jail, not him, and anyone who broke through the insulation in a suspicious manner risked getting knocked off.

If properly approached, Leuci kept saying, Bless would pay the bribe. But "properly" did not mean head-on. Detective Leuci could not ride the elevator up to Bless's apartment and ring the bell. Bless had to be reached in some devious manner that would seem to him natural. The tapes, or Leuci, or both, had to come to him with impeccable credentials. It had to be set up in some way, and this took time.

What, then, were Leuci's plans? He had none, except to wait. A hunter didn't stalk an animal, Leuci pointed out. An animal's senses were too acute. Instead the hunter put himself in a spot where the animal figured to pass by, and he waited. A detective was a hunter, and did the same.

Meanwhile, Leuci became ever more emotionally committed to Sheridan and Glazer. They were his partners. He was with them every day. He didn't want to know them or like them or hear their problems, but he couldn't help himself. It was especially difficult with Sheridan, who wanted so much to be friends, and couldn't understand why Leuci held him off. "You would respect me," the thirty-three-year-old Irishman said one day, "if only you would permit yourself to get to know me."

Leuci, each time he looked at Sheridan, thought: Every day is for you one less day of freedom.

It was Sheridan who warned Leuci about his so-called friends in SIU. These men were not truly his friends, he said, for they spoke against him behind his back. "You're too good, Bob," said Sheridan in his lilting brogue. "You don't see it. They really don't like you. They think that you were sent back into SIU for a reason. They are always talking bad things about you. I am more your friend than any of them. The bite of my tongue you will never hear."

One night, waiting for a case to be processed in night court, Leuci stood with Sheridan at a bar. When he glanced up, he saw DeStefano approaching.

"I'm glad those Knapp hearings are over," the fat bail bondsman said. "Jesus, you didn't testify much. Buy you a drink?" And smiling pleasantly, he added, "I still can't get over it," he said. "You never wear a fucking gun."

Sheridan, the veins standing out in his neck, put his face within inches of DeStefano's. Sheridan was a big rawboned man with heavy hands, clenched now into fists. "When he's with me," hissed Sheridan into DeStefano's face, "he needs no gun."

"Can't you guys take a fucking joke?" whined DeStefano.

"You're too good, Bob," said the Irishman, pushing DeStefano violently away. "I don't know why you deal with these greasy sons of bitches."

Leuci went to Scoppetta and began to plead in Sheridan's behalf. Sheridan was not really a bad man, he said. He didn't deserve the terrible things that were about to happen to him. Scoppetta had arranged for Hubert to be transferred to Intelligence. Why couldn't the same thing be done for Sheridan? Sheridan certainly wasn't the instigator of any of these corrupt deals. He was a tough, brave cop who went along with the others.

What about Stanley Glazer, Scoppetta replied. What about Sergeant Cohen? Was Leuci going to behave this way with everyone? Scoppetta's voice was full of sympathy: "Are you going to fall in love with each guy?"

Then he shook his head. There was nothing he could do. "We know you have this problem," he said. "We understand that it is only going to get worse. Please believe that we'll be with you. We'll stay with you till the end. We'll get you through it."

Leuci's other problem, making contact with Jacques Bless, was solved by Bless himself. Imagining himself possibly implicated in the Corso case, Bless sent a lawyer to DeStefano, and DeStefano came straight to Leuci. Could Leuci find out, DeStefano asked, if there was any heat on Jacques Bless?

"I have news for you," replied Leuci. "There's a lot of heat on Jacques Bless." And he began to describe the tapes he and his partners had made of Bless talking to Peter Corso. The tapes put Bless solidly into the conspiracy, Leuci said, but they were for sale for $50,000.

DeStefano nodded. Bless was a big-time guy and would pay that much money, he said, and he promised to send Lamattina back to the lawyer with Leuci's proposition. Lamattina had worked with the lawyer before and would know how to handle it.

And so Leuci once again began meeting regularly with Lamattina and DeStefano at Ruggerio's Restaurant in Brooklyn. They were convivial meetings. There was going to be money for everyone. Lamattina had met Bless's lawyer. If the tapes were for real, Lamattina said, the dope dealer was willing to pay $50,000 to have them.

At length Leuci agreed to gather his tape spools together and hand them over to Lamattina. Lamattina would listen to them to corroborate their validity. He would then turn them over to Bless's lawyer, and the money would be paid.

The next day Leuci and Lamattina met outside the Fourteenth Precinct station house, and the tapes were transferred from Leuci's car to Lamattina's. When Lamattina asked for something to put them in, Leuci plucked from his briefcase a brown manila envelope that seemed to be empty. Lamattina stuffed the tapes into the envelope and went home for the weekend.

In fact, the envelope was not empty. It had been given to Leuci by Scoppetta and still contained a memo from

Scoppetta to TPF-1 (Leuci's code name), requesting a report on Lamattina, DeStefano, and the Jacques Bless case. Leuci had not been doing his paperwork and he was being gently chided for it. Now Scoppetta's memo, crumpled up under the tapes, was on its way to Jacques Bless.

That Sunday, sitting at home on Staten Island, the thirty-eight-year-old Lamattina decided to listen to the tapes, and he spilled them out of the envelope onto a table. Scoppetta's memo fell out with them. Lamattina read it. It was a single sheet of unlined paper bearing no letterhead. It had been tapped out by Scoppetta himself, with many strikeovers. It was unsigned.

Lamattina telephoned DeStefano, and they hurriedly met. Both instinctively believed that the memo was exactly what it seemed to be. TPF-1 must be Leuci. They had been involved with Leuci now for well over four months.

They began to make telephone calls that became increasingly frantic. Was Leuci an informant? What were people's feelings about Leuci at this time?

One call went to Detective Nunziata. Nunziata would know about Leuci. Whatever he said could be both believed and acted upon. From Leuci's point of view, DeStefano and Lamattina could not have shown Scoppetta's memo to a more fortuitous choice. For Nunziata, above all else, was loyal to his friends.

When he had read the memo, Nunziata began to laugh. "If Leuci is a rat, my mother is a rat," he said. "Don't you know Leuci? He's flaky. He's trying to drive you crazy, and that's what he's done. You've been leaning on him, and now he wants to get even. He gives you the tapes, but he puts the letter in there. It's a joke. You probably owe him money."

Nunziata patted both of them on the back and left. DeStefano and Lamattina were not entirely certain, but they doubted this joke. The memo looked authentic to them.

On Monday morning Lamattina phoned Leuci and set up a meeting for dinner that night. Leuci sensed that something was wrong, and he brooded about it all day.

That night, when the three conspirators sat down to dinner in the restaurant, Leuci saw at once that the other two men were grim. Lamattina was about Leuci's height and weight. DeStefano was taller, and at least 100 pounds heavier. He sat there, stared at Leuci a moment, and then threw the memo across the table, saying, "Read this, and tell me what it is."

Leuci, looking down at Scoppetta's memo, blanched. He had only a few seconds to think up an acceptable explanation, but none came to mind. Nunziata had already provided him with one, but he did not know it. He had one reaction, and one only: I'm caught.

Could he lie his way clear yet again? An idea came to him.

"This is apparently Glazer's work," he said. "I knew that fucking Jew was a rat the moment I saw him."

Lamattina's face brightened at once, but DeStefano turned to him and said with disgust, "Are you a fucking moron, or what? Do you see the dates on that goddamn thing? Some of them are long before Glazer was even working with this guy. Some of these meetings Glazer was never at." He turned back to Leuci. "I want an explanation, and I want it fast."

Leuci pushed the memo back across the tablecloth. "I don't know what the hell it could be," he answered. "It's not mine."

"We're going to search you," said DeStefano.

"Go ahead," said Leuci. What was one more pat-down? And he stood up, holding his arms away from his body.

"Not out here, in there," snarled the fat man, jerking his thumb toward the rest room behind him.

"I'm not wearing a wire," said Leuci.

"We'll see," said DeStefano grimly.

In the toilet Leuci stood docilely while they stripped off his jacket, his tie, his shirt.

"See, what did I tell you," said Leuci. "You guys are crazy."

But it made the other two men, if possible, more frantic than ever. Nothing made sense to them, nothing. What is all this about, Bobby? they demanded. Who are you cooperating with? What are you trying to do to us?

DeStefano read the memo aloud, date by date, begging for explanation. Leuci chose not to respond. He ceased to say anything at all. When DeStefano came to the end of the memo, he looked up and said in an anguished voice, "This is not funny."

"You're right," Leuci said, "it's not funny. You guys are in a lot of trouble."

DeStefano turned to Lamattina and said, "Whack him. Kill him." But neither moved.

"What do you mean, kill him?" cried Leuci angrily. "I have seventy-five agents outside with machine guns. They'll blow both of you away."

All of a sudden, the fat bondsman, the crooked cop did not seem dangerous. For months they had seemed very vicious men. Often they had spoken about killing people or having them killed, about breaking informants' legs. But that was over. They were both, now, terrified.

"Relax, I can get you a deal," Leuci told them. But he wanted to get them outside where his backup agents were. "I can help both of you get out from under this thing. Let's get out onto the street and talk about it."

They followed him out of the restaurant, where they began to whine. "Oh , Bobby," DeStefano said. "We're in a lot of trouble."

Standing on the sidewalk, Leuci searched for his backup team. He saw no one. He began scratching his head—the agreed-upon danger signal. He scratched and scratched. But no backup agents ran up.

"What is that?" said DeStefano suddenly. "A signal of some kind?" the fat bail bondsman had begun to calculate. His mood had become dangerous again. Leuci's incriminating tapes would be worthless in court without the detective's testimony. There was no sign of seventy-five agents with machine guns. There was no sign of any agents at all. If Leuci was alone, then perhaps they still had a chance. Dispose of Leuci and they were clear.

Leuci's backup agents tonight were two IRS men and one cop, the cop he had been begging for, Patrolman Vinny Murano, who lived across the street. They had been driving round and round the block, and now, cruising past the restaurant again, they saw Leuci's signal.

"He's in trouble," said Murano.

But the IRS agent at the wheel was not sure. Perhaps Leuci was only scratching an itch, he said. They couldn't risk blowing his cover. Though Murano told him to stop, the agent drove by.

"He's in trouble," said Murano, lunging across the seat and turning off the ignition. As the car jerked to a stop, he sprang to the street.

Leuci was still scratching his head as Murano strolled up out of the darkness, stopped, and asked cautiously, "Hey, don't I know you?"

"Yeah, you know me," said Leuci. "Now arrest these two guys."

DeStefano and Lamattina were taken to the U.S. Attorney's office on Foley Square, where Scoppetta and Shaw offered them a chance to cooperate with the investigation. They wanted to cooperate, both said. They were frightened and bewildered. They wanted to think about it. Both promised not to blow Leuci's cover.

The Leuci investigation had lasted now almost a year. Scoppetta and Shaw felt it should be closed down that night. It was far too risky to let Leuci continue. They could not take the chance of sending him back onto the street.

Leuci, however, wanted to keep going, and he argued that Lamattina and DeStefano were in no position to blow his cover. How could they claim they had caught him out, when they were still out on the street themselves? It would be clear that they must be cooperating also. They could not afford to blow Leuci's cover.

Many conferences followed. At last the prosecutors agreed to accede to Detective Leuci's wishes. The investigation would continue.

From then on, Leuci became progressively more hot. Bit by bit Lamattina and DeStefano began to talk, to drop hints, and those to whom they talked, including some targets Leuci was still working on, began to put the pieces together, and to see the picture clearly.

Leuci believed he would be surfaced soon. He was treading a fine line, and it was getting finer every day.

17

THE RUMORS reached Mikey Coco.

Of all the mobsters Leuci had met, the one he cared about most and respected most was Mikey Coco. Coco had always been totally honest with him, and had never backed off from his word. If asked for a favor he would go to the ends of the earth to perform it. He seemed to trust Leuci absolutely, and if Leuci had gathered evidence against him, this was to a large extent his own fault. Leuci had been unable to avoid him. If he had been able to avoid Coco, he told himself, he would have done so. But Coco was a nosy, curious kind of guy, and he liked cops, particularly Leuci.

But now Coco had heard the rumors everyone else was hearing, and he kept phoning Leuci.

"Bobby, this is Sidney."

Coco wanted Leuci to meet him at once. Leuci, making one excuse after another, kept postponing this meeting.

At last, feeling that he had no choice if he was not to blow his cover completely, the detective agreed to meet Coco, and he arrived at the Baychester Diner, their usual meeting place, wearing his wire transmitter, and tailed by backup agents. He got into Coco's car.

Without even turning on his headlights, Coco sped out of the parking lot with a squeal of tires, made a U-turn, and was gone. He had again shaken the backup agents.

The headlights came on. Coco reduced speed. Leuci was alone with him.

"You have avoided me a couple of times," Coco said carefully. "You are nervous when you talk to me. You were never nervous before. I hear rumors you are wired all the time. I'm going to drive you somewhere, and I'm going to search you. And if you're wired—"

It was possible that the backup agents were still close enough to pick up Leuci's transmission. If he screamed for help, a great many patrol cars might be mobilized to search for him. But he did not do this. Instead he decided to brazen it out.

"You don't have to search me, Mike. I'm wearing a wire."

Leuci began lying fast. He was involved in an investigation. His home phone was tapped. The prosecutors he worked for knew about tonight's meeting with Coco, and had ordered Leuci to come wired. He disconnected one of the wires and showed it. "It's off, Mike. You can say what you want to say. Mike, trust me that I wouldn't hurt you."

Coco muttered, "I trust you. But people force people to do things they don't want to do."

Coco stopped in front of a restaurant on City Island, and they got out of the car. As they walked in past the bar, Leuci studied Coco's body, trying to see if the mobster had a gun. Coco was famous for not carrying a gun, but if he did have one, then whoever was with him was in trouble.

As they waited to be served dinner, Leuci continued to lie. His investigation had to do with cops and lawyers. "You people are separate," he said earnestly. "You have your own law. I'm not involved with you."

Leuci looked across into the hard, pockmarked face.

"You're lying to me," said the gruff-voiced mobster. "I've been in jail half my life. Do you think I'm fucking worried about going to jail? What did I do? I bribed you. They'll give me a year. Don't lie to me. Tell me the truth."

"Look, Mike, don't get angry."

"They caught you doing something, didn't they? If they caught you doing something, and you didn't come to us for help, then you deserve to get killed. Because you trust them more than you trust us."

Leuci said in a low voice, "No one caught me doing anything." This to Leuci was always the bottom line. No one had caught him. A man who squealed because he was caught was a rat. But Leuci, who had not been caught, was not.

He was a cop, Leuci told Coco. He had always been a cop. He didn't know how he had ever become involved with men like Mikey Coco. But to move freely within organized crime circles, to go to dinner with men like Coco had, at the beginning, excited him. He had felt a certain need to be wanted and needed by men who he knew were bad guys. "Do you understand all this, Mike?"

"No."

The waiter put plates down in front of them. When he was gone, Leuci began trying to explain about meeting Scoppetta, and talking with Scoppetta. "He got to me at a time when I felt that my world, all that I ever knew and believed in, had all gone down the tubes. I wanted to do something to show that I was a good guy, not a bad guy."

"Bobby, I never had any doubt that you were a good guy. Who were you being a good guy to?"

Leuci spoke about his father, who had always been so proud of him, and about his brother who had become a heroin addict.

Coco was surprised, "I didn't know that."

"Mike, I talked to you about my brother before. Your recommendation was that I break both his legs, and tie him to a chair. That wasn't the answer, Mike."

Neither was eating.

After a moment Coco pushed his plate away. "How bad am I going to be hurt?" he asked. "Don't tell me there's no case against me. There's got to be. I met that fucking Geik. Did you have a wire on that night? How long am I going to jail for?"

What was Leuci to answer to this? "I don't know, Mike. You're not going to get hurt that bad."

Coco called for the check.

"What's not bad by you? Five years? Ten years?"

Coco laid money in the dish on top of the check.

Leuci said, "I think the worst thing that could happen is that you get a year." The detective watched carefully, waiting for Coco's reaction. He didn't expect to get into a fight with him here in the middle of a crowded restaurant, but it was possible that, once back in the car, Coco would drive him off to where people were waiting. Coco could have set that up in advance.

But all Coco said was, "I could do a year standing on one hand. A year is nothing. Are you sure I'll get no more than a year?"

"I'm not sure," Leuci admitted. "I'm not a judge. As far as I'm concerned, you got extorted by Bernie Geik. You were the victim."

Abruptly, Coco laughed. "I've been a victim of you fucking cops since I started talking to you." Then studying Leuci, he asked in a softer voice, "And what's going to happen to you when this is over?"

"Perhaps they'll turn on me, and lock me up too. If they want to prosecute, there are things there."

"They are going to make you a hero," said Coco flatly. "But what they've really done is to make you a rat. Your father is going to be embarrasssed. Your cousin I don't want to even think about. Your cousin is going to have to explain to a lot of people how you got involved in this thing. Is anyone going to get hurt because of me? Bobby, that's very important. I introduced you to a few people. I vouched for you."

"I give you my word, Mike," Leuci said. "No one is going to get hurt because you vouched for me, or introduced me to someone."

They had been talking more than two hours, and this latest subject seemed the most dangerous so far. Leuci pushed back from the table and stood up. He did not want to give Coco time to consider who might be prosecuted because Coco had vouched for Leuci.

Coco said, "Sit down, Bobby. These people have turned you into a rat. You're not going to be able to live with yourself." He thought about it for a minute, then said, "I'm going to save your life. You meet me tomorrow morning at Kennedy Airport. I'll give you $75,000. You go anywhere in the world you want, and you get word back to me through your cousin or someone we can trust, and I'll send you another $75,000. You can start a new life. You won't be a rat."

There was no one in law enforcement willing to give Leuci $150,000 to start a new life.

"Mike, where in the world could I go?"

They left the restaurant and started back to where

Leuci's car was parked. As he drove, Coco was silent. Finally he said, "I'll drop you off a couple of blocks away. I'll find a nice dark street." He looked across at Leuci.

Leuci said, "Mike, you kill me, and you're fucking dead."

Coco grinned, "Bobby, why do you talk like that? You worry too much. That's why you are in all this trouble. Ever since I knew you, you were a fucking worrier."

Leuci got out of the car and walked away without looking back.

18

TARTAGLINO'S TARGET was still corruption within the court system. The conduit was still to be Sergeant Perrazzo. Tartaglino's idea was to equip still another agent with plenty of money and a dazzling cover story, and to arrange for this man to be arrested by Sergeant Perrazzo. Perrazzo would process the agent in state court. Once inside the court system, the agent would begin bribing. He would bribe his way as close to the top as he could get.

To Scoppetta, to Shaw, to Leuci, this latest plan by Tartaglino seemed a bit complicated, perhaps unworkable, but as soon as Tartaglino, speaking in his quiet, immaculate way, had sketched in the details, all their skepticism disappeared, and they were once again filled with awe.

To begin with, the agent would be Carlo Dandolo. Dandolo was an Italian—this much seemed certain—but the rest of his life and past was murky. He had lived in France, spoke French, and had owned a café in Marseilles. He had lived in Turkey and in Syria, and at present lived in Lebanon and kept a café in Beirut. He was not a federal narcotics agent. Rather he was a frequent freelance employee of the bureau. If he had a criminal past, Tartaglino did not know about it. The man had worked for him on many major narcotics cases in Europe, and when Dandolo worked on a target, that target went to jail. Dandolo, Tartaglino said, was the consummate undercover agent, the consummate actor. He was the best the bureau had access to. He was very likely the best in the world, and he would be able to bribe any corrupt official he tried to bribe.

Tartaglino began now carefully to outline his plan.

Agent Dandolo would fly into New York and take a room at the Americana Hotel, and Sergeant Perrazzo would be informed both that he was there and that he worked for a rival Mafia family. Agent Dandolo, who would have money, would be ripped off by Sergeant Perrazzo, and then arrested.

It was better to keep Detective Leuci to the side this time, Tartaglino explained. A lot of people were suspicious of Leuci now. Perrazzo might be one of them.

Agent Dandolo would have to be arrested for something serious, but not too serious. A small amount of narcotics, perhaps. The kind of trouble that a habitual offender could reasonably expect to buy his way out of. He should seem to be a major narcotics dealer with connections all over the world. Tartaglino was hoping to catch one or several assistant district attorneys and judges who were willing to let such a man go for money.

So Agent Dandolo flew into Kennedy Airport, and checked into the Americana Hotel. Sergeant Perrazzo was notified. Perrazzo, as expected, selected two detectives he could trust, and explained what they would do.

But one of these detectives immediately refused to take part. "We're assigned to Queens robbery," he said. "How do we show up at a hotel in Manhattan and lock up a junk dealer? We can't do it."

This argument seemed sound to Sergeant Perrazzo, who said, "Okay, I got a guy I can call who has citywide jurisdiction."

He began to dial Leuci's number, but the other detective stopped him, "Don't call Leuci. I hear stories about Leuci. Call anybody but Leuci."

Still needing a detective with citywide jurisdiction, Perrazzo thought of Joe Nunziata, and phoned him. About midnight, the former mounted cop, the former SIU superstar, went with his partner to the Americana and knocked on Dandolo's door.

Within minutes Detective Nunziata was in a state of intense excitement. He had found Dandolo's passport. It was stamped with cities like Marseilles, Rome, Beirut. He had found Dandolo's little black book. In it were listed major Mafia drug traffickers from New York to California. It even had the home phone numbers of certain political figures with Italian names.

He had found an ounce of heroin sewed into the lining of Dandolo's suit. The markings on the envelope were in Turkish. He had found, he believed, one of the biggest dope dealers ever to have fallen into the hands of any cop.

But Detective Nunziata worked now not for the Police Department but for the Joint Task Force, and so he took Dandolo not to state court but to federal court.

Tartaglino's scenario was already in ruins—wrong arresting officer, wrong courthouse—but he decided not to abandon it yet. Instead, he summoned the two cops and their prisoner to Washington.

Leaving Nunziata and his partner outside, Tartaglino spoke to Dandolo alone.

"I can make these two cops," Dandolo told him. "These two cops are corrupt cops," Dandolo said. "I sense it."

Though the target was supposed to be district attorneys and judges, Tartaglino nodded. "Go ahead and do it if you can." His decision was made. The case would continue.

A moment later Detective Nunziata stood in front of Tartaglino's desk. "This Dandolo is a major drug guy," Tartaglino told him. "When he makes bail, I want you to stick close to him. Maybe he'll lead you to whoever he does business with."

Dandolo did make bail, using money Tartaglino gave him. As a condition of his release he was confined to the jurisdiction of the Southern District of New York State, and his passport was confiscated.

About two weeks then passed. In New York there were constant meetings between Dandolo, Scoppetta, Leuci, Shaw, and Tartaglino. Nunziata is a straight guy, Leuci kept telling the others, for he was terrified for his friend. To Leuci, Dandolo was a time bomb. Nunziata is an honest detective, Leuci insisted. Let's cut Dandolo into somebody important. Get him off Nunziata. Working on Nunziata is a waste of time.

Nunziata, as instructed by Tartaglino, did stick close to

Dandolo, and they had a number of meetings. Dandolo would return from each one and report. They were exploring the idea, he said, that Nunziata would allow him to bring in large amounts of narcotics. In his heavily accented English, Dandolo would quote lines and phrases he said Nunziata had spoken.

"That's not the way Joe talks," Leuci kept protesting. "Joe is a straight guy. Let's cut Dandolo into someone else."

Dandolo was meeting the detective regularly in a midtown restaurant called Friar Tuck, and then hurrying up to the investigation's cover apartment on the East Side to report to Tartaglino. It was a luxuriously furnished apartment in a luxurious building. Briefings, debriefings, and conferences were held there. It was the place Leuci went to put his wire on, or take it off afterwards. The phones were in use constantly on official business, and the assigned federal agents often slept there. Leuci kept urging Dandolo to be careful when he came to this apartment, because Nunziata was doubtless trying to tail him.

Dandolo was insulted. He had been worked on by the best, he boasted. Even the Gestapo had been unable to tail him. No one could tail him.

Leuci said, "Well, let me tell you something, my friend. If you keep coming here, Joe is going to follow you here."

Again Leuci turned to Scoppetta. "I want to see this guy record Nunziata. Let me hear those conversations he says he's having with Nunziata."

Scoppetta saw Leuci's anguish, but turned away from it. "If your friend is an honest cop, Bob, you have nothing to worry about."

Detective Nunziata, meanwhile, had attempted to follow Dandolo away from every one of their meetings at the Friar Tuck restaurant. Dandolo had never once led him back to the Americana Hotel. Instead Dandolo had each time shaken the tail. This led Nunziata to the conclusion that the Americana was a cover, and that Dandolo kept another apartment somewhere. He became convinced that if he could locate this other apartment, he might be able to drop Dandolo's entire drug operation, and seize an important quantity of heroin.

But where was this cover apartment? How to find it?

Nunziata studied Dandolo, searching for a weakness. At last he found one—a waitress at the Friar Tuck who had caught Dandolo's eye. Nunziata went to the girl and gave her money to go with Dandolo. "You can go anywhere he wants to take you," he told her, "except to the Americana Hotel. All I want to know is where he takes you."

Dandolo took her straight to the investigation's cover apartment and bedded her.

Minutes after he learned this address, Nunziata was on the phone to Detective Carl Aguiluz, the best wireman in SIU, and shortly after that the two of them were in the basement attaching devices to the telephone box.

Upstairs, Leuci and the federal agents continued using the phone. Nunziata's tape recorder recorded every conversation.

Dandolo now offered Tartaglino a plan. It was urgent that he return to France, he would tell Nunziata. He would promise Nunziata to set up big arrests and an important seizure of drugs as soon as he got back. All this in exchange for his passport for two weeks—that's all he needed—two weeks in France. In addition, he would offer Nunziata $4000.

Dandolo looked around the room as if expecting applause. Tartaglino nodded thoughtfully. Basically the plan pleased him.

"Nunziata is not going to take that money," Leuci said. But there was a pleading note in his voice. "To Nunziata you are the biggest dope dealer he has ever dreamed of having. If he is just interested in money, it's better to wait. You can give him the biggest arrests he's ever had, and once he makes the arrests, he can sell the case for really big money, if money is what he wants. Why should he take $4000 from you now?"

"He'll take the money," said Dandolo smugly.

Dandolo would have to wear a wire, Tartaglino insisted in his soft, careful voice.

"Okay," said Dandolo, and he stripped to the waist and they taped it on him.

Tartaglino handed his agent the bribe money, $4000 in marked bills.

Dandolo buttoned his shirt back up, tied his tie, flashed his smug smile around the room, and went out the door.

Leuci had driven straight home, and there he blurted out the whole story to Gina. There was no doubt in Leuci's mind that if Dandolo came across to Nunziata the way he had said he would, if he ran the Sons of Italy routine—we're both Italians, trust me because I'm Italian—then Nunziata was going to fall for that, and probably he would take the money. Dandolo would find a way to get him to take the money.

Gina listened aghast.

Leuci wanted to phone Nunziata, warn him he was walking into a trap. But suppose Nunziata panicked, and did something crazy?

Leuci himself would be blown, together with many of the cases he had so carefully built up. That was the first certainty. A second certainty was that Tartaglino would have him prosecuted.

Leuci picked up his telephone, determined to phone Nunziata anyway, but he put it down again. Several times more he went to the phone, but he did not call his friend. Finally he left the house, went down to the beach, and sat on a bench facing out at the dark sea.

He remembered the day, looking nervous and very young, he reported to an office to be interviewed for possible transfer into the Narcotics Division. Several others also waited, including Nunziata. He was the only one not nervous. He was conservatively, expensively dressed. It was only the second time Leuci had ever met him.

Nunziata, waiting, began to tell horse stories—how once, when a suspect he was chasing tried to escape down into the subway, he had ridden his horse down the staircase after the guy, and had made the arrest.

Soon the waiting cops were laughing so hard their

nervousness was forgotten. A number of the clerks there had crowded around to listen to Nunziata. People always crowded around Nunziata.

The horse, he continued, was the dumbest creature living. The only way to teach a horse anything was with a left hook between the eyes. That was the way to make a horse respect you.

Leuci, watching the dark waves crash in, remembered all this and more.

In the Williamsburg section of Brooklyn where he had grown up, Nunziata had been a kind of mayor of his block. Little kids would cluster around him, would walk down the street beside him calling: Joey, Joey, Joey. Sometimes he played stickball with the kids. He could hit a stickball a mile. If teenage gangs of nonwhites came through knocking over garbage cans or beating up neighborhood boys, Nunziata would take them all on at once. He would thrash them, and they would not come back.

In the macho police society, cops often went out together at the end of a tour, and often enough they picked up women and did not go home. Not Nunziata, who was always in a hurry to get home to his wife Ann.

He was from a large family of working-class people, and this entire family looked to him as its leader. It had always been his ambition to save enough money to move out of the old neighborhood, and to live among educated people. He was very impressed by people who were educated. Recently he had bought a house in Great Neck.

A few years earlier the stars of SIU, and even of the Police Department as a whole, had been Sonny Grosso, and Eddie Egan, who had made the French Connection case. Egan and Grosso had since been transferred to other assignments—even as the film about it was playing in New York—just as Nunziata had since been transferred to the Joint Task Force, but when famous SIU detectives were spoken of, the three names were often mentioned interchangeably.

The three names had been inseparable also in the mind of Andrew Tartaglino. When first informed that Dandolo had been arrested not by Perrazzo but by Nunziata, Tartaglino had recognized the name instantly, and had dipped back into old files to refresh his memory. Tartaglino had then moved steadily, implacably forward.

And so on this particular night, with Leuci staring in despair at the sea, with Dandolo hurrying confidently through the streets toward Friar Tuck's restaurant, it was Gina Leuci who still had to act. The others—Tartaglino, Dandolo, Nunziata, her husband—all were acting out their roles with a kind of Calvinistic predetermination. Free will, it appeared, began and ended with herself.

After hesitating in an agony of indecision, she went to the telephone and dialed Nunziata's house, for she saw no other way out. It had become her job by default to save not only Nunziata, who was a friend, but also her husband. If Nunziata fell into Tartaglino's trap, it was her husband who would not survive.

He had betrayed already the Police Department code of silence, and also that code of silence that had its origins in the mountains of Sicily, and that had been brought to America by Leuci's own forebears, among others, remaining to this day a deeply rooted instinct in the breast of every young man of Italian origin. Silence and honor were the same. Now, in addition to betraying this ideal, he would also be betraying the cop whom he respected above all others.

As Gina waited for Nunziata's phone to be picked up, she had thought out, insofar as she was able, all possible consequences of her actions. She would explain to Nunziata's wife, or to Joe himself if he chanced to answer, that he must on no account meet with Dandolo tonight. Then she would hang up. Whatever happened, her husband would be clear. Tartaglino could give him a lie detector test tomorrow and he would pass it. She would never, never tell him what she had done, not tonight, not ever.

But there was no answer. She waited ten minutes, pacing, then dialed again. During the next hour she tried several times more, but there was still no answer.

Gina was a strong young woman, an Italian young

woman. She did not begin to weep. Though suffering intensively over what must now happen to both Nunziata and her husband, she accepted the decree of God, or fate, or whatever it was. She could do no more. What would happen now would happen, and it would be her job to glue the pieces of her husband back together again afterward, if she could.

19

IN THE NOISE AND BUSTLE of the Friar Tuck restaurant, Dandolo, speaking in low, urgent Italian, begged Nunziata for his passport. He needed just a few days in Marseilles, he pleaded. When he came back he would hand Nunziata an important case. He would inform on a Frenchman, or a Syrian, or on some black bastard. He would betray any of these rivals to his friend Nunziata, but he was not an informant, he was an Italian, and would never betray any fellow Italian. Nunziata knew that. Italians could trust each other.

The deal, on whatever level he may have considered it, sounded very good to Nunziata. Inevitably, this is how one did business when enforcing the drug laws. One made deals with scum like Dandolo. A detective learned to give up one case in exchange for another that was bigger.

"And now I want you to take this four thousand dollars," said Dandolo.

Nunziata, Dandolo's tape later proved, had at first protested. He did not want the money. They were both Italians. They trusted each other.

Afterward, certain members of the prosecution team scoffed at Nunziata's protestations. To them it was obvious from the tone of his voice, from its very unctuousness, that his initial refusal was a formality only, that he always intended to take the money. Others maintained that he took it only because Dandolo kept forcing it on him.

Nunziata handed $2000 to his partner, Detective Louis D'Ambrosia, and pocketed the rest. "The money is an expression of how I feel about you," said Dandolo, and he jumped up and embraced Nunziata, kissing him on both cheeks.

Nunziata then decided to check out his wiretap. It was

about one o'clock in the morning when he went down into the basement of the luxurious building on East Forty-ninth Street. He had not yet been back there, for it was Aguiluz who was supposed to monitor the tape from time to time.

In fact, Aguiluz had attempted to do so only once. He had gone downstairs into the basement and through the laundry room, walking right past a federal agent who was doing his wash there. This man watched, stupefied, as Aguiluz entered the storeroom where his tape recorder was hidden and began to move things around. The agent confronted Aguiluz and demanded to know who he was.

Aguiluz ran.

He ran upstairs and out of the building, with the agent in hot pursuit. The agent didn't know who Aguiluz was, and Aguiluz didn't know who the agent was. But both were cops, both knew something was not the way it should be. Both were not thinking, only reacting. Aguiluz sprinted down the street, into a crowded building, and out the other side. He dodged through hundreds of people, and at last when he looked back the agent was no longer chasing him.

This kind of thing had happened before to cops who installed illegal wiretaps. Usually the person in pursuit was the building superintendent or some busybody of a tenant. Nonetheless, the rule was never to go back to such a wiretap. It was too risky. Leave the gear in place forever. Abandon it.

Aguiluz was faithful to this rule. It was his gear he was abandoning. It was his job to check out the wiretap. It never occurred to him that Nunziata would go back there without him.

Nunziata, having descended to the basement, glanced around, listening carefully. The place seemed empty. He moved confidently toward the concealed tape recorder.

But the basement was not empty.

Upon losing Aguiluz in the crowd, the agent had called telephone company security, and what happened next was standard procedure. Telephone Security informed the Manhattan District Attorney's office that an illegal tap existed, and detectives from the D.A.'s squad were sent up to stake out the basement around the clock.

These detectives, as Nunziata reached for the tape recorder, were still staked out, and they grabbed Nunziata. He showed his shield and tried to laugh it off, one cop to another. It was a tap on a dope dealer. He expected them to let him go.

But too many superiors were involved, and they couldn't let him go. They made the proper notifications, and the superiors rushed in from all over, one of them Scoppetta.

Scoppetta and Nunziata had never met before. Scoppetta was grim. "You're in serious trouble," he told the detective.

Again Nunziata tried to laugh it off. "For what?" he demanded. "For an illegal wiretap? You must be kidding. This is the biggest case any of us have ever had."

"Not for an illegal wiretap, Joe," Scoppetta told him. "But for taking four thousand dollars."

In an instant, Nunziata's whole world crashed down around him.

Nunziata was allowed to go home. He was allowed several days in which to contemplate arrest, prison. He was the leader of his family. He was the hero of all the kids on the block. It was not possible for him to be arrested. So he had to seriously consider cooperating, consider denouncing cops he had worked with. The idea nauseated him. It made him crazy.

He called up various SIU detectives, though never Detective Robert Leuci, ranting unintelligibly into the telephone. A number of detectives, Aguiluz principal among them, went to his house, but he refused to let them in or to respond to the offers of money or the expressions of solidarity that they tried to shout to him through the door. At the end of two days, Nunziata was scarcely rational.

Strictly speaking, this was Scoppetta's show, but Tartaglino happened to be in town that week, so Scoppetta invited him to attend what was expected to be a showdown meeting with Nunziata in a motel room near LaGuardia Airport.

Detective D'Ambrosia was called in first. He was a young cop who had never been in trouble before. He was terrified, and willing to do almost anything to stay out of jail and perhaps save his Police Department career. Unfortunately, he was too new, he knew too little, there was no partner or superior he could give up in exchange for a break from the prosecutors, and they told him so. They told him that his only chance was to convince Nunziata to talk, for Nunziata knew plenty. Nunziata, if he agreed to cooperate, could perhaps save them both.

Then it was Nunziata's turn. He came into the motel room. His face was gray. The former SIU superstar was not visible, nor the hero of the Williamsburg section of Brooklyn, nor the tough, tough cop. He began to protest that he had never been in trouble before, that this was the only compromising situation in which he had ever been involved. Appearances were misleading here, he said, trying in a choked voice to convince these grim-faced prosecutors.

He had accepted the money only in order to make a solid bribery case against Dandolo. The money was still intact. He could turn it over to the prosecutors right this minute, and in fact wished to. He had believed Dandolo to be a major drug trafficker, and as soon as the Italian returned to New York Nunziata had planned to arrest him for bribery. With a solid bribery case against Dandolo, Nunziata had hoped to turn Dandolo, to force him to cooperate, to learn the names of his connections and the locations of his heroin drops.

Nunziata was pleading for his life.

Tartaglino had listened without emotion. He looked cool, immaculate. When he spoke, his voice was so low and soft that it was difficult to hear him. "Let's assume you're telling the truth, Joe," he said. "I think you might be telling the truth. You say you are."

Tartaglino paused. He spoke, as always, with meticulous care. "I'm going to give you a test," he said.

"Anything," said the anguished Nunziata. "What do I have to do?"

"Do you really want to cooperate?" said Tartaglino.

"Let's see whether you do. This first test I'm going to give you is a tough one. You get the tough ones first, and everything after that will be easy."

Tartaglino studied him.

"You have to do a good job, Joe. If you don't do a good job, then you're not helping us. You are an experienced cop, like I am. There are three things you have to do. I'll tell you what they are. The first thing is this. You go into a public phone booth, and you call Detective Sonny Grosso. You tell him to go out, get on a public phone, and call you right back."

Tartaglino studied the slack-jawed, ashen-faced detective.

"We're going to give you something written on a piece of paper," Tartaglino said. "When he calls you back, you are going to read it to him. It will say something like this: 'Sonny, I just found something out. The feds are on to us.' Then you are going to read him a statement of two or three lines."

Tartaglino paused. "I want to hear what Sonny's reaction is, Joe. If his reaction is 'But Joe, we haven't done anything wrong,' then we'll believe you. But if his reaction is 'Joe, you and me and Eddie Egan better get together and talk about it,' then I think some of us are going to decide you are lying to us."

For a moment the two men only looked at each other. Then Nunziata sprang to his feet. "I won't do it," he croaked. His voice fell amost to a whisper. "I can't take the test."

In the same quiet emotionless voice Tartaglino said, "You wanted a chance, Joe. You don't want to go to jail. Well, we've given you a chance. Sit down, Joe. Let me tell you something about yourself. You're a whore, Joe. You've been a whore since you put that uniform on, and all this business of you being a big hero is nonsense. You're a whore, and a thief.

"As far as I'm concerned," Tartaglino continued, "you have very few choices left. You can cooperate with us, or you can go to jail, or you can go out of here and shoot yourself."

The last alternative Tartaglino added almost as an afterthought. He was an expert at trying to turn a witness. Today, as always, he was using every argument that came to hand. As far as he was concerned, he had given Nunziata a better chance than Nunziata had sometimes given others.

"You decide what you are going to do," Tartaglino concluded quietly, "and you let us know tomorrow."

Nunziata went home, where he prepared a long rambling letter that proclaimed his own innocence, and especially D'Ambrosia's. D'Ambrosia was totally honest and had done nothing wrong, Nunziata wrote.

He spoke to his wife. He told her about the letter. In the morning he left the house.

He had an appointment to meet with Scoppetta to give his decision. He picked up D'Ambrosia, and the two detectives drove through the streets of Brooklyn with D'Ambrosia trying to convince Nunziata to cooperate, to save them both. Nunziata promised that he would not let his partner get hurt. "I'll see to it," he said.

They were already late for Scoppetta, but Nunziata had turned into the Williamsburg section of Brooklyn where he had grown up, and had begun driving up and down streets he had played in as a boy. D'Ambrosia supposed he was merely postponing as long as possible the inevitable meeting with Scoppetta. He was relieved when Nunziata at last pulled to the curb and instructed D'Ambrosia to telephone Scoppetta from that candy store there, to tell him they were on their way in to the federal building.

As soon as D'Ambrosia had entered the candy store, Nunziata withdrew his service revolver from his belt, pressed the muzzle to his chest, and shot himself in the heart.

Leuci was told on the steps of the courthouse. His stomach went into convulsions. Turning away, he began to vomit. When this ended, he entered a room where Scoppetta and other officials had been waiting for Nunziata to appear. Scoppetta asked the other men to leave, then said, "How did we get into this, Bob?"

They faced each other across the rug.

Leuci said, "I don't know. You did it."

Turning away, Scoppetta started to cry. Leuci started to cry. They stood apart, facing in opposite directions, weeping.

At last Leuci said, "Look, I'm just going to go away now. I'm going to go see Joe's wife."

It was SIU Detective Jack McClean who handled the wake for Ann Nunziata. McClean was everybody's Irish uncle. He had been a police kid—nearly every male in his family had been a cop, and he was an integral part of the Irish Mafia within the detective division. He was a first-grade detective who had lived through this kind of thing more than once. Now all that had to be done for Ann and for Nunziata's two kids Uncle Jack McClean took care of, and he also hosted the wake. It was Jack McClean who brought Leuci up to the coffin and stood with him there.

All the old SIU detectives were at the wake, Sonny Grosso, Eddie Egan, everyone. It was like an old family reunion, except that one of their number felt like a viper among them.

Much, much later it was discovered that the French Connection heroin, which had been kept as evidence in sacks in the police property clerk's office, was no longer heroin at all. The investigation showed that between 1968 and Nunziata's death in the spring of 1972, this heroin had been withdrawn from the property clerk's several times for presentation in court, and during one or more of these withdrawals someone had substituted pancake flour. On five of the withdrawal slips Nunziata's name appeared—apparently forged—and further investigation showed that the idea of such a ripoff had been Nunziata's also. Three years before his death he had gone to Robin Moore, author of *The French Connection,* and had suggested such a ripoff as the plot for a novel. He had hoped to share in the profits of this novel, but Moore declined to write it.

20

A YEAR and four months had gone by. Leuci had made more than a hundred clandestine tape recordings—not only with defense lawyers, but also with district attorneys, not only with Mafia drug dealers but also with bail bondsmen, not only with cops but also with federal narcotics agents. He had hurt only a handful of cops in all, none of them men he had cared about in the past. It was going to be possible to prepare more than thirty indictments.

But Nunziata was dead, and Leuci, it was clear, was close to the breaking point. At times he babbled. At other times, for no apparent reason, he wept.

He was also extremely hot. Rumors at SIU headquarters had grown ever more detailed and intense. Leuci was so hot as to be on fire.

Many times in the past the Harvard-educated Shaw had argued in private conferences with Scoppetta that the investigation should be cut short—it was too dangerous for Leuci. Always Scoppetta, the street fighter from the slums of New York, had argued otherwise—they were engaged in a dirty business, and such risks had to be taken—and always Scoppetta had prevailed. Now, in May 1972, both were in agreement. The danger was a factor, of course. But the main thing was that Leuci was played out. Emotionally he could go no further.

So the two prosecutors planned to pick up those few of Leuci's subjects who they imagined would agree to cooperate with the prosecution at once, the first being Sergeant Perrazzo. It was hoped that Perrazzo, once confronted with the evidence against him, would agree to wear a wire and to work undercover in his turn. The Leuci investigation would end, and the Sergeant Perrazzo investigation might begin.

The thing to do, they decided, was to come down on Perrazzo hard and quietly. Shock him. Bring him in immediately, lay the evidence out quickly, then show him the opening. Show him that he could save himself if he would agree to wear a wire and move against corrupt assistant district attorneys in Brooklyn and Queens.

All right, where should they pick him up? One possibility was to summon him to the offices of the U.S. attorney for the Southern District. Another was to arrest him at the detective squad where he worked. Instead, for maximum shock value, they decided to arrest him where he felt most secure, at home, and in the middle of the night. Two detectives from Internal Affairs went with Scoppetta to do the job. They had German names, and were not only considered professional hatchet men within the department, but were sometimes called The Gestapo.

While Scoppetta waited in the car, they knocked on Perrazzo's front door. He opened it.

"We want to talk to you."

Perrazzo, in pajamas, stared out at two men in topcoats. When they showed their shields, he said, "Come on in."

"I'm sure you don't want us to talk to you inside and wake up your family," they told him ominously.

Perrazzo got dressed and came outside. By then, terror already showed in his face. "Am I in trouble?"

"You have never been in more trouble, my friend. Did you ever hear of Bob Leuci? You're going to jail."

Perrazzo began to babble. "Why me? What did I do?" Standing in front of his own front door, he began screaming. "Why me? Why me? Why me? Why me? Why—"

By the time the two detectives and Scoppetta had got Perrazzo into the city, he had frozen up, and wouldn't—or couldn't—talk at all. After that, every time anyone tried to question him, he would begin to whimper, "Why me?" and then to scream in an anguished voice, "Why me? Why me?"

Later he was judged insane.

The secret investigation, it was clear, would not remain secret much longer. Shaw and Scoppetta were playing for time—time enough perhaps for one last case to be made, the biggest of all. The target was the office of the district attorney of Queens County.

But Leuci became obsessed with the notion that he would soon be blown, and that once this happened it would become impossible for him to explain his side of the story of Nunziata's death to those SIU detectives he cared about. It was Leuci himself who could keep the secret no longer. He decided to meet with several detectives, the most important being Carl Aguiluz. Nunziata had been Aguiluz's mentor too. In fact, Aguiluz had been closer to Nunziata than any other detective except for Leuci himself.

There was a restaurant on Twenty-third Street were SIU detectives often congregated. Leuci, knowing other detectives would also be present, arranged to meet Aguiluz there for dinner.

By this time, on explicit orders from Scoppetta, Leuci was accompanied everywhere by Vinny Murano, the cop who lived across the street. Murano had been ordered never to leave Leuci's side. To Scoppetta, Leuci was on the verge of a crackup. He was as fragile as a pane of glass. "Don't let him out of your sight," Scoppetta told Murano.

To meet Aguiluz, Leuci had first to get rid of Murano, or so he thought. Leuci begged his friend and bodyguard to let him meet with Aguiluz alone. But Murano refused. His orders were formal. How could he explain letting Leuci go to dinner with Aguiluz, he asked.

Leuci had a lie ready. He had lied so much he could hardly think straight any more. "Just tell them you dropped me off at the SIU office and then lost me," Leuci told him, adding, "I'm in great shape."

Murano said, "You tell me you're in great shape. You look awful. I don't know what goes on in your head."

Murano relented. He dropped Leuci off at the SIU office, then looked the other way.

Leuci went directly to the restaurant, where he sat

down at a table with Aguiluz and three other SIU detectives. Two he knew slightly. The third was new, and unknown to him.

The five detectives began to drink and talk and laugh. There was warmth and friendliness around that table, and Leuci talked of the old days when Nunziata used to be there with them.

The drinks worked on him. He began to relax, to feel really good. He was almost out from under this thing. In a few more days it would end, but before that he was going to tell his story to these men, his true friends. He was going to tell them tonight. He was going to tell them it wasn't his fault that Nunziata killed himself. He had had nothing to do with Joe's death.

Leuci went on drinking. Soon he was drunk enough that his vision of himself no longer hurt. Nothing hurt. He could talk to these men without being ashamed or afraid.

Finding himself alone with Aguiluz, Leuci said, "Carl, I'm going to tell you something. It will be a little hard for you to understand. But I want you to understand something." He paused. Even drunk it was proving harder to speak than Leuci had expected. "Some time in the near future you are going to hear all kinds of things."

Aguiluz said, "I know all that stuff."

"What do you know?" asked Leuci, shocked.

The story had been around forever, the Honduras-born detective told him. The story that Leuci was cooperating with prosecutors, that Leuci was supposed to be doing all sorts of strange things. Aguiluz watched him. "Everyone talks about you being a wreck," he said. "You must think we believe those rumors. Look, our friend Joe never believed them. Till the last day, he never believed anything bad about you. I don't believe it either. We know you. We know you would never do anything like that."

But Leuci was shaking his head into his drink. "Well," he said, "that's not entirely true."

Aguiluz turned white.

Leuci scarcely noticed this. He was closed in on his own pain. At last he was going to unburden himself to a man who cared about him, who would understand. He was going to unburden himself to SIU.

"I did some things—" He nodded drunkenly at Aguiluz, then added hurriedly, "I did nothing to hurt you. I did nothing to hurt Joe. Joe found himself in a situation that I had nothing to do with. I want you to understand what happened."

Now the words spilled out, a vast jumble of them: names, dates, cases. Most of this made no sense to Aguiluz. Leuci spoke of Dandolo, of Tartaglino coming up from Washington, of how he had once met Scoppetta, and had conceived the notion of trying to purify his own sins by moving against bigger sinners than himself, namely, the lawyers. He had wanted absolution, wanted to go back to the sacraments. But they had turned him against cops anyway.

The conversation had moved out of the restaurant. Aguiluz and Leuci were standing by Leuci's car in the street. Aguiluz was terrified. "I don't believe any of this," he said. "You are making this all up. Joe assured us you would never do anything like this."

The drunken Leuci had lied for months and months and been believed. Now he was telling the truth, but he could not, it seemed, make himself believed. Opening the trunk of his car, he ripped out the phony wall partition. Aguiluz stared at the tape recorder secured at the side of the car.

"I don't know what to say to you," said Aguiluz. After a moment he added, "You are telling me you had nothing to do with Joe. I believe you. How about us?"

"None of you guys are involved."

"I don't know how you are sleeping, but you better get home and get some sleep now. Do you want me to take you home?"

The other detectives had come out of the restaurant. They were clustered around.

"Can we help you in any way?" they asked. "Do you need any money? Do you need anything?"

Leuci said, "I'm not under arrest." Then he began screaming. "I didn't do this because they caught me! Don't you understand what happened here?" He was screaming, and in between phrases he was gulping for air. "I had nothing to do with Joe's death!" he screamed.

"You've got to believe that! I had nothing to do with Joe's death!"

"Take it easy," Aguiluz said. "You'll make yourself crazy."

The other detectives were trying to calm him down. "You'll do the same thing Joe did."

"I'm not going to do that!" Leuci screamed.

"How about giving us your gun," said Aguiluz.

"I'm not giving you my fucking gun!" Leuci screamed.

"We went through this with Joe," Aguiluz said. "He looked like you. He sounded like you. Are you going to do the same fucking thing? How bad is this thing?"

"Bad enough."

"How long has it been going on?"

"I don't know," Leuci whispered, close to tears. "A couple of years now."

"Let us take you home," Aguiluz said. "Give me your fucking gun."

"I'm all right," wept Leuci. "I can make it home."

He got into his car and drove away.

The next day Aguiluz called a meeting of SIU detectives and told what he knew. With so many men now in on the secret, inevitably the story reached the newspapers. There were headlines: a major investigation was about to break, and there was a Detective Leuci at the center of it.

The following day Bill Federici of the *New York Daily News* printed a story outlining each and every case. On Scoppetta's orders Leuci was immediately scooped up by detectives and put in protective custody in New York. He was not allowed to go home. Heavily armed agents from Tartaglino's office, together with detectives from Internal Affairs, surrounded Leuci's house in King's Park. But when they began to observe suspicious cars cruising by, it was decided to abandon the house and to keep Gina and the kids under guard in a hotel.

"A hotel?" Leuci asked, when he learned the decision. "What hotel? For how long?"

He would be testifying for the next two years or more, he pointed out, and perhaps he would not be safe even after that. Putting his family in a hotel was not the answer, he pleaded. He owned a cabin in the woods in the Catskill Mountains. He wanted permission for his wife and kids to go there to wait for him.

Scoppetta and Shaw mulled this over. Who knew about Leuci's cabin in the woods? they demanded.

"No one," Leuci lied. He had gone hunting there in the past with his former partners Mandato and Wolff, and other SIU detectives knew about the cabin also. But these men were his friends and would not hurt him, he believed.

Within hours Gina and the kids and all the belongings they could carry were convoyed upstate under guard to the rustic, half-finished cabin. Gina had loved her house on Long Island. She had lovingly polished many times every floor, every tile. She would never see it again. Even now federal agents were emptying it out. It was put on the market—to be bought, eventually, by another New York cop.

In a garage underneath the courthouse, federal marshals met Leuci. From now on they would be charged with his protection. Two unmarked government cars waited, together with six men carrying submachine guns. Leuci was exhausted and merely gazed at them. He wanted to know where his wife and kids were, he wanted to know if they were happy, if they were comfortable, and he wanted someone in law enforcement to understand what he had been through, how much he had suffered.

The chief marshal introduced himself: John Partington. He put his arm around Detective Leuci and led him to the government car. "I'm in charge of your security. You did your job for the past year and a half. From now on, until it's all over, it will be my job to take care of you and your family. I want you to forget about everything else."

A second marshal introduced himself: Ed Scheu. He was carrying a submachine gun. "Take my word for it," he said, "nobody is going to fuck with you when you're with us. They told us about you upstairs. We understand what you did. We think you have a hell of a lot of balls. From today on you have nothing to worry about except your wife and kids. We'll worry about everything else."

There were three marshals in the lead car, and Leuci

and three other marshals in the second car: the two cars as they started upstate were in radio contact at all times. Constantly they exchanged positions, and a short distance beyond the city limit two other cars were waiting, and a changeover was made. Marshal Partington kept up a steady stream of friendly conversation. Leuci should start thinking about where he wanted to live. "Pick a nice place where it's warm, because I'm going to come with you," said Partington. "Whatever you need, we are going to get for you." He knew the names of Leuci's kids. He knew Leuci's wife's name. "Anthony is fine," he said. "I spoke to Anthony. I spoke to Gina. She's fine. She's cooking you a spaghetti dinner.

When the two cars pulled up in front of the cabin in the woods, Gina came out, and they embraced. She said, "Did you see the people that are there?"

It was too dark to see anything.

Gina said, "Whatever direction you look, there's a man with a rifle. It makes me very nervous."

Partington assured her that none of the marshals would come into the house. They would stay outside.

Leuci said, "You are welcome to come into my house. There is not much room inside, but you are welcome."

The house was small. On the first floor were two bedrooms, and a living room-kitchen. There was a spiral staircase leading up to the second floor, which was an unfinished loft. Leuci had bought the property four years before, and had built the house himself, aided by his father-in-law and some friends who would come up for weekends. Now this cabin in the woods was home.

The next morning Partington phoned at 6 A.M. Apologizing for calling so early, he asked to come over. When he arrived, he explained that he had been up all night. He showed Leuci plans he had drawn up of the house, its access roads, and the points where marshals would stand guard. He also wanted a list of men Leuci felt might be threats. Leuci gave him the names of Mikey Coco, Sergeants Cohen and Perrazzo, John Lusterino, the lawyers Salko, Caiola and Rosner, and several others.

Later Partington came back with pictures of all these

men. "I know that this is going to upset your wife a bit," he said. "But we want her to carry these pictures. The marshal who will be with her at all times will have a set also. We're going to find out where these men are, and what they are doing, and we'll watch them."

Gina's house was gone, her life was constricted, but she never complained. She had been six years old when she became a refugee during World War II. She had owned nothing. Her parents owned nothing. Growing up, she had lived in a single room. She had come to the United States and had found work as a domestic. She had lived in a furnished room for a time, and for a time she had shared a two-room apartment with her aunt in Queens.

The house in Kings Park had meant a lot to her. Everything she had ever wanted in a house was in that house. It was hers. But now it was gone. Now this cabin in the woods was her home, and she was sharing it with a total of eighteen marshals. They had promised not to come into the house, but at night it was like Siberia up there, and she was not the woman to keep them outside.

There was only one bathroom in the cabin, and it was in the basement. She and her husband slept in the loft, and sometimes in the middle of the night she would have to come down the rickety spiral staircase that her husband had built. The staircase would shake and squeak. There would be marshals sitting downstairs watching television, and she would have to walk into the bathroom that was open on top and had no lock on the door, and she would die.

When morning came the marshals would take her son to school. They carried machine shotguns. This was an incredible weapon. The barrel was about eighteen inches long. The handle was short so that it could be fired from the waist like a pistol. These shotguns were loaded with double O buckshot, and it was said they were powerful enough to turn over a car. Each morning Gina would watch her young son go off to school with such men.

Leuci meanwhile was housed in a military barracks on Governors Island in New York harbor, commuting to the cabin only on weekends. Special grand juries had been impaneled, and he was testifying before them nearly every day. When it came time to testify in trials he was going to be cross-examined about his own previous misconduct, and he did not know what he was going to say. He was certain only that his old life was over, and that his future, in whatever direction he looked, was bleak.

Book Two

1

THE 100TH PRECINCT, Queens. On a hot summer day, two young cops patrol the Rockaway Beach boardwalk in a police jeep when their radio barks news of a cardiac arrest two blocks inland. They speed there. The house is a white bungalow with green shutters. They can hear a woman screaming. They dash into the house, and into the kitchen.

An old man. An old woman. The old woman, screaming, has her hands clasped to her head. The old man, half propped against the stove, gags and collapses.

One young cop rushes out to the radio to call for help. The second rookie straddles the old man, who has turned gray, and whose mouth is bubbling with spittle. He presses his lips—lips that have kissed girls—to the lips of this old man he has never seen before this minute, and who is dying.

The old woman is still screaming.

He has the old man's nose pinched closed. His other hand massages the bony old chest. He keeps breathing into the nearly toothless, spittle-soaked mouth. He is trying to breathe life into a corpse.

The kiss goes on and on, but resuscitates no one. The young cop's uniform becomes soaked with sweat. His fingers cramp on the ancient beak. His arm is numb but still massaging. His eyes burn. Sweat drips down his face and into his eyes.

Two blocks away, people frolic at the edge of the sea.

What seems like an hour passes. At last two older cops from Emergency Service Division burst into the kitchen. A hand falls gently on the young cop's back. The old man is dead, he is told.

But the young cop continues mouth-to-mouth resuscitation. "I can feel something moving inside his chest," he gasps.

The two emergency service cops pull him to his feet. "He's been dead at least ten minutes," one says. And then, "This is your first one, isn't it?"

The rookie patrolman, Robert Leuci, aged twenty-two, stares down on the old man whose last breath he has shared.

The emergency service cop has his arm around the rookie. "You done good, kid," he says, trying to comfort him. "You done all you could."

2

CERTAIN TAPES among the hundred Leuci had made with more than forty individuals were more than four hours in length. Voices were sometimes unidentified or obliterated by background noises, but these tapes would stand as the principal physical evidence in the trials to come, and a task force of nine police stenographers was brought in. Wearing earphones, they sat in banks day after day, roughing out first drafts.

A second task force of assistant federal attorneys had been assembled under Scoppetta and Shaw to sift through the individual cases. These men were faced with an embarrassment of riches—too many defendants, too much evidence—and therefore with a bewildering assortment of decisions. There were going to be, potentially, thirty or forty trials. Where to start? Whom to indict? In what order? Under which statutes?

Each morning, surrounded by bodyguards, the chief government witness was brought in from Governors Island to the Federal Courthouse, and each night he was brought back again. He was more a prisoner than any defendant. Though each now waited to learn his fate, at least all were still free. Leuci was not free. He was not allowed to leave the building.

Once inside the courthouse, the prisoner became king and held court. He was crucial to every case, and every day prosecutors and stenographers vied for his favors.

Leuci had never been busier. His ego swelled. The trials could not take place without him. All these men needed him. They were nice to him every day. No one else had ever done what he had done, they told him. This was true, and it was also what he wanted to hear. They worked hard. He worked harder. He would work as late as anyone

171

wanted to work, or come in as early. Indictments began to come down.

He was almost happy. The future—when some or all of his new friends might turn on him—was still some months off. He had survived this far, he told himself. Whatever happened, he would be able to think of something. He was smarter than these prosecutors, smarter than any defense lawyer. He would find a way to save himself, no matter what.

In the meantime he was worried about Wolff, Mandato, and Cody, and about Vinny Russo, who was still another former partner. He was worried about Sheridan and Glazer too, knowing how they must be agonizing. Well, there was nothing he could do about Sheridan and Glazer, but he wanted to contact the others, who might be agonizing too—in their case, needlessly.

Unable to leave the courthouse, he telephoned Mandato. The conversation was very short.

"Do I have anything to worry about?" asked Mandato.

"No, you don't, Frank."

Silence.

Mandato had been a cop thirteen years. He had proven himself shrewd, calculating, and physically brave. He was also, like most detectives of his age and experience, worldly, cynical, fatalistic. If Leuci had truly gone over to the other side—far enough over to testify against him—then there was nothing he could do about it. He remembered meetings with Leuci during the past year and a half. Had Leuci taped them? He didn't know. Had anything incriminating been said? He didn't remember. What had Leuci told the prosecutors about their five years together before that? He didn't know this either.

Nor could he ask any of these questions. This was a telephone conversation, and one never knew who might be listening, either with Leuci's concurrence or without.

"Okay," said Mandato, "see you around." And he hung up.

This abortive conversation threw Leuci into black depression, and he began to beg the prosecutors to allow him to meet some friends in a restaurant from time to time. He was not a criminal, not a prisoner. They had to allow him to meet some old friends.

When this boon was not accorded him, he arranged to meet Wolff and Cody anyway, inducing his bodyguards to stop one evening at a steak house on the upper East Side. The bodyguards, two burly ex-motorcycle cops, were willing enough, for it meant a good meal paid for by Leuci, and they were sick of taking him to the movies every night. Inside the steak house, they took a table with their backs to the wall, from which they could, like Wild Bill Hickok in an earlier age, watch the entire saloon.

The three old friends ordered drinks. "I'm going to tell you right now," Leuci began, "neither of you have anything to worry about."

Wolff's reaction in person was the same as Mandato's by telephone. Perfect trust was gone. Question: Why had Leuci requested tonight's meeting? Question: Was Leuci wired even now? Question: Who else was listening to this conversation?

"I don't want you to start asking me anything," said Leuci. "None of this concerns you guys."

Wolff, studying him, said nothing.

But a big grin had come onto Cody's face. The older man socked Wolff in the arm. "I told you, Les. Bob wouldn't hurt us. Les, don't worry about it."

"Dave," said Wolff soberly, "you never worry about anything. You don't worry about whether you have your shoes on or not. I have to do the worrying for both of us."

The dinner was strained, and only Cody, who had had a few drinks, failed to notice it. Wolff's discomfort was so strong that presently, despite himself, he began to probe. How far was this investigation going to go, he asked, and in which directions?

But each question was interrupted by Cody, "Les, there's nothing to worry about, Bob would never hurt us."

"No further than it's gone already," said Leuci to Wolff.

Wolff, watching Leuci's face, nodded.

Partners spend eight hours a day in each other's presence for week after week, year after year. They interrogate subjects together, kick in doors together, go to court together, sit on endless surveillances together. They become, when the relationship is a good one, closer than brothers, closer than husband and wife. There are things one can't tell a wife. There is nothing one can't tell a partner, and the love of a cop for cop which exists everywhere, transcending all jurisdictional boundaries, is only an extension of the strongest love most cops have ever experienced, the love of partner for partner.

Similarly, to lose a partner can be a cop's strongest grief.

Outside on the sidewalk in the night the three detectives shook hands, and when Wolff and Cody had gone off together, Leuci stepped back into the custody of his bodyguards and went off alone.

3

LEUCI'S FIRST PARTNER is Jerry Schrempf. The two young cops who are straight out of the Police Academy patrol Rockaway Beach: sunstroke cases and rowdy teenagers in summer; in winter, nothing.

"You'll love it here," an older cop has told them. "You get the same check as the guy working Harlem. But there's nobody out here looking to take your head off, like in Harlem, and there's no money here, like in Harlem, either. Where there is money, there is bickering. One squad doesn't talk to another squad. One sergeant doesn't talk to another sergeant. But out here we have picnics. We have softball teams. You get sand in your shoes, and everybody loves each other."

But Leuci and Jerry want to feel themselves real cops. Both apply for transfers to the Tactical Patrol Force. TPF cops move about the city in squads, saturating high-crime zones.

However, as TPF cops the partners are split up. Schrempf is assigned to Brooklyn, Leuci to Manhattan. They meet often, though. "What am I doing wrong?" Schrempf complains. "I'm not making any more collars than a precinct cop. I'm looking for arrests, and I can't find them."

"Work the rooftops, Jerry," counsels Leuci. "You got all the junkies on the rooftops, and from up there you can watch the fire escapes for burglars." Imagination, cunning. These qualities come to other cops after years of experience. Somehow Leuci seems to have been born with them. "And Jerry, you stop cars. You ask for license and registration. You run plate checks. If it comes back bad, you can search the guy. You can search the car. Then you start coming up with guns, knives, drugs."

But Schrempf, who believes in civil liberties, is against stopping cars for no reason.

"It's legal, Jerry," Leuci points out. "And if you stop cars, you make collars."

One night Leuci's home phone rings at 3 A.M.

"Jerry Schrempf's been hurt. He stopped a car, and—"

"Is he okay?"

"We got the guy who did it."

"Is Jerry hurt bad?"

"He's dead, Bob."

Leuci goes back toward the bed. "Dead," he tells Gina. "I was with him yesterday, and he was fine. He's dead." He bursts into tears. "Jerry's dead."

Gina holds him in her arms in the dark. He sobs and sobs.

4

DESPITE THE FAILURE of his conversations with Mandato, Wolff, and Cody, there was one more former partner whom Leuci felt obliged to reassure, and this was Vinny Russo.

Good undercover detectives were rare, and were much in demand. One of the best, perhaps the best of all eight years before, had been Detective Vinny Russo. But Russo wanted to work only in Manhattan. Manhattan had the most dealers and biggest cases.

In addition, no skilled undercover liked to work with inexperienced detectives like Leuci. Undercovers were rated not according to how many buys they made, but how many arrests these buys resulted in, and inexperienced arresting officers often proved unable to find the sellers once the buy had been made. If this happened too often, the undercover began to lose ground in the monthly ratings.

Russo had agreed to work with Leuci in Brooklyn only after surviving a savage in Manhattan.

He had stepped into a hallway with three black men to buy drugs. Russo was an effective undercover because he did not look like a cop. He was small, almost frail. The three blacks led him up a narrow, malodorous staircase. There was no reason for this, so he realized he was about to be ripped off. Then the three men grabbed him. Russo had not gone for his gun soon enough.

The three men kicked and punched him. One took out a straight razor, and began slashing. The razor sliced through Russo's pants. They fell down. His gun fell out. Another grabbed up the gun, held it to Russo's head, and pulled the trigger. But the automatic was on safety. The man tried to cock the gun, but didn't know how.

All three men began kicking and beating Russo. They kicked in ribs. They slugged him with their fists, and with his own gun. They found his shield and tried to break his arm off at the shoulder. Russo was screaming for them to kill him.

A black woman, opening her door onto the hallway grabbed Russo and dragged him into her apartment, slamming the door on the three assailants.

"It's over for me," Russo had said, when Leuci visited him in the hospital. "I can't go in the street any more. I'm afraid, Bob. I'm too afraid. I've been beaten up too many times."

"Come back to Brooklyn with me," urged Leuci. "I'll take care of you."

"I don't want to be an undercover cop any more," said Russo through puffed lips. "I want to be able to tell people I'm a cop. I want to be able to walk up to somebody and say: you fuck, you, you're under arrest."

But Leuci talked to him persuasively for a long time. In Brooklyn he would be safe. No matter what happened, Leuci would be there to protect him.

And so for a number of years Russo had worked as Leuci's undercover, had communicated to the younger man not only his own techniques, but also his personal vision of the street and of street people. Eventually both men—Mandato too—had been promoted to SIU, where their success had continued.

Now Leuci wanted to see Russo. Although Russo was the more experienced detective, still Leuci had protected him from harm for so many years that he felt almost fatherly to him. He wanted to convince him that he had nothing to worry about from Leuci or from the prosecutors Leuci now worked for.

But Russo was an emotional, excitable kind of man, and Leuci found himself afraid to call him. Russo might imagine that his former partner was recording him, was trying to set him up.

So Leuci asked Gina to call Maria Russo, and from their cabin in the Catskills, Gina dialed the number.

The conversation at first sounded fine. The two women

asked about each other's children, about their husbands.

All of a sudden Gina began weeping. "Bob promises me he would never hurt Vinny under any circumstances," sobbed Gina.

"What are you doing?" cried Leuci, grabbing the phone out of her hand. "How do you know who could be listening?"

The constant police fear. Perhaps his own phone was tapped. Hurt Vinny? That single phrase might be enough to aim investigators at Russo.

"Why do you say such things?" demanded Leuci.

"Well, what do you want me to say?" sobbed Gina.

"Maria," said Leuci into the phone.

"Bob, don't be afraid," said Maria Russo. "Vinny wants to see you. You're welcome in my house any time."

Then Russo came on. "How are you? Are you okay? Will you come to my house? Do you have bodyguards out there? Bring them. We'll feed them all."

Leuci, hanging up, felt terrific. Russo was an SIU guy and still his friend. The perfect undercover agent was still his friend, and he looked forward to an Italian dinner at Russo's house next week.

Leuci's bodyguards escorted him there. But Russo stood in the doorway barring it. He stared at the two bodyguards.

"I don't want these IAD creeps in my house," he said.

The vast police brotherhood does not extend to cops who work for Internal Affairs Division, investigating other cops. Russo had his horn-rimmed glasses on. He seemed to have aged five years in the last few months.

"You're welcome in my house any time, Bob. But I don't know these guys."

"They're regular cops. They're my bodyguards."

"I don't want them in the house."

"Oh, Vinny."

"All right. Tell them to come in."

They came in. Once he started talking to them, Russo realized his mistake. Patrolman John Farley was a motorcycle cop. Patrolman Artie Monty was a childhood friend who had been in Leuci's wedding party. Russo poured out wine. In Russo's living room, the four cops talked about other cops, and about the department. But presently the bodyguards, realizing that this was a private meeting, went out to have dinner.

Once they had left, Russo said, "How did this all happen, Bob?"

"I couldn't begin to explain it to you. I don't want to talk about it. I want to enjoy my time here with you."

"Bob, from the day I met you, you were constantly giving out the deep sighs. I knew there was something wrong. What the hell was it?"

"It's too complicated. I don't want to talk about it."

Russo's son Jimmy came in. He was a big boy now, practically a man, Leuci told him. Russo bragging about his son's school work. "He's smart," said Russo. "He don't take after me, he takes after Maria." Then Russo bragged of his other son, who played football on the school team. He was proud of his two boys and his girl.

Dinner was served. Maria kept bringing out Sicilian dishes while Russo poured more wine. It got late. The kids were in bed. The three adults were all laughing and relaxed.

"Vinny, listen to Bob," said Maria. "Bob, Vinny is giving himself an ulcer. He's afraid something is going to happen."

"Nothing is going to happen," insisted Leuci. "Can't you believe nothing is going to happen? Do you think I would hurt you? Under any circumstances, do you think I would hurt you?"

"People make people do strange things," said Russo. "I don't know. What can you hurt me about? I'm a schmuck. Look, I've got cement on my hands." It was true. The foundation was cracking on the side of his house, and he had been trying to fix it himself because he couldn't afford to pay a mason to do it.

"Are you trying to convince me you're a hard-working guy? Not a money guy?"

"Bob, do you want to see my car? I've got an old, beat-up car. I can't pay for this goddamn house. I've got no money. Why would they be interested in me? I was never like you."

"What does that mean?"

"You were different."

"I was an arresting officer. You were an undercover officer. We worked together."

This remark caused a rather long silence.

"Those SIU guys treated me like I was kid," said Russo after a moment. "They would send me out for coffee and things like that."

"You were a better detective than the whole bunch of them put together."

"Yeah, but I had no imagination. I couldn't put a case together. You guys were able to put those cases together. You and Nunziata and these other guys were incredible." He said, "Are any of the other guys in trouble?"

"Nobody's in trouble other than what you have read in the papers."

"Is anybody going to get—"

"Vinny, you're never going to get in trouble from me."

"I believe you. I really believe you."

"I want you to relax, enjoy your home. You have Maria, you're a second-grade detective. You're out of Narcotics now."

Russo, no longer undercover, had been transferred to a detective squad, where he investigated whatever crimes occurred each day.

"I love doing squad work," he said. "I can tell people finally: You are under arrest. All the years I was undercover and getting beat up, I wanted more than anything else to be able to tell people I was a cop. You're under arrest."

Monty and Farley were waiting downstairs by the car. Russo walked out to the car with his guest.

"Bob, I got three kids and a wife," Russo said. "I've got three years to do. I want to get out of this job in one piece."

"Vinny, you've got nothing to worry about."

They shook hands.

"My house is always open to you." Russo said. "At least you can relax here. I can see you laugh."

The car drove away. When it had covered a short distance Monty, whom Leuci had grown up with, turned and said to Leuci in the back seat, "You're never going to hurt that guy, are you?"

"Why should I have to hurt him? He has nothing to do with anything."

"He's worried. He's really worried, Bob."

"Those prosecutors," said Farley, "I don't trust those pricks. You are talking to them every day. You don't know when to keep your mouth shut. This guy seemed like a real nice guy."

Leuci stared out the window into the night. "If they ever come and take me, Bobby," Russo had said an hour ago, "they are never taking me to jail. I ain't going to jail. I got to whack myself out." After a moment he had added, "The only thing I want to do is see my kids grow up," and he had gazed searchingly into Leuci's eyes.

5

MIDNIGHT. A rooftop in a Bronx ghetto. Patrolman
Leuci, aged twenty-three, watches two men lifting objects
out of an apartment window onto the fire escape below.
Burglars.

Patrolman Leuci's flashlight beam encapsulates them.
One has a Vandyke beard. "Police officer. Stay where you
are."

Leuci goes over the wall onto the ladder. But its steel
moorings break loose from the mortar, and it swings out
into space. Leuci rides it, trying to get back to the wall.

The two burglars sprint down the fire escape.

The terrified Leuci manages to drop onto the top fire
escape. The burglars are already in the courtyard, running
away. Leuci fires a shot down into the courtyard into
pitch darkness.

"The fuck shot me," a voice screams. But the burglars
keep running and escape.

When superior officers arrive, Leuci is standing beside
a stack of loot, trembling. An investigation into the
shooting begins at once. It is a legal shooting, but a bad
one, and Leuci knows it. A shooting is morally justified in
the presence of deadly physical force only. There was
none here. The burglars were perhaps not even armed. In
this precinct there is a cop known as "The Silver Bullet."
He has killed three teenage kids in the last few months,
each with one shot in the head. The precinct is bubbling.

The hospitals. He must check every hospital in the
precinct until he finds his victim. In the first emergency
room he comes to, doctors are taking a bullet out of the
leg of a fifteen-year-old kid.

"Are you all right?" cries Leuci, grabbing the kid by the
hand.

"You is some shot, man," says the kid, grinning. He is pleased to have been shot. His emotion is pride. Leuci's is overpowering relief.

The kid's mother rushes into the emergency room and begins to embrace the young patrolman. With tears in her eyes, she thanks him for not shooting to kill. She doesn't know about the dark courtyard. She imagines he shot her son in the leg on purpose.

The shaken Leuci leaves the hospital having resolved never to fire his gun again unless he is being shot at. Once he becomes a detective, he will carry this resolve one step further, and rarely even wear it.

6

THERE HAD BEEN, some months previously, a single meeting between Police Commissioner Patrick V. Murphy and Detective Second-Grade Robert Leuci. Leuci had insisted on it. He could go no further, he had said, without knowing that his boss approved of what he was doing. He wanted to hear this from the P.C.'s own lips.

Few cops had day-to-day contact with the Police Commissioner, and some never encountered one in person in their entire careers. The P.C. stood as a kind of god figure in their lives. He was the personification of all they stood for, and their attitude toward him was not far from the reverence and awe that other Americans accord to the President of the United States.

The meeting took place in a conference room in the Federal Building downtown. Scoppetta had told Leuci to wear a suit. This offended the detective.

"You don't have to tell me that. I know."

Murphy was late. Leuci sat with his back to the door. Scoppetta sat next to him, and U.S. Attorney Seymour next to Scoppetta. On the opposite side of the table sat Shaw, by himself. They waited for Murphy.

The door opened, and all stood up. Seymour was even taller than Shaw—about six feet six—and Murphy was a small man.

Leuci, in the presence of the Police Commissioner, feared that he would freeze up and be unable to speak, but Murphy, as he shook hands with them all, appeared scared too, like a father being called to the principal's office to defend a truant son.

Murphy sat in the chair opposite Leuci and would not look at him. He looked at Seymour or Scoppetta or Shaw when one or the other spoke. The rest of the time he looked at the table.

One by one, the prosecutors described the Leuci investigation. It was going terrifically well, they said. Terrifically well, to Murphy, meant that these men, this single second-grade detective, were knocking over his Police Department.

Murphy had been a New York cop more than twenty years, he said at last. He knew about corruption. Why, when he was a patrolman, the precinct cops used to get their police cars washed for nothing, rather than doing the job themselves. But he had put an end to that little practice. Police cars could now be driven directly to car wash garages and be washed professionally, and the city would pick up the tab.

Presently enough time had gone by, or so Murphy seemed to feel. Rising to his feet, he said, "I'm behind you one hundred percent," and he shook Leuci's hand. There was still no eye contact of any kind. During the final handshake Leuci, who had sat for twenty minutes unable to say a word, expected Murphy's gaze to meet his own. Perhaps some secret police message would flash across the void. But there was nothing. Murphy had walked out of the room.

Shortly afterward, however, Murphy appointed Three-Star Chief Sydney Cooper to head a new office monitoring the Leuci investigation and the cases that would arise out of it. The office was set up in a downtown office building, not only outside police headquarters, but even outside the normal police orbit.

Cooper at that time was fifty-two years old, and one of only four three-star chiefs in the department—there was a single four-star chief inspector—and he had commanded both the Inspections and Internal Affairs Divisions. He considered his new job, with its small staff and secret office, to be a demotion. Murphy didn't care about this. The Leuci investigation, to Murphy, was critical, and Cooper was the best and most reliable man he had.

Cooper was a big heavy man, with a bald head, a big nose, and a loud voice. He could be extremely funny, though most often his wit had a cutting edge to it. He seemed by far the smartest of the top cops around Murphy, and he had the most credentials, including a law degree. He had had management and computer training as well, and the previous year had begun the laborious job of computerizing Police Department personnel records. With no personal life to speak of, he regularly put in sixteen-hour days. He was known as a fierce corruption fighter—fiercer by far than Murphy himself.

Cooper had long ago terrorized the Police Department as a whole. No one, it seemed, had anything on Syd Cooper. He went where the evidence led him, and he was merciless. Cooper would not only lock up cops, he even seemed to enjoy it. Cops saw him as a shark swimming through their ranks. Although an amiable fellow to those who knew him well, Cooper was to cops in general the most hated and feared figure in headquarters.

But now he had been, to all outward appearances, banished, reduced in importance if not in rank. Murphy had even given out the cover story that Cooper was seriously ill and had been given this minor new office—its nature was kept vague—to tide him over while he waited out retirement.

His only job was what Murphy called "this Leuci business." However, there had been for many long months no Leuci business to occupy Cooper at all. He was not privy to the prosecutors' decisions, nor even to their knowledge. They would not let him close to the case. His vast energies were being wasted. Frustrated, deceived, he brooded constantly about headquarters. He longed to get back there, back inside the councils of power. He kept looking around for some means to do so, and at last he found what he was looking for. If he could not have "this Leuci business," then he would find a Leuci of his own. Arrests, headlines would all follow.

And he did exactly that.

Scoppetta telephoned Leuci with the news, "Cooper's got Frank Mandato."

7

TWO DAYS before his twenty-sixth birthday Leuci gets his gold shield—he is now a detective—and shortly after that he gets a new partner, Patrolman Frank Mandato, thirty-one, who has spent the last five years driving a radio car through the streets of the Seventy-seventh Precinct.

Mandato is six feet tall, weighs 185 pounds, and begins immediately to grow his sculptured black beard. Mandato is dark-complexioned, and his piercing black eyes seem to notice everything. His street sense, nurtured in the Bedford-Stuyvesant high-crime ghetto, is as acute as Leuci's, and by midsummer they are bringing ten felony narcotics arrests per month into the court system. By fall Mandato has his gold shield too.

One other fact about Mandato is not obvious at first: Mandato knows about money. The Seventy-seventh Precinct, like all ghetto precincts, teems with illegal bottle clubs, with street gamblers, with merchants willing to pay for additional police protection. The Seventy-seventh Precinct is a hotbed of payoffs to cops.

Although Mandato is five years older, Leuci was there first. It is Leuci who is team leader, and principally this is because the network of informants he has developed in Narcotics is his, personally. Most are addicts. The male addicts sometimes deal, and the female addicts are usually prostitutes. Their number fluctuates between six and ten, and their faces change. Some get arrested by other detective teams and go to prison. Some become terrified and no longer inform. Some disappear, and some die. Toward their informants, Leuci and Mandato obey the same rules all detectives obey. A junkie who gives up a street dealer is left alone. The street dealer who gives up a wholesaler is left alone. Any criminal is allowed to continue whatever his business may be provided he gives up someone worse than himself.

"Listen, these guys want to give me money," says Mandato one day. "They're junkies, but they are also selling dope themselves. Do you know how much money they make?"

"It all goes into their arms. They don't have any money."

One informant, a small-time street dealer and junkie, owns a candy store. His name is Nicky Conforte. He is standing in the back of his store when Leuci and Mandato enter. When they question him, he informs on his new wholesaler—name, address, location of the next drop. The wholesaler is a street-level guy, too. Still, it will make a nice arrest.

"Listen," says Mandato to the informant, "Bobby's short. Could you loan us a couple of dollars?"

The candy store owner hands $100 to Leuci and $50 to Mandato.

The amazed Leuci puts the money in his pocket.

The following week the two detectives call on the candy store owner again, and when they have finished questioning him he hands over another $100 without being asked.

There is a second informant who, to support his own habit, sometimes sells nickel bags out of his bodega. Leuci goes to question him, and afterward says, "I'm short. Can you lend me any money?" The words prove easier to speak than he had supposed.

"Why didn't you ask me? Any time you're short, Bobby." The informant rings up a "no sale" and hands across $100.

From then on, both informants pay regularly. Without being asked, too. This seems important. It is no shakedown. There is no extortion. It is not even a bribe, Leuci and Mandato tell themselves, for they give nothing in exchange. It is more like a loan they don't have to pay back.

The money is spent. Leuci is buying better clothes, eating in better places. The big thing is to be able to buy equipment—or so the two detectives tell themselves—to buy tape recorders, to buy eavesdropping gear. To buy a new car so that you can chase somebody in it.

Nunziata notices Leuci's new affluence. All the older detectives notice. Leuci realizes that he has crossed a threshold, that he is now one of them. He is accepted by other narcotics detectives for the first time.

Nunziata invites him to dinner, and when they have ordered, remarks, "You've earned a few dollars."

"Yes," says Leuci proudly. He is elated to have won Nunziata's approval. When he describes what happened, Nunziata laughs. "You're incredible. With your information and my brains, I'd be a millionaire."

This is a sixty-dollar dinner for two in an Italian restaurant on the lower East Side. It is Nunziata who picks up the check.

Leuci basks in his new acceptance by his fellow detectives. The important thing is to be able to make your cases, to make arrests, and to live a decent life, all the detectives seem to feel. Putting their heads on the line for everybody and going home with seventy-five cents in their pockets makes no sense. It's stupid guys who do that, or kids who don't know better. Now that Leuci has graduated, or suddenly gotten older, they see the change in him, and they like him much better because he is not only a good cop but also smart enough to earn money.

Nevertheless, Leuci continues, as is his way, to brood about all this. It has made a wound in his psyche that is trying to heal, but he won't let it. He keeps picking at the scab. In his heart he sometimes feels ashamed. He wonders if all the other detectives are secretly ashamed also.

He wishes he could talk to Nunziata about it, but knows he can't. It isn't done. He has never heard any detective talk about it. He imagines all the other detectives rationalize their conduct just as he does, telling themselves: As long as we all do it together, it isn't really so bad.

8

MANDATO WAS ALWAYS immaculately groomed, and his possessions were always immaculate also. It was because of this meticulousness that he fell into the hands of Chief Cooper.

He had left his car off at a body shop to have a dent knocked out and repainted—any car Mandato drove had to look sharp. The black man working on the car became conscious of the odor of marijuana. He searched the interior of the car but found nothing. Opening the trunk, he found what he was looking for. He was staring down at a bale of marijuana. It looked as though it weighed about ten pounds.

The black man went to the phone and called the police. A radio car team responded, contemplated the bale of marijuana, and matched the car to Detective Third-Grade Frank Mandato.

In any cop's lexicon of crimes, marijuana ranked at the very bottom, and in addition the rule said that you gave another cop a break. But this was a case the two radio car cops did not dare bury. For one thing, the black man's call had been logged in, marijuana had been mentioned, and the complainant was standing there, looking at them. For another, the Police Department, because of the Knapp Commission, was in the grip of a kind of corruption hysteria. No one knew who was investigating whom anymore, and the bale of marijuana perhaps had nothing to do with this Detective Mandato. Perhaps the target here was not Mandato but themselves.

And so they played it safe. They called IAD, and when Mandato came to pick up his car later, two IAD detectives were standing beside it.

Routinely Chief Cooper was notified. "Mandato is

mine," he said, and began rubbing his hands together with glee.

Mandato, who at this time worked out of Tenth District Burglary-Larceny, claimed under interrogation that the bale of marijuana was evidence he had seized in an earlier case. He had "forgotten" to turn it in to the property clerk's office.

This was perhaps true. By regulation, evidence had to be vouchered with the property clerk on the day seized, and returned there immediately after each court appearance, but the property clerk was in distant Manhattan, and Brooklyn detectives were constantly getting in trouble for letting their evidence stockpile.

Chief Cooper ordered all of Mandato's cases examined; this inquiry showed that certain packages of seized heroin had not been turned in to the property clerk either. Mandato promptly produced what he said were these packages. He had always intended to turn them back in, he said. They had lain "forgotten" in a locked trunk in his basement for months.

Cooper ordered the packages analyzed by the police lab. One contained more heroin now than when analyzed the first time. To Cooper, it was obviously not the same heroin.

Cooper had been a cop since 1941—thirty-one years—and believed he knew cops. It seemed clear to him that Mandato had intended to hold this evidence back indefinitely—until he retired, perhaps longer. If ever anyone called for it, then he would of course produce it. If no one called for it, then many years from now he would—do what? Sell it, perhaps, thought Chief Cooper.

And Mandato had been Leuci's partner, brooded Cooper. Mandato was an insider too. He would know the same crooked cops, the same Mafia hoodlums that Leuci knew. Mandato, if Cooper could only apply sufficient pressure, could become Cooper's Leuci.

Cooper had all the leverage needed, or at least he thought he did. Although criminal charges against Mandato probably would not stick—no jury, Cooper supposed, would send him to jail for what could be made to sound like administrative oversights—still he was clearly guilty of serious breaches of Police Department regulations, and for these Cooper could have him dismissed. Mandato had thirteen years in; two more and the first stage of his pension would be secured, three-quarters of half pay for life. How much money, Cooper asked himself, were we talking about here? If you accorded Mandato a generous life span, then the answer came back at around a quarter of a million dollars. Mandato need only to hang on another two years, and all that money would be his.

Mandato would cooperate, Cooper decided grimly, or throw away $250,000. Mandato, cooperating, would give up corrupt cops, detectives, and bosses. He would perhaps give up Leuci, too. The prosecutors were still insisting that Leuci was guilty of only three corrupt acts. Mandato would know better, and perhaps could be made to confirm Cooper's own suspicions.

Any success at all would sweep Syd Cooper back into Headquarters, perhaps at an even higher level than before.

Cooper had dealt with hundreds of corrupt and suspect cops, and he planned to crack Mandato with the same classic techniques that had always worked in the past.

Technique number one was to order cops to his office, and then leave them sitting in chairs in an anteroom for eight hours straight, without taking any notice of them whatever. At the end of the day Cooper would allow them to sign out and go home. On the second day the same scenario would be repeated, and on the third, the fourth, the fifth—for however many weeks or months it took until the cop cracked, and babbled forth whatever information Cooper sought. Cooper had never known this technique to fail.

But Mandato, summoned to Cooper's office, arrived with coffee and a bagel in a paper bag, and with books to read. He sat down in the anteroom, took out a book, and calmly read all day long. At the end of eight hours he signed out and went home.

The following day he returned with another paper bag

containing coffee and a bagel plus the same book, or perhaps another. And he quietly turned pages for eight hours. Cooper took no notice of Mandato, and Mandato—apparently—took no notice of Cooper.

Every day Cooper walked past Mandato several times. Normally Mandato did not even look up. Weeks went by. Cooper waited for Mandato to pace the floor, to ask anxious questions of the clerks and secretaries, to show fear. But he never did.

Finally it was Cooper who cracked. Becoming increasingly aggravated, Cooper began, when passing Mandato's chair, to attempt to bait him. Mandato, as always, was smartly dressed; his sharply creased slacks must have cost forty dollars, perhaps more. His shoes were hand-stitched.

"How can a piece of shit like you afford to wear such expensive clothes?" demanded Cooper.

Mandato only smiled. "My wife is very frugal. I'm sure, if you wanted to, you could afford to buy some decent clothes."

Cooper, fuming, went into his office and slammed the door. Though used to cops who trembled—literally trembled—in his presence, he was finding it impossible to intimidate Mandato, and he could not understand why.

But Mandato, however cool he may have seemed to Cooper, was badly frightened, and when Leuci one night rang his bell, he was glad to see his former partner.

"You can save your job, Frank," Leuci said.

"How?" asked Mandato. "Just tell me how."

"You can talk to these people."

"What should I talk to them about? Should I tell them what you and I did? Should I tell them what Les Wolff and I did? Should I tell them what Nunziata did with other people?" He shook his head. "I've got nothing to tell them."

The two ex-partners gazed at each other.

"Do I have anything to worry about?" asked Mandato. "Tell me. Is there something I should be concerned about? What have you told them?"

"I told Scoppetta I had done three things, and that's all

I ever intend to tell anybody, and those three things concerned only me. That's it. That's all they'll ever get from me."

"Then I have nothing to tell them," said Mandato.

"Maybe I can work something out. Let me think about it."

It was Leuci, via Scoppetta, who brought Deputy Commissioner McCarthy into the case. Mandato found Cooper crude, Leuci told Scoppetta. McCarthy seemed a sensitive man. If he would interview Mandato, then perhaps communication would be easier.

"I'll talk to McCarthy," said Scoppetta, and he did.

Deputy Commissioner William McCarthy was a former chief of traffic cops whom Murphy had brought back from retirement. During his police career, McCarthy had assiduously avoided not only corrupt cops, but also corrupt situations. He had rarely ever been tempted. Now, recalled as a deputy commissioner, he had proven to be a man of advanced management ideas, but underneath this veneer his personality was as rigid and unbending as ever.

In the presence of Cooper and two of Cooper's aides, McCarthy did meet with Mandato, but the conversation went nowhere, and very soon McCarthy became exasperated. "Tell me every bit of corruption you have ever seen," he demanded of Mandato.

"I've heard about a lot of corruption," said Mandato, "but I've never seen any."

"You have thirty seconds," said McCarthy.

"I don't know what you want to know," said Mandato. "I have never seen any corruption."

McCarthy rose from his desk and strode to the door, where he turned to Chief Cooper and said, "Suspend him. Take his shield and gun." And McCarthy walked out of the room.

Cooper in turn strode toward the door. "Suspend him," said Cooper to his subordinate, Lieutenant George Ahrens. "Take his shield and gun."

Cooper walked out of the room.

Lieutenant Ahrens turned to Dave Powers, a sergeant.

"Suspend him, take his shield and gun," ordered Ahrens, and he too walked from the room.

Mandato stood holding his gun and shield in his hands. "Is there anyone left, sarge?" said Mandato. "There's only you and me now. I think you got to do it." And he handed his gun and shield to the sergeant.

A short time later, forced to resign from the Police Department or be dismissed for cause, Mandato moved to Florida. There he experienced every cop's withdrawal symptoms—he felt for his shield a dozen times a day, and it wasn't there. This meant he was now alone in the world. Walking in the street, he kept hitting himself in the back pocket. All the time. He would get in his car, and realize he was not sitting on it. His shield was gone, and he could not get it back.

One day a police car pulled him over for speeding. He jumped out of his car imagining that he had nothing to worry about. His hand went to his back pocket. He would show the cop his shield and—

Oh.

The trooper came over. "License and registration."

He had been a cop himself, Mandato told him. Thirteen years. But he had just retired.

"They give you a card when you retire," said the cop. So Mandato told him the truth.

The cop nodded. "License and registration," he said, and wrote out a ticket.

Mandato phoned Leuci in New York and recounted this story. "It's awful, awful," he said. "You got to beat them, Bobby. It's worth whatever it costs. You got to beat them. You got to hang in there."

9

TO MAKE ten felony arrests a month—sometimes fourteen or fifteen—takes all of the young detective's time. Leuci, now twenty-six, is in the streets of south Brooklyn day and night, or else in court with prisoners.

One night while cruising, looking for someone to arrest, he spies a beautiful Hispanic face. She looks fourteen or fifteen years old. A child. She wears a raincoat. Her long black hair is tied into a ponytail. Great round alabaster face, enormous black eyes, full lips. A beautiful face. He is sure she doesn't realize how beautiful she is. She walks the same block prostitutes walk.

Leuci pulls over. "You shouldn't be here. It's dangerous here."

She smiles. "I can take care of myself. You're a cop, right?"

He doesn't like the way she says: You're a cop. But it does not necessarily make her a bad girl.

"You're Babyface, aren't you?" She calls his name in a kind of shout, alerting the neighborhood to his presence.

"You fool around?" asks Leuci, after a moment.

"No, I don't fool around."

"What are you doing out here then?"

She smiles. "I'm just waiting for somebody."

So Leuci drives off, but he comes back via a side street and parks where he can look onto the avenue. She is tricking. Men come up and she talks to them. Here comes some crewcut kid. Leuci becomes terribly depressed. She puts her arm in the kid's and off they go. Twenty minutes later she is back.

Leuci gets out of his car, grabs her, and drags her into a hallway.

"Open your purse."

She becomes nasty. "Who the hell do you think you are?"

He empties her purse out on the floor. He is angry at her, and doesn't know why.

"Take off your coat," he orders. When she resists, he yanks it off her.

And he sees the needle marks.

But it makes him more depressed than ever, because he finds her gorgeous. Black hair and eyes. White teeth. One rarely sees addicts with good teeth.

"How long have you been fooling around?"

"If it's any business of yours, since I was twelve."

"How old are you now, fifteen?"

"I'm nineteen."

"Have you ever been busted before?"

"Twice."

She puts her stuff back in her bag. She is looking up at him. "I'm warning you, Babyface. You leave me alone."

"I'll see you around. I catch you and you're going."

"You got to catch me first, smart guy."

A few days later, early in the morning, Leuci drives down Pacific Street toward court. There she is in the same raincoat on the same corner. Pulling the car to the curb, Leuci watches her from some distance away. When a black man walks up to her, Leuci pulls out into traffic and approaches very slowly. He sees him hand something to her, after which he starts to walk away.

Leuci pulls to the curb, gets out, and starts running. As he closes in on the girl, she smiles and shouts her greeting, "Hello, Babyface." Again she has alerted the neighborhood.

She has her hand closed. He grabs her hand and forces it open. Two bags of heroin.

The black man has run into a brownstone. Leuci takes her junk, cries, "You wait right here," and runs into the building after him. She may run, but he thinks she will probably wait, hoping he might give her back her junk.

In the brownstone, Leuci pauses to get his bearings. It's a rooming house. He runs up the stairs. When he gets almost to the second landing, he spies the black man.

Then a dresser drawer comes down the stairs at him. It goes over him, knocking him down. The black man runs up onto the roof. By the time Leuci gets up there, he is gone, either onto another roof or down a fire escape.

Scared and angry, Leuci goes back downstairs and outside. The girl is sitting on the stoop with her head in her hands.

"You're under arrest. Get in the car."

He processes her in the 78th Precinct, then takes her to court. All morning she screams and curses him. But wherever they go, he notices, people stare at her because she is so beautiful. This only depresses Detective Leuci. She could be anything, this girl, he thinks. With any brains at all she could go someplace.

She has a foul, filthy mouth. Her name is Maria. She is a nasty little bitch, but he cannot take his eyes off her.

Once in court, her fear becomes apparent. Her yellow sheet has come back. Leuci sees she has never been arrested before. Never gone to jail before.

"Do you know what it's going to be like for me in the Women's House of Detention?" she asks. "You are going to send me there. They are going to hurt me. There are bull daggers in there. The guards are bull daggers."

She is petrified and he is petrified for her.

"Get me out of here. I'm scared."

Leuci approaches the assistant D.A. "Listen, this girl wants to cooperate with me. Can I get her out?"

But the judge has left the courtroom. Leuci hurries to his chambers.

"Judge, I want a recall on my case."

But the judge, wanting to get home, refuses. Leuci goes back to the girl. She is sitting there, and is in tears.

"How bad is your habit?" he asks.

She starts screaming at him. "Fuck you and your medication. I don't need any medication. I'll get through this night without you. I'll get through this night."

Leuci goes home. All night long he thinks about her. He can't get her beautiful little face out of his mind. What is it like for her tonight in that prison full of lesbians?

The next morning he gets to Brooklyn early, and looks

to make sure her case is on the calendar. Eventually the truck comes. The prisoners file out of it.

She glares at him.

"Do you want to get out of here? Would you work with me? We'll make some cases."

"I'm not a rat."

"Do you want to go back in there tonight?"

"Just get me out."

At Detective Leuci's request, the assistant D.A. makes the standard approach to the judge. "The police officer has apprised me that the defendant will cooperate with the police Narcotics division. She has information about dealers."

As the judge listens, the girl reaches over and grabs Leuci's leg. She gives him a squeeze, and a warm childish smile.

Quickly Leuci straightens out her papers. When he comes out of the courthouse she is waiting by his car.

"Get in, I'll drive you home." After a moment, he asks, "What kind of habit do you have?"

"I don't mainline or skin pop. I haven't got a habit."

"All right. How about if I see you tonight? Get dressed up and I'll see you tonight."

"You would take me out?"

"Of course I'd take you out."

"You're terrific."

He goes to his office and talks it over with Frank Mandato. "She's a gorgeous girl, Frank."

"What are you going to do with her?" asks Mandato.

"I'm going to take her out."

"Why don't you just take her to a hotel and screw her? She's a fucking pross. Are you crazy? Do you want to take her to the movies? Buy her an ice cream soda? This is a Puerto Rican prostitute. So she's nineteen and pretty. In two years she'll have no teeth and seventeen needle scars in her arms."

"Frank, you've got to see her. She's like a saint. She is a beautiful thing. Where will you be tonight?"

Mandato plans to have dinner with several other detectives at an Italian restaurant near the courthouse.

"I'll see you there," says Leuci.

"Are you losing your mind? There are cops—all the guys in the office—"

That night he goes to pick her up. She is dressed all in black in a lace dress. A lace shawl comes up over her hair.

But when he tells her where they will go for dinner, she says, "That's where all the cops hang out."

"Yeah, there will be some cops there."

"You're not ashamed of me?"

"Of course I'm not ashamed of you."

All heads turn as they enter the restaurant. Leuci beams with pride. Mandato, who stands at the bar with four other detectives, comes over and introduces himself. "I heard about you," she tells him.

He looks at her, smiles at Leuci, and walks back to the bar shaking his head.

Joe Nunziata walks over and introduces himself, and after him, one by one, all the other detectives. From the bar they stare over. They can't stop looking at her. They are also giggling and drinking, making cracks no doubt, amusing themselves with their wit. Leuci doesn't care.

"What are we going to have?" he asks. "Some wine?"

"I'm very nervous in here. I don't like these guys. They are making fun of us."

"They are not making fun of us. Nobody would make fun of you."

"I have to go to the ladies' room."

When she has left the table, Nunziata walks over and says to Leuci, "Is your name Angel?"

"Joe, what's so funny?"

"Apparently this girl is in love with a guy named Angel. When she comes back, take a good look at her."

She comes back and sits down. "Do you know somebody by the name of Angel?" asks Leuci.

"Yes, my old man. How do you know that's his name? Oh, you saw my thing."

"What?"

As she turns he sees the word Angel tattooed across the muscle of her upper arm. But it is a tattoo done in the street. It is not a professional tattoo.

"Who did that to you?"

"Angel did it to me."

He almost starts laughing. By the time he has paid the check he has convinced her—or thinks he has convinced her—that she should work with him. He will bring in a female detective to walk with her in the street. They will make all sorts of buys, providing himself and Mandato with many arrests. Although afraid, she has said, "If you are with me, I will do it."

But when he calls for her the next day at her mother's house, she isn't there. Her mother has no idea where she is. He looks for her in the streets but can't find her. At length he gives up looking.

A week passes. At two o'clock in the morning Leuci and Mandato finish processing a prisoner, and leave the station house. As they walk toward their cars, a taxi cab stops nearby. Out step three passengers: Maria, another girl whom Leuci recognizes as a prostitute, and the black man who pushed the bureau drawer down the stairs on him two weeks earlier.

To Mandato, Leuci says quietly, "That's the son of a bitch who got away from me the day I locked up Maria."

The detectives start walking fast toward the three street people. Maria, spotting Leuci, again attempts to alert the neighborhood: "Hey B—"

Leuci slaps her, cutting off her voice, and Mandato grabs the black man, hustling him into a hallway.

In the hallway, Leuci has the suspect by the throat. "You're the guy that got away from me," he shouts. "You're under arrest."

Maria, next to him, is shouting that this is not the same man. The suspect is struggling, the two girls are shouting, and Mandato gives a sudden gasp. "Bobby, he has a gun."

The prostitute screams, "Hey, man, no guns," and gives a kind of strangled scream as the gun appears. Close to his head Leuci hears the trigger pulled twice, two loud clicks, no explosion.

Mandato pushes Leuci out of the way. He is on top of the suspect on the floor, gripping the gun hand. Leuci tears the gun loose. Mandato picks the guy up. Leuci is shaking so much he can only stand there, holding the gun. Mandato, gripping the suspect, is shaking also.

"He pulled the fucking trigger on me," Leuci says.

He gets his handcuffs out, but is shaking so much that, handcuffing the suspect, he cuts himself with the cuffs.

They walk the suspect into the station house. It's nearly three o'clock in the morning and the place is empty. The girls have gone, faded into the night. Upstairs they empty the gun out. Leuci stares at the bullets. "Regular fucking bullets," Mandato mutters.

Attempted murder of a detective is a heavy crime. The paperwork will take hours. After locking the suspect in the cage, Leuci and Mandato go out for coffee and pastry to sustain them through what is left of the night.

When they return, the desk officer stops them. "I don't see walking a guy in here that tried to kill a cop. You carry the fuck in, or you send him to the hospital, or you send him away in a box."

On the staircase they meet the squad detectives coming down. One says, "Let me tell you something, Leuci. If you don't teach that prick a lesson, the next cop he runs into he's going to blow him away."

Leuci apologizes. It was over so fast.

"Well, he's upstairs," the detective says.

Upstairs, the suspect lies in a heap in the corner of the cage. Froth and blood bubble from his mouth.

"Oh, shit, Frank, the guy is dead."

Rushing into the cage, they lift the prisoner up, wash him off, plead with him not to die. A lieutenant arrives, and looks down at him.

"I understand beating a guy up on the street," he says. "But in the station houses it don't make any sense."

By morning the suspect is well enough to appear in court. Later he is sentenced to one to three years for attempted felonious assault. His gun goes to ballistics that same afternoon. The ballistics detective identifies it by name. "He pulled the trigger on me twice," says Leuci.

The ballistics detective nods. "These cheap guns never go off."

But when he aims it into a test-fire box and pulls the

trigger, it fires perfectly. The room fills up with the noise and smoke of the explosion. Leuci and the ballistics detective stare at each other.

From time to time after that, Leuci parks his car down the block and sits there watching Maria patrol her street corner, tricking. He does not again try to use her as an informant.

10

THE FIRST TRIAL approached—*The United States of America* v. *Edmund Rosner, Nicholas DeStefano, and Nicholas Lamattina*—and with it would come the moment Leuci dreaded, the moment when he would be asked under oath to describe his own previous misconduct.

It was not this particular trial that caused now his sleepless nights, or the perpetual tightness around the region of his heart. Rather it was the realization that from now on, in his role as chief government witness, he himself would be on trial too. The defendants would not take the stand. Only the witness would take the stand, and once he was there his credibility would become the issue, not their guilt. Prosecutor and defense lawyer both would hammer. What was he going to say?

To lie on the stand was perjury. But the truth would impeach his credibility to such an extent that this trial—and future trials too—would be compromised, probably lost. If the truth were once spoken, then the Police Department would have no choice but to dismiss him, the government no choice but to prosecute him, a jury no choice but to send him to jail—and with him would go all the detectives he would have implicated: Mandato, Wolff, Cody, Vinny Russo, and many, many others. Or so he believed.

The whole world would despise him, his new friends as much as his old. If he answered truthfully, he would bring down on himself and those he loved calamities without number. The truth would condemn him to death. It was lies, and lies only, that could set him free. And so he resolved in advance that he would lie. He would say nothing.

He worked every day with the assistant U.S. attorneys who would prosecute the case.

Weekends, in the Catskills, he would go out of the house, walk into the woods, and brood. He would try to think it all through. But he was never alone. Always at least two heavily armed marshals trailed him and sometimes, not understanding his need to be alone, his absolute need to think this thing through, they would stride along at his side chatting about the weather, or about football. Then the weekend would end, and Leuci would go back to New York, to his bare barracks room by night, to the corridors and offices of the Southern District Courthouse on Foley Square by day.

An all-out effort to convict Lawyer Rosner, Bailbondsman DeStefano, and Detective Lamattina had been ordered. As many as three assistant U.S. attorneys were assigned to help prepare the case at one time. Leuci worked at their sides, and this work went on literally night and day.

Leuci had made twelve recordings with one or another of the defendants. The transcripts had to be absolutely accurate, for the defense could be expected to challenge every line, and the various background noises made this difficult. The transcripts went through draft after draft until each line, each incriminating statement, was as accurate as they could make it.

After that, the prosecution's case had to be virtually memorized both by the lawyers and by the chief witness. Day after day, week after week, all these men studied, tightened, honed their case.

Scoppetta and Shaw, busy on other cases, were not involved in trial preparations, and so Leuci, ostensibly to keep them informed, took to dropping into their offices several times each day. They were his sole emotional support, although they didn't know this. They perceived neither the nature of his dilemma nor the extent of his suffering. What was he going to admit on the stand?

He had never asked for nor been promised immunity from criminal prosecution, much less immunity from Police Department charges. He had not needed immunity, because he had not been charged with anything. There was no evidence against him. To get immunity now he would first have to admit to the prosecutors that he needed it. He would first have to confess to actions they did not suspect. Nor was there hope under any circumstances of acquiring immunity for his former partners.

From Scoppetta and Shaw, who cared about him, he needed answers to questions he could not pose, legal advice that he dared not ask for. Scoppetta and Shaw were prosecutors. The law was inflexible. Leuci's questions alone would reveal the guilt he was concealing. They would be obliged by law to take action against him or be guilty of crimes themselves.

No, he would have to lie.

Leuci's only comfort was that they were there. They had strength, and to stand near them gave him the illusion of strength—enough, at least, to get through each day.

"I think I'm going to be leaving soon," said Scoppetta one morning. "I think I'm going to be given an important appointment." He was elated, and trying to keep from grinning.

Leuci did not grin.

Scoppetta was about to be appointed New York City's Commissioner of Investigations—the man charged with investigating corruption in any and all New York City agencies. This was a cabinet level post, equal in rank and salary to the Police Commissioner.

"I'm very happy for you, Nick," said the stricken Leuci.

A few days later, when Scoppetta's appointment was confirmed, the prosecutor came out from behind his desk and embraced Leuci, saying, "I've got it."

Scoppetta beamed with happiness, and held the detective by both shoulders.

Leuci went back to work.

The chief prosecutor in the Rosner case was a young lawyer named Elliot Sagor, and as the trial date neared he had begun working fourteen to fifteen hours a day, and weekends as well.

Around eleven o'clock one night, while editing tapes with Sagor, Leuci wanted to go to Vinnie's Clam Bar in Little Italy. Sagor told him this was crazy. It was too dangerous, and besides, they had to go on working. Probably they would have to work all weekend.

Frustrated from hours and hours of listening to the same tapes over and over, Leuci lost his temper.

For a moment they glared at each other. Then Leuci grabbed up Sagor's tape recorder and threw it down on the desk. Yanking Sagor's jacket off the coat tree, he tried to tear it in two. He upended Sagor's desk. "And furthermore, I'm going home this weekend."

Leuci's bodyguards had burst into the room, which was a shambles. Leuci was trying to get at Sagor. The two cops grabbed Leuci, and pulled him off.

"If you can find a way to get home and get back here by Sunday," said Sagor, "I'll let you do it."

From the next room Leuci phoned Marshal Partington, who arranged to put a customs helicopter at his disposal. On Friday evening Leuci was driven to the Wall Street heliport, and the machine took off into a clear night, flying up the East River over the bridges. He was going home to the north woods, and there he would try to store up in two days enough strength to get through next week. From the helicopter the view of his city at night was breathtakingly beautiful. He saw this beauty, but was too much involved with his own problems to enjoy it. Scoppetta was gone, but at least he still had Shaw.

And then Shaw too received an important new appointment. He was named head of the New York office of the Justice Department's Joint Stike Force Against Organized Crime. He cleaned out his desk and moved across the plaza to new offices—and new concerns.

Every day the strain on Leuci built higher. Every day the time when he would testify—and be cross-examined—came closer. Every day Shaw telephoned: "Are you all right?"

From time to time Leuci was still invited to dine with Shaw and Margaret in the couple's Brooklyn Heights apartment, and it was there one night that Shaw said suddenly, "I need a good Jewish undercover detective. Do you know anyone?"

Shaw in his new job had begun to put together a

scheme designed, if it worked, to break organized crime's stranglehold on New York's heavily Jewish garment industry. The Jewish detective would be furnished with money with which he would buy a garment business in partnership with a garment executive who had come to Shaw for help. Once installed in the garment business, the detective would become subject to and take part in shakedowns, shylock operations, truck hijacks. The investigation would last at least two years. And the detective would be in grave danger most of that time.

"I can't tell you about the case," said Shaw, "except to say that if I can find the right Jewish detective, it can be a great case."

"I think," said Leuci after a moment, "that the guy you're looking for is Les Wolff."

Shaw nodded. "Does he have any skeletons I should be warned about?"

Again the pull in two directions at once. But Wolff was a great detective. More important than that, with Shaw behind him, he would be safe from such people as Chief Cooper.

"No, none," answered Leuci. "Les Wolff is your man."

The Rosner-DeStefano-Lamattina case was almost ready for trial. "The only thing left to prepare is your cross-examination," said Sagor. "Get a good night's sleep tonight. Tomorrow come in early, and we'll start on that."

Now it comes, thought Leuci. He had only hours left in which to decide. How much was he going to tell?

He communicated his decision to Sagor the following morning. He would admit nothing. "What are you telling me?" The prosecutor responded. "That you now admit no misconduct of any kind? What about what you told Scoppetta?"

Leuci attempted a confident laugh. "I was bullshitting."

Sagor stared at him.

"It wasn't me," said Leuci. "I was talking about somebody else."

Sagor nodded his head up and down. "You'll have to

excuse me," he said, and strode toward the door. "Have your lunch brought in here. Order it sent up."

He went out.

Leuci's bodyguards came in from the outer office. "What are you going to do?" asked one. "Are you going to tell him you did something? You have to be out of your fucking mind. You'll lose your job. You can't tell him anything."

This was the conclusion Leuci had come to also.

"Don't tell them anything," advised the other cop.

Into the office walked Mike Shaw. He was wearing jeans and a sweater. He said to the two cops, "Will you excuse us?"

The two cops, looking surprised, left the room.

"Bob, I want to tell you something," began Shaw earnestly. "I couldn't care less if you sold junk. I couldn't care less what you've done in the past. I know you for what you are now. What you were three years ago, two years ago, even one year ago—that's not what you are now. You're a different man now. You've changed your life. But if you allow yourself to take the stand, and then perjure yourself—I understand why you might want to do that, but if you do it, you would lose me as a friend. I would know that you had lied. You would force me into a position where I would have to take the stand and testify against you, because I know that you've done things. You've told Nick that you did things."

Shaw paused. A pleading note came into his voice. "You're not going to put me in that position, are you, Bob?"

"Mike, why do I have to pay that price? Why do I have to get on the stand and tell what I've done. Tell me, why?"

"Because it's the truth. It's as simple as that. That's the difference between us and Rosner, because we're going to get on the stand and tell the truth."

The phone rang. Shaw picked it up, spoke for a moment, then handed the receiver to Leuci. "Talk to him. It's Nick."

"Bob, you've gone too far to turn back now," said

Scoppetta. "You've told me what it is. It's not so terrible. People will understand."

"I'm embarrassed, Nick. I'm ashamed."

When Leuci had hung up, Shaw called in Sagor and his boss, Robert Morvillo, head of the Criminal Division. "This guy is going to be the best witness you ever had," Shaw said.

"If he tells the truth he'll be the best witness I ever had," said Morvillo.

Shaw turned back to Leuci. "Margaret is waiting for me. I've got to go home." He turned to the two prosecutors. "Prepare him well. Let him know what he can expect." Shaw turned back to Leuci. "See you soon."

"See you soon, Mike."

Morvillo sat down at the desk, smiled at Leuci, and said, "Okay, detective, tell us about your misconduct."

"It's so hard."

"Let's make it easy for you. What did you tell Scoppetta? Start from the top."

"What was the first time?" said Sagor.

"The first time?"

"Tell us about it."

And so Leuci told the following story to the two prosecutors—the same story he would later tell in open court.

"It coincided with my cousin getting out of jail," he began haltingly.

11

IT IS four years ago, 1968. A lieutenant, Aaron Mazen, arranges to meet Leuci secretly in a restaurant. There he tosses a case folder onto the table. "Something's wrong with this case," he says.

Leuci begins to go through the folder. It is a narcotics investigation involving wiretaps. Leuci recognizes the names of the targets: Mikey Coco, Stanley Simons, Louie Legs, and the Indelicata brothers, Joseph and Sonny Red. Mazen wants Leuci to find out why the detective in charge made no arrests, and to decide whether the case is worth pursuing by a new team of detectives.

A day or two later Leuci is sent by his parents to his Aunt Rosa's house, because John Lusterino has just got out of jail. Perhaps they need help over there.

Leuci has not seen his cousin in thirteen years. Lusterino is now thirty-nine, but his blond hair is gray and he looks forty-nine. He is solidly built. In jail he spent half his time in the library studying law, and the other half in the gym lifting weights. He has been out two weeks but already sports a beautiful tan.

Lusterino's conversation is predictable. He is shocked to learn that Detective Leuci sometimes operates against Italians. "There's a million niggers out there selling junk," he says. "There ain't enough niggers for you? You have to work your own people?"

They go for a ride in Lusterino's new car. "Putting people in jail ain't going to put bread on your table, Bobby," Lusterino says. "It's better you sit down with them. See what you can work out. You help people out with a problem, they won't forget you."

For some minutes Leuci broods over the import of

these words. At last he decides to risk an exchange of information with his cousin. After exacting a promise that Lusterino will not burn him, Leuci shows his cousin photos of the targets of the investigation that has somehow gone bad.

"Johnny," he says hesitantly, "if you know any of these people, I just want to know three things about them. Are they in junk? Are they in it now? Can I make a case against them? All I want to do is avoid wasting time."

Lusterino laughs. "You're with me a day, and you're trying to make a rat out of me."

But later Leuci's home phone rings. It is Lusterino.

"Be at the corner of Elizabeth and Kenmare at six o'clock sharp on the button. Legs will be there and Joseph Indelicata. They want to talk to you."

"Wait a minute, wait a minute," cries Leuci. His head pounds. "You're making a big problem for me, Johnny. If the feds have a tail on these people, and I meet them—"

But at six o'clock Leuci is at the corner of Elizabeth and Kenmare. Louie Legs leads him into Charlie's Oyster Bar. They are joined by Joey Indelicata, who begins to curse.

"This fucking spic. What does this whore motherfucker want from us? What has he got?"

This is the first Leuci realizes that he is on a shakedown. The detective who has the case is threatening to arrest these hoodlums unless they pay.

"I don't want to be in the middle," Leuci says. "You want to talk to the guy, I'll try to get him down here."

"We're going to kill him. He don't know it yet, but this whore is going to get three in the head."

Leuci gets up from the table, finds a phone, and calls the detective at home.

"For these two pricks you're going to pull me out of my house?" he answers grumpily. "All right. All right. Give me half an hour."

Leuci is worried about safety. "These are bad people," he says when the detective arrives.

"They're scumbags. They're all scumbags. You don't

have to worry about them or nobody like them. Where are they?"

Although the detective is thirty-four, his deeply tanned face is as smooth as a boy's. His wavy hair is prematurely gray. He wears a double-vented blue blazer with gold buttons. There is a knife-edge crease in his tapered tan gabardine slacks.

The two detectives enter the bar. Leuci expects Legs and Indelicata to curse the detective to his face. Instead their manner is conciliatory.

"A beautiful guy like you," says Legs. "Ain't you got anything better to do than go around making up stories? I think it's time you cut the shit. You gave us a figure and it's a big figure. It's a fucking outrageous figure. What have you got to give us a figure like that?"

"Louie, we aint' got you good, we got you beautiful. All you fucking clowns talk too much. We've been sitting on your telephone for a month. We got a warrant. It's all legal. All nice stuff for the D.A. We've got an earful of you, we've got Sonny Red and—"

Indelicata jumps up, enraged. "You spic bastard. You motherfucker. My brother Sonny has got nothing to do with nothing. Don't you dare. Don't you dare bring his name into this. He's not in this. He's not in nothing."

The detective laughs. "Your brother's in this real good. He's in it up to his guinea ass. What's more, as a man on life parole for murder, he's not supposed to associate with you criminals. If we can't work something out, I go to the parole board with my notes off the wiretap, and that will be it for your brother. Back in the can for good. Seventy-five grand or you can say bye-bye to Sonny."

Legs and Indelicata are furious. "Who you think you're dealing with here?" cries Indelicata. "You think you got women here who you lay a lot of bullshit on?"

"Your brother is on life parole," says the detective. "Life parole."

Indelicata looks drained. "I'd sooner kill you tonight than have my brother go back into the can for nothing."

The detective, annoyed, gets up from his chair.

"You fuck," cries Legs. "That fucking shield you've got

ain't no bulletproof vest, and don't you forget it."

The detective gives a disgusted wave of his hand, and walks out.

Leuci jumps up. This is a fellow cop they are threatening. "Watch your mouth. You hear me?"

The two detectives leave the restaurant.

"These guys are killers," says a worried Leuci.

"They talk a lot of shit," snaps the other man. "They're tough. We're tougher. We've got the biggest fucking gang in the world. There are thirty-two thousand of us." Leuci looks at him in awe.

A few minutes later Leuci reenters the bar and sits down with Indelicata and Legs.

Indelicata says, "I don't want that spic bastard making moves against Sonny Red. My brother ain't got nothing to do with this. Nothing. And that spic knows it."

"Let's talk numbers," Leuci says. "He says he wants seventy-five grand. What's the best you guys want to do?"

"If he promises on the heads of his kids that he'll stay away from my brother, if we never hear from him again—" The two Mafiosi look at each other. "You tell that motherfucker we'll give him seventy-five hundred not to see his face again."

Leuci goes across the street to the bar where the detective waits. "Seventy-five hundred," he reports.

The other smiles. "We'll take it. What do you want, half?"

Leuci is bewildered. Is it that simple? Can an SIU detective simply walk in on big people like this and score $7500?

After a moment Leuci replies, "I'll take two thousand and the name of your stool." The detective is said to have the best informant in the city.

"You pick up the money and bring it to me," he agrees, "and I'll give you the stool."

The money is paid in two installments. "You took care of a real headache for us, kid," Leuci is told. "Sonny Red knows what you done for him. If you ever need a favor from Sonny Red, you got it."

Three years later the favor comes back. On a street

corner in Little Italy, Sonny Red tells DeStefano, "If you kill him, you better be sure he's a rat, because he's a friend of ours."

This was Leuci's story to the prosecutors. It was unsupported, and the other detective was one of the most decorated cops in Police Department history. His commendations, among them the Medal of Honor, covered two full pages, and they attested not only to his shrewdness, but also to his bravery. No criminal prosecution against him was ever initiated on Leuci's charges, for the alleged crime was already five and a half years in the past, and no corroborating evidence or witnesses could be found.

He was, however, brought up on charges in the Police Department trial room in 1975, eight years after the alleged crime, and Leuci's testimony was taken. Although trial commissioner Philip Michael wrote in his opinion that he did not disbelieve Leuci, nonetheless he noted that he could not convict an officer with such a record on the unsupported testimony of a fellow officer. The detective was permitted to retire from the Police Department with full pension rights.

12

"THAT WAS the first time?" asked Morvillo.

"The first big score, yes." It was his first meeting with his cousin after thirteen years, and his first meeting with the legion of Mafia hoodlums who became his contacts within organized crime and, in some cases, his friends.

"What else?" demanded Morvillo.

Leuci described selling, for $10,000, a botched case that Bernie Geik, who was an SIU detective at the time, had been trying to put together against Mafia drug dealer Stanley Simons.

There was a cynical half-smile on Morvillo's face, and his head nodded up and down. "How much did you get for that?"

"Twenty-five hundred dollars," said Leuci.

"That makes forty-five hundred so far. What else?"

Leuci described accepting $1000 for putting Mikey Coco together with Detective Dick Bell.

Morvillo nodded. "What did you do with all this money?"

Well, he had bought three cars in two years, he had bought fancy clothes, he had gone into expensive Italian restaurants with other SIU detectives. His eyes were on the floor, and his voice had dropped so low it was almost a whisper.

Nodding, Morvillo strode to the door, but when he had grasped the handle he turned abruptly. "You want to know something?" he said. "You're a fucking crook."

"I know that."

"You should be in jail."

"I know that."

Morvillo's voice rose. "Why aren't you in jail? You tell me why you aren't in jail."

"Because no one caught me," Leuci said. "What I just told you, you weren't good enough to catch me at."

"Oh?" said Morvillo, and a big smile came onto his face. "Is that what you are going to say on the witness stand? Because when you testify, you're going to be asked that question. The reason you are not being prosecuted is not because no one caught you. Because, in fact, once you told us, we caught you. The reason you are not being prosecuted is because we see fit not to prosecute you." Warmth came into his voice. "Because what you did is something special." He paused. "It's not going to be easy, Bob."

"I know it's not going to be easy."

"When you're on the stand, there will be a lot of name-calling. You're going to have to try to explain these three situations. That's all there were? Three?"

Leuci was not under oath, and he could go no further today.

All the following week, Sagor and Morvillo, who had now decided to try the case himself, worked late into the night preparing Detective Leuci for cross-examination. Over and over again they hammered at him, trying to trick him or trap him exactly as the defense lawyer was sure to do.

"What else have you done, detective?"

But Leuci remained firm.

With the trial now less than a week away, the defense lawyer, Albert Krieger, asked to interview Leuci.

"You have to give your permission," Morvillo advised him. "If you don't want to do it, you don't have to."

Leuci thought about it.

"He wants to size you up, I suppose," said Morvillo. "But it's also a chance for you to size him up."

The meeting took place in Morvillo's office. Leuci, as was his way, examined the man sartorially first, and after that examined his manicure, his scent, the hair in his ears. Krieger had a totally shaved head. He was beautifully, expensively dressed. His fingernails were lacquered, his after-shave lotion pungent.

Krieger's questioning was low-keyed, almost gentle. It

focused immediately on Leuci's past misconduct. Each question seemed carefully thought out in advance. Each was delivered in a soft, calm voice. Leuci answered the same way.

Morvillo, seated behind his desk, said nothing. When the questioning had gone on for some time, Krieger glanced toward Morvillo. "This Detective Leuci is a very charming guy," he said. "I believe we are in a lot of trouble."

"I know you are," answered Morvillo with a smile.

Krieger stood up, closed his briefcase, and prepared to leave.

"You're very disarming, Mr. Krieger," said Leuci. "I hope you are going to be this kind to me in court."

"You can bet that I won't be," answered the lawyer. "We're dealing here with a man's career, and with his life. Eddie Rosner is not such a terrible man."

"That's open to conjecture," said Morvillo.

Krieger peered at Leuci. "Three acts of misconduct, eh, detective? Three acts in eight years? I want you to know that I've done a great deal of work in the narcotics area. I've defended narcotics users, narotics dealers. I defended Detective Kelly a few years ago. Did you know Detective Kelly?"

Kelly had been an SIU detective. "I know Kelly," said Leuci.

"I know you know Kelly. And Kelly knows you. I've spoken to a number of addicts who have come forward and who will testify during this trial. They say they know you too. They say that maybe you are guilty of more acts of misconduct than you admit to."

"Well, they're lying."

"They very possibly could be. It's not unusual for someone to come in and lie about someone else. But when we get into court, I want you to understand that I'll be asking you questions about specific people."

Morvillo had jumped to his feet. "Hey, Al, let's not get carried away here. Okay, Al?"

"I just want Bob to know what to expect."

As Krieger walked out of the office, Leuci's eyes were

fixed on the back of the lawyer's bald head. Morvillo's eyes were fixed on Leuci.

"Bob, look at me," the prosecutor said. "I want to ask you one last time. I promise you I won't ask you again. Is there anything else in your past besides these three acts of misconduct?"

Morvillo and Leuci looked intently at each other. Elliot Sagor glanced from one to the other.

"What are you asking me, Bob?" asked Leuci.

"I'm asking you if there is anything else besides these three situations?"

After a moment Leuci said, "There is nothing else."

Morvillo nodded several times. "There fucking better not be, because if that man comes into court and proves that there is, then you're going to get locked up for perjury."

A perceptible choke had come into Leuci's voice. "Suppose he brings in a witness to testify that I've done something else?"

"He can walk in a hundred junkies, a hundred dope dealers. That's not what I mean."

There was a moment of heavy silence. "I understand what you are saying," mumbled Leuci.

"Okay, I'll see you at the trial."

Leuci went out of the office. Addicts. His mind was churning. Which ones had Krieger got his hands on?

13

A FREEZING COLD NIGHT in February. Leuci has just driven home to Kings Park, fifty miles from the city, when his phone rings. It is his informant, Johnny, and he is sobbing. "Bobby, I'm sick, I can't sleep."

They have worked all day together, making buys, setting up arrests, and in the morning will work together again. When Leuci left him two hours ago, he had had one bag of heroin to get him through the night.

"Whatever it was, Bobby, it wasn't heroin. It made me sick, Bobby."

Gina is sitting up in bed.

Johnny starts crying. "Bobby, I can't sleep."

"Johnny, can't you go out in the street and see anybody around? What about your girl?"

"She's gone. Oh, Bobby, please come back and get something for me."

In the middle of the night Leuci gets in his car and drives back into Brooklyn. Johnny lives in Red Hook, not far from the piers. Leuci rings his bell, and he comes out. His nose is running, his eyes are tearing, and he's retching.

"Get in the car, John. We'll ride down to the Union Street station house. I may know a detective in the squad."

Leuci parks outside the station house. Upstairs in the squad room he finds a detective he knows slightly.

"Listen, do you have any stuff around?" Leuci asks. "I need it for a stool of mine."

"I'm not in Narcotics," says the detective. "I don't know if I have anything in my locker or not." But in a moment he returns with a crumpled glassine envelope. Leuci looks at it. Thanking the detective, he goes down to Johnny. Right away Johnny grabs the envelope. A big grin comes into his face. He holds the envelope to the light, flicks it with his finger, taps it. "Yeah," he says, "there is stuff here. Come on, Bobby, take me down by the water."

As he drives, Leuci glances into the back seat. On the seat, Johnny has his works already laid out. His hypodermic is an eye dropper with a needle attached. His bottle cap and string are ready. He's rubbing his arm.

Leuci has parked. In the back seat of the car Johnny is heating his bottle cap. Suddenly he screams. Leuci, who is trying not to watch, turns sharply in his place. The "heroin" is fizzing up like Alka-Seltzer.

"I don't know what this is," sobs Johnny. He throws it down. "What am I going to do, Bobby?"

Near the piers lives a man named Pollock who sells nickel bags out of his house. Leuci drives there and parks out front.

"You gotta buy me something, Bobby."

But Leuci has no money.

So he studies Pollock's house. It sits by itself amongst the piers. Up the street Leuci spies someone coming—by his walk, obviously a junkie. Hands in his coat against the freezing wind, the junkie goes into Pollock's building.

In the back seat, Johnny is sobbing. "Oh Bobby, you gotta buy me something."

Leuci says, "Johnny, when that guy comes out I'm going to take him. I'll take whatever he just bought off Pollock and give it to you."

"Good, man," says Johnny. His tears stop. He is bouncing up and down with glee.

"Get down out of sight," snaps Leuci.

The junkie comes out of Pollock's house, and as he passes the car Leuci, who has slumped down, sits bolt upright. Immediately the junkie starts to run. Leuci springs from his car and runs after him. Behind him Johnny is running too. They run through the piers. Leuci, furious, catches up to the junkie and dives at him, a flying tackle that knocks him down. As he buckles, Leuci punches him as hard as he can in the face. He can feel the junkie's nose crunch. The junkie screams, but the scream becomes a whimper. "Don't hurt me, Babyface. Don't hurt me."

Leuci is sitting on his chest. Behind him Johnny is screaming, "Kill him, kill him."

"Johnny, go back to the car."

This junkie's name is Vinny. Leuci knows him—a kid from the neighborhood. Now his nose is shattered, he's bleeding, and he's shaking like an infant.

"Where is your junk?" snarls Leuci.

"Don't take my junk. Please don't take my thing. I've been out all day stealing, man. I made twenty-five dollars, enough to buy a spoon."

A spoon is five bags.

"I've got to take it, or lock you up. One or the other."

"Take half of it, don't take all. Please let me go home. Don't lock me up."

"Wait right here," orders Detective Leuci. Clutching the spoon bag, he goes back to the car. The night is freezing cold, and Johnny cowers now in the back seat.

"Do you have it, Bobby? Give it to me."

Leuci is consumed by an almost overpowering hatred. He hates both of these addicts. Opening the spoon bag, Leuci pours half of it into the envelope the detective gave him.

"Here. Now take your fucking works and go home." Johnny lives three blocks away. "Run the fuck home. If you get locked up, you're on your own. I'll see you in the morning."

"Thanks, Bob. Thanks a lot, man. You did good, man. You have some left hook, man."

Leuci returns to Vinny, who is sitting on the curb crying and bleeding. Blood from his nose is all over his face, his clothes.

"My nose is broken," he sobs. "I'm sick."

Leuci hands him the bag of heroin that contains now only two shots. "Get in the car. I'll take you home."

A young woman opens Vinny's front door. She looks from him to Leuci and back again.

"Don't worry," says Vinny proudly. "I have something."

At once she has forgotten Leuci. "Oh, thank God, thank God, where is it?"

He gives her the bag containing two shots, and at the

sink washes his face. "I'm sick," he says. "I'll be all right, though. As long as she's okay."

She comes out of the bedroom. "Did you save me anything?" asks Vinny anxiously.

She wears a kind of half-smile. "I blew my first shot," she says.

"You fucking liar," screams Vinny.

"I had to take two," she whines. "I blew the first one."

"Oh, you liar. Didn't you even leave me enough so I can get through the night?"

Leuci almost bolts for the door. But Vinny runs after him. "Bobby, do you have anything in the car? Can't you give me something, Bobby. Bobby, please. Bobby—"

On his way home, Leuci reaches Exit 40 and starts seeing trees again, starts seeing a whole other world.

14

MORVILLO RARELY TRIED cases himself, but this
one had turned very big. Media interest in Leuci was
high—*Life* magazine had devoted a full-scale profile to
him—and there was equally intense interest in the fate of
the clean-cut lawyer, Rosner, partly because of the two
characters, DeStefano and Lamattina, with whom he
seemed to have associated himself. In the days preceding
the trial, Morvillo was obliged to devote considerable
time to dealing with the press.

Ten times a day other prosecutors, stopping by his
office, volunteered to help him with any unfinished tasks.
Morvillo himself began to feel anxiety. He began to talk
frequently about how good a lawyer Al Krieger was, and
about how much Krieger must be costing Rosner.

His one nagging worry was Leuci. He didn't know how
Leuci would behave on the stand, under pressure. He
didn't know if the jury would believe Leuci. Several times
he considered giving his star witness a lie detector test, but
when he talked it over with his assistant prosecutors, all
advised him not to risk it—not because they doubted
Leuci, but because he had lived a double life for so long
and because he seemed to them now so emotionally
fragile that the apparatus would not be able to test him
fairly. Hook his blood pressure, his pulse rate, and his
sweat glands to the machine, and very likely he would
register a lie the moment you asked him his name. The
polygraph instrument, under certain conditions, was
virtually infallible, Morvillo believed. However, in no
way did Detective Leuci match these conditions, or so it
seemed to him.

In addition, he and his aides understood and
sympathized with the ever-tightening strain under which

Leuci lived. He was now, in a certain sense, a man without a country. He would never be able to go back to his past. He had become a man without a past. He had no future anyone could discern—certainly not as a cop in New York—and his present was bleak as well, inasmuch as he had no real home and could draw little sustenance from his wife and children, whom he saw only on weekends. No wonder he sometimes seemed to them close to a breakdown. To question his credibility now, Morvillo decided, might throw him over the edge. If that happened, not only would Detective Leuci be destroyed, but so would the case against Rosner, DeStefano, and Lamattina.

As jury selection began, Lamattina abruptly pleaded guilty to two of the seven counts against him. Two days later DeStefano also capitulated, and Morvillo found himself rushing to restructure his case against Rosner as sole remaining defendant. Before testifying, Leuci would be obliged to confess in open court to past misconduct of his own. Morvillo had wanted Rosner on trial with the other two men. Leuci would have seemed like a choirboy by comparison. Also, Rosner would surely have seemed tainted when standing in the same dock with two such men.

So now what?

Morvillo could perhaps use Lamattina and DeStefano as corroborating witnesses for the prosecution, but if he did so, they would taint only Leuci. The jury, with three admittedly corrupt law enforcement officers arrayed against him, might sympathize entirely with Rosner.

Morvillo decided he would call Leuci only.

With this decision made, Morvillo's nervousness left him. And on the appointed day he strode into a courtroom that was as packed and as tense as a football stadium. Sagor, in his opening statement to the jury, described Detective Leuci as a thirty-two-year-old police officer who almost two years ago had come forward of his own volition, had confessed to several past acts of mild misconduct, and then had conducted a sixteen-month undercover investigation at great risk and peril to himself.

Krieger then made his own opening statement, asking the jury to understand what had happened to this young lawyer—Rosner was then thirty-six—who had been under indictment by the federal government, and who had been very worried about that indictment. And then who should come forth, continued Krieger, but this super-slick detective with his offer to save Rosner's life. This super-slick detective offered to provide Rosner with information outlining how the government had framed him in that pending case. Would any human being not buy such information? Throughout the trial Krieger would continue to ask the jury to compare the life and the lifestyle of Eddie Rosner, whose pregnant wife could be seen in the front row of the courtroom, to the life and lifestyle of the main witness against him, corrupt Detective Robert Leuci.

Calling Leuci to the stand, Morvillo began by asking the same questions that the detective had already answered hundreds of times when testifying against defendants he had arrested. Will you tell us by whom you are employed? And in what capacity? And for how long? Then Morvillo said, "Now, Detective Leuci, while you were employed by the New York City Police Department, did you engage in any acts of misconduct? Will you tell the jury generally what those acts were and when they took place?"

Leuci on the witness stand was terrified, but so far he appeared only very nervous. Morvillo calmed him down, and suddenly Leuci felt comfortable. He was a cop on the witness stand, and this was nothing new to him. He was a member of the New York Police Department. Morvillo kept calling him "Detective Leuci," soothing words to him, until at last Leuci was able to convince himself of the one central fact: I'm not on trial here, Rosner is.

With that, a great calm came over Leuci, and he began to explain the three situations already described to Morvillo in private, in which he had taken money. As he spoke he tried to judge the reaction of the jurors. He thought he could see them nodding with sympathy, as if they understood how he had been put in a compromising spot—how he had been offered money, how in a moment of weakness he had taken it.

Leuci looked out over the crowded courtroom. Every seat was taken. There were standees in the aisles. Except for arraignment court at night, he had never before testified in a full courtroom. He had never before looked out on rows of reporters taking notes.

"In addition to these situations," asked Morvillo, "did you ever engage in any other misconduct of any kind?"

The courtroom had gone silent. The jurors leaned forward expectantly, and when Leuci had answered several sat back nodding their heads in agreement.

"No, sir," said Leuci in a clear voice.

And so the focus of the trial moved to the defendant, who sat with his head down, while Leuci described the wearing of transmitters into restaurants, and the passing of documents to DeStefano in exchange for money.

Sometimes Leuci studied notes before replying. Often he coughed nervously, or sipped from a glass of water. Then the jurors donned earphones, were handed transcripts, and the incriminating tapes were played—four hours of them.

DeStefano: "Are you going to get me those grand jury papers?"

Leuci: "If there's any way possible, I'll get them."

DeStefano: "Here you go." And he had handed Leuci an empty pack of cigarettes containing $1150.

Leuci: "What's here?"

DeStefano: "Eleven and a half."

In the tense courtroom another tape was threaded onto the machine.

Leuci: "All right, all right, all right, so listen. I'll put that—I'll put that to him. Fifteen hundred dollars for the grand jury minutes, and aside from that, more important, a thousand I'm getting, you know."

Rosner: "How long will it take to get them?"

Leuci: "Well, let's find out. Like I said to him, you know—"

DeStefano: "We don't get it pronto, then we don't need them."

Rosner: "Doesn't do us any good to get it at the last minute."

The jury also listened to a conversation in which Rosner took part, about a missing narcotics informant Leuci was asked to find; Leuci expressed reluctance for fear the informant would be killed.

Now Defense Attorney Albert Krieger, shaven head shining, advanced toward Leuci in the witness box and cross-examination began. Krieger started slowly, calmly, underplaying his role, taking Leuci step by step back to the three admitted acts of misconduct, probing for details, asking the same questions over and over again, seeking through repetition to discredit the witness.

Krieger: "At this point, did you believe yourself to be committing a crime?"

Krieger: "So from the time you went to contact Mr. Simons, you knew that you were committing a crime?"

Krieger: "Did these detectives know at that time that you would be receptive to the proposition of selling evidence?"

The witness became increasingly nervous.

Krieger: "What did you do with the money?"

Krieger: "Where did you count the money?"

At the end of the first day of cross-examination, Leuci was standing glumly in a little room beside the courtroom, when Shaw came in.

"You were fantastic," said Shaw. "You were calm, quiet. The jurors were looking at you and we sensed that they feel sorry for you."

Well, maybe.

The trial continued. Turning to the tapes, Krieger read certain conversations from the transcripts, for he wanted the jury to hear again the vicious, sometimes obscene language employed by the chief government witness. He wanted the jury to hear again how Leuci had described Rosner on tape as "that cheap Jew," and again as "that goddamn cheap Jew."

The presiding judge, Arnold Bauman, was Jewish. There were Jews on the jury. Later Krieger made a short speech to the effect that we don't need Buchenwald or

Auschwitz—we have Leuci.

Some defense attorneys not only scream, but also call witnesses vile names. Krieger's technique was far more subtle. Leuci was now on the stand for the third straight day, and Krieger's approach was still low-keyed, almost intellectual.

In predictable sequence came his next series of questions. Apart from these three corrupt situations to which Leuci had just admitted in open court, had Leuci committed any other corrupt acts? Nothing? In eleven years as a cop? In eight years as a narcotics detective? Come now, detective. Had he never perjured himself in court? Never made an illegal wiretap? Never taken money from informants? Never given drugs to informants? Never sold drugs himself? Never?

Leuci had convinced himself of his own righteousness. He was telling the absolute truth about Edmund Rosner.

And so to each of Krieger's direct questions, Leuci answered: No.

Krieger focused in on informants.

"You never gave heroin to informants?"

"No, never."

"You're telling me now that in all your years in narcotics, you never gave a piece of narcotics to anyone?"

"I never did."

"Do you know a man named Richie Carti?"

"He's an informant of mine."

"Did you ever give Carti heroin?"

"I never gave Carti heroin."

"Did you ever give Carti heroin to sell?"

"I never gave Carti heroin, period."

"Do you know a man named Frank Reggio? Did you ever give Reggio heroin?"

15

INFORMANTS LIKE REGGIO can be used for a month, three months if they are lucky. Despite instructions to the contrary, they stay in their own neighborhoods most times. They take the undercover detective to dealers they know—who, when arrested, know right away who the informant was. The dealer or his lawyer reads the affidavit and they figure it out: I sold to only three guys that day, to my brother, to my brother-in-law, and to this fucking Reggio and that guy that was with him that looked like a fucking cop, and that I've never seen since or before.

Informants become exhausted from getting beaten up. They become petrified of the street, but they have the sickness. They have habits that they have to take care of every day, and now the only people who will give them drugs are cops.

This adds up in Brooklyn alone to twenty-five or thirty addicts at a time who can no longer go in the street, can no longer buy narcotics, and who now count on policemen. They will work with any cop, cops from Safe and Loft, cops from local precinct squads. They become informants. That's the only thing they do, and they aren't even good informants.

They go down to the courthouse every day. They know which detectives are there, and they wait outside by their cars. Most detectives will give heroin even to another detective's informant. If he has anything, he will give it to them. This is no longer in exchange for work. These guys are finished as informants. The heroin is given away out of pity.

Narcotics detectives are paid every two weeks at the First Precinct. On payday hundreds congregate from all over the city. From a junkie's standpoint these are hundreds and hundreds of bags going into the station house to be paid, and they line up and stand there begging.

Some detectives laugh and walk by. Some mock them. Most, like Leuci, give. This is illegal, but not hard to justify. The junkie is probably twenty years older than I am, the detective thinks, and how does a man deal with another man who cries and begs? Impossible. I just can't deal with it. I do whatever he wants me to do. I give him something that costs me nothing, that he needs.

There is no fear to walking around with junk in their pockets. Nor in asking another detective for some bags. Yet some detectives are very careful. One has an old diary; he keeps bags in the cut-out pages of this diary in his pocket. Others have magnetic key boxes that they stick under the dashboard or hood of their cars.

Some are less careful. Once Leuci gets a call from the cleaner, who has found three bags of heroin in his pocket.

"What the hell is this? Is it heroin? I know you are a cop, but there has to be something wrong."

"Yeah, it's heroin." Leuci takes the bags and goes home. He is not afraid of arrest. Who is going to arrest him, IAD? The IAD guys are focused on gambling corruption, and so far have left narcotics alone.

Inevitably, addict-informants become almost part of Leuci's family. They are as dependent on him as his own children. He becomes convinced it is his responsibility to take care of them. After a day's work, each addict crawls back into some hovel. It seems heartless to leave him without anything, to be sick, when he has been with you for weeks.

Often in the middle of the night his home phone rings. The informant may be sitting in the Waldorf Cafeteria, or some such all-night place, alone or in a group, and he is high, stoned out. He wants to talk to a relative, or to somebody who cares about him, to say that he is feeling good. It is a different kind of talk, quiet, relaxed. Addicts' lives seem to have some kind of normalcy when they are high.

"You know, I used to have a house," one tells Leuci one night.

16

"DID YOU EVER give Reggio heroin?"

At times Reggio would shine and wax Leuci's car for hours, and when Leuci finally came out of the station house, or out of court, Reggio would greet him with a big grin, hoping to be rewarded with a bag of heroin.

The names kept spilling out of Krieger's mouth, even the street names, names like Pale Face, Blood, Young Blood.

"No. Never."

"All right," said Krieger.

Later, he began calling each of the named addicts to the stand. One by one they were walked into the courtroom, sworn in, and interrogated. Some were high, and stoned, and sick. Each testified to heroin deals with Leuci.

At last Judge Bauman asked Krieger how many more such witnesses he intended to call. A good number, Krieger replied, for Leuci—Babyface—was infamous, and such witnesses as these were available in a line that would stretch out around the block.

"They have smelled up my courtroom for the last day and a half," Judge Bauman said. He remarked that he had sat in judgment or otherwise dealt with narcotics addicts and dealers for years, and found them to be totally venal, totally unbelievable. Any jury, he believed, would feel the same.

Leuci had convinced himself still again that he had told the jury the truth. Whether, as a corrupt detective, he was involved in three situations, or three thousand, didn't matter. He had been able to face Rosner and say: I was a corrupt cop. Therefore he was being totally honest with Rosner and with the jury, and the jury now should judge the facts of the case, based on the recordings that he had made, and on the fact that he had been honest in admitting his own wrongdoing.

And so the jury retired to deliberate.

"Are you angry with me?" asked Leuci. He and Morvillo were waiting it out in Morvillo's office.

"No, I'm not angry with you. You did a great job. I just hope I didn't forget anything. I hope my summation was okay."

The verdict, after twelve hours of deliberation, was guilty on five of the seven counts.

In Morvillo's office, a kind of euphoria broke out. Every attorney in the building seemed to want to shake Morvillo's hand, to pat him on the back.

"You did it!" they cried. "You did it!"

But Morvillo said softly, "Not me, him," and he pointed to his chief witness. "He did it."

"I'd just like to get home now," said Leuci.

Shaw was there. "You were a great witness," he said.

Scoppetta telephoned. "Congratulations, Bob. Keep going. This is only the beginning."

Only the beginning. Leuci had already realized this for himself.

"It's not over for Rosner," said Morvillo, who stood with his arm around the government's chief witness. "There are going to be appeals and motions."

"What do you mean?" asked Leuci, alarmed. "He was convicted by a jury."

"He has money to spend. He's not going to sit still for this. He's going to ask for a new trial."

"Based on what?"

"New evidence. Don't forget, you admitted to only three acts of misconduct."

"That's right."

"Rosner apparently doesn't believe that, and neither does Krieger. They'll try for a new trial. You can expect a lot of motion papers."

"It's not important to me what Rosner believes," said Leuci. "What's important to me is what you and Sagor believe."

Leuci and his bodyguards went downstairs and out of the building.

Another trial came with a rush—the two detectives who had accompanied Sergeant Perrazzo to the hotel room to rip off the supposed drug courier, Federal Agent Sandy Bario. Leuci took the stand and was sworn in. Same questions, same answers. Better, rougher lawyer, who hammered the witness until his mind numbed, and he began to fear that in a moment he would crack, and begin to babble.

On to the next cases. More tapes to study and restudy, commuting to the Catskills weekends. More facts and details to dredge up out of memory. Shoveling snow away from the door of the cabin. More testimony to prepare. More prosecutors to fend off, to win over.

In an unstable world, prosecutors' offices were and are unstable at ten times the national average, a hundred times. The criminal justice system moves with the speed of a glacier, an inch at a time, but prosecutors move on like lightning. Most come in as assistant D.A.'s assistant U.S. attorneys at the age of twenty-four or so, fresh out of law school, at ridiculously low salaries. A year later they are trying major cases against defense lawyers of thirty years' experience, who earn sometimes hundreds of thousands of dollars a year. Some young prosecutors are naturally gifted, and win cases right away. Most are not and don't. Either way they learn their trade, and in less than five years resign to become rich lawyers in their turn. To say this is not a condemnation, merely a description, and five years of public service is more than most men give.

Scoppetta and Shaw had moved on. Morvillo was about to go into private practice, with Whitney North Seymour close behind him, and Detective Robert Leuci at the start of the new year, 1973, was handed over to a new young prosecutor, Richard Ben Veniste, twenty-nine. Ben Veniste would not last long. Within a few months he would move to Washington to direct the investigation into the Watergate coverup, passing Leuci on to still another assistant U.S. attorney.

Each of these shifts was, to the detective, as painful as a

divorce, but there was never time to grieve. Instead, with each change he set out immediately to court the replacement. He wanted each of these men, in effect, to fall in love with him. Only then would they want to protect him when—when what?—when whatever was going to happen finally happened. Leuci didn't know what this would be, or how soon. But he sensed perfectly well that it would be dreadful.

In fact, each of these men in turn did fall in love with him. They found him intelligent, observant, extremely perceptive too, and these are admirable qualities in any man. Furthermore, they believed that what he had done and continued to do required uncommon courage.

But more than all this, his entire being seemed turned toward them. He was tremendously open and vulnerable.

On the fourth floor of the Southern District Courthouse Leuci's telephone rang. One of his bodyguards picked it up. With his hand over the mouthpiece, he said to Leuci, "Hey, there's a guy on the phone. It sounds like he's not a cop. He says he's The Baron."

"That's my stool," said Leuci. "I'll talk to him." The Baron, he knew, had been working as an informant for the Bureau of Narcotics at a salary that may have reached at times $1000 a week. He was an outstanding informant.

Leuci put the phone to his ear. "They cut me off the program about three weeks ago," said The Baron. "I'm going to blow my house, I'll probably blow my boat. My car is in hock. I'm in all kinds of problems."

"Larry, what are you trying to tell me?" Leuci had gone weak with the sudden onrush of terror.

"You understand, Bobby. I'm flat broke. I've got kids, I've got a wife. I've got the same kinds of problems you've got."

"Larry, I don't know what you're trying to tell me," said Leuci. "Do whatever you've got to do. Just don't lie." The terror was making him babble. "I'll be seeing you around, Larry."

"Yeah, I guess so," said The Baron, and he hung up.

Someone's paying him to testify against me, Leuci told himself. Who's paying him? What will he say? Will it be believed? Leuci was trying to think, trying to consider his options.

An hour later he reported the conversation to Ben Veniste. The lawyer, apparently unimpressed, told him to make a memorandum about it and put it in the files.

"He'll come in and say I did all sorts of things, maybe," said Leuci.

"Let him come in and prove it to me," said Ben Veniste. "Fucking creep."

Leuci, smoking incessantly, waited and worried. It was too late to do anything else.

Allegations charging Leuci with perjury, and other crimes as well, were even now being prepared. In a few hours they would reach Morvillo's desk.

17

LEUCI, aged twenty-eight, is brand-new in SIU, and The Baron is the first SIU informant he has ever seen. Until now he has known only street informants, most of them addicts.

The Baron, whose name is Richard Lawrence, has come to him as part payment for the shakedown of the Indelicatas. Having been given The Baron's phone number, Leuci calls and introduces himself, and they arrange to meet on Houston Street and Avenue D. Though the other detective has promised him to Leuci, the decision will be made by The Baron himself, who is probably auditioning a number of new narcotics teams.

It is said that The Baron can work with any narcotics team he chooses. He is a fantastic informant who works off and on for the Bureau of Narcotics, for the Treasury Department, and for the Police Safe and Loft Squad, as well as for Police Narcotics. Leuci will have to sell himself to this man.

At last The Baron's car pulls up—an oil-green Eldorado with a black vinyl top and a telephone on the back shelf—and The Baron steps out. A tall, forty-two-year-old black man, he wears a full-length fur coat, though it is summer, plus a green fedora that matches the color of his car. His shoes and socks are green also. He is a strange-looking dude, Leuci thinks. He has a scar that runs from behind his ear across his cheek and over to his chin. Another scar runs from behind the other ear straight across his throat.

"Some scars," says Leuci.

"Combat marks, man. Combat marks."

Both men climb into The Baron's Cadillac. As he

drives, The Baron puts on his stereo. They ride up and down the streets of the East Village. "Can you get me some goods?" asks The Baron.

"What are you talking about? What kind of goods?"

"Can you get me some goods? You know what I'm talking about."

Leuci thinks about it.

"Larry," he says presently, "I don't know you, you don't know me. I know you worked this road for years. Let me tell you where it's at, as far as I'm concerned. I'll work day and night with you, and I'll make any kind of worthwhile case. You get in any kind of trouble, I don't care if it's homicide or what, and I guarantee you within an hour after you're locked up I'll get you out."

Leuci pauses. "There is only one difference between you and me. You are a connection. You are a dope dealer, and I'm a cop. We ain't going to switch them roles. You are not going to become the cop, and I'm not going to become the dope dealer. You want to do something in the street, you do it. I'll be there to protect you. But don't ask me to become a fucking dope dealer. Are you a junkie, Larry?"

"Am I a junkie? Do I look a fool to you?" The Baron's face has darkened. He pulls to the curb, leans across and pushes open Leuci's door. "What did you ask me here for? The kind of deal you offer I can get from anybody. I can work for any team, for any detective or federal agent in the city. What the fuck do I need you for? You're going to keep me out of jail. Big deal. I need somebody I can get stuff from all the time."

"Larry, here's my home phone number, I'll work with you. I want to work with you. But those are the conditions. You're not turning me into any fucking dope pusher."

"The kind of cases that I make, there is a lot of money around, man."

"You are talking about something different now. If there is money there, you are an equal partner."

"I'll think about it, and let you know," says The Baron.

A pensive Leuci watches the Eldorado drive away. He

is convinced he has blown the audition. He will never hear from The Baron again.

Back at SIU, Leuci recounts the story.

"This guy is not some jerk from Harlem," remarks another detective. "He's a connected guy. Promise him anything he wants. If you have to promise him a package to get him, then promise it."

"You promise it," retorts Leuci. "This guy works for the feds, he works for the D.A.'s office. He's a professional stool pigeon. If you think I'm going to put my life in his hands, you're crazy. I'm not looking to do twenty-five years."

"All right," said the other detective. "But if you could have got him, you would have been in fantastic shape."

Two weeks later, Leuci gets a call at home about eleven o'clock at night. He can hear music in the background. "Bobby? This is Larry. Same place, same time tomorrow, right?"

Leuci phones Mandato at once. "Hey, The Baron called me."

The next day The Baron gets out of his car wearing a big grin. It is as if the previous conversation never took place.

"I have a guy up in the Bronx," The Baron says. "An Italian kid. Thinks he's a big-time connection. I think I can buy a thousand-dollar package off him."

"How about you just talk to the guy?" suggests Leuci.

"I don't go around talking to people. I'm The Baron." Then he adds, "What is the reason for me to talk to some guinea in the Bronx? If I go talking, I'm talking about buying a package."

"What are you telling me, Larry?"

"Give me a thousand dollars."

"Go fuck yourself."

But Leuci seeks to persuade The Baron to meet this connection. "At least let us take a look at him," he pleads.

Finally The Baron agrees—and then he spends the next hour lecturing Leuci on how to put the case together. He knows where the Italian comes from, how he operates, and suspects who his Mafia contact must be.

Leuci listens with his mouth open, marveling at The Baron's knowledge and skill. No wonder all the teams want him as an informant!

After a couple of days Leuci receives another call. "I'm going to meet this guy tomorrow up in the Bronx near the Concourse Plaza Hotel."

Leuci and his team set up surveillance across the street in the park. From the park they watch this amazing actor who is The Baron take over. He sticks his finger in the guy's face—a tough Italian guy, supposedly—then turns his back on him, walks away, comes back, smiles, cajoles. The connection has his head down. He looks up, he shrugs. What do you want from me? The Baron steps back and yells at him. Finally The Baron gives a disgusted wave of his hand and strides away.

The detectives have a prearranged meeting place down by Yankee Stadium. When The Baron arrives, he beckons them to join him in his Eldorado, "I don't want to sit in your cramped piece of shit."

For the next several weeks they watch The Baron operate. He keeps bargaining for bigger and bigger loads, moving upward in rank from connection to connection. He requires very little direction. Evidence stockpiles.

Finally Leuci and Mandato make arrests. They grab two men and an eighth of a kilo of heroin. They are in the station house processing the arrests when The Baron calls. Leuci meets him outside.

"Do these guys have any money?" The Baron asks.

"They have no money."

After a moment The Baron says, "I have to see something out of this. This thing has taken eight or nine weeks of my time."

"We got a good case going," responds Leuci. "This thing can go higher. We are into some major Mafia junk dealers."

"So don't you think I ought to see something?"

"There's no money here. At the end of the case maybe there is going to be some money."

"Maybe."

They stare at each other.

"Let me go back and talk to my partners," says Leuci.

Back in the station house he huddles with Mandato and two other detectives assigned to the case. "We have an eighth of a kilo, maybe a little bit more, of evidence," he begins. "I'm petrified of giving him anything. Let's throw in some money together." But the others refuse. They vote unanimously to pay off The Baron by giving him a piece of the package.

Leuci gets an evelope and pours into it about an ounce of evidence, worth maybe $6000 on the street. Then he walks outside and gets into The Baron's car. They sit side by side.

"Man, you better find someone else to work with you," says The Baron. "I'm not going through all this bullshit for nothing. Working for the feds I can get a thousand a week, five hundred a week to do this shit."

"Larry, you did a great job, I want to thank you," says Leuci, and he steps out of the car, leaving the envelope behind him on the seat.

The Baron's electric window comes down. "Hey brother, nice day today, isn't it?" he says, He is grinning.

"It's going to be a good day," agrees Leuci. He is thinking: He's smart enough not to say anything about it. It's over now. I did it.

But back in the station house he begins to worry. He has heard of some sort of atomic test that can trace the route of a package. It can match a kilo of junk to other junk found elsewhere and can determine that both came from the same original package. This fuck could be working for the government, Leuci worries, and if they come up here and seize our evidence, they will prosecute me. Leuci is not worried about the heroin going into some black kid's arm, he is worried about twenty-five years in Attica. If The Baron turns on him—

As a young man The Baron was twice convicted of armed robbery; he spent eleven and a half years in jail. Today he owns a gypsy cab company, a laundromat, a beauty parlor. He has a wife and five kids and lives in the suburbs. He is also a street wholesaler. He has street dealers working for him, making him not quite a major narcotics mover. He operates with impunity because a legion of law enforcement agents, including Leuci now, have chosen not to arrest him in exchange for information.

As time goes on, The Baron constantly pressures Leuci for junk. Leuci becomes increasingly afraid of him, but at the same time more and more dependent on his information. The Baron is at the root of all his major cases. The Baron knows who's dealing and where the junk is coming from. He can cut into any operation. Leuci's instinctive fear increases in direct proportion to The Baron's demands for junk.

About twice a year The Baron gets arrested by other teams. Each time Leuci rushes to court, speaks to the district attorney and judge. The Baron gets out on parole, and they go back to work.

18

AND SO The Baron's allegations, purporting to describe his past dealings with Leuci, duly reached Morvillo. Morvillo and his aides were stunned. The allegations laid out names, places, and dates, and described crime after crime in detail. If true—and the details were so precise that they had the ring of truth—then Leuci was one of the most devious felons of all time, and they themselves had been gulled.

Morvillo's first reaction was personal: How is this going to look in the newspapers? How am I going to look? His second reaction was outrage. "I'll lock him up myself," he muttered to Sagor and the others. "I'll try the case myself."

Only after that did a certain calm obtain, and they began to study the charges. The Baron was alleging that illegal narcotics deals took place between himself and Leuci from 1968 up to and including the summer of last year. That is, Leuci had been buying and selling heroin during all of the time he was also working undercover for the government, according to The Baron.

The Baron, or whoever had written this script, had broken these deals down into four categories. He charged first that, several times a month, from 1968 through 1971, Leuci had supplied him with heroin which he diluted and sold; he had then paid Leuci for the cost of these packages. Second, on numerous other occasions Leuci had given him portions of the narcotics seized in cases in which he had assisted Leuci in setting up the arrests, in exchange for which he gave Leuci money and three automobiles. Third, he had been personally involved in transactions where Leuci had sold heroin to three other individuals known as "Slim," "Cornbread," and "The

Saint." Fourth, after Leuci and The Baron had profited financially for most of 1971 from supplying a Buffalo group with heroin, Leuci had arranged the buyer's arrest; the heroin seized at the arrest was the same heroin Leuci had supplied.

1971 was the undercover year. The prosecutors felt sick. They wished to read no further, but had to.

"Another 1971 case in which I received seized narcotics directly from Leuci," they read, "involved the arrest of three people at a Spanish grocery store on the southeast corner of 122nd Street and Lexington Avenue. I had given Leuci information concerning "Cadillac" Joe. When the narcotics arrived in a van, the arrests were made: seven ounces were seized from "Cadillac" Joe, and one ounce from each of two people in the store. Leuci and I later met at Houston Street and Leuci passed me an ounce in his car while we conversed.

"In another case I informed Leuci that I had seen seven kilos of heroin at a particular house on Atlantic Avenue in Brooklyn. Mr. Hershey from the Brooklyn district attorney's office called me to check the information in order to get a search warrant. Four persons were arrested that night, including a woman known as "Clementine" (who subsequently was sentenced to 15 years). A seizure was made at the house of heroin, narcotics paraphernalia, and guns. Leuci gave me three to four ounces of heroin from the seizure."

Now The Baron described meeting Leuci near Broome Street, which was the site of the police property clerk's office, where Leuci handed over heroin still contained in Police Department evidence pouches. The so-called French Connection ripoff of some 300 pounds of heroin evidence from the property clerk's office had come to light only a few weeks previously. Obviously The Baron, or The Baron's ghost writer, was suggesting that Leuci was involved in the ripoff.

"If this is true," muttered Morvillo, "then all our cases will be bad."

"Over the course of my dealings with Leuci," the allegations read, "I regularly gave him money. For a long period of time I gave Leuci approximately $100 a week. I also purchased and gave to Leuci three automobiles in 1969 and 1970: a 1966 yellow and red Oldsmobile (purchased at Fair Motors, Mount Vernon) for Leuci's brother; a 1966 or 1967 blue Plymouth (purchased also at Fair Motors, for about $500–$1000) for Leuci's wife; and a 1966 or 1967 blue Ford Country Squire station wagon (purchased at Manor Lincoln Mercury, Mall Street, White Plains, for approximately $1100) for Leuci's wife. Leuci did not reimburse me for these automobiles; nor did I ask him to.

"To my personal knowledge, Leuci supplied heroin to many other individuals. During the course of my relationship with Leuci I was personally involved in Leuci's transactions with three of these individuals: "Slim," "Cornbread," and "The Saint." I was involved in the "Slim" transactions in two ways: for a period of time Leuci supplied packages of heroin for Slim and me to divide; and sometimes I also helped Slim sell some of the heroin that Slim had received from Leuci. Slim had a barbecue store on Fulton Street, one block north of Washington Street, Brooklyn. Slim and Leuci, I was told, had been friends for years. Leuci introduced me to Slim and then Slim and I worked together making cases for Leuci in Brooklyn.

"During this period, Leuci moved around with New York City Detective Frank Mandato. On at least half a dozen occasions, Leuci and Mandato notified me along with Slim at Slim's store that they had a package of heroin for us. Slim then sent a woman named Jesse or her husband, whose name was also Jesse, to pick up the package. Slim and I then divided up the package on a table in a small room behind the kitchen, which we entered through a hole behind the stove. Slim took about a whole kilo each time for which he paid approximately $32,000. After dividing up the heroin, Slim and I would separate and then a day or so later we would meet with Leuci or Mandato to settle prices. When Slim gave me part of his portion of the heroin to sell I paid Slim the money for it. On several occasions Slim, myself, and

Leuci sat in Leuci's car and discussed these transactions. I was present on two occasions when Slim paid Leuci thousands of dollars for the cost of the heroin."

"This is sickening, sickening," said Morvillo, and he gave orders for The Baron to be brought in and interrogated.

This was done. Under severe questioning The Baron stuck to his story. He would be glad to get on the stand and testify against Leuci, he said, and would do this for nothing. He also wanted to work steadily as an informant for a fee of $5000. He was advised to go fuck himself.

But the prosecutors were worried, and they began trying to check the details of the allegations. When some of the cases and individuals mentioned proved not to exist, they became cheerful, but when the three cars had been traced, they became terrified. Because two proved to be registered in the name of Gina Leuci.

The Baron was advised that if he would take a lie detector test, and if he passed it, the government would be glad to pay him the $5000 he had requested. At this news, The Baron's scar-crossed face broke into a broad grin, and he agreed.

He was flown to Washington and driven to the offices of True Security in Alexandria, Virginia, where he was hooked up to the polygraph sensors. The results were sealed and sent back to Morvillo in New York by courier on the first shuttle the following morning.

Leuci had spent the night, as usual, on Governors Island, and his bodyguards, as usual, had telephoned the office after breakfast to say they were starting in. But a lieutenant got on the phone, demanded to speak to Leuci personally, and then ordered him to report to Morvillo's office forthwith. "Forthwith" was the most curt—and the most urgent—command in the police lexicon.

The detective had become a kind of human seismograph. He was able to measure at once any eruption that occurred in his life, no matter how small, no matter how distant.

Forthwith. Immediately came the terrible tightening in Leuci's stomach. He and his bodyguards got on the ferry and crossed to Manhattan. It could be any number of things, Leuci told himself. Inside the Federal Building he walked down the hall past people with whom he had exchanged smiles every day for months. Today there were no smiles. No one came out of his office to say hello. They all know, Leuci thought. Whatever it is. They all know something terrible is going to happen.

As he neared Morvillo's office on the fourth floor, fear came on strong, and he said to himself, "I'm not going to survive this fucking thing. There is just too much out there. I'm never going to be able to get through this. But I've got to get through this. Whatever it is, I've got to get through it."

He walked into Morvillo's waiting room. The prosecutor's secretary was an Italian girl who always claimed to be looking for an FBI Irish husband. Other mornings Leuci had kidded her. Today she gave him a queer expression, told him to take a seat, and after that wouldn't look up.

Leuci sat down on the couch. Presently Morvillo came out of his office, said nothing, not even good morning, and walked past Leuci into the hall.

"What the hell is going on?" said Leuci to the secretary.

"I don't know," she said vaguely, avoiding his eyes. "He is screaming in there all morning. It has something to do with a lie detector test."

Leuci's panic became total. He is going to make me take a lie detector test. How am I going to get through this thing? How am I going to get through this day?

Morvillo, crossing back into his office, glanced at Leuci, then at the envelope in his hands.

"I haven't opened this envelope yet," he said. "In it are the results of a lie detector test. I want to tell you something. If they are positive, I'm going to prosecute you myself."

"For what?"

"Did you ever hear of the crime of perjury?"

"Do you want to tell me what this is all about?"

"You'll know in a minute." He went inside and slammed the door.

Leuci waited.

The secretary's console buzzed. She said, "Go in. He wants to see you."

Morvillo was sitting at his desk.

"I want you to read this material," said Morvillo, and he tossed The Baron's allegations across the desk.

Reading, Leuci said automatically, "This is bullshit."

"All of it?" said Morvillo. "What if I told you we checked and found that the car part of it is true."

Leuci started to say, "Give me a break," but when he looked up Morvillo was grinning.

"They came to us, I want you to know, five days ago with this thing," said Morvillo. "We didn't know what to do. The Baron came in. We offered him money if he passed a lie detector test. We gave him a series of tests and he failed them all."

Leuci's heart was pounding, but he had started to sense that he was all right. "What did you ask him?"

Morvillo pushed across the questions. There were only about a dozen. The polygraph can measure only yes or no answers. All questions must be phrased with great specificity so as to demand a single yes or no response. Whoever had phrased these had confined himself exclusively to the most serious of The Baron's charges.

Did you and Leuci sell narcotics together?

Did you ever share money with Leuci from the sale of narcotics?

Did Leuci ever give you heroin in evidence vouchers near the property clerk's office?

Each time that The Baron answered yes to these questions, the graph needle had gone off the page.

Morvillo now was ecstatic. "I feel terrific, Bob," he said. "Bob, I felt sick for five days."

"Why didn't you tell me about it?"

"Tell you? Bob, we were deciding on how we were going to lock you up. How was I going to look in the paper?"

These are not my friends, Leuci was telling himself. Tomorrow they could prosecute me and never think twice about it. I have lost all my friends on the other side by now. I have nobody. Then he thought: Sooner or later these people are going to turn on me. There is no escaping this thing.

"By the way," said Morvillo," we want you to explain these cars. We find that both are registered in your wife's name."

"Those cars are mine," said Leuci, "but I never gave him narcotics for them. I paid for both of them. One was an old bomb, and the other was better. I probably paid in cash for them. I don't know."

"So you actually have those cars?" said Morvillo. "How the hell can you take cars from an informant?"

"This happened a long time ago," said Leuci. "The guy owned a taxi cab company. He owned a fleet of cars. I got cars from him for a couple of hundred dollars. I would have had to pay seven or eight hundred some place else."

"He's an informant," said Morvillo. "You don't take things from informants."

"Look, I paid for those cars," said Leuci, and he telephoned his wife, who soon called back to say she had found a canceled check endorsed by The Baron, paying for one of the cars.

Morvillo was jubilant. So was Leuci. They were patting each other on the back.

When Leuci came out of Morvillo's office, his bodyguards read the news on his face. "You did it again," one said. "You got out of it, whatever it was, didn't you?"

Nodding, Leuci thought: But for how much longer?

19

ENTERING the cocktail lounge, three men approached the table where the owner, John Lusterino, sat alone. One threw a newspaper down. It landed hard and split open in front of him.

The bar went instantly silent. In the world in which Lusterino moved this was already an insult. Lusterino was known to have a violent temper.

However, he only locked eyes with his visitors, proving to onlookers both that he knew them, and that they had weight.

Voices were raised. One of the men was thumping a particular article—it concerned Leuci's role in an upcoming trial—with his thumb. Lusterino shook his head several times.

All three visitors stomped out of the lounge.

Lusterino went to a phone and started a message via his mother through his aunt's household to his cousin. Leuci should phone him at once on a matter of great urgency.

Several days passed before the message reached its destination, and a telephone connection was made. Some men had been in his place, Lusterino told Leuci. "They're looking to hurt you, Bobby."

There was a short silence while Leuci digested this news.

"They think you should be hit," Lusterino continued. "I agreed with them. Do you expect me to defend you? I'm not your lawyer, Bobby."

Leuci began to ask quick, nervous questions. Who were the men, did he know them?

"They wanted me to do it," Lusterino interrupted bluntly. "I said, hey, the kid's my cousin. He's my uncle's son. I said I wouldn't do it." After a moment Lusterino added, "I also said I wouldn't interfere. I feel I owe you this much. I owe you a warning and that's all I owe you. Watch yourself, Bobby."

The conversation lasted some time longer. Leuci said he was sorry if he had embarrassed Lusterino, or put him in a position where he would be looked on with less respect than in the past. It was a way of saying: I hope you're not going to be killed because of me.

But Lusterino only laughed. "Listen, anyone I ever introduced you to, anyone that ever wanted to meet you, I always told them you were a cop. Fuck them." And he hung up.

Leuci's protection was already tight. With so many trials depending on him, his life was a valuable commodity to the government. Up to eighteen marshals working three eight-hour shifts guarded the cabin in the Catskills, and six cops guarded Leuci in New York. All these men had been screened for their integrity, for a wrong guard could have sold rights to his life for a lot of money.

Next a private investigator from Los Angeles came forward with information about a plot to assassinate Leuci by attaching a bomb to his car. The private investigator was a former New York police lieutenant. In a Las Vegas casino he had chanced to overhear the plot being discussed by three men. Even the name of the technician who would attach the bomb had been mentioned.

Leuci became paranoid. In the street the sound of a car starting could cause him to shudder, and he approached his own car each time with fear. I'm the guy that's supposed to start the car, he would tell himself, inserting the key. I'm the guy responsible. He always started the car himself. His bodyguards, meanwhile walked to the corner and stood with their fingers in their ears. This usually broke the tension, and everybody laughed.

In the Catskills the cabin stood at the end of a long dirt lane off an already isolated country road. The access lane, with heavily armed men posted along it, wound through the woods to a clearing where the house was. It was an expensive place to guard and an uncomfortable place to live—both for the marshals and for the Leucis. In winter the snow drifts piled to the windows, and in spring the mud rose up over the children's shoes. Because of the isolation, the marshals were rotated every three weeks or so. Gina and the kids were not rotated, nor was Leuci, who had to be driven up there every weekend by bodyguards, a minimum six-hour round trip.

Pressure to move the family became strong.

"I love being up in the mountains in our place," Gina told her husband one Friday night. "But I want our family in a home. This is a summer cottage. I look out the window and my kids are always by themselves. Or else they are playing with men with guns. I want them to be in a neighborhood where there are other children. I want to put a bedroom set together. I want to put a living room set together." Her voice got wistful. "I want a home."

She didn't know about the active investigations into threats against her husband's life, only that the government now decided to relocate the Leucis in northern Virginia. Leuci was flown down there one weekend. He saw and bought a house. The following weekend Gina was flown down and shown the house, and some time after that they moved in. There were no guards on the family in Virginia.

Nothing else changed. Leuci continued to live in the barracks on Governors Island, continued to commute home on weekends, although now it was via Eastern Airlines shuttle; his bodyguards now drove him to the airport every Friday night, and picked him up there every Monday morning. Usually the bodyguards arrived at the terminal an hour early to check out the waiting room first.

One Monday morning they spotted a man who, to their eyes, looked bad. They didn't like the hard-eyed stare with which he scrutinized every arriving passenger. And from the moment Leuci came out the gate, this individual's eyes never left him.

There were three bodyguards that morning: Bill Fritz, Artie Monty, and John Farley, all patrolmen in plain-clothes.

Leuci's bag came off the plane. He picked it up and walked toward the exit doors. When he glanced back the man was following. Monty and Farley were walking beside him. Fritz had gone to get the car.

"We'll walk to the parking lot," said Leuci. "When the car comes up we'll jump in and take off. Let's see what he does."

As Bill Fritz pulled up in the car, they saw the man running to his own car.

Leuci looked out the back window. He watched a late model green Chevy spin out of the parking lot and come up behind them. Everyone tensed up. They drove out of La Guardia onto the Grand Central Parkway. The green Chevy was still with them.

"This guy has got to be crazy," said Leuci. "He's all by himself. There are four of us here. He knows I'm a cop, so I've got a gun. He's got to believe you guys are cops. You all have guns. We got four guns facing one guy."

Monty tried a joke, "Maybe he's got a machine gun under the front seat."

Fritz was hitting eighty. They raced down the parkway. The other car, weaving in and out of traffic, stayed with them.

They sailed up an exit ramp, sped along the service road, and jumped the stop sign. The green Chevy did likewise.

"This fucking guy is chasing us," said Leuci.

They pulled into the next street, stopped the car, threw open the doors and sprang out, guns in their fists, seeking cover. Leuci was behind one car door, Monty behind the other. Farley and Fritz both left the car and ran to the sidewalks, where they crouched behind whatever protection was there.

The Chevy spun around the corner into a residential street blocked by their car. The driver hit his brakes and slid to a stop ten feet away. As he did so the four cops came at him from four different directions, their guns pointed at him.

He put his hands on his head and his head on his steering wheel. Farley pulled him out of the car. The guy sailed out on the fly, his feet never touching the ground.

They searched him. He was not armed. They searched the car but found nothing. He seemed terrified, and he began to claim that he was a horse player. He waited by the shuttle every Monday. Horse trainers would fly up from Virginia and Maryland, go into the city and place enormous bets at the offtrack betting. He would follow them, stand on line behind them, and dump down whatever money he could scratch together on whatever horses they bet.

The four cops threw him into their car. All the way to the Southern District courthouse he pleaded that he had nothing to do with any crime they thought he was doing.

Seeing Leuci come off the plane wearing a leather jacket and boots and a pair of brown slacks, the man insisted, he had taken him for a horse trainer. He kept mentioning a particular trainer's name. "You look just like this guy," he insisted, over and over again.

Leuci said, "You better be right. I better look just like this guy."

The man was thrown into the grand jury, where he swore that he didn't know Leuci, had never heard of Leuci.

Two members of the Police Commissioner's Special Force drove him to his home in Queens. They found an apartment that was empty except for a bed, a table, one or two chairs and a very sad woman who was the man's wife, and who told the story of her husband's sickness. He had long since gambled away all their savings. He was in debt to everyone in her family, in debt to everyone in the neighborhood. He had at one time owned his own taxicab. He had sold his taxicab, sold his medallion. The apartment was cluttered with thousands and thousands of scratch sheets everywhere. So maybe his story was true. Or maybe, in his desperation, he had accepted a hit

contract he was incompetent to carry out. He had an
Italian name and low-level Mafia connections.

The attitude of Leuci's bodyguards changed dramati-
cally. From then on they treated their jobs as serious
business. Whenever they moved they moved professionally.

In the end, the only hit contract carried out was on
Lusterino.

Lusterino had grown up in the Brownsville section of
Brooklyn in a neighborhood that now, in 1973, was
almost entirely black. In his childhood it had been heavily
Italian and most of the families had emigrated from the
same few Sicilian villages.

Lusterino's father, Marino, was a mason trying to
support six children. They lived in a railroad flat that
always smelled strongly of cooking oil and tomato paste.
All the Lusterinos were big and fair-skinned, and Johnny
was a blond with strong arms and a barrel chest.

His first arrest occurred April 1, 1948—grand larceny,
auto. The charge was dismissed. The car thief became a
burglar. Three years and only two arrests later he was sent
to Elmira, his first time inside. When he came out he
graduated to membership in a ring hijacking truckloads
of furs. Others were caught, not him, but someone
informed and, after fighting the case for almost two years,
and having been arrested twice more on gun charges in the
interim, he was sentenced to ten to fifteen years for first
degree robbery. In prison he played on the same football
team as Mikey Coco and Sonny Red.

By then he was what the Mafia world knows as a
"made guy." He had been taken into full-fledged
membership. He was one of the fortunate few. He had
proven himself early, and so when he came out of jail he
would be given things outright. He would be given
money, and the opportunity to make money. Of course he
would have to keep paying the men who made him.

Lusterino had a clear perspective on life.

"A man who hasn't spent time in prison and is in street
life is not a complete guy," he said once. "It's in prison that
you get your real education."

To Johnny there was white and there was black. One might think that men who had stayed out of jail would be called bright, but in Lusterino's world it was the opposite. "So and so is okay," he would say, "but he's never done a day's time." There were no gray areas. A man who hadn't been to prison was probably an informant.

Lusterino believed in rules that were simple to follow. There was nothing he would not do to help a friend—or to hurt an enemy.

When he came out this last time after so long, he was like a man lost. He was amazed at the progress of the world in his absence. The year he left for jail the girls had worn skirts to their ankles. Now they were in miniskirts. He would sit in his lounge watching the young people dance. "It's hard to believe," he would say, shaking his head. He married a go-go dancer from his lounge, a sweet, beautiful young girl named Bea—she was nearly twenty years younger than himself—and very quickly he fathered two children.

He was constantly hustling to make money, and he was constantly on the verge of going to war. People who had been in prison with him came into his lounge, and he gave them money. He often handed his "kid cousin" hundred-dollar bills for no reason.

But one day a friend asked Johnny if he had access to counterfeit money; after making a few calls, Lusterino found a suitcase full of it, which he handed to his friend over the bar. The friend then went to meet his buyer, who was a federal informant accompanied to the meeting by a Secret Service agent. Not only was the friend arrested, but so was Lusterino who had tailed along behind to watch the sale go down.

Whenever Johnny was on the street, law enforcement watched him closely. In the various Mafia albums kept by the police, the FBI, and others, Lusterino had a page to himself marked "at large." It was not clear what he did in organized crime, and so, although most albums called him a captain in the Colombo family, at least one rated him no higher than soldier.

He had moved his mother out of the railroad flat and

set her up in a semidetached house in a quiet street in Queens. It was there that men came to get him one night in March 1973. He had just kissed his mother good night on the porch. There was a brief struggle. A gun appeared. Lusterino got into a car with them, and was never seen again.

Rosa Lusterino had witnessed this, but she told detectives investigating the case that she had recognized no one, knew nothing. They got nothing more out of her.

Though Johnny's body was never found, and though no one was ever brought to trial, the detectives had little difficulty amassing information. As was usual after Mafia hits, the underworld seethed with conversation, and they soon learned the names of two of the three men involved. They also concluded that Lusterino was unquestionably dead.

He was forty-four. He left his wife Bea, who was twenty-six, and two sons, aged three and one, and a shaken cousin.

"Was Johnny killed over me?" Leuci asked himself. When he lay in bed in the dark, he was already seeing faces: Nunziata, Sheridan, Perrazzo. Now, night after night, his cousin's face was there, too, head thrown back, laughing. When in a temper, Lusterino didn't scream or shout, he laughed. He had a crazy, scary laugh, and no one ever laughed back.

Night after night, lying in the dark, Leuci asked himself: Who took him? But any of those men who used to frequent his bar could have done it. What was more difficult to understand was how Lusterino had let it happen. Lusterino would have seen them coming—he bragged that he could always see an enemy coming. Always look for a guy with a smile on his face, Bobby, he used to say. Look for a guy who's smiling, who never smiled before.

Did they torture him before they put him to death? Whenever the police found bodies in the trunks of cars, the guy had usually been tortured first in some grotesque way. Leuci had met a number of the men who performed such tasks.

From then on, Leuci worried about being captured. If a car pulled up and men opened fire on him, or if a bomb went off when he turned the ignition key, it would all be over in an instant. But if they captured him, it would last a very long time.

Mike Shaw realized how much the Lusterino hit had upset Leuci. "You're not holding yourself responsible, are you?" inquired the prosecutor.

"No," Leuci insisted.

"You're blaming yourself," said Shaw. "You're not responsible for other people's actions."

But in the night Leuci continued to see Lusterino's face laughing. He continued to worry too. If they take you, he told himself, you can't talk your way out, or buy your way out. These people don't want an explanation.

For months Leuci continued to ask about Bea and the kids. He asked his mother—he found he couldn't call Bea directly. Rosa Lusterino, Leuci was told, had urged her daughter-in-law to begin dating again, but Bea so far had refused, saying, "Not until I'm positive." But the day came when she announced to the family that she had begun going out with men again. "I want to find a father for my children."

That night in the dark Leuci again saw Lusterino's face, head thrown back, laughing.

20

THAT SPRING still another young prosecutor, Assistant U.S. Attorney Rudy Giuliani, twenty-nine, took over the Leuci cases, and he began to prepare the witness for his next important trial: *The United States of America* v. *Benjamin Caiola*. It was a good strong case. The recordings were unequivocal. The Mafia lawyer had clearly attempted to bribe Detective Leuci.

But Giuliani was troubled nonetheless. Leuci's testimony might be a problem. Giuliani had studied all Leuci's previous testimony, particularly in the Rosner case, and now, every day, he was studying Leuci in person. He saw an emotional young man who wanted everyone to like him, even his natural enemies. If he met Caiola right now he would want Caiola to like him, even as his testimony sent the lawyer to jail.

Leuci was also, Giuliani saw, guilt-ridden, worried, easily upset. Why so guilty? What was he worried about? He displayed a tremendous need to explain why he did what he did, but the explanation never entirely satisfied the young prosecutor. Because Leuci, despite such limited previous misconduct of his own, had made a major commitment to do dangerous, dirty undercover work for the government over a long period of time. He had accepted an enormous burden that was—or so Giuliani perceived—inconsistent with his personality. Why? Now, afterward, he was still deeply troubled. Why?

To Giuliani there had to be a better explanation for Leuci's conduct than the one advanced—a crisis of conscience—and what other explanation could there be than fear of prosecution. Leuci had admitted three acts of misconduct, but he could not have feared prosecution on any one of them. The only witnesses were Mafia men who would never testify.

So what else had he done that he feared being arrested on?

Up close, Giuliani found Leuci an extremely complicated man. He was enormously sensitive to other people and to their problems. He was a sympathetic listener, a charming talker. He was, Giuliani sensed, a man of integrity.

Yet he was deeply troubled. None of it added up. His personality didn't match with the facts.

Studying the Caiola case, Giuliani came up with still more questions, but no answers. Caiola had operated with impunity for years. Law enforcement considered him as evil and as dangerous a man as Rosner, but had never been able to make a case against him.

Then along comes Leuci. He goes straight to Caiola and elicits a bribe. Why was the lawyer so off guard? So sure of Leuci?

Just how much did this cop, Leuci, know?

Giuliani's suspicions were strong only at night when he was alone. In Leuci's presence he succumbed to the warmth and openness of the detective's personality. He believed his assurances.

"I wouldn't commit perjury. Are you crazy?"

Face to face, Giuliani found Leuci one of the most credible persons with whom he had ever dealt. Nonetheless, as he began to prepare Leuci's cross-examination, Giuliani resolved to try to break him down. To make him admit anything he might be concealing. He believed he could do this where Morvillo and Sagor had failed. Morvillo had prepared the Rosner case at night while running the Criminal Division in the daytime. Sagor did not have the right background and personality to understand Leuci.

But Giuliani had himself been brought up in an Italian family, and had spent time on the streets. Later Giuliani had graduated magna cum laude from both Manhattan College and New York University Law School.

The prosecutor realized that if he broke Leuci down, if other acts of misconduct came out, this would prove perjury, which would upset the Rosner verdict and probably make a successful prosecution of Caiola impossible as well. Still, he would have to do it if he could. His oath of office demanded it.

All this time Giuliani had also been negotiating with Caiola's lawyer, and now the defendant suddenly decided to plead guilty to conspiracy to use interstate facilities to further the crime of bribery. He was sentenced to a maximum term of three years in jail.

This was a great relief to Giuliani, whose suspicions of Leuci became moot. He watched Leuci prepare, with other prosecutors, many additional cases. But none ever came to trial. The detective never took the stand, and this was a relief to Giuliani, too.

Bail bondsman Dominic Marcone, an associate of DeStefano, pleaded guilty without trial. He got two years.

Drug dealer Mikey Coco pleaded guilty also, and went to jail for three years. Case after case was disposed of similarly.

Queens Assistant District Attorney Norman Archer did go on trial. Marked bribe money had been found in his safe. Leuci was not needed as a witness, and was not called.

As for Leuci, the only cloud on his horizon, and it seemed a small one then, was the Rosner appeal. Rosner was on bail, his appeal pending. Meanwhile the ex-lawyer had submitted two post trial motions to trial judge Arnold Bauman, requesting formal hearings. The motions were granted, but Leuci was not required to testify either time. Now, as the year ended, the Court of Appeals handed down its ruling. Rosner's conviction stood. The defendant, it seemed, would go to jail at last.

After him would go many, many others, for these cases were so strong that nearly every defendant could be expected to plead guilty: the Mafia hoodlums Marchese, Tomasetti; the Tolentinos Senior and Junior; the lawyer Salko; and the many compromised cops.

For Leuci this was a time of almost total security, and

it lasted many serene months. He was the hero of the Southern District Courthouse—look how easily all these bad people were being put out of circulation—and for month after month his credibility was not questioned.

He was the hero, in fact, of the entire criminal justice system. Partly because of the official corruption he had revealed on all levels, Governor Rockefeller had appointed a Special Prosecution Force headed by Maurice Nadjari to watchdog the entire justice operation. For the first time in history an attempt was going to be made to clean up not just the station houses, but the courthouses as well.

Nadjari was a firebrand—unpredictable, capricious, and blindly tenacious once he fastened on a scent—and this Leuci realized, could one day be a problem for himself. But mostly Leuci exulted that he was there, a lawyer whose principal function was supposed to be to investigate his own kind. Because credit for this went directly to Detective Second-Grade Robert Leuci.

It was possible, some days, to imagine himself the hero he had always wanted to be.

Meanwhile, his home life was good. In northern Virginia, Gina was happy with her new house, their children played in playgrounds with other kids, and Leuci was there every weekend without fail.

His friends were doing well. He met Les Wolff for dinner several times. In the garment district, Undercover Detective Wolff had penetrated the Mafia at an extremely high level. Major indictments were coming. Wolff was pleased with Leuci for having got him the job, and no longer distrusted his former partner. Mike Shaw, still directing the Federal Strike Force, was thrilled with Wolff.

And Assistant U.S. Attorney Giuliani, whom Leuci considered now an extremely close friend, had been promoted to head the Special Prosecution Section, and then the Narcotics Section as well. Still only thirty, he was now the third most powerful prosecutor in the U.S. Attorney's office.

Leuci even had, for the first time since his conversations with Scoppetta, a viable long-term future, or so it seemed, for in Washington he now met regularly with Tartaglino. The Bureau of Narcotics had recently changed its name to the Drug Enforcement Administration, but Tartaglino was still Number Two man there, and he too seemed to have succumbed to Leuci's warmth, his charm, his obvious vulnerability, his desire to be liked. The federal official talked often now of the detective's future—something Leuci had scarcely dared think of himself—when all these cases would be over.

"We are going to work out something for you," Tartaglino promised.

Once he showed him a written agreement he had negotiated with Police Commissioner Murphy. As soon as Leuci's cases ended, he would be picked up by the Drug Enforcement Administration; his salary would continue to be paid by the New York Police Department, his pension would continue to build up, he would still be a cop.

This sounded like a dream to Leuci.

Tartaglino talked about assigning Leuci to a task force he would form and send to Trieste. Or maybe Leuci should go to Syria and Turkey to make buys of opium. Maybe buy it all up for the government. "I have all sorts of ideas for you," he promised. "So don't be concerned about your future. You've done your job and you are going to be okay."

But he doesn't know the whole story, Leuci would think. Other times he would tell himself: He's so much smarter than the others that of course he knows. But he doesn't care as long as I never tell him.

One day Tartaglino spoke of still another task force. He was collecting agents from all over the country to go to the Mexican border. "It's not the nicest kind of assignment in the world, but it's not bad," he said. "You would work on the border with the Mexican police."

"Mr. Tartaglino," said Leuci, "I'll do whatever you ask me to do. My big fear is that I will embarrass you."

"You have said that to me before and I don't want to hear it anymore," answered Tartaglino. "You are going to get me thinking that you may embarrass me. Why do I have to think about that? There is no reason why you should embarrass me. You've told them everything. Are you going to tell them any more? No? Then that's it."

21

THERE WAS no keystone which, plucked out of the arch, caused the entire edifice to collapse. There was not even the steady undermining of any foundations. The collapse was sudden and total, and not even particularly dramatic.

It began with a series of events that apparently were not related.

First, the Baron's allegations reappeared as a formal affidavit. This time it was deposed in the proper form and place, and duly sworn. It was a legal masterpiece. the work of Rosner's new lawyer, the renowned constitutional scholar Alan Dershowitz of Harvard. This affidavit swayed Judge Bauman, who agreed to accord Rosner a hearing, and set a date for it. Detective Leuci would be obliged once again to take the stand. Once again he would be questioned under oath about himself.

Then, too, although Leuci had admitted during Rosner's trial to only three acts of misconduct, a memo out of the files of Tartaglino now came to light that outlined a fourth. At dinner at Shaw's apartment two or more years ago Tartaglino had badmouthed cops to such a point that Leuci had angrily described almost the first corruption he ever saw, because it was by federal agents. After executing a search warrant with the two agents, he and Mandato had met them in a bar, where $200, taken by one of the agents, was split four ways. The two cops had not even known until the split that money had been taken.

Tartaglino had made a memo of this conversation—fifty dollars' worth of corruption by Leuci—then had forgotten about it. So had Shaw. So had Leuci. But Assistant U.S. Attorney Elliot Sagor, obliged to answer so many questions by Rosner and others, had sent formal requests to every federal agency for any and all information on Leuci that their files might contain.

When the Tartaglino memo came back, Sagor was furious, and he summoned Tom Taylor and George Carros to his office. Taylor and Carros had both served in the Leuci investigation. Both had been promoted by Tartaglino as a result; they were now among the highest-ranking Drug Enforcement officials in New York. But they had gotten no publicity out of the investigation, had come to resent Leuci, who had made headlines.

Now in Sagor's office Carros and Taylor were scared. This oversight would seriously embarrass Tartaglino. It could subject the Justice Department to ridicule.

If Sagor reported them to Tartaglino, then their civil service futures might be in jeopardy. They would suffer while the crooked cop, Leuci, got off scot-free once again.

When they left Sagor's office, Leuci was waiting to go in. They cursed him. After that, knowing that success would remove all heat from themselves, they launched their own investigation into past misconduct by Leuci.

A third event in the series at this time was Special State Prosecutor Maurice Nadjari's announcement to the press that he had solved the ripoff of 300 pounds of heroin from the police property clerk's office. He hadn't, but it now became incumbent upon him to do so, and fast, and rumors began to circulate that Detective Second-Grade Robert Leuci was a solid suspect in the case. These rumors were fed by Leuci's appearance at Nadjari's offices day after day for interrogation.

And finally, SIU Detective Carl Aguiluz was indicted for perjury and offered a deal if he would cooperate.

Leuci had been informed of Aguiluz's arrest in advance. Assistant U.S. Attorney Wally Higgins called him in. "I sat through the Rosner trial, and I think you were great," Higgins began. "I'm going to ask you a favor. We are going to lock up a detective from SIU."

"Who?"

"Carl Aguiluz. Do you know him?"

Leuci's head began churning. So did his stomach. "Yeah, I know him."

"We're going to take him in the next couple of days. We

thought you might talk to him. He might do the kind of thing that you did."

It's coming to an end, Leuci thought. Aguiluz. Who else do they have? What other investigations do they have going on that I don't even know about?

"He testified in the grand jury," explained Higgins. He was pleased with himself, and totally unaware of the turmoil he had created inside Leuci. "We are sure he's committed perjury. So we got him. We can indict him and have him locked up. After that we're going to try to turn him. Maybe you can help us convince him to cooperate."

As Leuci left Higgins's office, the names of every SIU detective he had ever known flashed like file cards through his head. Who had Aguiluz worked with? Which of these detectives had Leuci also worked with? Who, if compromised, could finger whom? But he knew Aguiluz. Aguiluz was not going to cooperate. Then he thought about the Rosner hearing coming up, and about The Baron's affidavit, and about Nadjari's investigation, and about Carros and Taylor, who were interrogating The Baron and trying to move their investigation under the aegis of the U.S. Attorney's office in Brooklyn, because Leuci had no friends there who might protect him. Now Aguiluz.

It was all closing in on him at last.

"Things are getting really bad," he told Gina that weekend.

"What's so bad?" she asked. "We've gone through it. It's over now. I never thought we would survive it, but we did."

"What if I told you there was a chance I would be arrested?"

"What?"

"Because I never told them all the things I did."

"What does that mean? Who is going to arrest you? Scoppetta and those people? Bob? After all this, you could be arrested by the same people who got you to do it?"

From then on Leuci lived in a state of steadily mounting terror.

22

SPECIAL PROSECUTOR NADJARI was not the only man investigating the French Connection heroin ripoff. Eight other prosecutors also wanted to solve it: the elected district attorneys sitting in each of the five boroughs; the special narcotics prosecutor whose jurisdiction covered the entire city; the U.S. attorney for the Southern District whose jurisdiction covered Manhattan, the Bronx, and Staten Island; and the U.S. attorney for the Eastern District, whose jurisdiction covered Brooklyn, Queens, and Long Island.

The French Connection ripoff was the most celebrated crime any of these men might ever hope to solve, and all had active investigations going. So did the Police Department itself.

All these investigations proceeded along the same lines. At the start, investigators assigned to the job merely went around asking questions of persons active on the narcotics scene—the range extended from street junkies to detective commanders—and one of the first questions asked was always this one: who do you think did it?

The name Leuci was mentioned often. Again and again investigators were urged to take a close look at him. Surely he was involved in the ripoff in some way. Only a crime of this magnitude would explain why, when they had had nothing on him, he had volunteered to cooperate with the prosecutors in the first place. His sixteen months undercover was no doubt an attempt to save his neck in advance. All the prosecutors knew he had had the best organized-crime connections of any SIU detective. He could have used these connections to funnel the heroin back into the street.

Motive plus opportunity. To the cynical police mind, this equaled not logic but proof. The next step was to locate hard evidence against Leuci, and a great many investigators began digging. Apparently the heroin had been withdrawn over a period of months. Leuci's movements during these months were scrutinized. A search was begun for secret bank accounts. Samples of his handwriting were surreptitiously obtained and matched by handwriting experts against the withdrawal vouchers.

All this time the name Carl Aguiluz was mentioned frequently also. Detective Aguiluz was probably not involved himself, investigators were told. But he was a key guy in SIU. If anyone could unlock the French Connection case, Aguiluz could. Was there any way to make Aguiluz "cooperate"? Could he somehow be forced to talk?

In the offices of the U.S. attorney for the Southern District, Rudy Giuliani was not yet listening to the rumors about Leuci, for whom he still felt enormous sympathy. But the rumors about Aguiluz sounded good to him, and he pondered them. There had been for a long time a possible perjury case pending against Aguiluz. It was a weak case. There was enough to indict, not to convict, and the case had nothing whatever to do with the French Connection ripoff. But an indictment would be a hook into Aguiluz. It might be enough to make him talk.

Cops feared indictment far more than ordinary citizens, and they had good reason. Once indicted, they were immediately suspended from the Police Department. Emotionally, this meant moving about the city stripped of gun and shield. Financially, it meant their pay stopped. They were out of work during all the months and sometimes years that the indictment pended.

In addition, an indictment, even one that resulted eventually in acquittal, always resulted in a second trial by the Police Department. In the Police Department trial room, hearsay testimony, co-conspirator testimony, and other such evidence became fully admissible, and conviction became almost a foregone conclusion. Conviction meant, usually, dismissal without pension rights. It meant going out into the streets to find a job, and who would hire an ex-cop dismissed for corruption? Indictment to a cop meant his life was ruined.

At length the decision was made to indict Aguiluz and make him sweat. Scare him enough and he might crack. He might give up information on the French Connection ripoff.

The perjury case centered around an informant of Aguiluz's named Frank Ramos, who was maître d'hôtel at a midtown Spanish restaurant. Through Ramos, and through illegal wiretaps which Ramos had allowed him to install in the restaurant, the detective had learned of the imminent arrival of a major shipment of heroin. But when he went to stake out the site of the drop, he was recognized by federal agents, who protested that this was their case, and that Aguiluz must leave the scene at once. The dispute was carried to higher levels, and a political accommodation was made. Police Department brass ordered Aguiluz off the case.

Furious, anxious about his informant, Aguiluz went to a telephone and warned Ramos to stay away from the drop area. When the feds subsequently blew their arrests, they blamed Aguiluz, claiming he had warned the suspects they were there, and a grand jury investigation was opened into these charges. One of the first witnesses called was Frank Ramos.

Previously, a federal undercover agent had made two narcotics buys off Ramos, who was, therefore, in serious trouble. When told that he could lighten his sentence if he gave up Aguiluz, Ramos did not hesitate. Only a small part of his testimony proved critical. He put Aguiluz in his bar at a certain hour, and Aguiluz, testifying before the same grand jury, denied it.

Several other witnesses were found who corroborated Ramos's testimony—sort of. They put Aguiluz in the bar just before the time specified by Ramos and denied by Aguiluz. Thus the alleged perjury was a considerable distance removed from any crime Aguiluz may or may not have committed, and it was unlikely that any jury would ever vote to send the detective to jail for it.

Nonetheless the indictment came down, and late on a Friday night in January he was arrested and brought to an undercover office that federal prosecutors sometimes used. During the next several hours various prosecutors and agents attempted to question Aguiluz. Some spoke softly to him. Some railed at him. All attempted to persuade him that he should, and must, cooperate.

But Aguiluz continued to insist that he was an honorable cop and an innocent man. The perjury case against him was persecution, pure and simple, he said. It would never stick. Furthermore, there was nothing to cooperate about. He had committed no corrupt acts himself, and knew no detective who had. He knew nothing about the French Connection ripoff.

Leuci, who had been summoned to the cover office shortly after the interrogation of Aguiluz began, had since been cooling his heels in an anteroom. He was there, supposedly, to help persuade Aguiluz to cooperate, but three hours passed before the exhausted questioners, withdrawing, invited him to take his turn. "He's not going to turn," they asserted, "but see what you can do."

And so Leuci stepped into the office in which Aguiluz waited, closed the door, and sat down opposite him. Aguiluz, he saw, was terrified.

Leuci's own motivation at this time was not clear to him. If he could convince Aguiluz to talk, he would be in for another round of praise and handshakes. His friendships with the prosecutors would become firmer than ever. he would be the hero of the Southern District once again, and perhaps his friends—Giuliani and others—would urge the city's other prosecutor to leave him alone. Some of the heat would be off him.

On the other hand, if Aguiluz cracked and began to name names, it could be dangerous. Still, Leuci felt one step removed from whatever Aguiluz might reveal, for they had never worked a single case together.

He studied the man across the desk from him, and tried to decide how to start.

"You have to live with yourself and what you've done," burst out Aguiluz. "I'm not you. I'll never give up my partners and the guys I've worked with."

This was the start of a vitriolic outburst against "the feds" that lasted ten minutes. Leuci's first job was to separate himself in Aguiluz's mind from the men he so bitterly denounced.

"Carl, you're in bad trouble. You have to tell them whatever they want to know. It's the only way you can save yourself. We're cops. If I were in your position I'd have to do the same!"

Aguiluz continued to rant. There were federal agents as deeply involved as he was in this Ramos case. When they had rousted him from the drop site they had made him leave all his illegal gear in place, and had continued the wiretap themselves.

It made Leuci think that Aguiluz's problems could be limited to this one case, and he began urging him to name these specific federal agents. But Aguiluz only cursed the men outside this room. He would never cooperate, he said.

Leuci knew what a brilliant detective Aguiluz was. He knew that Aguiluz loved being a detective, and had no other life. And so he began to bring up some of the great cases Aguiluz had made hoping to appeal to the Hispanic detective's pride. Aguiluz, listening, fell silent, and stared at the floor.

Leuci said, "Is this the way it ends, Carl? Do you want to go to jail? To West Street, tonight? They're going to put you in jail, Carl, tonight."

"Why does everybody hate cops?" asked Aguiluz. "Why do they turn on us? Why do they persecute us?" It was a cry from the heart of every cop everywhere.

"I spoke with them," Leuci said. "They told me they would take it easy on you."

The desperate Aguiluz was thinking only of prison. "Can you come to West Street with me?" he begged. "Can you stay with me tonight? I'm not Nunziata. I can handle it. All I need is someone to help me get through tonight."

Leuci left the room to report. "He's going crazy in there. Let me leave with him now," Leuci told the prosecution team. "Give him his gun back and his shield. Let me take him out of here as a policeman. Don't take him out of here as a prisoner. Give him time to think about doing this as a policeman."

They agreed. An amazed Aguiluz took back his gun and shield.

Leuci took him to a restaurant on Long Island. Leuci's bodyguards sat apart while he and Aguiluz ordered drinks at the bar. They talked about Nunziata. Why had he done what he did? Look at the mess he had left Ann in, and the kids. Why had he let them beat him? Aguiluz mustn't let himself be beaten by them in his turn.

"Just tell them what they want to know," Leuci said. "When it's over, they'll relocate you in another part of the world. You can start a new life."

Aguiluz did not look up from his drink. "If I was to agree to cooperate," he said in a low voice, "I would tell them everything."

Oh God, Leuci thought. "Great," he said out loud. "Tell them everything." Just tell them a few things, he silently pleaded.

By the time Aguiluz got home he was calmer. Leuci had made some good points, and now Aguiluz pursued thoughts of his own. The feds were onto him, he reasoned, and they would never let him go. If he got out of this indictment, there would be another close behind it on something else. They would hound him till they got him.

Finally, having made his decision, he came in to the Southern District and began to tell his story. His debriefing lasted three days, and the prosecutors were amazed by it. None of them had ever before dealt with a cop who held nothing back. Aguiluz told the worst things first, and he solidly implicated his partners, Peter Daly and Joe Novoa; if they had been like brothers to him, it did not show. Aguiluz, Daly and Novoa had not seized 100 kilos of heroin and cocaine, it seemed, but 105 kilos. Aguiluz had held five back, and sold it. He and his partners had stolen tens of thousands of dollars from drug dealers. They had sold prisoners their freedom in exchange for tens of thousands of dollars more. Aguiluz's recital was so shocking that his "minor" crimes, by the time he got to them, seemed hardly worth noting down.

Yes, he had perjured himself in court—twenty or more times, in fact. He had given junk to informants hundreds of times, had planted dozens and dozens of illegal wiretaps.

Aguiluz seemed a cold man, at least this was the mask he had assumed: much of his tale was uttered in a monotone, without any emotion. But at other times he tried to justify his conduct. Every narcotics detective he had ever known gave junk to informants, he said. The informants were sick, and no man with any compassion could turn his back on them. As for perjury in court, this was mandated by the stupid search and seizure laws, and by the need to put drug dealers in jail. The wiretap laws were equally stupid, for without illegal wiretaps most cases could never be made.

Some of the prosecutors debriefing Aguiluz nodded in sympathy at such reasoning. It was true that the laws might be written better, and now was not the time to argue that each law, right or wrong, was sacred—to argue, that is, that the law was the law. Abstract concepts had never yet convinced a street detective, and the important thing was to keep Aguiluz talking.

Stealing money from junk dealers was, to Aguiluz, justifiable also. Most would be out on the street on bail before the arresting detective was, and right back dealing again. Most would have no difficulty whatever fixing their cases at some stage of the system. They would buy bondsmen, district attorneys, judges. They were so rich they could buy anybody. Most could be hurt, could be put out of business, in one way only, and that was by stealing all their cash at the moment of arrest. As for selling them freedom, for the most part this was done only when, because of a scarcity of evidence, a legal arrest could not be made anyway.

Aguiluz had an explanation for holding back five kilos out of his monumental seizure. He had been so euphoric to have made such a case, to stare down at so much junk, that he had scarcely known what he was doing, he said.

He had held the five kilos out. Afterward he could never explain why, even to himself.

Once he found himself stuck with the junk, he did not know what to do with it. He couldn't turn it in—he would go to jail for having held it back in the first place. He found he couldn't flush it down the toilet either, for it was worth too much money, and his partners knew he had it. Daly and Novoa wouldn't believe he had flushed it away. They would think he was holding out money.

For weeks he drove around with five kilos of narcotics stashed in the trunk of his car. Finally he, Daly, and Novoa got together, talked it all out, and decided to get rid of the junk. All three got into the car and drove down to the river. They had resolved to empty the sacks out, spill dust onto the current. The junk would float away. They would be rid of it.

But once they stood on the embankment they couldn't bring themselves to do it, and they talked the subject out once more. Together they had done what no one else they knew had ever done. They had been through The Door. It should have changed their lives, but on the other side was —nothing. A newspaper clipping.

Like most SIU detectives, they had become used to money at the end of a big case, and this one was much more than a big case. This one was "The Door." And there was no money there. There was no reward of any kind. All they were left with was these sacks of junk that they had unthinkingly, almost inadvertently, held back. At their feet the water rushed by fast enough to carry away all the drowsy misery in the city.

They turned away, put the sacks back into the trunk, and drove off. A day or so later Aguiluz had begun disposing of their merchandise. He sold it in installments for safety's sake, and shared the money with Daly and Novoa. What difference did five more kilos make going into the New York narcotics market—none. Or so he told himself. So all three told themselves.

It was a dirty story, but also a sad one, because Aguiluz had been not only a great detective, but even, at the start of his career, as idealistic as most other young cops.

One other quality came through Aguiluz's long recital—his extreme bitterness toward Leuci. Bob Leuci was lying to them, he advised the prosecutors again and again. They should not be so shocked at what Aguiluz was telling them, because their star witness had done the same or worse.

Clearly he blamed Leuci for plenty—for Nunziata's death, for provoking the entire investigation into SIU detectives, even for having persuaded Aguiluz himself now to cooperate. Aguiluz, having made his deal with the prosecutors, was going to be obliged to plead guilty to felony charges twice, once in the Eastern District, once in the Southern. Leuci, meanwhile, had not yet even been indicted. Why the hell was Leuci getting away with all this shit, while he, Aguiluz, was required to plead guilty? He would do it, he said, but he didn't like it, and he wanted them to know that this character Leuci wasn't the angel they thought he was.

The listening prosecutors kept demanding that he give specific facts of misconduct by Leuci, but Aguiluz said he didn't have any. Leuci had kept his deals to himself, he explained. Contrary to what people seemed to think, detectives did not sit around in a circle describing the scores they made. The only people who knew specifically what you were doing were your own partners, and he had never worked a case with Leuci. Leuci had worked on Italian organized crime, while Aguiluz concentrated on Hispanics. Still, it had been clear to everyone in SIU that Leuci was making money.

In the absence of specific information, Giuliani and the other Southern District prosecutors decided that they were not really interested in Leuci at this point. They were interested in corroborating Aguiluz's other revelations. So they picked up his brother-in-law, Sal Buteria, who was not a cop; and his sergeant, Jim Sottile; and a young Spanish-speaking detective named Luis Martinez. All three cracked quickly; they corroborated Aguiluz's stories, and they agreed to cooperate themselves.

Using the dates Aguiluz had provided, the prosecutors subpoenaed the bank records of his supervisor, Lieutenant John Egan. These records showed that Egan, on the day following virtually every score, had made substantial deposits to one or another of his many savings accounts.

It remained now to nail Aguiluz's partners, Daly and Novoa. One score, according to Aguiluz, had been divided up in a room in the Taft Hotel. So the Taft's records were subpoenaed. These showed that the room in question had been registered in the name of Detective Peter Daly. On the day following another score, Detective Novoa had bought a new car for cash.

Giuliani and his assistants were too busy to think about Leuci. In a single day some two dozen SIU detectives were indicted and arrested, so many that the prosecutors had to meet with them almost in groups. All were offered deals if they would cooperate. Many of them, at that point, brought Leuci's name into the conversation: "Give me the same deal you gave Leuci, and sure I'll cooperate. Just give me the same free ride he's getting."

Aguiluz, meanwhile, was sent across into Brooklyn to be interrogated by Eastern District prosecutors under Tom Puccio. His revelations were equally juicy there, and Puccio ordered other SIU detectives brought in and questioned.

At once Puccio in Brooklyn began listening to the same anguished voices as Giuliani was hearing in Manhattan.

"I'm not admitting that I did anything," said each detective he talked to. "But if I did do something it wasn't any worse than what Leuci did."

Puccio decided to meet with Giuliani. As they talked there seemed to be an echo in the room, and both heard it. "Leuci is as bad as we are. Leuci is lying to you. You are closing your eyes to it, because he's your pal."

But Leuci was no pal of Puccio's. They had never dealt with each other. Remarking that he had a few ideas he might try, Puccio left the meeting and went back to his own office. From then on the belt began to tighten around Leuci.

Giuliani summoned him. All the detectives were saying that Leuci was guilty of more than three things, the prosecutors began. Giuliani was troubled and it showed.

He cared about what happened to the detective opposite him. "Are you sure there's nothing you want to tell me?" Giuliani's tone was kindly. When Leuci, wearing his most sincere smile, insisted that there was nothing to tell, Giuliani showed him out.

Puccio summoned Leuci to Brooklyn. Leuci, who arrived nervous, was soon at ease, for this new prosecutor seemed at first as casual and friendly as all the others.

But there was method to Puccio's casualness. He began by praising Leuci and Aguiluz almost interchangeably. Both were brave, both were admirable. As for Aguiluz, the prosecutors were going to do for him whatever they could.

Leuci did not like to be equated to Aguiluz. Aguiluz had been caught, and he had given up his partners. Leuci himself had done neither. However, Leuci kept silent while Puccio prattled on.

Suddenly the prosecutor's smile vanished, and his voice went hard. "You're Babyface," said Puccio, "aren't you? We've come upon an old allegation against you, and the witness is sitting outside."

Puccio, watching Leuci carefully, noted a sudden tightening of the brows, and he wondered if this indicated guilt, or only surprise at the abrupt change in mood.

Leuci said he didn't know what case Puccio might be talking about.

So Puccio described it. Some years before, Leuci and his team had executed a fugitive warrant. They had kicked in a door and arrested the narcotics dealer inside. While they were processing the dealer in the station house, his partner and the partner's wife had arrived with a $5000 bribe. So all three were charged with attempted bribery as well.

"Oh, I do remember the case," said Leuci. He was smiling. He remembered the case with pride.

Suddenly Puccio said, "There was four hundred dollars taken at the scene of the arrest, according to this allegation."

Puccio was under heavy pressure from Taylor and Carros. It was they who had dug up this old case. They wanted Leuci indicted on it. They had the dealer himself outside willing to testify.

It would be a pretty flimsy indictment.

Puccio was trying to decide what to do. He was trying to read guilt or innocence in Leuci's face. The job of a prosecutor was no exact science, and bluffs sometimes broke cases wide open. The Aguiluz perjury indictment had been largely a bluff, and look at the result. But he didn't want to bluff a guiltless man.

"Who took the four hundred dollars?" Puccio demanded.

Leuci at first did not comprehend. "The guy offered us five thousand, and we locked up all three people for it."

Puccio said coldly, "Sometimes it's hard to tell who is lying, and who isn't. But it's my feeling that the four hundred dollars happened. There is no reason for the guy to lie about it."

"Even if it happened, Mr. Puccio," Leuci said, "don't you think it's possible that I wouldn't know anything about it?"

"No. I don't think it's possible."

Leuci hardly realized he had just been accused of a crime, for he had perceived something much worse: Puccio's plan—to make a case against him—any case—so as to turn him into an Aguiluz.

"Carl Aguiluz is not the same guy I am, Mr. Puccio," said Leuci, angrily. "Aguiluz is implicating his friends and his partners. People who trusted him, lived with him. Before I would do that, I'd kill myself."

A triumphant smile came onto Puccio's face. Leuci saw it, realized its significance, and was appalled at himself. Up to now, Puccio had not been certain. But his doubts had just been removed.

"What are you telling me?" Puccio demanded. "You're telling me flat out that you've done more than you have admitted to."

Shocked, frightened, Leuci made the additional mistake of calling Aguiluz a fucking rat.

"But you're not a rat, is that what you're saying?" said Puccio, nodding thoughtfully.

Leuci made no reply.

"I have a lot of respect for those prosecutors over at the Southern District," said Puccio coolly. "I don't know how they handled you. I don't know what they promised you or didn't promise you. I do know that if you were working for me, there is no way in the world you could get away with whatever you think you are getting away with. If you're not telling the truth, we'll find out. Half the SIU will be coming in here. And they will all cooperate."

"They are not going to cooperate."

"Nearly all of them will cooperate. They're cops. In their hearts, they want to admit their guilt. That's the way cops are. You know that as well as I do."

Leuci was sweating. "Can I leave now?"

Puccio smiled. "I'll be seeing you again."

The next day Giuliani, having spoken to Puccio, called Leuci in once more. "Puccio is about to indict some more people. Do you know a detective named Les Wolff?"

It was a moment before Leuci could speak at all.

"We were partners," he said in a choked voice.

"I know you were partners. Are you sure there's nothing more you want to tell me?"

Leuci shook his head, "No."

"So far," said Giuliani, "every allegation against you, by The Baron and everyone else, is unsupported. But just let one cop come in here and corroborate one dope dealer, and you'll go to jail. There will be no way anyone can save you." After a moment Giuliani added, "What do you think Les Wolff might tell Puccio?"

23

WOLFF, who was then thirty-nine years old, stood six feet tall and was a wiry, well-built man. He had dark, curly hair, and his dark face, somewhat pockmarked from childhood acne, was striking, and full of character. This character was set off by the way Wolff carried himself. He seemed a rather cold man, and he had a strong sense of self.

He came from a Bronx working-class family, went into the army, and served in West Germany. As a Jew in Germany, he was extremely uncomfortable, but he had loved, he often said, German girls. After military service he became a patrolman in the Twenty-fifth Precinct in Harlem.

From the beginning he saw the Police Department as a career. His ambition was to go further in life than his parents had gone, and so he worked harder than most of the cops around him. He made good arrests. He put in overtime. He was also fearless. in Harlem in the middle of the night he thought nothing of checking out cellars, alleyways, backyards alone, his flashlight out, his gun holstered. "These people don't scare me," he often said.

His promotion into the detective division had come after only six years in uniform—faster than most detectives, not as fast as some. As a detective he stayed in Harlem for about three years more, with Dave Cody as his partner, until in 1969, at the age of thirty-four, he was moved up into SIU, and assigned to the Leuci-Mandato team. He had been the leader of every team he ever worked on, he informed Detective Leuci at once, and though he accepted the leadership of Leuci, who was only twenty-nine, he did not like it. He was a competitor. From then on he competed for the job of team leader in almost every case that the newly composed four-man team worked.

To Wolff, being a detective was a business. You did it the best you knew how. It was Wolff who sought to master any new gear that came into the team's possession, principally electronic listening devices and cameras. He became an expert photographer. His paperwork was always perfect. He always had to be the best. He had to win.

After three years in SIU his career had made another upward leap—he had taken on the dangerous undercover assignment for Mike Shaw and the Federal Strike Force, and official reports about his work had been, he knew, glowing.

The fact was, Puccio was not aware of whatever Wolff's current job might be, for the Strike Force's investigation, code-named Project Cleveland, was known to very few men. For most of two years Wolff had worn a wire while recording incriminating conversations with many of the shylocks, extortionists, and hijackers who dominated the garment district, often meeting such men alone in the night in isolated places. His work much resembled what Leuci's had been, except that his target was organized crime rather than official corruption.

Wolff had been given a false name—Les Dana—and a cover apartment on West Ninth Street. Since he was supposedly second in command of a small trucking company, he had demanded appropriate clothes, and was given $300 to buy them. He spent the money and began wearing open shirts with chains around his neck and a lot of chest showing. He looked now not like a cop but like a Jewish hoodlum, and he acted not like a cop but like a trucking company executive. The role was congenial to him, and he began running the trucking company as a business, installing controls, and figuring out ways to cut overhead while improving profits. The detectives who covered him he assigned to unload rolls of merchandise from his trucks. It was the heaviest work imaginable. It was mule work. After one day they wanted off. So Wolff, business being business, unloaded his trucks himself, day after day, and complained to no one.

Whenever he wore his wire into hazardous meetings with hoodlums, he was so cool that no one ever suspected him. He was never patted down. Each time, showing no sign of nervousness, he got his recordings, then left the meetings and went home.

Once a week Mike Shaw held debriefings in the board room at the Morgan Guaranty Trust company on Broad Street. Wolff's manner, while giving his reports, was crisp, direct, totally professional. Shaw admired him. He considered Wolff an absolutely superb undercover detective.

So the first irate citizen Puccio had to contend with was Shaw. By indicting Wolff, Puccio had endangered Project Cleveland, on which the government had already spent hundreds of thousands of dollars. Shaw spoke to Puccio politely, lawyer to lawyer, but he was furious—particularly after he had studied the indictment and seen how thin the case against Wolff appeared to be.

The case dated from November 19, 1970, some three and a half years previously. Together with Aguiluz and five other SIU detectives, Wolff had entered at gunpoint the apartment of a South American drug dealer named Olate. There were three people inside, Olate, his wife, and a friend. A bag of cocaine was seized, evidence enough to arrest all three, but only the friend was taken away under arrest.

It was the details that changed the nature of the case. Puccio had these details from Aguiluz, and they had been verified by two other members of the team who were also cooperating. The seven-man team had fastened onto Olate through illegal wiretaps. They had raided his apartment expecting to find a heavy load of heroin. Instead they had found only money, about $80,000 in all, which they stole. In exchange for this money, the drug dealer and his wife were granted provisional freedom—twenty-four hours in which to leave the country.

Neither Aguiluz nor the two corroborating detectives claimed to have shared money with Wolff, whose portion had allegedly been paid him by one of the three remaining detectives who, so far, had refused to cooperate.

Olate was brought in, and a line-up was hastily arranged. The South American had no difficulty picking Aguiluz and certain other detectives out of this line-up.

But he failed to identify Leslie Wolff.

With that, Puccio had virtually no case against Wolff. However, for the moment the indictment stuck. Wolff had been arrested and stripped of gun and shield, and Shaw was obliged to drop him from Project Cleveland.

Wolff's anger at what he considered "the government" was so overt that Shaw worried that he might choose to endanger the work he had done under cover, but he never did. Nor did he ever threaten to. He was set to work in an office typing transcripts of the tapes he had made, and all waited hopefully for the indictment to be dismissed.

But when Puccio seemed in no hurry that this should come to pass, the furious Wolff stormed into Puccio's office and threatened to throw the prosecutor out the window. Puccio replied that Wolff could easily avoid trial, possible conviction, prison. All he had to do was cooperate. Tell what he knew.

Leaving Puccio's office, Wolff telephoned Leuci, and requested an urgent conference. They met on the sidewalk in front of Leuci's mother's house in Queens. It was about nine o'clock at night. With Leuci's bodyguards trailing about twenty paces behind, the two former partners walked round and round the block under the budding spring trees.

He would never, never cooperate, asserted Wolff. "I didn't do this. This indictment is bullshit."

"Les, take a lie detector test," pleaded Leuci. "You didn't do it."

Wolff stopped walking and stared at Leuci. "You take the lie detector test. Bob, that Spanish son of a bitch never put a dime in my hand."

As they walked on, Leuci was left to digest the two possible meanings of this statement. Either someone else had handed Wolff the money, or no one had.

"I'll never cooperate," Wolff repeated. But again he

stopped and fixed an anxious glance on his ex-partner's face. They must be pressuring Leuci to cooperate too, he said. What was Leuci going to do?

But his eyes said much more. The two partners were equally vulnerable. Together they were relatively safe. No one could give them up but each other.

"Les, they can cut me up in little pieces. I'm not telling them nothing. That's it. They've had their fun with me."

A cool March wind blew through the night, through the streets of Queens. Round and round the block they walked, but the message they had for each other never changed, and at the end they embraced. They had never done this before. They stood in the street hugging each other until it seemed that, through their overcoats, they could feel each other's heart beating.

As he moved off into the night, Wolff turned and called out, "Bob, I've never felt closer to you than I do right now."

Once Wolff was out of sight, the bodyguard Art Monty came mincing forward and in a kind of falsetto repeated Wolff's curtain line word for word: "I've never felt closer to you than I do right now." Then Monty counseled Leuci, "Don't trust him. He's going down the tubes."

It was perhaps what Leuci himself was thinking. How long could Wolff resist Puccio's pressure? How long could he himself resist it? Which of them would give up the other first?

24

DAY BY DAY the prosecutors, all working independently of each other, bounced Detective Leuci from one office to the next.

Nadjari's men grilled him about the French Connection ripoff. Tell us, detective, was it usual just to sign in with the property clerk and walk out with your evidence? Could you get it just by calling out your name from the back of the line? Is it true that clerks would pass the evidence to you over people's heads, and sign your name to the voucher? What about this affidavit by The Baron that you gave him junk in property clerk envelopes? Invariably they would ask him to leave the room.

"Wait outside, please, detective."

Waiting in the anteroom, pacing the hallway, he would wonder what was happening inside. What were they trying to pin on him now?

Called back in, he would be asked what he thought about this or that cop. "Which one of you fuckers do you think pulled this ripoff?" At last would come the curt dismissal: "You may go, detective."

Puccio took to summoning him every Friday afternoon, the phone ringing just as Leuci, anxious to get home to his family for the weekend, was about to leave for the airport. While Leuci dreamed of escape to Virginia, the prosecutor would engage him in leisurely, aimless conversations.

Puccio knew exactly what he was doing. He would seem friendly. "Bob, I need your help. We have a ton of work here. We've indicted all these detectives. We have to figure out what to do with all these guys. I want you to tell me what kind of men they are."

Shuttle after shuttle took off for Virginia.

"Look, Mr. Puccio, it's Friday night. I haven't seen my family in a week. Would you mind if I went home now?"

"If you prefer, you can come in tomorrow morning. We can finish our conversation then."

When Leuci kept silent, Puccio laughed. "Bob, you'll turn sooner or later."

Back to the Special Prosecutor's office. This time he was interrogated by Nadjari himself, the most feared prosecutor in the city. Leuci, entering his office, was petrified.

But Nadjari proved interested in the French Connection ripoff only. His investigators had focused on former SIU detective Frank King as mastermind. King had been close to Nunziata. Leuci had been close to Nunziata. Therefore Leuci and King—

But Leuci interrupted. "Mr. Nadjari, you want Frank King. You want people who can give you the French Connection case. I've never worked with any of those detectives. I can't give you them. If you don't believe that, I'll take a lie detector test right now. I had nothing to do with the French Connection case. I'm sure you know that."

After a moment, Nadjari said, "We also know that there's more you could tell us."

"How do you know that?" It seemed to Leuci that if he could get past Nadjari, he was safe. "I'm telling you I can't make a case against King. I can't make a case against his partner Jack McClean, who will give you Frank King."

Nadjari looked at him.

"I never worked with McClean," insisted Leuci. "I know nothing specific about him."

Nadjari saw the anguish in Leuci's eyes, but there was a message printed there too, and perhaps Nadjari was able to read it.

Leuci, without speaking a word, was begging Nadjari to receive and understand all that could not be spoken.

Yes, there's more in my past, Mr. Nadjari. But I can't admit to it. I would if I could give you Frank King, or Jack McClean. But what I am concealing concerns only me, and one or two partners. Nothing that is going to mean anything in your picture. Why do you want me to destroy myself? Why do you want me to come in and say the kinds of things Aguiluz is saying. I'll never do it. I'll never hurt Mandato. I'll never hurt Wolff or Cody. I'll never hurt Vinny Russo. Those were my partners. I'm not going to do it.

All this Leuci tried to tell Nadjari with his eyes.

"All right, that's enough for today," said Nadjari, and he showed the tormented detective to the door.

Giuliani summoned him. The Rosner hearing was coming up soon, he said. Leuci would be obliged to respond under oath to each of The Baron's charges. Leuci should begin to think about this.

It was clear to Giuliani that Leuci was losing control.

Giuliani felt sure now that Leuci had committed perjury in the Rosner case, that he was guilty of far more than three acts of misconduct. Clearly Leuci did not know what to do about it. He saw no way out. He was being torn apart, not only at the prospect of testifying against his former partners, but also at the thought that the new friends he had developed—Scoppetta, Shaw, Whitney North Seymour, Giuliani himself—would turn on him.

As for Leuci, the pressure was so constant that he became punchy. He couldn't keep his food down. He couldn't sleep. Fridays were a special nightmare. The call from Puccio. The long wait in Puccio's anteroom, the interview with Puccio, who was in no hurry ever, and who laughed at Leuci's barely concealed terror while one shuttle after another took off, until finally, each week, Leuci would be forced to beg, "Can I go now, Mr. Puccio?"

At last Leuci would board the plane. It would break up through the clouds into the sun, and he would sit back and try to think about going to Virginia. For an hour he would relax—more or less. But on Monday morning, as soon as he boarded the plane for the trip back, the terror would clamp down on him once again. What is waiting for me up there? There were too many people after him now— Puccio, Giuliani, Nadjari. What do I tell them, he asked himself. What don't I tell them? Through the porthole he watched the city as it came up to meet him.

His mind would not stand still. If I go in and tell them,

then I've got to tell the whole story. I can't pick and choose. And if I can't pick and choose, then I can't protect Mandato, I can't protect Wolff, I can't protect Cody. I can't protect Vinny Russo, who is a gentle, honest guy in the true sense of the word, and a decent little guy, and how can I burn Vinny Russo, who really broke me into narcotics? How can I do that to Vinny and to his wife and children?

For the time being, Leuci's resolve remained firm: I'm not going to do it. I'm not going to tell them anything.

The Sergeant Peter Perrazzo case came to trial in the Police Department trial room. Perrazzo, fifty-three, still confined to a mental institution, was to be judged in absentia. The object of the trial was to dismiss him on charges of corruption, because otherwise he would retain rights to his pension, amounting to about $14,000 a year for life. It was incumbent upon the department now to strip these funds from the madman's account.

The trial, before trial commissioner Phillip Michael, lasted about two hours. The chief prosecution witness was Detective Leuci. Only a few people were present, among them Perrazzo's court-appointed guardian and his middle-aged wife, who sat in the front row weeping quietly during the whole of the proceedings. She looked to Leuci like an Italian woman who had sat through a three-day wake and funeral. She resembled any one of his nine aunts, and he was furious with whoever had brought her there. Why should this woman have to hear her husband defamed, he asked himself. Why does she have to know all this?

Perrazzo was convicted and dismissed from the department. Leuci stumbled out of the room, asking himself: What have I done to these people, what have I done?

Another summons from Giuliani. Did Leuci know a detective named Vinny Russo?

Russo, when questioned about a certain illegal wiretap, had denied knowing about it, lying to protect the detectives involved. The plan now was to throw him into the grand jury. If he lied there, then he would be indicted for perjury.

Or did Leuci want to try to talk to him first?

When Leuci phoned Russo at home, it was Maria Russo who came on.

"Maria," he began, "I hate to bother you—"

"You're not going to hurt my Vinny."

"I'm not going to hurt Vinny."

Russo himself took the phone. "What do you want from me?"

"I'll meet you at Sweet's Restaurant next to the fish market."

Russo agreed to this meeting, but when he reached the site, he refused to come any closer to Leuci than the other side of the street. Standing on his side he shouted across to Leuci on the other, "You bastard! What do you want? You want to hurt my family. You want to hurt my kids. You want to hurt me. Why do you want to do this to me? You're here to hurt me."

"I'm not here to hurt you, Vinny," Leuci called across the street. "I want you to come in and talk to them about the wiretap."

"I'm not telling nothing," cried Russo. "What am I going to do? I don't know nothing. I don't know enough that they're going to help me. What am I going to tell them? That I know about a $300 score one time, a $200 score some other time? When I was in SIU, I used to follow a guy for three days. That's all I ever did. I did tails. When the case was over, they'd tell me to go home. I used to go home. I don't know enough. They're not going to help me."

When Leuci reported the results of this meeting, the prosecutors reverted to their original plan—the grand jury for Russo, followed by indictment. Although Leuci pleaded for his friend, the prosecutors remained adamant.

Nunziata, Sheridan, Lusterino, Wolff, Perrazzo, Russo

Leuci went to church because he could think of nowhere else to go. He did not go to the bright modern church in Virginia with its American flags and longhaired priests. That was no good. It was like a Protestant church. Instead he went back to his old neighborhood in

Queens, back to where all the priests talked with Italian accents. He wanted to see candles, to smell incense, to look up at saints. He wanted to talk through a screen to someone who might understand.

Standing in the gloom, he remembered as a child waiting on line outside the confessional on Saturday afternoons. He remembered entering the dark cubicle, confessing his childish sins through the screen, and then coming out into the sunlight again feeling the greatest liberation he had ever known before or since—almost wishing to be killed by a bus immediately, because he was friends with God again and would go straight to heaven.

The confessional he entered now was the same he used to enter as a boy. But when he knelt in the dark and tried to explain to the priest all that tormented him he found that the man didn't want to spend time on it.

We all have our crosses, the priest told him.

Leuci described Nunziata's death, his own remorse.

God decided for Nunziata, the priest told him. It wasn't your fault.

The detective attempted to talk about perjury, but the priest had no clear understanding of the legal meaning of the word. "Did your testimony put an innocent man in jail?" he inquired.

"No."

"It doesn't sound like perjury to me."

When Leuci stepped out of the box into the sunlight, there was no feeling of liberation. He was not consumed with a sense of his own goodness. The old feeling was not there. Nothing was there but emptiness and fear.

Every night now he was relying on Valium to get to sleep. But most nights it did not work well, and some nights it did not work at all.

25

PUCCIO at this time was subject to pressure of his own. It came principally from the Drug Enforcement Administration, in the persons of agents Carros and Taylor, who had come up with a plan. They wanted to threaten Leuci with indictment. Under such a threat, they assured the prosecutor, the detective would crack.

The prosecutor murmured that he had nothing to indict Leuci on. The case of the $400 bribe that they had brought him was not enough. However, he gave permission for the threat to be tried.

And so Leuci was summoned—forthwith—to the DEA offices off Columbus Circle. There he was made to wait in an anteroom. Pacing, he watched people come and go. They wore I.D. cards clipped to their pockets. They walked with great purpose. Leuci was duly impressed. These were powerful people. They were the federal government. He knew who they were, and what they could do to him.

At length Carros came out, ordered the two body-guards to remain in the anteroom, and led Leuci back to Taylor's office. Taylor had graduated from the Leuci investigation. He was now an assistant regional director. He sat behind his big desk attempting to look important. An American flag stood in the corner. The office, a big one, had a view overlooking much of the city. Carros stood at the window peering out.

From behind his desk, Taylor called Leuci a liar. "I not only think you're a liar, I know you're a liar, and I'm passing on to you a message from Puccio. If you don't tell us everything—what you've done and who you've done it with—by five o'clock this afternoon, Puccio is going to indict you. Do you have anything to say?"

The interrogation, if that was what it was, ran downhill from there. Taylor praised Aguiluz. Obviously Leuci had had this same knowledge. He could have made the same cases.

"Aguiluz has to live with himself for the rest of his life," cried Leuci. "I have to live with myself." Sure he could have made cases against some of those same detectives, he said. But why should he make cases against his friends, when he could make cases against so many other people elsewhere in the system who were equally corrupt—or more corrupt. Aguiluz had shown that there were corrupt detectives in SIU. Leuci had shown there was corruption in every part of the system.

Taylor accused Leuci of caring only about his prosecutor friends in the Southern District. These people had coddled him for years. But he was a crook. Taylor knew it, and so did Puccio in the Eastern District. Either Leuci would reveal all they wanted to know by five o'clock this afternoon, or he would be indicted.

Carros continued to gaze out the window.

Taylor and Leuci began to shout at each other. Taylor called Leuci a liar, a perjurer, a criminal. Leuci called Taylor a buffoon, a jerkoff, a fraud.

"You were a New York City cop for nine years," Leuci said. "And what did you do during those nine years? You bragged about it to me. You hid out in firehouses studying so you could go through college. You got paid by the city for nine years, and then you became an IRS agent, and now you are a big DEA boss. Who are you?"

"I'm the guy that could put you in jail."

"You're the boss of the guys who lost me all the time when they were my backup agents. You don't even know what cases we made. You never even read the memorandums on the cases you were working on."

Back at the offices of the Southern District, Leuci burst in on Giuliani and blurted out his tragic news: "They are going to indict me at five o'clock."

But Giuliani's face failed to register enough surprise. "You knew they were going to run this game on me, didn't you?" Leuci cried. "You didn't give a shit either, did you?"

Giuliani phoned Puccio, and, after a short conversation, hung up. "Puccio tells me that they are not going to indict you today after all," Giuliani reported.

"I'm leaving, I'm getting out of here. I'm going home to Virginia."

"Bob, you have a lot to think about," said Giuliani after a moment.

"Are they going to lock me up, or aren't they? What is going on here?"

"Bob, look at you. You're a nervous wreck. Maybe you better tell me the truth."

Leuci rushed off to Brooklyn Heights to see Shaw. "Mike, what should I do?"

Shaw lay full length on his couch, the lower part of his legs hanging over the far end. "Don't you understand the dilemma I'm in?" Shaw asked. "I can't advise you. I'm a prosecutor. If you make any admissions to me now, I would have to take action."

Shaw could offer nothing but sympathy. "Bob, the only thing I can tell you is that you've got to tell the truth."

Leuci left Brooklyn Heights. It was time for a changeover of bodyguards, Monty and Farley going off, Fritz and Bonifide coming on. "What do you guys think I should do?" asked the tormented Leuci.

The five men were sitting in a car on the same quiet street in Queens where every night the changeover took place. Farley and Monty were Leuci's age. Fritz and Bonifide were older. The younger men advised Leuci to tell the prosecutors nothing: "Those guys are looking to put you in jail."

The older patrolmen advised the opposite. Apparently there was more stuff there, they said. If so, he had best put all his trust in the prosecutors, and quickly. As far as cops in general were concerned, Leuci was already a rat. He had made cases against cops. He was finished. Protecting his former partners was not going to help him with other cops, and he could never go back into the Police Department. He would have to pick sides, and obviously he had better pick the prosecutors' side. It was his only chance. Otherwise sooner or later he would be indicted and arrested.

"They are going to get one guy who worked with you,

and he's going to give you up," said Bonifide. Fritz agreed, saying, "You are the first guy everyone wants to give up, if they have to give up anybody."

They all hate you, the older patrolmen told him. The Internal Affairs people hate you, the DEA agents hate you, the cops hate you, and all the prosecutors hate you, except perhaps for Giuliani.

They told him this with their heads down, not meeting his eyes. He ought to be thinking of one thing, and one only: Gina and the kids. There was no one else who cared about him.

The distraught Leuci ordered himself driven to the airport, and he fled home to Virginia.

The next day Giuliani and Leuci spoke by telephone. The detective's voice was choked, and he was clearly under terrific strain. His reasoning was convoluted, and most of his sentences broke off with their meaning only half complete. But his emotional state was clear to Giuliani. Leuci kept mentioning Nunziata. The decision that was being forced upon him, he said, was one he could not make, and he understood Nunziata's suicide better now. It was perhaps the only way out, not only for Nunziata, but also now for himself.

Giuliani said he would get down to Washington as soon as he could—on the next shuttle. Accompanied by Assistant U.S. Attorney Joe Jaffe, Giuliani rushed to La Guardia Airport and boarded the plane. He was terrified that he would reach Washington too late, but waiting at the exit gate, to his immense relief, was Leuci.

They drove straight to Leuci's house in northern Virginia. Jaffe was left with Gina, who was already preparing dinner. The prosecutor and the detective went for a walk, during which Leuci continued to insist that he was not going to turn on his partners. No one could make him turn on his partners, not Giuliani, not anyone. He wasn't going to do it.

"Don't you see," Giuliani asked, "that what you have just said is already an admission—that there were other acts of misconduct by you, in which your partners were involved? Let me go back, and with your permission, tell them that you are going to come in and tell us everything."

"You're asking me to put to death my best friends," said Leuci, and Giuliani thought he had never heard such anguish in a human voice.

What was Giuliani to answer, except what he took to be the truth—that Leuci's partners, had the situation been reversed, would do the same. Like Leuci, they would have no choice in the matter.

"No, no," Leuci insisted. "They wouldn't do it to me. That's the difference between you and them. They wouldn't do it to me. That's the fact of it. They wouldn't do it to me."

Giuliani told him that he would have to decide either to stick it out alone, or to cooperate completely. He couldn't go down the middle.

When they returned to the house, Gina served dinner, and a good deal of wine was poured, which, for a time, seemed to make everything better. After dinner the prosecutor and the detective descended to the playroom in the basement.

"If I were not a lawyer but a surgeon," Giuliani began, "and you came to me with cancer, and I told you, Bob, let me remove the cancer—what would you do? Because that's what you've got. You've got a cancer. It's eating you up, and if you don't let me take it out, you're going to die. And a lot of people will dance on your grave, good guys and bad guys."

More than three years ago, Giuliani continued, Leuci had set this whole chain of events in motion. He had decided to switch sides. He had come over onto the side of the government; whether he did it for good reasons or bad no longer mattered. Now that he was on this side, he had to play by the rules this side obeyed. "The side you are on," said Giuliani, "is the side where you have got to tell the truth."

When Gina and Jaffe came downstairs into the playroom, Giuliani and Leuci fled upstairs to continue their discussion. When Gina and Jaffe soon followed, they went out of the house and walked along under the trees.

Giuliani said he would love to be able to forget about this matter. He had no desire to force Leuci to reveal information that would overturn the conviction of a miserable son of a bitch like Eddie Rosner. But Rosner was irrelevant now. They had to follow a simple and direct approach. They had to find out what all of the truth was, and publish it. Perhaps Leuci never should have told Scoppetta anything, never should have worked undercover, never should have made any of these cases, never should have agreed to serve as witness. But he had done all that. There was no way now that he could erase the past three and a half years. He was going to have to tell the story of the rest of his misconduct.

At last Leuci began to ask Giuliani specific legal questions. What would happen to him if he revealed things like giving junk to informants or illegal wiretaps? Suppose he revealed that he had made a good many more scores, stolen a good deal more money than he had previously admitted? What would happen to the people he cared about who might have been involved with him? Could they be given immunity?

To all these questions Giuliani had no firm answers and said so. Leuci might be indicted, or he might not. Giuliani would certainly argue strongly against it. Leuci had performed an enormous public service at terrible cost to himself. The Police Department was to a large extent a different place now because of what he had done, the criminal justice system as a whole was cleaner and better, and his credit for this was so tremendous that perhaps he was entitled to make a couple of mistakes along the way. Giuliani would try hard to see to it that Leuci was not indicted. He didn't know. He didn't know how Puccio would react, for instance. He admitted that the Drug Enforcement Administration—Taylor and Carros—was hot after him, and wanted to see him hurt. Those two men could perhaps be calmed down, or held off. He just didn't know.

What would happen to his partners, Leuci wanted to know.

This also was out of Giuliani's control. Mandato,

Wolff, and the others would certainly have to be charged with crimes. There was no way around that. But perhaps something could be worked out, assuming they were willing to cooperate with the prosecutors.

"You set all that in motion when you first went to work undercover," Giuliani said. "Anybody who told you different was misleading you. They were so overwhelmed with what you could do that they never really focused on this part of it. But when you put yourself in the position of being a witness, from that moment on it became certain that everything had to come out."

It was four o'clock in the morning before Giuliani and Jaffe were shown a bedroom. Small beds. The kids' beds, probably. They got into them, and slept for several hours. Then Gina made breakfast, and after breakfast Giuliani and Leuci were alone again and the discussion continued. Giuliani marshaled his final arguments.

"Whether you tell us or don't tell us, we are going to get that information. Just about every detective who ever worked in SIU is going to go to jail. So if you don't tell us about whatever it is you're concealing, then someone else will tell us. Someone else will testify against the partners you're trying to protect, and against you, and the net result will be the same. They'll go to jail. And you'll go to jail."

Around three o'clock in the afternoon, Leuci drove Giuliani and Jaffe to the airport. Just before the two prosecutors boarded the plane, the detective, staring at his shoes, mumbled that tomorrow he would come into the office and tell everything. Giuliani breathed a sigh of relief. They all shook hands, and the two prosecutors walked down the ramp.

Leuci watched them go. By then he had decided to kill himself.

When he reached home, Leuci went for a walk with his son. He wanted to get some sense of how far the boy had come, what he would understand about his father. What did he think about being moved to the Catskills, moved to Virginia? What did he think about having men with machine guns for playmates?

But nothing much had registered on the child's mind. Men with machine guns were good playmates, and were not otherwise significant. The little boy understood nothing at all. He was seven years old. Kneeling, Leuci embraced him, saying goodbye.

He got into his car. I can't just blow myself away like Nunziata, he told himself. What I've got to do is crash my car, so my family can collect the insurance.

He was on the George Washington Parkway, driving fast, trying to figure out how to do it. Hit some other car head on? He couldn't risk killing some nice guy and his family coming the other way. He would have to crash into an abutment. Driving up and down the parkway, he began looking for a good one. He drove past one abutment, past two more. He was driving seventy miles an hour, then eighty, ninety, and a police car came up alongside and pulled him over.

Leuci jumped out of the car, showing his shield. "I'm a New York City cop."

The other cop, as it happened, was an Italian too. The two cops leaned their rumps against the fender and talked. The Washington cop had been in Narcotics once, he said, but he had got out quickly. Narcotics was a crazy scene. He wanted no part of it. He had read about all the Narcotics detectives getting locked up in New York. Were any of Leuci's friends in trouble?

"Yes," said Leuci, "some of my friends are in trouble."

They exchanged home phone numbers. The other cop invited Leuci to the Redskins' games in the fall. He had season tickets. "I got them on the arm," he said.

"Of course," said Leuci, "what else?"

In Florida, Mandato's phone rang. It was Leuci. "How are you doing?" asked Mandato.

"Not very well, Frank."

Mandato knew what this meant.

"Frank, I'm going up to the city tomorrow and—"

It was a call, Mandato realized, that he had half expected for a long time.

"You don't have to tell me. You're going to give us up."

"Yeah, Frank."

"Just call me when you get there," said Mandato, and he hung up. After a moment he turned away from the phone.

26

EARLY THE NEXT MORNING Leuci flew up to New York. It was a holiday. The streets of the city were empty. Foley Square in downtown Manhattan was deserted, no traffic, no people. To Leuci the downtown area had always been a scary place when it was empty like that. It was cold, and not nice—especially today.

He entered the Federal Courthouse and went directly to Giuliani's office. Giuliani and Jaffe were already there. The three men sat down. Giuliani said that Detective Leuci should tell them the worst thing first. When this suggestion was greeted by a heavy silence, he said, "I mean, what do you see as the worst thing you've ever done?"

"That's difficult to say," answered Leuci. "I mean, your perception of what is the worst thing, and my perception of the worst thing are, maybe, different."

"You know what we're asking you?" said Giuliani.

"What are you asking me?"

"Did you kill anyone?"

"No, I never killed anyone. And I didn't have anything to do with the French Connection ripoff, either."

The two prosecutors were relieved. Leuci said, "You guys thought I had something to do with that?"

"It's always possible," said Giuliani.

"I had nothing to do with it."

"That's terrific," said Giuliani. He was ebullient, and for the moment not thinking like a lawyer. But he caught himself at once, and his voice again became stern. "Did you ever sell narcotics?"

"I never sold narcotics."

"What narcotics dealings did you have? Maybe we should talk about The Baron's affidavit first."

"No, let's not do it that way."

It was not going to be easy for him to speak after all. He realized this now, and so did Giuliani.

"Tell us the first thing you ever did," said Jaffe.

"Start from the day you became a policeman," said Giuliani.

And so the long tangled tale at last came out. He described his rookie year in the Rockaway Beach Precinct. No corruption there that he ever witnessed. There was only one bookmaker in the precinct, and if he gave two dollars to a cop once in a while, that was the extent of it. In the Tactical Patrol Force there was no corruption at all. Then he had gone to Narcotics, and had been there for perhaps a year and a half before he began giving nickel bags of heroin to his informants.

The prosecutors wanted numbers. How often had he done this? As often as they had needed narcotics, Leuci answered. Dozens of times. Maybe hundreds of times. Every gift bag had been a sale under the law. Had Leuci known that?

Yes, he had known that.

"All right," said Giuliani, "what was the biggest score you were ever involved in?"

Leuci began to describe what became known as the Riverdale Motel case. This was in early 1968. He and Mandato were brand-new in SIU and had just been assigned to their first detective team. As it happened, the team was a large one, ten detectives in all, including two sergeants. The target was a major drug operation involving both blacks and South Americans, and so the detective team had been split in two. Leuci's team was assigned to work the blacks, while the other team, led by Detective Dominick Butera, had worked the South Americans. Butera's team made such fast progress that it became necessary to put the South Americans under surveillance for seventy-two hours straight, for a heavy package was supposed to arrive at any moment. But the package did not arrive, and with the detectives on surveillance exhausted, part of the Leuci team—Leuci, Mandato, and another detective—was ordered to spell them for a single night.

So the three relief detectives drove to the motel in two cars, then sat in one of them and watched the walls of the motel. Parked out front were two identical Cadillac Eldorados. Presently a South American wearing a cowboy hat got into one of the Eldorados and drove away. Leuci and the third followed. They tailed him into Manhattan, where he moved from bar to bar.

Leuci phoned the SIU duty officer. Was there any word from Mandato in Riverdale?

There was indeed. Mandato had reported that the other South American was loading the other Eldorado. He was carrying suitcases out of the motel room. Clearly the two men were planning to leave town.

Leuci phoned Detective Butera at home, waking him up. What should they do?

Take them, Butera said.

Mandato had left a phone number. Leuci called him back. Was the other South American alone? Well then, could Mandato take him by himself? Mandato laughed. Of course he could. Don't worry about it.

A few minutes later the first South American exited from a bar, took three steps, and found Leuci's arm around his throat, and Leuci's gun in his back.

Leuci handcuffed him, searched him. He also searched the Eldorado. No guns, no drugs. He drove the Eldorado back to the Riverdale Motel, with the prisoner protesting all the way.

Inside the motel room, Mandato sat watching the other South American, whom he had handcuffed to a chair. Mandato too had made a thorough search. He had found no drugs. He did find a gun and he also found something else. "Go take a look in the closet," he told Leuci.

In the closet in a suitcase was the most money any of them had ever seen.

They waited for Butera, the two sergeants, and the rest of the team to arrive. Soon the room was full of detectives, and there were a number of whispered conversations. The South Americans were offering half the money in the closet in exchange for their freedom.

Well, no drugs had been found. One South American could not be held at all and the other could be held only on a gun charge that would probably get thrown out of court tomorrow.

Leuci was sent into the adjoining room to count the money. He spilled stacks of money out of the suitcase onto the bed. Money covered the entire counterpane.

The gun and half the money were returned to the South Americans, and they were ordered to leave the city at once. Later the detectives met to count and divide the score. They had taken $40,000, which had to be split ten ways, including a share for a team member who was off that day—for the number one rule among cops then and always was that a partner got an equal share, no matter what. Cops had their own ten commandments, and the first of them was this: If you are walking along the street and find a dime, your partner gets a nickel.

So Leuci and Mandato the following night took the surprised partner out to dinner and handed him $4,000. He remarked that he had just had a new kitchen put into his house; he had been wondering how he was going to pay for this kitchen. Now you can pay for it, Leuci and Mandato told him.

In accepting the money the partner became guilty of a felony crime, though it was difficult in any sort of realistic world to imagine what else he might have done. The ripoff was over. He had not taken part. He could not give the money back to the South Americans—they were gone. He could not, lacking corroboration, make a case against his partners, even if he wanted to, for it would be nine voices against one. All he could do, if he chose to refuse the money, was to destroy himself before his peers. When the partner faced charges in the Police Department trial room later, Trial Commissioner Luis Neco, citing the foregoing arguments, acquitted him. But Police Commissioner Michael Codd overturned the verdict, cashiered him, and forfeited his pension. The partner has been litigating to get back in the Police Department ever since.

"Let's have the rest of the scores," prodded Giuliani gently.

Leuci recounted about fifteen scores in all, most of them similar, though the money involved now diminished steadily. The principal emotion evoked in the listening prosecutors was not horror, but sadness.

Soon after the Riverdale Motel Case, Wolff and Cody had come into SIU, and had been assigned to the now experienced Leuci and Mandato as partners, and from then on, according to Leuci, all four detectives had shared every score. The "victims" in almost every case were Hispanic drug dealers. Santiago Valdez: drugs seized, arrested, robbed of $12,000. Jose Vasserman: drugs seized, arrested, robbed of $3600; Manual Noa, no drugs found, no arrest, robbed of $20,000. And so it went.

Sometimes the four detectives operated with others, and scores had to be split into extra shares. In all, Leuci said, he had pocketed between twenty and thirty thousand dollars as his share during those years.

The first interrogation of Leuci lasted all morning. no notes were taken, and Leuci's recital was interrupted many times by his need not so much to justify, as to explain. Contrary to what people thought, he insisted over and over again, heroin seized by SIU detectives did not normally go back onto the street. There were two terrible exceptions, the French Connection ripoff, and the five kilos sold by Aguiluz. Apart from that he never heard of a single SIU detective selling heroin.

Nor, the prosecutors realized to their surprise, had they.

SIU detectives, Leuci insisted, arrested more pushers, seized more narcotics than any other agency by far. The SIU guys were great detectives, who committed corrupt acts once in a while. It was just something that happened. It just was there one day, and then it grew.

During the years 1968 to 1971 the Mafia moved out of narcotics—who knew why?—and South Americans took it over. These people didn't speak English. They seemed to consider themselves immune to the law—and most often they were right. They were the flashiest individuals the SIU detectives had ever seen. Their women were literally dripping with jewelry, and wore mink coats to the floor. The men wore heavy gold chains around their necks, and solid gold bracelets on their arms, and gold wristwatches thin as subway tokens.

They had so much money that once they reached court they almost always managed to fix the case, or at least to go free on bail. If necessary, they'd put up enormous amounts of cash bail, a hundred thousand dollars or more, anything just to get out onto the street again, and once there they simply disappeared. They forfeited the bail. Presumably they went back to wherever they came from, and some other dope dealer flew in to take their place.

The SIU detectives, Leuci explained, having conceived an overpowering hatred for these people, began to dispense their own justice. Sometimes they talked of killing one or another prisoner, though this had never been done to Leuci's knowledge. Instead, they simply began to rob them. They would take whatever money the dope dealer had, order him on to the next plane to South America, and applaud themselves for accomplishing what no court seemed able to accomplish, a heavy fine followed by instant deportation.

The only trouble was, it was stealing. But since they were all doing it together, it didn't seem so bad. They were not closely supervised. For the most part they were not supervised at all. There were never older and supposedly wiser superiors there to counsel them. Instead, the hierarchy of the Police Department preferred to close its eyes to what was happening, or even, in many cases, to accept an equal share.

Leuci's recital continued—and it dwindled away an hour or more later with the admission that twice he had given Detective Vinny Russo about two hundred dollars for minor scores in cases where Russo had not been present. "You can't hurt Vinny," Leuci pleaded. "He wasn't even there."

Russo's name was noted.

Giuliani stood up. It was not yet noon, but he was exhausted. They all were. Since it was a holiday, nothing more could be done today. Giuliani told Leuci to go home to Virginia. "We appreciate what you've done," he said, a banal remark that nobody thought was banal at the time. "When you come back, we'll have DEA and IRS people sit down with you and debrief you."

"I want to call Mandato," Leuci said. "I want him to have the opportunity to come in and cooperate."

The prosecutors looked at each other.

"I want to call Cody."

"You can't call everybody, Bob."

"I want to call as many as I can."

"Do you want to get yourself killed?" said Jaffe.

"I want to call my closest partners. I want to call Mandato and Cody, and Wolff."

"Definitely not Wolff." Puccio's indictment against Wolff was still pending.

There was a brief discussion. Finally they decided they would permit him to call Mandato. Cody they wanted to think about. Wolff was out of the question. Leuci should go home now and try to relax. Try to rest. Next week was going to be bad.

From Virginia, Leuci phoned Mandato. "I've told them everything, Frank. If you come up and tell them everything—the truth—you'll be okay."

"Oh? What are they going to do, put me back in the Police Department? What do you mean I'm going to be okay?"

But presently Mandato agreed to fly to New York. "What about Dave and Les?"

"I'm going to talk to both of them."

Mandato said, "All four of us are going to walk in hand in hand, right?"

"That's right, Frank."

"What did you tell them?"

"I told them everything."

"Everything? But Bob, we've done things with people that are dead."

"I told them everything."

"Okay," said Mandato, and hung up the phone without saying goodbye.

The next time the two men spoke was in the corridor in

the Southern District offices. The prosecutors had kept them separated, and were accompanying them even to the bathroom lest they meet and confer. Inevitably they passed each other in the hallway.

"I guess you told them everything, Bob," said Mandato. "These are really nice guys. I can really understand why you would want to tell them everything."

Mandato was not under arrest, and each night he was allowed to go home. He was living in his sister's house on Staten Island.

The prosecutors were playing their cards carefully and well. Not until they were certain that Mandato would cooperate did they permit Leuci to telephone Cody. The idea was to confront Cody with two of his three former partners, proving to him it was useless to fight. He too would begin to make admissions, after which Wolff would be brought in. Once Wolff comprehended that all three partners were prepared to testify against him, he would be forced in his turn to confess, and to cooperate in whatever future trials the U.S. attorney's office might care to prosecute.

Cody was at first amenable. He appeared crushed, and he began to make the admissions of past misconduct that the prosecution team was looking for. He agreed to come back the following morning, and to "cooperate" even more fully. He asked only one favor. Wolff was to be called in the following day. Cody asked permission to talk to Wolff first.

This favor was accorded him, and he left the Southern District offices looking sad, but resigned.

Cody was now forty-seven years old, a frail, gentle kind of man who had lived with his mother most of his life. She had recently died, and he lived alone. His life was centered around cop bars. He met with other cops in bars night after night, exchanging war stories, often drinking himself into oblivion and being driven home by other cops. He had no one else. Apart from his partners—apart from cops—he was alone in the world.

He was forty before he became a detective and was assigned to the Harlem narcotics group, and it was there that he met, became friendly with, and eventually the partner of Detective Leslie Wolff. Wolff was the team leader. Wolff was Cody's strength. It was Wolff who told Cody where to be the next day and what to do when he got there.

For a cop, Cody was an amazingly gentle person. He felt only pity for junkies, whom he likened to alcoholics. He called them sick people. He was never unkind to anyone, not even prisoners, and none of his partners ever saw him angry, even in combat street situations. He was tall and skinny, and looked almost emaciated from years of too much drinking, too many years of improper diet.

That day he met Wolff, and urged his partner to cooperate. Perhaps he used the same words Mandato had used. If the four partners went through this holding hands, they would survive it.

Wolff, however, had no intention of cooperating. Not then, not ever, he told Cody, no matter how many of his friends betrayed him. Wolff was not coming in.

There was no way Cody could handle news like this. If Wolff was going to fight, then Cody would be put in the position of testifying against him in court.

Cody was too weak a man. If he was not able to speak harshly of dope dealers he had arrested, how would he be able to walk into open court and denounce Les Wolff, whom he loved?

He left Wolff, went into a bar, and started drinking. When he was drunk enough, he went across into the park near his apartment in the north Bronx, withdrew his .38 caliber Smith and Wesson Chief from its holster, and fired one shot into his left temple. It was 4:19 in the afternoon.

Within minutes the news swept through the offices of the Southern District. Someone said to Leuci, "By the way, Cody just killed himself."

Leuci had a tube of Valium in his pocket. He gulped down its entire contents, every pill, fifteen of them, maybe more. He wanted his head out of there.

It took him only seconds to lose the bodyguards assigned him that day. He made a right, a left, another right, found himself in front of the judge's elevator, and pushed a button. The doors opened, disclosing a small, middle-aged judge whose expression, as soon as he glanced into Leuci's face, turned to fear. Leuci stepped into the elevator. The judge backed to the rear wall and stood there, saying nothing.

In the street, walking dazedly away from the Federal Courthouse, Leuci asked himself over and over again: What have I done, what have I done?

Someone saw him heading for the Brooklyn Bridge, and rushed up to tell Giuliani. Giuliani knew Leuci was missing. He had already sent agents into the street to find him. Now he sent others rushing toward the bridge. "We've pushed him too far," he told Jaffe.

Giuliani, until recently, had prosecuted corrupt cops with no more compunction than he would accord a bank robber. But his attitude had changed. He could not look at one anymore without compassion. These were men of conscience who had erred, almost every one, and even though they had committed crimes, their consciences remained intact. It was their consciences that, once they were caught, caused them—and the prosecutors—so much trouble. All moral philosophers argued that each man must obey his own concept of good and evil, that his own conscience was paramount. The problem was that each cop's strongest moral principle was loyalty to other cops, particularly partners. It was this principle that the prosecutors forced them to abjure, forcing them to commit, therefore, what were, morally speaking, unspeakably evil acts. Rather than commit such acts, two cops had already killed themselves, one was insane, and Leuci was headed for the Brooklyn Bridge.

Giuliani, though a minor figure early in the Leuci undercover period, had nonetheless been involved—it was he who had driven the car out to arrest Perrazzo. He could no longer be objective. If Leuci went off that bridge, then a part of Giuliani would go with him.

Leuci, by this time, was standing in the middle of the bridge, staring down at the water far below. He didn't remember how he had got there, nor why he had come.

Perhaps he was crying, for he could not see the water very well. He put his hands on the rail. I should do it, he told himself. I'd be doing everybody a favor if I did it. He thought of Mandato, whom he considered more fragile than himself. Frank, when he heard, would definitely whack himself out. No, he would have to go out to Staten Island to save Frank.

Across the bridge was Shaw's house. Shaw would know what to do. He began to stumble on toward Brooklyn. He became confused. A different choice seemed offered to him. He had forgotten jumping, and the pills had only made him stupid. A woman takes pills, he thought. For him it would have to be a bullet.

An hour later he was in the streets of Brooklyn Heights, standing under a theater marquee. Though he still wanted to get to Shaw, he no longer knew the way. A woman passed who looked at him strangely. A moment later she had him by the elbow. It was Margaret Shaw.

Upstairs, Shaw poured strong coffee down him, and made him bathe his fevered face with cold washcloths. Shaw also phoned the Southern District, for they were frantic there, and his most immediate job was to call off the search.

After that he could do little more than listen, and nod sympathetically, as the whole terrible story came spilling out of Leuci.

"Don't you see?" Leuci said, "we're not criminals. We're policemen, and we can't cope with being criminals. When was the last time a Mafia guy committed suicide because he got in trouble? It isn't criminals who kill themselves, it's cops."

"This is such a horror," Shaw said. "This whole thing is so sad, so sad."

Leuci's concern switched to Mandato. Mandato might do something terrible, he said. He wanted to go there, tell Mandato himself.

The doorbell rang, and in walked Assistant U.S. Attorney Joe Jaffe and a federal marshal. It was Jaffe and the marshal who drove Leuci out to Mandato's sister's house on Staten Island. Leuci walked across the lawn and rang the bell.

Mandato himself opened the door. He looked from Leuci to Jaffe and back again. "What's the matter?"

While Jaffe and the marshal waited outside, Leuci entered the house with Mandato. Mandato was alarmed. "Are you okay?" he asked. "You look terrible. Are you okay?"

"Cody killed himself, Frank."

Mandato let out a half-muted scream, and then: "Oh God, Dave, Dave, Dave."

A moment later, the two detectives walked outdoors. Mandato was half leaning on Leuci, half hugging him. They began walking fast up and down the sidewalk. Mandato alternately moaned and screamed Cody's name.

The two detectives were walking so quickly that Jaffe behind them could not keep up. They could hear him muttering, "I will never get involved in this kind of thing again. I will never get involved with cops again." The federal marshal was sitting on the curb across the street watching.

An hour passed. The two detectives patrolled the sidewalk, still clinging to each other.

Jaffe decided to put an end to this meeting. "You've said enough," he told them. "Let's get in the car, Bob."

In the light of the street lamp Mandato studied his former partner. He was beginning to get himself under control, but Leuci, he saw, was as brittle as ever. "Are you okay, Bob? You're not going to do anything, crazy, are you? You're not going to harm yourself, are you? You're not going to leave me to get through this by myself, are you?"

Mandato watched Leuci climb into the car.

Jaffe too was worried. Mandato no longer had a gun, but Leuci did, and the prosecutor, turning in his seat, demanded to know where it was.

"I don't carry my gun. It's in my attaché case." But he refused to give it to Jaffe.

With the marshal at his heels, Leuci stumbled through

the night. He met with Giuliani in one bar, and for a time he sat in another trying to drink himself into a stupor, while the federal marshal watched him nervously from nearby. For a time he may have dozed sitting up in a parked car. Morning came. Unshaven, wearing the same clothes as the night before, he moved through the corridors of the Southern District Courthouse demanding to see Mandato. But his former partner was in an office being interrogated by one prosecutor and three DEA agents, he was told, and a man stood at the office door, barring it and him. Leuci flung the man aside and kicked the door open.

Five startled men looked up at him. It was clear from his face that he was out of control. Nonetheless, the DEA agent nearest the door said, "What the hell do you think you're doing, busting in here like this?"

"Get up out of that chair, and I'll fucking kill you," shouted Leuci.

A stunned silence filled the room. Then Mandato stood up. "I'll take care of him," he said gently, and moved to Leuci's side.

He began to walk Leuci up and down the hall, talking to him in a soft voice.

"I just want to get out of here," Mandato told him. "I want to go back home to Florida. I'm going to tell them what they want to know, and then I'm getting the hell out of here. It's too late to do anything else."

"Frank, I'm not doing it. It's over. I'm calling up Les."

Shaking Mandato off, Leuci went to a phone and dialed Wolff's home number. When Wolff came on, Leuci, in a broken voice, gave way to the grief and remorse that afflicted him.

"Bob," Wolff said, interrupting harshly. "I did my crying last night. I'm done crying for Cody. I'm done crying for you. Fuck you, fuck him. He was a drunk. No one would have believed him anyway." In Wolff's voice Leuci sensed one emotion, and one only, hatred—hatred for the prosecutors, hatred for Leuci and Mandato as well. "If the prosecutors want to believe the ramblings of a drunk, if they want to believe you, let them. They can believe whatever they like, but I'm not coming in there. They're not doing to me what they've done to you guys."

Leuci felt a kind of befuddled admiration for Wolff. He was proud of him. Wolff would defy the entire United States Government.

"Les, you don't have anything to worry about from me, because as far as I'm concerned, you and I never did anything together."

"Don't tell me that," said Wolff coldly. "Tell that to the people you work for." And he hung up.

Leuci stood there a moment, goofy with pride about Wolff. Only slowly did the degree of Wolff's hatred sink in, so that suddenly he saw how it all would end. Wolff would stand fast all right, but he himself would not. When the trial came, Les Wolff would stand in the dock, and Detective Second-Grade Robert Leuci would be sworn in as a principal witness against him.

Leuci went back to the office where the prosecutors waited. Seeing the state he was in, they told him to go home. Mandato was allowed to walk him to the elevator. As he stepped into it, Leuci turned to his former partner and said, "Don't hate me, Frank."

Just as the doors closed, Mandato answered, "Bob, I'll never hate you."

27

GIULIANI, meanwhile, had two problems. The first was how to turn the new Leuci material over to the court, and the second was whether or not Leuci should be indicted.

The first problem was more quickly resolved than the second. Leuci's admissions, including the many counts of perjury, were gathered together by Jaffe and bound into a kind of booklet. The booklet, eighty-four pages thick, was a masterpiece of duplication, cross references, and overkill. Defense lawyers in every subsequent trial would be delighted with it, not only because it would make cross-examination of Leuci so easy, but also for the heavy, satisfying thud it made when tossed contemptuously, theatrically onto a table top, or into the principal government witness's lap. Copies of this booklet were turned over to Rosner's new lawyer, Alan Dershowitz, and to Judge Bauman, who had presided at the original trial, and who would also preside at the hearing he had ordered into The Baron's affidavit.

The compiling of the booklet was a painful thing for Leuci, for he was made by those interrogating him to go over and over acts that were by now up to seven years into his past. He was a different man today than he had been then, or at least he hoped he was, and it was painful for him to be forced to confront the man he had been then—the detective known as Babyface. To talk about Babyface nauseated him. Babyface was his enemy. And yet he remembered the sense of purpose with which Babyface had approached his work in those years— Babyface was never completely evil, or so Leuci wanted to believe, and to repudiate Babyface now, which he had to do and wanted to do, was like repudiating his brother, or his father.

The hearing began. Leuci walked into court, and Judge

Bauman, who had been so friendly and understanding during the Rosner trial, now refused to look at him. Every time the witness, Leuci, looked up at him during the course of the interrogation, the judge swiveled his chair around so that he was facing in the other direction.

The interrogation by Dershowitz went on and on. The lawyer played up each situation, each incident, forcing the witness to provide every detail, to wallow in his own shame.

After a time, afraid he might actually vomit, the witness asked to be excused, and he rushed to the men's room in the hall. When he came out, he found himself suddenly alone in the corridor and face to face with Edmund Rosner. This shocked him, but he dropped his eyes and started to walk past.

"Hey, I'm sorry," said Rosner. "I wish all this had never happened."

Leuci looked at him, "You and me both, pal."

"Can I shake your hand?" asked Rosner.

"Sure." The two men shook hands.

"Good luck," said Rosner.

"Good luck to you," said Leuci.

Then he was back on the stand again. When he looked out into the courtroom, it was to recognize men from Internal Affairs, all wearing half-smiles, notebooks open on their laps, ballpoints busy, taking down every name Leuci divulged. Looking at them was, for Leuci, like looking into a mirror: all the things he had sworn he would never do, he was now doing in open court for posterity forever.

His testimony ended. The hearing ended. And Judge Bauman retired to deliberate. Was Rosner entitled to a new trial?

Even as Judge Bauman studied the new testimony by Leuci and pondered his decision, other arguments resounded up and down the corridors of the Southern District Courthouse. What to do about Leuci? Should he be indicted, or not? There seemed to be three camps, only one of them pro-Leuci. The other two wanted him in jail, though for different reasons.

The Drug Enforcement Administration, as represented by Tom Taylor and George Carros, not only urged that Leuci be indicted, they virtually demanded it. The two agents despised and hated Leuci, that much was clear. Of all the men the detective had dealt with over the past three and a half years, these appeared to be the only two he had not won over.

As they urged his indictment, their voices were loud and their faces sometimes contorted, but their arguments could not, on these grounds, be discounted, for in the everyday functioning of the U.S. attorney's office they were important men. It was they who assigned the agents who did the leg work as many of the cases under investigation were put together. Furthermore, many of their arguments made sense. "How can you not indict Leuci?" they would demand. How could Leuci's crimes be allowed to go unpunished? How could others reasonably be prosecuted for lesser offenses?

A good many assistant U.S. attorneys were also pushing for indictment. Their arguments were altogether intellectual, and for that reason more powerful. The government, they pointed out, was here faced with a clear and overwhelming case of perjury. In the Rosner trial alone, Leuci had lied dozens of times, and that verdict was now in jeopardy. There had been only one other trial—that of Perrazzo's two confederates—in which his perjury had been identical. Add to this perjury the hundreds of other crimes—the giving of heroin to informants, the illegal wiretaps, the scores—to which Leuci had now confessed. These prosecutors too asked, "How can you not indict him?"

Though most of the lawyers attempted to keep their emotions separate from their deliberations, this proved to be difficult. Perjury always made a prosecutor angrier than any other crime. For one thing, it was the only crime that, normally, a prosecutor witnessed. For another, it struck at the root of the prosecutorial system itself. The courthouse was a kind of concrete temple in which resided the god of justice, but this temple was built upon the most fragile of underpinnings, namely the testimony of witnesses. These fragile underpinnings were protected by one thing only, the sworn oath. Perjury, they argued, must be dealt with everywhere and always as the most terrible of crimes, because that was what it was.

For purely tactical reasons also, it was argued, Leuci ought to be indicted. It might save the Rosner case. It might save some of the future cases as well, for many had not yet come to trial. It would defuse arguments by Rosner and others that the government had had knowledge of Leuci's perjury and had kept silent. It would prove that the government was furious with its principal witness, and all its arguments before Judge Bauman and others would seem more honorable, more substantial, more convincing.

The decision would be made by the new U.S. attorney, Paul Curran, who knew very little of Leuci personally. He had not been present during the heroics of the undercover phase of Leuci's activity, nor during the indictment and trial of Rosner, nor during the subsequent indictments of so many others. He had no prejudices one way or the other. He looked to his aides for advice, and more advice had come in than he had counted on, much of it conflicting. The weight of it, however, seemed clearly against Detective Leuci. Of his closest, highest-ranking aides, only Giuliani argued firmly for no indictment.

Then Curran's predecessor, Whitney North Seymour, marched through the door. Seymour was a giant of a man, not only in physical stature, but in prestige as well. In the law enforcement community Seymour was a heavyweight, and he argued now in Leuci's behalf. His arguments took the form of a description of the services Leuci had performed for the government. To Seymour, Leuci had tried to do the right thing from the moment he first came forward. Even in lying on the witness stand he had been obeying the dictates of his conscience—he had been trying to protect his partners. This was no doubt reprehensible, but it was certainly understandable, and it was possible even in condemning it to see Leuci's perjury as an act of intergrity.

In calm, measured tones, Seymour underwrote Leuci's character.

He was followed into Curran's office in succeeding days by Scoppetta, and then by Shaw. Shaw, in fact, came twice. The arguments of both men much resembled those of Seymour. Both were trying to keep their counsel on a professional, intellectual plane insofar as possible, but Shaw, finally, was unable to do so.

Inside the U.S. attorney's office, Shaw had always been considered a distant, intellectual kind of man. Often his colleagues went to him with legal problems and he solved them instantly, and they thought of him always as a first-class legal mind. Now, as his plea on behalf of Leuci became personal, even emotional, everyone was surprised.

Shaw was distressed at the way things were leaning in this office, he began. Sure there were rational arguments why Leuci should be indicted, and there were irrational ones too. He categorized the conduct of Carros and Taylor, in threatening Leuci with indictment, as unspeakably evil. Shaw himself had been exposed to Leuci from the very beginning, and to what he had done, and to what it all had cost him. Although Curran hadn't witnessed all this himself, nonetheless he ought to respect it. As the tall, thin lawyer saw on the sofa in Curran's office, the emotions that he usually kept strongly checked rose to the surface. If you appreciated how it started, Shaw said, and what it accomplished, and how understandable his lies were, you couldn't conscientiously bring charges against him. It would not be a fair treatment of this human being.

Giuliani was present during both of Shaw's visits, and from time to time other assistant U.S. attorneys also, and all were surprised at Shaw's understanding of Leuci's character, for on the surface the Harvard-educated rich man's son and the street cop from Queens had nothing in common. "Bob Leuci is one of my heroes," said Shaw.

The decision finally would be Curran's alone. If he decided to indict, whether for perjury or for any other of Leuci's past acts of misconduct, then conviction, given Leuci's confessions, would automatically follow. Curran, as far as Leuci was concerned, was a one-man judge and jury, and on his verdict rode in many respects the rest of

Leuci's life. Indictment would mean at the very least dismissal from the Police Department; it would mean exclusion from any future job within law enforcement as well. To indict Leuci would be to ban him forever from the only world he knew or cared about.

In the American criminal justice system, prosecutors within their jurisdictions are granted absolute discretion. They may prosecute or not prosecute, as they choose. The two decisions, Curran's and Judge Bauman's, were handed down almost simultaneously, though the prosecutor's came first.

The government declined to prosecute Detective Leuci, ruled Curran. The additional Leuci testimony about his own misdeeds had been collateral, ruled Judge Bauman. Collateral is a legal term meaning apart from the central issue, and therefore of no consequence. Rosner's conviction stood.

28

THERE CAME a day when Assistant U.S. Attorney Rudolph Giuliani, trying to put together a major narcotics investigation with new narcotics detectives newly assigned to him, realized that they were all inept. They couldn't tail a suspect without getting made. They couldn't contact a surveillance without calling in that they were lost. They never played hunches.

A great detective, Giuliani thought, should be a man of imagination and fearlessness. A man with a sense of adventure, a man not limited by procedure. In his new detectives, all these qualities were absent, so that he asked himself almost in despair: Where have all the great detectives gone? The answer that came back to him was this one: I put them all in jail.

By then the SIU had been disbanded. Of the approximately seventy men who served in the small, elite unit between 1968 and 1971, fifty-two were indicted. Even this latter figure does not tell the whole story. Nunziata and Cody were never indicted, nor was Bermudez, nor Hubert, nor Leuci himself. Many others were implicated but, for one reason or another, not prosecuted.

Among these was Detective Vinny Russo. It was unlikely, the prosecutors felt, that any jury would send Russo to jail for accepting $150 on one occasion or another, or even for lying in an attempt to protect other cops. Besides, one of the witnesses against him would have to be Leuci. "If you prosecute Vinny Russo," Leuci had told them over and over again, "you'll have another Dave Cody on your hands." Looking at Leuci, as he pleaded for his friend, the prosecutors were struck by the strain that showed in his voice and in his eyes. If they prosecuted Vinny Russo, they might have two more Dave

Codys on their hands. Russo, was, however, forced to retire from the Police Department.

Very few of the detectives against whom charges were brought were acquitted. Aguiluz, after testifying in eight trials, after pleading guilty to felony tax fraud both in the Southern and Eastern Districts, received a suspended sentence and was relocated—no one knew where. His two partners, the Irishman Peter Daly and Joe Novoa, found legally guilty of Aguiluz's five kilo sale, went to Atlanta Federal Penitentiary to smash rocks for ten years.

Novoa had been offered a chance to cooperate; at the last minute he refused it. He was not going to turn on his partners and friends, and he was not going to admit to his children that he was a dope dealer. Aguiluz testified against him, Giuliani prosecuted, and he was convicted. A year or so later he was brought back to New York by the prosecutors to be questioned about another matter; by then he no longer looked like a cop. His shoulders were stooped, he walked with his head down, and he no longer raised his eyes when people addressed him.

Peter Daly had somehow foreseen all that would happen from the moment that Aguiluz was summoned to testify before the grand jury. Daly fled to Ireland at once, for he was safe there. No extradition treaty between Ireland and the United States existed which would touch him. He had made it back home, and he was free. Once he sent a picture of himself to Aguiluz. He was sitting by a handsome lake, wearing a crewneck sweater, waving. There was a pier nearby, and gorgeous Irish countryside in the background.

But his sister got beaten up by her husband in England—and Daly did what any cop would do for his sister—he flew there twice to try to help her. A priest informed on him. During his first visit, Scotland Yard detectives missed him. The second time they did not.

He was flown back to New York with a Scotland Yard detective seated on either side, and in the course of the long flight, one of them asked him the size of the largest seizure of narcotics he had ever made. "One hundred and five kilos," remarked Peter Daly proudly. But only 100 kilos had been vouchered. So at Daly's trial not only did Aguiluz testify against him, but so did the two Scotland Yard detectives. Guilty on all four counts. Ten years.

Detective Jack McClean, everybody's Irish uncle, who had hosted the Nunziata funeral, was sentenced to nine years, along with his partners Ray Viera and Medal of Honor winner Eddie Codelia, for ripping off Hispanic drug dealers. Later their sentences were reduced to four years. Most of the rest of the detectives were prosecuted for income tax evasion, for that was easiest, and the most usual sentence meted out, whether the detectives went to trial or pleaded guilty, was two and a half years.

One or two, among them Sheridan, were made to cooperate in other cases, then were allowed to plead guilty to misdemeanors. At the end Sheridan received a suspended sentence, and escaped jail.

Hardly any detective survived SIU with reputation intact. Imagination, fearlessness, a sense of adventure, a disregard for procedure—SIU men had these qualities in abundance. They were great detectives. Of course it was these same qualities that got them into trouble.

The trials went on month after month—there were so many of them—and the last of these on the schedule was the trial of Detective Leslie Wolff.

29

ON THE NIGHT BEFORE he was to testify against his former partner, Leuci lay in bed in the dark, and remembered how much he had learned to care for Les over the years.

He remembered when his cabin in the Catskills was finished, and it was time to bring a load of old furniture up there. He was in the office complaining about what a hassle this would be, renting a van, loading and unloading the furniture, the long lonely drive up and back. Without being asked, Wolff said, "I'll call you in the morning. We'll go get the van. We'll drive up there together. We'll have a nice day."

He remembered the first time Les and Sandy came to his house for dinner. Les arrived bearing a hand-carved wood head of Christ that he had picked up in an antique shop in Germany when he was in the army there. It was obviously valuable, and Leuci was so surprised that he said, "Les, you must let me pay you for this."

Wolff said, "No, I want you to have it. It's no big deal."

He remembered another dinner at Wolff's house. When dinner was over the Wolffs' daughter, who must have been about twelve that year, played the classical guitar for them all.

He remembered meeting Wolff outside his mother's house after Wolff's indictment by Puccio. Leuci had begun by putting his arm around Wolff's shoulders, at the same time surreptitiously feeling for a wire, so that Wolff, giving his half-smile, said, "Are you searching me? You are the most paranoid guy."

"Are you wearing a wire?"

"No, are you?"

"No. Do you want to search me?"

Again the half-smile. "No, I don't want to search you. I take your word for it."

And then the way the meeting ended: first the embrace, and then, "Bob, I've never felt closer to you than I do right now."

Wolff rarely showed affection. He rarely laughed either. He was always worried about what people thought of him. Which was probably why he had chosen to go to jail. If convicted he could always claim he had been framed. But to plead guilty would be to admit to his two children, who were now teenagers, that he had been a corrupt cop.

And so tomorrow Leuci would be forced to give testimony that might send Les to jail. Leuci got out of bed, felt his way to the bathroom, spilled Valium out into his hand, and gulped down the pills in the dark.

But back in bed he still could not sleep, and the old faces began to parade before his tightly closed eyes: Nunziata, Cody, Lusterino, Butera, Hourigan. Butera had taken part in the Riverdale Motel score, had been arrested, indicted, suspended, his gun and shield taken from him, and then for six months the prosecutors had pounded him. He dropped dead of a heart attack one day while on his way to meet the prosecutors of the Eastern District. He was forty-two years old. Hourigan had taken part in one of the ripoffs for which Wolff would go on trial tomorrow. Once arrested, he had begun to drink, and before the year was out had drunk himself to death. He too was forty-two years old.

These were the dead, but in the dark Leuci kept visualizing the faces of the living whom he had ruined, as well. Poor crazy Perrazzo, Vinny Russo, Mandato, and now Les Wolff.

The Valium was no help. He could not sleep, and at last he got up and paced until morning came. Haggard, exhausted, he drove to the courthouse, where he swallowed more Valium and then stepped into court, mounted the witness stand, and was sworn in.

The prosecutor was Tom McDermott, and he was another in the long line of those who, almost despite themselves, now cared very deeply about Detective Leuci.

Leuci and Wolff were staring at each other across thirty feet of intervening courtroom. Both faces, to an outsider, would have appeared expressionless, but McDermott thought he could discern a thousand messages flashing back and forth between the former partners. Stepping into the line of sight, he interrupted this anguished exchange, and began his questioning.

Step by step he led Leuci back over the three events for which Wolff was now on trial.

1. Armed with warrants, Leuci, Mandato, Cody, Wolff, a lieutenant, a sergeant, and the lieutenant's driver raided the bar and apartment of a major narcotics dealer named Santiago Valdez. They arrested him and seized his drugs. While Leuci was searching the bar, Wolff came down and said he had found money in the apartment upstairs. The sergeant, who had seen the money too, suggested that they skim off a couple of hundred dollars to cover legitimate expenses incurred in making the case—the Police Department reimbursed no expenses ever. According to Leuci, Wolff said, "There's a hell of a lot of money up there, and I'm not giving it to this dope pusher."

So they worked out a way to get the money out of the house. They synchronized their watches. Wolff went back upstairs. After precisely 90 seconds, Leuci stepped out onto the sidewalk, and the money came flying out of the upstairs window in a hatbox, Leuci caught the hatbox, walked to his car and drove off. Later the seven detectives split $12,000.

2. Leuci and his teammates obtained a warrant for the arrest of Jose Vasserman, another major narcotics importer. Again their work was flawless. Vasserman was supposedly armed and dangerous, and his door was surely barricaded. Hit that door with shoulders, and two things would happen. The drugs would go down the toilet, and one or more detectives might get shot. So Leuci and his team talked the building superintendent into shutting off Vasserman's water and electricity simultaneously. When Vasserman peered out into the hallway to see

if the building lights were out too, the detectives grabbed him without a struggle.

Inside the apartment they found that Vasserman had been packaging heroin in the presence of a second man they didn't know. Under the law the second man, who had not been part of the investigation, was as guilty now as Vasserman—who promptly offered them $3600 to let the man go. After talking it over, they accepted the money. They then arrested Vasserman, and seized and vouchered his drugs.

About two weeks later Leuci got a phone call from Lusterino, who said that Mikey Coco wanted to see him. Leuci and Mandato met Coco in the Holiday Inn on Fifty-seventh Street. The mobster said, "There's a bail bondsman who has got $20,000 to fix this case for Vasserman."

The two detectives said there was no way Vasserman could beat the case.

"Take this $10,000," said Coco. "If the guy goes to jail, give it back to me, because I'm going to have to vouch for this money. If the guy beats the case, you get another $10,000."

Leuci and Mandato took the money, and the next day talked it over with Cody and Wolff. Leuci said, "If Vasserman goes to jail, we're going to have to give this money back, because Coco is vouching for it." He added, "I don't want to be in the position of owing a guy like that money."

According to Leuci, Wolff said, "Let him sue me. Fuck him."

Vasserman was sentenced to seven years. Coco's $10,000 was not returned.

3. The four detectives had been trying to make a case against Manuel Noa, another major narcotics mover. But Noa never touched drugs unless paid in advance. The detectives decided to order the drugs themselves, then arrest Noa for possession. But for this they needed $9,000 front money. The Police Department did not have that kind of money. If they went to the feds for it, the feds would take over their case—and probably blow it. To SIU

detectives, federal narcotics agents were one and all buffoons. So they went to an informant—a second major dealer—who agreed to order the drugs and put up the money.

At length Noa informed the informant that the shipment was in. The informant informed the detectives, who drove up to Noa's West Forty-ninth Street apartment armed with warrants. Inside, they found drug paraphernalia and records of drug transactions, but no drugs, though they tore the apartment apart. They did find a picnic basket full of money, an enormous amount of money, a hundred thousand dollars or more, and they owed their informant $9000.

Negotiations ensued. The five detectives (Leuci's team plus Sergeant Hourigan) left the apartment with a paper bag full of money. They returned the $9000 to their informant and shared the rest, which came to about $2000 each.

30

ALTOGETHER Leuci was on the stand for two full days.
As soon as Prosecutor McDermott was finished with him,
Wolff's defense attorney, Paul Goldberger, rose and
approached the stand. From the defense table, Wolff
watched passively while Leuci, under cross-examination
by Goldberger, was accused—and accused himself—of
the acts for which Wolff was being tried. The case—
Leuci's whole life—had come full circle, and sitting before
the jury in the thirteenth floor courtroom, he seemed to be
fulfilling two roles at once: he was prosecutor and
defendant both.

Goldberger started with nicknames. Did Leuci have a
nickname? Was Babyface his nickname?

Leuci: "Babyface was a common nickname given to
young-looking narcotics detectives. When I was first
starting in the Narcotics Division I was a lot younger than
I am now—"

Goldberger: "Detective Leuci, will you answer the
question? Did anybody call you by the nickname of
Babyface?"

Leuci: "Junkies in the street used to call me Babyface,
yes. No detective would refer to me as Babyface,
counselor."

Goldberger: "Why, because they were afraid of you?
Were you a tough guy in the street? Did you use a lot of
physical force in the street?"

Goldberger: "You used to carry narcotics around with
you in Brooklyn, didn't you? As a matter of fact, you had
a little magnetic box that used to hook up under the
dashboard, and you used to keep some bags of narcotics
in it, is that right?"

Leuci: "A little key case that I used to keep narcotics in for my informants, that's correct."

Goldberger: "You used to carry something else with you, some other white powder occasionally?"

Leuci: "I used to carry packages occasionally of pancake flour."

Goldberger: "And with the pancake flour you threatened to flake some junkie in the street, is that right?"

Leuci: "I would threaten to put it in his pocket if he tried to swallow some narcotics on me when I approached."

Goldberger: "So where did you carry this white powder, in your pocket?"

Leuci: "Sometimes."

Goldberger: "Felony weight?"

Leuci: "It was pancake mix, counselor."

Goldberger: "Would it have been felony weight if it had been drugs?"

Leuci: "It could have made twenty pancakes."

Goldberger: "But your testimony is that you never did flake anybody? Never framed anybody?"

Leuci: "Much too easy to arrest them."

Goldberger: "Now, would you say it's a fair statement that from time to time you and Mandato would cover for each other?"

Leuci: "Yes."

Goldberger: "Mandato was in the habit of taking a lot of time off when he was supposedly on the job, wasn't he? Mandato would wind up at a motel with some girl as opposed to being on the job on some occasion? Wouldn't he?"

McDermott: "Objection, your honor."

Goldberger: "Are you familiar with the Jade East Motel in Queens?"

Leuci: "Am I familiar with it?"

Goldberger: "Yes."

Leuci: "Yes."

Goldberger: "Mandato been there?"

Leuci: "I heard Mandato was—I heard Mandato mention the Jade East Motel to me."

Goldberger: "Were you ever at the Jade East Motel when you were supposed to be on duty?"

The Court: "May I make a suggestion, Mr, Goldberger? I may be a little obtuse. I don't at this point think that the sexual—"

Goldberger: "I'm not at all interested in the sexual appetite, judge."

The Court: "—have any relevance to these proceedings."

Goldberger: "Mandato, from time to time, had psychiatric problems, is that correct?"

The question, according to the rules of courtroom procedure, demanded only a yes or no answer, so Leuci was obliged to reply in the affirmative. He looked across at a jury that was already hostile to him, that had not even met Mandato yet, but already despised him, and he wanted to explain that Mandato, when forced out of the Police Department, had experienced a depression so deep and long-lasting that he had not known what else to do besides trying a psychiatrist.

But Goldberger had already begun a new line of questioning. "Did you come to know a person by the name of Jacobs? And did you come to know a person by the name of Johnny Ryan? Did you give Johnny Ryan heroin to simonize or wash your car in front of the Brooklyn Supreme Court?"

Leuci: "I don't remember giving heroin to Johnny Ryan at the Brooklyn Supreme Court. I had given heroin to Johnny Ryan many times around the Narcotics Bureau headquarters downtown, and he washed my car along with all the other detectives' cars in Narcotics. That was the only way Johnny Ryan would ever get drugs. Johnny Ryan was a burnt-out informant. Our cars may have been washed the day before. We didn't need it. He had to feel he was doing something. He was a guy that just hung around the Narcotics Division and he couldn't buy drugs in the streets any more and narcotics detectives took care of his habit as best we could."

Goldberger: "And when you gave drugs to Ryan, or gave drugs to Jacobs, did you understand that you were committing a crime at that time?"

Leuci: "Did I understand that to be a crime, the fact of giving drugs to someone? At that time? Yes, I guess so, I guess so."

Goldberger: "You guess so?"

Leuci: "Yes, I guess so. I'll give you that, counselor, sure. I knew it was a crime."

Goldberger: "So when you gave drugs to Johnny Ryan, and to Joe Jacobs, you were selling them drugs under the law, is that right? So the answer is yes, you had sold drugs?"

Leuci: "No, I did not sell drugs. I never gave anyone drugs for money, and that's what you are saying, counselor. I never did that."

Goldberger: "How many times would you say that under the law you sold drugs?"

Then Goldberger started a new line of questioning: the scores to which Leuci had just admitted in open court, and for which Detective Wolff, sitting silent and unmoving at the defendant's table, was on trial.

Goldberger: "And the money you made was cash money, right? Green dollar bills, is that right? You took them home with you?"

Leuci: "Yes."

Goldberger: "You built a trap in your house in Kings Park?"

Leuci: "I had a trap. That was built into my house in Kings Park to put my guns in, Counselor. I had two little children and I had a trap built into the house and there was also money in there, but it was a very tiny little trap."

Goldberger: "A tiny little trap that got filled up with lots of money."

McDermott: "Objection."

Goldberger: "Do you take medication before you testify?"

Leuci: "At times."

Goldberger: "Did you take some tranquilizers yesterday?"

Leuci: "Yes."

Goldberger: "What kind of tranquilizers do you take before you testify?"

Leuci: "I take a Valium every once in a while. I

don't—yesterday I did. I took a Valium yesterday."

Goldberger: "Did you take a Valium this morning?"

Leuci: "Yes."

Goldberger: "It calms you down before you testify?"

McDermott: "Objection."

The Court: "Sustained."

Goldberger went off in still another direction. Did Mandato or Wolff or Cody or Hourigan or O'Brien speak Spanish? Leuci answered that they did not.

Goldberger: "So pretty much you are the man. If there was a Spanish drug dealer to talk to, and he could only speak Spanish, he'd pretty much have to talk to you, is that right?"

Leuci: "Plenty of Spanish dealers were ripped off by guys who couldn't speak Spanish, my friend."

Goldberger: "I ask that that be stricken, judge, as unresponsive to the question."

Night came. Again Leuci lay awake in the dark. He could not stop thinking about Les, and about the trial. This cross-examination, which would continue in the morning, was the most savagely personal he had yet undergone—the nickname, the pancake flour, the trap, the Valium, the Jade East Motel. Goldberger had been supplied with information only a partner could know. To be subjected to such a cross-examination was a sickening experience. But he didn't blame Les. Les was fighting for his life.

I'm doing this for my family, Leuci told himself, for my kids. Then he thought: Does Les love his children any less than I love mine?

Lying there, he realized how much he still cared for Les Wolff. He wanted Les to come out of this trial okay. At the same time, he didn't want to lose the trial, because this would mean he had gone through these years, this trial all for nothing. His thoughts were a jumble. He didn't want Wolff convicted, and yet if Wolff were acquitted, then would not the jury, in effect, be condemning him in Wolff's place?

When dawn came he was still trying to work it out.

Later he was back on the witness stand, his questions

unresolved, his emotions no clearer, his brain foggy from two nights of no sleep.

Goldberger: "And what of your testimony yesterday that Detective Wolff went over to the picnic basket and put his hands in, and he says something like: 'This is for us,' or 'This is for me?'"

Leuci: "The picnic basket is opened up. The defendant walked over to the basket, reached in, and it was—with a smile on his face, and I was laughing. We were all laughing. We thought it was kind of funny. Noa didn't think it was so funny, I don't think. He said, 'We're going to take this money,' and Noa said, 'No, no, no,' and we smiled, and the defendant put the money back in the basket."

Goldberger: "Is it a fact, sir, is it the best of your recollection that you never testified at a grand jury concerning Les Wolff going over and picking up any money out of a picnic basket?"

McDermott: "Objection."

The Court: "Sustained."

From time to time Leuci glanced over at the jury. He saw no sympathy there, no understanding of any kind. At the defendant's table, Wolff watched him impassively, while his wife Sandy, in the first row of the courtroom, mouthed curses in the direction of the witness stand.

At last Leuci was allowed to step down and former detective Frank Mandato was sworn in in his place. Under questioning by Prosecutor Joel Cohen, Mandato's descriptions of the three ripoffs differed from Leuci's in no significant detail. His cross-examination by Goldberger was also almost identical. The former detective testified in a flat, emotionless voice, and when he gazed across at Wolff from time to time he too seemed to be trying to send messages, one of which seemed to be: Perhaps I can do you more good up here than I could sitting beside you in the dock.

Other witnesses followed, including Domingo Coca, the informant who had put up the $9000, Wilfredo Risco, José Vasserman's friend, who had bought his freedom for $3600, and Manual Noa's ex-wife. Coca had just pleaded guilty in a drug sale case, and had been sentenced to five years in prison. Risco, whom they had let go, was a worse man than Vasserman by far, though they hadn't known this. Risco had shot one cop in Ecuador, had bribed his way out of prison there, was currently in jail for armed robbery, and was about to go on trial for the murder of another cop in Puerto Rico.

When the turn of the defense came, Goldberger called only character witnesses, a series of them, the most important being William Aronwald, who had succeeded Shaw as head of the Strike Force. Aronwald testified that Wolff had an outstanding reputation for honesty and integrity. As for Leuci, he was "not worthy of belief." A second Strike Force attorney, Steven Frankel, testified that Leuci "has an awful reputation for truthfulness . . . you can't believe the things he says to you."

The trial was halted while a second group of prosecutors was brought in to praise Leuci. Scoppetta, now a deputy mayor, came. Whitney North Seymour came. E. Michael Shaw came. Rudolph Giuliani, now an associate deputy attorney general, flew up from Washington. Their presence, as well as their words testified to the extremely rare thing Leuci had done in coming forward of his own accord, testified to his truthfulness, testified to his integrity. Yes, he had perjured himself in two trials, but only to save his partners—to save Leslie Wolff.

It was no longer a trial of facts. It was Leuci against Leslie Wolff, partner against partner. The jury was asked to choose one partner or the other. It filed out and began deliberations. It was, Leuci realized, six years almost to the day since Leuci's first conversations with Scoppetta. Had those six years atoned for anything?

Leuci himself seemed to be hoping for a verdict that would justify not only his testimony against Wolff, but his testimony against everyone else, too—a verdict beyond the competence of this jury or any other.

It was 2:05 P.M. the next day when the jurors filed back into the courtroom and took their seats.

The verdict was not guilty on all counts.

As it was announced, Sandy Wolff leaped to her feet,

screaming and clapping. Wolff himself smiled faintly at the jury. Otherwise he showed no emotion.

A few days later, Wolff stood trial on the same charges in the Police Department trial room before Deputy Commissioner Francis Looney. There were few witnesses, few spectators. Looney's verdict, later endorsed by Police Commissioner Michael Codd, was guilty on all counts. Detective Third-Grade Leslie Wolff was ordered dismissed from the Police Department, and his pension forfeited.

There was one final meeting between Leuci and Wolff.

Leuci was assigned at this time to the First Deputy Commissioner's Special Force in an office at 280 Broadway, across Police Plaza from headquarters. When a call came in summoning him to headquarters, he glanced around for someone to walk him over. But there was no one available, and he realized suddenly that he had not walked alone in the city in over four years.

The commanding officer of the Special Force, Deputy Inspector Harold Hess, told him he could wait, or else he could go alone. "Sooner or later you're going to have to go out alone," said Hess.

On the elevator, going downstairs alone, Leuci was in the grip of a sudden fear which he did not understand, and he wanted to turn back. Instead he began walking fast across Police Plaza, head down. When he looked up, who was coming toward him on an intersecting path but Les Wolff. Leuci saw that he had very few choices. He could stop in his tracks, he could go back to 280 Broadway, or he could continue on to Police Headquarters. But if he did continue, he would come face to face with Les Wolff in the middle of this vast open plaza.

A quick glance showed that Wolff had changed neither speed nor direction. Abruptly, Leuci decided that he wouldn't either. He also decided that when their paths intersected, he would let Wolff speak first. But his feet became leaden. Glancing up, he saw that Wolff had slowed also.

And so they came together. They looked at each other, and for a moment Leuci thought that Wolff began to smile. An instant later he realized he was wrong. That crease on the side of Wolfe's cheek was not a smile. Leuci looked straight into Wolff's eyes, and saw only coldness there, only hatred. Then Wolff's eyes dropped. Shaking his head from side to side, he walked on.

Some months later, when asked to describe Wolff, Leuci said, "Les Wolff was tough, strong—much stronger than I am—calculating, devious. Les Wolff had ice water in his veins. I don't believe for a second he ever cried for Dave Cody. Les Wolff never cried for anyone but Les Wolff. He was the coldest man I've ever met. I respect Les, and—" A catch came into Leuci's voice: "—and I miss him."

31

LEUCI WAS OFFERED a new name and relocation, but he chose to remain instead a New York City cop. Even before the trials were finished, he had sold the house in northern Virginia and bought another in a distant New York suburb. From then on he commuted to work by Volkswagen, unaccompanied by bodyguards.

But he remembered to carry his attaché case on his person more often than in the past, and he tended also never to zip it shut. He tried not to think of further attempts on his life. Mikey Coco was still in jail, but would be getting out soon. The lawyer Benny Caiola was already out. Edmund Rosner, his last appeal exhausted, had just gone in, so presumably he was no longer a threat, if in fact he ever had been. On the other hand, the various ex-policemen had begun now one by one to trickle back into the sunlight again. Were any of them threats? Leuci chose to think not.

The undercover phase of his life had lasted sixteen months. The trials had lasted four and a half years after that, and though they marked the end of many lives, they could be said to have signaled the beginning of his. It would be a long road back, and he knew this. He did not expect it to be easy. But if only he could remain a cop, he believed he could get through it. Being a cop was a part of his physical protection. To kill him would be to kill a cop, and no one would do that lightly but a crazy man. But being a cop was part of his psychic protection too.

Only if he could remain a cop was there any hope to build a new Bob Leuci, or so he believed.

It would not be easy.

In the midst of the trials he had been assigned to a newly formed integrity unit, The First Deputy Commissioner's Special Force. This unit was staffed to a large extent by integrity-minded officers who had already served for many years in the Internal Affairs Division. Leuci had never hoped to be received by such cops as these with open arms, but surely they would grant him at least a grudging acceptance.

They had not done so. When he came into the office the first day no one welcomed him. No one even smiled at him. Men looked up from their work, stared at him, and then looked away. Leuci was assigned to a lieutenant and to a sergeant. There was no warmth there, none of the camaraderie that he had always sought and found in other police units in the past. He had never experienced such coldness before, and he did not know how to cope with it.

Deciding to try to win them over, he began to come in mornings carrying containers of coffee on the lid of a box, or he went out in mid-morning and brought coffee back. He put a container down on the desk of each of the men he worked with, and the containers stood there untouched, all day. There even were times when men got up from their desks and came back a few minutes later carrying coffee containers of their own. They sat down and drank from these, without a word to Leuci.

Finally he had decided to attempt a man-to-man talk with the two lieutenants and the sergeant whom he considered the most influential officers in the unit. But as he led the three men into a small office, he had no idea what he was going to say to them.

They sat down and asked him what this was all about.

His life was difficult enough, Leuci told them. He lived in a kind of no man's land. He thought maybe they would have some kind of empathy for him. Apparently they didn't. At least he needed to know why they felt about him the way they evidently did. Perhaps it would help if they understood where he was coming from and why he had acted the way he had.

The middle-aged sergeant, James Meehan, said, "Leuci, I don't give a fuck about you. I don't give a shit what your story is."

"I think maybe you misunderstand me," said Leuci hesitantly.

Sergeant Meehan cut him off. "You are a fucking rat. I don't like rats." He got up and left the room.

The two lieutenants remained a short time longer. One explained that he had spent twenty-six years in the Police Department, and that, while assigned to the Special Force, he would do his job. He would never judge Leuci for what he had done. On the other hand, Leuci should not expect to be treated as his friend. And he left the room.

The lieutenant who remained was the best educated of the three. He wore an enormous college ring. His approach was more philosophical. He didn't know Leuci's whole story, he admitted. He understood that no one had caught him, that he had "cooperated" of his own accord—which was all to the good, he supposed. Now Leuci should do his job here, and if he did it well, no one would bother him. "But if you're here to make friends," the lieutenant concluded, "you may as well forget it."

"What am I supposed to do?" asked Leuci, "come in here and not talk to anybody? I can't go through every day like that."

"Your life is away from the Police Department now," said the lieutenant. "It's not part of the department any more." And he walked out.

Left behind, Leuci tried to convince himself that he was not as evil as these men seemed to think. He would win them over. There were good people in the Police Department. He wanted to be part of them, to feel the affection and closeness that he had known in the old days as a patrolman in TPF—and that he had known as a corrupt detective in SIU, too.

From then on, if a job had to be done that no one else wanted, Leuci would say, "Look, I'll do it." Although he was not a drinker, he would stand with them in bars at the end of the working day, buying rounds of drinks, listening to their conversation, rarely taking part except, sometimes, to agree with them. As the months passed he began to win smiles from time to time. They had problems being nice to him, but eventually couldn't help themselves.

The day came when Sergeant Meehan's son, a young patrolman in the Ninth Precinct, was indicted.

Sergeant Meehan believed passionately in many right-wing causes. He believed in the American flag. He played Sousa marches on the phonograph in his office, and "The Stars and Stripes Forever" was one of his favorites. His son was his pride and joy. After distinguishing himself in combat in Vietnam, the kid became a cop, and he was his father's image. He worked in one of the toughest precincts in the city, he survived a gun fight, he received commendations. Like his father, he was a rugged street guy, a tough, tough cop who, however, would never curse in front of a woman.

James Meehan, Jr., was exactly what his father had wanted.

But Internal Affairs had been conducting an investigation of corruption in the Ninth Precinct, and six cops were quietly indicted. Sergeant Meehan was never told that his son was among them until the day came when Jimmy Meehan, Jr., was to be arrested.

Sergeant Meehan by this time had reached the stage where he was willing to engage in long conversations with Leuci. He could understand cops making money, he said, for he had seen it happen many times in his years in the job. What he couldn't believe was that any cop would take money from a dope dealer.

Leuci tried to explain. An erosion took place that was exactly similar to what happened to cops who worked against known gamblers, and who got caught up in the corruption of taking money from the gamblers. In fact, probably the gamblers' money came from junk, Leuci said. The cops who took the money never thought that far.

Usually these discussions ended with Meehan walking out, slamming the door behind him. To take money in a narcotics case was the lowest thing in the world. How could any cop do that, and call himself a cop?

It was the job of Inspector Hess, who headed the unit,

to inform Sergeant Meehan that his son was to be arrested. Meehan walked in the door that morning, a big smile on his face, wearing a plaid suit, with a red and green tie that didn't match the suit, and big heavy brown shoes. Hess said, "Jimmy, I have to tell you something."

As he listened to Hess, the blood drained from Sergeant Meehan's face.

"My son's no thief," Meehan cried, when Hess had concluded. "I know he's not."

He began to talk about lawyers. He would hire his son the best lawyer in the country.

Leuci said to him, "Jimmy, whatever you need, just ask me. Anything I can do to help."

For a moment Meehan only stared at him. Then his arm went around Leuci's shoulder and he said, "Don't worry, I take care of my own children."*

Leuci's acceptance by members of the Special Force dated from that day. It had taken, literally, years.

After Wolff's trial, it became necessary to reassign Leuci elsewhere. If, in the upper echelons of the Police Department, any deep thinking was done on the subject, it was never made public. In a routine change, he was transferred to Internal Affairs, a unit that had always been, within the department, a separate place, cut off from the mainstream, cut off from other cops. He was assigned a desk, and regular working hours, and he began teaching courses in surveillance as part of the training program which Internal Affairs conducted.

When he stood up in front of his first class of students, he was introduced only as a man with eleven years of detective experience, an expert on surveillance techniques. He began to speak about leapfrogging, and block-squaring. To conduct a proper surveillance, Leuci explained, one needs four cars ideally and—

In the middle of the classroom a hand shot up. "What did you say your name was?"

"Detective Leuci."

---

*James Meehan, Jr. was later acquitted, and was ordered reinstated as a police officer.

"Are you *the* Detective Leuci?"

"I'm Detective Leuci."

"I don't think I have anything to learn from you," said the student, who was a detective lieutenant. He got up and walked out of the classroom and did not come back.

Of course certain cops told Leuci they were proud of what he had done. And many others were new, and had never heard of him.

He was a policeman again, he told himself. It was his opinion that a man could only be a policeman if he was accepted as such by other policemen. These men accepted him here. He was back in the Police Department, more or less. He missed the street, believing that that was where he operated best, and he realized that probably the department would never trust him in the street again. He went on teaching. I'm not in combat, he told himself, but not everyone can be.

Deep down he wanted to believe, and he wanted the world to believe, that he had done what he had done because he was a policeman, because he had seen evil growing before his eyes, evil that he himself was part of, and he had moved to end it by the only means open to him. He had come forward not as a rat, but as a cop. He had acted not calculatingly, but emotionally. And of all those he had destroyed, he had destroyed the old Bob Leuci most of all.

His most recurrent nightmare is this one: that he should be asked to leave the Police Department. To remain a cop, moving among other cops, is the only life for him that he can conceive, and he is taking it one day at a time.

"The twelfth Charlie Parker novel that John Connolly has intrigued, scared, and tortured us with . . . *The Wolf In Winter* delivers [a] powerful, supernatural punch."

—*Mustard Seed Thoughts*

"The creepy feeling of a good *X-Files* episode."

—*Tzer Island*

THE WRATH OF ANGELS

"Connolly writes seamlessly about an array of forces both criminal and supernatural, killings, and torture alongside the plethora of more prosaic human failings that he delineates so compassionately."

—*Library Journal* (starred review)

"Few thriller writers can create a sense of menace and evil as deftly as Connolly does. Compelling."

—*The Irish Independent*

"An exciting fusion of the occult and the hard-boiled . . . a gruesomely entertaining ride."

—*Publishers Weekly*

"The best kind of book for long winter nights."

—*Newsday*

"It's Evil versus Good versus an entity indifferent to both."

—*Booklist*

THE BURNING SOUL

"Harrowing and memorable."

—*Kirkus Reviews* (starred review)

"A complex story leading to an explosive and terrifying end game."

—*The Irish Independent*

"The blurring of worlds is what Connolly specializes in. His Parker books are populated by the usual denizens of crime thrillers: serial killers, mobsters, corrupt cops, assassins. But intruding on this world are ghosts, supernatural creatures, and Evil with a capital E."

—*Centre Daily Times*

And all the Charlie Parker thrillers

"Speeds us through a harrowing plot to a riveting climax."
—*New York Times* bestselling author Jeffrey Deaver

"Unfailingly compelling."

—*New Orleans Times-Picayune*

"For Connolly, the 'unknown' remains unknown, lending an air of mystery and tension that's as unrelenting as it is unsettling. [He] truly understands both horror and crime fiction, and his deft blend . . . makes for a powerful and heady brew, resulting in one of the most potent and emotionally wrenching P.I. series in recent memory. His characterizations are so sharp they could draw blood."

—*The Thrilling Detective*

"A unique voice."
—*New York Times* bestselling author Michael Connelly

"Powerful, disturbing prose."

—*Omaha World-Herald*

"He writes like a poet about terrible horrors. . . . His words sing."

—*Houston Chronicle*

"One of the best thriller writers we have."
—*New York Times* bestselling author Harlan Coben

"Leaves unshakable images lurking on the edge of the reader's consciousness."

—*Booklist*

THE WOLF
IN WINTER

A CHARLIE PARKER
THRILLER

JOHN CONNOLLY

POCKET BOOKS
New York   London   Toronto   Sydney   New Delhi

Pocket Books
An Imprint of Simon & Schuster, Inc.
1230 Avenue of the Americas
New York, NY 10020

Copyright © 2014 by John Connolly

All rights reserved, including the right to reproduce this book or portions thereof in any form whatsoever. For information, address Atria Books Subsidiary Rights Department, 1230 Avenue of the Americas, New York, NY 10020.

First Pocket Books paperback edition August 2015

POCKET and colophon are registered trademarks of Simon & Schuster, Inc.

For information about special discounts for bulk purchases, please contact Simon & Schuster Special Sales at 1-866-506-1949 or business@simonandschuster.com.

The Simon & Schuster Speakers Bureau can bring authors to your live event. For more information or to book an event, contact the Simon & Schuster Speakers Bureau at 1-866-248-3049 or visit our website at www.simonspeakers.com.

Manufactured in the United States of America

10 9 8 7 6 5 4 3 2 1

ISBN 978-1-4767-0319-0
ISBN 978-1-4767-0320-6 (ebook)

For Swati Gamble

1

HUNTING

He fled in fear and reached the silent fields
And howled his heart out, trying in vain to speak.

Ovid, *Metamorphoses*

I

The house was studiedly anonymous: not too large or too small, and neither particularly well kept nor in any sense dilapidated. Situated on a small patch of land not far from the outskirts of the city of Newark, Delaware, in the densely populated county of New Castle, the town had taken a hit when Chrysler's Newark assembly plant closed in 2008, along with the nearby Mopar distribution center. However, it was still the home of the University of Delaware, and twenty thousand students can spend a lot of money if they put their minds to it.

Newark was an unsurprising choice of location for the man we were hunting. It was close to the borders of three states—Pennsylvania, New Jersey, and Maryland—and only two hours from New York City by car. Then again, it was just one of any number of rat's nests that he had established for himself, acquired over the years by the lawyer who protected him. The only distinguishing feature of this property lay in the degree of power consumption: the utility bills were steeper than for the others we had discovered. This one looked as if it was used regularly. It was more than a storehouse for elements of his collection. It was a base of sorts.

He called himself Kushiel, but we knew him as the Collector. He had killed a friend of ours named Jackie Garner at the end of the previous year. The Collector would have called it an eye for an eye in his version of justice, and it was true that Jackie had made an appalling error—one that resulted in the death of a woman who was close to the Collector. In revenge, the Collector had shot Jackie down without mercy while he was unarmed and on his knees, but he had also made it clear that we were all under his gun now. We might have been hunting the Collector for what he had done to one of ours, but we also knew that it was only a matter of time before he decided we might be less of a threat to him with six feet of earth above our heads. We intended to corner and kill him long before it came to that.

A light burned in one room of the house. The others were all dark. A car stood in the driveway, and its arrival had alerted us to the possibility of the Collector's presence. We had placed a dual wireless break-beam alert system in the undergrowth halfway up the drive. The system was timer-based, so an alert would be sent to our phones only if the two beams weren't broken twice within a ten-minute period. In other words, it allowed for deliveries, but a vehicle that entered the property and remained on it for any length of time would trigger the alarm.

Of course, this assumed that the Collector would not arrive on foot, or by cab, but we figured that he had too many enemies to leave his escape routes to chance, and he would keep at least one well-maintained vehicle. A windowless garage stood to the right of the house, but we had not risked breaking into it when we first discovered the existence of the property. Even planting the little wireless infrared transmitters was a calculated gamble, and had been undertaken only after a sweep of the yard revealed no similar alarm system beyond whatever was used to secure the house itself.

"What do you think?" said Louis.

His dark skin caught something of the moonlight, making him seem even more a creature of the night than usual. He wore dark cotton trousers cinched at the ankles, and a black waxed-cotton Belstaff jacket from which all the buckles and buttons had been removed and replaced with non-reflective equivalents. He looked cool, but then he always looked cool.

"My legs are cramping up, is what I think," said Angel. "If we don't make a move soon, you'll have to carry me in there on a sedan chair."

Angel didn't care about cool. His clothing was functional and unlabeled. He just preferred things that way. His gray hair was hidden beneath a black beanie. Without the cap, he looked his years. He was older than Louis and me, and had grown quieter and more cautious in recent times. Mortality shadowed him like a falcon mantling its wings over dying prey.

We squatted in the grass by the side of the road, Angel to my left and Louis to my right, each of us armed with a suppressed Glock 9mm loaded with subsonic ammunition. We'd lose something in velocity, but if we found the Collector we'd be working at close range. There were properties to the east and west of the house, and the area was quiet. We didn't want to bring local law enforcement down on our heads by replicating the sound of the Gunfight at the O.K. Corral. All three of us also carried Russian-made anti-fog gas masks. They cost less than Louis's boots, but they hadn't let us down yet.

"You two take the back," I said. "I'll cover the front."

Louis reached into the pocket of his jacket and produced a tear-gas grenade. Angel had a second, and I had two more.

"Try not to get shot before you've thrown them," Angel told me.

"I'll try not to get shot after I've thrown them as well," I said.

It wasn't an ideal situation. We'd need to break glass to

get the grenades into the house, and hope that we didn't take fire in the process. If the Collector was cornered and chose to take his chances inside, then Angel and Louis would have to go in and get him, or flush him out to where I would be waiting. Grenade launchers might have been more effective, but your average grenade launcher tended to attract a certain amount of attention in the suburbs, and was hard to hide under a jacket, even one as expensive as Louis's. The other option might have been to try and break down the doors and come in shooting like gangbusters, but we risked looking kind of stupid—and kind of dead—if the doors were reinforced or booby-trapped in any way. The Collector was very protective of his health.

This was the third of the Collector's nests that we had targeted, and we were becoming almost accomplished by this point. We went in fast, and hit both sides of the house simultaneously, the panes of three windows shattering as one. The grenades delivered a combination of military-grade pepper spray and tear gas, and could cover a range of more than 20,000 cubic feet in less than a minute. Anyone who was in those rooms when they exploded wouldn't be staying there for long.

I was edgy before the first grenade went in, but I was doubly so as I prepared to toss the second. If shots were going to come, they would come now, but there was no re-action from inside the house. After a minute, I heard more glass shattering. Angel and Louis were going in through a window, not through the door. It was a calculated risk: expose yourself while climbing in through the busted frame, or try the door and hope that it wasn't wired. They'd opted for the former. I pulled back from the front of the house and took cover behind the car in the drive. It was a midsize Chevy sedan, the kind that an accountant might drive. The interior was pristine, and the seats were bare.

Nothing happened. There were no shouts, and no gun-shots. I could hear doors banging open in the house, but no more than that. After three minutes, my cell phone rang. It was Louis. He was breathing heavily. Behind him I could hear Angel coughing.

"He's gone," said Louis.

WE ALLOWED THE GAS to disperse before heading back inside. This house was better furnished than the others we had seen. There were books on the shelves—political biographies and modern histories, for the most part—and an effort had been made to decorate the rooms. The wood floors were partly covered with cheap but tasteful rugs, and abstract prints hung on some of the walls. The kitchen closets contained canned goods, rice, pasta, a couple of jars of instant coffee, and a bottle of Martell XO cognac. A small portable refrigerator hummed on the floor. Inside were candy bars, fresh milk, and a six-pack of diet soda. A TV in the living room was hooked up to a DVD player, but there was no cable connection. A copy of that day's *Washington Post* lay on the floor by the single armchair. Beside it was a mug of coffee, still warm. We must have missed him by minutes, seconds.

My eye caught an object hanging from the reading lamp by the chair. It was a bear-claw necklace. The Collector had taken it from Jackie's truck either before or after he killed him. It had once hung from Jackie's rearview mirror. It was his good-luck token, but his luck had still run out. In the end, everyone's luck does.

The Collector always kept souvenirs of his kills. He had not abandoned this one lightly. It was a message for us: a taunt, or perhaps a gesture of recompense, depending upon how one chose to take it.

I stepped carefully to the window and risked a glance

at the small backyard. Two houses backed onto this one, and in the distance I saw the lights of Newark. I could feel him out there. He was watching us. He knew that we wouldn't come after him on foot over unfamiliar ground, and at night. He was waiting to see what we would do next.

"We got more trinkets," I heard Angel say.

He joined me at the window, his back to the wall. Even in the darkness, he didn't want to make a target of himself. In his gloved hand he held a gold charm bracelet, a photograph of a young woman in an ornate silver frame, and a baby shoe that had been cast in bronze, each a token of a life taken.

"How did he get out?" I asked.

"Through the back door?"

"It's still locked from the inside," I said. "The front door was the same way. And you had to break a window to get in. They only open at the top, and a child could barely fit through the gap."

"In here," said Louis from the main bedroom.

We joined him there. Like all the other rooms in the house, it had a low ceiling. A hole for an AC unit had been cut in the wall by the main window, but there was no unit in place, and the hole appeared to have been boarded up. A chair was nearby. Louis stood on it and tested the board. It was hinged at the top, and moved like a pet door with the pressure of his hand. The hole looked small, but then Louis flipped up the frame surrounding it, and suddenly the space was big enough to allow an average-sized man to squeeze through.

"Bet the board on the other side is hinged too," said Louis. "He crawled out of here like the bug that he is."

He stepped down from the chair. The night was clear. No clouds obscured the moon.

"He's out there, isn't he?" he said.

"Probably."

"Can't go on like this. Eventually he's going to get tired of running."

"Maybe. Who knows how many of these bolt holes he has. But somewhere there's one that matters more than the others, more even than this one. That's where he's keeping the lawyer."

The lawyer Eldritch steered the Collector in the direction of those who had, in his eyes, forfeited the right to life—perhaps even the right to their immortal souls. He presented the case for the prosecution, and the Collector took care of the punishment. But Eldritch was injured in the same incident that had killed the woman and brought the Collector down on Jackie, and the Collector had spirited the old lawyer away. Who knew, Eldritch might even be dead. If that was the case, the Collector would be off the leash entirely. If nothing else, Eldritch held his hunting dog in some form of check.

"We going to keep looking for this refuge?" asked Louis.

"He killed Jackie."

"Maybe Jackie brought it on himself."

"If you believe that, then we all bring it on ourselves."

"That might just be true."

Angel joined us.

"Why hasn't he hit back? Why hasn't he tried to take us out?"

I thought that I had the answer.

"Because he believes that he violated his own code when he killed Jackie. Jackie's life wasn't his to take, whatever mistakes he might have made. Somewhere in what passes for his conscience, the Collector suspects that we may have earned the right to come after him. It's like Louis said: maybe we all bring it on ourselves.

"And then, like us, the Collector is just a pawn in a greater game. He might know more about the rules of the game than we do, but he has no idea of the state of play, or how close anyone is to winning or losing. He's afraid to kill us in case it tips the balance against him, although I don't know how long that situation will continue."

"What about us?" said Angel. "If we kill him, will there be blowback?"

"The difference is that we don't care," I said.

"Oh," said Angel. "I must have missed that memo."

"Basically, it said 'Fuck 'em if they ain't on our side,'" Louis explained.

"Yeah, I would have remembered seeing that one," said Angel. "So we keep hunting him until we corner him, or until he just rolls over and dies?"

"We hunt him until he tires, or we tire," I said. "Then we'll see how it plays out. You got anything better to do?"

"Not lately. Not ever, to be honest. So what now?"

I looked again into the darkness beyond the house.

"If he's out there, let's give him something to watch."

WHILE ANGEL WENT TO retrieve our car, Louis and I broke into the Chevy and pushed it against the door of the house. I could already smell the gas from the stove in the kitchen as Louis doused the interior of the Chevy with the Collector's cognac, saving about a third of the liquid. He stuck a kitchen rag into the neck of the bottle and shook it to soak the material. When Angel was sure that the road was clear, he signaled Louis with his headlights, and Louis lit the rag, tossed the bottle into the car, and ran.

The Chevy was already burning as we drove away, but the two explosions—the first from the car, the second from the house itself—came sooner than anticipated and occurred almost simultaneously, catching us by surprise. We didn't stop to watch the fireball rise above the trees. We just kept driving, taking Telegraph Road into Maryland as far as the intersection with Route 213, then headed north into Pennsylvania. We handed the car over to a woman in Landenberg, took possession of our own vehicles, and separated without another word, Louis and Angel heading for Philly while I drove north to the Turnpike.

ON THE OUTSKIRTS OF Newark, a man in a dark coat watched fire trucks pass. The sleeve of his coat was torn, and he limped slightly as he walked, favoring his right leg. The lights of the trucks briefly illuminated his thin face, his dark, slicked-back hair, and the thin trickle of blood that ran from his scalp. They had come close to catching him this time, so very close. . . .

The Collector lit a cigarette and inhaled deeply as his house burned.

II

The wolf was a young male, alone and in pain. His ribs stood out beneath his rust-brown fur, and he limped as he drew closer to the town. The wolf's pack had been annihilated by the shores of the St. Lawrence River, but by then the urge to roam had already taken him, and he had just begun moving south when the hunters came. His had not been a large pack: a dozen animals in all, led by the alpha female that was his mother. They were all gone now. He had escaped the slaughter by crossing the river on winter ice, flinching at the sound of gunfire. He came across a second, smaller group of men as he neared the Maine border, and sustained an injury to his left foreleg from a hunter's bullet. He had kept the wound clean, and no infection had set in, but there was damage to some of the nerves, and he would never be as strong or as fast as he once had been. The injury would bring death upon him, sooner or later. It was already slowing him down, and slow animals always became prey in the end. It was a wonder that he had come so far, but something—a kind of madness—had driven him ever onward, south, south.

Now spring was approaching, and soon the slow melting of snow would commence. If he could just survive the remainder of the winter, food would become more plentiful. For the time being, he was reduced to the status of a scavenger. He was weak from starvation, but that afternoon he had picked up the scent of a young deer, and its spoor had led him to the outskirts of the town. He smelled the deer's fear and confusion. It was vulnerable. If he could get close enough to it, he might have enough strength and speed left to take it down.

The wolf sniffed the air, and picked up movement among the trees to his right. The deer stood motionless in a thicket, its tail raised in warning and distress, but the wolf sensed that he was not the cause of it. He tested the air again. His tail moved between his legs, and he drew back, his ears pinned against his head. His pupils dilated, and he exposed his teeth.

The two animals, predator and prey, stood united in fear for a moment, and then retreated, the wolf heading east, the deer west. All thoughts of hunger and feeding had left the wolf. There was only the urge to run.

But he was wounded, and tired, and winter was still upon him.

* * *

A SINGLE LIGHT BURNED in Pearson's General Store &
Gunsmithery. It illuminated a table around which sat four
old men, each of them concentrating on his cards.

"Jesus," said Ben Pearson, "this is the worst hand I've
ever seen. I swear, if I hadn't watched it dealt myself I'd
never have believed it. I didn't even know cards went this
low."

Everybody ignored him. Ben Pearson could have been
holding four aces dealt by Christ himself and still he'd have
bitched. It was his version of a poker face. He'd developed
it as a way of distracting attention from his regular features,
which were so expressive as to give away his every passing
thought. Depending upon the story that one was telling,
Ben could be the best or the worst audience a man might
wish for. He was almost childlike in his transparency, or so
it seemed. Although he was now in his seventies, he had a
full head of white hair, and his face was comparatively unlined. It added to his air of youthfulness.

Pearson's General Store & Gunsmithery had been in
Ben's family for four generations in one form or another,
and yet it wasn't even the oldest business in the town of
Prosperous, Maine. An alehouse had stood on the site of
what was now the Prosperous Tap since the eighteenth
century, and Jenna Marley's Lady & Lace had been a
clothing store since 1790. The names of the town's first
settlers still resounded around Prosperous in a way that
few other such settlements could boast. Most had roots
back in Durham and Northumberland, in the northeast of
England, for that was where Prosperous's first settlers had
originally come from. There were Scotts and Nelsons and
Liddells, Harpers and Emersons and Golightlys, along with
other more singular names: Brantingham, Claxton, Stob-
bert, Pryerman, Joblin, Hudspeth. . . .

A genealogist might have spent many a profitable day scouring the town's register of births and deaths, and some had indeed journeyed this far north to investigate the history of the settlement. They were received courteously, and some cooperation was offered, but they invariably left feeling slightly dissatisfied. Gaps in the town's annals prevented full and thorough research, and making connections between the settlers of Prosperous and their ancestors back in England proved more difficult than might first have been expected, for it seemed that those families which departed for the shores of the New World had done so in their entirety, leaving few, if any, stray branches behind.

Of course, such obstacles were hardly unfamiliar to historians, whether amateur or professional, but they were frustrating nonetheless, and eventually the town of Prosperous came to be regarded as a dead end, genealogically speaking, which perfectly suited the inhabitants. They were not unusual in that part of the world in preferring to be left untroubled by strangers. It was one of the reasons their forefathers had ventured so far into the interior to begin with, negotiating treaties with the natives that held more often than not, giving Prosperous a reputation as a town blessed by the Lord, even if its inhabitants declined to allow others to share in their perceived good fortune, divinely ordained or otherwise. Prosperous did not invite, or welcome, new settlers without specific connections to the northeast of England, and marriages outside the original primary bloodlines were frowned upon until the late nineteenth century. Something of that original pioneering, self-sufficient spirit had transmitted itself down the generations to the present population of the town.

Now, in Pearson's General Store, cards were exchanged, and bets were placed. This was nickel-and-dime poker in the most literal sense, and it was a rare evening when any man went home with his pockets more than a dollar or two lighter or heavier. Still, bragging rights for the rest of the week could be gained from a good run of cards, and there had been times when Ben Pearson's fellow players had chosen to avoid his store for a couple of days in order to let Ben's triumphalism cool a little.

"I'll raise you a dime," said Calder Ayton.

Calder had worked alongside Ben Pearson for the better part of half a century, and envied him his hair. He owned a small share in the store, a consequence of a brief period of financial strife back in the middle of the last century, when some of the townsfolk had allowed their attention to wander, what with the war and all, and ancient, careful habits had been set aside for a time in the hope that they might eventually be abandoned altogether. But folk had learned the foolishness of that way of thinking, and the older inhabitants had not forgotten the lesson.

Thomas Souleby pursed his lips and gave Calder the cold eye. Calder rarely went above a nickel unless he had a straight at least, and he'd flipped his dime so fast that Thomas was certain he was holding a flush or better. They always played with one-eyed royals as wild cards, and Thomas had caught a glimpse of Calamity Jane squinting at him from Calder's hand—Thomas not viewing it as cheating if someone was careless enough to display his hand to all and sundry. It was what had made him a good businessman in his day, back when he worked in corporate acquisitions. You took whatever advantage came your way, and you milked it for all it was worth.

"I'm out," said Luke Joblin.

At sixty he was the youngest of the quartet, but also the most influential. His family had been in real estate ever since one caveman looked at another and said to himself,

"You know, his cave is much bigger than mine. I wonder if he'd see his way to moving out. And if he doesn't see his way to moving out I'll just kill him and take his cave anyway." At which point some prescient seed of the Joblin clan had spotted an opportunity to make a percentage on the deal, and perhaps prevent some bloodshed along the way.

Now Luke Joblin made sure that real estate in Prosperous stayed in the right hands, just as his father and his grandfather and his great-grandfather had done before him. Luke Joblin knew the state's zoning and land-use regulations backward and forward—not surprising, given that he'd helped write most of them—and his eldest son was Prosperous's code-enforcement officer. More than any other family, the Joblins had ensured that Prosperous retained its unique character and identity.

"The hell do you mean, you're out?" said Ben Pearson. "You barely looked at those cards before you dropped them like they was poisoned."

"I got nothing but a hand of cultch," said Luke.

"You got nearly a dollar of mine from the last eight hands," said Thomas. "Least you can do is give a man a chance to win his money back."

"What do you want me to do, just hand your money over to you? I got no cards. This is a game of strategy; you gamble when you're strong, you fold when you're weak."

"You could try bluffing," said Thomas. "You could at least make some kind of effort."

It was always like this between them. They liked each other well enough, but the pleasure each derived from the other's company was directly proportionate to the degree of pickle he could give over the course of an evening.

"I brought the whisky," Luke pointed out. "It wasn't for me, you'd be drinking Old Crow."

There were murmurs of agreement.

"Ayuh, this one's a sippa," said Calder, laying on the accent with a trowel. "Wicked good."

Each man took it in turn to provide a bottle for the weekly poker night, although it usually sufficed for two evenings, and it was a point of pride to bring along something that satisfied all tastes to a degree. Luke Joblin knew Scotch better than any of them, and that night they were drinking an eighteen-year-old from Talisker, the only distillery on the Isle of Skye. It was a little spicy for Thomas's palate, but he had to admit that it was far superior to The Glenlivet, which had been his selection some weeks earlier. Then again, Thomas had never been one for hard liquor, preferring wine. He gave the whisky a second swirl from habit, and took a small mouthful. He was starting to like it more and more. It certainly grew on a fella.

"Maybe I'll let you off this once," said Thomas.

"That's generous of you," said Luke.

In the end, Calder took the pot with a flush, just as Thomas had anticipated. Thomas was enduring a mauling that night. If things kept going the way they were, he'd have to break another dollar.

By unspoken consent, they rested for a while. Talk turned to local matters: business dealings, rumors of romances, and problems in the town that needed to be addressed. Tree roots were just about coming through the sidewalk on Main Street, and the Town Office needed a new boiler. A dispute had also arisen over the old Palmer house, with three families seeking to acquire it for their children. The Palmers, a private couple even by the town's standards, had died without issue, and represented the end of their line in Prosperous. The proceeds of their estate were to be dispersed among various charities, with a portion going also to the town's central fund. But living space was at a premium in Prosperous, and the Palmer house, though small and in need of repair, was much coveted. In any ordinary community, market forces would have been allowed to prevail, and the house would have gone to the highest bidder. Prosperous, though, didn't operate that way. The decision on the sale of the house would be made according to who was owed it, who had the best claim upon it. Discussions would be held, and a consensus reached. The family that eventually acquired the house would make some reparation to the others. Luke Joblin would get his commission, of course, but he would earn it.

In effect, the poker night functioned as an unofficial meeting of most of the board of selectmen. Only Calder Ayton didn't contribute to the discourse. Meetings bored him, and whatever Ben Pearson decided was always fine with him. Old Kinley Nowell, meanwhile, was absent on this occasion, laid up in the hospital with pneumonia. There was a general feeling that Kinley didn't have long on this earth. Possible replacements had to be considered, and Ben now raised the matter with his fellow selectmen. After a little back-and-forth, they decided that some younger blood wouldn't hurt them. They'd approach the elder Walker girl, Stacey, once the chief selectman had given her consent. Hayley Conyer—she didn't care to be called a selectwoman, didn't approve of that kind of nonsense—was not one for poker games or whisky evenings. Ben Pearson said that he would talk to Hayley in the morning and sound her out, but he told the others that he didn't anticipate any refusal, or any problems with the nomination. Stacey Walker was a clever girl and a good lawyer, and it never hurt to have lawyers on call.

Thomas Souleby wasn't so sure. He felt certain that Hayley Conyer would object, and she retained a rarely used power of veto when it came to nominations to the board. Conyer was a strong woman who preferred the company of men, and had no particular sense of obligation to others of her sex who might be a threat to her position. She wouldn't welcome the arrival of someone as young and vibrant as Stacey Walker, and Thomas believed that, in the case of the Walker girl, Conyer might well have a point. He had ambitions of his own to lead the board once Conyer was gone, whenever that might be, and had worked long and hard to ensure that he had as little competition as possible. Stacey Walker was just a mite too clever, and too ambitious, for Thomas's liking. While he frequently clashed with Conyer, he would not object to her using her veto to shoot down the Walker nomination. Someone more suitable could be found; someone more substantial, more experienced.

Someone more malleable.

Thomas stretched and took in the old store, with its curious mix of expensive artisan products alongside the regular items that you could buy for half the price in a Hannaford or a Shaw's. Ben certainly wasn't shy with his pricing, Thomas would give him that, but there was also the matter of convenience, and exchanging gossip, and supporting local businesses to consider. It was important that money stayed within the town's precincts wherever possible. Once cash started leaking out, Prosperous would be financially sound in name only. For the early settlers, the name had been part prayer, part aspiration. Now it was a reflection of the reality of the town's situation: it had the highest per capita income in Maine, a fact that might not have been immediately apparent were a visitor to judge it on appearances alone. Prosperous maintained a low profile, and did not call attention to itself.

The four men were seated at the western side of the store, where Calder had set up some tables beside a picture window that looked out on his yard and on the woods beyond. In summer there were picnic benches at which to sit, but now icy snow still lay on the grass, and the air was pierced by a damp chill that made an old man's bones hurt. To Thomas's left, a locked door led into the gun shop, and behind that was the gunsmithery itself. A tattered and yellowed sign on the door advised that a deposit of thirty dollars was required for each weapon accepted for service, with a further twenty-five levied if the weapon was presented without the required magazine. Thomas didn't even know why the sign was still in place. The only people who presented Ben Pearson with weapons to be serviced were locals, and they were hardly likely to forget that they'd left them with Ben. Similarly, if they neglected to bring along the magazine, they could just drop by with it later in the day.

Thomas's wife, Constance, used Ben's services occasionally—she had been a competitive rifle shooter for most of her life, and hadn't been far shy of Olympic standard as a young woman, although, at that level, the gap between what she could do and what was required might as well have been as deep and wide as an abyss—but she was one of the exceptions in Prosperous. Even allowing for those who hunted, the town had one of the lowest rates of gun ownership in the state. The gunsmith element of Ben Pearson's business was little more than a hobby for him. He kept only a small range of rifles and pistols for sale, mostly high-end stuff, but he seemed to enjoy the metalwork aspect of the job, the threading and fluting and jeweling. He was also reputed to make very fine custom-built stocks, if that was what floated your boat.

Thomas yawned and checked his watch. The whisky had gone to his head, and he was wishing for his bed. He glanced to his right. The light from their table illuminated only a few feet of snow on the yard outside. Beyond was darkness.

Something pale flickered in the shadows. It looked like a moth. As Thomas watched, it grew larger and larger. It took on the form of a young woman wearing a stained white dress, the color of it nearly lost against the snow, so that he thought he might almost have been dreaming her. Her feet were bare as she ran, and there were leaves caught in her dark hair. Closer and closer she came. Thomas opened his mouth to speak, but no words emerged. He rose from his chair just as the girl impacted against the glass, shaking it in its frame. Her fingernails were torn. They left trails of blood on the window.

"Help me," she cried. "Please help me."

Her words turned to clouds on the air, and the wind snatched them away and bore them into the listening woods.

III

Miles to the south, in the city of Portland, a homeless man was dying.

His name was Jude—no last name, just Jude— and he was well known both to his fellow street people and to those in law enforcement. He was not a criminal, although there were some in Portland who seemed to regard being homeless as a criminal act, punishable by the withdrawal of services and support until death took care of the problem. No, Jude had always been law-abiding, but he had been on the streets so long that he knew every nook and cranny of the city, every crack in the sidewalk, every raised brick. He listened carefully to the reports from others of his kind—the appearance of strangers among them, men of vicious demeanor, or the news of abandoned properties that had previously provided some shelter and were now being used by dealers of narcotics—and traded that information with the police. He did not do so for his own benefit, although there were times when the nights were cold and he was offered the comfort of a cell in which to rest, or even a ride to South Portland or farther afield if a cop was feeling particularly generous or bored.

Jude functioned as a kind of father figure to the homeless of Portland, and his relationship with the police allowed him to intervene on behalf of men and women who sometimes found themselves in trouble with the law for minor infractions. He also acted as a go-between for the operators of the city's homeless services, keeping an eye on individuals who were most at risk, and therefore least likely to maintain a consistent relationship with anyone who might be in a position to help them. Jude knew where everyone slept, and at any time he could name the number of homeless in the city to within a handful of people. Even the worst of them, the most violent and troubled, respected Jude. He was a man who would rather go a little hungrier himself, and share what he had with a brother or sister, than see another starve.

What Jude declined to share with others was much of his own history, and he rarely sought anything beyond the most basic assistance for his own needs. He was clearly an educated man, and the backpack he wore on his shoulders always contained a book or two. He was well versed in the great works of fiction, but preferred history, biography, and works of social commentary. He spoke French and Spanish, some Italian, and a little German. His handwrit-

ing was small and elegant, not unlike its practitioner. Jude
kept himself clean, and as neatly turned out as his situation
allowed. The Goodwill stores on Forest Avenue and out
by the Maine Mall, and the Salvation Army on Warren
Avenue, all knew his sizes by heart, and would often put
aside items that they thought he might appreciate. By the
standards of the streets, one might even have said that Jude
was something of a dandy. He rarely spoke of any family,
but it was known that he had a daughter. Of late, she had
become a topic of conversation among Jude's few intimates.
It was whispered that Jude's daughter, a troubled young
woman, had fallen off the radar again, but Jude spoke little
of her, and refused to bother the police further with his
private concerns.

Because of his efforts, and his decency, the city's advo-
cates for the homeless had tried to find Jude permanent
housing, but they soon learned that something in his
character rendered him ill suited to settling down. He
would stay in his new home for a week, or a month, and
then a social worker would respond to a complaint and
find that Jude had given up his apartment to four or five
others, and had himself returned to the streets. In winter,
he would seek a bed at the Oxford Street Shelter or, if
no such bed was available, as was often the case when
the weather turned harsh, he would lie down on a thin
mat on the floor of the nearby Preble Street community
center, or take a chair in the lobby of Portland's general-
assistance office. On such nights, with the temperature at
seventeen degrees and the wind so cold that it penetrated
his layers of wool and cotton, of newspaper and flesh,
right down to his bones, he would wonder at those who
claimed that Portland was too attractive to the homeless,
because it found a place for anyone who sought shelter.
But he would consider, too, the flaws in his own personal-

ity that rendered him unable to accept the comforts that he sought for others. He knew that this meant he would die on the streets. He was not surprised, therefore, by the fact that death had now come for him at last, but merely by the form it had taken.

He had been living in the basement of a run-down and gutted condo near Deering Oaks for a week or more. He was eating little, apart from what he could scavenge and what the shelters provided, trying to balance the need to save money with the basic requirements of staying alive.

He would be of no use to her if he died.

Was it genetic? Had he passed on his own flaw, his destructive love affair with the streets, to his only daughter? In his colder, more logical moments, he thought not. He had never had difficulties with drugs or alcohol. Substance addiction was not in his nature. His daughter, by contrast, started using shortly after Jude left home, or so her mother had told him before all communication between them ceased. His wife had died hating him, and he could hardly blame her. She would tell him that she did not know what she had done wrong, what grave offense she had given that caused her husband to leave her and their child, for she could not accept that she had done nothing. Something had broken inside him, that was all. He had walked away from everything—his job, his family, even his dog—because, had he not done so, he would have taken his own life. His was a psychological and emotional disturbance of untold, awful depth, mundane and yet tragic in its very ordinariness.

He had tried talking to his daughter, of course, but she would not listen. Why would she? Why should she take lessons in life from a man who had been unable to come to terms with happiness, with being loved? She threw his failings back in his face, as he knew she would. If he had stayed, if he had been a true father, then perhaps she too might have remained where she was, and this beast would not have taken her in its clutches and slowly drained the life from her. You did this to me, she said. You.

But he had done what he could for her, in his way. Just as he kept careful watch on those in his charge on Portland's streets, so others did the same for his daughter, or attempted to. They could not save her from herself, for she had a self-destructive urge that was kin to her father's fractured nature. Whatever had come from her mother's estate went into her arm or the arms of others, or briefly lined the pockets of boyfriends who were one step above pimps and rapists.

Now she had traveled north. He had heard reports of her in Lewiston, and Augusta, then Bangor. The news from an old homeless woman, traveling south, was that his daughter was clean and seeking somewhere to live, as a place of her own would be the first step toward finding a job.

"How did she look?" Jude asked.

"She looked well. She's pretty, you know that? Hard, but pretty."

Yes, he thought. I know that. Pretty, and more than pretty.

She is beautiful.

So he took the bus north, but by then all trace of her was gone. There was talk, though. She had been offered a job. He learned that a young woman living and working at the Tender House, a shelter for homeless mothers and their children in Bangor, had spoken with her. His daughter had seemed excited, or so Jude was told. She had money in her hand. She was going to take a shower, buy some new clothes, maybe get a haircut. There was work for her. A couple, a nice older couple, needed someone to help maintain their house and their big yard, perhaps cook a meal or two as well, or drive them places when the need arose. For the sake of their own security, and to calm any concerns that the girl might have, they told her that they'd drop by the local police department on the way to the house, just so that she could confirm that they were on the level and meant her no harm.

"They showed me a picture of their house," Jude's daughter told the young woman from the Tender House. "It's beautiful."

What was the name of this town? Jude asked his informant.

Prosperous.

Its name was Prosperous.

But when Jude traveled to Prosperous, and went to the police department, he was told that no such girl had ever passed through its doors, and when he asked on the streets of the town about his daughter he was met with professions of ignorance. Eventually, the police came for him. They drove him to the town limits, and told him not to return, but he did. The second time he got a night in a cell for his troubles, and it was different from the cells in Portland or Scarborough, because he was not there of his own volition, and the old fears came upon him. He did not like being shut in. He did not like locked doors. That was why he roamed the streets.

They drove him to Medway the next morning, and escorted him onto the bus. He was given a final warning: stay out of Prosperous. We haven't seen your daughter. She was never here. Quit bothering people, or next time you'll be up before a judge.

But he was determined not to stay away. There was something wrong in Prosperous. He felt it on that first day in the town. Living on the streets had made him sensitive to those who carried a bad seed inside them. In Prosperous, one of those seeds had germinated.

He shared none of this with others, and certainly not with the police. He found excuses to remain silent, although one in particular came more naturally than others: his daughter was a drifter, an addict. Such people routinely disappeared for a while before turning up again. Wait. Wait and see. She'll come back. But he knew that she would not return, not unless someone went looking for her. She was in trouble. He sensed it, but he could not bring himself to speak of it. His vocal cords froze on her name. He had been on the streets for too long. The illness that caused him to leave his family had left him unable to open himself up, to express weakness or fear. He was a locked box inside which tempests roiled. He was a man enshadowed by himself.

But there was one whom he trusted, one to whom he might turn: an investigator, a hunter. He worked for money, this man, and with that realization came a kind of release for Jude. This would not be charity. Jude would pay him for his time, and that payment would buy Jude the freedom he needed to tell his daughter's story.

This night, his final night, he had counted his money: the handful of notes that he had hidden in a box in the damp earth of the basement; the small savings he had entrusted to one of the social workers, reclaimed that day; and a bag of filthy bills and coins, just a small fraction of the loans that he had given out to others and now repaid at a quarter on the dollar by those who could afford to do so.

He had just over a hundred and twenty dollars, enough to get him beaten up by some, or killed by others.

Enough, he hoped, to hire the detective for a couple of hours.

BUT NOW HE WAS DYING. The rope, suspended from a ceiling beam, was tightening around his neck. He tried to kick, but his legs were being held. His arms, previously restrained by his sides, were released, and he instinctively raised his hands to the noose. His fingernails were ripped from his flesh, but he barely felt the pain. His head was exploding. He felt his bladder release, and knew that the end was coming. He wanted to cry out to her, but no words came. He wanted to tell her that he was sorry, so sorry.

The final sound that he made was an effort to speak her name.

IV

It was left to Thomas Souleby to calm the girl down. He had four daughters of his own, and they, in turn, had so far gifted him only with female grandchildren, so he had more experience in placating women than anyone else in the room. This particular woman needed more placation than most: her first act, after they had let her in through the back door of the store, was to grab the nearest knife and keep them at bay. None of Thomas's offspring had ever pulled a knife on him, although he wouldn't have put it past one or two of them during their teenage years.

"Easy, honey," he said. He stayed out of range of the knife, and spoke as softly as he could. "Easy, now. What's your name?"

"Annie," she replied. "Call the police. Please, just call the police."

"We will," he said. "But we just—"

"*Now!*" she screamed, and the sound just about busted Calder Ayton's hearing aid.

"Okay, we're calling them," said Thomas. He motioned to Ben, who already had his cell phone in hand. "But what are we supposed to tell them?"

"You tell them that some bitch and her fucker husband locked me in a basement and fattened me up like a pig for slaughter," she said. "That's what you tell them."

Thomas looked at Ben and shrugged.

"You maybe don't have to use those exact words," Thomas told him.

Ben nodded, and started dialing.

"Put it on speaker, Ben," said Thomas. "Just so Annie here knows we're on the up and up."

Ben tapped the screen on his phone and turned the volume to maximum. They all listened to it ring. On the third tone, a voice broke in.

"Chief Morland," it said.

The girl seemed to relax at the sound of the voice, but Thomas could still see her casting glances over his shoulder, staring out the picture window in the direction from which she had come. She couldn't know how long it would be before her captors noticed that she was gone and came looking for her. She didn't trust four old coots to keep her safe.

"Lucas, this is Ben Pearson over at the store. We got a girl here in some distress. She says her name is Annie, and that someone has been holding her in a basement. I'd appreciate it a whole lot if you could get here real soon."

"On my way," said the chief. "Tell her to sit tight."

The connection was cut.

"How far away is the police station?" asked Annie.

"Less than a mile, but I called the chief on his cell phone," said Ben. "He could be closer than that, or a little farther away, but this isn't a big town. It won't be long before he's here."

"Can we get you something, honey?" said Thomas. "You want water, or coffee? We got whisky, if that helps. You must be freezing. Ben, find the girl a coat."

Ben Pearson moved to the rack to get one of the men's coats. His motion brought him almost within reach of the knife, and the girl slashed at the air in warning.

"Jesus!" said Ben.

"You stay back!" she warned. "All of you, just keep back. I don't want anyone to come near me—not until the police get here, you understand?"

Thomas raised his hands in surrender.

"Anything you say, but I can see that you're shivering. Look, Ben will go to the rack and slide a coat across the floor to you. None of us will come near you, okay? Seriously, nobody here is in a hurry to get cut."

The girl considered the offer, then nodded. Ben took his big old L.L.Bean goose-down parka from the rack and slid it across the floor. The girl squatted and, never taking her eyes from the four men, slipped her left arm into the sleeve. She rose, and in one quick movement changed the knife from her right hand to her left so that she could put the parka on fully. The men remained completely still while she did so. The girl then moved sideways across the room to the poker table, poured herself a glass of the whisky, and tossed it back in one gulp. Luke Joblin looked slightly pained.

"These people who held you captive," said Thomas. "Did you get a look at them?"

"Yes."

"Do you know their names?"

"No." The girl relented, and soon the words were tumbling from her lips. "They weren't the ones who brought me here first, though. They were an older couple, David and Harriett Carpenter, if those were even their real names. They showed me some ID when we first met, but what do I know about IDs? As soon as we got to the outskirts of this shithole, they handed me over to another couple, younger than them. They were the ones who kept me in their damn basement. I know their faces. They didn't even bother to keep them hidden from me. That's how I knew they were going to kill me in the end. Others came too. I caught them looking at me through the slit in the door. I pretended to be asleep, but I saw some of their faces as well."

Thomas shook his head in disbelief, and sat down heavily. Ben Pearson looked toward the woods, just as the girl had done, waiting for figures to appear out of the gloom, hell-bent on dragging her back to captivity. Luke Joblin watched the young woman, his expression unreadable. Calder Ayton's attention was drawn to the wrinkles on his hands. He traced them with the tips of his index fingers—first the left, then the right—as though surprised to find this evidence of his aging. No further words were spoken, no more reassurances given. This was Morland's business now.

Annie walked over to the register, where she could keep an eye on the parking lot outside the store. Blue lights shone in the distance. The police were on their way. She watched the four men, but they seemed stunned into inaction. She was in no danger from them.

An unmarked Crown Vic pulled into the lot, a flashing blue light on its dashboard. Although Ben had killed the outside spots when he closed the store, there were motion-activated lights above the porch. Those lights now illuminated the lot, bathing Chief Morland in their glow as he stepped from the car.

"I feel sick," said Annie. "I need to go to the bathroom."

"The chief has just arrived, honey," said Thomas.

"It's the whisky," said the girl. "It's done something to my stomach."

She bent over, as if in pain.

"I need to puke or shit—I don't know which."

Ben didn't want her to do either in his place of business, so he directed her to a door at the rear of the store. It led into his private quarters, where he sometimes stayed the night, particularly if he was working late in the gunsmithery. His house was less than a mile away, but since the death of his wife it had felt too big and empty for him. He preferred the store. That was his place now.

"It's the second door on the left," he said. "You take your time. You're safe now."

She headed toward the back of the store, her hand over her mouth, seconds before the chief entered. He was a big man, six feet three and topping out at about two hundred pounds. He was clean-shaven, and his eyes were gray, like the cold ashes of old fires. He had been Prosperous's chief of police for nearly a decade, and had taken over the job from his father. Before that, he served his apprenticeship in the Maine State Police. That was how he always described it: "my apprenticeship." Everyone knew that Prosperous was the only place that mattered. He walked with the slightest of limps, a consequence of a car accident near Augusta back in the day. No one had ever suggested that his injured limb might affect his ability to carry out his job, and the chief had never given anyone cause to do so.

"Where is she?" he asked.

"In the bathroom," said Ben. "She wasn't feeling good."

Morland had been in Pearson's store often enough to know it nearly as well as he did his own house. He went straight through to the bathroom and knocked on the door.

"Miss?" he called. "My name is Lucas Morland, and I'm the chief of police here in Prosperous. Are you okay in there?"

There was no reply. A cold breeze flipped the ends of Morland's trousers against his shoes and legs. It was coming from under the bathroom door.

"Shit!" he said.

He stepped back, raised his right foot, and kicked hard against the lock. The lock held, but the jamb broke on the second attempt. The door opened to reveal an empty bathroom. The small window above the toilet gaped open. Morland didn't even waste time trying to look out. The girl would already be seeking the cover of darkness.

Thomas Souleby had followed behind the chief, and was almost bowled over by him as he moved back into the store.

"What is it?" he asked, but Morland didn't answer. He was trying to hide the pain in his left leg. This damn weather always played hell with it, and he'd be glad when summer came. He stomped into the parking lot and turned left at the corner of the store. Pearson's was close to the intersection of two roads; the front faced north on the main road into Prosperous, while to the west was the highway. Morland's eyesight was good, even in the dark, and he could see a figure moving fast between two copses of trees, making for the highway. The road crested a hill at Prosperous's western boundary. As he watched the girl, the lights of a truck appeared on the hill.

If she reached it, he was lost.

ANNIE RAN.

She'd been so close to safety, or so she'd thought, and

then the cop had appeared. She'd recognized him at once: the shape and size of him, but most of all the way that he limped. She'd seen him twice before. The first time was just after the handover, when she was brought to the base- ment. She'd fought against them as they carried her from the truck, and the cloth across her eyes had slipped a little. The cop had been there, supervising the operation, follow- ing behind as they took her to her cell. The second was on one of the occasions when they permitted her to shower, although they always kept her hands and feet manacled. She had glanced to her right as she left her basement cell, and caught a brief glimpse of the man with the gray eyes at the top of the stairs before the door closed. On neither oc- casion had he been in uniform, otherwise she would have known better than to let the old geezers call the cops.

The couple had kept her well fed. That, at least, was something. She had strength, perhaps more than she'd had in many years. There was no alcohol in her system, and she was clean of drugs. Her own speed surprised her.

Annie saw the truck at the same time that Morland did. If she could get to the highway in time, she could stop it and beg for a ride to another town. There was a chance that the cop might come after them, but any truck driver in his right mind would be able to see her bare, bloodied feet and her tattered nightgown, and know that something terrible had befallen her. If that wasn't enough to convince him, she was sure that her story would do the rest. He—or she, if she was lucky enough to be picked up by a woman—could take her to the cops in Bangor, or to the nearest state police troop house. The truck driver could haul her to the FBI in Washington, DC, for all Annie cared. She just wanted to get away from this godforsaken town.

The ground began to slope upward as she neared the road. She stumbled slightly as her feet hit a rock, and there was a terrible, sharp pain. She'd broken the big toe of her right foot. She was sure of it. It slowed her down, but it didn't stop her. The truck was still some distance away, but she would reach the highway long before it passed her spot. She was prepared to stand in the middle of the road and risk being hit if that was what it took. She'd rather die quickly under its wheels than be taken back to that basement.

Something pushed her from behind, and she fell to the ground. An instant later, she heard the shot, and there was a pressure in her chest, followed by a burning that set her lungs on fire. She lay on her side and tried to speak, but only blood flowed from between her lips. The truck passed barely an arm's length from where she lay, the driver oblivious of her dying. She stretched her fingers toward it, and felt the breeze of its passing. The burning inside her was no longer fiery but cold. Her hands and feet were growing numb, the ice spreading inward to the core of her being, freezing her limbs and turning her blood to crystals.

Footsteps approached, and then two men were looking down at her. One was the limping cop, the other the old man who had given her his coat. He was holding a hunting rifle in his arms. She could see the rest of his friends following behind. She smiled.

I got away. I escaped. This wasn't the ending that you wanted.

I beat you, you fuckers.

I . . .

BEN PEARSON WATCHED THE life depart the girl, her body deflating as its final breath left it. He shook his head in sorrow.

"And she was a good one too," he said. "She was

scrawny, but they were fattening her up. If we were lucky, we could have got ten years or more out of her."

Chief Morland walked to the road. There were no more vehicles coming their way. There was no chance that they would be seen. But what a mess, what a godawful mess. Somebody would answer for it.

He rejoined the others. Thomas Souleby was closest to him in height. These things mattered when you were dealing with a body.

"Thomas," he said, "you take her arms. I'll take her legs. Let's get this all cleaned up."

And together the two men carried the remains of Annie Broyer, lost daughter of the man named Jude, back to the store.

V

They saw the cars pull into their drive and knew that they were in trouble.

Chief Morland was leading, driving his unmarked Crown Vic. The dash light wasn't flashing, though. The chief wasn't advertising his presence.

The chief's car was followed by Thomas Souleby's Prius. A lot of folk in Prosperous drove a Prius or some other similarly eco-conscious car. Big SUVs were frowned upon. It had to do with the ethos of the town, and the importance of maintaining a sustainable environment in which to raise generations of children. Everybody knew the rules, unofficial or otherwise, and they were rarely broken.

As the cars pulled up outside the house, Erin gripped her husband's hand. Harry Dixon was not a tall man, or a particularly handsome one. He was overweight, his hair was receding, and he snored like a drill when he slept on his back, but he was her man, and a good one too. Sometimes she wished that they had been blessed with children, but it was not to be. They had waited too late after marriage, she often thought, and by the time it became clear that the actions of nature alone would not enable her to conceive they had settled into a routine in which each was enough for the other. Oh, they might always have wished for more, but there was a lot to be said for "enough."

But these were troubled times, and the idyllic middle age they had imagined for themselves was under threat. Until the start of the decade, Harry's construction company had weathered the worst of the recession by cutting back on its full-time employees and paring quotes to the bone, but 2011 had seen the company's virtual collapse. It was said that the state had lost forty-eight hundred jobs in March of that year alone, which contributed to making Maine the nation's leader in lost jobs. They'd both read about the arguments between the Maine Department of Labor and the Maine Center for Economic Policy, the latter basing its figures on higher Bureau of Labor Statistics job loss figures that the former refuted. As far as the Dixons were concerned, that was just the state's Department of Labor trying to sweep the mess under the carpet. It was like telling a man that his feet are dry when he can feel the water lapping at his chin.

Now Harry's company was little more than a one-man operation, with Harry quoting for small jobs that he could complete with cheap labor, and bringing in skilled contractors by the hour as he needed them. They could still pay their mortgage, just about, but they'd cut back on a lot of luxuries, and they did more and more of their buying outside Prosperous.

Erin's half sister, Dianne, and her surgeon husband had helped them out with a small lump sum. They were both hospital consultants, and were doing okay. They could afford to lend a hand, but it had hurt the couple's pride to approach them for a loan—a loan, what's more, that was unlikely to be repaid anytime soon.

They had also tapped the town's discretionary fund, which was used to support townsfolk who found themselves in temporary financial trouble. Ben Pearson, who was regarded as one of the board's more approachable members, had taken care of the details, and the money— just over two thousand dollars—had helped the Dixons out a little, but Ben had made it clear that it would have to be paid back, in cash or in kind. If it wasn't, the board would start delving more deeply into their situation, and if the board started snooping it might well find out about Dianne. That was why the Dixons had agreed, however reluctantly, to keep the girl. It would serve as repayment of the loan, and keep their relationship with Dianne a secret.

Erin had only discovered her half sister's existence some three years earlier. Erin's father had left Prosperous when she was little more than an infant, and her mother had subsequently remarried—to a cousin of Thomas Souleby's, as it happened. Her father hadn't been heard from again, and then, at the end of 2009, Dianne had somehow tracked Erin down, and a tentative if genuine affection had sprung up between them. It seemed that their father had created a whole new identity for himself after he left Prosperous, and he never mentioned the town to his new wife or to their child. It was only following his death, and the death of her mother, that Dianne had come across documents among her father's possessions that explained the truth about his background. By then she was on her second marriage—to a man who, coincidentally or through the actions of fate, lived in the same state that had spawned her father, and not too far from the town and the life that he had fled.

Erin had professed complete ignorance of the reasons that their father might have gone to such lengths to hide his identity, but when Dianne persisted she hinted at some affair with a woman from Lewiston, and her father's fear of retribution from his wife's family. None of it was true, of course—well, none of the stuff about the affair. Her father's fear of retribution was another matter. Nevertheless, she made it clear to Dianne that it would be for the best if she kept her distance from Prosperous and didn't go delving into the past of their shared father.

"Old towns have long memories," Erin told Dianne. "They don't forget slights."

And Dianne, though bemused, had consented to leaving Prosperous to its own business, aided in part by her half sister's willingness to share with her what she knew of their father's past, even if, unbeknownst to Dianne, Erin had carefully purged all the information she offered of any but the most innocuous details.

So Erin and Harry were the poor relatives, bound to Dianne and her husband by the shade of a father. They were content to play that role, though, and to keep the existence of Dianne and her husband hidden from the citizens of Prosperous. Unspoken between them was the fact that they might have need of Dianne at some point in the future, and not only for money, for the Dixons wanted nothing more than to leave Prosperous, and that would be no easy task. The board would want to know why. The board would investigate. The board would almost certainly find out about Dianne, and the board would wonder what secrets Erin Dixon might have shared with her half sister, the daughter of a man who had turned his back on the town, who had stolen its money and, perhaps, whispered of the deal it had made to secure itself.

Keeping all their fears from Dianne and her husband wasn't easy. To further complicate matters, Harry and Erin had asked that the money be paid in cash. She could still remember the look on Dianne's face: puzzlement, followed by the dawning realization that something was very wrong here.

"What kind of trouble are you two in?" Dianne asked them, as her husband poured the last of the wine and gave them the kind of disapproving look he probably reserved for patients who neglected to follow his postoperative advice and then seemed surprised when they started coughing blood. His name was Magnus Madsen, and he was of Danish extraction. He insisted on the pronunciation of his first name as "Mau-nus," without sounding the "g," and had resigned himself to correcting Harry's literal pronunciation whenever they met. Harry just couldn't seem to manage "Mau-nus," though. That damned "g" kept intruding. Anyway, it wasn't as if Magnus Madsen was fresh off a Viking longship. There were rocks that hadn't been in Maine as long as the Madsens. His family had been given plenty of time to learn to speak English properly, and drop whatever airs they'd brought with them from the Old Country.

"We'd just prefer it if people in Prosperous didn't know that we were having serious difficulties," said Harry. "It's a small town, and if word got out it might affect my chances of bidding successfully for work. If you pay us in cash, then we can make pretty regular lodgments into our account until we find our feet again, and nobody will be any the wiser."

"But surely any dealings you have with your bank are entirely confidential," said Magnus. "Couldn't you ask your bank manager for an extended line of credit? I mean, you're still working, and you must have paid off the bulk of your mortgage by now. That's a nice house you have, and it's worth a fair sum, even in these difficult times. It's hardly like asking for an unsecured loan."

There was so much that Harry wanted to say at that point, but it could have been summarized as "You and I do not live in similar worlds." Those words "unsecured loan" bit at him as well, because that was precisely what they were asking of Magnus and Dianne, but mostly he knew that Magnus had no conception of the way the town of Prosperous worked. If he did, it would turn his hair white.

And, shortly after that, he'd be dead.

Magnus and Dianne gave them the money in the end, and Harry used it to pump up the deposits being made at the bank, but the borrowed cash was almost gone now, and he didn't think that his in-laws could be tapped again. In any normal situation, Harry and Erin would have sold up and moved on. Sure, they'd take a bit of a hit on the house, but with a little luck they might come out of it with a high five- or low six-figure sum once the mortgage was paid off. They could start again, maybe rent for a while until the economy recovered.

But this wasn't a normal situation. They knew that they probably weren't the only ones in the town who were suffering; there were rumors, and more than rumors. Even Prosperous wasn't entirely immune from the vagaries of the economy, just as, throughout its history, it had never been completely protected from conflict, or financial turmoil, or the wrath of nature. Yet it had always been better protected than most. The town took steps to ensure that this was the case.

"What do you think happened?" Erin now whispered to her husband, as they watched the men approach. "Did she get away?"

"No," said Harry. "I don't believe she did."

If she had escaped, these others wouldn't be here on their doorstep. There were only two possibilities. The first was that the girl had been captured before she could leave Prosperous, in which case the chief was going to be mad as hell with them for failing to keep her locked up, and they could only hope that the girl had sense enough to keep any suspicions about the ease of her escape to herself. The second possibility was that she was dead, and Harry found himself wishing that the latter was true. It would be easier for all of them.

They didn't give the chief time to knock on the door. Harry opened it to find Morland with his fist raised, and he flinched instinctively in anticipation of the blow. There was a doorbell, but it wouldn't have been like Lucas Morland to use it under the circumstances. Psychologically, a sharp knock was far more effective.

Harry stepped aside to admit them, the chief with his face set hard and Thomas Souleby looking more disappointed than angry, as though Harry and Erin were errant teenagers who had failed some crucial parental test.

"We know why you're here," said Harry.

"If you know why we're here," said the chief, "then why didn't you call to tell us about the girl?"

"We only just found out she was gone," said Erin. "We were about to call, but—"

She looked to her husband for help.

"But we were frightened," he finished for her.

"Frightened of what?"

"That we'd let you down—that we'd let the whole town down. We knew you'd be angry."

"Did you try looking for her?"

"Sure," said Harry. "I mean, no, not yet, but we were about to. See, I'd put my boots on." He pointed at his feet, which were, indeed, booted. He never wore footwear in the house—Erin bitched about the carpets—but he'd put his boots on that night, just in case it all went to hell. "I was ready to head out when you arrived."

"Did you find her?" asked Erin. "Please tell me that you found her."

She was good, Harry gave her that. It was just what she should have said, just what the chief would have expected to hear.

Morland didn't reply. He was leaving them to stew for a while, waiting to see what they might reveal to him. They'd have to step carefully now. What would the girl have said when she was caught? What would she have told them?

Nothing, Harry figured. She'd have kept quiet. That was why he and Erin had simply left the doors mostly unsecured and gone about their business. If the girl was caught, they'd have deniability.

Morland leaned against the kitchen table and folded his arms.

"How did it happen?" he asked.

"It was my fault," said Erin. "I left the door unlocked. I didn't mean to. Sometimes, if I knew she was asleep, I'd just shoot the bolt and let the shackle hang loose on the mechanism. I was tired, though, and I may have forgotten to put the padlock on. She must have worked the bolt free from the inside. I found a piece of cloth on the floor that she could have used. Maybe she tore it from her nightgown."

"How did she know that you hadn't locked the door?" asked Souleby.

Damn you, thought Harry. I always felt you were too

smart for anyone's good. Souleby, the miserable bastard, reminded Harry of an old stork: all beak and limbs.

"I don't know," said Erin. "My guess is that she never gave up trying to escape. She probably tested the door every time I left the room, and this time she just got lucky."

"Got lucky, huh?" said Morland.

He permitted himself a little smile.

"Show me the door," he said. "Explain it all to me again."

They went down to the basement, and Erin showed him the cell, and the bolt, and the padlock. Just as she had told him, there was a piece of white material on the floor, stained with grease from the bolt. The chief examined it, and toyed with the bolt and the padlock for a while.

"Get inside," he said to Erin.

"What?"

"Go on. Get inside that cell." He handed her the strip of cloth. "And take this with you."

She did as she was told. The chief closed the door on her and slid the bolt, but did not secure it with the padlock.

"Now," he said, "open it."

The saliva dried up in Harry's mouth. He would have prayed, but he had long since stopped believing in God. The continued existence of Prosperous was one of the strongest arguments he could come up with against the possibility of a benevolent deity watching over humankind.

After a couple of attempts, Erin managed to get the cloth through the gap between the door and the frame, and over the bolt. There was, though, no way that she could pull the other end back in. Harry closed his eyes. This was it.

A thin shaft of broken wood poked through the gap, caught the strip of cloth, and pulled it back through to the other side of the cell door. Slowly, Erin began to twist it back and forth. The bolt moved: not by much, but it moved. With some perseverance, it would be only a matter of time before Erin managed to unlock the door from the inside, as she claimed the girl had done.

Morland stared at Harry. Despite what he had witnessed, Harry knew that the chief still didn't quite believe what he'd been told. If he was expecting Harry to crack, though, he would be disappointed, unless he resorted to torture, and even Morland was probably above that.

"Let her out," he told Souleby, and Souleby pulled the bolt.

Erin stepped out of the cell, flushed but triumphant.

"Where did you get the wood?" said the chief.

"It was on the floor by the girl's bed," she said. "I saw it when I was trying to figure out how she did it."

She handed him the fragment of pine. The chief tested it with his finger, then went to the bed and found the spot from which it had been taken.

"Looks new," he said.

"She hasn't been gone but an hour," said Erin.

"Uh-huh." Chief Morland took the stick in both hands and snapped it. It was the first outward demonstration that he had given of the rage he was feeling.

"You still haven't told us if you found her," said Harry.

"Oh, we found her all right," said the chief.

"Where is she?"

"In the trunk of my car."

"Is she—?"

"Is she what?"

"Is she . . . dead?"

The chief didn't answer immediately. He closed his eyes and wiped his face with his right hand. His shoulders sank. That was when Harry knew that they were okay, for now.

"Yes, she's dead," said Morland finally. "Just not the right kind of dead. You got a shovel?"

"Sure," said Harry. "In my toolshed."

"Good," said the chief. "Because you're going to help me bury her."

VI

I had a ticket for the 8:55 P.M. flight with US Airways out of Philadelphia, if I chose to use it, but I realized that I would either kill myself trying to make it or end up with a ticket for speeding. Neither possibility particularly appealed to me, so I changed my flight to 9:30 A.M. the following morning and checked into a motel off Bartram Avenue. I had dinner in a bar that was one step up from eating food off the street, but I didn't care. Once the adrenaline had stopped flowing after the events in Newark, I experienced a comedown that left me shaking and nauseated. It didn't matter what I ate: it would have tasted foul anyway, but I thought I needed something in my stomach. In the end, I left most of the food on the plate, and what I ate didn't stay in my system for long once I was back in my room.

In truth, such reactions were becoming increasingly common as the years went on. I suppose I had always been frightened as I faced situations like that night's—anyone who has found himself looking down the barrel of a gun, or confronting the possibility of injury or death, and claims to have done so without fear is either a liar or insane—but the more often you do it and survive, the more aware you become that the odds are inevitably swinging against you. If cats could count, they'd start getting nervous around the time they put paid to their fifth life.

I also wanted to watch Sam, my daughter, grow up. She was long past those early years when children, though cute, don't do a whole lot except babble and fall over, much like a certain type of really old person. I found her endlessly fascinating, and regretted the fact that I was no longer with Rachel, her mother, although I didn't think Rachel was about to move back in just so that I could spend more time with Sam. Then again, I didn't want Rachel to move back in, so the feeling was mutual. Still, with Rachel and Sam in Vermont, and me in Portland, arranging to spend time with my daughter took some planning. I supposed that I could always move to Vermont, but then I'd have to start voting socialist, and finding excuses to secede from the Union. Anyway, I liked Portland, and being close to the sea. Staring out over Vermont's Lake Bomoseen wasn't quite the same thing.

I checked my cell phone messages as I lay on the bed. There was only one, from a man in Portland named Jude. He was one of a handful of the local street folk who'd proved helpful to me in the past, by providing either information or the occasional discreet surveillance service, as people tended not to notice the homeless, or pretended not to. Naturally there was no callback number for Jude. Instead, he had suggested leaving a message with the folk at the Portland Help Center or on the bulletin board at the Amistad Community on State Street to let him know when I might be available to meet.

I hadn't seen Jude around in a while, but then I hadn't really been looking out for him. Like most of Portland's homeless, he did his best to stay off the streets in winter. To do otherwise was to risk being found frozen in a doorway.

Me, I wasn't doing so badly. Work had picked up over the winter because I'd developed a nice sideline in process serving. It wasn't glamorous work, but it paid reasonably well, and occasionally required the exercise of more than a handful of brain cells. The day before I headed down to Newark to join Angel and Louis, I'd cashed a check for two thousand dollars, including a goodwill bonus payment, for just one job. The subject of the subpoena was an investment analyst named Hyram P. Taylor, who was involved in the initial stages of serious and hostile divorce proceedings with his wife, who was represented by my lawyer—and, for the most part, my friend—Aimee Price. Hyram was such a compulsive fornicator that even his own lawyer had privately acknowledged the possibility of his client's possessing a penis shaped like a corkscrew, and eventually his wife had just become tired of the humiliation. As soon as she filed for divorce, Hyram set about hiding all records relating to his wealth, and moving said wealth as far as possible from his wife's reach. He even abandoned his office in South Portland and tried to go to ground, but I tracked him down to the apartment of one of his girlfriends, a woman called Brandi, who, despite having a stripper's name, worked as an accountant in New Hampshire.

The problem was that Hyram wouldn't so much as pick up a piece of paper from the street for fear that it might be attached to an unseen piece of string ending in the hand of a process server. He didn't go anywhere without Brandi in tow, and she was the one who paid cash for newspapers, groceries, and drinks in bars. Hyram didn't put his hand on anything if he could help it. He probably had Brandi check him before he peed in the morning, just in case someone had attached a subpoena to his manhood while he slept.

His weakness—and they all have a weakness—was his car. That was how I found him. He drove a six-liter black

Bentley Flying Spur Speed: ten miles to the gallon in the city, 0–60 in 4.8 seconds, and $200,000 worth of vehicle, at the very least. It was his pride and joy, which was probably why he stood up so suddenly that he spilled coffee over himself when I walked into the Starbucks on Andrews Road and asked if anyone owned a hell of a nice Bentley, because I'd just knocked off the wing mirror on the driver's side.

Hyram wasn't a slim man, but he could move fast when the need arose, even with hot coffee scalding his thighs. He went past me at full sail and arrived at his car to find that, sure enough, the mirror was hanging on to the body of the car only by wires. It had been harder to knock off than I'd anticipated, requiring two blows from a hammer. The Bentley may have been expensive, but it was clearly built well.

"I'm real sorry," I told him when I found him stroking the car as though it were a wounded animal that he was trying to console. "I just wasn't looking. If it's any help, I got a brother who runs an auto shop. He'd probably give you a good deal."

Hyram seemed to be having trouble speaking. His mouth just kept opening and closing without a sound. I could see Brandi hurrying across the parking lot, still trying to struggle into her coat while juggling her coffee and Hyram's jacket. Hyram had left her in his wake, but she'd be with us within seconds. I needed to hook Hyram before she got here, and while he was still in shock.

"Look," I said, "here are my insurance details, but if you could see your way clear to just letting me pay cash to cover the damages I'd surely be grateful."

Hyram reached out for the paper in my hand without thinking. I heard Brandi cry out a warning to him, but by then it was too late. His fingers had closed on the subpoena.

"Mr. Taylor," I said, "it's my pleasure to inform you that you've just been served."

It said a lot about Hyram P. Taylor's relationship with his car that he still seemed more upset by the damage to it than he was by being in receipt of the subpoena, but that situation didn't last long. He was swearing at me by the time I got to my own car, and the last I saw of him was Brandi flinging her coffee at his chest and walking away in tears. I even felt a little sorry for Hyram. He was a jerk, but he wasn't a bad guy, whatever his wife might have thought of him. He was just weak and selfish. Badness was something else. I knew that better than most. After all, I'd just burned a man's house down.

I made a note to get in touch with Jude, then turned out the light. The post-adrenaline dip had passed. I was now just exhausted. I slept soundly as, back in Portland, Jude twisted on his basement rope.

VII

Harry Dixon and Chief Lucas Morland drove to the burial site in Morland's car. There wasn't a whole lot of conversation between them. The last body Harry had seen was that of his own mother, and she was eighty-five when she passed on. She died in a hospice in the middle of an October night. The call had come to Harry at 3 A.M., informing him that his mother's last hours on earth were approaching and perhaps he might like to be with her when she went, but by the time he got to her she was already dead. She was still warm, though. That was what Harry remembered the most, the nurse telling him that he ought to touch her, to feel his mother's warmth, as though warmth equated to life and there might still be something of her inside that shell. So he placed his hand on her shoulder, for that appeared to be what was expected of him, and felt the heat gradually leave her, the spirit slowly departing until at last there was nothing left but cold.

He had never, he realized, seen anyone who wasn't supposed to be dead. No, that wasn't right, but he couldn't put it any better to himself. It had been his mother's time to go. She was sick, and old. Her final years had mostly been spent sleeping, misremembering, or forgetting entirely. Only once in her last months of life could he recall her speaking with any lucidity, and then he had just been thankful that they were alone together in the room. He wondered if, in her dementia, she had spoken of such matters to the nurses. If she did, they must have dismissed them as the ravings of an old woman on her way to the grave, for nobody had ever mentioned them to him. Those words came back to him now.

"I saw them do it once," she had said, as he sat beside her in an uncomfortable hospice chair. "I wanted to look. I wanted to know."

"Really?" he replied, only half listening, practiced in the art of nodding and ignoring. He was thinking of his business, and money, and how it had all gone so wrong for Erin and him when it continued to go well for so many others, both within and beyond the boundaries of Prosperous.

After all, he and Erin played their part in the business of the town. They did as they were asked, and did not complain. How come they were suffering? Weren't the benefits of living in Prosperous supposed to be distributed equally among all? If not, what was the point of being part of the community in the first place?

And now his mother was rambling again, dredging up some inconsequential detail from the mud of her memories.

"I saw them take a girl. I saw them tie her up and leave her, and then—"

By now he was listening to her. Oh, he was listening for sure, even as he cast a glance over his shoulder to make sure that the door was closed.

"What?" he said. "Then what?" He knew of that which she spoke. He had never seen it himself, and didn't want to see it. You weren't supposed to ask; that was one of the rules. If you wanted to be certain, you could become a selectman, but selectmen in Prosperous were chosen carefully. You didn't put yourself forward. You waited to be approached. But Harry didn't want to be approached. In a way, the less he knew, the better. But that didn't stop him wondering.

"Then—"

His mother closed her eyes. For a moment he thought that she might have fallen asleep, but as he watched a tear crept from her right eye and her body began to shake. She was crying, and he had never seen his mother cry, not even when his father died. She was a hard woman. She was old Prosperous stock, and they didn't show frailty. If they had been frail, the town would not have survived.

Survived, and bloomed.

"Mom," he said. "Mom."

He took her right hand in his, but she shook it away, and

only then did he realize that she wasn't crying but laughing, giggling at the memory of what she had witnessed. He hated her for it. Even in her slow dying, she had the capacity to horrify him. She stared at him, and she could see by his face how appalled he was.

"You were always weak," she said. "Had your brother lived, he would have been stronger. He would have become a selectman. The best of your father's seed went into him. Whatever was left dribbled into you."

His brother had died in the womb three years before Harry was born. There had been a spate of miscarriages, stillbirths, and crib deaths during the same period, a terrible blight upon the town. But the board of selectmen had taken action, and Prosperous had been blessed with only healthy, live children for many years thereafter. Harry's mother had never ceased to speak of his dead brother, though. Earl: that was the name she had given him, a melancholy echo of the status he might have attained had he lived. He was the Lost Earl. His royal line had died with him.

There were times in her dotage when Harry's mother called him Earl, imagining, in her madness, a life for a son who had never existed, a litany of achievements, a great song of his triumphs. Harry suffered them in silence, just as he had endured them throughout his life. That was why, when his mother's end approached at last, he had left Erin in bed, put on his clothes, and driven for two hours to get to the hospice on a miserable fall night to be with her. He simply wanted to be certain that she was dead, and few things in their relationship had given him greater pleasure than feeling the warmth leave her body until just the withered husk of her remained. Only consigning her to the flames of the crematorium had been more rewarding.

"You still awake there?" said Morland.

"Yes," said Harry. "I'm awake."

He didn't look at the chief as he spoke. He saw only his own reflection in the glass. I resemble my mother, he thought. In Prosperous, we all look like our parents, and sometimes we look like the children of other folks' parents too. It's the gene pool. It's too small. By rights it shouldn't be deep enough to drown a kitten, and every family should have a drooling relative locked away in an attic. I guess we're just blessed, and he smiled so hard, and so bleakly, at his choice of the word "blessed" that he felt his bottom lip crack.

"You're very quiet," said the chief.

"I never had to bury anyone before."

"Me neither."

Now Harry did look at him.

"You serious?" he said.

"I'm a cop, not an undertaker."

"You mean nothing like this has ever happened before?"

"Not to my knowledge. Seems this may be the first time."

It didn't make Harry feel any better. There would be repercussions. This trip with the chief was only the beginning.

"You didn't tell me what happened to the girl," said Harry.

"No, I didn't." The chief didn't speak again for a time, stringing Harry along. Then: "Ben Pearson had to shoot her."

"Had to?"

"There was a truck coming. If she'd stopped it—well, we would have had an even more difficult situation than the one we're currently in."

"What would you have done?" asked Harry.

The chief considered the question.

"I'd have tried to stop the truck, and I'd have been forced to kill the driver."

He turned his gray eyes on Harry for a moment.

"And then I'd have killed you, and your wife too."

Harry wanted to vomit, but he fought the urge. He could taste it at the back of his throat, though. For the first time since he had gotten into the car with Morland, he felt frightened. They were in the darkness out by Tabart's Pond, just one of many locations around Prosperous that was named after the original English settlers. There were no Tabarts left now in Prosperous. No Tabarts, no Mabsons, no Quartons, no Poyds. They'd all died early in the history of the settlement, and the rest had seemed set to follow them before the accommodation was reached. Now Harry was about to dig a grave in a place named after the departed, the lost, and a grave could accommodate two as easily as one.

"Why?" said Harry. "Why would you have killed us?"

"For forcing me to do something that I didn't want to do. For making life harder than it already is. For screwing up. As an example to others. You take your pick."

The chief made a right turn onto a dirt road.

"Maybe I'll have another look at that lock on your basement when we're done," he said. "Something about all this doesn't sit quite right with me. Kinda like the lock itself, it seems."

He grinned emptily at Harry. The beams of the headlights caught bare trees, and icy snow, and—

"What was that?" said Harry. He was looking back over his right shoulder.

"Huh? I didn't see nothing."

"There was something there. It was big, like an animal of some kind. I saw its eyes shining."

But the chief was paying him no attention. As far as Morland was concerned, Harry's "something" was just a ruse, a clumsy attempt to distract him from the business of the basement door. But Morland wasn't a man to be turned so easily. He planned to walk both Harry and his wife through their versions of the escape. He'd do it over and over until he was either satisfied with their innocence or convinced of their guilt. He'd been against entrusting the girl to them from the start, but he was overruled. He wasn't a selectman, even though he could sit in on the board's meetings. No chief of police had ever been a selectman. It was always felt that it was better to have the law as an instrument of the board's will.

The board had wanted to test Harry and Erin Dixon. Concerns had been raised about them—justifiable concerns, it now appeared. But it was a big step from doubting the commitment of citizens of Prosperous to taking direct action against them. In all the town's history, only a handful of occasions had arisen when it became necessary to kill one of their own. Such acts were dangerous, and risked sowing discontent and fear among those who had doubts, or were vulnerable to outside influence.

Morland now regretted telling Harry Dixon that he might have killed his wife and him. He didn't like Dixon, and didn't trust him. He'd wanted to goad him, but it was a foolish move. He'd have to reassure him. He might even have to apologize and put his words down to his justifiable anger and frustration.

But the test wasn't over. The test had only just begun. Harry Dixon would have to make amends for his failings, and Morland was pretty sure that Harry Dixon wouldn't like what that would entail, not one little bit.

"So what was it that you thought you saw?" said Morland.

"I believe I saw a wolf."

VIII

The ground was hard. Not that Harry should have been surprised; he'd lived in Penobscot County long enough to have no illusions about winter. On the other hand, he'd never had to dig a grave in any season, and this was like breaking rocks.

Morland left him to his own devices at the start. The chief sat in his car, the driver's door open but the heat on full blast, and smoked a series of cigarettes, carefully stubbing each one out in the ashtray. After a while, though, it became clear that Harry would be hacking at the ground until summer if he was forced to dig the grave alone, and so Morland opened the trunk of his car and removed a pickax from it. From where he stood, Harry caught a glimpse of something wrapped in transparent plastic sheeting, but he didn't look for long. He figured he'd have seen more than enough of it by the time the night was over.

Morland broke the ground with the pickax, and Harry cleared the earth away with the shovel. They worked without speaking. They didn't have any energy to spare. Despite the cold, Harry felt sweat soaking into his shirt.

He removed his coat and was about to hang it on the low branch of a tree when Morland told him to put it in the car instead. Harry assumed it was because the car would keep his coat warm, until Morland made it clear that Harry's health and well-being were the last things on his mind.

"With luck, she'll stay down here and never be found," said Morland. "But you never know. Prepare for the worst and you won't be disappointed. I've seen crime scene investigators put a man behind bars for the rest of his life on the basis of a thread left on a branch. We take no chances."

Morland wasn't concerned about leaving tracks on the ground. It was too hard for that. Neither was he worried about being seen. Nobody lived nearby, and anyone who might be passing would, in all likelihood, be a citizen of Prosperous, and would know better than to go sticking a nose into Chief Morland's affairs even if he or she was foolish enough to come and investigate in the first place. Anyway, by now news of what had happened to the girl would have been communicated to those who needed to know. The roads around Prosperous would be quiet tonight.

They continued to dig. When they got to three feet, they were both too exhausted to go farther. The chief was a big, strong man, but Harry Dixon was no wilting flower either; if anything, he'd grown fitter over the previous year, now that he was required to be more active on his construction sites than he had been in decades. That was one of the few good things to come out of the financial mess in which he found himself. He had spent so long supervising, and ordering, and taking care of paperwork, that he had almost forgotten the pleasure of actual build-ing, and the satisfaction that came with it—that, and the blisters.

Morland went to the car and took a thermos of coffee

from the back seat. He poured a cup for Harry, and drank his own directly from the neck. Together they watched the moon.

"Back there, you were kidding about the wolf, right?" said Morland.

Harry was wondering if he might have been mistaken. At one time, there had been wolves all over Maine—grays and easterns and reds—and the state had enacted wolf bounties until 1903. As far as he could recall, the last known wolf killing in the state was back in 1996. He remembered reading about it in the newspapers. The guy had killed it thinking it was a large coyote, but the animal weighed more than eighty pounds, twice the size of the average coyote, and had the markings of a wolf, or a wolf hybrid. There had been nothing since then, to his knowledge: sightings and rumors, maybe, but no proof.

"It was a big animal, and it had a doglike head. That's all I can say for sure."

Morland went to light another cigarette, but found that the pack was empty. He crushed it and put it carefully into his pocket.

"I'll ask around," he said. "Wouldn't be a wolf, but if there's a coyote in the woods we'd best let folk know, tell them to keep a watch on their dogs. You done?"

Harry finished the last of the coffee and handed the cup back to the chief. Morland screwed it back on and tossed the thermos to the floor of the car.

"Come on, then," said Morland. "Time to put her in the ground."

THE TRUNK LIGHT SHONE on the plastic, and the girl inside it. She was lying on her back, and her eyes were closed. That was a mercy, at least. The exit wound in her chest was massive, but there was less blood than Harry might have expected. The chief seemed to follow the direction of his thoughts.

"She bled out on the snow of Ben's yard," he said. "We had to shovel it up and spread some more around to hide what we'd done. Take her legs. I'll lift from the head."

It was difficult to get her out of the trunk. She hadn't been a big girl, which was why they'd decided to fatten her up first, but for the first time Harry understood what was meant by "dead weight." The heavy-duty plastic was slippery, and Morland struggled to get a grip. Once she was out of the car, he had to drop her on the ground, put his foot under her to raise her upper body, and then wrap his arms around her chest to carry her, holding her to him like a sleeping lover. They stood to the right of the grave, and on the count of three tossed her in. She landed awkwardly, in a semi-seated position.

"You'd best get down there and straighten her," Morland told Harry. "If the hole was deeper I'd be inclined to let it go, but it's shallow as it is. We don't want the ground to sink and have her head peeping up like a gopher's."

Harry didn't want to get into the grave, but it didn't seem as though he had much choice. He eased himself down, then squatted to grip the ends of the plastic. As he did so, he looked at the girl. Her head was slightly lower than his, so that she seemed to be staring up at him. Her eyes were open. He must have been mistaken when he first saw her lying in the trunk. Perhaps it had been the reflection of the internal light, or his own tiredness, but he could have sworn . . .

"What's the problem?" said Morland.

"Her eyes," said Harry. "Do you recall if her eyes were open or closed?"

"What does it matter? She's dead. Whether we cover her up with her eyes wide open or squeezed shut is going to make no difference to her or to us."

He was right, thought Harry. He shouldn't even have been able to see her eyes so clearly through the plastic, but it was as though there was a light shining inside her head, illuminating the blue of her irises. She looked more alive now than she had in the basement.

He shook the thought from his head and pulled sharply on the plastic, dragging the girl's body flat. He didn't want to see her face again, so he turned away from it. He'd tried. She'd been given a better chance than any of the others, of that he was certain. It wasn't his fault that Ben Pearson had put an end to her hopes.

Suddenly, all the strength was gone from his body. He couldn't haul himself from the grave. He could barely raise his arms. He looked up at Morland. The chief had the pickax in his hands.

"Help me up," said Harry. But the chief didn't move.

"Please," said Harry. His voice cracked a little, and he despised himself for his weakness. His mother was right: he was half a man. If he'd been gifted with real courage, he'd have put the girl in his car, driven her to the state police in Bangor, and confessed everything to them, or at least dropped her off in the center of the city, where she'd be safe. Standing in the grave, he imagined a scenario in which the girl agreed to keep quiet about what had occurred, but it fell apart as soon as he saw himself returning to Prosperous to explain her absence. No, he'd done the best that he could for her. Anything more would have damned the town. Then again, it was already as close to damnation as made no difference.

He closed his eyes and waited for the impact of the pickax on his head, but it never came. Instead, Morland grabbed Harry's right hand, leaned back, and their combined strength got him out of the grave.

Harry sat on the ground and put his head in his hands.

"For a second, I thought you were going to leave me down there," he said.

"That would be too easy," said Morland. "Besides, we're not done yet."

And Harry knew that he wasn't referring to the filling in of the grave alone.

THE GIRL WAS GONE, covered by the earth. The ground had clearly been dug up, but Morland knew that whatever remained of the winter snows to come would take care of that. When the thaw came in earnest, the ground would turn to mire. As it dried, all traces of their activity would be erased. He just hoped that they'd buried the girl deep enough.

"Shit!" he said.

"What is it?" said Harry.

"We probably should have taken her out of the plastic. Might have helped her to rot quicker."

"You want to dig her up again?"

"No, I do not. Come on, time to go."

He wrapped the blade of the shovel and the head of the pickax in plastic bags, to keep the dirt off the trunk of his car. Tomorrow he'd clean it inside and out, just to be sure.

Harry had not moved from his place beside the grave.

"I have a question," he said.

Morland waited for him to continue.

"Isn't there a chance that she might be enough?" said Harry.

Morland might have called the look on Harry's face hopeful, if the use of the word "hope" weren't an obscenity under such circumstances.

"No," said Morland.

"She's dead. We killed her. We've given her to the earth. Why not? Why can't she be enough?"

Chief Morland closed the trunk before he replied.

"Because," he said, "she was dead when she went into the ground."

IX

It was just after five on the evening after my return to Portland when I arrived at the Great Lost Bear on Forest Avenue. The bar was buzzing, as it always was on Thursdays. Thursday was showcase night, when the Bear invited a craft brewery to let folks taste its wares, always at a discount and always with a raffle at the end. It really didn't take much to keep customers loyal, but it always amazed me that so many businesses couldn't work up the energy to make the minimal extra effort required.

I found Dave Evans, the Bear's owner, marshaling the troops for the assault to come. I hadn't worked there in a while. Like I said, business had been good for me in recent months, maybe because, like the Bear, I tended to go the extra mile for my clients. In addition, some ongoing litigation relating to the purchase of my grandfather's old house on Gorham Road had been settled in my favor, and a lump sum had found its way into my accounts. I was solvent, and likely to remain so in the foreseeable future. Still, I liked to keep my hand in at the Bear, even if it was only once or twice a month. You hear a lot from people in bars.

Admittedly, most of it is useless, but the occasional nugget of information creeps through. Anyway, my presence would allow Dave to take the rest of the night off, although he was strangely reluctant to leave.

"Your buddies are here," he said.

"I have buddies?"

"You used to. I'm not sure if the word still applies where those two are concerned."

He indicated a corner of the bar that was now looking significantly smaller than it usually did, thanks to the addition of two massive men in polyester jogging suits: the Fulci brothers. I hadn't seen them since Jackie Garner's funeral. His death had hit them hard. They had been devoted to him, and he had looked out for them as best he could. It was hard for men so large to keep such a low profile, but somehow they'd managed it during the months since Jackie's death. The city might even have breathed a bit easier for a while. The Fulcis had a way of sucking the oxygen from a room. They had a way of knocking it from people too. Their fists were like cinder blocks.

Dave's concern was therefore understandable. But despite their appearance, and an undeniable propensity for violence that seemed resistant to all forms of pharmaceutical intervention, the Fulcis were essentially brooders by nature. They might not brood for very long, but they did tend to take some time to consider which bones they might enjoy breaking first. The fact that they'd stayed away from me for so long meant that they'd probably been considering the fate of their friend with a certain degree of seriousness. That boded either well or very badly for me.

"You want me to call someone?" said Dave.

"Like who?"

"A surgeon? A priest? A mortician?"

"If they've come here to cause trouble over Jackie, you may need a builder to reconstruct your bar."

"Damn, and just as the place was coming together."

I worked my way through the crowd to reach their table. They were both sipping sodas. The Fulcis weren't big drinkers.

"It's been a long time," I said. "I was starting to worry."

To be honest, I was still worrying, and maybe more than before, now that they'd shown up at last.

"You want to take a seat," said Paulie.

It wasn't a question. It was an order.

Paulie was the older, and marginally better adjusted, of the two brothers. Tony should have had a lit fuse sticking out of the top of his head.

I took the seat. Actually, I wasn't too worried that the Fulcis might take a swing at me. If they did, I wouldn't know a lot about it until I woke up, assuming that I ever did, but I'd always gotten along well with them, and, like Jackie, I'd tried my best to help them whenever I could, even if it meant just putting in a word with local law enforcement when they stepped over the line. They'd done some work for me over the years, and they'd put themselves in harm's way on my behalf. I liked to think that we had an understanding, but Timothy Treadwell, that guy in the Herzog documentary who was eaten by the grizzlies he'd tried to befriend, probably felt the same way until a bear's jaws closed on his throat.

Paulie looked at Tony. Tony nodded. If things were going to turn bad, they would do so now.

"What happened to Jackie, we don't blame you for it," said Paulie.

He spoke with great solemnity, like a senior judge communicating a long-considered verdict.

"Thank you," I said, and I meant it, not only because

my continued good health appeared assured but because I knew how important Jackie was to them. I wouldn't have been surprised if they'd held some residual grudge against me, but it appeared there would be none. With the Fulcis, it was all or nothing. We had a clean slate. "Jackie done something very bad," said Tony, "but that didn't mean he should have been shot down from behind because of it."

"No," I said.

"Jackie was a good guy," Tony continued. "He took care of his mom. He looked out for us. He—"

Tony choked. His eyes were tearing up. His brother patted him on a muscled shoulder.

"Whatever we can do," said Paulie, "whatever help you need to find the man who did this, you let us know. And, anytime you want us to step up for you, you just call. Because Jackie would have stepped up, and just because he ain't around no more don't mean we ought to let these things slide, you understand? Jackie wouldn't have wanted that."

"I hear you," I said.

I reached out and shook their hands. I didn't even wince, but I was relieved to get the hand back.

"How's his mom doing?" I asked.

Jackie's mother had been given a diagnosis of Creutzfeldt-Jakob disease the previous year. Her illness was the only reason Jackie had committed the acts that led to his death. He just needed the money.

"Not so good," said Paulie. "Even with Jackie she would have struggled. Without him . . ."

He shook his head.

Jackie's insurance company had invoked a clause in his life-insurance policy relating to criminal activity, arguing that his death had resulted from participation in a criminal enterprise. Aimee Price was fighting the case on a pro bono basis, but she didn't believe the insurance company was going to modify its position, and it was hard to argue that it didn't have a point. Jackie was killed because he screwed up: he was careless, somebody died, and vengeance fell. I made a mental note to send a check to Jackie's mother. Even if it helped only a little, it would be something.

The Fulcis finished their drinks, nodded their goodbyes, and left.

"You're still alive," said Dave, who'd been keeping one eye on proceedings and another on his bar, in case he didn't get to see it again in its present form.

"You seem pleased."

"Means I get my night off," he said, as he pulled on his overcoat. "Would have been hard to leave otherwise."

I ENJOYED THAT EVENING in the Bear. Perhaps it was partly relief at not having incurred the wrath of the Fulcis, but in moving between the bar and the floor I was also able to empty my head of everything but beer taps, line cooks, and making sure that, when Dave returned the next morning, the Bear would still be standing in more or less the same condition it was in when he left it. I drank a coffee and read the *Portland Phoenix* at the bar while the night's cleanup went on around me.

"Don't tax yourself," said Cupcake Cathy, as she nudged me with a tray of dirty glasses. "If you strained something by helping, I don't know how I could go on living."

Cathy was one of the waitstaff. If she was ever less than cheerful, I had yet to see it. Even as she let off some steam, she was still smiling.

"Don't make me fire you."

"You can't fire me. Anyway, that would require an effort on your part."

"I'll tell Dave to fire you."

"Dave just *thinks* we work for him. Don't disillusion him by making him put it to the test."

She had a point. I still wasn't sure how the Bear operated, exactly; it just did. In the end, no matter who was nominally in charge, everyone just worked for the Bear itself. I finished my coffee, waited for the last of the staff to leave, and locked up. My car was the only one left in the lot. The night was clear, and the moon bright, but already there was a layer of frost on the roof. Winter was refusing to relinquish its hold on the Northeast. I drove home beneath a sky exploding with stars.

OVER BY DEERING OAKS, the door to Jude's basement opened.

"Jude, you in here?"

A lighter flared. Had there been anyone to see, it would have revealed a man layered in old coats, with newspaper poking out of his laceless boots. The lower half of his face was entirely obscured by his beard, and dirt was embedded in the wrinkles on his skin. He looked sixty but was closer to forty. He was known on the streets as Brightboy. He once had another name, but even he had almost forgotten it by now.

"Jude?" he called again.

The heat from the lighter was burning his fingers. Brightboy swore hard and let the flame go out. His eyes were getting used to the dark, but the basement was shaped like an inverted "L," which meant that the moonlight penetrated only so far. The dogleg to the right remained in darkness.

He hit the lighter again. It was a cheap plastic thing. He'd found a bunch of them, all still full of fluid, in a garbage can outside an apartment building that was being vacated. In this kind of weather, anything that could generate heat and flame was worth holding on to. He still had half a dozen left.

Brightboy turned the corner, and the light caught Jude's brown boots dangling three feet above the floor. Brightboy raised the flame slowly, taking in the reddish-brown overcoat, the green serge pants, the tan jacket and waistcoat, the cream shirt, and the carefully knotted red tie. Jude had even managed to die dressed like a dandy, although his face was swollen and nearly unrecognizable above the knot in his tie, and the noose that suspended him above the floor was lost in his flesh. A backless chair was on its side beneath his feet. To its right was a wooden box that he had been using as a nightstand. His sleeping bag lay open and ready next to it.

On the box was a plastic bag filled with bills and coins.

The lighter was again growing hot in Brightboy's hand. He lifted his thumb, and the flame disappeared, but the memory of its light danced before his eyes. His left hand found the bag of money. He put it carefully into his pocket, then dragged Jude's pack into the moonlight and rifled it for whatever was worth taking. He found a flashlight, a deck of cards, a couple of pairs of clean socks, two shirts fresh from Goodwill, and a handful of candy bars just one month past expiration.

All these things Brightboy transferred to his own pack. He also took Jude's sleeping bag, rolling it up and tying it to the base of his pack with string. It was better than his own, newer and warmer. He didn't even think about Jude again until he was about to leave. They had always got along okay, Brightboy and Jude. Most of the other homeless people avoided Brightboy. He was untrustworthy and dishonest. Jude was one of the few who tried not to judge him. True, Brightboy had sometimes found Jude's obsession with his appearance to be an affectation, and he suspected that it helped to make Jude feel superior to his brothers and sisters on the streets, but Jude had been as generous with Brightboy as he had been with everyone else, and rarely had a harsh word passed between them.

Brightboy thumbed the lighter and held it aloft. Jude seemed frozen in place. His skin and his clothing were spangled with frost.

"Why'd you do it?" said Brightboy. His left hand dipped into his pocket, as though to reassure himself that the money was still there. He'd heard that Jude had been calling in loans. Brightboy himself had owed Jude two dollars. That was one of the reasons he'd come looking for him; that and a little company, and maybe a swig of something if Jude had it to spare. Someone had said that Jude wanted the money urgently, and it was time to pay up. Jude rarely asked for anything from the rest of his kind, so few resented him calling in his debts, and those that had it paid willingly enough.

So why would a man who had succeeded in putting together what Brightboy guessed to be at least a hundred dollars suddenly give up and take his own life? It made no sense, but then a lot of things made no sense to Brightboy. He liked his street name, but he had no conception of the irony that lay behind it. Brightboy wasn't smart. Cunning, maybe, but his intelligence was of the lowest and most animal kind.

Whatever had led Jude to finish his days at the end of a rope, he had no need for money where he now was, while Brightboy was still among the living. He walked to St. John Street, ordered two cheeseburgers, fries, and a soda for five dollars at the drive-through window of McDonald's, and ate them in the parking lot of a Chinese restaurant. He then bought himself a six-pack of Miller High Life at a gas station, but it was so cold outside that he had nowhere to drink the beers. With no other option available, he headed back to Jude's basement and consumed them while the dead man hung suspended before him. He unrolled Jude's sleeping bag, climbed into it, and fell asleep until shortly before dawn. He woke while it was still dark, gathered up the bottles for their deposit, and slipped from the basement to seek out breakfast. He stopped only to make a 911 call from a public phone on Congress.

It was the least that he could do for Jude.

Jude died without enough money to pay for his own funeral, so he was buried by the city at taxpayers' expense. It cost fifteen hundred dollars, give or take, but there were those who resented spending even that much to give a decent burial to a man who seemed to them to have been nothing but a burden on the city for most of his life. The only consolation they could derive was that Jude was unlikely to trouble them for a handout again.

He was interred in an unmarked grave at Forest City Cemetery, in South Portland, when the medical examiner had finished with his body. A funeral director recited a psalm as the coffin was lowered into the ground, but, unlike most city cases, Jude did not go to his rest unmourned. Alongside the cemetery workers stood a dozen of Portland's homeless, men and women both, as well as representatives of the local shelters and help centers who had known Jude. I was there too. The least that I could do was acknowledge his passing. A single bouquet of flowers was laid on the ground above him once the grave had been filled in. Nobody lingered. Nobody spoke.

The medical examiner's opinion was that Jude's injuries were consistent with asphyxiation, with no indication of a suspicious death. The investigation was ongoing, though, and the police and the attorney general were under no obligation to accept the ME's opinion as gospel. Still, in this case it was unlikely that the Portland PD would reject it. When a homeless man died at the hands of another, it was usually in a brutal manner, and there was little mystery to it. Jude, despite the care that he took with his appearance, was a troubled man. He suffered from depression. He lived from meal to meal, and handout to handout. There were more likely candidates for suicide, but not many.

If there was anything unusual about this case, it was that the medical examiner had found no trace of drugs or alcohol in Jude's system. He was clean and sober when he died. It was a minor detail, but one worthy of notice. Those who choose to take their own lives often need help with the final step. Either they set out with the intention of killing themselves, and find something to relax them in those last hours and minutes, or the mood induced by alcohol or narcotics is the trigger for the act. Suicide isn't easy. Neither, whatever the song might say, is it painless. Jude would have learned that as he kicked at the air from the end of a rope. I don't know how much help booze might have been under the circumstances, but it couldn't have made his situation any worse.

To be honest, I let Jude slip from my mind after the funeral. I'd like to say that I was better than everybody else, but I wasn't. He didn't matter. He was gone.

LUCAS MORLAND PULLED UP in front of Hayley Conyer's home on Griffin Road. It wasn't the biggest house in Prosperous, not by a long shot, but it was one of the oldest, and, being partly built of stone, conveyed a certain authority. Most of it dated from the end of the eighteenth century, and by rights it should probably have been listed on the National Register of Historic Places, but neither generations of Conyers nor the citizens of Prosperous had seen fit to nominate the house. The town didn't need that kind of attention. The old church presented them with enough problems as it was. Anyway, the Conyer house wasn't particularly noteworthy in terms of its situation or its design, and had no interesting historical associations. It was just old, or at least old by the standards of the state. The leading citizens of Prosperous, cognizant of their heritage, of their links to a far more ancient history back in England, took a more nuanced view of such matters.

Hayley Conyer's Country Squire station wagon stood in the drive. There seemed to be even more bumper stickers on it than Morland remembered: "Obama/Biden"; a "No Tar Sands in Maine" protest badge; "Maine Supports Gay Rights" over a rainbow flag; and a reminder that sixty-one percent of the electorate had not voted for the current governor of the state. (Blame the state's Democrats for that, thought Morland; trust them to split their own vote and then act surprised when it came back to bite them on the ass. Jesus, monkeys could have handled the nomination process better.) The station wagon was so ancient that it was probably held together by those stickers. He'd heard Hayley arguing with Thomas Souleby about the car, Souleby opining that the old gas-guzzler was causing more environmental pollution than a nuclear meltdown, and Hayley responding that it was still more environmentally friendly that investing in a new car and scrapping the old one.

Morland's own Crown Vic had been acquired from the Prosperous Police Department back in 2010, while it was still in perfect running order. By then, Ford had announced that it would cease production of the Police Interceptors in 2011, and Morland decided to secure one of the department's Crown Vics for himself before his officers drove the fleet into the ground. The Crown Vic had two tons of rear-wheel drive, and a V8 engine under the hood. If you crashed in a Crown Vic, you had a better chance of walking away alive than you did in a lighter patrol car, like the increasingly popular Chevy Caprice. The car was also spacious, and that meant a lot to a big man like Morland. The sacrifice was getting only thirteen miles to the gallon, but Morland reckoned the town could afford that small gesture on his behalf.

Hayley appeared on her porch as Morland sat musing on his car. She was still a striking woman, even as she left seventy behind. The chief could remember her in her prime, when men had circled like insects, flitting around her as she went about her business and did her best to ignore them or, if they grew too persistent, swatted them away with a flick of her hand. He had no idea why she had never married. That rainbow bumper sticker on her car might have caused some folk to suggest an explanation, but Hayley Conyer was no lesbian. She was, if anything, entirely asexual. She had committed herself to the town: it was hers to have and to hold, to love and to cherish.

She had inherited her duty to it, for more members of the Conyer family than any other in Prosperous had served on the board. Hayley herself had been the first selectman for more than four decades now. There were those who whispered that she was irreplaceable, but Morland knew better. Nobody was irreplaceable. If that were true, Prosperous would never have thrived for so long.

But in the dark corners of his mind Morland was starting to feel that it might be for the best if Hayley Conyer made way for another. It would take her death to do it, for she would never relinquish control while there was breath in her body, but it was time that the Conyer reign came to a close. There was a lot to be said for the discipline of married life. It forced one to learn the art of compromise, and to remedy the flaws in one's nature. Morland himself was still a work-in-progress after two decades of marriage, but he liked to think that his wife might be as well. Hayley Conyer, on the other hand, simply grew more resolute in her self-belief, more intransigent in her views, and more ready to embrace the use of diktats to get her way. She was helped by the rules of the board, which gave the first selectman the equivalent of two votes. It meant that, even if the board was evenly divided on an issue, Hayley's side would triumph, and she could force a stalemate with only one other selectman on her side. It was also a simple fact that the rest of the board combined had less testosterone than she did. It was increasingly left to Morland to try to deal with Hayley, and to encourage her to moderate her behavior, but he had been having less and less success in recent months. A body left hanging in a Portland basement was testament to that.

"I was just admiring your car," said Morland.

"You going to tell me that I need to replace it too?" she said.

"Not unless pieces of it start coming off on the highway and injuring folk, although that's starting to seem increasingly likely."

She folded her arms over her chest, the way she did at meetings when she wanted to let people know that she had done listening to their arguments and her decision was made. She wasn't wearing a brassiere, and her breasts hung low beneath her shirt. With her flowered skirt and her sandaled feet, and her long gray hair held back by a scarf, she came across as the typical earth mother, all bean sprouts and wheatgrass and organic milk. It wasn't entirely inapt, even if it didn't hint at the hardness beneath.

"It's mine," she said, "and I like it."

"You're only holding on to it because the Thomas Soulebys of this world keep telling you to get rid of it," he said. "If they started stroking it and admiring it, you'd sell it for scrap in a heartbeat."

Her scowl softened. Morland had a way of disarming her that few others could lay claim to. His father had enjoyed the same gift. Daniel Morland's relationship with Hayley Conyer had been almost flirtatious, at least when his wife wasn't around. Whether Hayley chose to embrace sexual activity or not, she was an attractive woman, and Alina Morland wasn't about to stand by and let her husband play patty-cake with her just to ensure the smooth running of the town. Neither had Alina been concerned by the power that Hayley wielded as chief selectman, because that was all politics and this was about a wife and her husband. The town could have decided to make Hayley Conyer its official queen, and Alina would have knocked her crown off for stirring even the slightest of sexual feelings in her husband.

This demonstrated one of the curious truths about Prosperous: in most things it ran pretty much like any other town of similar size. It had its rivalries, its intrigues. Men cheated on their wives, and wives cheated on their husbands. Hugo Reed didn't talk to Elder Collingwood, and never would, all because of an incident with a tractor and a garden gate some forty years earlier. Ramett Huntley and Milisent Rawlin, although superficially polite to each other, were obsessed with their bloodlines, and both had made regular pilgrimages back to the northeast of England over the years in an effort to trace their lineages to royalty. So far neither had been successful, but the search went on. In Prosperous, business as usual was the order of the day. The town differed in only one crucial way from the rest, and even that had become a version of normal over the centuries. It was surprising what folk could accustom themselves to, as long as they were rewarded for it in the end.

"You want some tea, Lucas?" said Hayley.

"Tea would be good."

In Prosperous, you were more likely to be offered tea than coffee. It was a hangover from the Old Country. Ben Pearson was probably the only store owner for fifty miles who regularly ran out of loose-leaf Earl Grey and English Breakfast, and Yorkshire Tea teabags. And, damn, was there trouble when he did.

Inside, Hayley's home resembled a Victorian house museum: dark-wood antique furniture, Persian rugs, lace tablecloths, overstuffed chairs, and wall upon wall of books. The chandeliers were late-nineteenth-century reproductions by Osler & Faraday of Birmingham, based on classic eighteenth-century Georgian design. Morland thought them excessively ornate, and ill suited to the house, but he kept that opinion to himself. Still, sitting at Hayley's dining table always made him feel as if he were preparing for a séance.

Hayley boiled some water and set the tea to brew. The teapot was sterling silver, but the tea would be served in mismatched mugs. China would have been too much of an affectation. She poured milk into each of the mugs, not bothering to ask Morland how much he wanted, or whether he might prefer to do it himself. By now she knew his habits and preferences almost as well as his wife did. She added the tea, then found some shortbread biscuits and emptied four onto a plate. Biscuits, not cookies; it said so on the packaging, which was also decorated with Highland cattle, tartans, and ancient ruins.

They sipped their tea, nibbled the shortbread, and spoke of the weather and the repairs that would have to be made to the town office once winter was gone, before moving on to the real business of the afternoon.

"I hear they buried that hobo," said Hayley.

Morland wasn't sure that the man named Jude had been a hobo, strictly speaking. As far as he knew, hobos were migratory workers. Technically, Jude had been a bum.

"Apparently so," said Morland.

"Has there been any fuss?"

"Not that I've heard."

"I told you there wouldn't be. I had to listen to all that bitching and moaning for nothing."

Morland didn't dispute the point. He had done all his arguing when the board's decision was communicated to him, but by then it was too late. He'd tried to talk Hayley around, but on that occasion she had proved immune to his charms.

"It would have been preferable if he'd just disappeared," said Morland.

"That would have cost more—a lot more. Books have to be balanced."

"It might have been worth it. I don't think anyone would

have come looking for a missing homeless man, and it's hard to prove the commission of a crime without a body."

"Nobody's trying to prove that a crime was committed. A hobo hanged himself, and that's the end of it."

Not quite, thought Morland. Hayley was thinking like a selectman, Morland like a lawman.

"The problem, as I see it, is that we now have two dead bodies to no good end," said Morland.

"Ben told me that he had no choice but to shoot the girl. You agreed."

Yet I didn't agree to the killing of her father, Morland was about to say, but he stilled the words before they reached his tongue.

"This town has survived, and flourished, by being careful," he said.

"You don't have to tell me that!" said Hayley. A little blood found its way into her pale cheeks. "What do you think I've been doing all these years? Every decision I've made has been with the best interests of the town at heart."

I've made, he noticed, not *we've* made. He wondered if this was how all despots began. At some point, someone had to speak truth to power. Then again, those who did frequently ended up with their heads on stakes.

"I'm not questioning your commitment to the town, Hayley. Nobody is. But two dead from the same family could attract attention."

"One dead," she corrected him. "There's one body, not two. Has the girl even been reported missing yet?"

"No," he conceded.

"And she won't be either, because the only one who might have been concerned about her is now in the ground. By acting as we did, we solved the problem—or we would have if that damn fool Dixon hadn't let the girl go."

"That's an interesting choice of words," said Morland.

He hadn't raised his suspicions with Hayley before. He wanted to let them percolate some before he started pouring them out. Hayley nibbled on her shortbread, her tiny white teeth chipping away at it with the actions of a hungry rodent.

"You think he's telling lies about what happened?" she said.

"I went to their house and tried using a scrap of material to open the bolt from the inside, like he and Erin claimed the girl did."

"And?"

"It worked."

"So?"

"It took a while, and I had to use a piece of wood to pull the cloth in and form a loop, just as Erin Dixon did when I put her in the basement and asked her to demonstrate how the girl might have escaped. She told me she'd found the wood on the floor, and that the girl must have broken it off the bed. She showed me the bed, and there was a long splinter of wood missing that matched the piece in Erin's hand."

"I'm waiting for a 'but.'"

"But there was blood on the floor by the bed when I let Erin out, and it was fresh."

"Could it have been the girl's? She couldn't have been gone for but an hour by then."

"If it was, the blood would have congealed."

"If it was Erin's blood, maybe she cut herself when she was examining the wood."

"Maybe."

Hayley set her shortbread down by her mug. She seemed to have lost her taste for sweetness.

"Why would they let her go?"

"I don't know. There are rumors about Harry's business."

"I've heard. I've been concerned since they took that loan."

"The paintwork on his house needs a new coat, and that old truck of his might just be the only vehicle in Prosperous that's in worse shape than yours. I didn't have time to take a good look around his kitchen when I visited, but I saw that some groceries had been unpacked and hadn't yet been put away. They're buying cheap bread, generic pasta, a couple of packs of chicken joints that were about to expire but would be okay if you froze them, that kind of thing."

"They could have been for the girl. They weren't going to be feeding her filet mignon."

"It just doesn't sit right with me." He regarded her closely. "It sounds to me like you're trying to defend them."

"I'm not defending anyone," said Hayley. "I'm trying to understand. If what you're suggesting is true, we have a major problem on our hands. We'll have to act, and that could cause unrest in the town. We don't turn on our own."

"Not unless our own start turning on us."

"I still can't figure out why they'd want to release her."

"Pity? Guilt?"

"It's not like we were asking them to kill her," said Hayley. "They just had to take care of her until we were ready. She was too thin. All this might have been avoided if Walter and Beatrix hadn't brought us a junkie."

"It's been a long time since we've had to find someone," said Morland. "It's harder now. The safest way is to take the vulnerable, the lost, the ones that nobody will miss. If that means junkies and whores, then so be it."

"Junkies and whores may not be good enough."

"It's been many years, Hayley. Some people are wondering if it might not be necessary at all."

She flared up.

"Who? Tell me!" Her eyes grew sly. "The same ones who are whispering about my 'commitment' to the town?"

He should have stepped more carefully. She heard everything, turning the details over in her mind and examining them the way a jeweler might consider gemstones before deciding which to keep and which to discard.

"I know there are some who are starting to doubt me," she said.

Hayley stared at Morland, as though willing him to confess that he himself had been guilty of such thoughts, but he did not. She leaned over the table and grasped his hand. Her skin was cold, and its look and feel reminded him of the cheap cuts of chicken at the Dixon house.

"That's why this is so important," she said. "If I'm to go, I want to leave knowing the town is secure. I want to be sure that I've done all that I can for it."

She released her grip on him. She had left marks on the back of his hand, as if to remind him that she was still strong and should not be underestimated.

"What do you suggest?" he said.

"We talk to the Dixons. We tell them to find us another girl, fast. And no junkie either; we want someone clean and healthy. If they come through for us, we'll see what more the town can do to help them out if they're in trouble."

Morland had more to say about the Dixons, but he kept it to himself, for now.

"And if they don't?"

Hayley stood and started clearing the table. She was tired of talking with him. The discussion was over.

"Then they're a threat to the security of the town. There's still money in the discretionary fund, thanks to the decision not to disappear the hobo instead of just leaving him to be found.

"And," she added, "our friends will be grateful for the work."

XI

I was sitting at a table in Crema Coffee Company, on Commercial, when the man who called himself Shaky found me. It was just after nine in the morning, and while a steady stream of people kept the baristas busy, most of the tables remained empty. It was that time of day when folk wanted to order and go, which suited me just fine. I had a nice sun-dappled spot by the window, and copies of the *New York Times* and the *Portland Press Herald*. Crema had one of the best spaces in town, all bare boards and exposed brickwork. There were worse places to kill an hour. I had a meeting later in the morning with a prospective client: trouble with an ex-husband who hadn't grasped the difference between keeping a protective eye on his former wife and stalking her. It was, depending upon whom you asked, a thin line. Neither did he appear to understand that if he really cared about his wife he should pay her the child support that he owed. On such misunderstandings were hourly rates earned.

Shaky was wearing black sneakers, only slightly frayed jeans, and an overcoat so big that it was just one step away from being a tent. He looked self-conscious as he entered Crema, and I could see one or two of the staff watching him, but Shaky wasn't about to be dissuaded from whatever purpose he had in mind. He made a beeline for my table.

It wasn't just Shaky who called himself by that name. Apparently, everyone on the street did. He had a palsied left hand that he kept close to his chest. I wondered how he slept with it. Maybe, like most things, you learned to get used to it if you had to endure it long enough.

He hovered before me, the sunlight catching his face. He was clean-shaven, and smelled strongly of soap. I may have been mistaken, but it struck me that he'd tidied himself up and dressed in his best clothing to come here. I remembered him from the funeral. He was the only one present to shed a tear for Jude as he was lowered into his grave.

"You mind if I sit down?" he asked.

"Not at all," I said. "Would you like a coffee?"

He licked his lips, and nodded. "Sure."

"Any preference?"

"Whatever's the biggest, and the warmest. Maybe sweet too."

Since I was mainly a straight-filter kind of guy, I had to rely on the girl behind the counter to guide me on warm and sweet. I came back with a maple latte and a couple of muffins. I wasn't too hungry, but Shaky probably was. I picked at mine to be polite while Shaky went back to the counter and loaded up his latte with sugar. He tore into the muffin as soon as he resumed his seat, then seemed to realize that he was in company, and nobody was likely to try and steal the snack from him, so he slowed down.

"It's good," he said. "The coffee as well."

"You sure there's enough sugar in there for you?" The stirrer was pretty much standing up by itself in the coffee.

He grinned. His teeth weren't great, but the smile somehow was.

"I always did have a sweet tooth. I guess it's still in there somewhere. I done lost most of the rest."

He chewed some more muffin, holding it in his mouth for as long as he could to savor the taste.

"Saw you at the cemetery," he said, "when they put Jude in the ground. You're the detective, right?"

"That's correct."

"You knew Jude?"

"A little."

"What I heard. Jude told me that he did some detecting for you, couple of times."

I smiled. Jude always did get a kick out of being asked to help. I could hear some skepticism in Shaky's voice, just a hint of doubt, but I think he wanted it to be true. He kept his head down as he stared up at me, one eyebrow raised in anticipation.

"Yes, he did," I said. "Jude had a good eye, and he knew how to listen."

Shaky almost sagged with relief. Jude hadn't lied to him. This wasn't a wasted errand.

"Yeah, Jude was smart," he said. "Wasn't nothing happened on the streets that Jude didn't know about. He was kind too. Kind to everyone. Kind to me."

He stopped eating, and for an instant he looked terribly lonely. His mouth moved soundlessly as he tried to express emotions that he had never shared aloud before: his feelings for Jude, and about himself now that Jude was gone. He was trying to put loss into words, but loss is absence, and will always defy expression. In the end, Shaky just gave up and slurped noisily at his latte to cover his pain.

"You were friends?"

He nodded over the cup.

"Did he have many friends?"

Shaky stopped drinking and wiped his mouth with the back of his hand.

"No. He kept most people at a distance."

"But not you."

"No."

I didn't pursue it. It was none of my business.

"When did you last see him alive?"

"Couple of days before he was found in that basement. I was helping him to collect."

"Collect?"

"Money. He was calling in the debts he was owed, and he asked me to help. Everyone knew that me and him was close, and if I said I was working on his behalf then it was no word of a lie. He put it all down on paper for me. As I'd find someone I'd cross the name off the list and record how much they'd given me."

He reached into one of his pockets and produced a sheet of paper, which he carefully unfolded and placed before me. On it was a list of names written neatly in pencil. Beside most of them, in a considerably messier hand, figures were scrawled: a dollar or so, usually, and no sum more than two bucks.

"Sometimes I'd get to a person after he did, and maybe they'd already have paid up, and maybe they wouldn't have. Jude was soft, though. He believed every hard-luck story, because it was his way. Me, I knew some of them was lying. As long as they was breathing, they was lying. I made sure that, if they could, they paid."

I took the piece of paper and did a little rough addition on the numbers. The total didn't come to much: a hundred dollars and change. Then I realized that, while it wasn't much to me, that kind of sum could get a man beaten to a pulp if he fell in with the wrong company. It might even be enough to bring death upon him.

"What did he want the money for?" I said.

"He was looking for his daughter. Told me she used to be a junkie but she was straightening out. Last he heard she was up in Bangor looking for work, and seems like she found some. I think—"

He paused.

"Go on."

"I think she'd come up here because she wanted to be near him, but not so near that it would be easy for him," said Shaky. "She wanted him to come find her. Jude had abandoned her momma and her way back, and he knew that the girl blamed him for everything that had gone wrong in her life since then. She was angry at him. She might even have hated him, but when there's blood involved love and hate aren't so different, or they get all mixed up so's you can't tell one from the other. I guess he was considering moving up to Bangor and having done with it. But Jude didn't like Bangor. It's not like here. They tore the heart out of that city when they built the mall, and it never recovered, not the way Portland did. It's a bad place to be homeless too—worse than here. But Jude wanted to make up to the girl for what he'd done, and he couldn't do it from Portland."

"How long did it take you and Jude to get the money together?"

"A week. Would have taken him a month if he'd been working alone. I ought to get me a job as a debt collector."

He used the forefinger of his right hand to pull the scrap of paper back to him.

"So my question is—" he began, but I finished it for him.

"Why would a man who had just spent a hard week calling in his debts, and who was fixated on mending his relationship with his daughter, hang himself in a basement just when he's managed to get some cash together?"

"That's right."

"So, what: he was going to give his daughter the money, or use it to move to Bangor?"

"Neither," said Shaky. "If I understood him right, I think he was hoping to hire you to find her."

He seemed to remember that he still had his coffee. He

drank half of what remained in one go, and turned an eye to the muffin on my plate. I pushed it toward him.

"Go ahead," I said. "I'm not as hungry as I thought."

WE SPOKE FOR AN hour, sometimes about Jude, sometimes about Shaky himself. He'd served in the military, and that was how he had come by his bad arm; it was nerve damage of some kind, caused by a jeep tire exploding.

"Not even a proper wound," as Shaky told me. "I used to lie about it to make myself sound brave, but it just don't seem worth the effort no more."

At the end of our conversation, two things were clear to me: Shaky knew Jude better than almost anyone else in Portland, and he still didn't really know him at all. Jude had shared only the barest of information about his daughter with him. To Shaky, it seemed as though the more troubles his friend encountered the more reluctant he was to seek help with them, and that was how men ended up dying alone.

I bought Shaky another maple latte before I left, and he gave me instructions for how best to reach him. As with Jude, he used the Amistad Community and the good folk at the Portland Help Center for such communications. I then drove to South Portland to meet my prospective client at her home, and she gave me details of where her husband was working, where he was living, just how much of an asshole he now was, and just how much of an asshole he didn't used to be. For her children's sake, she didn't want to involve the police, and she hated her lawyer. I was the least bad of the remaining options, although she did ask if I knew someone who would break her husband's legs once I had made it clear that this wasn't something I was prepared to take on—or not without a better reason.

Since I had nothing else to do, I went to visit the errant husband at his office in Back Cove, where he was a partner in some hole-in-the-wall financial advice and investment business. His name was Lane Stacey, and he didn't look pleased when he discovered that I wasn't there to give him money to invest. He did some hollering and grandstanding before it became clear to him that I wasn't about to be intimidated back onto the street. A calm demeanor always helped in these situations—calmness, and having a good forty pounds on the man on the other side of the argument.

Like the Bentley-owning Hyram P. Taylor, Stacey wasn't a bad guy. He wasn't even as priapic as Hyram. He was lonely, he missed his wife and kids, and he didn't think anybody else would be willing to have him. His wife had just fallen out of love with him, and he, to a lesser degree, with her, although he had been more willing to keep things going as they were in order to secure a roof over his head and have someone around to nurse him when he caught cold, and maybe sleep with him occasionally. Eventually I ended up having lunch with him at the Bayou Kitchen, where I explained to him the importance of not stalking his wife, and of paying to support his children. He, in turn, confessed that he'd been hoping to force her to take him back by starving her—and his kids—into submission, which went some ways toward explaining why his fears that he might not find anyone else to put up with him had some basis in truth. By the time lunch was over I'd secured some guarantees about his future behavior, and he'd tried to sell me on a short-term bond so risky that it was little more than a personal recession waiting to happen. He took my rejection on the chin. He was, he said, "optimistic" about the country's financial future, and saw only great times ahead for his business.

"Why is that?" I asked.

"Everybody loves the promise of a quick buck," he said. "And the sucker store never runs out of stock."

He had a point.

After all, I'd just paid for lunch.

XII

A couple of calls gave me the name of the detective whose name graced the file on Jude's case. It came as both good and bad news. The good news was that I knew the detective personally. The bad news was that I had once kind of dated her. Her name was Sharon Macy, and "dated" might have been too strong a word for the history between us. She'd come into the Bear a couple of times when I was bartending, and we had dinner once at Boda, on Congress, which wasn't far from her apartment on Spruce Street. It had ended with a short kiss, and an agreement that it might be nice to do it again sometime soon. I wanted to, and I think she did too, but somehow life got in the way, and then Jackie Garner died.

Sharon Macy was an interesting character, assuming you were content to accept the Chinese definition of "interesting" as resembling a kind of curse. Some years earlier, she was temporarily stationed on an island called Sanctuary, out in Casco Bay, when a group of hired guns with a grudge came calling, and a lot of shooting had resulted. Macy came through unscathed, but she bloodied herself along the way, and had acquired no small degree of respect as a cop with clean kills. As a result, she hadn't been destined to stay in uniform for long, and no one was surprised by her move to detective. She worked in the Portland PD's Criminal Invesigation Division, and was also heavily involved in the Southern Maine Violent Crimes Task Force, which investigated serious incidents in the region.

Macy's cell phone was off when I called her number, and I didn't bother to leave a message. She wasn't at her apartment when I went by, but a neighbor said that she had gone to drop off her laundry at the eco place on Danforth. The guy at the Laundromat confirmed that she'd been in, and said that he thought she might be waiting in Ruski's while he did a fast wash-and-fold for her.

Ruski's was a Portland institution, opening early and serving food until late. It had long been a destination for those whose working hours meant that breakfast was eaten whenever they happened to want it, which was why Ruski's served it all day. On Sundays it was a magnet for regulars, including cops and firefighters from anywhere within an easy drive of Portland who wanted somewhere dark and friendly in which to kill an afternoon. It boasted darts, a pretty good jukebox, and a shortage of places to sit, and it never changed. It was what it was: a neighborhood bar where the prices were better than the food, and the food was good.

Macy was sitting by the window when I walked up, drinking and chatting with a patrol cop named Terrill Nix. I knew Nix a little because one of his brothers was a cop out in Scarborough. Nix was in his late forties, I guessed, and probably already thinking about cashing out. His hair was thinning, and his face had assumed a default expression of pained disappointment. The remains of a hangover special—hash, toast, eggs, home fries—lay on the plate beside him, but he didn't look as if he was trying to beat down a hard night. His eyes were bright and clear. He could probably see all the way to retirement.

Macy looked like Macy: small, dark, with quick eyes and an easy smile. Damn. I tried to remember why I hadn't called her again. Oh, yeah. Life, whatever that was. And some dying.

Nix spotted me before Macy did, as she had her back to the door. He nudged Macy's left leg with his right foot to alert her. It didn't look as though there was anything between them, just two cops who happened to cross paths in Ruski's, where cops crossed paths with one another all the time. Anyway, Nix's wife would have emasculated him and left him to bleed out before decorating the hood of her car with the pieces if she even caught a whiff of another woman off him, not to mention the fact that Nix's brother had married Nix's wife's sister. The whole family would have helped weigh down his corpse in the Scarborough marshes.

"Charlie," said Nix. "Detective Macy, do you know Charlie Parker, our local celebrity PI?"

Macy's initial surprise at seeing me gave way to a lop-sided grin.

"Yes, I do. We had dinner once."

"No shit?" said Nix.

"Mr. Parker never called for a second date."

"No shit?" Nix said again. He clucked at me like a disappointed schoolmarm. "Hurtful," he opined.

"Uncouth," said Macy.

"Maybe he's here to make amends."

"I don't see any flowers."

"There's always the tab."

"There is that," said Macy. She hadn't taken her eyes off me since I'd come in. She wasn't flirting, but she was enjoying herself.

"So if he's not here to apologize for blowing you off, why is he here?" said Nix.

"Yes, why are you here?" said Macy.

"He's going to put trouble on someone's plate," said Nix.

"Are you going to put trouble on someone's plate?" said Macy.

"Not if I can help it," I said, just happy to be getting a word in at last now that Nichols and May had paused for breath. "I had a couple of questions about the Jude case. Your name came up in connection with it."

Nix and Macy exchanged a look, but Nix left it up to Macy to comment if she chose. She was, after all, the detective.

"Small world," said Macy.

"Really?" I said.

"Nix was first responder," said Macy. "And there is no 'Jude case'—unless," she added, "you know different."

"It was a nice, clean hanging," said Nix, and I knew what he meant. You took those when they came along. They were paperwork, and not much else.

I pointed at their bottles, which were mostly suds. "You want another?"

Nix was drinking a Miller High Life. There was something about Ruski's that made people want to do strange stuff like drink High Life. Macy was on Rolling Rock. Both of them agreed to let me spend my money on them, and Nix wondered aloud if buying a drink constituted a second date in my world. I ignored the peanut gallery and ordered the drinks, along with a Rolling Rock for myself as well. I tried to remember the last time I ordered a Rolling Rock, but couldn't. I suspected a fake ID might have been involved.

Nix, I noticed, had the sports section of the *Press Herald* beside him, open to the basketball page.

"You a fan?" I asked.

"My kid's a Yachtsman," he said.

The Yachtsmen were Falmouth High's basketball team. The previous season they'd taken the kind of beating from their local rivals, Yarmouth, that usually requires years of therapy to overcome: 20–1 in the regional final. They had looked dead and buried, but so far this season they'd been beaten only once, by York, and had won their first sixteen games by an average margin of more than twenty points. Now they had the state final in their sights, and Coach Halligan, who had also taken Falmouth to nine state soccer titles in his twenty-six-year career, was considered a candidate for sainthood.

"Better season than last," I said.

"They got stronger kids this year," said Nix. "My boy plays soccer too, and he skis. Kid is built like a racehorse, and he's got another year left. He's ready for the move to Class A."

He took a long tug on his beer. Once again, he was leaving it to Macy to do the heavy lifting.

"So, what do you want to know about Jude?" said Macy.

"How was he found?"

"Nine-one-one call from a public phone on Congress. No name given. We figure it was one of his homeless buddies."

"Anything odd about it?"

She looked to Nix, who thought about the question. "It was an unfinished dirt basement, L-shaped, so kind of split in two by the angle of the walls. It looked like someone else had slept in there that night. There was a depression in the earth, and we found a couple of beer caps. Whoever it was had also taken a dump, and used a copy of that day's newspaper to clean himself off. But the ME's report said that Jude had been dead for at least thirty-six hours when we found him. You do the math."

"Somebody spent a night with the corpse."

"They maybe slept with their back to it, but yeah. You know, it was wicked cold, and if you don't have anywhere else to go . . ."

"What about his possessions?"

"Sleeping bag was gone," said Macy. "And it looked like his pack had been rifled for valuables."

"Any money found?"

"Money? Like what kind of money?"

"More than a hundred dollars. Not much in the normal scheme of things, but a lot to a guy like that."

"People have died for less."

"Amen."

"No, there was no money. What, you think he might have been killed for it?"

"Like you said, people have died for less."

"Sure," said Macy, "but it's hard to hang a man who's struggling against it, and harder still to make it look like a suicide. The ligature marks were consistent with the downward momentum of the body, and the ME found no excessive injury to the neck. The victim did scratch at the rope, but that's not unusual."

"Any idea where the rope might have come from?"

"Nope. It wasn't new, though. Like Jude, it had been around the block a couple of times. It had been cut to size to make the noose."

"At the funeral, I heard that he had no alcohol or narcotics in his system."

"That's right."

"Which *is* unusual."

"Depends on how you read it," said Nix. "If you're talking Dutch courage, then, yes, you might have expected him to take something to ease the pain. On the other hand, if you're looking for evidence of a homicide made to look like a hanging suicide, then some drugs or alcohol might be useful if you wanted to subdue the victim first."

I let it go.

"The money is the other thing," I said.

"How come?" said Macy. She was interested now. I could see it in her eyes. A lot of detectives wouldn't have cared much to have a snoop question a neat, closed case, but Macy wasn't one of them. I doubted that she had ever been that kind of cop, and whatever happened out on Sanctuary had done nothing to change her. If anything, it had simply strengthened that aspect of her character. She hadn't told me much about what occurred on the island beyond what was in the official record, and I hadn't pressed her on it, but I'd heard stories. Sanctuary was a strange place, even by the standards of this part of the world, and some of the bodies from that night had never been found.

"Jude went to a lot of trouble to collect it," I said. "It seems that he was worried about his daughter. Her name was Annie—ex-junkie, trying to go straight, living in a shelter up in Bangor. He was trying to reestablish a relationship with her when she disappeared. He was worried about her. The money was to help him search for her. In fact, I think he might even have hoped to hire me with the cash."

"What would it have bought him?" said Nix. "A couple of hours?"

"I'd have given him a discount."

"Even so."

"Yeah."

Nix took another hit on his beer. "Well, chances are that whoever slept in the basement and cherry-picked Jude's possessions also took the money. I don't think they'd have gone to the trouble of trying to stage it as a suicide, though. A homeless person would have been more likely to use fists, or a blade. It wouldn't have taken much to put Jude down. He wasn't a strong guy."

"It still doesn't explain," I said, "why a man who has gone to the trouble of calling in his debts, and who's concerned about his daughter, should end it all in a basement and leave her to whatever trouble she was in. And, as you said, Jude wasn't a strong man. A breeze could have lifted him off the street. A big man, or two big men, could have held him long enough to hoist him up on a chair, put a rope around his neck, and kick the chair out from under him. They'd have left marks on his body, I guess. Couldn't not have."

I was thinking aloud now. Macy set aside her beer unfinished.

"You got a couple of minutes?" she said to me.

"Sure."

"You want to head down to Rosie's, I'll join you there for one more. I got some laundry to pick up along the way."

Nix decided to stay at Ruski's for another beer. He knew better than to tag along, regardless of any history between Macy and me. If she chose to share more about Jude's death with a PI, then that was her business. He didn't want, or need, to know.

I did cover his tab, though, including his drink for the road. He sighed theatrically as I left.

"And I bet you won't even call," he said. "I just feel so . . . *used.*"

XIII

Harry and Erin Dixon were deep in discussion when they heard the car approach.

"We have to leave," said Erin.

"And go where?" said Harry.

"I don't know. Anywhere. We could promise not to tell if they just let us go and didn't follow."

Harry tried not to laugh, but he couldn't stop himself. The idea that Prosperous had survived for so long just by allowing those who were uncomfortable with its edicts to leave was so preposterous as to be beyond belief. Erin, of all people, should have known that. They had hunted her father, Charlie Hutton, for years, and they had never given up. He had been clever, and lucky. He was also a teller at the bank, and he didn't leave with his pockets empty: he raided the town's discretionary fund before he ran. The money bought him time, and some room to maneuver. It allowed him to set himself up with a new identity and a new life, but Harry was sure that he spent his days fearing every knock on the door and searching the faces on the street for the gaze that lingered too long.

Charlie hadn't been afraid that they'd set the police on him. That wasn't the way Prosperous worked. Anyway, the money that he stole didn't officially exist, and the fund was used for purposes about which it was better that the law knew nothing. What had always stayed with Harry was that Erin's father had never told. He could have gone to the police and tried to explain the nature of Prosperous, but it was so fantastic that he would have risked being dismissed as a madman. Even if they had chosen to believe him, there were no bodies to which he could point, no shallow graves to be dug up and bones to be exhumed. Harry wondered how deep you'd have to go to find the victims of Prosperous, if anything of them truly remained at all. Any searchers would have given up long before they first struck rock, and some of the bodies probably lay even deeper than that. And then there was the fact that rarely did it happen more than once every twenty or thirty years, and those responsible kept the secret of it to themselves. To descry any kind of pattern would be almost impossible, and the names of those who had been taken were forgotten as soon as they were belowground. In many cases, they had never been known at all.

But there was another probable reason that Erin's father had remained silent, a deeper reason: he was bound to Prosperous, and one didn't slough off one's loyalties to a place so old, and so strange, with any ease. He stayed loyal to the town even as he sought to put as much distance between him and it as possible, for he couldn't deny the truth, even if he wanted no further part in it.

But the town learned from what had happened with Charlie, and steps were taken to ensure that it wouldn't occur so easily again. It kept a close watch on its inhabitants in the guise of caring for their well-being, and it bound them together with bonds of matrimony, familial and business loyalties, and fear.

"You want to be like your father?" said Harry, once his laughter had ceased. He hadn't cared much for the sound of it. It held a distressingly lunatic tone. "You want to be hunted all your life?"

"No," she said softly. "But I don't want to stay here either."

But Harry wasn't listening to her. He was on a roll now.

"And he had money. We have nothing. You don't think they're watching our spending habits, our patterns of deposits and withdrawals? They *know*, or at least they suspect. We're vulnerable, and that means they're concerned about how we might act. No, we have no choice. We have to wait this out. We have to hope that our situation improves. When it does, we can start putting money away. We can plan, just like Charlie must have done. You don't leave Prosperous on a whim. You don't—"

And then there came the sound of the car. Lights washed over the house, and the words died in Harry Dixon's mouth.

XIV

Rosie's wasn't too dissimilar from Ruski's, but your chances of getting a seat at Rosie's were greater than at Ruski's simply because Rosie's had more chairs. I didn't want another beer, so I ordered coffee instead, and watched the cars go by on Fore Street. Music was playing, a song that I thought I recognized, something about seas of charity and unchosen exiles. I called Rachel while I waited, and she put Sam on. We chatted for a while about events in elementary school, which seemed to involve a lot of painting, and a certain amount of argument with a boy named Harry.

"His mom and dad named him after Harry Potter," Sam explained. She didn't sound as though she approved. A whole generation of adults who had dressed up as wizards when they should have known better now seemed destined to inflict whimsy on their offspring. I wasn't a big fan of whimsy. Whimsical people were the type who got run over by cars without anybody really noticing or caring that much beyond the damage to the vehicle, which was usually minimal anyway, whimsical folk being kind of lighter than most.

"He draws lightning on his forehead," said Sam.

"Does he?" I said.

"Yeah. He says it's real, but it comes off when you rub hard."

I decided not to ask how she knew this, although I was pretty certain that, however she'd discovered it, the boy named Harry had been an unwilling participant in the experiment. Talk moved on to the trip to Florida that she was taking the following weekend, where she and Rachel would join Rachel's parents in their new winter vacation home. Rachel's current boyfriend, Jeff, wouldn't be going along with them, Sam informed me.

"Oh," I said, keeping my voice as neutral as possible. I didn't like Jeff, but it didn't matter. Jeff liked himself enough for both of us.

"Daddy!" said Sam. "You don't have to pretend you're sad." Jesus.

"Are you sure you're just in elementary school?" I said. "You're not studying psychology on the side?"

"Mom knows psycottagy," said Sam.

"Yes, she does." Not enough of it to avoid dating a jack-ass like Jeff, but solving other people's problems was often easier than taking care of your own. I considered sharing that insight with Rachel but decided against it. Maybe I was learning at last that discretion was the better part of valor. "Just put your mom back on. I'll see you when you get back."

"Bye. Love you," said Sam, and my heart broke a little.

"Bye, hon. Love you too."

I chatted with Rachel for a minute or two more. She seemed happy. That was good. I wanted her to be happy. If she was happy, Sam would be happy. I just wished Rachel could be happy with someone other than Jeff. It reflected badly on her good taste, but then there were those who might have said the same about her time with me.

"What are you working on?" asked Rachel.

"Nothing much. Process serving. Errant husbands."

"Is that all? It won't keep you out of mischief for long."

"Well, there's this thing with a homeless guy too. He hanged himself, and I can't figure out why."

"I'll bet he didn't pay you in advance."

"You know, it's funny you should say it, but someone in this city might have the money that he would have used to hire me."

"Do I need to tell you to be careful?"

"No, but it always helps."

"I doubt that, but for the sake of your daughter . . ."

"I'll be careful."

"You in a bar?"

"Rosie's."

"Ah. A date?"

Macy arrived. She had some photocopied pages in one hand and a mug in the other. Like me, she had sought coffee.

"No, I wouldn't say that."

Rachel laughed. "No, you wouldn't, would you? Go on, get lost."

I hung up. Macy had been hanging back in an effort

to give me privacy. Now she stepped forward and laid the papers on the table as she sat.

"You can read," she said, "but I'm not leaving them with you, okay?"

"Understood."

It was the ME's report on Jude's body. I could probably have bargained a look at it out from the ME's office, but this saved me the trouble of a trip to Augusta. The rope used in the hanging was cotton, with a running knot placed above the occipital region. Some rope fibers and remnants had been found on a table nearby, along with marks in the wood that were consistent with the cutting action of a sharp knife.

"Did you find a knife at the scene?" I asked Macy.

"No, but it could have been with the other possessions that were taken."

"I guess."

Rigor mortis and postmortem staining on both legs, distal portion of upper limbs, and area of waist above the belt line. Both eyes partially open; conjunctiva congested and cornea hazy. Mouth partially open, tongue protruding.

I moved on to the ligature mark. The ME found that it encircled the whole neck, apart from a small gap beneath the knot, consistent with the drag weight of the body. The ligature ran backward, upward, and toward the occipital region. The ligature marks were slightly wider on the left of the neck than on the right, but only by about a fifth of an inch. Dissection of the neck revealed no evidence of fracture of the thyroid cartilage or hyoid bone, as is often the case in forced strangulation, which seemed to rule out the possibility that Jude had been attacked. Likewise, there was no extravasation—forced flow—of blood in the neck tissues. The ME had concluded that the cause of death was asphyxia due to suicidal hanging by ligature.

The only other noteworthy inclusion in the report was a list of bruises, scars, and abrasions to Jude's body. They were considerable enough to make me wince. As if to compound the issue, Macy slid another sheet of paper across the table. It was a color copy, and the quality wasn't great. This was a small mercy, given what the two photographs on it revealed about the battering that Jude had taken over the years. Falls, fights, beatings: all were recorded on a map of skin and flesh, and all were concealed beneath the trappings of a thrift-shop dandy. Anyone who was dumb enough to imagine that life on the streets of Portland was some kind of state-funded outdoor vacation needed just one look at the picture of Jude's torso and limbs to be set straight.

"The ME says some are recent, but most are pretty old," said Macy. "One or two might have been received in the hours prior to his death. These here are interesting."

She pointed to marks on Jude's upper right and left arms.

"What are they?"

Macy handed over a final sheet. She had a flair for the dramatic. The pictures showed enlargements of the marks.

"They look like grips," I said, "as though someone held him hard from behind."

"That's what I thought," said Macy. "But it doesn't mean they're connected to his death. This was a man who took knocks on a regular basis."

"You going to ask around?"

"I wasn't until you showed up. Look, I still think he took his own life, but I'll admit that you've raised enough questions to make me wonder again about why he did it.

Might be useful if we could find the contents of his pack, though—or, better still, talk to whoever made that call. You never know what we might learn."

"You try asking around?"

"Nix did, as best he could. If anybody knew anything, they were keeping quiet. But if I came across a dead man, and then rifled his belongings and stole what little money he had, I'd probably keep quiet about it too."

Macy gathered up the photocopies and finished her coffee.

"So, you doing much pro bono work these days?"

"No, but I hear it's good for the soul."

"Which is why you'll keep on this—for the good of your soul, and the fact that you think you might owe Jude some hours?"

"Whatever I owe him, it's not hours," I said.

"You still have my number?"

"Yes."

"Good. I thought you might have lost it, seeing as how you never called and all."

"I'm sorry about that."

"Don't be. It was a good dinner, and you did pay for it."

"It was, but I still should have called. I don't know why I didn't."

"I do," she said. "The same things that stopped me from calling you. Life. Death."

She stood.

"You know how to find me," she said. "I'd appreciate a heads-up if you learn anything."

"Done," I said.

She turned back briefly as she walked away.

"It was good seeing you again."

"And you," I said.

I watched her go. A couple of other guys did too.
Damn.

XV

Morland sat on one side of the kitchen table, Hayley
Conyer to his right. Harry and Erin sat on the
other side, facing them. The Dixons had never
entertained Hayley in their home before. They had never
entertained her anywhere. Neither had they ever set foot in
her house. They had heard that it was beautiful and ornate,
if gloomy. Erin was secretly pleased that, while their own
home might not have been anything special, it wasn't lacking in cheer. The kitchen was bright, and the living room
that connected to it was even brighter. There was a shadow
over all of it now, though. Hayley Conyer seemed to have
brought something of the night in with her.

"You have a lovely home," she said, in the manner of one
who was surprised at how far the little people could stretch
a nickel but still wouldn't want to live like them.

"Thank you," said Erin.

She had made coffee. She had a vague recollection that
Hayley Conyer preferred tea, but she deliberately hadn't
offered her any. She wasn't even sure that there was tea in
the house. If there was, it had been there for so long that
nobody would want to drink it.

"I noticed that the paintwork on your windows is flaking," said Morland. "You ought to do something with it before it gets much worse."

Harry's smile didn't waver. It was a test. Everything was a test now, and the only thing that mattered in a test was not failing.

"I was waiting for winter to pass," he said. "It's hard to paint a window frame when your hands are shaking with cold. You're liable to end up with windows that you can't see much out of."

Morland wasn't about to let it go.

"You could have taken care of it last summer."

Harry was finding it hard to keep his smile in place.

"I was busy last summer."

"Yeah?"

"Yeah."

"Doing what?"

"Making a living. Is this an interrogation, Chief?"

Hayley Conyer intervened.

"We're just worried about you, Harry. With this downturn in the economy, and the way it's hit construction—well, you're more . . . *vulnerable* than most. Businesses like yours must be suffering."

"We're getting by," said Erin. She wasn't going to let her husband be cornered alone by these two. "Harry works hard."

"I'm sure he does," said Conyer.

She pursed her lips, and then pulled from memory the semblance of a concerned expression.

"You see, it's the job of the board to protect the town, and the best way we can do that is by protecting the *people* of the town."

She didn't look at Harry. She had her eyes on Erin. She spoke to Erin as though to a slow child. She was goading

her, just as Morland had goaded Harry. They wanted a reaction. They wanted anger.

They wanted an excuse.

"I understand that, Hayley," said Erin. She didn't allow
even a drop of sarcasm to pollute her apparent sincerity.

"I'm glad. That's why I asked Chief Morland here to look
into your affairs some, just to be sure that all was well with
you."

This time, Erin couldn't conceal her anger.

"You *what*?"

Harry placed a hand on her arm, leaning into it so that
she felt his weight.

Calm, calm.

"Would you mind explaining to me what that means?"
said Harry.

"It means," said Morland, "that I talked to some of your
suppliers, and your subcontractors. It means that, when
the mood has struck me, I've followed you around these
last few weeks. It means that I've had a meeting with Allan
Dantree at the bank, and we had a discreet conversation
about your accounts."

Harry couldn't help but close his eyes for a moment.
He'd tried so hard, but he'd underestimated Morland, and
Hayley Conyer, and the board. He wasn't the first to
have tried to hide his difficulties, and he wouldn't be the
last. He should have known that, over the centuries, the
town had learned to spot weakness, but he had exposed
himself by applying to the town's fund for that loan. Perhaps they'd all just been more alert than usual to strange
patterns, blips in behavior, because of the economy. So
many folk were struggling in the current climate. That
was why the board had acted. That was why they had
taken the girl.

"Those are our private affairs," said Erin, but her voice

sounded hollow even to her. In Prosperous nothing was private, not really.

"But what happens when private difficulties affect all?" said Hayley, still speaking in that maddeningly reasonable, insidiously patronizing tone. God, Erin hated her. It was as though cataracts had been removed from her eyes, the old clouded lenses replaced with ones that were new and clear. She saw the town as it really was, saw it in all its viciousness, its self-regard, its madness. They had been brainwashed, conditioned by centuries of behavior, but it was only when it arrived at their own door, in the form of the girl, that Harry and Erin realized that they could no longer be a part of it. Releasing the girl was an imperfect solution, the action of those who were still not brave enough to take the final step themselves and hoped that another might do it for them. The girl would go to the police, she would tell her story, and they would come.

And what then? The girl would have been able to give the police a description of Walter and Beatrix, and of Harry and Erin. All four would have been questioned, but Walter and Beatrix wouldn't have buckled under interrogation. They had been responsible for finding and taking the last two girls, but they were now nearing death. They were as loyal to the town as Hayley Conyer was, and they weren't likely to roll over on it in the final years of their life. At best, it would have been their word against that of Harry and Erin.

They threatened us. They told us to get them a girl or they'd burn our house down. We're old. We were frightened. We didn't know what they wanted with the girl. We didn't ask. . . .

And Hayley Conyer, and the selectmen, and Chief Morland? Why, there'd be nothing to connect them to the girl, nothing beyond the word of Harry and Erin Dixon, who'd kept her trapped in their basement before leaving a door unlocked, and it could be that they did so only because they'd lost the courage to follow through on whatever it was they had planned for her. They would have been liable to felony charges of kidnapping and criminal restraint—a Class A crime, or a Class B if the prosecution accepted that they'd voluntarily released the victim alive and in a safe place, and not suffering from serious bodily injury. It was the difference between ten years behind bars and thirty years, but it would still have been more time than either of them wanted to spend in a cell.

And maybe, just maybe, someone might have believed their story.

But no, that was the greatest fantasy of all.

"Harry? Erin? You still with us?"

It was Morland speaking.

Erin looked at her husband. She knew that their thoughts had been running along similar lines.

What if, what if . . .

"Yes," said Harry. "We're listening."

"You're in financial difficulties—far more serious difficulties than you chose to share with Ben when you asked for a loan—and you tried to keep them from us."

There was no point in denying it.

"Yes, that's true."

"Why?"

"Because we were ashamed."

"Is that all?"

"No. We were frightened as well."

"Frightened? Frightened of what?"

There was no going back now.

"Frightened that the town might turn against us."

Now Hayley Conyer spoke again.

"The town does not turn against its own, Harry. It protects them. That's the reason for its existence. How could you doubt that?"

Harry squeezed the bridge of his nose with the index finger and thumb of his right hand. He could feel a migraine coming on.

"I don't know," he said. "With all that was going on, with all our problems . . ."

"You lost faith," said Conyer.

"Yes, Hayley, I suppose we did."

Conyer leaned across the table. Her breath smelled of mints and dying.

"Did you let the girl go?" she asked.

"No," said Harry.

"Look me in the eye and tell me true."

Harry took his hand away from his nose and stared Conyer down.

"No, we did not let the girl go."

She didn't want to believe him. He could see that. Like Morland, she had her suspicions, but she couldn't prove them, and the town wouldn't allow her to move against them without proof.

"All right, then," she said. "The question is, where do we go from here? You'll have to make amends, both of you."

The pain was pulsing in Harry's head now, and with it came the nausea. He knew what was coming. He'd known from the moment Morland arrived at their house with the body of the girl in the trunk of his car. He wanted to tell them of the dreams he'd been having, but he bit back the words. He hadn't even told his wife about them. In his dreams, the girl wasn't dead. They'd put her in the grave alive, because dead girls didn't open their eyes. She was alive and scratching at the plastic, and somehow she had managed to tear through it and dig her way out of the ground, except that when she emerged she really was dead. She was a being transformed, a revenant, and when she opened her mouth she spewed darkness, and the night deepened around her.

"What do you want us to do?" said Harry, but he asked only because it was what was expected of him. He might as well have been reading from a script.

Hayley Conyer patted his hand. It was all he could do not to yank it away at her touch.

"Find us another girl," said Conyer. "And quickly."

XVI

I got to the Preble Street Soup Kitchen just as the dinner service was coming to an end. A woman named Evadne Bryan-Perkins, who worked at the Portland Help Center, a mental health and community support facility off Congress, had directed me to the kitchen. Shaky had given me her name as a contact person, but she told me that she hadn't seen him in a day or two, and suggested that he might drop by Preble Street for a bite to eat.

Preble Street served three meals per day not only to the city's homeless but to seniors and families who were struggling to get by on welfare. That added up to almost five hundred thousand meals per year, but the meals were just a starting point. By getting people in the door, the staff was in a position to help them with housing advice, employment, and health care. At the very least, they could give them some clean, warm socks, and that meant a lot during winter in Maine.

One of the volunteers, a young woman named Karyn, told me that Shaky had been through earlier in the evening, but had finished his meal and headed back out almost immediately after. This was unlike him, she said. He was more sociable than some, and he usually appreciated the company and warmth of the shelter.

"He hasn't been the same since his friend Jude died," she said. "They had a bond between them, and they looked out for each other. Shaky's talked to us a little about it, but most of it he's kept inside."

"Do you have any idea where he might have gone?"

Karyn called over another volunteer, a kid of about college age.

"This is Stephen," she said. "He was one of the coordinators of this year's homeless survey. He might be able to help you."

She went back to cleaning tables, leaving me with Stephen. He was a tall young man. I pretty much had to lean back just to look him in the eye. He wasn't as open as Karyn had been. He had his arms crossed as he spoke to me.

"Can I ask why a private detective is looking for Shaky?" he said.

"He came to talk to me about Jude's death. I think he set tumblers falling in my mind. If I'm to take it any further, there are some questions that he might be able to help me answer. He's in no trouble. I give you my word on that."

I watched him consider what I'd told him before he decided that I wasn't about to make Shaky's existence any more difficult, and he loosened up enough to offer me coffee. Between the beer I'd had at Ruski's and the coffee at Rosie's, I was carrying more liquid than a camel, but one of the first things I learned when I started out as a cop was always to accept if someone you were trying to talk with offered you a coffee or a soda. It made them relax, and if they were relaxed they'd be more willing to help you.

"Karyn mentioned something about a survey," I said, as we sipped coffee from plastic cups.

"We're required by the Department of Housing and Urban Development to do a census of the homeless each year," said Stephen. "If we don't know how many folk need help, we can't work out budgets, staffing, even how much food we're likely to require over the months to come. But it's also a chance to make contact with the ones who've avoided us so far, and try to bring them into the fold."

I must have looked puzzled.

"You're wondering why anyone who's hungry would pass up the chance of a hot meal, right?" said Stephen.

"I guess it doesn't make much sense to me."

"Some people who take to the streets don't want to be found," he said. "A lot of them have mental health issues, and if you're a paranoid schizophrenic who believes that the government is trying to kill you the last thing you're going to want to do is turn up at a shelter where someone might start prying into your business. Then there are others who are just plain scared. Maybe they've gotten into a fight with someone in the past, and they know that there's a knife out there looking to sink itself into them, or they've had a bad experience with the authorities and prefer to keep their heads down. So, for one night of the year we go out in force, looking under bleachers and behind Dumpsters, and we try to reach them all. I mean, we're out there at other times of the year, too, but the sustained focus of survey night, and the sheer weight of volunteers on the streets, means that we get a hell of a lot done in a few hours."

"So where does Shaky hang out?"

"Shaky likes to come into the shelter, if there's a mat available to sleep on. He hasn't been in so much since Jude died, which means that he's either set up camp somewhere off the interstate, probably around Back Cove Park, or he's sleeping at the rear of one of the businesses on Danforth or Pleasant, where the cops can't see him. That's where I'd look."

He toyed with his coffee cup. He wanted to say more. I didn't hurry him.

"Did you know Mr. Jude?" he eventually asked.

I'd never heard anyone call Jude "Mister" before. He was always just Jude. It made me warm more to the kid.

"A little," I said. "I'd sometimes put money his way if I needed someone to watch a car or an address for a while. He never let me down."

"He was a smart man, and a good one too," said Stephen. "I could never quite figure out how he ended up in the situation he was in. Some of the men and women here, I can see it. There's a trajectory you can reconstruct. But not in Mr. Jude's case. The best I can tell, there was a weak bolt in the machinery, and when it broke the whole mechanism ground to a halt."

"You're not an engineering student by any chance, are you?"

He grinned for the first time. "Know a man by his metaphors."

"You sound as though you liked Jude," I said.

"Uh-huh, I did. Even in the midst of his own troubles, he still had time for others. I tried to follow his lead by helping him in turn."

"You're talking about his daughter?"

"Yeah, Annie. I was kind of keeping an eye on her for him."

"Really?"

"Because of my work with the shelter here, I was in a position to talk to others in the same business. I made an occasional call to the Tender House in Bangor, where Annie was staying, just so I could reassure Mr. Jude that she was doing okay. When she disappeared, I—"

He stopped.

"You felt responsible?"

He nodded, but didn't speak.

"Did Jude say anything to make you believe he felt the same way?"

"No, never. It wasn't in his nature. It didn't help, though. It didn't make me feel any less guilty."

Stephen was clearly a good kid, but he had the egotism of youth. The world revolved around him, and consequently he believed that he had the power to change how it worked. And, in the way of the young, he had made another's pain about himself, even if he did so for what seemed the best of reasons. Time and age would change him; if they didn't, he wouldn't be working in soup kitchens and shelters much longer. His frustrations would get the better of him and force him out. He'd blame others for it, but it would be his own fault.

I thanked him and left my cell phone number, just in case I couldn't find Shaky, or he chose to come into the shelter for the night after all. Stephen promised to leave a note for the breakfast and lunch volunteers as well, so that if Shaky arrived to eat the next day they could let me know. I used the men's room before I left, just to ensure that my bladder didn't burst somewhere between the shelter and Back Cove. An old man was standing at one of the sinks, stripped to the waist. His white hair hung past his shoulders, and his body reminded me of the images I'd seen of Jude's poor, scarred torso, like some medieval depiction of Christ after he'd been taken down from the cross.

"How you doing?" I said.

"Livin' the dream," the old man replied.

He was shaving with a disposable razor. He removed the last of the foam from his cheek, splashed water on his face, and rubbed his skin to check that it was smooth.

"You got any aftershave?" he asked.

"Not with me," I said. "Why, you got a date?"

"I haven't been on a date since Nixon was president."

"Another thing to blame him for—ruining your love life."

"He was a son of a bitch, but I didn't need no help on that front."

I washed my hands and dried them with a paper towel. I had money in my pocket, but I didn't want to offend the old man. Then I thought that it was better to risk hurting his feelings. I left a ten on the sink beside him. He looked at it as though Alexander Hamilton might bite him if he tried to pick it up; that, or I might ask him to bite me as part of some bizarre sexual fetish.

"What's that for?" he said.

"Aftershave."

He reached out and took the ten.

"I always liked Old Spice," he said.

"My father wore Old Spice."

"Something stays around that long, it has to be good."

"Amen," I said. "Look after yourself."

"I will," he said. "And, hey?"

I looked back.

"Thanks."

XVII

It's a full-time job being homeless. It's a full-time job being poor. That's what those who bitch about the underprivileged not going out there and finding work fail to understand. They have a job already, and that job is surviving. You have to get in line early for food, and earlier still for a place to sleep. You carry your possessions on your back, and when they wear out you spend time scavenging for replacements. You have only so much energy to expend, because you have only so much food to fuel your body. Most of the time you're tired, and sore, and your clothes are damp. If the cops find you sleeping on the street, they move you on. If you're lucky, they'll give you a ride to a shelter, but if there are no beds free, or no mats available on the floor, you'll have to sleep sitting upright in a plastic chair in an outer office, and the lights will be on full, because that's what the fire code regulations require, so you go back out on the streets again, because at least there you can lie down in the dark, and with luck you'll sleep. Each day is the same, and each day you get a little older, and a little more tired.

And sometimes you remember who you once were. You were a kid who played with other kids. You had a mother and a father. You wanted to be a fireman, or an astronaut, or a railroad engineer. You had a husband. You had a wife. You were loved. You could never have imagined that you would end up this way.

You curl up in the darkness, and you wait for death to kiss you a final, blissful good night.

*   *   *

SHAKY WAS BACK ON the streets. He'd been tempted to stay at one of the shelters and find a mat on which to sleep. His arm ached. It always pained him in winter, leaving him with months of discomfort, but it had been hurting more since Jude died. It was probably—what was the word? He thought and thought—*psychosomatic*, that was it. It had taken him a good minute to recall it, but Jude would have known the word instantly. Jude knew about history, and science, and geography. He could tell you the plot of every great novel he'd ever read, and recite whole passages from memory. Shaky had once tested him on a couple, and had jokingly remarked that, for all he knew, Jude could have been making up all those quotations off the top of his head. Jude had responded by claiming that Shaky had impugned his honor—that was the word he'd used, *impugned*—and there had been nothing for it but for the two of them to head down to the Portland Public Library on Congress, where Shaky had pulled *The Great Gatsby* from the shelves, along with *The Adventures of Huckleberry Finn*, *Lolita*, *The Grapes of Wrath*, *As I Lay Dying*, *Ulysses*, and the poems of Longfellow and Cummings and Yeats. Jude had been able to quote chunks of them without getting a word wrong, without a single stumble, and even some of the librarians had come over to listen. By the time he got on to Shakespeare, it was like being in the presence of one of those old stage actors, the kind who used to wash up in small towns when there were still theaters in which to perform, their costumes and props in one truck, the cast in another, and put on revues, and comedies, and social dramas, or maybe a condensed Shakespeare with all the dull parts removed, leaving only the great moments of drama: ghosts, and bloodied daggers, and dying kings.

And there was Jude in his old checked suit and two-tone shoes, the heels worn smooth and cardboard masking the holes in the soles, surrounded by curious readers and amused librarians. He was lost in words, lost in roles, someone other than himself for just a little while, and Shaky had loved him then, loved him as he basked in the glow of pleasure that emanated from Jude's face, loved him as his eyes closed in reverie, and he said a prayer of gratitude for the presence of Jude in his life even as he wondered how one so clever and so gifted could have ended up scavenging in Dumpsters and sleeping on the streets of a city forever shadowed by winter, and what weakness in Jude's being had caused him to turn away from his family and his home and throw himself to the winds like a leaf at the coming of fall.

Shaky's pack weighed heavily on him. He thought again about the shelter. He could have left his belongings there—even if there was no bed for him, someone might have been willing to look after them—and returned to pick them up later, but increasingly he found the presence of others distressing. He would look at the familiar faces, but the one he sought was no longer there, and the presence of the rest only reminded him of Jude's absence. How long had they been friends? Shaky couldn't remember. He had lost track of the years a long time ago. Dates were of no consequence. He was not marking wedding anniversaries, or the birthdays of children. He left the years behind him, discarded without a thought, like old shoes that could no longer fulfill even his modest needs.

He was near Deering Oaks. He kept returning there, back to the place in which Jude had breathed his last. He was a mourner, and a pilgrim. He stopped outside the house, its windows boarded. Someone had placed a new lock and bolt on the basement door since Jude's death: the police, maybe, or the owner, assuming it was still owned by a person and not a bank. Crime scene tape had been placed across the door, but it was torn now. It drifted in the night's breeze.

Shaky felt no sense of Jude at the house. That was how he knew that Jude had not taken his own life. Shaky didn't believe in ghosts. He didn't even believe in God, and if he turned out to be wrong, well, he and God would have some words about the dog-shit hand that Shaky had been dealt. But Shaky did have a certain sense about people and places. Jude had it too. You needed it if you wanted to survive on the streets. Shaky knew instinctively whom to trust, and whom to avoid. He knew the places in which it was safe to sleep and the places, though empty and apparently innocuous, in which it was best not to rest. Men and women left their marks as they moved through life, and you could read them if you had a mind to. Jude had left his mark in that basement, his final mark, but it didn't read to Shaky like the mark of a man who had given in to despair. It read to Shaky like the mark of one who would have fought if he'd had the strength, and if the odds had not been against him.

He walked down to the basement door and took the Swiss Army knife from his pocket. It was one of his most valuable possessions, and he maintained it well. There was one blade that he kept particularly sharp, and he used it now to make two signs on the stonework beside the door. The first was a rectangle with a dot in the center, the old hobo-alphabet symbol for "danger." The second was a diagonal line joined halfway by a smaller, almost perpendicular line. It was the warning to keep away.

He spent the rest of the night asking questions. He did it carefully, and discreetly, and he approached only those whom he trusted, those he knew would not lie to him or betray him. It had taken him a while to figure out what he should do. Talking to the detective had crystallized things for him. Someone had taken Jude's money, and the contents of his pack. It might have been those responsible for his death, but it didn't seem likely that they'd then call in his hanging corpse to the cops. Neither would they have taken the money if they wanted his death to appear as a suicide. Anyway, from what Shaky had learned, Jude had been dead for a day or more before his body was found.

All this suggested to Shaky that the person who had called in the killing, and the person who had taken the money and rifled Jude's belongings, were one and the same, and it seemed to Shaky that it might well be one of their own, a street person. One of the city's homeless had either stumbled across Jude's sleeping place by accident or, more likely, had gone looking for Jude to begin with. The word was out: Jude was calling in his loans. He needed money. The unknown person could have been seeking Jude out in order to pay his debts, but, equally, there were those on the street who would not be above hunting Jude down in order to steal whatever cash he had managed to accumulate. It didn't matter; either way someone had found Jude hanging in that basement and looted his belongings in the shadow of his corpse.

Shaky well knew that a hundred and twenty dollars was a lot of money for someone who struggled by on a couple of bucks a day. The instinct would be to celebrate: booze, or perhaps something stronger; and fast food—bought, not scavenged. Alcohol and narcotics made people careless. Rumors would start to circulate that one of their own had enjoyed a windfall.

By the time he returned to his tent at Back Cove Park, Shaky had a name.

Brightboy.

XVIII

The next morning, Shaky didn't join the line for breakfast at the shelter. He kept his distance, and fingered the note in his pocket. It had been pinned to the bulletin board at Preble Street. The detective wanted to talk. Shaky had memorized the number, but he kept the note, just in case. He knew that the years on the streets had addled his brain. He would sometimes look at a clock face, and see the hands pointing at the numbers, and be unable to tell the time. He could be in a store, the price of a six-pack or a bottle of liquor clear to read on the sign, his change laid out in his hand ready to pay, and fail to make the connection between the cost of the booze and the money in his possession.

Now, as he stood in the shelter of a doorway on Cumberland Avenue, he repeated the cell phone number over and over to himself. He had considered calling the detective and telling him what he knew, but he wanted to be sure. He wanted to present the detective with hard evidence. He wanted to prove himself, both for his own sake and for Jude's, so he stood in the shadows and watched his fellow homeless gather for breakfast.

IT DIDN'T TAKE HIM long to spot Brightboy. He arrived shortly before eight, his pack on his back. Shaky's keen eyes were drawn to Brightboy's boots. They were tan Timberlands, better than what Brighboy usually wore. It was possible that he'd found them, but, equally, they were the kind of Goodwill purchase that even a moron like Brightboy might have the sense to make while he had money in his pocket. A good pair of boots would keep your feet warm and dry, and make days spent walking the streets a little easier. He watched Brightboy exchange greetings with those whom he knew, but for the most part he kept to himself. Brightboy had always been a loner, partly out of choice, but also because he couldn't be trusted. There were those with whom one could leave a pack and know that it would be safely looked after, that its contents would not be searched and its valuables—socks, underwear, a candy bar, a can opener, a permanent water bottle—looted. Brightboy was not such a man, and he had taken beatings in the past for his thievery.

Shaky had learned that Brightboy had been on a drunken tear these past few days, and a serious one too: Mohawk Grain Alcohol 190 and Old Crow bourbon, bottle after bottle of it. As was his way, Brightboy had declined to share the contents of his portable liquor cabinet. Had he done so, there might not have been quite so many whispers of discontent.

Shaky didn't follow Brightboy into the shelter, but instead waited on the street and nibbled on a bagel from the previous day. Shaky was known in most of the city's bakeries and coffee shops, and rarely left them without having something to eat pressed upon him. He was careful to spread his lack of custom evenly, and by now he had his weekly routine down: this place on Monday morning, this one Tuesday, this one Wednesday . . . They had grown to expect him, and if he missed a visit questions would be asked of him when he returned. What happened? Were you ill? You doing okay? Shaky always answered honestly. He never played sick when he wasn't, and he never lied. He didn't have very much, which made retaining some semblance of dignity and honor all the more important.

Brightboy emerged an hour later. Shaky knew that he'd have eaten, and used the bathroom. He would probably have half a bagel, or a piece of toast, wrapped in a napkin in his pocket for later. Shaky let Brightboy get some distance ahead of him, then followed. When Brightboy stopped to talk to a woman known as Frannie at Congress Square Park, Shaky slipped into the Starbucks across the street and took a seat at the window. With his damaged arm, and the slight stoop that came with it, he felt like the unlikeliest spy in the world. Undercover Elephant would have been less conspicuous. Fortunately, it was Brightboy he was following. Brightboy was dumb, and self-absorbed. He was nearly as bad as the regular folk in his failure to notice what was going on around him.

Portland was changing. The old Eastland Hotel was being renovated by a big chain—Shaky had lost count of the number of new hotels and restaurants the city had added in recent years—and it looked as if part of Congress Park, the old plaza at Congress and High, would be sold to the hotel's new owners. A Dunkin' Donuts had once stood at the corner of Congress Park, and it became a gathering spot for the city's homeless, but it was long gone now. The businesses that had occupied the space over the years sometimes seemed to Shaky as transient as some of those who frequented its environs. It had been a laundry, a Walgreens, the Congress Square Hotel, and, way back, a wooden row house. Now it was a brick-and-concrete space with a sunken center and a few planting beds, where people like Brightboy and Frannie could conduct their business.

Brightboy's encounter with Frannie ended with the woman screaming abuse at him, and Brightboy threatening to punch her lights out. Shaky wished him luck. Frannie had been on the streets for a decade or more, and Shaky didn't even want to think about the kind of treatment she'd endured and survived in that time. The story was that she'd once bitten off the nose of a man who tried to rape her. This was subsequently described as an exaggeration: she hadn't bitten off all of his nose, said those who knew of such matters, just the cartilage below the nasal bone. Shaky figured that it must have taken Frannie a while, because she didn't have more than half a dozen teeth in her head worth talking about. He had a vision of her holding on to the guy by his ears, gnawing away at him with her jagged shards. It gave him the shivers.

He kept after Brightboy for two hours, watching him search for coins in pay phones and around parking meters, and halfheartedly rummaging through garbage cans. At the intersection of Congress and Deering Avenue, Brightboy took a detour on Deering past Skip Murphy's sober house. He lingered outside for a time, although Shaky didn't know why. Skip's accepted only those who were in full-time employment, or students with some form of income. More to the point, it took in only those who actually wanted to improve themselves, and Brightboy's best chance of improving himself lay in dying. Maybe he knew someone in there, in which case the poor bastard in question would be well advised to give Brightboy a wide berth, because Shaky wouldn't have put it past Brightboy to try and drag someone who had embarked on a twelve-step back down to his own level. It was the only reason Brightboy might offer for sharing a drink. Misery loved company, but damnation needed it.

Brightboy moved on, Shaky trailing him, and at last they came to Brightboy's stash, where he kept the stuff that he couldn't, or didn't want to, carry. There were some who used a shopping cart to haul their possessions, but they were mostly the ones who tried to make a bit extra by scavenging. Brightboy didn't have that kind of resolve. He had hidden whatever was worth keeping behind a warehouse on St. John Street, stashing it in the bushes beside a Dumpster that looked as if it hadn't been emptied since plastic was invented. He was crouched over the bushes when Shaky turned the corner, so intent on whatever he was doing that he didn't hear Shaky approach.

"Hey," said Shaky.

Brightboy was squatting with his back to Shaky. He looked over his shoulder, but didn't try to get up. Shaky could see his right hand moving in the bushes.

"Hey," said Brightboy in reply. His hand kept searching. Shaky knew that it had found what it was seeking when he saw Brightboy smile. Glass flashed in the sunlight as Brightboy withdrew his hand. He started to rise, but Shaky was too quick for him. Some might have called him a cripple behind his back, but he was far from it. His left foot was forward, his right moving in a strong arc to join and then pass it. The toe of his boot caught Brightboy in the side of the head. Brightboy gave a single yelp and fell sideways. The empty bottle of Old Crow fell from his hand and rolled across the ground. Shaky aimed a second kick at Brightboy, just to be sure, and because he wanted to. He had never liked Brightboy. Jude hadn't cared much for him either, even if his personal code of ethics forbade him to turn his back on him. Jude's attitude toward Brightboy was proof positive to Shaky that his late friend had not been without flaw.

This time, Shaky landed a glancing blow to Brightboy's chin. Brightboy started to crawl away, and Shaky finished him off with a toe to the groin from behind. Brightboy stopped moving and lay on the ground, cupping himself with his hands as he moaned softly.

The previous night's breeze was no more, and the day

was still. Shaky began to search Brightboy's possessions. It took him only a minute to find Jude's old canvas bag. Jude had used it to transport what he called his "essentials": wipes, toothbrush, comb, and whatever book he happened to be reading at the time. It was small enough to carry easily, and big enough to take any treasures he might scavenge along the way, while he left his main pack in a locker at Amistad. Brightboy must have swept Jude's valuables into it before he left the basement.

Shaky sank down against the Dumpster. The sight of the bag, the feel of it in his hands, brought home to him with renewed clarity that Jude was gone. Shaky started to cry. Brightboy looked up at him from the ground. His eyes were glazed, and he was bleeding from the mouth.

"You took this from him," said Shaky. "You took it from him while his body was still warm."

"His body weren't warm," said Brightboy. "It was cold as shit."

He tried to sit up, but his balls still hurt. He lay down again, rocking with pain, but managed to keep talking.

"Anyway, Jude would have wanted me to have it. He couldn't take it with him. If he could've talked, he'd have told me so."

God, Shaky hated Brightboy. He wished that he'd kicked him hard enough to drive his balls up into his throat and choke him.

"Even if he'd given this to you, you wouldn't have deserved to have it," Shaky told him.

Inside the bag he found the last of Jude's money—forty-three dollars, still wrapped in the same rubber band—and Jude's toothpaste and comb. The wipes were gone. Strangely, the book Jude had been reading at the time of his death, an architectural history of early churches in England, was also among the books stolen by Brightboy. Jude had ordered it specially, Shaky remembered. The people at Longfellow Books had found a paperback copy for him, and refused to accept payment for it. Jude had picked it up days before he died, just after returning from his most recent trip north. Shaky had put the selection down to another manifestation of Jude's magpie intellect, but his friend had been different about this book. He hadn't wanted to discuss it with Shaky, just as he hadn't wanted to tell him exactly where he had gone when he left Portland those final two times.

"Bangor?" Shaky had pressed him.

"It doesn't matter."

"Your daughter still up there, you think?"

"No, I believe she went . . . someplace else."

"You find her?"

"Not yet."

Jude had begun to mark the pages as he read. Shaky flipped through them, and some bus tickets fell out. He tried to grab them, but at that moment the wind came up again from out of nowhere and snatched the tickets away. It blew them into some briars, and Shaky tore the skin on his right hand trying to retrieve them. He almost gave up, but he hadn't come this far to let anything slide that might help the detective. He knelt down and reached into the bush, ignoring the pain and the damage to his coat.

"Damn you," he whispered. "Damn bushes."

"No," said a voice behind him. "Damn you, you fuck!"

The sunlight caught the bottle of Old Crow again. This time it didn't roll away, but shattered against Shaky's skull.

SHAKY CAME BACK TO consciousness as the paramedic tended his wounds. Later he would learn that a driver had come into the lot to turn, and spotted him lying on the ground. The driver thought he was dead.

"We'll need to get you stitched up," said the paramedic.

He and his colleague wore blue plastic gloves that were stained with Shaky's blood. Shaky tried to rise, but they held him down.

"You stay there. We got you."

Shaky felt something in his right hand. He looked and saw the bus tickets crumpled in his fist. Carefully he put them into the pocket of his coat, and felt his fingers brush against the piece of paper with the detective's number on it.

"You got someone we can call?" said the paramedic, and Shaky realized that they didn't know he was homeless. He had laundered his clothes only a day earlier, and showered and shaved at Amistad while they were drying.

"Yes," said Shaky, and despite the blow to the head he recited the detective's cell phone number from memory before promptly losing consciousness again.

XIX

By the time I got to Maine Medical, a doctor had picked the shards of glass out of Shaky's scalp and stitched him up. He was woozy from the mild sedative they'd given him, but he wasn't going to be kept overnight. X-rays had revealed no sign of skull fracture. He'd just have a hell of a headache, and his scalp looked as if it had been sewn together by Victor Frankenstein.

He silently pointed me to his possessions, which were contained in a plastic bag. The nurse told me that, before his lights went out behind the warehouse, he insisted that the medics retrieve his book. That was in the bag as well.

"A history of early English churches?" I said, waving it at Shaky as he lay on the gurney, his eyes heavy. "I have to say that I'm surprised."

Shaky swallowed hard and gestured toward the water pitcher nearby. I poured him a glass and held it to his mouth. He only dribbled a little.

"It was a friend's," he said.

"Jude's?"

He nodded, but it clearly made his head hurt, because he winced and didn't try to do it again.

"Coat," he said.

I went through the pockets of his coat until I found the bus tickets, along with the scrap of paper containing my cell phone number. The tickets were for two Portland–Bangor round-trips with Concord, and then two further onward round-trips on the Cyr Bus Line that connected Bangor to Aroostook and points between, this time from Bangor to Medway, in Penobscot County.

"Where did he get the money for these tickets?" I asked Shaky. "From earlier loans he called in?"

"Guess so," said Shaky. "And bottles and cans."

Portland's homeless, like most people in their position, made a little money by scouring the trash for drink containers. Tuesday evenings were particularly profitable, since Wednesday was pickup day for recycling.

"Did he say why he wanted to go to Medway?"

"No."

"But it must have been something to do with his daughter?"

"Yeah. Everything had to do with his daughter these last few weeks."

I looked again at the tickets. The main reasons to go to Medway were hunting, fishing, snowmobiling, and skiing, and I couldn't see Jude doing any of those, whether they were in season or not. Perhaps his daughter had ended up there, but at this time of year there wasn't a whole lot happening. Eventually the snow would melt, but a lull would follow before the summer tourists began arriving.

I flicked through the book. There was something there, something that I couldn't quite grasp. It danced at the edge of my awareness. Maine and English churches.

Then it came to me: a town with an ancient church, an English church.

"Prosperous," I said aloud, and a nurse gave me a curious glance. "But what the hell would Jude be doing in Prosperous?"

IT DIDN'T TAKE LONG for the police to find Brightboy. He'd bought himself a half gallon of Caldwell Gin and found a quiet spot in Baxter Woods in which to drink it. He hadn't even bothered to ditch the items that he'd taken from Jude's basement. After they cuffed him and put him in the back of the car, Brightboy told them, without prompting, that he wasn't sorry for hitting Shaky with the empty Old Crow bottle.

"I'd have hit him with a full one," he said, "if'n I could have afforded to."

When he was questioned at Portland PD headquarters, once he'd sobered up some, Brightboy could add little to the sum of knowledge about Jude's death, and Shaky didn't want to press charges over the assault, arguing that "Jude wouldn't have wanted me to." Then again, Jude was dead, and he wasn't the one who'd been smacked over the head with the Old Crow.

A bed was reserved for Shaky at one of the shelters, and the staff had agreed to keep an eye on him for any signs of concussion. He looked comfortable when I spoke to him about Brightboy, but an emergency shelter didn't seem the best place in which to try to recover from a head injury. As good fortune had it, Terrill Nix was one of the respondents to the initial assault, and between us we agreed to see if something could be done to move Shaky up the housing-placement list in return for his efforts in tracking down Brightboy.

The police continued to question Brightboy about Jude, and what he might or might not have seen in the basement. Brightboy didn't prove too helpful on that count—not out of unwillingness but because he had seen nothing beyond Jude's corpse and the consequent open season on his possessions. The cops could have charged Brightboy with both petty theft, for the total value of the cash and other items taken from the basement was less than five hundred dollars, and with interfering with a possible crime scene, but in the end they decided just to put him back on the streets. The court and the prison systems were overburdened as it was, and a spell behind bars was unlikely to have much of an impact on Brightboy one way or another.

Macy joined Nix while I was at the hospital, and I mentioned the bus tickets to her, and the book on church architecture.

"What the hell would someone like Jude be doing in Prosperous?" she said.

"You know," I replied, "those were almost exactly my own words."

"I've talked to my lieutenant," said Macy, "and his view is that all this is just complicating what should be kept simple. We have enough to keep us busy for the next twelve months without adding Jude to the list. He thinks we should let it slide for now. I'll keep an open mind on it, though. If you find out anything solid, you let me know. Terrill?"

She looked to Nix for his view. I had to admire the way she worked. There were detectives who wouldn't have bothered to cut a patrolman in on a discussion like this, let alone seek his opinion. The potential downside was that it could make the detective look indecisive, or lead to a situation where patrol cops might feel they had the right to drop in their two cents' worth without an invitation, but I got the impression Macy wouldn't have those problems. She didn't give too much. She gave just enough.

Nix took the path of least resistance.

"The more I sleep on it, the more it looks like Jude took the drop of his own free will. I spoke to one of the psychiatrists at the Portland Help Center. He said that Jude suffered from depression most of his life. It was one of the reasons he couldn't hold down the permanent housing they tried to find for him. He'd just get depressed and head back to the streets."

I understood their position. Jude wasn't a pretty USM sophomore, or a nurse, or a promising high school student, and the narrative of his death, however incomplete, had already been written and accepted. I'd been there myself, once upon a time.

"Did someone ask Brightboy about a knife?" I said. I was still wondering how Jude had cut the rope, assuming that he had even done so himself.

"Shit!" said Macy.

She slipped away and made a call. When she returned, she looked troubled.

"Brightboy had a penknife in his possession when we picked him up, but he says it's his own. He didn't recall seeing a knife at the scene. He could be lying, though, and he admits that he was out of his skull most of the time he was in that basement. I don't think Brightboy remembers much of anything, even at the best of times."

But she seemed to be talking more to convince herself than to convince me. I let it go. The seed had been planted. If it took root, all the better.

Macy left with Nix. I watched her go. A passing doctor watched her too.

"Damn," he said.

"Yeah," I replied. "My sentiments exactly."

The next time I saw Macy, I was dying.

A pall hung over the house of Harry and Erin Dixon after the departure of Chief Morland and Hayley Conyer. A visit from either of them would have been enough to unnerve the Dixons at the best of times, for they were the two most powerful citizens in Prosperous, even allowing for the fact that Morland didn't sit on the board. But a visit from both of them, especially under the circumstances, was sufficient to push Harry and Erin to breaking point.

They had let the girl go because they wanted to be free of this madness—and perhaps because she reminded them of the daughter they had never had, but for whom they had always wished—and now they were being drawn deeper into the town's insanity just because they had tried to do the right thing. In a way, Erin thought, it might be the shock to the system that they needed. Something of their torpor, their acquiescence to the town's edicts, had already been challenged, or they could not have acted as they had in freeing the girl. Now, faced with the prospect of kidnapping a replacement, any remaining illusions they had were being profoundly dissipated.

As their vision grew clearer, so too did their desperation to get away from Prosperous increase, but neither had yet spoken about what was being asked of them. To a greater (in the case of Harry) or lesser extent (in the case of his wife), they were like children, hoping that by ignoring the problem it might go away, or that some other solution might present itself. Harry, in particular, had sunk into denial. He found himself almost wishing that some stray girl—a waif, a runaway—might pass through Prosperous, or be picked up at the side of the road by one of the selectmen: a safe, older man like Thomas Souleby or Calder Ayton, who would offer her a ride into town and buy her soup and a sandwich at Gertrude's. He would excuse himself to go to the men's room, and a conversation would ensue behind closed doors. A woman would approach the girl, a mother figure. Concern would be expressed for her. A place to stay would be offered, if only for a night or two until she had a chance to clean herself up. There might even be work for her at Gertrude's, if she wanted it. Gertrude's was always shorthanded. Yes, that would work; that would do it. That would take the pressure off Harry and Erin, and they could continue to plan for their eventual escape. Yes, yes . . .

A day went by. Harry avoided speaking with his wife, finding excuses to be away from her. That was not how their marriage had survived for so long. True, Harry might sometimes be a reluctant participant in conversations about feelings, hurt or otherwise, but he had come to accept their value. While Erin could not know the direction of his thoughts, she understood him well enough to guess them.

Father, if thou be willing, remove this cup from me . . .

He sometimes quoted that particular piece of Scripture—Luke 22:42, if she remembered correctly—in times of mild difficulty, like when she asked him to take out the trash if it was raining or, occasionally (and annoyingly) when they were about to make love. Her husband had his weaknesses. She had no illusions about them, just as, she assumed, he was aware of hers in turn, although she liked to think that hers were venal, and of less consequence. Harry disliked confrontation, and was poor at making serious decisions. He preferred to have responsibility for the latter taken from him by circumstance, for then he would not be blamed if the consequences were negative. Erin had never said so aloud, but, had her husband demonstrated a little more backbone, a pinch more ruthlessness, some of their financial problems might have been avoided.

But would she have loved him as much if he had? Ah, there was the rub.

Like her husband, she attended church every Sunday. Most of the people of Prosperous did. They were Baptists, and Methodists, and Catholics. Some had even embraced roadside churches whose denominations were unclear even to their adherents. They believed, and yet did not believe. They understood the difference between the distant and the immanent, between the creator and what was created. But Erin derived more consolation from the rituals than her husband did. She could feel him zoning out during services, for he had little or no interest in organized religion. Sunday worship was a form of escape for him, though only in the sense that it gave him some peace and quiet in which to think, daydream or, occasionally, nap. But Erin listened. She didn't agree with all that she heard, but so much of it was unarguable. Live decently, or what was the point in living at all?

And the people of Prosperous did live decently, and in most matters they behaved well. They gave to charity. They cherished the environment. They tolerated—no, embraced—gays and lesbians. Entrenched conservatives and radical liberals all found their place in Prosperous. In return, the town was blessed with good fortune.

It was just that, sometimes, the town needed to give fortune a push.

But had her husband listened a little more attentively to what was being said at services, and perhaps read the Bible instead of just picking up random quotations from it, he might have recalled the second part of that verse he so loved to throw her way as she began to nuzzle his neck late at night.

. . . nevertheless not my will, but thine, be done.

It was the town's will that had to be done.

"We need to talk about it," said Erin as they sat at the table to eat an early dinner. She had made a pot roast, but so far neither of them had done more than pick at it.

"There's nothing to talk about," said Harry.

"What?" She stared at her husband with absolute incredulity. "Are you out of your mind? They want us to abduct a girl. If we don't, they'll kill us."

"Something will turn up," said Harry. He forced himself to eat some of the pot roast. It was strange—or maybe it wasn't strange at all—but ever since he and Chief Morland had buried the girl, Harry had experienced something of a turn against meat. He'd started consuming a lot of cheese, and bread smeared with peanut butter. The pot roast tasted so strong that he had to force himself not to spit it back onto the plate. Somehow he managed to chew it long enough to enable him to swallow. He separated the meat from the vegetables and the potatoes, and proceeded to eat them instead.

"They won't kill us," he said. "They can't. The town has survived by not hurting its own. The board knows that. If they kill us, others will start to fear that it might be their turn next. The board will lose control."

Or they'll tighten it, thought Erin. Sometimes it was necessary to make an example, just to keep the rest in line, and most of those in town—the ones who knew, the ones who participated—would have little time for anyone who placed the present and the future of Prosperous at risk. Any townsfolk who might have some sympathy for the Dixons' predicament were those most like them-selves, the ones who were secretly struggling. But there was no chance of them turning against Prosperous once the Dixons were gone, not as long as Chief Morland and Hayley Conyer didn't show up at *their* door and demand that they go hunting for a young woman. Young men didn't work as well. Prosperous had learned that a long time ago.

"You're wrong," said Erin. "You know you are."

He wouldn't look up at her. He speared half a potato with his fork and stuffed it into his mouth.

"What would you have me do?" he asked.

"We have to tell someone."

"No."

"Listen to—"

"*No!*"

She shrank back from him. Harry rarely raised his voice—not in joy, and certainly not in anger. That was one of the reasons she had been so attracted to him.

Harry was like a strong tree; he could be buffeted by storms, but he always remained rooted. The downside of his disposition was that tendency not to act but to react, and then only when no other option presented itself. Now he found himself in a situation that he had always hoped to avoid, and since he did not know how to extricate himself from it he had responded with inertia, coupled with a peculiar misplaced faith in a combination of good luck and the possibility of a change of mind on the part of the board.

"I'm dealing with it," he said.

His voice had returned to its usual volume. That brief flash of anger, of energy, was gone, and Erin regretted its passing. Anything was better than this lassitude.

Before she could continue, their doorbell ring. They had heard no car approaching, and had seen no lights.

Harry got up and went to the door. He tried not to think of who might be out there: Morland, asking to look at their basement again, querying further the manner of the girl's escape; or Hayley Conyer, come to check on their progress, to see if they'd started trawling the streets yet.

But it was neither of them. On the step stood Luke Joblin's son, Bryan. He had a bag at his feet. Bryan was twenty-six or twenty-seven, if Harry remembered correctly. He did some lifting work for his father, and was good with his hands. Harry had seen some furniture that Bryan had made, and was impressed by it. The boy had no real discipline, though. He didn't work at developing his gifts. He didn't want to be a joiner or a carpenter or a furniture maker. Mostly, he just liked hunting, in season and out; anything from a crow to a moose, Bryan Joblin was happy to try and kill it.

"Bryan?" said Harry. "What are you doing out here?"

"My dad heard that you might need some help," said Bryan, and Harry didn't like the gleam in his eye. He didn't like it one little bit. "He suggested I ought to stay with you for a week or two. You know, just until you get back on top of things again."

It was only then that Harry spotted the rifle case. A Remington 700 in .30-06. He'd seen Bryan with it often enough.

Harry didn't move. He felt Erin's presence behind him, and it was only when she put her hand on his shoulder that he realized he was trembling.

"There's no problem, is there, Mr. Dixon?" said Bryan, and his tone made it clear that there was only one right answer to the question.

"No, there's no problem at all," said Harry.

He stepped back to admit Bryan. The boy picked up his bag and gun and stepped inside. He greeted Erin with a nod—"Mrs. Dixon"—and the food on the table caught his attention.

"Pot roast," he said. "Smells good."

Erin had not taken her eyes off Harry. Now they looked at each other across the Joblin boy, and they knew.

"I'll show you to your room, Bryan," said Erin, "and then you can join us for a bite to eat. There's plenty to go round."

Harry watched her lead the boy down the hall to the spare room. When they were both out of sight, Harry put his face in his hands and leaned against the wall. He was still standing in that position when Erin returned. She kissed his neck and buried herself in the scent of him.

"You were right," he whispered. "They're turning on us."

"What will we do?"

He answered without hesitation.
"We'll run."

XXI

The wolf was in agony. His injury was worsening. In his earlier pain and fear, he had traveled far from the place of his pack's destruction, but now he was having trouble walking even a short distance. Somewhere in the depths of his consciousness the wolf recognized the fact of his own dying. It manifested as a gradual encroachment of darkness upon light, a persistent dimming at the edges of his vision.

The wolf feared men, dreading the sound and scent of them, remembering still the carnage they had wrought by the banks of the river. But where men gathered, so too was there food. The wolf had been reduced to scavenging among trash cans and garbage bags, but in doing so he was eating better than he had in weeks. He had even managed to take a small mongrel dog that had ventured too far into the woods. The wolf could hear the noise of men calling and whistling as he tore the dog's throat apart, but the prey's body was light enough to clamp in his jaws and carry away. He took it far from the sounds of pursuit, and consumed it until just fur and small bones remained.

But the wolf remained hungry.

Now it was night, and his nose was twitching. He smelled decaying meat. He came to the place where the scent was strongest, and found that the ground was soft and broken.

Ignoring the ache in his wounded leg, he started to dig.

2

TRAPPING

"We! Lord," quoth the gentyle knyght,
"Whether this be the Grene Chapelle?
Here myght aboute mydnyght
The Dele his matynnes telle!"

Sir Gawain and the Green Knight

XXII

Prosperous looked like a lot of Maine towns, except that those towns lay mostly Down East and were kept wealthy by tourists who didn't balk at spending fifty dollars on decorative lobster buoys. But Prosperous was well off the tourist trail, and its stores and businesses relied on local trade to remain solvent. Driving down Main Street, I took in the antique streetlamps, and the carefully maintained storefronts, and the absence of anything resembling a chain outlet. Both coffee shops were small and independent, and the pharmacy looked old enough to be able to fill prescriptions for leeches. The Prosperous Tap reminded me of Jacob Wirth, in Boston, even down to the old clock hanging above the sign, and the general store at the edge of town could have been dropped into the nineteenth century without attracting a single sidelong glance.

That morning I had done a little reading up on Prosperous in the library of the Maine Historical Society, in Portland, before making the journey northwest. Prosperous's home-ownership rate was as close to a hundred percent as made no difference, and the median value of property inside the town limits was at least fifty percent higher than the state average. So too was median household income, and the number of residents who held a bachelor's degree or higher. Meanwhile, if Prosperous had any black residents they were keeping themselves well hidden, and it was the same for Asians, Latinos, and Native Americans. In fact, if the census figures were correct, Prosperous had no foreign-born residents at all. Curiously, the number of residents per household was much higher than the state average as well: nearly four, while the average was 2.34. It seemed that kids in Prosperous liked to stay home with mom and dad.

There was one other strange fact that I discovered about Prosperous. Although its percentage of military veterans was roughly proportional to its size, none of the townsfolk had ever been fatally wounded while serving their country. Not one. All had returned home safely. This extraordinary feat had been the subject of an article in the *Maine Sunday Telegram* following the return of Prosperous's last serving soldier from Vietnam in 1975. The town's good fortune had been ascribed to the "power of prayer" by its pastor, a Reverend Watkyn Warraner. His son, Michael Warraner, was the current pastor. While there were various Catholic, Baptist, Methodist, and Presbyterian houses of worship in the surrounding area, the only church within the town limits was the tiny, and peculiarly named, Congregation of Adam Before Eve & Eve Before Adam, and it was of this flock that Michael Warraner was apparently shepherd.

Which was where things got really interesting: Prosperous's church, which was stone-built and barely large enough to hold more than twenty people, had been transported to Maine in its entirety from the county of Northumberland, in England, at the beginning of the eighteenth century. Each stone of the church had been carefully marked and its position in the structure recorded, then all were carried as ballast on the ships that brought the original congregation to Bridgeport, Connecticut, in

1703. From there, these pilgrims journeyed north to Maine and, over a period of decades, eventually founded the town of Prosperous and rebuilt their church, which had been placed in storage for the duration.

The reason they left England, and took their church building with them, came down to religious persecution. The Congregation, as it became known, was an offshoot of the Family of Love, or the Familists, a religious sect that emerged in sixteenth-century Europe. The Family of Love was secretive, and reputedly hostile to outsiders to the point of homicide, although that may just have been anti-Familist propaganda. Marriage and remarriage were kept within the sect, as was the precise nature of its followers' beliefs. As far as I could make out, the Familists believed that hell and heaven existed on earth, and that there was a time preceding Adam and Eve. In the seventeenth century, the majority of Familists became part of the Quaker movement, with the exception of a small group of Northumbrian members who rejected a formal rapport with the Quakers or anyone else, and continued to worship in their own way, despite efforts by King Charles II to crack down on nonconformist churches in England. All officials in towns were required to be members of the Church of England, all clergy had to use the Book of Common Prayer, and unauthorized religious gatherings of more than five people were forbidden unless all were members of the same family. The Familists were among those persecuted in this way.

But the sect proved hard to suppress. The Familists learned to hide themselves by joining established churches while continuing to conduct their own services in secret, and they maintained that charade during the worst years of the crackdown on nonconformism. Also, as intermarriage between families was common, they could easily circumvent the rule about religious gatherings.

In 1689, Parliament passed the Toleration Act, which gave nonconformists the right to their own teachers, preachers, and places of worship, but it seemed that some Familists had already made the decision to abandon the shores of England entirely. They may simply have grown weary of hiding, and had lost faith in their government. The only hint of a deeper discontent lay in the footnotes of an essay that I found titled "The Flight West: Nonconformist Churches and the Goodness of God in Early New England Settlements," in which the author suggested that the Familists who formed the Congregation had been forced out of England because they were so nonconformist as to be almost pagan.

This corresponded to a couple of paragraphs in Jude's book on church architecture, which stated that the Congregation's church was notable for its carved figurines, including numerous "foliate heads," part of a tradition of carving ancient fertility symbols and nature spirits on Christian buildings. Such decorations were routinely tolerated, even encouraged, on older houses of worship. They were a kind of tacit recognition by the early church fathers of the link between the people and the land in agrarian communities. In the case of the building that eventually found its way to Maine, though, the general consensus among the sect's opponents was that the heads were more than merely decorative: they were the object of Familist worship, and it was the Christian symbols that were incidental. As I parked just off Main Street, it struck me as odd that a congregation with a history of concealment should have placed enough value on an old church building to transport it across the Atlantic Ocean. This might be a church worth seeing.

The interior of the Town Office, housed in a nineteenth-century brownstone with a modern extension to the rear, was bright and clean. When I asked to see the chief of police, I was directed to a comfortable chair and offered coffee while a call was put through to his office. The coffee came with a cookie on a napkin. If I stayed long enough, someone would probably have offered me a pillow and a blanket. Instead, I passed the minutes looking at the images of Prosperous through the years that decorated the walls. It hadn't changed much over the centuries. The names on the storefronts remained mostly the same, and only the cars on the streets, and the fashions of the men and women in the photographs, gave any clues to the passage of time.

A door opened to my right, and a man in uniform appeared. He was taller than me and broader in the back and shoulders, and his neatly pressed dark-blue shirt was open at the neck to reveal a startlingly white T-shirt beneath. His hair was dark brown. He wore rimless bifocal spectacles, and a SIG as a sidearm. All things considered, he looked like an accountant who worked out most evenings. Only his eyes spoiled the effect. They were a pale gray, the color of a winter sky presaging snow.

"Lucas Morland," he said, as he shook my hand. "I'm chief of police here."

"Charlie Parker."

"I'm very pleased to meet you, Mr. Parker," he said, and he appeared to mean it. "I've read a lot about you. I see you've already been given coffee. You need a top-off?"

I told him I was fine with what I had, and he invited me to step into his office. It was hard to tell what color the walls might be, as they were covered with enough certificates and awards to render paint pretty much superfluous. On his desk were various photographs of a dark-haired woman and two dark-haired boys. Chief Morland wasn't in any of them. I wondered if he was separated. Then again, he may just have been the one taking the photographs. I was in danger of becoming a "glass half empty" kind of guy. Or a "glass emptier" guy.

Or maybe a "What glass?" guy.

"You have a nice town," I said.

"It's not mine. I just look out for it. We all do, in our way. You considering moving here?"

"I don't think I could afford the taxes."

"Try doing it on a cop's salary."

"That's probably how Communism started. You'd better keep your voice down, or they'll start looking for another chief."

He leaned back in his chair and folded his hands across his stomach. I noticed that he had a small belly. That was the problem with quiet towns: there wasn't much that one could do in them to burn calories.

"Oh, we have all kinds here," said Morland. "Did you notice the motto on the sign as you came into town?"

"I can't say that I did."

"It's easy to miss, I guess. It's just one word: 'tolerance.'"

"Pithy."

He looked out the window and watched a stream of elementary school kids waddle by, each with one hand clinging tightly to a pink rope. It was a clear day, but cold, and they were wrapped in so many layers that it was impossible to see their faces. Once the kids had disappeared from view, and he was content that nothing had befallen them, or was likely to, he returned his attention to me.

"So how can I help you, Mr. Parker?"

I handed him a copy of a photograph of Jude that I'd found at the Portland Help Center. It had been taken at a Christmas lunch the previous year, and Jude, wearing a tan suit and a white shirt accessorized with a piece of tinsel in place of a tie, was smiling. A pedant would have pointed out that the suit was too close to cream for the time of year, but Jude wouldn't have cared.

"I was wondering if you'd seen this man around Prosperous recently, or if he'd had any contact with your department," I said.

Morland wrinkled his nose and peered at the photograph through the lower part of his bifocals.

"Yes, I recall him. He came in here asking about his daughter. His name was . . ."

Morland tapped his fingers on his desk as he sought the name.

"Jude," he said finally. "That was it: Jude. When I asked him if that was his first or last name, he told me it was both. Is he in trouble, or did he hire you? To be honest, he didn't seem like the kind of fella who had money to be hiring private detectives."

"No, he didn't hire me, and his troubles, whatever they were, are over now."

"He's dead?"

"He was found hanged in a basement in Portland about a week ago."

Morland nodded.

"I think I recall reading something about that now."

The discovery of Jude had merited a paragraph in the *Press Herald*, followed by a slightly longer feature in the *Maine Sunday Telegram* about the pressures faced by the city's homeless.

"You say that he was asking about his daughter?"

"That's right," said Morland. "Annie Broyer. He claimed that someone at a women's shelter in Bangor told him that she was headed up this way. Apparently she'd been offered a job here by an older couple, or that was the story he'd heard. He wanted to know if we'd seen her. He had a photograph of her, but it was old. He described her well, though, or well enough for me to be able to tell him that no young woman of that description had found her way into this town—or none that I knew of, and I know them all."

"And was he happy with that?"

Morland's face bore an expression I'd seen a thousand times. I'd probably worn it myself, on occasion. It was the face of a public servant who just wasn't paid enough to deal with the unhappiness of those for whom the reality of a situation wasn't satisfactory.

"No, Mr. Parker, he was not. He wanted me to take him to every house in Prosperous that might be occupied by an older couple and have me show them the photograph of his daughter. In fact, he went so far as to suggest that we ought to *search* the houses of everyone over sixty, just in case they had her locked up in their home."

"I take it that wasn't an option."

Morland spread his hands helplessly.

"He hadn't reported his daughter missing. He didn't even know if she *was* missing. He just had a feeling in his bones that something was wrong. But the more we got into it the more apparent it became that he didn't really know his daughter at all. That was when I discovered that she'd been living in a women's shelter, and he was homeless, and they were estranged. It all got messy from there."

"What did you do in the end?"

"I made a copy of the photograph, put together a description of his daughter to go with it, and told him I'd ask around. But I also tried to explain to him that this wasn't the kind of town where people took in street women they didn't know and offered them beds in their homes. To be honest, I don't know a whole lot of towns where anyone would behave in that way. The story just didn't ring true. He gave me a couple of numbers for shelters and soup kitchens where a message could be left for him, and then I gave him a ride to Medway so he could catch the bus back to Bangor."

"Let me guess," I said. "The offer of a ride to Medway wasn't one that he could refuse."

Morland gave me the long-suffering public servant expression again.

"Look, it was a last resort. He said he was going to get a cup of coffee, and next thing I knew he was stopping folks on the streets to show them the picture of his daughter, and taping crappy photocopies to streetlights. I'd told him that I'd do what I could to help him, and I meant it, but I wasn't going to have a bum—even a well-dressed bum—harassing citizens and defacing public property. I like my job, Mr. Parker, and I want to keep it. Most of the time it's easy, and even when it's hard it's still kind of easy. I like this town too. I grew up here. My father was chief of police before me, and his father before him. It's our family business, and we do it well."

It was quite a speech. I'd have voted for him if he ran for office.

"So you drove Jude to Medway"—I resisted suggesting that Jude had literally been given the bum's rush—"but I'll venture that he didn't take the hint."

Morland puffed his cheeks.

"He started calling my office two or three times a day, asking if there had been any progress, but there was none. Nobody here had seen his daughter. He'd been given bad information. But he wouldn't accept that, so he came back. This time, he didn't pay me the courtesy of a visit, just went from house to house, knocking on doors and peering in win-

dows. Naturally, I started getting telephone calls from panicked residents, because it was getting dark. He was lucky he
didn't get himself shot. I picked him up and kept him in a cell
overnight. I told him I could have him charged with criminal
trespass. Hell, he even ended up in the cemetery more than
half an hour after sunset, like that fella in Dickens."

"Magwitch," I said.

"That's the one."

"What was he doing in the cemetery?"

"Trying to get into the church. Don't ask me why; we
keep it locked, and visits are only by appointment. We've
had incidents of vandalism in the past. Do you know about
our church?"

I told him that I did, and that I'd be curious to see
it before I left, if that was possible. Morland perked up
slightly at the prospect of my leaving town. He was tiring
of talking about the problems of dead bums and their
daughters.

"In conclusion, the next morning I drove him back to
Medway—*again*—and told him that if he showed his face
in Prosperous one more time he would be arrested and
charged, and he'd be no help to his daughter from a jail
cell. That seemed to get through to him, and, apart from
a phone call or ten, that was pretty much the last I saw or
heard of him, until now."

"And nobody in town knew anything about his
daughter?"

"No, sir."

"But why would his daughter have said that she was
going to Prosperous if someone hadn't given her reason to
do so? It sounds like an odd story to make up."

"She might have been trying to impress the other
street people. Worst case, she spoke to someone in
Bangor who told her they were from Prosperous when

they weren't. It may be that this Jude was right, and something did happen to her, but if so, it didn't happen to her here."

Morland returned the photo of Jude and got to his feet. We were done.

"So you want to see the church before you go?"

"If it's not too much trouble," I said. "At least you won't have to drive me to Medway after."

Morland managed a thin smile, but said nothing. As I stood, I let my arm brush one of the photographs on the desk. I caught it before it hit the floor, and returned it to its place.

"Your family?" I said.

"Yes."

"Good-looking boys. No girls?"

Morland gave me a peculiar look, as though I had intimated something unpleasant about him and the nature of his familial relations.

"No, no girls," he said. "I'm happy about that, I got to say. My friends with daughters tell me they're more trouble than boys. Girls will break your heart."

"Yes," I said. "Jude's daughter certainly broke his."

Morland took the photograph from me and restored it to its place on his desk.

"You had a daughter, didn't you?"

"Yes," I said. "She died," I added, preempting whatever might have followed. I was used to it by now.

"I know," said Morland. "I'm sorry. You have another little girl now, don't you?"

I looked at him curiously, but he appeared nothing but sincere.

"Did you read that somewhere too?" I asked.

"You think there's anyone in Maine law enforcement who doesn't know your history? This is a small-town state. Word gets around."

That was true, but Morland still had a remarkable memory for the family histories of men he had never met before.

"That's right, I have another little girl," I conceded.

Morland seemed on the verge of saying something, then reconsidered, contenting himself with, "Maybe if this man Jude hadn't walked out on his family his daughter might not have ended up the way she did."

Morland had a point—Jude, had he still been alive, might even have agreed with him—but I wasn't about to point the finger at Jude's failings as a husband and a father. I had my own guilt to bear in that regard.

"He tried to make up for it at the end," I said. "He was just doing what any father would have done when he came looking for her in Prosperous."

"Is that a criticism of how he was treated by my department?"

Morland didn't bristle, but he wasn't far off it. "My department," I noted, not "me."

"No," I said. "You just did what any chief of police would have done."

That wasn't quite the truth, but it was true enough. Maybe if Morland had a daughter of his own he would have behaved more compassionately; and if Jude hadn't been a bum, and his daughter a homeless ex-junkie, Morland would have tried a little harder—just a little, but sometimes that's all it takes. I didn't say any of this aloud, though. It wouldn't have helped, and I couldn't guarantee that, in his position, and with his background, I would have behaved any differently.

We walked from his office. Morland told the receptionist that he was heading out to the chapel. She looked surprised, but said nothing.

"This woman, Annie Broyer, you think she's dead?" asked Morland as we stepped outside.

"I don't know," I said. "I hope not."

"So you're going to keep looking for her?"

"Probably."

"And you've been hired to do this by whom?"

"I haven't been hired by anyone."

"So why are you looking for her?"

"Because nobody else will," I said.

Morland took this in, then told me to follow his car. He was still shaking his head as he pulled away.

XXIII

The Chapel of the Congregation of Adam Before Eve & Eve Before Adam, to give it its full title, was situated in the middle of a forest about half a mile northwest of Prosperous. A road marked PRIVATE, and secured with a lock and chain for which Chief Morland had a key, wound through the woods until it came to iron railings painted black, within which lay the town's original cemetery and the church. Morland parked his car on a narrow strip of grass beside the railings, and I parked on the road. There was a gate in the railings, also kept closed with a lock and chain, but it was already open when we arrived.

"I gave Pastor Warraner a call along the way and asked him to join us," said Morland. "It's just good manners. The church is in his care. I have a key, but it's only in case of an emergency. Otherwise, I leave all such matters to him."

I looked around, but I could see no sign of the pastor. The church was even smaller and more primitive than I had expected, with walls of rough-hewn gray stone, and a western orientation instead of the more usual eastern. I did one full circuit of the building, and it didn't take long. A heavy oak door seemed to be the only point of entry or exit, and there were two narrow windows on its northern and southern walls, sealed with glass from within and bars without. The wall behind what I presumed to be the altar was blank and windowless. The roof was relatively new, and appeared incongruous above the ancient stones.

The main decorative features, the faces for which the church was famous, were in the upper corners of each wall, creating a kind of Janus effect where they met, an impression compounded by the fact that the lengths of carved ivy and branches of which the decorations were composed flowed between the faces and continued along the upper lengths of the walls, so that the visages all appeared to spring from the same source. They had weathered over the centuries, but not as much as might have been expected. Intricate constructions of stone leaves formed a protective screen around them, from which the faces peered out. They reminded me of childhood, and fairy tales, and of the way in which the markings on the trunks of very old trees sometimes took on the appearance of contorted, suffering people, depending on the light and the angle at which they were examined.

But what struck me most was the sheer malevolence of the expressions on the carvings. These were not manifestations of gentle emotions, or signifiers of hope. Instead, they boded only ill for all who looked on them. To my mind, they had no more place on a church building than a pornographic image.

"What do you think?" said Morland, as he joined me.

"I've never seen anything like them before," I said, which was the most neutral reply I could offer.

"There are more inside," he said. "Those are just the opening acts."

As if on cue, the door to the chapel opened and a man stepped out.

"Pastor Warraner," said Morland, "this is Mr. Parker, the detective I told you about."

Warraner wasn't what I had expected of a cleric who had charge of a building that was almost a millennium old. He wore jeans and battered work boots, and a brown suede jacket that had the look of a garment long reached for instinctively when warmth and comfort were required. He was in his late forties, with heavily receding hair, and as we shook hands I saw and felt the calluses on his skin, and caught a faint smell of timber and wood shavings on him.

"Call me Michael," he said. "I'm glad I was around to say hello."

"Do you live nearby?" I asked. I hadn't seen any other vehicle when we arrived.

"Just the other side of the woods," he said, gesturing over his right shoulder with his thumb. "Five minutes on foot. Same time it takes me in my truck by the less scenic route, so it makes more sense to walk. May I ask what brings a private detective to our town?"

I stared at the church carvings, and they stared back. One had its mouth wide open, and a tongue poked obscenely from between its carved lips. It seemed to mock any hope I might have of finding Annie Broyer alive.

"A homeless man named Jude came to Prosperous recently," I said. "Chief Morland tells me that he may have trespassed on the church grounds in the course of one of those visits."

"I remember," said Warraner. "I was the one who found him here. He was very agitated, so I had no choice but to call Chief Morland for assistance."

"Why was he agitated?"

"He was concerned about his daughter. She was missing, and he was under the impression that she might have found her way to Prosperous. He felt that he wasn't getting the help he needed from the police. No offense meant, Chief."

"None taken," said Morland, although it was hard to tell if he was sincere, as he had kept his sunglasses on against the glare of winter sun on snow. I barely knew Morland, but I had already figured him for a man who guarded any slights jealously, nurturing them and watching them grow.

"Anyhow, I tried to calm him down, but I didn't have much success," said Warraner. "I told him to leave the grounds, and he did, but I was worried that he might attempt to break into the church, so I called the chief."

"Why would you think he'd want to break into the church?" I asked.

Warraner pointed at the faces looming above his head.

"Disturbed people fixate," he said, "and this wonderful old building provides more opportunities for fixation than most. Over the years, we've had attempts to steal the carvings from the walls, and to deface them. We've found people—and not just young ones either but folk old enough to know better—having sex on the ground here because they were under the impression it would help them to conceive a child, and, of course, we've been visited by representatives of religious groups who object to the presence of pagan symbols on a Christian church."

"As I understand it, this town was founded by the Familists, and it was originally their church," I said. "Their belief system strikes me as more than a complicated variation on Christianity."

Warraner looked pleasantly surprised at the question, like a Mormon who had suddenly found himself invited into a house for coffee, cake, and a discussion of the wit and wisdom of Joseph Smith.

"Why don't you step into my office, Mr. Parker?" he said, welcoming me into the chapel.

"As long as I'm not keeping you from anything important," I said.

"Just kitchen closets," he said. "I run a joinery service."

He fished a card from his pocket and handed it to me.

"So you're not a full-time pastor?"

Warraner laughed. "I'd be a pauper if I was. No, I'm really just a caretaker and part-time historian. We no longer have services here; the Familists are no more. The closest we have are some Quaker families. The rest are mainly Baptists and Unitarians, even some Catholics."

"And what about you?" I said. "You still keep the title of 'pastor.'"

"Well, I majored in religion at Bowdoin, and studied as a Master of Divinity at Bangor Theological Seminary, but I always did prefer woodworking. Still, I guess you could say that the theological gene runs in the family. I hold a weekly prayer group, although often I'm the only one praying, and there are people in town who come to me for advice and guidance. They tend to be folk who aren't regular churchgoers but still believe. I don't probe too deeply into what it is that they *do* believe. It's enough that they believe in some power greater than themselves."

We were in the church now. If it was cold outside, it was colder still inside. Five rows of hard wooden benches faced a bare altar. There were no crosses, and no religious symbols of any kind. Instead, the wall behind the altar was dominated by a foliate face larger than any that decorated the exterior. Two slightly smaller faces of a similar kind were visible between the windows.

"Do you mind if I take a closer look?" I said.

"By all means," said Warraner. "Just watch your step. Some of the stones are uneven."

I approached the altar along the right aisle of the church. As I passed, I glanced at the first of the faces. It was more detailed than the ones outside, and had a grinning, mischievous expression. As I looked at it more closely, I saw that all its features were made from stone re-creations of produce: squash, pea pods, berries, apples, and ears of wheat. I had seen something like it before, but I couldn't recall where.

"Wasn't there an artist who painted images like this?" I asked Warraner.

"Giuseppe Arcimboldo," he replied. "I've always meant to study up on him, but there never seems to be enough time. I imagine that he and the creators of these carvings would probably have had a lot to discuss, particularly the intimate connection between man and the natural world, had they not been separated by the ages."

I moved to the altar and stood before the carving on the wall. If the face on the right was almost cheerful—albeit in the manner of someone who has just watched a puppy drown and found it amusing—and evoked images of the earth's bounty, this one was very different. It was a thing of roots, thorns, and nettles, of briars, bare winter bushes, and twisting ivy. Branches bristling with spines poured from its open mouth and seemed both to form its features and to suffocate them, as though the image were tormenting itself. It was profoundly ugly, and startlingly, vibrantly present, an ancient being brought to life from dead things.

"It's the same visage, or the same god, depending upon one's inclination," said Warraner from behind me.

"What?"

He pointed to his right, at the face made from produce, to his left at another constructed from blossoming flowers, and finally at a fourth face that I had not noticed before, as it was above the door: a face composed of straw, and leaves that had just begun to wither and die.

"All versions of a similar deity," said Warraner. "In the last century, the name 'Green Man' was coined for him—a pagan god absorbed into the Christian tradition, a symbol of death and rebirth long before the idea of the resurrection of Christ came into being. You can see why a building decorated in such a manner would have appealed to the Familists, a sect that believed in the rule of nature, not God."

"And are you a Familist, Pastor Warraner?" I asked.

"I told you," he answered. "The Familists no longer exist. Frankly, it's a shame. They were outwardly tolerant of the views of others while repudiating all other religions entirely. They refused to carry arms, and they kept their opinions and beliefs to themselves. They attracted the elite, and had no time for the ignorant. If they were still around today, they'd regard most of what passes for organized religion in this country as an abomination."

"I read that they were accused of killing to defend themselves," I said.

"Propaganda," said Warraner. "Most of those allegations came from John Rogers, a sixteenth-century cleric who hated Christopher Vitel, the leader of the Familists in England. He called the Family of Love a 'horrible secte,' and based his attacks on depositions given by dissenting ex-Familists. There's no evidence that the Familists ever killed those who disagreed with them. Why should they? The sect's members were quietists; they didn't even identify themselves publicly, but hid among other congregations to avoid being identified and put at risk."

"Like religious chameleons," I said, "blending into the background."

"Exactly," said Warraner. "Eventually, they simply became what they pretended to be."

"Except the ones who traveled here to found Prosperous."

"And in the end even they vanished," said Warraner.

"Why did the Familists leave England?" I asked. "It wasn't clear from the little that I could find out about them. As far as I can tell, religious persecution was already dying when they departed. Why flee when you're no longer threatened?"

Warraner leaned against a pew and folded his arms. It was a curiously defensive gesture.

"The Familists entered a state of schism," he said. "Disagreements arose between those who advocated following the Quaker way and those who wished to adhere to the sect's original belief system. The traditionalists feared being named as something more dangerous than dissenters, particularly when it was suggested that the building we're in should be razed. They viewed this church as the wellspring of their faith, which was probably why those who had chosen to follow an alternative path so desired its destruction. A wealthy cadre of the faithful came together to save the church, and their sect, from annihilation. The result was an exodus to New England, and the founding of Prosperous."

He glanced at his watch.

"Now, I'm sorry," he said, "but I really do need to get back to my kitchen closets."

I took one more look at the largest of the faces on the wall, the image of a winter god, then thanked him and joined Morland, who had waited throughout by the door. We watched Warraner lock the chapel with a key from a heavy ring and check that it was securely closed.

"One last thing," I said.

"Yes?"

He sounded impatient. He wanted to be gone.

"Wasn't Christopher Vitel a joiner too?"

Warraner thrust his hands into his pockets and squinted at me. The sun was setting, and the air was growing colder, as though the chill inside the chapel had permeated the outside world while the door was open.

"You really have done your homework, Mr. Parker," he said.

"I like to keep myself informed."

"Yes, Vitel was a joiner. It was used against him by his enemies to suggest that he was nothing but a vagabond."

"But he was much more than that, wasn't he? I understand that he was also a textile merchant in the Low Countries, and it was there that he encountered the founder of the Familists, Hendrik Niclas, except at that time he was Christopher Vitell. He dropped the second 'l' when he returned to England to spread the doctrine of the Familists, effectively giving himself a new identity."

"That may be true," said Warraner. "Such changes of

spelling were not uncommon at the time, and may not even have been deliberate."

"And then," I continued, "around 1580, when the government of Queen Elizabeth was hunting the Familists, Vitel simply disappeared."

"He is not present in the historical record from that time on," said Warraner. "It's not clear why. He may have died."

"Or assumed another identity. A man who changed his name once could easily do so again."

"What are you suggesting, Mr. Parker?"

"Maybe preaching isn't the only talent you inherited from your genes."

"You should have been a historian, Mr. Parker. A speculative one, perhaps, but a historian nonetheless. But then isn't historical research a form of detection too?"

"I suppose it is. I hadn't really considered it."

"In answer to your suggestion, I have no idea if my line stretches back to Vitel, but I would consider myself blessed indeed if that were the case."

He tested the door one last time, and began walking toward the gate.

"It's been interesting talking to you, Mr. Parker," he called back just before he reached it. "I hope you get to visit us again sometime."

"I think I'll be back," I said, but only Morland heard me.

"It's a dead end," he said. "Whatever you're looking for isn't here."

"You may be right," I said, "but I'm not sure what it is that I'm looking for, so who's to know?"

"I thought you were looking for a missing girl."

"Yes," I said, as Warraner vanished into the woods without a backward glance. "So did I."

Morland escorted me from the churchyard and locked the gate behind us. I thanked him for his time, got into my car, and drove away. I thought he might have followed me to the town limits to make sure that I was leaving, but he didn't. When I turned right, he went left to go back to Prosperous. I kept the radio off and played no music as I drove. I thought about Jude, and Morland, and my time with Pastor Warraner. One small detail nagged at me. It might have been nothing, but, like a fragment of thorn buried in my flesh, it itched as I headed south, and by the time I reached Bangor it was impossible to ignore.

Warraner had not asked me anything more about Jude, or my reasons for visiting Prosperous, once we left the subject of Jude's intrusion on the cemetery. It might simply have been the case that Warraner wasn't curious about Jude or his missing daughter. He may have become distracted as we talked about his beloved chapel. Or there was a third possibility: Warraner didn't ask about Jude because he knew that Jude was dead, but if that was so, why not mention it? Why not ask who had hired me, or why I had come so far north to ask about a homeless man? Yes, Morland could have told Warraner the reason for my visit while I was following him to the churchyard, but if so, why would Warraner have bothered to ask me the same question a second time?

My headlights caught bare branches and twisted trees, and every shadow concealed the face of the Green Man.

XXIV

Morland drove to the outskirts of Prosperous and sat in his car, drinking coffee from his thermos and watching the cars enter and leave the town. His Crown Vic rested on a small hill partially concealed by trees, a site that he often used as the location for a speed trap when the mood took him. His father had shown him this location, pointing out to him the sweet spot, the perfect position from which to watch without being seen while also giving an unrestricted view of the road. On this occasion, Morland left the radar gun in its case. He didn't want to be disturbed. He wanted to think.

Hayley Conyer would have to be informed of the detective's visit, and it was better that Morland be the one to do it rather than Pastor Warraner. Who knew what poisons Warraner would pour into Hayley's ear? It was the pastor who had shouted loudest for the killing of the one named Jude, even as Morland tried to divert the board from a course of action that had now brought a dangerous man down upon them.

For the detective was dangerous, of that Morland had no doubt. The chief had not been busy when the detective arrived at the Town Office, and could have seen him immediately, but he had taken time to compose himself, to run through the possible reasons for the man's visit. Morland had been surprised when the detective mentioned Jude's name, but had hidden it well. He had struggled harder to retain his composure when the detective wanted to visit the chapel, but he shouldn't have: it was a perfectly understandable request to make, given the unusual nature of the building, although Morland had offered the detective an opening by mentioning that Jude had been arrested on church grounds. As for Warraner, he regularly received letters and emails from interested parties asking for permission to view the building, even if he was careful to limit such visits to those whose reasons were entirely without ulterior motive.

But Morland believed that the detective did *nothing* without an ulterior motive. He wasn't the kind of man to go sightseeing at an old church simply because he had time on his hands. He was looking for connections. Morland could only hope that he had left Prosperous without making any. The chief ran over the details of their conversation again and again, adding what he'd heard of the detective's discussion with Warraner. Morland tried to see the situation through the detective's eyes, and by the time the thermos was empty he had decided that there was nothing about the day's business that could have added to any half-formed suspicions the detective might have brought with him. It had been a fishing expedition, nothing more, and the hook had come back bare. Still, Morland hadn't liked the way the detective watched Warraner as the pastor departed, or his suggestion that the girl's disappearance might not be the sole purpose of his visit. The detective's first hook might not have caught on anything, but he had left others trailing.

Morland climbed from the car and went into the bushes to take a leak. It was dark now, but the moon shone silver on the small body of water known as Lady's Pond. This was where the women of Prosperous would go to congregate and bathe, undisturbed by their menfolk, in the early decades of the township. Morland wondered how many of them knew of the town's true nature, even then. Probably only a handful, he thought. More of the townsfolk understood Prosperous now, but far from all. Some chose to be blind to it, and others were deliberately kept in the dark. It was strange, thought Morland, how generations of Prosperous families had never been entrusted with the truth, yet still had reaped its benefits. It was stranger still that the town's secret had remained undiscovered by outsiders over the centuries, even allowing for the killings that had occurred in order to silence those who were ready to betray it. Perhaps it was a circular argument: the town was always at risk because it required murder to survive, but by spilling blood it accrued the blessings that enabled it to keep that risk to a minimum, and assure the town's continued prosperity. Put that way, it sounded simple, logical.

Morland wondered if, like his father and his grandfather before him, he had become such a monster that he almost failed to notice his own moral and spiritual deformity anymore.

The issue of betrayal brought him back to the Dixons. It had been Morland's decision to place Luke Joblin's son with them. He hoped that Bryan Joblin's presence would keep the Dixons in line and force them to act according to the board's wishes, but he had his doubts. If the Dixons actually managed to produce a girl to replace Annie Broyer, Morland would give up coffee for a year.

But there was a part of the chief that hoped Harry Dixon was right—that the fact of the girl's killing and the soaking of her blood into the soil of Prosperous might be enough. The town was hurting, but not as much as the rest of the state. People were getting by. Morland imagined a situation where Pastor Warraner informed the board that all was now well and the chapel remained quiet, so no further action was required. But Warraner was both fanatical and weak, and Morland had not yet decided whether the latter quality was useful or dangerous. It depended upon the circumstances, he supposed, but it meant that Warraner had a habit of attacking from behind when it came to disputes. He was no honest broker. Morland wished that Warraner's father were still alive and in charge of the chapel. Old Watkyn Warraner had been a cautious man by all accounts, but he steered the congregation for more than half a century without blood being spilt more than once. It was the longest such period of contentment the town had known.

Well, we're paying for it now, thought Morland. Two bodies—one here and one in Portland—and it appeared that they were not enough. Now a detective was asking questions, a strange man with a reputation for excavating long-buried secrets and annihilating his enemies. Under the circumstances, Warraner could argue that the spilling of blood was more necessary than ever, for only by blood would the town be saved, and the selectmen might well be inclined to agree. They were all old, and fearful—even Hayley Conyer, but she just hid her fear better than most. Younger people were needed on the board, but most of the town's youths weren't ready to take on the burden of protecting Prosperous. It took decades for the town to seep into one's soul, for the recognition of one's obligations to it to form. It was a kind of corruption, a pollution passed down through the generations, and only the oldest were corrupt and polluted enough to be able to make the tough decisions required to keep the town alive.

Morland used a bottle of water to wash his hands before drying them on the legs of his trousers. It was time to talk with Hayley Conyer. He called his wife and told her that he would be home late. No, he wasn't sure when. He knew only that a long evening stretched ahead.

Morland drove to the Conyer house and parked outside. The drapes were drawn on all the windows, but a sliver of light was visible from Hayley's mausoleum of a living room. He wasn't surprised to find her home. Unless she was out on board business, Hayley was always home. Morland couldn't remember the last time she'd left town for more than a couple of hours. She was afraid the place would collapse into the ground without her. That was part of the problem, of course.

"Bitch," he said softly, as he stepped from the car. The wind whipped the word away, and he found his right hand twitching involuntarily, as if it were hoping to catch the insult before it reached the ear of Hayley Conyer.

He rang the doorbell, and Hayley answered.

"I'm sorry to disturb you—" Morland began to say, but Hayley held up a hand to interrupt him.

"It's quite all right," she said. "I've been expecting you."

She invited him to step inside, then led him to the living room, where Pastor Warraner had already made himself at home in an armchair.

Shit, thought Morland.

XXV

The woman on desk duty at the Tender House in Bangor was named Molly Bow, and she looked as if she should have been fixed to the prow of a ship. She was big and weathered, but attractive in a matronly way, and at one point I had to take a couple of steps back to avoid being crushed by her breasts as she passed me to get to a filing cabinet in her office.

"Comin' through," she said as I flattened my back against a wall. She gestured toward her bosom. "I was born large. Backache apart, it's been useful in life. People make an effort to get out of my way."

Once again, I had an image of a schooner or, better still, a man-of-war cleaving a path through the waves, but I kept my eyes fixed on a neutral spot on the opposite wall, well above chest height.

The Tender House had no signs outside to mark its presence. It was housed in a pair of adjoining clapboard buildings surrounded by a white picket fence that was only slightly higher than those of its neighbors. Two cars were parked in the drive, which was secured by an automatically operated steel gate, also painted white. Inside the front door of the main building was a waiting room containing toys, a library of self-help books, boxes of tissues, large containers of secondhand clothes organized according to type and size, from infant to adult, and, in a discreet corner, toothbrushes, toothpaste, and toiletries. Behind the reception desk was a small playroom.

The Tender House wasn't a homeless shelter but, rather, a "crisis center" for women, where homeless-ness was only one of the problems it tackled. It catered to victims of domestic and sexual abuse, runaways, and women who simply needed a place to stay while they tried to improve their situation. Its staff liaised with the police and the courts, advising on everything from restraining orders to educational and job opportunities, but it gener-ally steered the long-term homeless toward other agencies and centers.

"Got it," said Bow, waving a file. She licked an index finger and flipped through some pages. "We had her for about eleven days, apart from the fifth night, when someone broke out a couple of half gallons of Ten High over by Cascade Park. We had some sore heads the next day, Annie's among them."

"Was she an alcoholic?"

"No, I don't think so. She'd been a user, but she claimed to be clean by the time she arrived at our door. We made it clear to her that we had a zero-tolerance policy when it came to drugs. If she got high, she'd be back on the streets."

"And alcohol?"

"Officially, we're down on that too. Unofficially, we give some leeway. Nothing on the premises, and no intoxication. Actually, I was disappointed when Annie came back to us all raw from the Ten High. I had her pegged as a young woman who was genuinely trying to change her life. We sat her down and had a talk with her. Turned out her estranged father had come looking for her, and his presence in town had thrown her. She was offered a sip or two to steady herself, and it all got sort of blurry for her after that."

"Did she say anything about her relationship with her father?"

Bow was clearly reluctant to share confidences. I could understand her reservations.

"Annie is missing, and her father is dead," I said.

"I know that. He hanged himself in a basement down in Portland."

I gave it a couple of seconds.

"He was found hanging in a basement in Portland," I corrected her. It was minor, but it was important.

Molly sat behind her desk. She'd been standing until then. We both had. As she sat, so did I.

"Is that why you're here—because you don't think it was suicide?"

"So far I don't have any proof that it wasn't," I said. "A couple of small details are just snagging like briars."

"Such as?"

"Such as the fact that he loved his daughter, and clearly wanted to reestablish contact with her. He had spoken of heading up here permanently to be closer to her. He'd also gone to a lot of trouble to pull together some money in the days before he died. He succeeded too. Those aren't the actions of a suicidal man."

"What was the money for?"

It struck me that I was on the wrong side of an interrogation: I should have been asking the questions, not her, but sometimes you had to retreat an inch to gain a foot.

"To support him as he tried to find his daughter. I think he was also hoping to hire me to help look for her."

"So how much money did he manage to collect?"

"More than a hundred dollars."

"Do you work that cheap?"

"Funny, you're the second person who's asked me that. I could have given him a couple of hours, or more if I took the time from some of my wealthier clients."

"Isn't that unethical?"

"Only if I don't tell them I'm doing it. They pay by the hour, even if the job only takes five minutes. I don't do fractions. Look, do you think *I* might get to ask a question at any point?"

Bow smiled. "You just did."

Hell.

She leaned back in her chair, like a reigning champ who had dispensed with another challenger to her crown, then threw me a bone of consolation.

"I'm joshing with you," she said. "You'd be surprised

how many people I get in here asking questions about the women in our care. I have to be careful, for their sakes."

"What kind of people?"

"Sometimes we have women who turn tricks when times are desperate, and a john will come looking for one of them just because he's a creep, or he's got a beef about the service he received, or he liked it so much he wants a second bite. We get husbands and boyfriends trying to take back their possessions, because the kind who come storming in here mostly regard women as chattel. Oh, they'll do their best to dress it up as nicely as they can—they want to talk things over, to give the relationship another try, and they're sorry for whatever it is that they've done, which usually involves a fist or a boot, often with a little domestic rape thrown in along the way—but I've developed a nose for the worst of them. It's not hard. As soon as you put an obstacle in their way the threats start to emerge, but those ones are usually pretty dumb along with it. They mooch around in the hope that they'll be able to snatch their woman off the street, but we have a good relationship with the Bangor PD, and they'll get here before I've hung up the phone.

"But we've had men try to break in, or beat up volunteers. Last year, one even tried to burn us down by starting a fire at the back door. At the same time, we try to keep channels of communication open between women and their families. This is a place to which women—and their children—come when they're desperate. It isn't a long-term solution. We make that clear to them from the start, but I've been seeing some of the women who pass through these doors on and off for the past ten years. They just get older and more bruised. There are times when I wonder how far we've come as a society where women are concerned. Whenever I turn on the TV to hear some jackass in a blazer bleating about feminists I want to set him on fire, and don't get me started on those dumb bitches who find themselves on the top of the pile only to reject the whole concept of feminism, as though their success wasn't built on the struggles of generations of women. I defy them to spend one day here with a forty-year-old woman whose husband has been stubbing out cigarettes on her for so long that he has to search for a spot where it still hurts, or a nineteen-year-old girl who has to wear diapers because of what her stepfather did to her, and tell me that they're not feminists."

What was strange about Molly Bow's speech was that, by the end of it, she was still leaning back in her chair and her voice hadn't grown even slightly louder. It was as though she had seen too much to want to expend valuable energy on useless rage. Better to direct it into more productive channels.

"And where did Annie fit into all this?"

Molly's fingers stroked the file, as if Annie Broyer were seated on the floor beside her and she was still capable of consoling her, of offering her some assurance that the world might be gentler with her in time.

"She was deserted by her father, and her mother died when she was a teenager. That doesn't mean she had to become an addict, and find herself on the streets, but she did. She wasn't weak, though. She had real strength to her. I don't like to use the word 'rescue,' or make out like I'm on some kind of mission to turn round the life of every woman who passes through our doors. It's just not possible, and we do what we can here, but there was something about Annie, something bright and untouched. It was why I let the drinking go, and the fact that she couldn't keep curfew to save her life—"

She suddenly stopped talking as she became aware of

the dual meaning of what she had just said. A spasm of pain convulsed her, and she looked away.

"But that's not what happened, is it?" I said. "She didn't vanish from the streets in the night."

"No," she said, once she was certain that her voice wouldn't break, although she still didn't look at me. "She came in the sunlight, and she packed her bags and left. I wasn't even here. She asked one of the other volunteers to thank me for what I'd done, but I hadn't done anything, not really."

She touched the file again.

"Do you think she's dead?" she asked.

"Do you?"

"Yes. I hate to say it, but yes; I have a feeling of absence. I have no sense of her in the world. Do you think—?"

"What?"

"Is it possible that her father might have hurt her— killed her—and then taken his own life out of remorse?"

I thought about what I knew of Jude.

"No, I don't believe so."

"Call me a cynic," she said, "but I had to ask. He wouldn't have been the first."

The office was very quiet for a time. The silence was disturbed by a young woman who appeared at the reception desk from somewhere upstairs. She wore a yellow T-shirt that extended to her thighs, and she was almost unbearably beautiful. She had hair so blond that it shone white, and her skin was without blemish. She held in her arms a girl of two or three who might have been her daughter or, given the youth of the woman who carried her, perhaps even her younger sister. The child had clearly been crying, but the sight of two adults silenced her. She laid her face against the young woman's neck and watched me carefully.

"I'm sorry," said the older girl. "She wants hot milk, but we finished our milk earlier. I was hoping—"

She proffered a plastic cup, the kind with a lid and a perforated mouthpiece.

"Sure, honey," said Molly, accepting the cup. "Just take a seat. I won't be but a minute."

Molly went to the refrigerator, removed a half-gallon container of milk, and disappeared into the little kitchen that adjoined the reception area. I could see the young woman from where I sat, and she could see me. I smiled at the child in her arms. She didn't smile back, but peered out from under the safety of the older girl's chin before burying her face in her chest. I decided not to bother either of them and went back to finding interesting spots on the wall at which to stare. Eventually Molly returned with the hot milk, and the two children—because that's what they were—vanished back upstairs.

"Do I even want to know?" I asked when Molly returned.

"It's bad," she said. "But we've had worse. There's always worse. That's the hell of it. And we don't usually allow men on the premises after five, so your presence here probably threw her some. Don't take it personally. Sorry, where were we?"

"Annie, and the day she left the shelter."

"Right."

"I'd like to talk to the woman who saw her last. Is she still here?"

Molly nodded.

"Candice, but she likes being called Candy."

"Will she speak with me?"

"Probably, but you'll have to be patient. She's special . . ."

*   *   *

CANDY WAS IN HER late thirties. She wore pink bunny slippers, oversized jeans, and a T-shirt that announced she would work for cookies. Her hair was red and unruly, and her chin was speckled with acne. Her eyes were slightly too small for her face, but she had a radiant smile. Had Molly not told me about her while we waited for her to come down, I might not have guessed that she had mild Down syndrome. Molly told me that women like Candy were often referred to as "high-functioning," but this was a phrase that was generally disliked in the Down community, as it implied a hierarchy among those with the condition. Candy was the daughter of the shelter's original founders. Both were now deceased, but Candy remained. She cleaned the rooms, helped around the kitchen, and provided company and consolation to those who needed it. As Molly put it, "Candy gives good hugs."

Candy took a seat on the couch in the office while Molly made her a mug of hot chocolate.

"Not too much marshmallow," warned Candy. "I'm watching my weight."

She patted her belly, but still looked disappointed when the hot chocolate arrived with a Weight Watcher's sprinkling of tiny marshmallows.

"Oh," she said. She poked disconsolately at the melting islands of pink and white. "Not many marshmallows."

Molly raised her eyes to heaven.

"You told me you were watching your weight," she said.

"I am watching my weight," said Candy. "But I'm not fat. It's all right. Don't worry."

She stuck out her lower lip and gave a long-suffering sigh. Molly went to the kitchen and returned with enough marshmallows to cover the entire surface of the hot chocolate and then some.

"Thank you," said Candy. "Very kind."

She slurped noisily at her drink, and surfaced with a chocolate mustache.

"Aaah. That's good."

Molly placed a hand on Candy's arm.

"Charlie here would like to ask you about Annie," she said.

"Annie?"

"Yes. You remember Annie."

Candy nodded.

"Annie was my friend."

Molly had said that Candy had been unusually fond of Annie, and that Annie, in turn, had been particularly good with Candy. Some of the women in the shelter found it harder to deal with Candy than others. They treated her like a defective, or a child. Annie did neither. She simply treated Candy as Candy.

"Do you remember when you saw her last?" I said.

"January twenty-second," said Candy. "A Tuesday."

"Can you tell me what you talked about?"

Candy's eyes welled up.

"She told me she was going away. Got a job. I was sad. Annie was my friend."

Molly patted her on the arm again.

"Did she say where the job was?" I asked.

"Prosperous." Candy struggled with the word slightly, so that it came out as "Prospuss."

"You're sure?"

"Yes. She said. She told me she was going to Prospuss. She had a job. Was going to clean, like Candy."

"And did she mention who had given her the job?"

Candy thought.

"No. They had a blue car."

"How do you know? Did you see them?"

"No. Annie told me."

"Candy is very interested in cars," Molly explained.

"I like to know colors," said Candy. "What color is your car?"

"I have two cars," I said.

"Two cars!" Candy said, clearly shocked. "What color?"

"One red, and one blue. I used to have a green car too, but—"

"Yes? But?"

"I didn't really like the color."

Candy considered this. She shook her head.

"I don't like green. Like red."

"Me too."

Candy grinned. We'd bonded. Clearly, anyone who preferred red cars to green could not be all bad.

"Annie didn't tell you the make of car, did she?" I said.

"No, just blue."

"And the people who owned it, did she tell you anything about them?"

"They were old."

She took another sip of her hot chocolate.

"How old?" I asked. "Older than I am?"

Candy giggled. "You're not old."

"So older?"

"I think so." She yawned. "Tired. Time for bed."

We were done. Candy stood to leave, carefully holding her mug of hot chocolate so that it didn't spill.

"Candy, is there anything else you can tell me about Annie?" I said.

The blue car was something, but it wasn't much.

"Annie told me she'd write to me," said Candy. "She promised. But she didn't write."

She turned her attention back to Molly.

"Must go to Prospuss," said Candy. "Find Annie. Annie's my friend."

"Charlie is going to look for Annie," said Molly. "Aren't you, Charlie?"

"Yes," I said. "I'll look for Annie."

"Tell her Candy said she must write," said Candy. "Mustn't forget her friend Candy."

With that, she trotted off to her room. Molly and I said nothing else until we were sure she was gone.

"She would have written," said Molly. "She wouldn't have wanted to disappoint Candy."

She swallowed hard.

"If I'd been here when she left, I'd have made sure that she gave us details of where she was going. I'd have asked to meet these people who were offering her work. But all the full-time staff were at a meeting that day with the Department of Health and Human Services over on Griffin Street, and we just had volunteers manning the shelter. Volunteers, and Candy."

Anything I might have said would have sounded trite, so I said nothing. Instead, I took one of my business cards from my wallet and handed it to her.

"If you or Candy can think of anything else that might help me, or if anyone else comes around asking about Annie, I'd appreciate it if you'd give me a call. Also . . ."

"Yes?"

"I don't think Candy should talk too much about that blue car. I think it might be better if she kept it to herself."

"I understand. We didn't lie to Candy, did we? You are going to keep looking for Annie? I mean, I'd hire you myself if I could afford to."

"You forget: I work cheap."

This time she didn't smile.

"Somehow, I don't believe that's true. What you charge and how you work are two different things."

I shook her hand. "I'll be in touch."

Molly showed me to the door. As she opened it, there

was movement behind us. Candy was sitting on the stairs, just out of sight of the office.

She was crying, crying beyond consolation.

I FOUND SHAKY IN his bed at the Oxford Street Shelter. They'd done their best to keep him comfortable while the injury to his head was healing. He still had a headache, and his scalp had begun to itch, but otherwise he was doing as well as could be expected for someone who had been hit over the skull with a liquor bottle. I put him in my car and took him to the Bear for a burger and a beer. When he was settled in his seat, with a rodeo burger on order and a Shipyard Old Thumper in a glass before him, and Cupcake Cathy had fussed over him some, I told him a little of the day I'd had. After all, I was working for him. I'd made him pay me a dollar while he was lying on the hospital gurney. One of the nurses had taken it amiss, and my reputation at Maine Medical was now probably lower than that of most ambulance chasers.

"So he definitely went to Prosperous?" said Shaky.

"He didn't just go there; he got run out of town. Twice. The first time politely, the second time less so."

"He could be a stubborn man," said Shaky.

"He was a bright one too," I said. "Brighter than I am, at least, because I'm still not sure what he was doing nosing around an old church."

"Do you believe what that cop told you?"

"I've no reason not to. The job Jude's daughter spoke of could have fallen through. She might have changed her mind about it, or that old couple, if they existed at all, could have reconsidered their Good Samaritanism while she left to get her bags. Or she might just have been unlucky."

"Unlucky?"

"She was a vulnerable woman living on the streets. There are men out there who'd regard someone like her as easy prey."

Shaky nodded and took a long sip of his beer.

"I know," he said. "I've met enough of them in my time, and they don't all sleep on mats on floors."

"You may be right," I said. "In my experience, the worst of them wear suits and drive nice, well-maintained vehicles. But one thing is certain: as far as the services in Bangor are concerned, Annie dropped off the radar on the day she spoke about that job. I went by the women's shelter on my way back down here, and nobody has seen or heard from her since then."

"And this woman, this Candy, she's certain Annie said she was going to Prosperous?"

"Yes, but that doesn't mean Prosperous is where she ended up."

"So what are you going to do?"

"Go back there. Look for a blue car. See what happens."

"Wow, good plan. You have it all worked out. And people pay you for that?"

"Not a lot," I said, pointedly. "And sometimes not at all."

XXVI

In the living room of Hayley Conyer's house, Morland steepled his hands over his face, closed his eyes, and made a prayer of thanks to a god in whom he did not believe. It was force of habit, and no more than that. It looked good for him to go to church on Sundays. All of the most influential citizens in Prosperous were members of one congregation or another. Some even believed. Just like their ancestors back in England who had carved faces into the walls of their church, their faith could encompass more than one deity. Morland was not of their kind. He no longer even knew what he believed in, apart from Prosperous itself. All he could say for sure was that no Christian god impinged on his consciousness.

He was weary from arguing, but at least his view had prevailed, for now. As the guardian of the church, it was Warraner and not Morland who had Hayley's ear in times of crisis, but on this occasion Morland had managed to sway Hayley. He had been helped by the absence of two members of the board: Luke Joblin was attending a Realtors' convention in Philadelphia, and Thomas Souleby was currently under observation at a sleep clinic in Boston, having recently received a diagnosis of sleep apnea. In times of crisis Hayley could act without a vote from the board, but Morland had convinced her that the situation wasn't that desperate. The detective was simply asking questions. There was nothing to link the death of the girl's father to the town, and the girl herself was no more. Unless the detective could commune with the deceased, he would find his avenues of inquiry quickly exhausted.

Hayley Conyer poured the last of her tea into her cup. It must have been cold and unbearably strong by now, but she wasn't one to let things go to waste. To her right sat Warraner, his face frozen. That was the other thing: Warraner had wanted them to take action, but he couldn't specify what kind of action. Killing the detective wasn't an option, and Warraner had no solution of his own to offer. He just didn't like seeing Morland get his way. Warraner would rather have been the king of nothing than the prince of something.

"I'm still not entirely happy," said Warraner. "This man is a threat to us."

"Not yet," said Morland, for what seemed the hundredth time. He removed his hands from his face. "Not unless we make him a threat."

"We'll discuss it again when Thomas and Luke have returned," snapped Hayley. She seemed as weary of Warraner as Morland was. "In the meantime, I want to be informed the moment he returns to Prosperous, *if* he returns here. I don't want to have to wait to hear it from the pastor."

Warraner's face thawed into a smile. Morland didn't react. He simply wanted to be gone from the house. He stood and took his coat from the chair.

"If he comes back, you'll know," said Morland.

He was hungry. Alina would have done what she could to save some dinner for him, but it would still be dried to hell and back by now. He'd eat it, though, and not just because he was hungry. He'd have eaten it even if Hayley Conyer had force-fed him caviar and foie gras during their meeting. He'd eat it because his wife had prepared it for him.

"Good night," said Morland.

"Just one more thing, Chief," said Hayley, and Morland stiffened as surely as if she'd inserted a blade into the small of his back.

He turned. Even Warraner seemed curious to hear what it was she had to say.

"I want the girl's body moved," said Hayley.

Morland looked at her as though she were mad.

"You've got to be kidding."

"I'm far from kidding. This detective's presence in Prosperous has made me uneasy, and if that body is discovered we'll all be fucked."

Warraner looked shocked. Even Morland was surprised. He hadn't heard Hayley Conyer swear in a coon's age.

"I want the girl's remains taken beyond the town limits," she continued. "*Far* beyond. How you dispose of her is your own concern, but get her gone, do you understand?"

In that moment, Morland hated Hayley Conyer more than he had ever hated anyone before. He hated her, and he hated Prosperous.

"I understand," he said.

This time, he didn't call her a bitch when he was alone again. He had a stronger word for her instead, and he used it all the way home. He'd dig up the body the next day, just as he had been told, but he wouldn't do it alone, because fucking Harry Dixon would be right there along-side him.

"Fuck!" shouted Morland, as he drove. "Fuck! Fuck! Fuck!"

He slammed the steering wheel hard in time with each use of the word, and the wind tugged at the branches of the trees as around him the woods laughed.

XXVII

There were three towns within a two-mile radius of Prosperous's limits. Only one, Dearden, was of any significant size; the other two were towns in the same way that Pluto used to be a planet, or a handful of guys standing at a crossroads counted as a crowd.

Every town has someone who is a royal pain in the ass. This role divides pretty evenly between the sexes, but the age profile is usually consistent: over forty, at least, and preferably older; usually single, or with the kind of spouse or partner who is either lost in hero worship or one step away from murder. If a meeting is held, they're at it. If change is in the air, they're against it. If you say it's black, they'll say it's white. If you agree that it's white, they'll reconsider their position. They've rarely held an elected position, or, if they once did, no one was crazy enough to reelect them. Their self-appointed role in life is to ensure that they're nobody's fool, and they want as many people as possible to know it. Because of them, things get done more slowly. Sometimes things don't get done at all. Very occasionally, they inadvertently do some good by preventing from happening that which might ultimately have proved to be unbeneficial or actively destructive to their community, but they manage to do so only on the basis that even a stopped clock is right twice a day.

If a town is sufficiently large, there may be many such persons, but Dearden was big enough to contain only a single such entity. His name was Euclid Danes, and even a cursory Internet search in connection with Dearden threw up Euclid's name with a frequency that might lead one to suspect that he was the only living soul in town. In fact, so omnipresent was Euclid Danes that even Dearden wasn't big enough to contain him, and his sphere of influence had extended to encompass parts of Prosperous too. Euclid Danes owned a number of acres between Prosperous and Dearden, and it appeared that he had made it his lifelong business to singlehandedly resist the expansion of

Prosperous to the south. His land acted as a buffer between the towns, and he had steadfastly and successfully fought every attempt by the citizens of Prosperous to buy him, or force him, out. He didn't seem interested in money or reason. He wanted to keep his land, and if by doing so he irritated the hell out of the wealthy folk up the road, then so much the better.

Euclid Danes's house was the original bad-neighbor nightmare: poorly kept, with a yard that was a kissing cousin to wilderness and littered with pieces of unidentifiable machinery that, with a little work and a lot of chutzpah, might even have qualified as some form of modern sculpture. An original Volkswagen Beetle was in the drive. In an open garage beyond stood the skeleton of a second Beetle, scavenged for parts.

I parked and rang the doorbell. From somewhere at the back of the house came the sound of excited barking.

The door was opened by a stick-thin woman in a blue housecoat. A cigarette smoldered in her right hand. In her left she held a small mongrel puppy by the scruff of the neck.

"Yes?" she said.

"I was looking for Euclid Danes."

She took a drag on the cigarette. The puppy yawned.

"Jesus, what's he done now?" she said.

"Nothing. I just wanted to ask him a few questions."

"Why?"

"I'm a private investigator."

I showed her my identification. Even the puppy looked more impressed by it than she did.

"You sure he's not in trouble?"

"Not with me. Are you Mrs. Danes?"

This provoked a burst of laughter that deteriorated into a fit of coughing.

"Jesus Christ, no!" she said, once she'd recovered. "I'm his sister. There's nobody desperate enough to marry that poor sonofabitch, or if there is, then I don't want to meet her."

I couldn't see a wedding ring on her finger either. Then again, she was so thin that it would have been hard to make one fit, or, if it did, the weight would have unbalanced her. She was so skinny as to be almost sexless, and her hair was cut shorter than mine. If it hadn't been for the housecoat, and the pale twig legs that poked out from under her skirt, she could have passed for an elderly man.

"So, is Mr. Danes around?"

"Oh, he's around somewhere, just not here. He's on his throne, holding court. You know where Benny's is?"

"No."

"Head into town and take the first left after the intersection. Follow the smell of stale beer. When you find him, tell him to get his ass home. I'm cooking meat loaf. If he's not sitting at the table when it comes out of the oven, I'll feed it to the dogs."

"I'll be sure to let him know."

"Much appreciated." She held the puppy up at eye level. "You want to buy a puppy?"

"No, thank you."

"You want one for free?"

The puppy, seeming to understand that it was the object of discussion, wagged its tail hopefully. It was brown, with sleepy eyes.

"Not really."

"Damn."

"What'll you do with it?"

She looked the puppy in the eyes.

"Feed it meat loaf, I guess."

"Right."

She closed the door without saying another word. I remained where I was for a few moments, the way you do when you've just had something that might have passed for a conversation if you weren't paying attention, then got back into my car and went to look for Benny's.

BENNY'S WASN'T HARD TO find. Dearden was no metropolis, and there was only one intersection of any size at the heart of town. It didn't even have a signal, just a quartet of stop signs, and Benny's was the sole business on its street. Actually, Benny's was the sole *anything* on its street. Beyond it lay only woods. Benny's was a squat redbrick building whose sign had been provided by the Coca-Cola Company at least thirty years earlier, and was now faded and yellowed. It also lacked a possessive apostrophe. Maybe Benny didn't like to boast. If so, it was a wise move.

A certain odor comes with a bar that isn't cleaned regularly. All bars smell of it a little—it's a product of spilled beer that has ingrained itself into the floors and storage spaces, along with whatever chooses to propagate in old yeast—but Benny's smelled so strongly of it, even from outside, that birds flying above were at risk of alcohol-induced disorientation. Benny's had added an extra component to the stink by combining it with rancid grease: the extractors at the back of the building were caked with it. By the time I got to the door, Benny's had put its mark on me, and I knew that I'd end up stinking of the place all the way home, assuming my arteries didn't harden and kill me first.

Curiously, it didn't smell as bad inside, although that would have been difficult under the circumstances. Benny's was more of a restaurant than a bar, assuming you were prepared to be generous with your definition of a restaurant. An open kitchen lay behind the counter to the left, alongside a couple of beer taps that suggested microbrews were regarded as a passing fad. A menu board on the wall above had adjustable plastic letters and numbers arranged into the kinds of prices that hadn't changed since Elvis died, and the kinds of food choices that had helped to kill him. The tables were Formica, and the chairs wood and vinyl. Christmas tree lights hung on all four walls just below the ceiling, providing most of the illumination, and the décor was old beer signs and mirrors.

And, you know, it was kind of cool, once my eyes had adjusted to the gloom.

Music was playing low: "Come Together," followed by "Something." *Abbey Road.* A big man in an apron stood at the grill, flipping burgers.

"How you doin'," he said. "Waitress will be with you in a minute. How is it out there?"

"It's cold. Clear skies, though."

"Weather Channel says it could go down to ten degrees tonight."

"At least you're warm in here."

He was sweating over the grill. Nobody was going to have to salt a hamburger.

"I always got insulation."

He patted his massive belly, and I instantly recalled Candy, back in the Tender House in Bangor, watching her weight and counting marshmallows. It reminded me of why I was here.

A compact middle-aged woman with huge hair materialized out of the darkness. I had already begun to make out half a dozen figures scattered around, but it would have taken a flashlight shined on their faces to discern their features.

"Table, hon?" said the woman.

"I was looking for Euclid Danes," I said. "His sister told me he might be here."

"He's in his office," she said. "Table at the back. She send you to bring him home?"

"Apparently she's cooking meat loaf."

"I can believe it. She can't cook nothing else. Get you a drink?"

"Coffee, please."

"I'll make it extra strong. You'll need it if you're going to stay awake listening to his ramblings."

Euclid Danes looked like his sister in male drag. They might even have been twins. He was wearing a shabby blue suit and a red tie, just in case he was suddenly required to interfere in someone else's business. The table before him was covered with newspapers, clippings, random documents, assorted pens and highlighters, and a half-eaten plate of french fries. He didn't look up as I stood over him, so lost was he in annotating a sheaf of reports.

"Mr. Danes?" I said.

He raised his right hand while the fountain pen in his left continued to scrawl across the page. His notes were longer than the report itself. I could almost hear the rise of frustrated sighs at some future meeting as Euclid Danes stood, cleared his throat, and began to speak.

A long time went by. My coffee came. I added milk. I took a sip. Oceans rose and fell, and mountains collapsed to dust. Finally, Euclid Danes finished his work, capped his pen, and aligned it with the paper on which he had been working. He clasped his hands and looked up at me with young, curious eyes. There was mischief in them. Euclid Danes might have been the bane of life in Dearden, but he was smart enough to know it, and bright enough to enjoy it.

"How can I help you?" he said.

"You mind if I take a seat?"

"Not at all." He waved at a chair.

"Your french fries?" I said, pointing at the plate.

"They were."

"Your sister is going to be annoyed that you've eaten."

"My sister is always annoyed, whether I eat or not. Is she now hiring detectives to monitor my habits?"

I tried not to show surprise.

"Did she call ahead?"

"To warn me? She wouldn't do that. She's probably at home praying that you make me disappear. No, I read the papers and watch the news, and I have a good memory for faces. You're Charlie Parker, out of Portland."

"You make me sound like a gunfighter."

"Yes, I do, don't I?" he said, and his eyes twinkled. "So how can I help you, Mr. Parker?"

The waitress appeared and freshened my coffee.

"I'd like to talk to you about Prosperous," I said.

CHIEF MORLAND PICKED UP Harry Dixon at his home. He didn't inform Harry as to why he needed him, just told him to get his coat and a pair of gloves. Morland already had a spade, his pickax, and flashlights in the car. He was tempted to ask Bryan Joblin to join them, but instead told him to wait with Harry's wife. Morland didn't want her to panic and do something stupid. He could see the way she was looking at him while Harry went to fetch his coat, as if he was ready to put her husband in the ground, but it hadn't come to that, not yet.

"It's all right," said Morland. "I'll bring him back in one piece. I just need his help."

Erin Dixon didn't reply. She sat at the kitchen counter, staring him down. She won, or he let her win. He wasn't sure which. In either event, he simply looked away.

Bryan Joblin was sitting by the fire, drinking a PBR and watching some dumb quiz show. Bryan was useful because he didn't think much, and he did as he was told. A purpose could always be found for men like that. Empires were built on their backs.

"How long is he going to stay here?" said Erin, pointing at Bryan with her chin. If Bryan heard her, he didn't respond. He took another sip of his beer and tried to figure out on which continent the Republic of Angola was situated.

"Just until the next girl is found," said Morland. "How's that coming along?"

"I've driven around some, as has Harry," said Erin. "It would be easier if we could move without that fool tagging along with us everywhere."

Bryan Joblin still didn't react. He was lost in his show. He'd guessed Asia, and was smacking the arm of his chair in frustation. Bryan would never serve on the board of selectmen, not unless every other living thing in Prosperous—cats and dogs included—predeceased him.

Morland knew that Bryan alternated his vigils between Harry and his wife. He was currently helping Harry out with an attic conversion on the outskirts of Bangor. Bryan might not have been smart, but he was good with his hands once he worked up the energy to act. In practical terms, there wasn't much Bryan could do if either Harry or Erin decided to try something dumb while he was with the other spouse, but his presence was a reminder of the town's power. It was psychological pressure, albeit with a physical threat implied.

"As soon as we have a girl, he'll be gone," said Morland. "You brought him on yourselves. You brought all of this on yourselves."

THE WOLF IN WINTER   199

Harry had reappeared with his coat. He'd taken his time. Morland wondered what he'd been doing.

Harry patted his wife gently on the shoulder as he passed her. She reached out to grasp his hand, but it was too late. He had moved on.

"You have any idea how long we're going to be?" he asked Morland.

"Couple of hours. You got gloves?"

Harry removed a pair from his pocket. He always had gloves. They were part of his uniform.

"Then let's go," said Morland. "Sooner we get started, sooner we finish."

EUCLID DANES ASKED ME why I was interested in Prosperous.

"I'd prefer not to say," I told him. I didn't want the details to end up in one of Euclid's files, ready to be raised at the next meeting.

"You don't trust me?" said Euclid.

"I don't know you."

"So how did you find out about me?"

"Mr. Danes, you're all over the Internet like some kind of cyber rash. I'm surprised that the residents of Prosperous haven't paid to have you taken out."

"They don't much care for me up there," he admitted.

"I'm curious to know what your beef is with that town. You seem to be expending a lot of energy to insert splinters under the fingernails of its citizenry."

"Is that what they are—citizenry?" he said. "I'd say 'cultists' was a better word to use."

I waited. I was good at waiting. Euclid pulled a sheet of blank paper from a sheaf and drew a circle at the center of the page.

"This is Prosperous," he said. He then added a series of

arrows pointing out toward a number of smaller circles. "Here are Dearden, Thomasville, and Lake Plasko. Beyond them, you have Bangor, Augusta, Portland. Prosperous sends its people out—to work, to learn, to worship—but it's careful about whom it admits. It needs fresh blood because it doesn't want to start breeding idiots in a shallow gene pool, so in the last half-century or so it's allowed its children to marry outsiders, but it keeps those new family units at arm's length until it's sure they're compatible with the town. Houses aren't sold to those who weren't born in Prosperous, or businesses either. The same goes for land, or what little the town has left to develop. Which is where I come in."

"Because Prosperous wants to expand," I said. "And you're in the way."

"Give that man a candy bar. The original founders of the town chose a location bounded by lakes and marsh-land and deep woods, apart from a channel of land to the southeast. Basically, they created their own little fortress, but now it's come back to bite them. If they want their children to continue to live in Prosperous, they need space on which to build, and the town has almost run out of land suitable for development. It's not yet critical, but it's getting there, and Prosperous always plans ahead."

"You make it sound like the town is a living thing."

"Isn't it?" said Euclid. "All towns are a collection of organisms forming a single entity, like a jellyfish. In the case of Prosperous, the controlling organisms are the original founding families, and their bloodlines have remained unpolluted. They control the board of selectmen, the police force, the school board, every institution of consequence. The same names recur throughout the history of Prosperous. They're the guardians of the town.

"And, just like a jellyfish, Prosperous has long tentacles

that trail. Its people worship at mainstream churches, although all in towns outside Prosperous itself, because Prosperous only has room for one church. It places children of the founding families in the surrounding towns, including here in Dearden. It gives them money to run for local and state office, to support charities, to help out with donations to worthwhile causes when the state can't or won't. After a couple of generations, it gets so that people forget that these are creatures of Prosperous, and whatever they do aims to benefit Prosperous first and foremost. It's in their nature, from way back when they first came here as the remnants of the Family of Love. You know what the Family of Love is?"

"I've read up on it," I said.

"Yeah, Family of Love, my old ass. There was no love in those people. They weren't about to become no Quakers. I think that's why they left England. They were killing to protect themselves, and they had blood on their hands. Either they left or they were going to be buried by their enemies."

"Pastor Warraner claims that may just have been propaganda. The Familists were religious dissenters. The same lies were spread about Catholics and Jews."

"Warraner," said Euclid, and the name was like a fly that had somehow entered his mouth and needed to be spat from the tip of his tongue. "He's no more a pastor than I am. He can call himself what he wants, but there's no good in him. And, to correct you on another point, the Familists weren't just dissenters; they were infiltrators. They hid among established congregations and paid lip service to beliefs that weren't their own. I don't believe that's changed much down the years. They're still an infection. They're parasites, turning the body against itself."

This was a metaphor I had heard used before, under other circumstances. It evoked unpleasant associations with people who unwittingly sheltered old spirits inside them, ancient angels waiting for the moment when they could start to consume their hosts from within.

Unfortunately for Euclid Danes, his talk of jellyfish and parasites and bloodlines made him sound like a paranoid obsessive. Perhaps he was. Euclid guessed the direction of my thoughts.

"Sounds crazy, doesn't it?" he said. "Sounds like the ravings of a madman?"

"I wouldn't put it that strongly."

"You'd be in the minority, but it's easy enough to prove. Dearden is decaying, but compared to Thomasville it's like Las Vegas. Our kids are leaving because there's no work, and no hope of any. Businesses are closing, and those that stay open sell only stuff that old farts like me need. The towns in this whole region are slowly dying, all except Prosperous. It's suffering, because everywhere is suffering, but not like we are. It's insulated. It's protected. It sucks the life out of the surrounding towns to feed itself. Good fortune, luck, divine providence—call it what you will, but there's only so much of it to go around, and Prosperous has taken it all."

The waitress with the big hair came by to offer me yet more coffee. I was the only person in the bar who seemed to be drinking it, and she clearly didn't want to waste the pot. I had a long ride home. It would help me stay awake. I drank it quickly, though. I didn't think there was much more that Euclid Danes could tell me.

"Are there others like you?" I asked.

"Wackjobs? Paranoiacs? Fantasists?"

"How about 'dissenters'?"

He smiled at the co-opting of the word. "Some. Enough. They keep quieter about it than I do, though. It doesn't pay to cross the folk up in Prosperous. It starts with small things—a dog going missing, damage to your car, maybe a call to the IRS to say that you're taking in a little work on the side to cover your bar tab—but then it escalates. It's not only the economy that has led to businesses closing around here, and families leaving."

"But you've stayed."

He picked up his fountain pen and unscrewed the cap, ready to return to his papers. I glimpsed the name on the pen: Tibaldi. I looked it up later. They started at about four hundred dollars and went up to forty thousand. The one that Euclid Danes used had a lot of gold on it.

"I look like the crazy old coot who lives in a run-down house with more dogs than bugs and a sister who can only cook meat loaf," he said. "But my brother was a justice of the Massachusetts Supreme Judicial Court, my nephews and nieces are lawyers and bankers, and there's nothing anyone can teach me about playing the markets. I have money, and a degree of influence. I think that's why they hate me so much: because, except for an accident of birth, I could have been one of them. Even though I'm not, they still feel that I should side with wealth and privilege, because I'm wealthy and privileged myself.

"So Prosperous can't move against me, and it can't frighten me. All it can do is wait for me to die, and even then those bastards will find that I've tied so much legal ribbon around my land that humanity itself will be extinct before they find a way to build on it. It's been good talking with you, Mr. Parker. I wish you luck with whatever it is that you're investigating."

He lowered his head and began writing again. I was reminded of the end of *Willy Wonka & the Chocolate Factory*, when Gene Wilder dismisses Charlie and tries to lose himself in his papers until the boy returns the Everlasting

Gobstopper as a token of recompense. I hadn't shared all that I knew with Euclid, because I was cautious. I had underestimated and misjudged him, although I thought Euclid might have done the same with me.

"A homeless man named Jude hanged himself down in Portland not long ago," I said. "He was looking for his daughter before he died. Her name was Annie Broyer. He was convinced that she'd gone to Prosperous. There's still no trace of her. I think she's dead, and I'm not alone in believing it. I also think that she may have met her end in Prosperous."

Euclid stopped writing. The cap went back on the pen. He straightened his tie and reached for his coat.

"Mr. Parker, why don't you and I take a ride?"

IT WAS ALREADY DARK. I had followed Euclid Danes to the northwestern limit of the town of Dearden. His fence marked the boundary. Beyond it lay woodland: part of the township of Prosperous.

"Why haven't they built here?" I asked. "The land's suitable. It would just be a matter of knocking down some trees."

Euclid took a small flashlight from his pocket and shined it on the ground. There was a hole in the earth, perhaps eighteen inches in diameter, or a little more. It was partly obscured by undergrowth and tree roots.

"What is it?" I asked.

"I don't know. I've found three of them over the years, but there may be more. I know for sure that there are a couple around that old church of theirs. I haven't seen them myself for some time—as you can imagine, I'm persona non grata in Prosperous—but I have it on good authority from others who've been there."

"You think the ground is unstable?"

"Might be. I'm no expert."

I was no expert either, but this wasn't karst terrain, not as far as I was aware. I hadn't heard of any Florida-style sinkholes appearing in the area. The hole was curious, unsettling even, but that might have been a vague atavastic dread of small, enclosed places beneath the earth, and the fear of collapse they brought with them. I wasn't claustrophobic, but then I'd never been trapped in a hole below the ground.

"What made it?"

Euclid killed the flashlight.

"Ah, that's the interesting question, isn't it?" he said. "I'll leave that one with you. All I know is that I have meat loaf waiting, with a side of indigestion to follow. I'd ask you to join me, but I like you."

He began to walk back to his car. I stayed by the fence. I could still make out the hole, a deeper blackness against the encroaching dark. I felt an itching on my scalp, as though bugs were crawling through my hair.

Euclid called back a final piece of advice when he reached his car. He was driving a beautiful old '57 Chevy Bel Air in red. "I like them to know I'm coming," he had told me. Now he stood beside its open door, a chill breeze toying with his wispy hair and his wide tie.

"Good luck with those people up there," he said. "Just watch where you put your feet."

He turned on the ignition and kept the Chevy's lights trained on the ground in front of me until I was safely back at my own car. I followed him as far as his house, then continued south, and home.

ON THE OUTSKIRTS OF Prosperous, Lucas Morland and Harry Dixon were staring at another hole in the ground. At first Harry had been struck by the absurd yet terrible thought that the girl had actually dug herself out, just as he had dreamed, and what had crawled from that grave was something much worse than a wounded young woman who could name names. But then their flashlights had picked out the big paw prints on the scattered earth, and the broken bones, and the teeth marks on them. They found the head under an old oak, most of the face gnawed away.

"I told you," said Harry to Morland. "I told you I saw a wolf."

Morland said nothing, but began gathering up what he could retrieve of the remains. Harry joined him. They couldn't find all of the girl. The wolf, or some other scavenger, had carried parts of her away. There was an arm missing, and most of one leg.

Evidence, thought Morland. It's evidence. It would have to be found. For now, all he could do was put what they collected of the girl into more of the plastic sheeting, dump it in the car, and refill the grave. Nothing like this, nothing so terrible, so unlucky, had happened in Prosperous for generations. If the girl hadn't run . . . If Dixon and his bitch wife hadn't let her escape . . .

Morland wanted to punch Harry. He wanted to kill him. It was the Dixons' fault, all of it. Even if Harry and Erin located a suitable girl, Morland would find a way to make them pay. Hell, if Erin herself wasn't so fucking old and worn they could have used her. But no, the town didn't feed on its own. It never had. Those from within who transgressed had always been dealt with in a different way. There were rules.

They taped up the plastic, forming three packages of body parts. After that they drove north for an hour, far beyond Prosperous, and reburied what was left of the girl. The stench of her stayed with them both all the way to town. Later, back in their own homes, both men scrubbed and showered, but still they could smell her.

Erin Dixon knocked at the bathroom door fifteen minutes after the shower had stopped running, and her husband had still not emerged. Bryan Joblin had fallen asleep in the armchair by the fireplace. She had thought about killing him. She was thinking about killing a lot lately.

"Harry?" she called. "Are you okay?"

From inside the bathroom she heard the sound of weeping. She tried the door. It was unlocked.

Her husband was sitting on the edge of the tub, a towel wrapped around his waist and his face buried in his hands. She sat beside him and held him to her.

"Can you smell it?" he asked her.

She sniffed him, inhaling the scent of his hair and his skin. She detected only soap.

"You smell fine," she said. "You want to tell me what happened?"

"No."

She went to the bathroom doorway and listened. She could still hear the sound of Joblin snoring. She closed the door and returned to her husband, but she kept her voice to a whisper, just in case.

"Marie Nesbit called me earlier on my cell phone, while that asshole was snoring his head off," she said.

Marie was Erin's closest friend. She worked as a secretary at the Town Office, and was from one of the founding families, just like the Dixons. Her husband, Art, was an alcoholic, but gentle and sad, for the most part, rather than violent. Erin had long provided her with a sympathetic ear.

"She told me that a detective came to town asking about the girl."

Harry had stopped weeping.

"Police?"

"No, a private investigator, like on TV."

"Did she say who had hired him?"

"No. She only overheard the start of what he had to say. She didn't want to be seen spying."

"What was his name?"

"Parker. Charlie Parker. I googled him on my phone, then erased the history. He's been in the newspapers."

So that's why Morland wanted the girl's body moved. The detective had come, and Morland had gotten scared. No, not just Morland. He might have been chief, but Morland did what he was told to do by the board. The order to dig up the corpse had probably come from Hayley Conyer herself, but a wolf had reached it first. First the girl, then the detective, now the wolf. The town was starting to unravel.

"Harry," said Erin. "I've decided: I'm not going to find them another girl."

He nodded. How could they, after setting the last one free? How could a couple who had wished for, but never been given, their own daughter collude in the killing of someone else's child?

"They'll be monitoring the detective," said Harry. "That's how they work. We can't contact him, not yet. Maybe not ever."

"So what will we do?"

"It's like I said. We'll leave, and soon. After that, we'll decide."

Erin gripped his hand. He squeezed hers in return.

"When?"

"A couple of days. No more than that."

"Promise?"

"Promise."

She kissed him. His mouth opened beneath hers, but

before they could go any further they were disturbed by a knock on the door and Bryan Joblin said, "Hey, are you two in there?"

Erin went to the door and unlocked it. Joblin stood bleary-eyed before her, smelling of his cheap beer. He took in Erin, and Harry standing behind her, his towel around his waist, his body angled to hide his now diminishing hard-on.

"Havin' some fun?" said Joblin. "Shit, you got a bedroom. We all got to use this room, and I need to take a piss."

XXVIII

Chief Morland rarely dreamed. He was curious about this fact. He understood that everybody dreamed, even if they didn't always remember their dreams when they woke, but they could retain details of some of them at least. His wife dreamed a lot, and she had a recall of her dreams that bordered on the exhaustive. Morland could bring to mind only a handful of occasions on which he had awakened with some memory of his dreams. He couldn't associate them with any particularly difficult or traumatic periods in his life. It wasn't as though his father died, and that night he dreamed, or he was plagued by nightmares, following the time he nearly sent his car into a ditch at high speed after skidding on black ice, and was certain that his moment had come. He couldn't pinpoint that kind of cause and effect.

But he dreamed on the night that he and Harry Dixon found the girl's scattered remains. He'd gone to bed late because he'd been thinking about the wolf. He should have believed Dixon on that first night, when he claimed to have seen an animal on the road. He should have connected the sighting with the reports that had come to him of garbage bags torn apart, and Elspeth Ramsay's missing dog, but his mind was on other matters, like a girl with a hole in her chest, and the Dixons and their tales of bolts and wood splinters, and the slow decline in the fortunes of his town that had to be arrested.

And it had been decades since a wolf was last seen in the state. The St. Lawrence formed a natural barrier, keeping them in Canada, and that suited Morland just fine. He was aware that some in Maine were in favor of the reintroduction of wolves, arguing that they'd been an important part of the ecosystem until they were slaughtered out of existence. You could make the same argument for dinosaurs and saber-toothed cats, as far as Morland was concerned, but that wasn't a reason to bring them back. What might happen to a kid who got lost in the woods, maybe separated from parents who were hiking the trails? What about an adult stumbling and breaking a leg, and suddenly finding himself surrounded by a wolf pack—what would happen then? The same thing that happened to Elspeth Ramsay's pet, perhaps, or the same thing that happened to the girl, except that at least she was dead when the wolf started to gnaw on her. The world was full of do-gooders, but it was left to men like Morland to clean up their mess.

He poured himself a finger of bourbon. Just as he rarely dreamed, so too he only occasionally consumed hard liquor. He wondered if the two might not be connected. Didn't matter. Tonight was different. Tonight he'd gone to dig up a body and found that a wolf had done it for him, forcing him to scrabble in the dirt for bone, and rotting meat, and scraps of plastic and cloth. He'd seen dead bodies before—suicides, accidental shootings, traffic collisions, and the regular actions of mortality that called for the local cops to break a window or kick in a door because someone had been selfish enough to pass away without giving prior notice to his friends, relatives, and neighbors. Morland had never killed anyone himself, unlike his old man, but Daniel Morland had prepared his son well for the responsibility that would eventually pass to him when he became chief of police, and Morland had been surprised at how dispassionately he'd viewed the girl's body following the shooting. It reminded him of the sense of passing sadness he felt upon looking down at a deer felled during the course of a hunt.

He took a mouthful of bourbon—not a sip, a mouthful. This wasn't a night for sipping. He closed his eyes and briefly tried to pretend that he was chief of police in a normal town, but it didn't take. A "normal town"—his own words made him laugh aloud, and he covered his mouth like a child who feared being caught doing something naughty. The only thing normal about Prosperous was the way it proved that, over time, individuals could habituate themselves to the most appalling behavior. So many of the townsfolk, even the ones most closely involved in its secrets, regarded themselves as "good" people, and not without reason. They looked after their families, and they abided, for the most part, by the law. Politically, Prosperous was the most liberal town in this part of Maine: Proposition 1, to allow same-sex marriage in the state, had passed by as much of a majority in Prosperous as it had in

Portland, and the town leaned slightly Democrat or liberal independent in elections. But the older citizens of Prosperous understood that the town was built on a lie, or a truth too terrible to be named. Some of them preferred to pretend not to know, and nobody begrudged them their show of ignorance. They weren't suited to leadership. In the end, it always came down to the original families, to the founders. They looked after the town for all.

Morland finished his drink. He should have called Hayley Conyer to tell her about the wolf and the turmoil at the grave site, but he didn't. He'd had his fill of Hayley. The call could wait until morning. Tomorrow he would see about putting together a hunting party, and they'd find the wolf and kill it quietly. Thomas Souleby had an old hound that might be useful in picking up the wolf's scent. Morland didn't know much about hunting wolves, apart from what he'd learned that evening from Google, but opinion seemed to be divided on the usefulness of packs of dogs in a hunt. Some said that a wolf would run from them, but in Wisconsin a couple of hundred dead hunting dogs said otherwise. Elspeth Ramsay's missing mongrel suggested that this wolf wasn't above taking down a domestic animal if it had the chance. No matter; Prosperous wasn't overflowing with the kinds of dogs that might be useful in a confrontation with a wolf anyway, not unless he had missed a news flash about the hidden strength of labradoodles. Trapping seemed the most effective way to deal with the animal, but they might be lucky enough to get it under their guns first, although right now luck was in short supply.

He went to bed. He kissed his wife. She mumbled something in her sleep.

He dreamed.

In his dream, Prosperous was burning.

*   *   *

THE HEADLINES IN THE newspapers in the days that followed were all very similar: "Triple Tragedy Strikes Small Town," "Maine Town Mourns Its Dead," "Trouble Comes in Threes for Close-Knit Community". . . .

In Afghanistan, a UH-60 Black Hawk helicopter carrying four U.S. "military advisers" and crew went down in Kandahar. Three of the men survived the crash, which was caused by a mechanical failure, but they didn't survive the firefight with the Taliban that followed. In the shadowy corners of the Internet, a photograph circulated of three severed heads placed in a line on the sand. Two of them were identified as Captain Mark Tabart and Staff Sergeant Jeremy Cutter, both natives of Prosperous, Maine.

On the same day that the two soldiers died, a woman named Valerie Gillson rounded a bend between Dearden and Prosperous and saw a wounded fawn lying in the middle of the road. The animal appeared to have been struck by a vehicle, for its back legs were twisted and broken. It scrabbled at the road with its front hooves and thrashed its head in agony. Valerie stepped from her car. She couldn't leave the animal in distress, and she couldn't run it over to put it out of its agony: she'd never be able to drive her car again. She took out her cell phone and called the police department in Prosperous. Chief Morland would know what to do. The number rang, and Marie Nesbit, who was on dispatch duty that day, picked up the call.

"Hi, Marie? This is Valerie Gillson. Yes, I'm fine, but I'm about a mile south of town and there's a wounded deer in the middle of the road. It's in a lot of pain, and I don't—"

She stopped talking. She had just noticed that there was something tangled around the back legs of the deer. It looked like wire. No, not wire: roots, or thick briars—she wasn't sure which. They extended into the undergrowth. It was almost as if the wounded deer had been placed there as bait. Instinctively, she raised her phone and took a photograph of the deer's legs.

She heard Marie's voice asking if she was okay.

"Sorry, Marie, I just noticed—"

Valerie Gillson never got to tell Marie what she had just seen, because at that moment a logging-company truck took the bend behind her just a fraction too fast. The driver swerved to avoid the car and struck Valerie instead, killing her instantly. Her cell phone was recovered in the aftermath. On it was the last photograph that Valerie had taken: the hindquarters of a fawn, its legs entwined with dark roots.

But of the animal itself there was no sign.

And in the gunsmithery at the back of his store Ben Pearson was carrying his favorite hunting rifle to the workbench. The gun was the same one that he had used to kill Annie Broyer. Chief Morland had advised him to get rid of it, and Ben knew that it made sense to do as Morland said. The bullet had gone straight through the girl, and Ben hadn't been able to find any trace of it, try as he might. The rifle linked him to murder, and it didn't matter how much time and effort he'd put into customizing it so that there wasn't a gun to rival it for miles; it had to be taken apart and destroyed.

He had been thinking a lot about the dead girl. He didn't regret what he'd done. If she'd escaped, that would have been the end for all of them, but he had a lingering sense of transgression. The girl hadn't been his to kill. She had been sourced for a particular reason. She was the town's girl. She belonged to Prosperous, and her life was the town's to take. By killing her, he had deprived the town of its due. That had never happened before, not in the long history of the community. Ben feared that if another girl wasn't found soon there could be repercussions. He would bury the rifle in the woods. It would represent his own small sacrifice, an act of recompense.

For the first, and last, time, Ben stumbled in his workshop, a place that he had known for decades. As he fell, his finger slipped inside the trigger guard. The rifle should not have been loaded. As far as Ben was concerned, the rifle *could* not have been loaded. He was obsessively careful about such matters, and never left a round chambered.

The bullet tore through his chest, nicking his heart.

And he held his beloved rifle in his arms as he died.

XXIX

I had been anticipating the call from Euclid Danes ever since the first reports began to link the deaths of the soldiers in Afghanistan to the town of Prosperous. A traffic fatality and an apparently accidental shooting in the same town in the space of twenty-four hours would have been unlikely to attract quite the same degree of media interest, but the addition of the military casualties, and the manner in which the soliders had died, brought attention to Prosperous, and not just from the local and state outlets. The nationals turned their gaze on the town, and it was featured on the Web sites of the *New York Times* and *USA Today*. The task of dealing with the media fell to

Hayley Conyer, as the head of the board of selectmen. (One unfortunate local TV reporter inadvertently referred to it as the board of "selectpersons" within earshot of Conyer, and was lucky to escape with his life.) She handled her role well. She was polite, dignified, and distant. She gave the reporters just enough to keep them from prying further, but in repeating the same sound bites over and over, along with ongoing pleas for privacy, she managed to dull their curiosity. Prosperous weathered the storm of attention for a few days, and then subsided into a traumatized calm.

Euclid Danes called me on the third day, when Prosperous was already starting to slide from prominence in the bulletins.

"Looks like Prosperous has emptied its barrel of good fortune," he said. He didn't sound triumphant, but concerned.

"It happens," I said.

"Not to Prosperous."

"I guess they'll just have to deal with it."

"That's what worries me. I received a call early this morning. There was no caller ID. The voice was male, but I didn't recognize it. He told me that my bullshit wasn't going to be tolerated any longer, and if I didn't keep my mouth shut I'd be put in a hole in the ground, and my bitch sister too. His words, not mine. I like my sister, apart from her cooking. I was also warned not to go shooting my mouth off to strangers in Benny's."

"Somebody ratted you out."

"Money's scarce in Dearden, so I wouldn't be surprised if someone was being paid a little on the side to keep an eye on me, but I thought you should know about the call. With all that's happened over the last day or two, Prosperous is going to be in pain, and wounded animals lash out."

"I'll bear that in mind. Thank you, Mr. Danes."

Euclid Danes said goodbye and hung up.

I waited until the remains of the soldiers were repatriated, and the bodies laid in the ground, before I returned to Prosperous.

IT WAS PASTOR WARRANER'S daughter who alerted him to the presence of a man in the cemetery.

Warraner had almost finished the final detailing on the last of the kitchen cabinets. It was an out-of-town order from a banker and his wife in Rockland, and they hadn't even blinked at his estimate, even though he'd added a premium of twenty percent to what was already an expensive quote. The recent tragedies, and their implications for the town, would not force him to miss his deadline. He was already a week ahead when the deaths occurred, for which he was grateful; he could not work well with fear in his heart, and his pace had slowed during Prosperous's recent troubles.

The board was scheduled to meet the following evening, now that the media circus had collapsed its tents and departed to seek out new miseries and misfortunes. Warraner had pressed for an earlier conclave, but Hayley Conyer had resisted. The presence of the newspapers and TV cameras, and the unwelcome attention they brought on Prosperous, had disturbed her, adding to her shock and grief at the four deaths. She and Ben Pearson had been close, even though their personalities had differed vastly. There was an element of the Brahmin to Hayley, while Ben had been an earthy Mainer through and through. Unlike so many others in Prosperous, Ben Pearson had no fear of Hayley Conyer, and she had admired his independence of thought. It made her respect his opinion more than those of the other board members, and she usually tended to listen when he disagreed with her, and adapt her views and actions accordingly.

Now there was a vacancy on the board. Under ordinary circumstances, the remaining members would have come up with the names of suitable candidates and presented them to the townsfolk for rubber-stamping, but Prosperous was in crisis and this was not the time for an election. The board would continue with only five members, and Morland and Warraner would remain as observers who could offer advice and arguments but were still not entitled to vote.

The soldiers, along with Valerie Gillson and Ben Pearson, were buried in the new cemetery to the south. Nobody had been interred in the grounds of the old church since the end of the last century, not even deceased members of the senior families, whose surnames already adorned so many stones in the churchyard. It was Warraner's father who had decreed that the cemetery was now closed to interments, and nobody had questioned his decision. The only reason he had given was this:

Why risk disturbing what is at rest?

In recent days his son had issued an even more restrictive edict. The cemetery and church were out of bounds to all. Nobody was to trespass there, and while the media was in town Morland and his deputies—aided by the most trustworthy of the younger citizens—had maintained a twenty-four-hour vigil to ensure that visitors and reporters were kept away. Had Warraner been asked for a reason, he would have given this one:

Why risk disturbing further what is no longer at rest?

Now here was his youngest daughter telling him that a man was walking among the stones, and taking photographs of the church with his phone. Warraner was so incensed that he didn't even go to the house to get a coat but ran in his shirtsleeves through the woods, ignoring the cold, ignoring, too, the branches that pulled at him even as he recalled the final photograph on Valerie Gillson's cell phone, the image of a deer with its legs bound by briars, a deer that had been crippled and laid out as bait. . . .

He burst from the woods and saw the intruder.

"Hey!" he cried. "That's private property, and sacred ground. You've no right to be in there."

The stranger turned, and at the sight of him Pastor Warraner immediately understood that the town's troubles had just increased considerably.

I WATCHED WARRANER AS he came to a halt at the iron railing that surrounded the cemetery. He was breathing heavily, and a scratch on his neck was bleeding into his shirt collar.

"What are you doing here?" he asked.

I walked toward him. He watched my progress carefully.

"Same as last time," I said. "Trying to find a missing girl."

"She's not in this place, and you're disturbing the peace of the dead."

I sidestepped a tilting stone cross. The names and dates on it were so old and faded as to be entirely illegible.

"Really? I've found that it takes a lot to wake the dead, unless some were never quite asleep to begin with."

"This is neither the time nor the place for mockery, Mr. Parker. Our town has been through a difficult period."

"I'm aware of that, Mr. Warraner," I said. "And I'm entirely serious."

I was facing him now. His hands gripped the railing so tightly that his knuckles showed white against his skin. I turned to the right and continued walking, forcing him to keep pace with me.

"The gate is to your left," he said.

"I know. That's how I got in."

"It's locked."

"It *was* locked. I found it open."

"You're lying."

"I suppose you could call Chief Morland and ask him to dust it for fingerprints. Or you could just buy a better lock."

"I fully intend to call Chief Morland," said Warraner. "I'll have you arrested for trespassing."

His hands searched his pockets for his cell phone but came up empty. I offered him mine.

"Feel free to call, but I was planning to pay him another visit anyway, just as soon as I've finished here."

I saw that Warraner was tempted to take my phone, but even he could appreciate the absurdity of doing so. The threat of police involvement was of limited effectiveness if the person being threatened was only a middleman away from calling the cops on himself.

"What do you want, Mr. Parker?" he said.

I paused beside a hole in the ground. It was similar to the one that Euclid Danes had pointed out to me close to the edge of his own land.

"I was wondering what this might be?"

I had stumbled across the hole by accident—literally; I had almost broken my ankle in it.

"It's a fox den," he said.

"Really?"

I knelt and examined it. An active den usually retained signs of the animal's comings and goings, but this had none. The ground around it was undisturbed.

"It's big for a fox hole," I said. "And I don't see any sign of foxes."

"It's an old den," said Warraner. Hostility flowed from him in waves.

"Do you have many old dens around here?"

"Possibly. I've never taken the time to count them. For the last time, I want you to leave this place. Now!"

If we'd both been nine years old and in a schoolyard I could have asked him to make me, or inquired about what he might do if I refused, but that didn't seem appropriate in a cemetery, and I'd annoyed him enough for now. He tracked me back to the gate and examined the lock once I was back on the right side of the fence. I hadn't been forced to break the lock; two decades of friendship with Angel had taught me the rudiments of picking. Warraner wrapped the chain from gate to fence and secured it.

"Do you want to follow me to the police department?" I said.

"No," said Warraner. "I know you'll go there. You have more questions to ask, don't you? Why can't you just leave us in peace?"

"Questions always remain, even when things work out. It comes with the territory."

"With being a self-righteous prick who can't allow a town to mourn its dead undisturbed?"

He savored the word "prick." I'd been called worse, but not by anyone with a degree in divinity.

"No, with being human. You should try it, Mr. Warraner, or Pastor Warraner, or whatever title you've chosen to give yourself. Your dead are past caring, and your mourning will do them no good. I'm searching for a missing girl. If she's alive, she's in trouble. If she's dead, someone else is. As an individual who professes to be a man of god, I'd suggest that your compassion is currently misdirected."

Warraner plunged his hands into the pockets of his jeans as though he feared the damage he might otherwise inflict on me. He was a big man, and strong as well. If he got his hands on me, he'd do some harm. Of course, I'd shatter one of his knees before he got that close, but it wouldn't look good on my résumé. Still, all of his weight was on his left leg, which was ramrod straight. If he moved, I'd take him.

Warraner breathed deeply to calm himself and recover his dignity. The moment passed.

"You know nothing of my god, Mr. Parker," he said solemnly.

I looked past him and took in the ancient stones of his church, and the leering faces visible in the fading afternoon light.

"You may be wrong about that, Pastor."

He stayed at the gate as I drove away, his hands deep in his pockets, his gaze fixed on me, standing in the shadow of his church.

In the shadow of his god.

Chief Morland was looking out the window of his office as I pulled up outside his department. If he was pleased to see me, he was trying manfully to hide it. His arms were folded, and he stared at me without expression as I walked up the path. Inside there was a strained silence among the staff, and I guessed that, not long before, Chief Morland had been shouting into a telephone receiver at Pastor Warraner. Nobody offered me coffee and a cookie. Nobody even wanted to catch my eye.

Morland's door was open. I stood on the threshold.

"Mind if I come in?"

He unfolded his arms. "Would it matter if I did?"

"I can talk to you from here, but it seems kind of childish."

Morland gestured me inside and told me to close the door. He waited for me to sit before doing the same himself.

"You've been keeping my phone busy," he said.

"Warraner?"

"The pastor was just the most recent caller. We've had reports of a man in a car like yours casing properties, and I already sent a deputy out to take a look. If you'd been driving your fancy Mustang I'd have known it was you, but you seem to have left your toy automobile back in Portland today."

"I was trying to be discreet."

"The pastor didn't think so. Maybe you failed to notice the sign that read PRIVATE PROPERTY out by the cemetery?"

"If I paid attention to every sign that read PRIVATE PROPERTY or NO ENTRY, I'd never get anything done. Besides, I figured that after the last tour I was practically a member of the congregation."

"It doesn't have a congregation."

"Yeah, I've been meaning to ask about that. I still find it strange that a religious sect would go to the trouble of hauling a church across the Atlantic, rebuild it brick by brick, and then just shrug and walk off."

"They died out."

"You're speaking metaphorically, right? Because the descendants of the original settlers are still here. This town has more old names than the Bible."

"I'm no historian, but there are plenty of folk in this

town who consider themselves one," said Morland. "The Familists faded away. I've heard it said that the worst thing to happen to the Family of Love was leaving England. They survived because they were hunted and oppressed, and there's nothing more guaranteed to harden a man's convictions than to be told that he can't follow his own beliefs. With freedom to worship also came the freedom not to worship."

"And where do you worship, Chief?"

"I'm a Catholic. I go to Mary Immaculate down in Dearden."

"Are you familiar with a man there called Euclid Danes?"

"Euclid's a Methodist, although they'd disown him if they weren't so short on bodies to fill their seats. How do you know him?"

He didn't blink, didn't look away, didn't rub his left ear with his right hand or scratch his nose or whatever it is that men and women are supposed to do when they're lying or trying to hide knowledge, but he might just as well have. Morland was well aware that I'd been speaking with Euclid Danes. He wouldn't have been much of a chief of police if he weren't, not in a town like Prosperous. So he pretended, and I let him pretend, and each of us watched the other act.

"I found him on the Internet," I said.

"Looking for a date?"

"He's a little old for me, although I bet he cleans up nicely."

"Euclid's not very popular in this town."

"He wears it as a badge of pride. In his place, I might do the same. Are you aware that he's been threatened?"

"He's always being threatened. Doesn't do much good, though."

"You sound almost as though you approve."

"He's one stubborn man standing in the way of the expansion of a town and the money that would bring into the local economy."

"As you yourself said, there's nothing more likely to make a certain kind of man resolute than finding himself threatened for his beliefs."

"I don't think the First Amendment guarantees your right to be an asshole."

"I think that's precisely what it does."

Morland threw his hands into the air in despair. "Jesus, if I closed my eyes I could almost be talking to Danes himself, and you don't know how unhappy that makes me. So you talked to Danes? Go, you. I'll bet he told you all about how rich old Prosperous is bad, and its people are jerks just because they look after their own. I could give a fuck what Danes says. We're weathering the recession, and we're doing okay. You know why? Because we support one another, because we're close-knit, and that's helped us get through the bad times.

"In case you haven't noticed, Mr. Parker, this town has taken a kicking recently. Instead of busting into old cemeteries, you should go to the new one and pay your respects to the two boys we just buried there. Their crosses won't be hard to find. They have flags beside them. Close by you'll find fresh earth over Valerie Gillson's grave, and the messages her kids left on it for her. Look to your right and a pile of flowers marks where Ben Pearson is resting. Four dead in twenty-four hours, a town in mourning, and I have to deal with your bullshit."

He had a point. I just chose to ignore it.

"I'm looking for an older couple," I said, as though he had never spoken. "Sixties at least, at a guess, although you know how young people are; when you're in your twenties, everyone over forty looks old. This couple own a blue car.

I saw a few blue cars during my ride through your very clean town, but I resisted the impulse to start knocking on doors until we'd spoken. You could save me time by giving me the names and addresses of anyone who might fit the criteria."

I took a small hardback notebook from my pocket, slipped the minipen from the spine, and waited. I felt like a secretary poised to take dictation.

"What are you talking about?" said Morland.

"I have a witness who says that the people who took Annie Broyer to this town were an older couple in a blue car. I thought I might try talking to older couples with blue cars. Sometimes the simplest options are the best. You're welcome to come along, unless you're preparing some more stump speeches."

There was a knock at the door behind me.

"Not now," said Morland.

The door opened a fraction. I turned to see one of the secretaries poke her head in.

"Chief, I—"

"I said, 'Not now!' "

The door quickly closed again. Morland hadn't taken his eyes from me throughout the brief exchange.

"I told you when you came through last time that there's no evidence the woman you're looking for ended up in Prosperous."

"I think she did."

"Has she been reported missing?"

"No," I admitted.

"So you're looking for a street person, a former junkie, who has probably fallen back into her old ways, and you want me to help you accuse seniors of kidnapping her?"

"Seniors, and younger," I corrected. "And only ones with access to a blue car."

"Get out!"

I closed my notebook and restored the minipen to the spine.

"I guess I'll just have to go through the DMV."

"You do that. Nobody here fits your bill. That girl is not in Prosperous. If I see you within the town limits again, you'll be charged with trespass and harassment."

I stood. I'd filled my aggravation quota for the day.

"Thank you for your time, Chief," I said as I left the office. "You've been a big help."

He took it as sarcasm—I could see it on his face—but I was speaking the truth.

I had never told Morland that Annie Broyer was an ex-junkie.

THE WOLF CONTINUED TO circle the town. He had returned to the place in which he found the meat and bone belowground, but only the scent of it remained now. For a time, the streets had been filled with even more light and noise and men than before, and the activity had caused the wolf to flee into the woods, but his hunger had driven him back. He tore apart a garbage bag and fed on the chicken carcasses he smelled inside before slipping back into the woods. He remained thin, and even through the double layer of his fur, his ribs shone sharply carved. The temperature had started to drop again; that night it would plummet to minus seven. The wolf's thick subcutaneous fat had become depleted over the winter months as his body fed upon itself. The food from the town was sustaining him, but the damage had already been done. Instinct warned him to seek shelter from the cold, to find a dark, hidden place with warmth. In his youth, members of the pack had sometimes colonized abandoned fox dens, and the wolf now sought a hole in the ground in which to hide.

The pain was spreading through his body, and he could put no weight on his damaged limb.

South of the town, he picked up the smell of a deer. The spoor was old, but the wolf identified the pain and panic that had marked the deer's final moments. He paused, wary now. The deer had died in terror, and beneath the sweet stink of prey the wolf could detect another smell, one that was unfamiliar and yet set his senses jangling. The wolf had no predators, aside from man. He would even take on a grizzly in a fight for food, and his pack had once come upon, and consumed, a hibernating black bear. The fear that the wolf now felt reminded him of his fear of man. Yet this was no man.

The scent of the deer drew the wolf on. He flattened his ears against his head and arched his back as a car passed. The light vanished, the sound faded, and he continued to pick his way through the trees until at last he came to a clearing.

In the clearing was a hole. Beside it, almost hidden by roots and branches, lay the deer. The wolf narrowed his eyes and pulled back his ears. His tail pointed straight out, parallel to the ground. The threat came from the hole. Now the wolf snarled, and his fur bristled. He crouched in anticipation of an attack. His senses were flooded by the smell of the deer. He would fight to eat.

And then the wolf's tail moved, withdrawing fully between his legs. He thrust out his tongue and lowered his hindquarters, his eyes still fixed on the hole but his muzzle pointing up. His back arched again, just as it had when the car passed, but this time it was a gesture not of fear but of active submission, the repect that one animal pays to the dominant other. Finally, the wolf approached the deer while maintaining a careful distance from the hole. Briars entangled around the deer's hind legs came away easily as the wolf pulled at the remains. Despite his weariness and his hunger, he did not start to feed until he had managed to drag the deer as far from the hole in the ground as he could. The smell of danger grew fainter. The threat from the dominant animal was receding, moving farther away.

Moving deeper into the earth.

THE DOORBELL RANG IN Chief Morland's house. Morland's wife went to answer, but he told her that he would take care of it. He had barely spoken to her since coming home, and hadn't eaten dinner with the family. His wife said nothing, and did not object. Her husband rarely behaved in this way, but when he did he usually had good cause, and she knew better than to press him. He would tell her of his troubles in his own time.

Thomas Souleby stood on the doorstep. Beside him was a man whom Morland did not know. He wore heavy tan boots, and his body was hidden beneath layers of clothing. His red beard was thick, flecked here and there with gray. In his right hand he held a wolf trap on a length of chain.

The two visitors entered the house, and the door closed softly behind them.

3

KILLING

We humans fear the beast within the wolf because
we do not understand the beast within ourselves.

Gerald Hausman, *Meditations with the Navajo*

XXXI

THEY CONVENED AT THE home of Hayley Conyer, as they always did when issues of great import had to be discussed in private. The board of selectmen conducted public meetings on a regular basis, but the agenda for such gatherings was decided well in advance, and sensitive subjects were resolutely avoided. They were also open only to residents of Prosperous, following an abortive attempt by Euclid Danes to hijack one session. The late Ben Pearson had advocated killing Danes following that particular incident, and he had not been joking. If it had gone to a vote of the board, the motion would almost certainly have been passed unanimously.

Luke Joblin arrived first at Hayley's house, accompanied by Kinley Nowell. Kinley had checked himself out of the hospital following Ben Pearson's death. He was still weak, and his breathing was shallow and labored, but he walked into the house under his own steam, aided only by the walker that he had been using for the past decade or more. Joblin carried his ventilator for him. After them came Thomas Souleby, and then Calder Ayton. Hayley was most solicitous of Calder, whose grief at the loss of Ben was etched on his face. She whispered to him as he sat silently at the table, the chair to his right—the chair that had always been occupied by Ben—now empty.

Pastor Warraner arrived at the same time as Chief

Morland. Had Hayley not known of the animosity that existed between them she might almost have suspected them of collusion, but the two men stood awkwardly apart on the porch when she opened the door to them, their body language speaking volumes about their distaste for each other. She knew that Morland had been out in the woods that day, setting traps for the wolf with Abbot, the hunter brought by Souleby to the town. Morland looked exhausted. Good, thought Hayley: it would make him more pliable. She took him by the arm as he passed, indicating to Warraner that he should go on ahead into the dining room. Warraner did as he was told. He had no concerns about what Hayley Conyer might have to say to Morland in his absence. Even after their last meeting, when Hayley had sided with Morland against him, Warraner remained secure in his position as Hayley's spiritual adviser.

"Did you find the animal?" asked Hayley.

"No, not yet, but it's still around. We discovered a deer carcass. It was all chewed up. Abbot reckoned it had been dead for a while, but the damage to it was recent—not more than twenty-four hours. We've laid bait and set traps. We'll get it soon. Abbot says that it's wounded. He could tell by the tracks."

But Hayley was now more interested in the deer. Like the others, she had seen the photograph on Valerie Gillson's phone.

"The deer, was it—?"

"Maybe. There wasn't much of it left to identify. And there was a hole not far from where we found it."

She nodded. "Go inside. The others are waiting."

Morland joined them. The four surviving members of the board sat on either side of the dining table, with a chair left empty at the head for Hayley. Warraner sat at the other end of the table, leaving two chairs between himself and Kinley Nowell. Morland seated himself across from Warraner, leaving three chairs between himself and Calder Ayton. If he squinted, he could almost see the ghost of Ben Pearson occupying one of them, tearing open a pack of exotic cookies or passing around some British candy, because it was Ben who had always taken it upon himself to provide a small treat for the board and the observers. But the chair remained empty, and the table bare. There were no reports to be considered, and no notebooks lay open. No true record of this meeting would ever be kept.

Hayley turned off the lights in the hall and took her seat at the head of the table.

"All right," she said. "Let's begin."

HARRY DIXON KNELT INSIDE his bedroom closet and removed a section of baseboard. The house was quiet. Erin was at her quilting circle, where work had commenced on a quilt in memory of the town's recent dead. According to Erin, so many women wanted to participate that they had to bring in more chairs. Bryan Joblin had gone with her, although he would be drinking in a bar while Erin sewed. Harry wondered how long the board planned to keep up this farce of imposing Joblin on them: until he and Erin found another girl; until they proved themselves.

To that end, Harry had earlier gone out with Joblin, and together they had cruised the streets of Lewiston and Augusta, looking at women. It wasn't exactly difficult work. Harry figured that Joblin would have been doing something similar in his spare time anyway, even if it weren't a matter of some urgency. Hell, Harry had been known to cast a wistful eye at young beauties when his wife wasn't around, but he was nothing like Bryan Joblin. The Joblin boy had a reputation for being a pussy hound of the first order, to the extent that Hayley Conyer herself had taken Bryan and his father to one side following a chance encounter on Main Street and warned them that if Bryan didn't keep his pecker to himself, or at least limit its use to the vast swath of the United States beyond Prosperous, she would personally slice it off and hang it from the town's welcome sign as a warning to others who might be similarly tempted to screw around with the feelings and, indeed, bodies of Properous's generative future. Since then, Bryan Joblin had indulged himself largely in the relative fleshpots of Bangor, and still tended to cross the street in order to avoid any further confrontations with Hayley Conyer, as though fearing that the old woman might whip out a blade at any moment and make good on her threat.

That afternoon, Harry and Joblin watched schoolgirls, and young housewives. One of them would be ideal, Joblin said. He was in favor of snatching a girl right there and then—a young, athletic-looking brunette out by the mall in Augusta—but Harry dissuaded him. These things needed to be planned properly, Harry told him. Taking a woman in broad daylight was too risky. They looked at some of the homeless women, but they were all too old or worn. Fresher meat was needed.

"What about a child?" said Joblin. "It's gotta be easy to take a child."

Harry didn't reply. He just pictured Bryan Joblin dying in painful ways.

Joblin had bitched all the way back to Prosperous, but Harry knew he would inform his father that the Dixons looked as if they were at least trying to fulfill their obligations to the town, and Luke Joblin would, in turn, tell the board. To add to the deception, Harry set Joblin to trawling prostitution Web sites: twenty-five or younger, Harry had stipulated, and they should be from out of state. No tattoos, and no ID requirements from prospective johns. Independents too, not agency girls. Bryan had dived into the work wholeheartedly. He even printed off a list of possible candidates for Harry.

"You know they can trace all those searches back to our computer?" Erin told Harry, when she learned of what Bryan was doing. Her quilting bag was on the bed behind her, ready for use. They were whispering. They spent most of their days in near silence now because of their unwanted houseguest. It was like living in some kind of religious retreat.

"It doesn't matter," said Harry. "It's all just smoke anyway."

"Well, I still don't like it. It makes the computer seem dirty. I won't feel the same about using it."

Give me strength, thought Harry.

"The computer won't be coming with us," he said. "I'll buy you a new one when we get—"

"Get where?" she asked.

"Get to wherever we're going," he finished.

"When?"

"I don't know. "

"When?" she repeated. There were tears in her eyes. "I can't do this much longer. I can't stand having Bryan Joblin around. I hate the smell of him, the sound of him. I hate the way he looks at me."

"Looks at you? What do you mean?"

"Jesus, you see nothing. Nothing! It's like you can't imagine that another man might find me attractive."

And with that she stormed out to start work on the great quilt. Harry had watched Erin as she walked to her car, Bryan Joblin trailing behind her. Of course, she was still a good-looking woman. He knew that better than anyone. It shouldn't have surprised him that Bryan Joblin might appreciate her too.

Now he placed the section of baseboard on the carpet and reached into the space revealed. His hands came out holding a red fireproof box, a smaller version of the one in which he and Erin kept their passports and valuable documents. The key was in the lock. He had no fear of anyone finding the box, and he didn't want Erin coming across the key by accident and asking what it was. They didn't have many secrets from each other, but this was one of them.

Harry opened the box. Inside were five thousand dollars in tens and twenties: it was Harry's emergency fund. He had resisted dipping into the cash until that week, even when his business was at its lowest. Harry didn't know how long five thousand dollars would last once he and Erin started running, but their main priority would be to put distance between themselves and Prosperous. After that, he'd make some calls. He still had friends beyond Prosperous.

The box also contained a letter written and ready to mail. The letter was addressed to Hayley Conyer, and its contents could be summarized as a promise to keep quiet about Prosperous if he and Erin were left in peace. Even after all that had occurred, Harry remained loyal to the town. He didn't want to betray its secrets.

The final item in the box was a handgun, a five-shot Smith & Wesson 638 with a concealed hammer, a barrel length of less than two inches, and a weight of just fourteen ounces when empty. It had been acquired for him by one of his subcontractors, a plumber with a string of convictions who owed Harry, because Harry gave him work when nobody else would. Harry had been afraid to purchase a legal firearm. He was worried that word would get back to Chief Morland, and then questions would be asked, and with questions came suspicions. The gun fit easily into the pocket of his favorite jacket, and was powerful, accurate, and easy to fire, even for a neophyte like him. Erin didn't approve of guns and wouldn't tolerate them in the house. If she'd discovered that he had the S&W, he'd have found a quick use for the box of self-defense round-nose loads that sat alongside the pistol.

Now he transferred the entire contents of the box to a small black canvas sack and hid it on the top shelf of the closet behind a stack of old T-shirts. He hadn't told Erin, but preparations for their departure were almost complete. He had spoken to a used-car dealer in Medway and arranged a trade-in, with some cash on the side, for his truck. One morning, while Bryan Joblin was watching Erin, Harry had driven to the T.J.Maxx in Bangor with a list of his wife's measurements and bought various items of underwear and casual clothing and sneakers, along with a pair of cheap suitcases. He didn't need to buy much for himself; he'd hidden a plastic garbage bag filled with jeans, shirts, and a new pair of boots in the spare toolbox in his truck, and these he added to one of the suitcases. He then went to the Walgreens on Broadway and replicated as many as possible of the toiletries and cosmetics he had seen in their bathroom and on his wife's dressing table. When he was done, he paid a quick visit to Erin's sister and asked her to take care of the cases for him. To his surprise, she didn't ask any questions. That made him wonder how much she already knew, or suspected, about Prosperous.

Harry restored the empty box to its space behind the closet and replaced the baseboard. It seemed to him that by removing the cash and the gun he had made his decision. There was only one final step to take. After that, there could be no going back.

Harry drove to the post office and, with only a slight hesitation, mailed the letter to Hayley Conyer.

XXXII

Hayley was playing with him, Morland knew, trying to put him off guard and make him ill at ease. He had seen her do this more than once with those who displeased her, and his father had warned him about it when it came time for him to take over as chief of police.

"She's a clever one, you mark my words," his father said. "You watch yourself around her, and never turn your back on her. She's crossed swords over the years with a lot of men and women who thought they were smarter than she was, and she's left them all lying dead in the ground."

Even then, Morland had wondered if his father was speaking literally or metaphorically.

Now Morland made himself as comfortable as possible in the creaky old dining chairs, and did his best to keep his temper in check as Hayley baited him. Almost an hour had gone by, and she hadn't yet even alluded to the detective. She was building up to it, allowing the tension in the room to coalesce around Morland, constraining him so that when at last they came to the issue at hand he would be both wound tight internally and compressed by her implied disapproval of his actions, although he didn't know how else he might have reacted to the detective's interest in the missing girl. What did Haley expect—that he should kill anyone who so much as glanced curiously in the town's direction? Perhaps so; she had always been paranoid, although she tried to justify it by claiming that the fate of the town, and the responsibility for its citizens, lay in her hands. What was that line about power corrupting? Whatever it was, it was true, but also incomplete: power didn't just corrupt. After a time, it could also drive a person mad.

So it was that, over the past hour, Hayley had ignored Morland's interjections, even when it was clear that she had left space in the discussions for him to offer an opinion. If he remained quiet, she asked him to contribute and then ceased to listen almost as soon as he began speaking, until finally, while he was still in mid-flow, she would begin to talk over him, or turn to one of the others for an alternative view, or simply change the subject altogether, leaving Morland to wind down slowly into silence. It was humiliating, and Morland was certain that Hayley's ultimate intention was to drive him from the meeting entirely, but he refused to be forced into giving her what she wanted. It was crucial that he remain present. He guessed what she was planning to do, and he had to stop her. She hadn't met the detective, and didn't fully understand the danger that he represented. Even Warraner, who had twice encountered Parker, was guilty of underestimating him, but that was a function of Warraner's own misplaced sense of superiority. Morland had watched him with the detective in the chapel, behaving like some glorified tour guide, almost inviting Parker to draw conclusions about hidden knowledge that might or might not be true. But the detective was subtler and more cunning than Warraner had first assumed, and by the time Warraner came to that realization—with the detective's questions about the Familists and Vitel—it was too late.

And then the detective returned, with his talk of blue cars, baiting Morland and Warraner just as Morland himself was now being baited. He'd spoken to Danes too, and Danes was much more than a simple nuisance. He had the ear of people in the state legislature, although he didn't have much influence over the current governor, mainly because, as far as Morland could tell, the current governor didn't listen to anyone. But Morland and the board knew that Danes had managed to scatter seeds of suspicion about Prosperous down in Augusta. True, most people still dismissed him as a flake, but he was a flake with money, and money bought influence.

Morland recalled again the late Ben Pearson's rage at Danes's intrusion on the public meeting. The old bastard had been practically frothing at the mouth, and Souleby and the others weren't far behind him, howling for blood like the high priests before Pilate. On that occasion, it was Hayley who proved to be the voice of reason. They couldn't kill Danes, because who knew what trouble his death might bring on them if there was even a hint of foul play about it? They'd just have to wait for him to die naturally, but so far Danes had proved to be as stubbornly healthy as Hayley herself. Sometimes Morland even suspected that Hayley liked having Danes around. She seemed almost indulgent of his efforts to hamper the town's expansion, as though their intensity were a reflection of Prosperous's importance, and a vindication of her own stewardship.

Prosperous had influence in Augusta as well. It was natural in a town as wealthy as this one, and even though its citizens differed politically, they still recognized that contributions to politicians of all stripes served the common cause. But that influence had to be used subtly and carefully. Morland sensed that a time was coming when the town's investment in state politics might finally be required to yield profit. He would be happier if it could be saved for another moment, but he was growing increasingly ill at ease at this meeting. It was like watching a snake preparing to strike, unaware of the shadow of the blade behind it.

The board had almost concluded its discussion of the recent fatalities. Hayley asked about the families, and how they were coping, and Warraner gave her chapter and verse about his pastoral role, and each vied with the other to appear the more sympathetic, the more understanding, the more pained by the sufferings of others. It was quickly decided that a fund should be established to aid the families in their time of need. The selectmen immediately offered generous contributions, and Hayley matched their combined total. Once they had tapped the rest of the town for sums both big and small, it would represent a significant source of financial consolation for the families.

Call it what it is, thought Morland. Call it a bribe, a way of buying time and loyalty. There were already whispers among the townsfolk (for Morland was listening and, where possible, stoking the fires of discontent with the board). Why had this happened? Where had their protection gone? What was the board going to do about it? If the board could do nothing, or not enough, then it might be that it was time for others to step up and take the responsibility of running the town from these old men and this old woman who had served Prosperous so well for so long, but whose hour was now past.

And if any of them objected—and by "any" they could be referring only to one, Hayley Conyer—then, Morland thought, the town would understand if some bad luck were to befall her, for old women had accidents, and Prosperous would accept her passing as a different kind of sacrifice. So this was an important meeting, perhaps the most important in nearly a century. The town's survival might not have been at stake, not yet, but the survival of the current board certainly was.

"Well, so that's decided," said Hayley at last. She would write it all down the next day, creating inconsequential minutes for a meeting of great consequence. Let the town, and those whose eyes were upon it, see how it handled itself in times of strife. Meanwhile, the truth would be communicated in quiet words at gas stations, and on street corners, and in kitchens when the children were asleep. The whispers of doubt would be smothered. The board had acted. All would be well.

"That brings us to the main business of the evening."

There was shuffling around her. Heads turned toward Morland. He felt the wires tighten around him, and instinctively he breathed in, swelling his upper body, tensing his arms and hands against unseen bonds, making himself larger, gaining himself room to move.

Hayley sat back in her chair. It was a Carver, the only chair at the table that had arms. She rested her right elbow on one arm, her thumb beneath her chin, her index finger to her right temple, and stared thoughtfully at Morland, like a queen waiting for the courtier who had disappointed her to explain his way out of an appointment with the executioner.

"So, Chief Morland," she said. "Tell us about this detective. . . ."

XXXIII

Ronald Straydeer came by my house while I was once again reading through the material about the Familists culled from the archives of the Maine Historical Society. Ronald was a Penobscot Indian out of Old Town, north of Bangor. He had served with the K-9 Corps in Vietnam and, like so many men who fought in that war, he came back with a fracture running through his soul. In Ronald's case, that fracture was caused by the decision of the U.S. military to classify its war dogs as "equipment" and then leave them behind as "surplus to requirements" when the United States fled South Vietnam. Thousands of war dogs were either transferred to the South Vietnamese Army or euthanized, and many of the handlers, like Ronald, never quite forgave their country for its treatment of the animals.

The Vietcong hated the K-9 teams because they made surprise attacks almost impossible to carry out, and both the dogs and their handlers were hunted by the enemy with extreme prejudice. The bond between the K-9 soldiers and their dogs was immensely strong, and the emotional and psychological damage caused by the attitude of the U.S. Army toward the teams was impossible to quantify. A wiser military, one more attuned to the effects of combat on the psyche, would have allowed the men to adopt their dogs, but such legislation would not come into effect until 2000. Instead, the K-9 soldiers watched South Vietnam fall to the North Vietnamese, and they knew that their dogs would be slaughtered in revenge.

Now Ronald worked with veterans, but he did so almost entirely without the assistance of the U.S. government or its military. He wanted little to do with either. I think that was one of the reasons he sold pot. It wasn't so much that he cared one way or another about drugs; it was just a means of quietly socking it to Uncle Sam for sacrificing Elsa, Ronald's German shepherd, back in Vietnam. He was largely a recreational dealer, though; he probably gave away more than he sold, and smoked the rest himself.

I hadn't seen him in a while. Someone told me that he'd left town. His brother up in Old Town was ill, or so the story went, and Ronald was helping his family out. But, as far as I knew, Ronald didn't have a brother.

Tonight his eyes were brighter than usual, and he was wearing a blue sports jacket over jeans, a matching shirt, and off-white sneakers.

"You know," I said, "the denim shirt-and-jeans look only works if you're a country singer, or you own a farm."

Ronald gave me a hard look.

"Should I tell you of how, long before the white man came, my people roamed these lands?"

"In matching denim?"

"We move with the times."

"Not fast enough."

He followed me into my office. I offered him coffee, or a beer if he was in the mood, but he declined both. He took a seat in one of the armchairs. He was a big man, and he made the chair look too small for him. Actually, the way he had to squeeze himself into it made me start worrying about how we were going to get him out again when he tried to stand. I had visions of injecting Crisco down the sides from a pastry-icing bag.

"So, how have you been?" I asked.

"I stopped drinking," he said.

"Really?"

Ronald had never been a big drinker, from what I could recall, but he had been a steady one, although he stuck to beer, for the most part.

"Yeah. I quit smoking weed too."

This *was* news.

"You stop dealing as well?"

"I got enough money in the bank. I don't need to do that no more."

"You didn't fall off a horse on the road to Damascus, did you?"

"No, man. I don't like horses. You thinking of the Plains Indians. You ought to read a book, educate yourself."

Ronald said all of this with an entirely straight face. It was generally hard to tell if he was serious or joking, at least not until he started punching you in the gut.

"I heard you'd been out of town for a while," I said. "I guess now I know what you were doing. You were self-improving."

"And thinking."

"Mind if I ask what about?"

"Life. Philosophical shit. You wouldn't understand, being a white man."

"You look good for it, even to a white man."

"I decided it wasn't positive for me to be drinking and smoking and dealing when I was working with men for whom all of those activities might prove a temptation. If I was going to help them get straight and clean, I had to be straight and clean myself, you understand?"

"Absolutely."

"I kept up with the newspapers, though. You weren't in them. Looks like you haven't shot anyone in months. You retired?"

"I could be tempted to break my spell of gun celibacy, under the current circumstances. Are you just here to yank my chain, or is there something I can help you with?"

"I hear you been around the homeless shelters asking questions," said Ronald.

In his dealings with veterans, Ronald was often to be found working in the shelters, trying to form bonds with men and women who felt abandoned by their country once their period in uniform was over. Some of them even ended up staying with him on occasion. Despite his some-what stony demeanor, Ronald Straydeer had a seemingly infinite capacity for empathy.

"That's right."

"Veterans?"

Ronald had helped me out in the past with cases involv-ing soldiers or the military. It was his turf, and he was con-scious of protecting it.

"Not really, or only by association. You knew Jude, right?"

"Yeah. He was a good man. Dressed funny, but he was helpful. I hear he died. Suicide."

"I don't think he killed himself. I believe he was helped into the next world."

"Any idea why?"

"Can I ask why you're interested?"

"Someone's got to look out for these people. I try. If the city's homeless are being targeted for any reason, I'd like to know."

That was as good a reason as any.

"It's early," I said, "but I think he might have been killed because he went looking for his daughter. Her name was Annie, and she was following in her father's footsteps, in both senses of the term. She'd lost her way, and ended up on the streets. I believe she was trying to draw him to her, while at the same time keeping him at a distance. She was staying at a women's shelter in Bangor, but she's not there any longer. There's nobody around to report her missing, but I have a feeling that she might have been snatched. Jude was concerned about her before he died."

"And what's this to you?"

"A friend of Jude's, a man named Shaky, told me that Jude had saved up to buy a few hours of my time. Call it an obligation on my part."

"I know Shaky. Any idea who might have taken the girl?"

"You ever been to the town of Prosperous?"

"No. Heard of it. Don't think they have much time for the natives, or anyone who isn't white and wealthy."

"Annie told someone up in Bangor that she'd been offered a job by an older couple from Prosperous. She collected her things from the shelter before taking a ride with them, and that was the last anyone saw of her."

"The couple might have been lying," said Ronald. "It's easy to say you're from one place when you're actually from another."

"I had considered that."

"It's why you're a detective."

"That's right. I like to think of myself as wise for a white man."

"That bar is set low," said Ronald.

"Not for all of us, and perhaps not for Annie Broyer. I

get the sense, from the people I've spoken with about her, that she wasn't dumb. Otherwise she wouldn't have survived on the streets for as long as she did. I think she would have asked for some proof that these people were on the level. If she said she was going to Prosperous, then I believe that's where she ended up. Unfortunately, according to the local police there's no sign of her, and never has been."

I hadn't told Ronald anything that Shaky or the cops in Portland didn't already know, for the most part. Any other thoughts or suspicions, including the peculiar history of the Familists, I kept to myself.

Ronald remained seated silently in his chair. He appeared to be contemplating something, even if it was only how he was going to get out of the chair now that he'd found out what he wanted to know.

"How did the people who killed Jude find him?" said Ronald at last.

People: Ronald knew that it took more than a single person to stage a hanging, even one involving a man seemingly as weak as Jude.

"They watched the shelters," I replied. "He was, as you remarked, a distinctive figure."

"Someone might have noticed them. The homeless, the sharp ones, they're always watching. They keep an eye out for the cops, for friends, for men and women with grudges against them. It's hard and merciless at the bottom of the pond. You have to be careful if you don't want to get eaten."

Ronald was right. I hadn't asked enough questions on the streets. I had allowed myself to become sidetracked by Prosperous and what it might represent, but perhaps there was another way.

"Any suggestions as to whom I might talk with?"

"You go around using words like 'whom' and nobody will talk to you at all. Leave it with me."

"You're sure?"

"I'll get more out of them than you will."

I had to admit the truth of it.

"One thing," I said.

"Yes?"

"I'd be discreet about it. If I'm right, and Jude was murdered, the people who did it won't be reluctant to act if they have to cover their tracks. We don't need any more bodies."

"I understand."

Ronald rose to leave. As anticipated, he had some trouble extricating himself from his seat, but by pressing down hard with his arms he somehow managed it. Once he was free, he regarded the chair in a vaguely hostile manner.

"Next time, I will not sit," he said.

"That might be for the best."

He looked out the window at the moonlight shining on the marshes.

"I've been thinking about getting another dog," he said.

Ronald hadn't owned a dog since Vietnam.

"Good," I said.

"Yes," said Ronald, and for the first time since he arrived at my door he smiled. "Yes, I believe it is."

WHEN HE WAS GONE, I called Angel and Louis in New York. Angel answered. Angel always answered. Louis regarded telephones as instruments of the Devil. He used them only reluctantly, and his conversation was even more minimal over the phone than it was in person, which was saying something—or, in Louis's case, nothing at all.

Angel told me that he was working on finding more of the Collector's nests, but so far he'd come up empty. Maybe we'd taken care of all of them, and the Collector was now living in a hole in the ground like a character in a book I'd read as a boy. The man had tried to assassinate someone who might have been Hitler, and failed. Hunted in turn, he had literally gone underground, digging a cave for himself in the earth and waiting for his pursuers to show their face. *Rogue Male*—that was the title of the book. They'd made a movie of it, with Peter O'Toole. Thinking of the book and the movie reminded me of those holes in the ground around Prosperous. Something had made them, but what?

"You still there?" said Angel.

"Yes, sorry. My mind was somewhere else for a moment."

"Well, it's your dime."

"You're showing your age, remembering a time when you could make a call for a dime. Tell me, what did you and Mr. Edison talk about back then?"

"Fuck you, *and* Thomas Edison."

"The Collector's still out there. He can rough it, but the lawyer can't. Somewhere there's a record of a house purchase that we haven't found yet."

"I'll keep looking. What about you? Whose cage are you rattling these days?"

I told him about Jude, and Annie, and Prosperous, and even Ronald Straydeer.

"Last time I talked to you, you were process-serving," said Angel. "I knew it wouldn't last."

"How's Louis?"

"Bored. I'm hoping he'll commit a crime, just to get him out of the apartment."

"Tell him to watch a movie. You ever hear of *Rogue Male*?"

"Is it porn?"

"No."

"It sounds like gay porn."

"Why would I be watching gay porn?"

"I don't know. Maybe you're thinking of switching teams."

"I'm not even sure how *you* got on that team. You certainly weren't picked first."

"Fuck you again, and your team."

"Tell Louis to go find *Rogue Male*. I think he'll like it."

"Okay." His voice grew slightly fainter as he turned away from the phone. "Hey, Louis, Parker says you need to go find some rogue male."

I caught a muffled reply.

"He says he's too old."

"*Rogue Male*, starring Peter O'Toole."

"Tool?" said Angel. "That's the guy's name? Man, that's gotta be porn. . . ."

I hung up. Even "hung" sounded mildly dirty after the conversation I'd just had. I made some coffee and went outside to drink it while I watched the moon shine on the marshes. Clouds crossed its face, changing the light, chasing shadows. I listened. Sometimes I wished for them to come, the lost daughter and the woman who walked with her, but I had no sense of them that night. Perhaps it was for the best. Blood flowed when they came.

But they would return, in the end. They always did.

XXXIV

Morland told the board what he knew of the detective. He spoke of his history, and the deaths of his wife and child many years earlier. He told them of some of the cases in which the detective had been involved,

the ones that had come to public notice, but he also informed them of the rumors that circulated about other investigations, secret investigations. It was a delicate line that
Morland was walking; he wanted them to understand the
threat that the detective posed, but he did not want them to
feel concerned enough to act rashly. Morland was certain
that Hayley already knew most of what he had to say. His
performance was for the benefit of the rest of the board,
and Warraner too.

"You say that he has crossed paths with the Believers?"
said Souleby.

There was a rustle of disapproval from the others. The
board of selectmen had been in existence in Maine longer
than the sect known as the Believers, and it regarded them
with a mixture of unease and distaste. The Believers' search
for their brethren, for lost angels like themselves, was of no
concern to the citizens of Prosperous. On the other hand, neither did the town wish to attract the attentions of others like
the Believers, or those in whose shadows the Believers toiled.
The Believers were only one element of a larger conspiracy,
one that was slowly encroaching upon the state of Maine.
The board wanted no part of it, although unofficial channels
of communication with certain interested parties were kept
open through Thomas Souleby, who retained membership in
various clubs in Boston, and moved easily in such circles.

"He has," said Morland. "All I've heard are whispers, but
it's safe to say that they regretted the encounters more than
he did."

Old Kinley Nowell spoke up. He had to remove the
oxygen mask from his face to do so, and each word
sounded like a desperate effort for him. Morland thought
that he already looked like a corpse. His skin was pale and
waxen, and he stank of mortality and the medicines that
were being used to stave it off.

"Why has the detective not been killed before now?"

"Some have tried," said Morland. "And failed."

"I'm not talking of thugs and criminals," said Nowell. He put his mask to his face and drew two deep breaths before resuming. "I'm not even speaking of the Believers. There are others in the background, and they do not fail. They've been killing for as long as there were men to kill. Cain's blood runs in their veins."

The Backers—that was how Morland had heard them described. Men and women with great wealth and power, like the board of selectmen writ large. Souleby's people.

"If he's alive," said Souleby, as if on cue, "then it's because they want him alive."

"But why?" said Nowell. "He's clearly a threat to them—if not now, then in the future. It makes no sense for them to let him live."

Hayley Conyer looked to Warraner for the solution, not to Souleby. It was, in her view, a theological issue.

"Pastor, would you care to offer a possible answer to this conundrum?"

Warraner might have been arrogant and conniving, thought Morland, but he wasn't a fool. He gave himself almost a full minute before he replied.

"They're afraid to kill what they don't understand," he said, finally. "What do they want? They wish to find their buried god and release him, and they feel themselves to be closer to that end than they have ever been before. The detective may be an obstacle, or it may be that he has a part to play in that search. For now, they do not understand his nature, and they're afraid to move against him for fear that, by doing so, they may ultimately harm their cause. I have listened to what Chief Morland has to say, and I confess that I may have underestimated the detective."

This surprised Morland. Warraner rarely admitted

weakness, especially in front of Hayley and the board. It caught Morland off guard, so that he was unprepared when the blade was thrust into his back.

"That said," Warraner continued, "Chief Morland underestimated him as well, and should not have brought him to the church. The detective should have been kept far away from it, and from me. I was forced into a situation where I had to answer questions, and I dealt with them as best I could, under the circumstances."

Liar, Morland wanted to say. I saw you preening. You wretched man; I will remember this.

"Chief?" said Conyer. "Is this true?"

She was amused. Morland could see it. She enjoyed watching her pets snap at each other. He felt her willing him to grow angry. The small humiliations that she had aimed at him earlier hadn't been enough to make him lose his temper. It might be that she already had someone else in mind to succeed him, but Morland didn't believe she had thought so far ahead. She knew only that he was beginning to doubt her, and she wished to retain her position. If she had to sacrifice him in order to survive, she would.

But Morland said only "I did what I thought was best," and watched with some small satisfaction as disappointment clouded the old woman's face.

Souleby, ever the diplomat, chose that moment to intervene.

"Throwing blame around isn't going to help us," he said. "Chief Morland, the question is this: will the detective give up?"

"No, but—"

Morland thought hard about how he was going to phrase his next words.

"Go on," said Souleby.

"He has no evidence, no clues. He has only his suspicions, and they aren't enough."

"Then why did he return to the town a second time?"

"Because he's taunting us. In the absence of evidence, he wants us to act. He wants us to move against him. By acting, we'll confirm his suspicions, and then he'll respond with violence. He isn't just the bait but the hook as well."

"Only if he lives," said Nowell, filled with malice as the end neared, as though he were intent on expending all his viciousness before he passed on.

"He has friends," said Morland. "They would not allow any action against him to go unpunished."

"They can die too."

"I don't think you understand—"

"Don't!" cawed Nowell. He raised a withered finger, like an ancient crow clawing against the darkness. "I understand better than you think. You're afraid. You're a coward. You—"

The rest of his accusations were lost in a fit of gasps and coughs. It was left to Luke Joblin to secure the mask to Nowell's face and leave it in place. For now, the old man's contributions to the meeting, however worthless they might be, were over. Why don't you just die, Morland wished—die and free up a place for someone with an ounce of sense and reason left to him. Nowell eyed him over the mask, reading his thoughts.

"You were saying?" said Souleby.

Morland looked away from Nowell.

"The detective has killed," he said. "He has victims who are known, and I guarantee you there are just as many who are unknown. A man who has acted in this way and is not behind bars, or has not been deprived of his livelihood and his weapons, is protected. Yes, some on the side of law would be glad to see him removed from the equation, but even they would be forced to act if he was harmed."

There was quiet among the members of the board,

broken only by the tortured breathing of Kinley Nowell.

"Could we not approach the Backers and seek their advice?" said Luke Joblin. "They might even work with us."

"We don't ask the permission of others to act," said Hayley Conyer. "Their interests and ours are not the same, not even in this case. If they're unwilling to move against him on their own behalf, they won't do so on ours."

"And there's the matter of another girl," said Calder Ayton. They were his first words since the meeting began. Morland had almost forgotten that he was present.

"What do you mean, Calder?" asked Conyer. She too seemed surprised to hear him speak at all.

"I mean that we have received a warning, or four warnings, depending upon one's view of the current dilemma," said Ayton. "Our people are worried. Whatever threat this detective poses, another girl has to be found and delivered—and quickly. Can we take the chance of having this man nosing around at such a delicate moment in the town's history?"

"What news from the Dixons?" Souleby asked Morland. "Has there been progress?"

"Bryan is watching them," said Luke Joblin, answering for Morland. "He thinks they're getting close to finding someone."

But Morland had his own view of the situation.

"Bryan tells me that he's been out scouting with Harry, but—and please don't take this the wrong way, Luke—your son isn't the sharpest tool in the box. My view is that the Dixons aren't to be trusted. I think they're leading Bryan on. We should have given the job of finding a girl to someone else."

"But, Chief Morland, it was your suspicions that led us to test them with the hunt," said Conyer.

"There might have been better ways to satisfy ourselves as to their loyalty," said Morland.

"It's done now," said Conyer. "Your regrets are a little late."

Again, it was Thomas Souleby who intervened.

"But if they are leading Bryan on—and, by extension, the rest of us—they're doing so to what end?" he asked.

"I think they're planning to run," said Morland. .

His opinion went down badly. People did leave Prosperous. After all, it wasn't a fortress, or a prison, and a larger world existed beyond its boundaries. But those who left were secure in their loyalty to the town, and many of them eventually returned. Running was another matter, for it brought with it the possibility of disclosure.

"There is a precedent for it on Erin's side," said Ayton.

"We don't blame the children for the sins of the adults," said Conyer. "And her mother more than made up for the failings of the father."

She returned her attention to Morland.

"Have you taken steps?" she said.

"I have."

"Could you be more precise?"

"I could, but I would prefer not to," said Morland. "After all, I may be wrong about them. I hope that I am."

"But the detective," Ayton insisted. "What of the detective?"

"We'll vote on it," said Conyer. "Reverend, do you have anything to add before we start?"

"Only that I believe the detective is dangerous," said Warraner.

A nicely ambiguous reply, thought Morland. Whatever they decide, and whatever the consequences, no blame will fall on your head.

"And you, Chief?"

"You know my views," said Morland. "If you attack him and succeed in killing him, you will bring more trouble down on this town. If you attack him and fail to kill him, the consequences may be even worse. We should not move against him. Eventually he'll grow weary, or another case will distract him."

But Morland wondered if he was indulging in wishful thinking. Yes, the detective might leave them in peace for a while, but he would not forget. It was not in him to do so. He would return, and keep returning. The best they could hope for was that his visits might bring no reward and, in time, someone else might do them the favor of killing him.

Around him, the board meditated on what it had heard. He couldn't tell if his words had made any impact.

"Thank you both for your contributions," said Conyer. "Would you mind waiting outside while we make our decision?"

The two observers rose and left. Warraner wrapped his coat tightly around himself, thrust his hands into his pockets, and took a seat on the porch. It was strange, but Morland had the sense that something of his own words of warning had penetrated Warraner's carapace of blind faith and deluded self-belief. He could see it in the pastor's face. Warraner lived to protect his church. For him, the town's continued safety and good fortune were merely a by-product of his own mission. It was one thing for him to assent to the killing of a homeless man, one whom Warraner believed would not be mourned or missed; it was another entirely to involve himself in an attack on a dangerous individual which could well have negative consequences whether they succeeded in killing him or not.

"Bait," said Warraner.

"What?" said Morland.

"You said that the detective was prepared to use himself as bait. Why would a man put himself in that kind of danger, especially for someone he didn't even know?"

"A sense of justice, maybe. The world beyond the limits of our town isn't as entirely corrupt as we might like to believe. After all, look at how corrupt we ourselves have become."

"We do what is necessary."

"Not for much longer."

"Why do you say that?"

"Our ways can't continue in the modern world. In the end, we'll be found out."

"So you believe that we should stop?"

"We can stop, or we can be stopped. The former might be less painful than the latter."

"And the old god?"

"What is a god without believers? It is just a myth waiting to be forgotten."

Warraner gaped. To him, this was blasphemy.

"But what will become of the town?"

"The town will survive. It'll just be a town like any other."

Bile rose up and caught in Morland's throat, the acidity bringing tears to his eyes. How could Prosperous ever be such a town? The blood had permeated it too thoroughly. It was mired in redness and sin.

"No," said Warraner. "It can never be that."

And Morland was sure that Warraner had missed the point.

"You haven't answered my question," said Warraner. "Some vague concept of justice isn't sufficient to explain this man's actions."

"Justice is never vague," said Morland. "The law only makes it seem that way. And as for this man . . ."

Morland had been thinking about the detective a lot. In reading up on him, he believed that, on some level, he almost understood him. When Morland spoke again, he was talking as much to himself as to Warraner.

"I don't think he's afraid of dying," said Morland. "He doesn't seek out death, and he'll fight it until the end, but he's not frightened of it. I think he's in pain. He's been damaged by loss, and it's left him in agony. When death does come for him, it'll end his pain. Until then, nothing that anyone can visit on him will be worse than what he's already experienced. That makes him a formidable enemy, because he can endure more than his opponents. And the things he's done, the risks he's taken for others, they've won him allies, and some of them may be even more dangerous than he is, because they don't share his morals. If he has a weakness, it's that he's a moral being. Where possible, he'll do the right thing, the just thing, and if he does wrong he'll bear the guilt of it."

"You respect him."

"You'd have to be a fool not to."

"But you sound almost as though you like him."

"Yes," said Morland. "It may be that I like him even better than I like myself."

He stepped down into Hayley Conyer's garden and lit a cigarette. She wouldn't approve, but he didn't care. His position had been made clear—the inconsequentiality of his role in the town's affairs, the hollowness of his authority. After all this was over, he would have to resign. If he was fortunate, the board would accept his resignation and allow him to take his family and leave. Otherwise, it could force him to stay on, a pitiful figure good only for issuing parking violations and speeding tickets.

Although it could do worse.

He felt the end of things approaching, had felt it ever since the shooting of the girl. The arrival of the detective had merely compounded what he already knew. Even with the coming of spring there would be no rebirth, not for Prosperous. That might even be for the best.

He took a long drag on his cigarette, and thought of wolves.

*   *   *

THE WOLF SMELLED THE meat. The wind carried it to him. He had been resting in the shelter of a fallen tree, sleeping fitfully and feverishly through his pain when the scent of blood came. The wolf had only nibbled at the dead deer he had been permitted to take. The meat had tasted wrong, infected by the manner of the fawn's dying.

The wolf rose slowly. He was always stiff when he first stood, even if he had been lying down for only a short time, but the promise of fresh meat was enough to spur him on.

With the moon full in the sky, and blood in the air, he limped south.

XXXV

It was Thomas Souleby who summoned Morland and Warraner back inside. By then, Morland had finished one cigarette and started another. The curtains at the living room window moved, and he glimpsed a face peering out at him. It might have been Hayley Conyer, but he couldn't be sure. He stamped out the remains of the second cigarette on the gravel, and considered leaving it there for the old bitch to find in the morning, but thought better of it. There was no percentage in pettiness, even if it did offer a passing sense of satisfaction.

Souleby sniffed at him as he reentered the house.

"She'll smell it on you," said Souleby. "It's one thing smoking on the sly, another bringing the evidence into her home."

Morland didn't look at him. He didn't want Souleby to see his desperation, his grim sense that it was important, above all, to let the detective be. The more he had paced and smoked, the more he dreaded what was to come.

"She'll smell worse on me once all this is over," said Morland. "This whole town is going to stink of blood."

And Souleby didn't try to deny it.

MORLAND KNEW WHAT THEY had decided as soon as he entered the dining room. He supposed he had known even before he left them to their deliberations, but the vindictively triumphant expression on the portion of Kinley Nowell's face not obscured by his mask removed any lingering doubt.

Now that her victory was assured, Hayley Conyer was content to soften her attitude toward her chief of police—because that, of course, was how she thought of him: "her" chief of police, "her" board, "her" town. She waited for him to take his seat, and smiled in the manner of a prospective employer preparing to break bad news to an unsuccessful job candidate.

"We've decided to deal with the detective," she said.

"There will be repercussions," said Morland.

"We have taken that possibility into account. The finger of blame will point . . . elsewhere."

Morland noticed that Conyer now had a sheet of paper in front of her. While he watched, she took a pen from the pocket of her cardigan and drew a symbol on the page. Wordlessly, she passed it to him.

Morland didn't touch the sheet. He didn't have to, for he could see what she had drawn clearly enough, but neither did he *want* to touch it. Conyer had drawn a trident. It was the symbol of the Believers. An already difficult and dangerous situation was about to become potentially disastrous.

"They'll know that it was us," said Morland.

"He's right," said Souleby. He looked genuinely frightened. Clearly this element of Conyer's plan hadn't been discussed. "It goes beyond the bounds of common sense."

"They won't know if we're careful," said Conyer. "And we are always careful."

That was a lie, but Morland didn't call her on it. If they had been truly careful, the detective would never have set foot in their town.

Nowell pulled off his mask.

"And what matter if it becomes known that it was us?" he rasped. "The Believers weren't many to begin with, and the detective has taken care of the rest."

"We don't know that for sure," said Morland. "There may be others. They hide. It's in their nature. And then there's the matter of the Backers. They have always maintained links with the Believers. There may even be Believers among them. They could have acted against the detective, but they chose not to. Making the decision to remove him for them may not be appreciated."

"No blame will accrue to us," Conyer insisted.

"You can't be certain," said Morland.

He felt a migraine coming on. He rubbed at his temples, as though that might somehow ward off the pain and the nausea. He was weary. He should have just kept his mouth shut, because this was a pointless discussion. The battle was lost, and soon the war would be as well.

"You're right; I can't be certain," said Conyer.

Morland glanced up in surprise.

"But they can," she concluded.

Morland heard movement behind him, and two shadows fell across the table.

It had all been a farce—the meeting, the arguments, the final private discussion. The decision had been made long before. These two would not have been present otherwise. They didn't travel unless killing was imminent.

"You don't have to worry about the detective any longer, Chief Morland," said Conyer. "Our friends will take care of him for us. For now, though, the Dixons remain your responsibility. I want them watched. If they try to run, I want them stopped.

"And if they get beyond the town limits," she added, "I want them killed."

THEY DRIFTED FROM THE meeting. Nobody spoke. Morland went outside to smoke another cigarette, and watched them go. He didn't care what Hayley Conyer thought of his nicotine addiction now. It was the least of his worries. Anyway, his days as chief of police were now definitely numbered. She had emasculated him back in the living room, just as surely as if she had used on him the blade with which she had threatened to remove Bryan Joblin's manhood. It was then appropriate, somehow, that it was only Luke Joblin who lingered after most of the others had departed, Souleby leaving alone, Ayton taking responsibility for the fading vileness of Kinley Nowell.

Morland offered Joblin a smoke, and he accepted.

"I knew you hadn't really given up," said Morland.

Joblin had spent the last couple of months trumpeting the fact that he'd kicked cigarettes, although he boasted loudest when his wife was near.

"Barbara thinks that I have," he said. "I don't know which is costing me more, the cigarettes or the breath mints."

Together they watched the rear lights of the last car disappear as the vehicle turned onto the road and headed toward town.

"Something on your mind, Luke?" said Morland.

"I'm worried," said Joblin.

"About Bryan?"

"Jesus, no. You're right; he's not bright, but he can take care of himself. If you need help with the Dixons, you can rely on him. He's a stand-up young man."

Bryan Joblin wasn't a stand-up anything. He was borderline psychotic, with a deep wellspring of viciousness and sexual deviance from which to draw, but Morland kept that opinion to himself. He had few friends on the board, and he didn't need to alienate Luke Joblin too.

Joblin took a long drag on the cigarette. "No, it's the Backers. I don't understand why we didn't approach them. We don't want to cross them. They could crush us. We should have spoken to them before we acted, but Hayley shot down that idea as soon as it was raised. Why?"

"Because we worship different gods," said Hayley Conyer from behind them.

Morland hadn't even heard her approach. One second they were alone, and the next she had materialized at their backs.

"I'm sorry," said Joblin, although it wasn't clear whether he was referring to his criticism of the decision or the fact that he'd been caught smoking in Conyer's yard, or both. He looked for somewhere to put out the cigarette. He didn't want to drop it. Finally, he settled for lifting the sole of his left shoe and stubbing the butt out on the leather. It left a scorch mark. He would have to hide the shoe until he found time to get new soles made. His wife would wonder what a reformed smoker was doing stubbing out cigarettes on three-hundred-dollar shoes. Morland took the butt from him and put it in his now empty pack.

"Don't be," said Conyer. "It is at the root of all that we do here, all that we're trying to protect. We aren't like the Backers, and their god isn't like our god. Theirs is a wicked god, an angry god."

"And ours?" said Morland.

He saw Warraner standing on the porch steps, watching them. Behind him, two figures waited in the hallway.

Hayley Conyer laid a gentle hand on Morland's forearm. It was a peculiarly intimate gesture, equal parts consolation, reassurance, and, he recognized, regretful dismissal.

"Ours," she said, "is merely hungry."

THE WOLF HAD FOUND the meat: a slab of bloody venison haunch. He circled it, still wary despite his need, but at last he could no longer resist.

He took two steps forward, and the trap snapped shut upon his paw.

XXXVI

Founded in 1794, and located on the shores of Casco Bay where the Androscoggin River flowed into the sea, Bowdoin College was routinely ranked among the top colleges in America. Its list of alumni included

Henry Wadsworth Longfellow, Nathaniel Hawthorne, the explorer Robert Peary, and the sexologist Alfred Kinsey. Unfortunately, it did not appear to include Prosperous's own Pastor Warraner. An early morning call to the Office of Alumni Relations produced no record of a Michael Warraner among its former students, and a similar inquiry left at Bangor Theological Seminary also drew a blank.

While I was still sucking on a pencil and trying to figure out why Warraner would bother to lie about something that could so easily be checked, I received a follow-up call from a secretary at Bowdoin. Apparently, one of their associate professors was interested in meeting with me. He was free that afternoon, in fact, if I could find the time to "pop up" to the college.

"Did he really say that?" I asked.

"Say what?" said the secretary.

"'Pop up'?"

"That's how he speaks. He's from England."

"Ah."

"Yes. Ah."

"Please tell him that I'd be delighted to pop up."

Somewhere among Bowdoin's faculty of religion, the name Warraner had set a small alarm bell ringing.

PROFESSOR IAN WILLIAMSON LOOKED exactly as I'd always believed most academics should look but rarely did: slightly disheveled—but not so much as to raise too many concerns about his mental well-being—and fond of waistcoats and varieties of tweed, although in his case the potential fustiness of the cloth was offset by his choice of Converse sneakers as footwear. He was youthful, bearded, and cheerfully distracted, as though at any moment he might catch sight of an interesting cloud and run after it in order to lasso it with a piece of string.

As it turned out, Williamson was a decade older than I was, so clearly the academic life agreed with him. He'd been at Bowdoin for more than twenty years, although he still spoke like a weekend visitor to Downton Abbey. Frankly, if Professor Williamson's accent couldn't get him laid in Maine, then nothing could. He specialized in Religious Tolerance and Comparative Mystical Traditions, and his office in the lovely old faculty building was filled equally with books and assorted religious bric-a-brac, so that it was somewhere between a library and a market stall.

He offered me coffee from his own personal Nespresso machine, put his feet up on a pile of books, and asked me why I was interested in Michael Warraner.

"I could ask you the same thing," I said, "given that he doesn't appear to be one of your alumni."

"Ah, fencing," said Williamson. "Right. I see. Excellent."

"What?" I said, not seeing.

"Fencing." He made a parrying gesture with an imaginary foil and accompanied it with a swishing noise, just to make certain that I got the picture. Which I didn't.

"Sorry, are you challenging me to a duel?"

"What? No. I meant verbal fencing—the old thrust and parry. Philip Marlowe and all that. I say, you say. You know, that kind of thing."

He stared animatedly at me. I stared less animatedly back.

"Or perhaps not," said Williamson, and a little of his enthusiasm seemed to leach away. I felt as though I'd kicked a puppy.

"Let's say that I'm curious about Prosperous," I said. "And I'm curious about Pastor Warraner. He seems like a strange man in an odd town."

Williamson sipped his Nespresso. Behind him, on his otherwise empty desk, I noticed a trio of books with their spines facing toward me. All related to the Green Man. It couldn't have been a coincidence that they were displayed so prominently.

"Michael Warraner entered Bowdoin as a liberal arts student when he was in his midtwenties," said Williamson. "From the start, it was clear that his focus was on religious studies. It's a demanding regimen, and tends only to attract students with a real passion for the subject. A major consists of nine courses, a minor five, with two courses required: Introduction to the Study of Religion, or Religion 101, and Theories About Religion. The rest are composed of various options from Asian Religions, Islam and Post-Biblical Judaism, Christianity and Gender, and Bible and Comparative Studies. Clear enough?"

"Absolutely."

Williamson shifted in his chair.

"Warraner was not the most able of students," he said. "In fact, his admission hung in the balance for some time, but he had influential supporters."

"From Prosperous?"

"And elsewhere. It was clear that efforts were being made on his behalf. On the other hand, we were aware that space existed in courses for dedicated students, and . . ."

"Yes?"

"There was a certain amount of curiosity among faculty members, myself included, about Prosperous. As you're no doubt aware, it is a town founded by a secretive religious sect, the history and ultimate fate of which remain nebulous to this day. By admitting Warraner, it seemed that we might be in a position to learn more about the town and its history."

"And how did that work out?"

"We got what you might refer to as 'the party line.' Warraner gave us a certain amount of information, and we were also permitted to study the church and its environs, but we really found out very little about Prosperous and the Family of Love that we didn't already know. Furthermore, Warraner's academic limitations were exposed at a very early stage. He struggled to scrape together credits and D grades. Eventually, we were forced to let him go.

"Pastor Warraner, as he subsequently began to style himself, was later readmitted to this college as a 'special student.' Special students are people from the local community who, for whatever reason, desire to resume their education on a part-time basis. While they're assessed on their academic record, non-academic achievements are also considered. They pay course fees, and no financial aid is available to them. Their work is graded, and they receive a college transcript, but they are non-degree candidates, and therefore cannot graduate. Pastor Warraner took ten such courses over a period of about five years, some more successfully and enthusiastically than others. He was surprisingly open to issues of Christianity and gender, less so to Asian religions, Islam, and Judaism. Overall, my impression was that Warraner desired the imprimatur of a college education. He wanted to say that he had been to college, and that was all."

"I believe he also told me that he'd majored in religion at Bowdoin, and studied as a Master of Divinity at Bangor Theological Seminary."

"I suppose, if one were being generous-spirited enough, those statements might offer a certain latitude of interpretation, the latter more than the former. If you asked around, I bet you'd find that he approached Bangor at some point and was rebuffed, or tried to sit in unofficially on seminars. It would fit with that desire for affirmation and recognition."

"Any other impression he may have left on you?"

"He was a fanatic."

"Doesn't that come with the territory?"

"Sometimes. Warraner, though, could rarely string together more than a couple of sentences without referring to 'his' god."

"And what kind of god does he worship? I've met him, and I've seen his church, and I'm still not sure just what kind of pastor he is."

"Superficially, Warraner is a variety of austere Protestant. There's a bit of the Baptist in him, a sprinkling of Methodism, a dash of Quaker, but also a healthy dose of pantheism. None of it is particularly deep, though. His religion, for want of a better explanation, is his church—the bricks and mortar of it. He worships a building, or what that building represents for him. You say that you've seen it?"

"I got the grand tour."

"And what did you think?"

"It's a little light on crosses for my tastes."

"Catholic?"

"Occasional."

"I was raised in the Church of England—Low, I should add—and even I found Warraner's chapel positively spartan."

"The carvings apart."

"Yes, they are interesting, aren't they? Unusual here in the United States. Less so, perhaps, among the older churches of England and certain parts of Europe, although Warraner's are quite distinctive. It's a Familist church, of that there can be little doubt, but a Familist chuch of a particular type. This is not the element of the sect that fed into the Quakers or the Unitarians, infused with a spirit of peace and gentleness. It's something harsher."

"And Warraner—is he still a Familist?"

Williamson finished his coffee. He seemed to be considering making more, then thought better of it. He put his cup down.

"Yes, Mr. Parker," he said. "I believe that not only is Warraner a Familist but that Prosperous remains a Familist community. To what end, I couldn't say."

"And their god?"

"Look again at those carvings inside the church, if you get the chance. My suspicion is that, somewhere along the line, the link between God—the Christian deity—and the rule of nature has become lost to Warraner and those who share his religious convictions. All that's left is the carvings. For the people of Prosperous, those are the faces of their god."

I stood to leave. As I did so, Williamson handed me the books from his desk.

"I thought these might interest you," he said. "Just pop them in the post when you're done with them."

There he was again, "pop"-ing, and putting things in the "post." He caught me smiling.

"Did I say something funny?"

"I was just wondering how many dates you'd gotten in the United States because of that accent of yours."

He grinned. "It did seem to make me very popular for a while. I suspect I may even have married out of my league because of it."

"It's the residual colonial admiration for the oppressor."

"Spoken like a history major."

"No, not me, but Warraner said something similar when I met him. He drew an analogy between detection and historical research."

"But aren't all investigations historical?" said Williamson. "The crime is committed in the past, and the investigation conducted in the present. It's a form of excavation."

"Do you feel a paper coming on?"

"You know, I might do, at that."

I flicked through the first of the books. It was heavily illustrated with images and drawings.

"Pictures too," I said.

"If you color any of them in, we may be forced to have a long talk."

"One last question?" I said.

"Go right ahead."

"Why are so many of these faces threatening, or hostile?"

"Fear," said Williamson. "Fear of the power of nature, fear of old gods. And perhaps, too, the early Church found in such depictions a literal representation of a metaphorical concept—the *radix malorum*, the 'root of all evil.' Hell, if you choose to believe in it, is beneath our feet, not above our heads. You'd have to dig deep to find it, but it wasn't difficult for Christians with ancient links to the land to conceive of the influence of the maleficent in terms of twisted roots and clinging ivy, of faces formed by something buried far beneath the earth trying to create a physical representation of itself from whatever materials were at hand. But the god depicted on the walls of the Prosperous chapel has no connection with Christianity. It's older, and beyond conceptions of good and evil. It simply *is*."

"You sound almost as though you believe in it yourself."

"Perhaps I just sometimes find it easier to understand how someone could conceive and worship a god of tree and leaf, a god that formed as the land around it formed, than a bearded figure living on a cloud in the sky."

"Does that count as a crisis of faith?"

He grinned again. "No, only a natural consequence of the study of every shade of religious belief, and of trying to teach the importance of being tolerant in a world in which tolerance is associated with weakness or heresy."

"Let me guess—you and Michael Warraner didn't exactly see eye to eye on that subject."

"No. He wasn't hostile toward other forms of religious belief, merely uninterested."

"When I see him again, should I pass on your good wishes?" I said.

"I'd prefer if you didn't," said Williamson.

"Frightened?"

"Wary. You should be too." He was no longer distracted, no longer smiling. "One of the challenges I like to set my students for their first class is a word association game. I ask them to list all the words, positive or negative, that come to mind when they think of 'god.' Sometimes I get pages of words, at other times a handful, but Warraner was the only student who ever wrote just one solitary word. That word was "hunger." He and those like him worship a hungry god, Mr. Parker, and no good can ever come of worshipping a deity that hungers. No good at all."

XXXVII

I drove back toward Scarborough, but stopped off at Bull Moose Music's massive warehouse store on Payne Road and browsed the racks for an hour. It was part pleasure, part displacement activity. I felt that I'd reached a dead end as far as Prosperous was concerned, and my talk with

Williamson had served only to confirm my own suspicions about the town without opening any new avenues of inquiry.

I was no closer to finding Annie Broyer than I had been when I started out, and I was beginning to wonder if I might not have been mistaken in assuming that everything I had learned in the past week was useful or even true: an elderly couple, a blue car, a passing reference to a job in Prosperous made to a woman with the mental capacity of a child, and a homeless man's obsession with the carvings on an ancient church. Every piece of information I had gathered was open to question, and it was entirely possible that Annie Broyer would turn up in Boston, or Chicago, or Seattle in the days and weeks to come. Even Lucas Morland's passing reference to Annie as an "ex-junkie" could be explained away if he had made a simple phone call to Portland or Bangor after my first visit to the town. In the eyes of some, I had already violated the primary commandment of an investigation: don't assume. Don't create patterns where there are none. Don't conceive of a narrative and then force the evidence to fit it. On the other hand, all investigations involve a degree of speculation—the capacity to bear witness to a crime and imagine a chain of events that might have caused that crime to be committed. An investigation was not simply a matter of historical research, as Warraner had suggested. It was an act of faith both in one's own capacities and in the possibility of justice in a world that had made justice subservient to the rule of law.

But I had no crime to investigate. I had only a homeless man with a history of depression who might well have hanged himself in a fit of desperation, and a missing girl with a history of narcotic and alcohol abuse who had drifted for most of her life. Was I fixating on Prosperous because its citizens were wealthy and privileged, while Jude and his daughter were poor and suffering? Was I marking Warraner and Morland for simply doing what a pastor and a policeman should do, which was to protect their people?

And yet . . .

Michael Warraner wasn't quite a fraud, but something potentially much more dangerous: a frustrated man with a set of religious or spiritual principles that reinforced his inflated opinion of himself and his place in the world. It was also clear from the way Morland reacted to my unauthorized visit to the church that Warraner had a position of authority in the town, which meant that there were influential individuals who either shared his beliefs or didn't entirely discount them.

What—if anything—all that had to do with the disappearance of Annie and the death of her father, I did not know. Prosperous just felt wrong to me, and I'd grown to trust my feelings. Then again, Angel and Louis might have asked if I ever felt *right* about anything, and if I'd learned to trust those feelings too. I could have countered by replying that nobody ever asked for my help when there wasn't a problem, but I then found myself growing annoyed that I was having arguments—and, more to the point, losing them—with Angel and Louis even when they weren't actually present.

I headed into Portland, where I caught a movie at the Nickelodeon and then ate a burger at the Little Tap House on High Street. The building had once housed Katahdin before that restaurant's move to Forest Avenue. A tapas place had briefly occupied the location in the aftermath of the move, and now the Little Tap House had carved out a niche for itself as a neighborhood bar with good food.

I drank a soda and tried to read a little of the books with which Williamson had entrusted me. They traced the development of foliate sculpture from at least the first century AD, through its adoption by the early Church, and on to its proliferation throughout Western Europe. Some of the illustrations were more graphic than others. My server seemed particularly dismayed by a capital in the cathedral at Autun that depicted a man disappearing into the jaws of a leafed face. Many of the carvings, such as a thirteenth-century mask from Bamberg Cathedral, in Germany, had a kind of beauty to them, which rendered them even more sinister.

I did find a source for Williamson's Latin reference: the apocryphal gospel of Nicodemus, in which Satan was described as *radix omnium malorum*, "the root of all evil," alongside a picture of a tricephalos, a three-faced demon from the façade of San Pietro, in Tuscany. Coiling tendrils pushed through the mouths of the demons, extrusions from the original root, and the text described them as "blood-suckers" in the context of another fifteenth-century head from Melrose Abbey. Here too there was a reference to the relationship between the human and plant elements in the masks as essentially hostile or parasitic, although the general consensus seemed to be that they represented a type of symbiosis, a long-term interaction and mutually beneficial relationship between two species. Man received the blessings of nature's fruits, or the rebirth wrought by the changing of the seasons, and in return—

Well, that last part wasn't so clear, although the cathedral at Autun, with its images of consumption, offered one possible realm of speculation.

I closed the books, paid my tab, and left the bar. The weather had warmed up a little since the previous night—

not by much, but the weathermen were already predicting that the worst of winter was now behind us for another year; prematurely, I suspected. The sky was clear as I drove home, and the saltwater marshes smelled fresh and clean as I parked outside my house. I walked around to the back door to enter by the kitchen. It had become a habit with me ever since Rachel and Sam moved out. Entering by the front door and seeing the empty hallway was somehow more depressing than going in through the kitchen, which was where I spent most of my time anyway. I opened the door and had reached out to key in the alarm code when my dead daughter spoke to me from behind. She said just one word

daddy

and it contained within it the prospect of living and the hope of dying, of endings and beginnings, of love and loss and peace and rage, all wrapped up in two whispered syllables.

I was already diving to the floor when the first of the shotgun blasts hit me, the pellets tearing the skin from my back, the hair from my skull, the flesh from my bones. I burned. I fell to the kitchen floor, and found the strength to kick at the door, knocking it closed, but the second blast blew away the lock and most of the glass, showering me with slivers and splinters. The floor was slick with my blood as I tried to rise, my feet sliding in the redness. I somehow stumbled into the hallway, and now pistol shots were sounding from behind me. I felt the force of their impact in my back, and my shoulder, and my side. I went down again, but as the pain took hold I found it in myself to twist my body to the left. I screamed as I landed on the floor, but I was now halfway across the doorway of my office. My right hand found the corner of the wall, and I dragged myself inside. Again I kicked a door closed, and managed to seat myself upright against my desk. I drew my gun. I raised it and fired a round. I didn't know what it hit. I didn't care. It was enough that it was in my hand.

"Come on," I cried, and blood and spittle sprayed from my lips. "*Come on!*" I said, louder now, and I did not know if I was speaking to myself or to whatever or whomever lay beyond the door.

"Come on," I said a third time, to the approaching darkness, to the figures that beckoned from within it, to the peace that comes at last to every dead thing. Above it all sounded the wailing of the alarm.

I fired again, and two bullets tore through the door in response. One missed. The other did not.

"Come—"

THE WOLF LOOKED UP at the men who surrounded him. He had tried to gnaw his trapped paw off, but had not succeeded. Now he was weary. The time had come. He snarled at the hunters, the fur around his mouth wet with his own blood. A sharp, bitter scent troubled his senses, the smell of noise and dying.

He howled, the final sound that he would ever make. In it was both defiance and a kind of resignation. He was calling on death to come for him.

The gun fired, and the wolf was gone.

"HOLD HIM! HOLD HIM!"
    Light. No light.
    "Jesus, I can't even get a grip on him, there's so much blood. Okay, on three. One, two—"
    "Ah, for Christ's sake."

"His back is just meat. What the fuck happened here?"

Light. No light. Light.

"Can you hear me?"

Yes. No. I saw the paramedic. I saw Sharon Macy behind him. I tried to speak, but no words would come.

"Mr. Parker, can you hear me?"

Light. Stronger now. "You stay with me, you hear? You stay!"

Up. Movement. Ceiling. Lights.

Stars.

Darkness.

Gone.

XXVIII

The house, larger than most of its neighbors, lay on a nondescript road midway between Rehoboth Beach and Dewey Beach on the Delaware coast. Most of the surrounding homes were vacation rentals or summer places used by Washingtonians with a little money to spend. Transience was the norm here. True, a handful of year-round residents lived on the road, but they tended to mind their own business and left others to mind theirs.

A significant number of the homes in the area were owned by gay couples, for Rehoboth had long been one of the East Coast's most gay-friendly resorts. This was perhaps surprising, given that Rehoboth was founded in 1873 by the Reverend Robert W. Todd as a Methodist meeting camp. Reverend Todd's vision of a religious community was short-lived, though, and by the 1940s the gay Hollywood crowd were carousing at the DuPont property along the ocean. Then came the Pink Pony Bar in the 1950s, and the Pleasant Inn and the Nomad Village in the 1960s, all known to be welcoming to DC's more closeted citizens. In the 1990s, some of the town's less tolerant residents made a vain attempt to restore what were loosely termed "family values," in some cases by beating the shit out of anyone who even looked gay. But negotiations among representatives of the gay community, homeowners, and the police largely put an end to the unrest, and Rehoboth settled gently into its role as not only the "Nation's Summer Capital" but the "Nation's *Gay* Summer Capital."

The big house was rarely occupied, even by the standards of vacation homes. Neither was its care entrusted to any of the local Realtors, many of whom boosted their income by acting as agents for summer rentals, and taking care of houses during the winter months. Nevertheless, it was well kept, and local rumor suggested that it had been bought either as part of some complicated tax write-off (in which case the fewer questions asked about it the better, especially in an area swarming with Washingtonians who might or might not have connections to the IRS) or as a corporate investment, for its ownership apparently lay with a shelf company, itself a part of another shelf company, on and on like a series of seemingly infinite matryoshka dolls.

And now, with the hold of winter still upon the land, and the beaches largely empty and devoid of life, the house at last was occupied. Two men, one young and one old, had been noticed entering and leaving, although they did not socialize in any of the local bars and restaurants, and the older gentleman appeared somewhat frail.

But two men, of whatever vintages, living together was not so unusual in Rehoboth Beach, and so their presence went largely unremarked.

INSIDE THE HOUSE, THE Collector brooded by a window. There was no view of the sea here, only a line of trees that protected the house and its occupants from the curiosity of others. The furnishings were largely antiques, some acquired through clever investment but most through bequests, and occasionally by means of outright theft. The Collector viewed such acquisitions as little more than his due. After all, the previous owners had no more use for them, the previous owners being, without exception, dead.

The Collector heard the sound of the lawyer Eldritch coughing and moving about in the next room. Eldritch slept more since the explosion that had almost cost him his life, and had destroyed the records of crimes, both public and private, painstakingly assembled over many decades of investigation. Even had the old man not been so frail, the loss of the files would have seriously curtailed the Collector's activities. He had not realized just how much he relied upon Eldritch's knowledge and complicity in order to hunt and prey. Without Eldritch, the Collector was reduced to the status of an onlooker, left to speculate on the sins of others without the evidence needed to damn them.

But in recent days some of Eldritch's old energy had returned, and he had begun the process of rebuilding his archive. His memory was astonishing in its recall, but his recent sufferings and losses had spurred him still harder to force it to relinquish its store of secrets, fueled by hatred and the desire for revenge. He had lost almost everything that mattered to him: a woman who had been both his consort and his accomplice, and a lifetime's work of cataloging the mortal failings of men. All he had left now was the Collector, and he would be the weapon with which Eldritch avenged himself.

And so, where once the lawyer had been a check on the Collector's urges, he now fed them. Each day brought the two men ever closer. It reminded the Collector that, on one level, they were still father and son, although the thing that lived inside the Collector was very old, and very far from human, and the Collector had largely forgotten his previous identity as the son of the ancient lawyer in the next room.

The house was one of the newest of the Collector's property investments, but also one of the best concealed. Curiously, he owed its existence to the detective Parker. The Collector had arrived in Rehoboth as part of his exploration of the detective's past, his attempt to understand Parker. It was an element of Parker's history—a minor one, admittedly, but the Collector was nothing if not meticulous—and therefore worthy of examination. The house, modest yet handsome, drew the Collector. He was weary of sparsely furnished hideouts, of uncarpeted rooms filled only with mementos of the dead. He needed a place in which to rest, to contemplate, to plan, and so it was that, through Eldritch, he acquired the house. It remained one of the few in which he still felt secure, particularly since the detective and his friends had begun tracking him, seeking to punish him for the death of one of their own. It was off to Rehoboth that the Collector had spirited the lawyer once his wounds had healed sufficiently to enable him to travel, and now the Collector too was sequestered here. He had never known what it was to be hunted before, for he had always been the hunter. They had come close to trapping him in Newark: the recurrent pain from the torn ligaments in his leg was a reminder of that. This situation could not continue. There was harvesting to be done.

Worse, when night came the Hollow Men gathered at his window. He had deprived them of life and returned their souls to their maker. What was left of them lingered, drawn to him not only because they erroneously believed that it was he alone who had caused their suffering—the dead being as capable of self-delusion as the living—but because he could add to their number. That was their only comfort: that others might suffer as they did. But now they sensed his weakness, his vulnerability, and with it came a terrible, warped hope that the Collector would be wiped from the earth, and with his passing might come the oblivion they desired. At night they gathered among the trees, their skin wrinkled and mottled like old, diseased fruit, waiting, willing the detective and his allies to descend upon the Collector.

I could kill them, thought the Collector. I could tear Parker apart, and the ones called Angel and Louis. There was enough evidence against them to justify it, enough sin to tip the scales.

Probably.

Possibly.

But what if he was wrong? What might the consequences be? He had killed their friend in a fit of rage, and as a result he was now little better than a marked animal, running from hole to hole, the ring of hunters tightening around him. If the Collector were to kill the detective, his friends would not rest until the Collector was himself buried. If the Collector were to kill Parker's friends yet leave him alive, the detective would track him to the ends of the earth. And if, by some miracle, he were to kill all three of them? Then a line would have been crossed, and those who protected the detective from the shadows would finish what he had started and hunt the Collector to death. Whatever choice the Collector made would end the same way: the pursuit would continue until he was cornered and his punishment meted out.

The Collector wanted a cigarette. The lawyer did not like him to smoke in the house. He said that it affected his breathing. The Collector could go outside, of course, but he realized that he had grown fearful of showing himself, as if the slightest moment of carelessness might undo him. He had never before been so frightened. The experience was proving unpleasantly enlightening.

The Collector concluded that he could not kill the detective. Even if he were to do so and somehow escape the consequences of his actions, he would ultimately be acting against the Divine. The detective was important. He had a role to play in what was to come. He was human, of that the Collector was now certain, but there was an aspect of him that was beyond understanding. Somehow, in some way, he had touched, or been touched by, the Divine. He had survived so much. Evil had been drawn to him, and he had destroyed it in every instance. There were entities that feared the Collector, and yet they feared the detective even more.

There was no solution. There was no escape.

He closed his eyes, and felt the gloating triumph of the Hollow Men.

THE LAWYER ELDRITCH TURNED on his computer and returned to the task in hand: the reconstruction of his records. He was progressing alphabetically, for the most part, but if a later name or detail came to him unexpectedly he would open a separate file and input the new information. The physical records had been little more than aides-mémoire; everything that mattered was contained in his brain.

His ears ached. His hearing had been damaged in the explosion that killed the woman and destroyed his files, and now he had to endure a continuous high-pitched tinnitus. Some of the nerves in his hands and feet had been damaged as well, causing his legs to spasm as he tried to sleep, and his fingers to freeze into claws if he wrote or typed for too long. His condition was slowly improving, but he was forced to make do without proper physiotherapy or medical advice, for the Collector feared that if Eldritch showed himself it might draw the detective down upon them.

Let him come, thought Eldritch in his worst moments, as he lay awake in his bed, his legs jerking so violently that he could almost feel the muscles starting to tear, his fingers curling so agonizingly that he was certain the bones must break through the skin. Let him come, and let us be done with all this. But somehow he would steal enough sleep to continue, and each day he tried to convince himself that he could discern a diminution in his sufferings: more time between the spasms in his legs, like a child counting the seconds between cracks of thunder to reassure himself that the storm was passing; a little more control over his fingers and toes, like a transplant patient learning to use a new limb; and a slight reduction in the intensity of the noise in his ears, in the hope that madness might be held at bay.

The Collector had set up a series of highly secure email drop boxes for Eldritch, with five-step verification and a prohibition on any outside access. Telephone contact was forbidden—it was too easy to trace—but the lawyer still had his informants, and it was important that he remain in touch with them. Now Eldritch opened the first of the drop boxes. There was only one message inside. Its subject line was "IN CASE YOU DID NOT SEE THIS," and it was only an hour old. The message contained a link to a news report.

Eldritch cut and pasted the link before opening it. It took him to that evening's News Center on NBC's Channel 6, out of Portland, Maine. He watched the report in silence, letting it play in its entirety before he called to the man in the next room.

"Come here," said Eldritch. "You need to look at this."

Moments later, the Collector appeared at his shoulder.

"What is it?" he said.

Eldritch let the news report play a second time.

"The answer to our problems."

XXIX

G arrison Pryor was on his way to the chef's table at L'Espalier, on Boylston, when the call came through to his personal cell phone, the one that was changed weekly, and for which only a handful of people had the number at any time. He was particularly surprised to see the identity of the caller. Pryor hit the green answer button immediately.

"Yes?" he said.

There would be no pleasantries. The Principal Backer didn't like to linger on unsecured lines.

"Have you seen the news?"

"No, I've been in meetings all day, and I'm about to join some clients for a late dinner."

"Your phone has Internet access?"

"Of course."

"Go to Channel Six in Portland. Call me when you're done."

Pryor didn't argue or object. He was running late for dinner, but it didn't matter now. The Principal Backer didn't make such calls lightly.

Pryor hung up and found a spot against the wall by the entrance to the Copley T station. It didn't take him long to find the news report to which the Principal Backer had been referring. He went to the *Portland Press Herald*'s Web site, just in case it had further details, but there were none.

He waited a moment, gathered his thoughts, then called the Principal Backer.

"Are you at home?" asked Pryor.

"Yes."

"But you can talk?"

"For now. Was it one of ours?"

"No."

"You're certain?"

"Absolutely. Nobody would have made a move like this without consulting me first, and I would have given no such authorization. It was decided: we should wait."

"Make sure that we weren't involved."

"I will, but there's no doubt in my mind. The man was not short of enemies."

"Neither are we. There will be consequences for all of us if we're found to be anywhere near this."

"I'll send out word. There will be no further activity until you say otherwise."

"And get somebody to Scarborough. I want to know exactly what happened at that house."

"I'll make the call now."

There was silence on the other end of the line, then:

"I hear L'Espalier is very good."

"Yes." It took Pryor a second or two to realize that he had not told the Principal Backer where he was eating that night. "Yes, it is."

"Perhaps you should inform your clients that you won't be able to make it to dinner after all."

The connection was cut off. Pryor looked at the phone. He'd only had it for two days. He removed the battery, wiped it with his gloves, and tossed it in the trash. As he walked on, he broke the SIM card and dropped the pieces down a drain. He crossed Boylston, heading for Newbury. He stepped into the shadows of Public Alley 440, put the phone on the ground, and began grinding it beneath his heel, harder and harder, until finally he was stamping furiously on fragments of plastic and circuitry, swearing as he did so. Two pedestrians glanced at him as they passed down Exeter, but they didn't stop.

Pryor pressed his forehead against the wall of the nearest building and closed his eyes.

Consequences: that was an understatement. If someone had made an unauthorized hit on the detective, there was no limit to how bad things might get.

IN AN APARTMENT IN Brooklyn, the rabbi named Epstein sat before his computer screen, watching and listening.

It had been a long day of discussions, arguments, and something resembling slow progress, assuming one took a tectonic view of such matters. Epstein, along with two of his fellow moderate rabbis, was trying to hammer out compromises between the borough of Brooklyn and the local Hasidim on a lengthy series of issues, including the Hasidim's desire for the separation of the sexes on city buses and their religious objections to the use of bicycles, mostly with little success. Today, for his sins, Epstein had been forced to explain the concept of *metzizah b'peh*—the practice of oral suction from a baby's circumcision wound—to a disbelieving councilman.

"But why would anyone want to do that?" the councilman kept asking. "Why?"

And, to be honest, Epstein didn't really have an answer or, at least, not one that would satisfy the councilman.

Meanwhile, some of the young Hasidim apparently regarded Epstein with little more affection than they did the goyim. He even heard one of them refer to him behind his back as an *alter kocker*—an "old fart"—but he didn't react. Their elders knew better, and at least acknowledged that Epstein was trying to help by acting as a go-between, attempting to find a compromise with which both the Hasidim and the city could live. Still, if they had their way the Hasidim would wall off Williamsburg from the rest of Brooklyn, although they'd probably have to fight the hipsters for it. The situation wasn't helped by certain city officials publicly comparing the Hasidim to the Mafia. At times, it was enough to make a reasonable man consider abandoning both his faith and his city. But there was a saying in Hebrew, "We survived Pharoah, we'll survive this too." In the words of the old joke, it was the theme of every Jewish holiday: they tried to kill us, they failed, so let's eat!

With that in mind, Epstein was hungry when he arrived home, but all thoughts of food were gone now. Beside him stood a young woman dressed in black. Her name was Liat. She was deaf and mute, so she could not hear the news report, but she could read the anchorman's lips when he appeared onscreen. She took in the images of the police cars, and the house, and the picture of the detective that was being used on all the news reports. It was not a recent photograph. He looked older now. She recalled his face as they had made love, and the feel of his damaged body against hers.

So many scars, so many wounds, both visible and hidden.

Epstein touched her arm. She looked down at his face so that she could watch his lips move.

"Go up there," he said. "Find out what you can. I will start making inquiries here."

She nodded and left.

Strange, thought Epstein: he had never seen her cry before.

XL

It was Bryan Joblin who told them the news, just as he was running out the door. His departure at that moment, leaving them alone, seemed a godsend. Harry and Erin had been growing increasingly fractious with Joblin as his perpetual presence in their lives began to tell on them, while he had settled happily into his role as their watcher, houseguest, and sometime accomplice in a crime yet to be committed. He still pressed Harry to find a girl, as if Harry needed to be reminded. Hayley Conyer herself had stopped by the house that morning while they were clearing up after breakfast, and she had made it very clear to the Dixons that they were running out of time.

"Things are going to start moving fast around here pretty soon," Conyer said, as she stood at the front door, as though reluctant even to set foot once again in their crumbling home. "A lot of our problems are about to disappear, and we can start concentrating again on the tasks that matter."

She leaned in close to the Dixons, and Harry could smell on her breath the sour stink that he always associated with his mother's dying—the stench of the body's internal workings beginning to atrophy.

"You should know that there are folk in Prosperous who blame you for what happened to our young men in Afghanistan, and to Valerie Gillson and Ben Pearson, too," she said. "They believe that if you hadn't let the girl go"—Conyer allowed the different possible interpretations of that conditional clause to hang in the air for a moment—"then four of our people might still be alive. You have a lot of work to do to make up for your failings. I'm giving you three days. By then, you'd better produce a substitute girl for me."

But Harry knew that they wouldn't be around in three days, or, if they were, it would probably be the end of them. They were ready to run. Had Bryan Joblin not told them of what had occurred, then left them for a time to their own devices, they might have waited another day, just to be sure that everything was in place for their escape. Now they took his news as a sign: it was time. They watched him drive away, his words still ringing in their ears.

"We hit the detective," Joblin told them. "It's all over the news. That fucker is gone. *Gone!*"

And, within twenty minutes of Joblin's departure, the Dixons had left Prosperous.

HARRY MADE THE CALL on the way to Medway. The auto dealership closed most evenings at six, but Harry had the dealer's cell phone number and knew that he lived only a couple of blocks from the lot. He'd told the guy that, if it came down to the wire, he might have to leave the state at short notice. He had spun the man a line about a sick mother, knowing that the dealer couldn't have given a rat's ass if Harry's mother was Typhoid Mary, as long as he paid cash alongside the trade-in. So it was that, thirty minutes after leaving Prosperous, the Dixons drove out of the lot in a GMC Savana Passenger Van with 100,000 miles on the clock, stopping only at the outskirts of Medway to call Magnus and Dianne and let them know that they were on their way. The van was ugly as a mud slide, but they could sleep in it if they had to, and who knew how long they might be on the road, or how far they might have to travel? They couldn't stay with Harry's in-laws for long. Even one night would be risky. In fact, the closer Harry got to the house in Medway, the more he started to feel that perhaps he and Erin shouldn't stay with them at all. It might be wiser just to pick up their stuff, arrange some way of remaining in contact, and then find a motel for the night. The more distance they put between themselves and Prosperous, the better. He expressed his concerns to Erin, and he was surprised when she concurred without argument. Her only regret, as far as he could tell, was that they hadn't managed to kill Bryan Joblin before they left Prosperous. She might have been joking, but somehow Harry doubted it.

They pulled up in the driveway of the house. The lights were on inside, and Harry could see Magnus watching TV in the living room, the drapes open. He saw his brother-in-law stand as he heard the sound of the engine. He waved at them from the window. They were still getting out of the van when Magnus opened the front door.

"Come in," he said. "We've been worrying ever since we got your call."

"Where's Dianne?" said Erin.

"She's in the bathroom. She'll be right down."

Magnus stood aside to let Harry and Erin enter.

"Let me take your coats," said Magnus.

"We're not staying," said Harry.

"That's not what you told us."

"I know what I told you, but I think it's better if we just keep driving. They're going to come looking for us once they find that we've gone, and it won't take them long to make the connection to you and Dianne. We need to put ground between Prosperous and us. I can't tell you why. We just have to leave the town far behind."

Magnus closed the front door. Harry could still feel a draft on his face, though. It was coming from the kitchen. A gust of wind passed through the house. It blew open the dining room door to their left. Inside, they saw Dianne seated in the dark by the table.

"I thought you were—" said Erin, but she got no further.

Bryan Joblin sat across from Dianne. He held a gun in his right hand, pointing loosely at her chest. Behind him was Calder Ayton. He too held a gun, but his was aimed at the head of Dianne's daughter, Kayley.

Harry's hand slid slowly toward the gun in his jacket pocket, just as Chief Morland appeared from the living room. He laid a hand on Harry's arm.

"Don't," said Morland, and his voice was almost kindly.

Harry's hand faltered, then fell to his side. Morland reached into Harry's pocket and removed the Smith & Wesson.

"You have a license for this?" said Morland.

Harry didn't reply.

"I didn't think so," said Morland.

He raised the gun and touched it to the back of Erin's head. He pulled the trigger, and the cream walls of the hallway blushed crimson. While Harry was still trying to take in the sight of his wife's body collapsing to the floor, Morland shot Magnus in the chest, then advanced three steps and killed Dianne with a single bullet that entered her face just below the bridge of her nose.

It was Kayley's screams that brought Harry back, but by then it was all too late. Morland swept Harry's feet from under him, sending him sprawling to the floor beside his dead wife. He stared at her. Her eyes were closed, her face contorted in a final grimace of shock. Harry wondered if she'd felt a lot of pain. He hoped not. He'd loved her. He'd loved her so very much.

Morland's weight was on his back now. Harry smelled the muzzle of the gun as it brushed his face.

"Do it," said Harry. "Just do it."

But instead the gun disappeared, and Harry's hands were cuffed loosely behind his back. Kayley had stopped screaming and was now sobbing. It sounded as if there might have been a hand across her mouth, though, for the sobs were muffled.

"Why?" said Harry.

"Because we can't have a multiple killing without a killer," said Morland.

He lifted Harry to his feet. Harry stared at him, his eyes glazed. Morland's features formed a mask of pure desolation.

Calder Ayton and Bryan Joblin emerged from the second entrance to the living room, carrying Kayley between them. They walked through the kitchen to the back door. Shortly after that, Harry heard the trunk of a car closing, and then the vehicle drove away.

"What's going to happen to her?" he asked.

"I think you already know," said Morland. "You were told to find us a girl. It looks like you did your duty after all."

Bryan Joblin reappeared in the kitchen. He smiled at Harry as he approached him.

"What now?" said Harry.

"You and Bryan are going to take a ride. I'll join you both as soon as I can."

Morland turned to leave, then paused.

"Tell me, Harry. Did the girl really escape, or did you let her go?"

What did it matter, thought Harry. The girl had still died, and soon he would join her.

"We let her go."

The use of the word "we" made him look down at Erin, and in doing so he missed the look that passed across Morland's face. It contained a hint of admiration.

Harry felt as though he should cry, but no tears would come. It was too late for tears, anyway, and they would serve no purpose.

"I'm sorry it's come down to this," said Morland.

"Go to hell, Lucas," said Harry.

"Yes," said Morland. "I think that I probably will."

XLI

A day passed. Night fell. All was changed, yet unchanged. The dead remained dead, and waited for the dying to join their number.

On the outskirts of Prosperous, a massive 4WD pulled up by the side of the road, disgorging one of its occupants before quickly turning back east. Ronald Straydeer hoisted a pack onto his back and headed for the woods, making his way toward the ruins of the church.

XLII

The two-story redbrick premises advertised itself as BLACKTHORN, APOTHECARY, although it had been many years since the store sold anything, and old Blackthorn himself was now long dead. It had, for much of its history, been the only business on Hunts Lane, a Brooklyn mews originally designed to stable the horses of the wealthy on nearby Remsen and Joralemon Streets.

The exterior wood surround was black, the lettering on and above the window gold, and its front door was permanently closed. The upstairs windows were shuttered, while the main window on the first floor was protected by a dense wire grille. The jumbled display behind it was a historical artifact, a collection of boxes and bottles bearing the names, where legible at all, of companies that no longer existed, and products with more than a hint of snake oil about them: Dalley's Magical Pain Extractor, Dr. Ham's Aromatic Invigorator, Dr. Miles's Nervine.

Perhaps, at some point in the past, an ancestor of the

last Blackthorn had seen fit to offer such elixirs to his customers, along with remedies stranger still. A glass case inside the door contained packets of Potter's Asthma Smoking Mixture ("may be smoked in a pipe either with or without ordinary tobacco") and Potter's Asthma Care Cigarettes from the nineteenth century, along with Espic and Legras powders, the latter beloved of the French writer Marcel Proust, who used it to tackle his asthma and his hay fever. In addition to stramonium, a derivative of the common thorn apple, *Datura stramonium*, which was regarded as an effective remedy for respiratory problems, such products contained, variously, potash and arsenic. Now, long fallen from favor, they were memorialized in the gloom of Blackthorn, Apothecary, alongside malt beverages for nursing mothers, empty bottles of cocaine-based coca wine and heroin hydrochloride, and assorted preparations of morphine and opium for coughs, colds, and children's teething difficulties.

By the time the final Blackthorn was entering his twilight years—in a store that, most aptly, eschewed sunlight through the judicious use of heavy drapes and a sparing attitude toward electricity—the business that bore his family name sold only herbal medicines, and the musty interior still contained the evidence of Blackthorn's faith in the efficacy of natural solutions. The mahogany shelves were lined with glass jars containing moldering and desiccated herbs, although the various oils appeared to have survived the years with little change. A series of ornate lettered boards between the shelves detailed a litany of ailments and the herbs available to counteract their symptoms, from bad breath (parsley) and gas (fennel and dill) to cankers (goldenseal), cancer (bilberry, maitake mushroom, pomegranate, raspberry) and congestive heart failure (hawthorn). All was dust and dead insects, except on the floor, where regular footfalls had cleared a narrow path through the detritus of decades. This led from a side entrance beside the main door, through a hallway adorned with photographs of the dead, and amateur landscapes that bespoke a morbid fascination with the work of the more depressive German Romantics, and into the store itself by way of a door with panels decorated by graphically rendered scenes from the Passion of Christ. The path's final destination was obscured by a pair of black velvet drapes that closed off what had once been old Blackthorn's back room, in which the apothecary had created his tinctures and powders.

Now, as a chill rain fell on the streets, specks of light showed through the moth holes in the drapes, and they glittered like stars as unseen figures moved in the room behind. Evening had descended, and Hunts Lane was empty, apart from the two men who stood beneath the awning of an old stable, watching the storefront on the other side of the alley, and the vague signs of life from within.

Two days had passed since the shooting.

"He gives me the creeps," said Angel.

"Man gives everyone the creeps," said Louis. "There's dead folk would move out if they found themselves buried next to him."

"Why here?"

"Why not?"

"I guess. How long has he been holed up in that place?"

"Couple of weeks, if what I hear is true."

The location had cost Louis a considerable amount of money, along with one favor that he could never call in again. He didn't mind. This was personal.

"It's homely," said Angel. "In a Dickensian way—it's kind of appropriate. Any idea where he's been all these years?"

"No. He did have a habit of moving around."

"Not much choice. Probably doesn't make many friends in his line of work."

"Probably not."

"After all, you didn't."

"No."

"Except me."

"Yeah. About that . . ."

"Go fuck yourself."

"That would be the other option."

Angel stared at the building, and the building seemed to stare back.

"Strange that he should turn up now."

"Yes."

"You know what he was doing while he was gone?"

"What he's always been doing—causing pain."

"Maybe he thinks it'll take away some of his own."

Louis glanced at his partner.

"You know, you get real philosophical at unexpected moments."

"I was born philosophical. I just don't always care to share my thoughts with others, that's all. I think I might be a Stoic, if I understood what that meant. Either way, I like the sound of it."

"On your earlier point, he enjoyed inflicting pain, and watching others inflict it, even when he wasn't suffering himself."

"If you believed in a god, you might say it was divine retribution."

"Karma."

"Yeah, that too."

The rain continued to fall.

"You know," said Angel, "there's a hole in this awning."

"Yes."

"It's, like, a metaphor or something."

"Or just a hole."

"You got no poetry in your heart."

"No."

"You think he knows we're out here?"

"He knows."

"So?"

"You want to knock, be my guest."

"What'll happen?"

"You'll be dead."

"I figured it would be something like that. So we wait."

"Yes."

"Until?"

"Until he opens the door."

"And?"

"If he tries to kill us, we know he's involved."

"And if he doesn't try to kill us, then he's not involved?"

"No, then maybe he's just smarter than I thought."

"You said he was as smart as any man you'd ever known."

"That's right."

"Doesn't bode well for us."

"No."

There was a noise from across the alley: the sound of a key turning in a lock, and a bolt being pulled. Angel moved to the right, his gun already in his hand. Louis went left, and was absorbed by the darkness. A light bloomed slowly in the hallway, visible through the hemisphere of cracked glass above the smaller of the two doors. The door opened slowly, revealing a huge man. He remained very still, his hands slightly held out from his sides. Had Angel and Louis wanted to kill him, this would have been the perfect opportunity. But the message seemed clear: the one they had come to see wanted to talk. There would be no killing.

Not yet.

There was no further movement for a time. Angel's gaze alternated between the shuttered windows on the second floor of the apothecary and the entrance to Hunts Lane from Henry Street. Hunts Lane was a dead end. If this was a trap, there would be no escape. He had questioned Louis about their approach, wondering aloud if it might not be better for one of them to remain on the street while the other entered the alley, but Louis had demurred.

"He knows that we're coming. He's the last one."

"Which means?"

"That if it's a trap he'd spring it long before the alley. We'd be dead as soon as we set foot in Brooklyn. We just wouldn't know it until the blade fell."

None of this did Angel find reassuring. He had met this man only once before, when he sought to recruit Louis—and, by extension, Angel—for his own ends. The memory of that meeting had never faded. Angel had felt poisoned by it afterward, as though by breathing the same air as the man he had forever tainted his system.

Louis appeared again. He had his gun raised, aimed directly at the figure in the doorway. The giant stepped forward, and a motion-activated light went on above his head. He was truly enormous, his head like a grave monument on his shoulders, his chest and arms impossibly massive. Angel didn't recognize the face, and he would surely have remembered if he had seen such a monster before. His skull was bald, his scalp crisscrossed with scars, and his eyes were very clear and round, like boiled eggs pressed into his face. He was extraordinarily unhandsome, as though God had created the ugliest human being possible and then punched him in the face.

Most striking of all was the yellow suit that he wore. It gave him a strange air of feigned jollity, the product, perhaps, of an erroneous belief that he might somehow appear less threatening if he just wore brighter colors. He watched Louis approach, and it struck Angel that he hadn't yet seen the sentinel in the doorway blink once. His eyes were so huge that any blinks would have been obvious, like the flapping of wings.

Louis lowered his gun, and simultaneously the man at the door raised his right hand. He showed Louis the small plastic bottle that he held and then, without waiting for Louis to respond, tilted his head back and added drops to his eyes. When he was done, he stepped into the rain and silently indicated that Angel and Louis should enter the apothecary's store, his right hand now extended like that of the greeter at the world's worst nightclub.

Reluctantly, Angel came forward. He followed Louis into the darkness of the hallway, but he entered backward, keeping his eyes, and his gun, on the unblinking giant at the door. But the giant didn't follow them inside. Instead, he remained standing in the rain, his face raised to the heavens, and the water flowed down his cheeks like tears.

XLIII

Angel and Louis followed the trail through the dust, the interior lit only by a single lamp that flickered in a corner. The room smelled of long-withered herbs, the scent of them infused in the grain of the wood and the peeling paint on the walls, but underpinning it was a medicinal odor that grew stronger as they approached the drapes concealing the back room.

And there was another smell again beneath them all: it was the unmistakable reek of rotting flesh.

Louis had replaced his gun in its holster, and now Angel did the same. Slowly Louis reached out and pulled aside the drapes, revealing the room beyond, and a man seated at a desk lit only by a banker's lamp. The angle of the lamp meant that the man was hidden in shadow, but even in the darkness Angel could see that he was yet more misshapen than when they'd last met. As they entered he raised his head with difficulty, and his words were slurred as he spoke.

"Welcome," he said. "You'll forgive me for not shaking hands."

His twisted right hand reached for the lamp, its fingers so deformed that they appeared to have been lost entirely, the digits reduced to twin stumps at the end of the arm. Angel and Louis didn't react, except for the merest flicker of compassion that briefly caused Angel's eyes to close. It was beyond Angel's capacity not to feel some sympathy, even for one such as this. His response didn't go unnoticed.

"Spare me," said the man. "If it were possible to rid myself of this disease by visiting it instead on you, I would do so in an instant."

He gurgled, and it took Angel a moment to realize that he was laughing.

"In fact," he added, "I would visit it upon you anyway, were it possible, if only for the pleasure of sharing."

"Mr. Cambion," said Louis. "You have not changed."

With a flick of his wrist, Cambion moved the lamp so that its light now fell upon his ravaged face.

"Oh," he said, "but I have."

*   *   *

ITS OFFICIAL NAME WAS Hansen's disease, after the Norwegian physician Gerhard Armauer Hansen, who, in 1873, identified the bacterium that was its causative agent, but for more than four thousand years humankind had known it simply as leprosy. Multidrug therapies had now rendered curable what had once been regarded as beyond treatment, with rifampicin as the base drug used to tackle both types of leprosy, multibacillary and paucibacillary, but Cambion was one of the exceptional cases, the small unfortunate few who showed no clinical or bacteriological improvement with MDT. The reasons for this were unclear, but those who whispered of him said that, during the earliest manifestations of the disease, he had been treated unethically with rifampicin as a monotherapy, instead of in conjunction with dapsone and clofazimine, and this had created in him a resistance to the base drug. The unfortunate physician responsible had subsequently disappeared, although he was not forgotten by his immediate family, helped by the fact that pieces of the doctor continued to be delivered to them at regular intervals. In fact, it wasn't even clear if the doctor was dead, since the body parts that arrived appeared remarkably fresh, even allowing for the preservative compounds in which they were packed.

But truth, when it came to Cambion, was in short supply. Even his name was an invention. In medieval times, a cambion was the mutated offspring of a human and a demon. Caliban, Prospero's antagonist in *The Tempest*, was a cambion—"not honour'd with a human shape." All that could be known of Cambion for sure, confirmed by his presence in the old apothecary, was that his condition was deteriorating rapidly. One might even have said that it was degenerating, but then Cambion had always been degenerate by nature, and his physical ailment could have been taken as an outward manifestation of his inner corruption. Cambion was wealthy, and without morals. Cambion had killed—men, women, children—but as the disease had rotted his flesh, limiting his power of movement and depriving him of sensation at his extremities, he had moved from the act of killing to the facilitation of it. It had always been a lucrative sideline for him, for his reputation drew men and women who were at least as debased as he, but now it was his principal activity. Cambion was the main point of contact for those who liked to combine murder with rape and torture, and those who devoutly wished that their enemies might suffer before they died. It was said that, when possible, Cambion liked to watch. Cambion's people—if people they even were, as their capacity for evil called into question their very humanity—took on jobs that others refused to countenance, whether for reasons of morality or personal safety. Their sadism was their weakness, though. This was why Cambion's services remained so specialized, and why he and his beasts hid themselves in the shadows. Their acts had been met with promises of retribution that were at least their equal.

When Angel had last seen Cambion, more than a decade earlier, his features were already displaying signs of ulceration and lesions, and certain nerves had begun to enlarge, including the great auricular nerve beneath the ears and the supraorbital on the skull. Now the ravages of the disease had rendered him almost unrecognizable. His left eye was barely visible as a slit in the flesh of his face, while the right eye was wide but cloudy. His lower lip had swollen immensely, causing his mouth to droop open. His nasal cartilage had dissolved, leaving two holes separated by a strip of bone. Any remaining visible skin was covered with bumps that looked as hard as stone.

"What do you think?" said Cambion, and spittle sprayed from his lips. Angel was glad that he hadn't chosen to stand closer to the desk. After that first, and last, encounter with Cambion, he had taken the time to read up on leprosy. Most of what he knew, or thought he knew of the disease, turned out to be myths, including that it was transmitted by touch. Routes of transmission were still being researched, but it appeared to be spread primarily through nasal secretions. Angel watched the droplets of spittle on Cambion's desk and realized that he was holding his breath.

"Don't look like you're getting no better," said Louis.

"I think that's a safe conjecture," said Cambion.

"Maybe you ought to try—" Louis clicked his fingers and turned to Angel for help. "What's that shit you use? You know, for your scabies."

"Hydrocortisone. And it's not scabies. It's heat rash."

"Yeah, that's it," said Louis. He returned his attention to Cambion. "Hydrocortisone. Clear that shit right up."

"Thank you for the advice. I'll bear it in mind."

"My pleasure," said Louis. "You give what ails you to SpongeBob SquarePants outside too?"

Cambion managed to smile.

"I'll let Edmund know what you called him. I'm sure he'll find it amusing."

"I don't much care either way," said Louis.

"No, I don't imagine you would. As for what troubles him, he has a condition known as lagophthalmos—a form of facial paralysis that affects the seventh cranial nerve, which controls the orbicularis oculi, the closing muscle of the eyelid. It leaves him unable to properly lubricate his eyes."

"Man," said Louis, "you quite the pair."

"I like to think that Edmund's exposure to me enables him to put his own problems into some kind of perspective."

"It would, if you hired a bodyguard who can see right."

"Edmund's not just my bodyguard. He's my nurse, and my confidant. In fact"—Cambion waved his right arm, displaying the stumps—"you could say that he's my right-hand man. My left, though, continues to have its uses."

He displayed his left hand for the first time. It still had three fingers and a thumb. They were currently wrapped around a modified pistol with an oversized trigger. The muzzle of the gun pointed loosely at Louis.

"We was going to kill you, we'd have done it already," said Louis.

"Likewise."

"You were hard to find."

"Yet here you are. I knew you'd get to me eventually, once you'd exhausted all other avenues of inquiry. You've been tearing quite a swath through the city, you and your boyfriend. There can't be a stone left unturned."

It was true. Within hours of the shooting, Angel and Louis had begun asking questions, sometimes gently, sometimes less so. There had been quiet conversations over cups of coffee in upscale restaurants, and over beers in the back rooms of dive bars. There were phone calls and denials, threats and warnings. Every middleman, every fixer, every facilitator who had knowledge of those who killed for money was contacted directly or received word: Louis wanted names. He desired to know who had pulled the trigger, and who had made the call.

The difficulty was that Louis suspected the shooter—or shooters, for Louis believed that the combination of shotgun and pistol used pointed to a team—hadn't been sourced through the usual channels. He had no doubt that they were pros, or, at least, he had started off with that assumption. It didn't smell like amateur hour to him, not where Parker was concerned, and the likelihood of two gunmen reinforced that belief. If he was wrong, and it turned out that some enraged loner was responsible, then it would be a matter for the cops and their investigation. Louis might get to the shooter first if the information leaked, but that wasn't his world. In Louis's world, people were paid to kill.

But the detective's connections to Louis were well known, and nobody of Louis's acquaintance would have accepted the contract, either as the agent or as the trigger man. Nevertheless, it had been necessary to check, just to be sure.

There was also the distinct possibility that the hit was related to Parker's movements through darker realms, and with that in mind Louis had already made contact with Epstein, the old rabbi in New York. Louis had made it clear to him that, if Epstein discovered something relating to the hit and chose not to share it, Louis would be seriously displeased. In the meantime, Epstein had sent his own pet bodyguard, Liat, up to Maine. She was, thought Louis, a little late to the party. They all were.

A third line of investigation pointed to the Collector, but Louis had dismissed that possibility almost immediately. A shotgun wasn't the Collector's style, and he'd probably have come after Angel and Louis first. Louis suspected that the Collector wanted Parker alive unless there was no other option, although he still didn't understand why, despite Parker's efforts to explain the situation to him. If he ever did manage to corner the Collector, Louis planned to ask him to clarify it, just before he shot him in the head.

Finally, there was the case on which Parker had been working before the hit: a missing girl, a dead man in a basement, and a town called Prosperous, but that was all Louis knew. If someone in Prosperous had hired a killer, then it brought the hunt back to Louis. He would find the shooters and make them talk.

Which was why he and Angel were now standing before Cambion, because Cambion didn't care about Louis, or Parker, or anyone or anything else, and he dealt, in turn, with those who were too vicious and depraved to care either. Even if Cambion hadn't been involved—and that had yet to be established—his contacts extended into corners of which even Louis was not aware. The creatures that hid there had claws and fangs, and were filled with poison.

"Quite the place you have here," said Louis. His eyes were growing used to the dimness. He could see the modern medicines on the shelves behind Cambion, and a doorway beyond that, presumably, led to where Cambion lived and slept. He could not visualize this man making it up a flight of stairs. A wheelchair stood folded in one corner. Beside it was a plastic bowl, a spoon, and a napkin. A china bowl and a silver soup spoon sat on the desk beside Cambion, and Louis spotted a similar bowl and spoon on a side table to his right.

Curious, thought Louis: two people, but three bowls.

"I was growing fond of my new home," said Cambion. "But now, I think, I shall have to move again. A pity—such upheavals drain my strength, and it's difficult to find suitable premises with such a gracious atmosphere."

"Don't go running off on my account," said Louis. He didn't even bother to comment on the ambience. The apothecary's old premises felt to him only a step away from an embalmer's chambers.

"Why, are you telling me that I can rely on your discretion—that you won't breathe a word of where I am?" said Cambion. "There's a price on my head. The only reason you've got this close is because I know that you declined the contract on me. I still don't understand why."

"Because I thought a day like this might come," said Louis.

"When you needed me?"

"When I'd have to look in your eyes to see if you were lying."

"Ask it."

"Were you involved?"

"No."

Louis remained very still as he stared at the decaying man. Finally, he nodded.

"Who was?"

"No one in my circle."

"You're sure?"

"Yes."

Although it was only the slightest of movements, Angel saw Louis's shoulders slump. Cambion was the last of the middlemen. The hunt would now become much more difficult.

"I have heard a rumor, though. . . ."

Louis tensed. Here was the game. There was always a game where Cambion was concerned.

"Which is?"

"What can you offer me in return?"

"What do you want?"

"To die in peace."

"Looking at you, that don't seem like an option."

"I want the contract nullified."

"I can't do that."

Cambion placed the gun, which had remained in his hand throughout, on the desk and opened a drawer. From it he produced an envelope, which he slid toward Louis.

"Talking tires me," he said. "This should suffice."

"What is it?"

"A list of names—the worst of men and women."

"The ones you've used."

"Yes, along with the crimes for which they're responsible. I want to buy the contract back with their blood. I'm tired of being pursued. I need to rest."

Louis stared at the envelope, making the calculations. Finally, he took it and placed it in his jacket pocket.

"I'll do what I can."

"Those names will be enough."

"Yes, I think they will. Now, the rumor."

"A man and a woman. Married. Children. Perfect Middle Americans. They have only one employer. A handful of hits, but very good."

"Their motivation?"

"Not money. Ideology."

"Political?"

"Religious, if what I hear is true."

"Where?"

"North Carolina, but that may no longer be the case. It's all I have."

Behind them, the yellow-clad giant named Edmund appeared. He handed Louis a slip of paper. On it was written a cell phone number. The meeting was over.

"Soon I'll be gone from here," said Cambion. "Use that number to confirm that the contract has been rendered null and void."

Louis memorized the number before handing the paper back to Edmund. It vanished into the folds of the giant's hand.

"How long you got left?" he asked Cambion.

"Who knows?"

"Seems like it might be a mercy to let the contract run its course," said Louis, as Edmund stepped aside so that the two visitors could leave, and prepared to escort them out.

"You might think that," said Cambion, "but I'm not ready to die yet."

"Yeah," said Louis, as the drapes fell closed behind him. "That's a damn shame."

XLIV

Ronald Straydeer was not unfamiliar with sleeping outdoors. He'd bedded down in the jungles in Vietnam, the Great North Woods of Maine, and beside pot plantations in upstate New York during a period of misunderstanding with some rival growers, which came to an end when Ronald put one of them headfirst into a narrow hole and proceeded to fill it in.

Thus Ronald understood the necessity of good nutrition and proper clothing, particularly when it came to cold weather. He wore polypropylene, not cotton, next to his skin, because he knew that cotton trapped moisture, and the action of convection meant that cold air and damp drained the body's heat. A hat with earflaps covered his head, because when the head got cold the body began to shut off circulation to the extremities. He kept himself moving constantly, if only through the gentle shuffling of his feet and minute stretches of his arms, fingers, and toes, generating heat as a by-product. He had brought plenty of water, and an assortment of nuts, seeds, energy bars, jerky, and salami, as well as a couple of MREs—because sometimes a man needed a hot meal, even one that tasted as if it had been made for pets—and containers of self-heating soup and coffee. He didn't know how long he might be out in the wild, but he had packed enough food for four days, or more if he had to be abstemious. He was armed with a licensed hunting rifle, a Browning BAR Mark II Lightweight Stalker in .308. If it came down to it, he could claim to be hunting squirrels or hare, even coyotes, although the Browning wouldn't leave much of a varmint behind apart from bits of fur and memories.

He had been fortunate with this location. The woods around the ruined church were a mixture of deciduous and evergreen, but more of the latter. He bedded down in the thickest copse he could find and covered his sleeping bag with branches. He made a careful recce of his surroundings but did not enter the church grounds—not out of superstition but simply because, if Shaky was right, the church was important, and people tended to protect places that were important. He checked the gate and the fence, and saw nothing to indicate that the grounds were guarded electronically, but he still didn't want to risk setting off any kind of hidden motion sensor. Neither did he attempt an exploration of the town itself. Ronald was a striking, imposing man, and he attracted attention. Perhaps he would be seeing more of the town soon enough.

To pass the time, he read. He had brought with him a copy of *Bleak House*, by Charles Dickens, because he recalled the detective's recommending it to him once. He had bought it but never got around to reading it. Now seemed the appropriate time.

Shaky, like Jude before him, was convinced that Prosperous was rotten, and he had halfway managed to convince Ronald of the same thing, even before Ronald had ever come to the town. Shaky had accompanied Ronald around Portland and South Portland as he began quietly questioning the homeless about what they had seen in the days preceding Jude's death. Shaky had a way of calming folk. He was unthreatening, and generally well liked. It was, thought Ronald, a little like having a good dog with him— an old Labrador, maybe, something friendly and tolerant. He didn't share this with Shaky, though. He wasn't sure how it might be taken.

Despite their efforts, they learned nothing of worth until the end of a long day of searching and questioning. It came from an unlikely source: the woman known as Frannie, with whom Shaky had witnessed Brightboy arguing on the morning that Brightboy attacked him. Shaky usually did his best to avoid Frannie due to her intimidating nature, and the vision of a man having his nose gnawed off that she invariably conjured up, but Ronald Straydeer wasn't troubled by her in the least. He told Shaky that he knew Frannie from way back, when she still had most of her teeth.

"Is it true that she once bit a man's nose off and spit it out in front of him?" asked Shaky. After all, it seemed that Ronald Straydeer might be able to confirm the story, once and for all.

"No," said Ronald solemnly. "That's not true."

Shaky was relieved, but Ronald wasn't done.

"She didn't spit it out," he continued. "She swallowed it."

Shaky felt ill. During the subsequent conversation with Frannie, he found himself using Ronald's body as a bulwark between him and the woman. If she'd developed a taste for male flesh, she'd have to go through Ronald to get to him.

Frannie was pleased to see Ronald, although she was

less pleased when she learned that he was no longer dealing. Using mainly four-letter words, she expressed the view
that Ronald was a grave disappointment to her. Ronald accepted the judgment without complaint, and gave her the
name of someone who might be able to help her find some
pot, along with twenty bucks with which to treat herself.

In return, Frannie told them about the couple she'd seen
near Jude's basement.

Frannie wasn't a mixer. She avoided the shelters. She
was always angry, or briefly coming down from being
angry prior to getting angry all over again. She liked no
one, not even Jude. She'd never asked him for anything,
and he'd never offered, knowing better than to do so.
Shaky couldn't understand why she was opening up to
Ronald Straydeer, even allowing for the money and the
pot connection. It was only later that it dawned on him:
Frannie had been flattered by Ronald's attention. Ronald
spoke to her as he would to any woman. He was courte-
ous. He smiled. He asked about a wound on her arm, and
recommended something for it. None of this did he
do in a false manner; Frannie would have seen through
that in an instant. Instead, Ronald talked to her as the
woman that she once was, and perhaps, deep down,
still believed herself to be. How long had it been since
anyone had done that for her, thought Shaky. Decades,
probably. She hadn't always been this way and, like all
of those who ended up on the streets, never wanted it
for herself. As she and Ronald spoke, Shaky saw her
change. Her eyes softened. She wasn't beautiful—she
would never again be that, if she had ever been—but for
the first time Shaky saw her as something other than an
individual to be feared. She let her guard down while
talking to Ronald, and it struck Shaky that Frannie lived
her life in a state of perpetual fear, for, however bad it

was to be a homeless man, it was infinitely worse to be a homeless woman. He had always understood that, but as an abstract concept, and generally applied it only to the younger girls, the teenagers, who were more obviously vulnerable. He had made the mistake of imagining that somehow, for Frannie, it might have become easier over the years, not harder. Now he knew himself to be wrong.

So Frannie told Ronald Straydeer of how she had walked past Jude's place the night before he died, and seen a car parked across the street. And because she was always desperate, and asking was free, she tapped on the glass in the hope that a dollar might be forthcoming.

"They gave me a five," she told Ronald. "Five bucks. Just like that."

"And did they ask for anything in return?" said Ronald.

Frannie shook her head.

"Nothing."

"They didn't ask after Jude?"

"No."

Because they already knew, thought Shaky, and they were smarter than to draw attention to themselves by bribing a homeless woman for information. Instead, they paid her—enough to be generous, but not too generous—and she went away, leaving them to wait for Jude to appear.

Ronald asked what Frannie remembered about them. She recalled a silver car, and Massachusetts plates, but she admitted that she might have been mistaken about the plates. The woman was good-looking, but in that way of women who try too hard to keep themselves in condition as they get older and end up with lines on their tanned faces that might have been avoided if they'd resigned themselves to a little flesh on their bones. The man was balding, and wore glasses. He had barely looked at Frannie. The woman gave her the money, and responded to Frannie's word of thanks with the briefest of smiles.

Frannie's information wasn't much, but it was a small reward for their efforts. Ronald prepared to take his leave of Shaky and return home. He would call on the detective along the way, and share what he had learned with him. Instead, he and Shaky saw the detective's face appear on the television screen of a bar on Congress as they passed. Ronald bought Shaky a beer while he sipped a soda, and together they watched the news. Shaky told him that it had to be connected to Jude and his daughter. If that was the case, it was also connected to Prosperous, and if Prosperous was involved it had something to do with the old church, which was how Ronald came to be lying in the woods eating MREs and reading Dickens. Even if Shaky was mistaken, at least Ronald was trying to do something, but he had to give it to the little homeless man: Prosperous felt wrong, and the old church felt multiples of wrong.

There had been little activity since he arrived. Twice a police cruiser had driven up the road to the church, but on each occasion the cop had simply checked the lock on the gate and made a cursory circuit of the cemetery. Ronald had used the telescopic sight to pick out the cop's name on a briefly visible shirt tag: Morland.

The only other visitor was a tall man in his forties with receding hair, dressed in jeans, work boots, and a brown suede jacket. He arrived at the cemetery from the northwest, so that his appearance in the churchyard caught Ronald by surprise. On the first occasion, Ronald watched as he opened the church and checked inside, although he didn't remain there for long. Ronald figured him for the pastor, Warraner. Shaky had learned about him from the detective, as well as something of the chief cop named Morland. Both Jude and the detective had endured run-ins with each of them, according to Shaky. Ronald didn't follow Warraner when he left, but later he found the path that led from the churchyard to the pastor's house. Better to know where he was coming from than not.

The pastor returned shortly before sunset on the first day, this time with a rake and a shovel, and began clearing undergrowth from an area about forty feet from the western wall of the church. Ronald watched him through the scope. When Warraner was done, a hole just a little over two feet in diameter was revealed in the earth. Then, apparently content with his work, the pastor left and hadn't yet returned.

Now darkness had descended again, and Ronald was preparing to spend another night in the woods when the car arrived. It approached slowly, because it was driving without lights, and it stopped well before it neared the cemetery's railings. Two men got out. Ronald turned his Armasight night-vision binoculars on them. One was Morland, although this time he was out of uniform. The second was an old scarecrow of a man wearing a long coat and a felt hat. They didn't speak as Morland unlocked the cemetery gate, and the two men entered.

A second car, a station wagon, came up the road. Morland and the scarecrow stopped to watch it approach. It pulled up alongside the first vehicle, and an elderly woman emerged from the driver's side. Two more men climbed out of the back, although one of them needed the assistance of his companion and the woman to do so. He wore a small oxygen tank strapped to his back, and a mask covered his mouth. Supported by the others, he made his way into the churchyard.

Finally, from the northwest, came the pastor, but he

wasn't alone. There was a girl of eighteen or nineteen with him. She wore a padded jacket over what looked like a nightgown, and there were unlaced sneakers on her feet. Her hands were restrained behind her back, and tape covered her mouth. To her right walked another man, a decade or so older than the pastor. He held the girl's right arm above the elbow, guiding her so that she wouldn't trip over the old gravestones, whispering and smiling as he did so. The girl didn't struggle or try to run. Ronald wondered if she was drugged, for her eyes drooped slightly, and she dragged her feet as she came.

She was brought to the place by the western wall of the church from which Warraner had cleared the undergrowth earlier that day. Ronald tried to get closer to them, but he didn't want to risk making a noise and alerting the group below. He contented himself with shifting position slightly so that he might see more clearly what was happening. It was a still, quiet night, and the voices of the group carried to him if he listened carefully. He heard Warraner tell the girl to rest, that they were almost done. The man who held her arm assisted her as she sank to her knees, and the others formed a semicircle around her, almost obscuring her from sight. A blade appeared, and Ronald drew a breath. He put down the binoculars and switched to the night-vision scope on his rifle. It wasn't as powerful, and didn't give him such a wide view of proceedings, but if anyone tried to take the knife to the girl, then, cop or no cop, he planned to cut them down before the metal touched her skin. The Browning was self-loading, which gave him four shots before he'd have to pause.

But the knife was used only to cut the bonds holding the girl's hands. Ronald watched them fall loosely to her sides, and then the man who had been assisting her removed the padded jacket, leaving her with only the nightgown as protection against the cold. Through Ronald's scope she looked like a pale ghost in the churchyard. He fixed his sights on the man with the knife and waited, his finger not quite touching the trigger of the rifle, but the blade disappeared, and none of the others was holding a weapon.

They backed away from the girl, partially obscuring Ronald's view of her. He could still see her nightgown, though, white against the dark. He moved his sights from one back to the next, watching for movement, waiting for someone to produce a gun or knife, to make a move on the girl, but nobody did. Instead, they appeared to be waiting.

Ronald moved back to what he could see of the girl, and a finger of shadow crept across the pallor of her nightgown, as though the moon had suddenly shone on an overhanging branch.

But there was no branch, and there was no moon.

A second shadow came, and a third, like cracks on ice. There was a flurry of movement, a blur of white, and a single dull snap, as of a bone breaking. The watching elders came together, and for an instant the girl's form was entirely hidden from Ronald.

When they separated again, she was gone.

Ronald removed his eye from the scope and blinked. It wasn't possible. He scanned the ground, but there was no sign of the girl in the white nightgown. Even had it somehow been stripped from her, her naked body would have been visible on the ground, but Ronald could see nothing.

Now the group was dispersing. Warraner was heading back to his house, while the man who had come with him joined the others as they returned to their cars. Within minutes, the gates were locked once again, and the vehicles were making their way back down the road to the highway, still driving without lights.

Ronald waited for fifteen minutes, then headed for the cemetery. He climbed the railing, heedless now of any hidden sensors, and approached the spot where he had last seen the girl. He knelt, and discerned signs of disturbance. Clumps of earth had been dislodged from the dry ground, and there were marks in the dirt where something had briefly been dragged through it. They ended where the hole once lay, but it had now collapsed, leaving only a slight depression in the ground.

Ronald put his rifle aside and started to scrabble at the dirt with his bare hands. He dug until one of his fingernails cracked, but there was no trace of the girl, only earth and thick roots, although Ronald couldn't tell their origin, for there were no trees in the cemetery. He sat back on the ground, breathing heavily. Above him, the old church loomed.

A fragment of something pale caught his eye. Lodged against a small stone in the dirt was a piece of pale cloth about half an inch square. Ronald held it between his finger and thumb.

I am not mad, he thought. I am not mad.

He picked up his rifle and, using his boots, tried to hide his efforts at digging. When he felt that he had done all he could, he returned to his hiding place, gathered his belongings, and prepared to leave. He checked to make sure that he had not left behind any trash or possessions, even though he knew himself to be more careful than that. Still, it paid to take the time to be sure. When he was done, he started walking. It was not yet 11 P.M., and by traveling carefully he made it to the town of Dearden shortly before midnight, where he huddled down at the outskirts and made himself as comfortable as possible against a tree. He called just one number along the way, but it was not 911. He used a cup of coffee to warm himself, but it didn't stop his shivering, and his whole body was aching by the time the truck arrived. The Fulci brothers helped him inside, and drove him back to Scarborough.

XLV

Angel and Louis were parked close to the intersection of Amity and Henry, about four blocks south of Hunts Lane. They spoke as they walked, heads down against the rain.

"So?" said Angel.

"He's not telling us all he knows," said Louis.

"But you believed what he did tell us?"

"Yes."

"Why?"

"Because there was a percentage in keeping information back from us, but none in lying, and he's a man who works the percentages. He wasn't the middleman on the hit, but he has more information about who was responsible than he's shared with us."

"You could tell that just by looking in his eyes?"

"I understand him. And I know that he's scared of me."

"It's not a very exclusive club."

"No, but not everyone in it has the resources to make

a move against one of my friends. Cambion does, but he's smart enough to know that if he involved himself he'd have to take me out as well, and that didn't happen."

"Which means that the shooters either don't know about you or don't care."

"And you just know that it can't be the latter."

"God forbid. You'd have no reason left to live."

"Exactly."

"So what's Cambion holding back on the shooters?"

"Their names. Cambion doesn't trade in rumors. Maybe they crossed his path once. He might even have tried to recruit them."

"And, like you, they turned him down."

"But, unlike me, they sound like religious zealots."

"True. Nobody could ever accuse you of darkening church doors, not unless you were planning to shoot somebody from the shadows. So Cambion is waiting for you to get the contract voided, and then he'll give you more?"

"That would be my guess, theoretically."

"Can you do it? Can you burn the contract?"

"No. It's gone too far. There are too many people with an interest in seeing Cambion dead, either for what he's done or for what he knows."

"But if Cambion is as clever as you say, he must realize that."

"Probably."

"Then what's the game?"

"He's trying to buy time. Like I told you, he works the percentages. I think he knows exactly who we're looking for, so right now he's trying to figure if the people who were sent after Parker are more dangerous than I am. If they are, then he can sell me out to them in return for whatever it is he needs—money, a hiding place, or most likely the heads of some of those who are hunting him. If Cambion doesn't believe the shooters are good enough to take me out he'll feed them to us, but he'll wait until we have more to offer him. I don't think he was lying when he said he wanted to live out the rest of his days in peace. He wants a guarantee of protection, but he knows that's more than I alone can give him."

Angel considered this.

"Feds," he said, after a time. "He wants a government screen."

"Feds," confirmed Louis.

"But we only know one Fed."

"That's right."

"And he doesn't like you and me."

"No, but right now I'd say he's real interested in us."

"How can you be sure?"

"Because I reckon that's who's been following us for the last two blocks."

"The big blue Ford? I was wondering about that. Maybe he figures he's undercover."

"I don't think he cares."

Louis stepped out into the street in front of the creeping car, put his fingers to his lips, and gave a piercing whistle as it braked within feet of him.

"Yo, taxi!" he said.

Through the wipers and the rain, Special Agent Ross, of the Federal Bureau of Investigation, grimaced at him. His lips moved soundlessly as Angel joined Louis. Angel cupped a hand to his ear.

"Sorry, 'mother-what?'" said Angel.

The second time, Ross shouted the word, just to make sure.

THEY SAT TOGETHER IN Henry Public, at 329 Henry. Each ordered a Brooklyn Brown Ale. It seemed only right, given the neighborhood. They were almost alone in the bar, given the hour.

"I'll pay," said Ross, as the beers were brought to their table. "It's bad enough that I'm sitting with you. I don't want to be accused of corruption as well."

"Hey, wasn't this how that Fed in Boston got caught, the one who was tight with Whitey Bulger?" said Angel. "One minute you're just enjoying a drink with friends in Southie, the next you're doing forty years."

"To begin with, we're not friends," said Ross.

"I'm hurt," said Angel. "Now how am I going to get my parking violations fixed?"

"That's the fucking NYPD, knucklehead," said Ross.

"Ah, right," said Angel. He took a sip of his beer. "But suppose I get ticketed in DC?"

"Fuck you."

"You know, you swear more than the Feds on TV."

"I only swear under stress."

"You must be stressed a lot."

Ross turned to Louis.

"Is he always like this?" said Ross.

"Pretty much."

"I never thought I'd say it, but you must be a fucking saint."

"I believe so," said Louis. "He also has his uses."

"I don't even want to know," said Ross.

He took a long draft from his bottle.

"You been to see him?"

"Parker?" said Louis.

"No, the new pope. Who the fuck else would I be talking about?"

A look passed between Angel and Louis. Angel wanted to go up to Maine, but Louis had demurred. He believed they could be of more use to Parker in New

York. He was right, of course, but it still sat uneasily with Angel. He was deeply fond of the detective. If Parker wasn't going to pull through, Angel wanted to be able to say his goodbye.

"No," said Louis. "They say he's dying."

"That's what I hear."

"Is it true?"

"He's like a cat: he has nine lives. I just don't know how many of them he's used up by now."

They let that one sink in while they drank.

"What do you want, Agent Ross?" said Louis.

"My understanding is that you're turning the town upside down trying to find out who shot him. I was wondering how far you'd got."

"Is this an attempt at an information exchange?" said Louis. "If so, you're about to be gravely disappointed."

"I know who you were seeing in Hunts Lane," said Ross.

Louis's left eye flickered. For him, it was an expression of extreme surprise, the equivalent of someone else fainting. Ross caught it.

"How fucking inefficient do you think we are?" he said.

"Is that a rhetorical question?"

"You want to see my file on you?"

Louis let that one pass.

"How long have you been watching him?" said Angel.

"Ever since he got back into town," said Ross. "How's he looking? We haven't been able to get a clear shot of him. The last pictures we had of him, he wasn't doing so good."

"He's probably still having a little trouble dating," said Angel.

"Was he involved?"

Ross watched them both, and waited. He was very patient. A full minute went by, but he didn't seem perturbed.

"No," said Louis, eventually. "Or not directly."

"Were you planning on bringing him in?" said Angel.

"We've got nothing but stories. We do hear there's money for whoever pushes the button on him, though." His gaze flicked back to Louis. "I thought you might be looking to cash in."

"You got the wrong guy," said Louis.

"Clearly."

"Were you listening?"

"I wish. He hasn't left that old store since he took up residence. There's no landline. If he's using cell phones, they're throwaways. He conducts all his business away from the windows, which means we can't pick up vibrations, especially with all those drapes."

"So?" said Louis.

"My understanding is that he's been making informal approaches, looking to have the contract lifted. Is it true?"

Again Louis waited awhile before answering. Angel remained silent. If this was to be an exchange, it was for Louis to decide how much to give and what he wanted in return.

"That's true," said Louis. "You considering offering him a deal?"

"Our understanding is that he holds a lot of secrets."

"He'll bleed you for every one he reveals, and you'll never get him to testify."

"Maybe we don't want testimony," said Ross. "Maybe we just want details. It's not just about putting people behind bars. It's about knowledge."

Angel thought of the list of names now in Louis's possession. It might be worth something. Then again, it might be worth nothing at all. The truth, in all likelihood, lay somewhere in between.

Ross finished his first beer and held up the bottle, signaling the waitress for another round, even though Louis had barely touched his first drink.

"I heard he tried to bring you into his fold," Ross said to Louis. "Way back in the day."

"Not so far back," said Louis.

"You didn't bite?"

"Like you, he seemed to be confused about what I did for a living."

"And you didn't like him."

"There wasn't a great deal to like. Even less now, seeing as so much of him has rotted away."

The second beers arrived, but no one reached for them. Angel sensed that they had reached a crucial point in whatever negotiation was unfolding, although, as far as he could tell, there didn't seem to have been much obvious progress of any kind. Angel wasn't built for negotiation. That U.N. job just got further out of reach every day.

"I'll ask you again," said Louis. "What is it you want from me, Agent Ross?"

He fixed Ross with his gaze, like a snake mesmerizing an animal before striking. Ross didn't blink. He'd taken the "three guys having a beer approach," and that hadn't worked. He must have known that it wouldn't, but it never hurt to try. As Angel watched, he transformed himself, sitting up straighter in his seat, his face tightening, the years seeming to fall away from him. In that moment, Angel understood why Parker had always been so careful around Ross. Like Cambion, he was a creature of concealment, a repository of secrets.

"I came to warn you that I won't tolerate a campaign of vengeance, even for your friend. I won't tolerate it because I'm concerned that it might interfere with my own work, with the bigger picture. For every man or woman you kill, a potential avenue of inquiry closes. That's not how this thing works."

"And what is the 'bigger picture,' Agent Ross?" asked Angel. "What is 'this thing'?"

"The hunt for something that's been hidden away since before the appearance of life on earth," said Ross. "An entity, long buried. Is that big enough for you?"

Angel picked up his beer.

"You know," he said, "maybe I will have this second one after all."

He drained half the bottle.

"And you believe in the existence of this 'entity'?" said Louis.

"It doesn't matter what I believe. What matters are the beliefs of those who are looking for it, and the havoc they've created, and will continue to create, until they're stopped."

"So you want us to step back and do nothing?" said Louis.

"I'm not a fool," said Ross. "Doing nothing isn't an option where you're concerned. I want cooperation. You share what you find."

"And then you tell us if we can act on it?" said Louis. "That sounds like the worst fucking deal since the Indians got screwed for Manhattan."

"It also sounds like a good way to end up in jail," said Angel. "We might as well just sign a confession in advance. We tell you what we'd like to do, you say, 'Hey, that sounds like a fucking great idea. Be my guest!' and next thing we're all staring awkwardly at one another in front of a judge."

"He has a point," said Louis. "No deal."

To his credit, Ross didn't appear particularly sur-

prised or disappointed. Instead, he reached into his
pocket and removed a manila envelope. From it he slid
a single photograph and placed it on the table before
them. It showed the symbol of a pitchfork, crudely
carved into a piece of wood. Louis and Angel knew
it immediately for what it was: the sign of the Believers. Parker had crossed paths with them in the past,
Angel and Louis too. The Believers hadn't enjoyed the
encounters.

"Where was it taken?" said Angel.

"At Parker's house, immediately after the attack.
Now do you understand why I'm asking you to tread
carefully?"

Louis used the edge of his bottle to turn the photograph
so that he could see it more clearly.

"Yes," he said. "I understand."

It was Louis's turn to produce an envelope from his
pocket. He handed it to Ross without comment. Ross
opened it and glanced at a typewritten list of names, places,
and dates. He didn't need Louis to tell him what it meant.

"From Cambion?" said Ross.

"Yes."

"Why did he give it to you?"

"He thought I could act as the go-between in his contract difficulties."

"What did you get in return?"

"It doesn't matter."

Ross folded the list and returned it to the envelope.

"Why are you giving this to me?"

"It's what you wanted, right?"

"Yes."

"Now you don't need to cut a deal with him, and you
can call off your surveillance."

"Leaving him at your mercy."

"I don't have any mercy for him."

"Should that concern me?"

"I don't see why."

Ross balanced the envelope on the palm of his right hand, as though judging its weight against the cost to his soul.

"You went to Cambion because you thought he knew something about the hit on Parker," said Ross. "I'll bet a shiny new quarter that he gave you a taste of what he had, but you believe there may be more. Negotiating on his behalf was part of the deal. Don't bother telling me if I'm warm. I wouldn't want you to feel compromised."

"I'm a long way from feeling compromised, Agent Ross," said Louis.

"But now you've got nothing," said Ross.

"Except a clear run at Cambion, if I need it, right?"

The envelope stayed on Ross's palm for a few seconds longer, then vanished into his pocket.

"Right," he said. "And Parker?"

"If it leads us to the Believers, I'll let you know through the rabbi, Epstein. Otherwise, you stay out of our affairs."

"You're an arrogant sonofabitch, you know that?"

"At least you didn't call me uppity. That might have caused serious friction."

Ross stood and dropped a fifty on the table.

"It's been a pleasure doing business with you, gentlemen," he said.

"Likewise," said Louis.

"You're sure you can't help with parking violations?" said Angel.

"Fuck you," said Ross.

"I'll hold on to your number anyway," said Angel. "Just in case."

XLVI

Angel and Louis didn't speak again until they were back in their apartment, as Louis was concerned that Ross might have decided to cover himself by bugging their car. A subsequent sweep of the vehicle revealed nothing, though. It didn't matter; Louis hadn't survived this long by being careless, and Angel really didn't have anything better to do than sweep the car for listening devices, or so Louis told him.

They were greeted on their return by Mrs. Bondarchuk, the old lady who lived in the apartment below theirs. Mrs. Bondarchuk, in addition to being their sole neighbor, was also their sole tenant, the building being owned by one of Louis's shelf companies. Mrs. Bondarchuk kept Pomeranians, on which she lavished most of her love and attention, Mr. Bondarchuk having long since departed for a better place. For many years Angel and Louis had labored under the misapprehension that Mr. Bondarcuk was dead, but it had recently emerged that he had simply bailed in 1979, and his better place was Boise, Idaho—"better" being a relative term in an unhappy marriage. Mrs. Bondarchuk didn't miss him. She explained that her husband had left rather than be killed by her. The Pomeranians were a more than satisfactory replacement, despite their yappy natures, although Mrs. Bondarchuk raised exclusively male dogs, and made sure to have them neutered at the earliest opportunity, which suggested to Angel and Louis that she retained some residual hostility toward Mr. Bondarchuk.

Mrs. Bondarchuk defended the noisiness of her Pomeranians on the grounds that it made them good watchdogs, and hence they constituted a virtual alarm system of their own. Louis took this with good grace, even though the building had the kind of alarm system that governments might envy, and that usually only governments could afford.

Some years earlier there had been what Mrs. Bondarchuk continued to refer to as "the unpleasantness," during which an effort had been made to access the building through hostile means, an effort that ultimately concluded with the deaths of all those responsible. It was an incident that failed to trouble the police, once Angel had explained to Mrs. Bondarchuk, over milk and chocolate cake, the importance of sometimes avoiding the attentions of the forces of law and order, such forces perhaps not always understanding that there were times when violence could be met only with violence. Mrs. Bondarchuk, who was old enough to remember the arrival of the Nazis in her native Ukraine, and the death of her father during the encirclement of Kiev, actually proved very understanding of this point of view. She told a startled Angel that she and her mother had transported weapons for the Ukrainian partisans, and she had watched from a corner as her mother and a quartet of other widows castrated and then killed a private from the German police-battalion 'Ostland' who had been unfortunate enough to fall into their clutches. In her way, as a Jew whose people had been slaughtered at Minsk and Kostopil and Sosenki, she knew better than Angel the importance of keeping some things secret from the authorities, and the occasional necessity of harsh reprisals against degenerate men. Ever since then, she had become even more protective of her two neighbors than before, and they, in turn, ensured that her rent was nominal and her comforts were guaranteed.

Now, with Mrs. Bondarchuk greeted and the building secured, the talk turned once more to the events of that evening as Louis poured two glasses of Meerlust Rubicon from South Africa, a suitably wintry red. Flurries of snow obscured the view through the windows, but they were halfhearted and ultimately inconsequential, like the parting shots of a defeated army. Angel watched as Louis shed his jacket and rolled up his shirtsleeves. The shirt was immaculately white, and as smooth as it had been before it was worn. It never failed to amaze Angel how his partner's appearance could remain so pristine. If Angel even looked at a shirt, it started to wrinkle. The only way he could have worn a white shirt for an evening and returned home without evidence of grievous use was to add so much starch to it that it resembled the top half of a suit of armor.

"Why did you give Ross those names?" Angel asked. He spoke without a hint of accusation or blame. He was simply curious to know.

"Because I don't like Cambion, and I'll be happy when he's dead." Louis swirled the wine in his glass. "Did you notice anything odd about Cambion's little pied-à-terre?"

"If I knew what that was, I might be able to answer. I'll take a guess that you're talking about the apothecary."

"You have a lot of room for self-improvement."

"Then you have something to look forward to. And, in answer to your question, there was *only* odd when it came to Cambion's little whatever-you-said."

"I counted three soup bowls, one of them plastic. I didn't count but two people."

"One of the bowls could have been from earlier."

"Maybe."

"But you don't think so."

"The place was old, and weird, but it was tidy. Apart from those bowls."

"A plastic bowl," said Angel. "You think he has a child in there?"

"I don't know. I just don't think he and his boy Edmund are the only ones holed up in that old store."

"You planning on going back there to clarify the situation?"

"Not yet. We're prioritizing."

"On that subject: you gave Ross the list, but what did we get in return?"

"We know that the Believers had nothing to do with the hit."

Angel wondered if the wine and the two earlier beers had somehow interacted disastrously, destroying some of his already threatened brain cells. Ross had shown them a picture. Had Ross been lying?

"What about the photograph?"

"The photograph is meaningless. It's a false trail. These people, or whatever they are, they don't sign their names. That's for dime-store novels. You think I ever put a bullet in a man, then rolled up a business card and stuck it in the hole because it pays to advertise?"

Angel doubted it, but you never knew.

"You think Ross figures it's a false trail?"

"Ross don't care one way or the other. It's one more nail in their coffin, and it don't matter to him who hammered it in."

"Doesn't. It *doesn't* matter. You have inconsistent grammar, you know that?"

Louis's public and private personae were different, but sometimes he forgot which role he was supposed to be playing.

"Fuckin' Ross was right about you, you know *that*?" said Louis.

"Ross can't even get a parking ticket fixed. He said so

himself. So we go back to Cambion and tell him what—that we sold out his future to the Feds? Or do we just lie and make out like you're still trying to burn the contract?"

"Neither. I know people in the Carolinas. If there's a team of husband-and-wife shooters operating out of there, someone's got to have heard."

"Not if they're selective. Not if they don't work for money but out of some misguided sense of purpose."

"What, you mean like us?"

"Exactly like us, except without the religion."

"Yeah, and look how hard we were to find. It wasn't so long ago we had delivery men with explosives trying to blow our door off, and tonight Ross could have run our asses over if he'd felt like it. But we'll nail them, however long it takes."

"And then?"

"We make them talk."

"And after that?"

Louis tried the wine. It was good.

"We kill them."

LOUIS WAS CORRECT IN more than one of his assumptions. Even the most cautious of men can be found, if his pursuer has the commitment and the resources. The man who stood at the rain-soaked corner on the Upper West Side, where the poor were in sight of the rich and, more worryingly for those who feared imminent societal collapse, the rich were in sight of the poor, had spent a long time, and a not inconsiderable amount of money, trying to establish where Angel and Louis lived. In the end, it was the attack on the building—"the unpleasantness" over which Angel and Mrs. Bondarchuk had bonded—that brought them to his attention. Louis had made every effort to ensure that word of what happened didn't leak to the police, but the man on the corner represented a different form of law and justice, and such matters were very difficult to keep from him and his father.

The Collector cupped his hands over the match and held it to the cigarette at his lips, then smoked it with the butt held between the thumb and index finger, the remaining fingers sheltering it from the rain. He had arrived just as Angel and Louis entered the building. He did not know where they had been, but he could guess: they would be tracking those responsible for the attack on the detective. The Collector admired their single-mindedness, their focus: no mercy dash north to be at the detective's bedside, none of the fruitless beating at the darkness that comes from those who have grief without power, and anger without an object. They would even have set aside their pursuit of the Collector himself in order to concentrate on the more immediate matter. The Collector knew that most of that impetus probably came from Louis, but his lover was not to be underestimated either. Emotionless killers rarely survived for long. The trick was not to stifle the emotions but to control them. Love, anger, grief—all were useful in their way, but they needed to be kept in check. The one called Angel enabled Louis to do this. Without him, Louis would have died long ago.

But Angel was dangerous too. Louis would calculate the odds and, if the situation wasn't to his liking, back off and wait for a better opportunity to strike. The logician in him was always at the fore. Angel was different. Once he made the decision to move, he would keep coming at his target until one of them went down. He knew how to channel emotion as a weapon. That kind of force and determination wasn't to be underestimated. What most people failed to realize was that fights were decided in the opening seconds, not the closing ones, and there was something about facing an attacker of apparently relentless belligerence that could psychologically undo even a bigger, stronger opponent.

But what was strangest of all for the Collector, as he assessed these two men, was the realization that he had come to admire them. Even as they hunted him from nest to nest, and destroyed the hiding places that he had so carefully constructed for himself, he was in awe of their ferocity, their guile. Neither could he deny that he and these men, through their allegiance to Parker, were engaged in variations on the same work. True, the Collector had been forced to kill one of their number, but in that he had erred. He had let emotion get the better of him, and he accepted that he must pay a price for his lapse. The loss of his nests had been the price, but now he was tiring of the chase. He would give these two men what they wanted in order to secure a truce. If they did not agree, well, there was work to be done, and their pursuit of him was getting in the way of it. The distraction and threat that they posed, and the time and effort they were causing him to expend, enabled men and women of profound viciousness to continue to prey on those weaker than themselves. Judgments were waiting to be handed out. His collection needed to be replenished.

He called Eldritch from a pay phone. Over the old man's objections, the Collector had secured the services of a nurse for the period of his enforced absence. The Collector trusted the nurse implicitly. She was a niece of the woman who had kept Epstein's office in order, and put warmth in his bed, until her recent passing. She was discreet, and selectively deaf, mute, and blind.

"How are you feeling?" said the Collector.

"I'm well."

"The woman is taking good care of you?"

"I can take care of myself. She just gets in the way."

"Consider it a favor to me. It puts my concerns at rest."

"I'm touched. Have you found them?"

"Yes."

"Have you approached them?"

"No, but soon I'll have a message delivered to them. Tomorrow we will meet."

"They may not agree."

"One is a pragmatist, the other driven by principle. What I offer will appeal to both."

"And if it doesn't?"

"Then this goes on and, inevitably, more blood will be spilled. They will not want that, I guarantee it. I believe that they are as weary of it as I am. The detective is their priority—the detective, and those who pulled the trigger on him. And, who knows, I may manage to negotiate a little extra for us—a prize that you've been seeking for many years."

"And what would that be?"

"The location of a corrupted man," said the Collector. "The lair of a leper."

XLVII

Garrison Pryor's tame cop had experienced difficulty gaining access to the scene of the shooting. Not only was the Scarborough PD all over it; so were the Maine State Police's Major Crimes Unit and the FBI, which had immediately sent agents not just from its field office in Boston but from New York too. The house and its environs had been locked down from the instant the first patrol car arrived, and the flow of information was being tightly controlled amid threats of suspension and possible imprisonment for any breaches by police or emergency personnel.

But, despite all those precautions, Pryor's guy was able to talk to one of the ambulance crew, and—cops being cops—managed to piece together small details just by keeping his mouth shut and listening. Nevertheless, days went by before Pryor learned of the symbol that had been carved into the wood of the detective's kitchen door. The knowledge placed him in a difficult position: should he alert the Principal Backer immediately, or wait until he had clarified the situation? He decided to take the former course of action. He did not want to give the Principal Backer any cause to doubt him, and better to plead ignorance initially, and work to correct it, than be accused of withholding information, leaving himself open to suspicion.

As the morning sun tried to pierce the gray clouds over Boston, the Principal Backer listened in silence while Pryor communicated what he had learned. The Principal Backer was not the kind of man who interrupted, or who tolerated being interrupted in turn.

"Well, was this the work of Believers?" he said when Pryor had finished.

"It's possible," said Pryor. "But, if so, it's not any of whom we have knowledge. There's no connection to us."

He didn't need to mention that most of the Believers were dead. Only a handful had ever existed to begin with, and the detective and his allies had wiped most of those out. Although it had never been formally discussed, many of the Backers regarded the elimination of the Believers as something of a blessing. Each group had its own obsessions, its own motives, and while its ultimate aims sometimes intersected or followed a similar path, neither party entirely trusted the other. But generations of Backers had been content to use the Believers when it suited them. Some had even allied themselves to the Believers' cause. Connections existed.

"If someone is scratching the Believers' symbol into the woodwork of scenes of attempted murder, then there is potentially a connection to all of us," said the Principal Backer. "Any investigation could damage us."

"It may be the action of renegades," said Pryor. "If so, they could be difficult to find. We know the identities of the ones who have crossed Parker. Any others have kept themselves hidden, even from us. Ultimately, my instinct says that the symbol is a false trail. Whoever carried out the attack, or ordered it to be carried out, wants to divert attention from themselves."

"There are those who would willingly use even a suspicion of involvement to act against us. What of the detective?"

"His condition remains critical. Privately, the doctors are suggesting that he won't survive. Even if he does, he will not be the same man. Perhaps he has no part to play in what is to come after all."

"Perhaps not, or it could be that his role has simply changed."

Laurie, Pryor's personal assistant, knocked at his office door. He waved her away in irritation. How urgent could it be? If there was a fire, he'd hear the alarm bells.

But she persisted, and her face contorted into a rictus of anxiety.

"Sir, I may have to get back to you," said Pryor.

"Is there a problem?"

"I think so."

He hung up the phone, and Laurie immediately entered.

"I had asked—" he began, but she cut him off.

"Mr. Pryor, there are agents from the Economic Crimes Unit downstairs. Security is trying to delay them, but they have warrants."

The Economic Crimes Unit was the branch of the FBI's Financial Crimes Divison tasked with investigating securities and commodities fraud, among other areas. The Principal Backer's fears were being realized. The attack on the detective had given their enemies an opening. This might just be a fishing expedition, but through it a message was being sent to them.

We know of you.

We *know*.

WHILE GARRISON PRYOR PREPARED to confront the federal investigators, Angel called Rachel Wolfe. She had just returned to her home in Vermont, having spent a couple of nights in Portland to be close to the father of her child. Her daughter had not stayed with her. Rachel felt that it was important for Sam to continue her routines, and not be engaged in some ongoing deathwatch, but she had been permitted to see him briefly in the ICU. Rachel was worried about exposing Sam to the sight of her father lying broken and dying in a hospital bed, but the child had insisted. Jeff, Rachel's partner, drove Sam over to Portland, then took her home again. He might not have been particularly enamored of Rachel's former lover, but he had behaved sensitively since the attack, and she was grateful to him for it. Now Rachel spoke to Angel of tubes and needles, of wounds and dressings. One kidney gone. Shotgun pellets painstakingly removed from his skull and back, including a number perilously close to his spine. Potential nerve damage to one arm. Murmurs of possible brain injury. He remained in a coma. His body appeared to have shut down all but the most essential of systems in order to fight for survival.

"How did Sam do?" asked Angel.

"She didn't shed a tear," said Rachel. "Even Jeff looked broken up, and he doesn't even like Charlie. But Sam, she just whispered something to him, and wouldn't tell me what it was. Apparently she was quiet on the ride home. She didn't want to speak. Then, when Jeff looked back at her somewhere around Lebanon, she was fast asleep."

"You try talking to her about it since the visit?"

"I'm a psychologist—all I ever do is talk about things. She seems . . . fine. You know what she told me? She said she thought her daddy was deciding."

"Deciding what?"

"If he wanted to live or die."

And Rachel's voice broke on the last word.

"And how are you doing?"

He could hear her trying to control herself, trying not to cry.

"Okay, I guess. It's complicated. I feel disloyal to him, somehow, like I abandoned him. Does that make any sense?"

"It's guilt."

"Yes."

"For fucking an asshole like Jeff."

She couldn't help but splutter with laughter.

"You're the asshole, you know that?"

"I get that a lot."

"Jeff's been good, you dick. And, hey, you know what the weirdest thing about being at that hospital was?"

"I get the feeling you're going to tell me."

"You bet I am. It was the number of women who kept coming into the place asking about him. It's like waiting by the bedside of King Solomon. There was a little dark-haired cop, and a woman from that town, Dark Hollow. You remember it? You ought to. There was shooting."

Angel winced, not so much at the memory of the town itself but at the mention of the woman. Her name was Lorna Jennings, and she was the wife of the chief of police up in Dark Hollow. There was history there, the kind you didn't want to discuss with the mother of a man's child, even if they were now separated and he was dying in a hospital bed.

"Yeah, it rings a bell."

"Do you remember her?"

"Not so much."

"Liar. Did he sleep with her?"

"I don't know."

"Come on."

"Jesus, I don't know! I don't follow him around with a towel and a glass of water."

"What about the cop?"

That had to be Sharon Macy. Parker had told Angel about her.

"No, he didn't sleep with her. I'm pretty certain of that."

Angel tried to remember a more awkward conversation that he'd had, but failed.

"And there's another woman. She doesn't stray far from the ICU, and I get the impression she has police permission to be there, but she's no cop. She's a deaf mute, and she carries a gun. I've seen how she looks at him."

"Liat," said Angel. Epstein must have sent her to watch over Parker. She was a curious choice of guardian angel. Effective, but curious.

"He slept with her, didn't he? If he didn't, he should have."

What the hell, thought Angel.

"Yeah, he slept with her."

"Trust him to sleep with a woman who couldn't answer back."

"It was just once," said Angel.

"What are you, his personal apologist?"

"You've *made* me his apologist! I only called to see how you were. Now I'm sorry I asked."

Rachel laughed. It was genuine, and he was happy that he had given her that, at least.

"Will you come up to see him?" she asked.

"Soon," he said.

"You're looking for them, aren't you, the ones who did this to him?"

"Yes."

"Nobody ever got this close to him before. Nobody ever hurt him so badly. If he dies . . ."

"Don't say that. Remember what your daughter told you; he's still deciding, and he has a reason to come back. He loves Sam, and he loves you, even if you are fucking an asshole like Jeff."

"Go away," said Rachel. "Do something useful."

"Yes, ma'am," said Angel.

He hung up. Louis stood beside him, waiting. He handed Angel a Beretta 21 fitted with a suppressor that was barely longer than the pistol itself. The Beretta could now be fired in a restaurant and would make a sound only slightly louder than a spoon striking against the side of a cup. Louis carried a similar weapon in the pocket of his Belstaff jacket.

They were off to do something useful.

They were going to meet and, if necessary, kill the Collector.

XLVIII

Ronald Straydeer sat in the living room of his home near the Scarborough Downs racetrack. He held in his hands a photograph of himself as a younger man in uniform, his left arm encircling the neck of a massive German shepherd. In the picture, Ronald was smiling, and he liked to think that Elsa was smiling too.

He wished that he still smoked pot. He wished that he still drank. It would have been easy to return to doing one or the other, or even both. Under the circumstances, it would not have been surprising or blameworthy. Instead, he spoke to the picture, and to the ghost of the dog within it.

He was often asked, by those who didn't know any better, why he hadn't found himself another dog in the intervening years. He knew there were some who said that those who kept dogs had to resign themselves to their eventual loss because of the animals' relatively short lives. The trick—if "trick" was the right word—was to learn to love the spirit of the animal, and to recognize that it transferred itself from dog to dog, with each one representing the same life force. Ronald believed that there might be some sense in this, but he felt, too, that men might equally say the same thing about women, and vice versa. He had known plenty of women, and had even loved one or two of them, so he had a degree of experience in the matter. But some men and women lost a partner early in life and never managed to give themselves again to another. Ronald thought there might have been something of that catastrophic sense of loss to his feelings for his abandoned dog. He wasn't a sentimental man—although, again, some mistook his grieving for a dead animal as sentimentality. Ronald Straydeer had simply loved the dog, and Elsa had saved his life and the lives of his brother soldiers on more than one occasion. In the end, he was forced to abandon and betray her, and the sight of her, caged and scratching at the wire as she was taken from him, had torn at him every day since then. His only hope was that he might eventually be reunited with his dog in a world beyond this one.

Now he told the ghost of the dog about the church, and the girl, and the shadows that had encircled her before she was dragged beneath the ground. He could have gone to the police, but there was a policeman involved. And what could he have told them—that he saw a girl kneel by a hole in the earth and then disappear? All he had was a fragment of pale material. Could they extract DNA from it? Ronald didn't know. It depended, he supposed, on whether it had touched the girl's skin for long enough, if it had touched her at all. He had placed the material in one of the resealable bags that he used for food and waste. It was before him now. He held it up to the light, but he could see no traces of blood on it, and it seemed to be stained only by dirt. He didn't know her name, and he wasn't sure if he could have identified her from the glimpse that he caught of her in the greenish light of his night-vision lens. He knew only that she was not Jude's daughter. He had seen photographs of Annie. Jude had shared them with him, and Ronald retained an uncanny recall for faces and names. The girl swallowed by the churchyard was younger than Jude's daughter. Ronald wondered if Annie too lay somewhere in that cemetery, if her fate had been the same as that poor girl's. If so, how many others slept beneath the church, embraced by roots? (For those were not shadows that had wrapped themselves around the girl before she was taken. Oh, no . . .)

But Ronald also understood instinctively that, even if people were to believe him and a search was eventually conducted, men could dig long and deep in that church-yard without finding any trace of the girl. As he worked at the collapsed earth with his bare hands, hoping to reveal some sign of her, he had felt the presence of a perfect and profound hostility, a malevolent hunger given form. It was this more than any inability to keep digging that had caused him to abandon his efforts to find a body. Even now, he was glad that he had used the water in the Fulcis' truck to clean his hands of the soil from that place, and one of their towels to dry them, and had then disposed of the towel in a Dumpster so that it wouldn't be used again. He was grateful not to have contaminated his home with even a fragment of that cursed earth, and he kept sealed the bag containing the piece of material lest some minute particle of grit should fall from it and pollute all.

The detective would have known what to do, but he was dying. He had friends, though: clever men, dangerous men. Right now, those men would be looking for the ones responsible for shooting him. Ronald didn't find it hard to make a connection between the detective's inquiries into the disappearance of Annie Broyer and the sight of an unknown girl being dragged beneath the ground while a group of men and one woman watched. It wasn't much of a stretch from there to imagine a set of circumstances in which those same people might have seen fit to try and take the detective's life.

And if he was wrong? Well, the men who stood by the detective were more like him than perhaps even they knew, and they had wrath to spare. Ronald would find a way to contact them, and together they would avenge those trapped in uneasy rest beneath the dirt of Prosperous.

AS RONALD STRAYDEER SAT in contemplation and mourning, the bodies of Magnus and Dianne Madsen, and Erin Dixon, were discovered by the police after Magnus failed to appear as scheduled for his hospital duties. The Maine State Police informed Lucas Morland of the Prosperous Police Department once Erin's identity was established. With both Kayley Madsen and Harry Dixon apparently missing, a patrol car was immediately dispatched to the Dixon house, but there was no sign of Harry or his niece. Their faces duly began showing up on news channels, and an auto dealer in Medway came forward to say that he'd taken a trade-in on a GMC Passenger Van from Harry Dixon just a few days earlier. The van was soon found in a patch of woodland just outside Bangor, with Harry seated at the wheel and holes in his head where the bullet from the gun in his hand had entered and exited. On the seat beside him was a woman's shirt, stained with blood at the collar. Its size matched clothing found in Kayley Madsen's closet, and DNA tests would subsequently confirm that the blood was Kayley's, although no other trace of her was ever found.

"Prosperous: Maine's Cursed Town," read one of the more lurid newspaper headlines in the aftermath. Prosperous crawled with MSP investigators, but Morland handled them all well. He was diligent, cooperative, and unassuming. He knew his place. Only once did he experience a shred of alarm, and that was when an FBI agent named Ross visited from New York. Ross sat in Morland's office, nibbled on a cookie, and asked about the detective Parker. Why had he come to Prosperous? What did he want to know? And then he gave Morland a possible out: had Parker spoken to Harry

Dixon or his wife at any point? Morland didn't know, but he conceded that it was possible, although why Parker might have wanted to meet with the Dixons Morland couldn't say. But anything that linked Parker to the Dixons was good for Morland, and good for Prosperous. That was a dead end, and the FBI and the state police could spend decades peering into it for all Morland cared.

"Can I ask why the FBI is interested in the fact that a private detective was shot in Maine?" said Morland.

"Curiosity," said Ross. Then: "Your town seems to be having a bad time of it lately."

"Yeah," said Morland. "They say these things come in threes."

"Really?" said Ross. "I count, uh—" He worked it out on his fingers. "Six," he concluded. "Or nine, if you include the Madsens and their missing daughter. Or, wow, eleven allowing for that homeless guy in Portland and *his* missing daughter. That's a lot. More than three, anyway."

It wasn't the first time Morland had heard something of the kind. The MSP investigators had intimated as much, and now Morland replied to Ross just as he had responded to them.

"Sir, my reckoning is two killings by religious terrorists thousands of miles from here; one accidental self-inflicted gunshot wound on an elderly man; one automobile incident; and, to our shame and regret, an apparent murder-suicide involving two of our townsfolk. I can't speak to suicides in Portland, or missing girls. I just know what this town has endured. I can't say why Harry Dixon might have killed those people. I heard that he had money problems, but a lot of folk have money problems and don't take a gun to their family as a consequence. It could be that the town's troubles caused something in him to snap. I'm no psychiatrist. But if you can establish a connection between all those disparate events, then I'll never again question the amount of taxes our government plows into the bureau."

Ross finished his cookie.

"And the attempted murder of a private investigator," said Ross. "I almost forgot to add that."

Morland didn't respond. He was all done with the FBI for now.

"Can I help you with anything else today, Agent Ross?"

"No," said Ross. "I think that'll be all. I appreciate your time. And the cookie was very good. My compliments to the baker."

"My wife," said Morland.

"You're a fortunate man," said Ross.

He stood and buttoned his coat before heading out. There was still a chill in the air.

"And this is quite a town. Quite a town indeed."

THIRTY MINUTES LATER, MORLAND received a call from Pastor Warraner.

Ross had been out at the church.

XLIX

At first, Angel and Louis believed the missive from the Collector to be little more than a taunt. It was delivered by a bike messenger, and consisted of a padded envelope containing a single final bear claw from the neck-lace that had once belonged to their friend, the late Jackie Garner, and a business card from the Lexington Candy Shop on Lexington, the old soda-candy store and lun-cheonette that had been in operation at that location since 1925. It was only when Louis turned over the card and saw a date (that same day) and a time (11 A.M.—written on the back) that they understood that this might be different, although whether it would prove to be an olive branch or a trap they were not certain.

Even the Collector's choice of location for the meeting wasn't without resonance: the Lexington Candy Shop was where Gabriel, Louis's late master, would hold his meetings with clients, and sometimes with the operatives for whom he acted as a middleman, Louis among them. Perhaps, thought Louis, the distance between Cambion and Gabriel wasn't as great as Louis might have liked to believe. Gabriel was merely Cambion with a more highly developed moral sense, but that wasn't saying a whole lot. There were things breeding in petri dishes with a more highly developed moral sense than Cambion's. By extension, the distance between Louis and Cambion might well have been signifi-cantly less than it was comfortable to imagine. The differ-ence was that Louis had changed, while Cambion had not. Cambion didn't have a man like Angel by his side, but then a man like Angel would never have allied himself with one such as Cambion to begin with. It made Louis wonder if Angel had seen the possibility of redemption in him long before Louis himself had recognized it. Louis found this simultaneously flattering and slightly worrying.

The Collector's decision to nominate the Lexington Candy Shop as the venue for their meeting was his way of telling Louis that he knew all he needed to know about Louis and his past. It added another layer of peculiarity to the Collector's invitation. This was not the action of a man laying a trap but of a man willingly walking into one.

The only other customers at the diner when Angel and Louis entered were two male Japanese tourists excitedly taking photographs of the interior, with its gas-fired coffee urns and its ancient signage. The Collector sat at the back of the diner, near the door marked NO ADMITTANCE. STAFF ONLY. His hands lay flat on the table before him, resting on either side of a coffee cup. He was dressed as he nearly always was, in a long dark coat worn over dark pants, a dark jacket, and a tieless shirt that had once been white but now, like his nicotine-stained fingertips, had more than a hint of yellow about it. His hair was slicked back from his forehead and hung over the collar of his shirt, adding touches of grease to the yellow. He was, thought Angel, even more cadaverous than when last they'd met. Being hunted will do that to a man.

Once Louis and Angel were inside, a middle-aged woman moved from behind the counter, locked the door, and turned the sign to CLOSED. She then unhurriedly poured two cups of coffee and left through the private staff door without looking at them or at the man who sat waiting for them, stinking of cigarette smoke.

The two Japanese tourists laid down their cameras and turned to face the Collector. The younger of the men signaled almost imperceptibly to a pair of his countrymen watching from the southeastern corner of Lexington and Eighty-Third. One of them now crossed the street to cover the front of the store, while the other watched the side.

"You think I didn't notice them?" said the Collector. "I spotted them before they were even aware of my presence."

Louis sat at the table facing, but to the right of, the Collector, and Angel took a similar position to the Collector's left, forming a kind of lethal triangle. By the time they were seated the guns were in their hands, visible to the Collector but not to anyone glancing in casually from the street.

"We've been looking for you," said Louis.

"I'm aware of that. You must be running out of houses to burn down."

"You could have saved us a lot of gas money by just showing up here months ago."

"And maybe I could have marked the spot on my fore-head for the bullet to enter."

"You should have been more careful about your choice of victims."

Louis reached into his coat pocket with his left hand and withdrew Jackie Garner's bear claw necklace. The claws rattled like bones as he fed them through his fingers. In his right he held the final claw, broken from the necklace and included with the Collector's invitation.

"I might say the same about your late friend," said the Collector.

Slowly, precisely, so as not to cause the men before him to react, he picked up his cup and sipped his coffee.

"We can, if you choose, play the blame game until the sun starts to set, but none of us is that naïve," he said. "Mr. Garner miscalculated, and someone close to me paid the price. I reacted in anger, and Mr. Garner died. You'll for-give me if I refuse to allow someone like you, a man with the blood of both the innocent and the guilty on his hands, to admonish me about the appropriateness or otherwise of killing. Hypocrisy is a particularly galling vice."

Angel inclined slightly toward Louis.

"Are we being lectured by a serial killer?"

"You know, I do believe we are."

"It's a novel experience."

"Yes, it is. I still won't miss him after we kill him."

"No, me neither."

The Collector's hands were, once again, resting on the table. He showed no sign of unease. It might have been that he was not aware of how close he was to death, or he simply might not have cared.

"I hear that your friend, the detective, is dying," he said.

"Or still living," said Angel. "It's a matter of perspective."

"He is an unusual man. I don't claim to understand him, but I would prefer it if he survived. The world is more colorful for his presence. He draws evil to him like moths to light. It makes its practitioners easier to dispose of."

"You come here to deliver a get-well-soon wish?" said Louis. "We'll be sure to pass it on. And if he does die, well, you may just be in a position to express your regrets to him personally."

The Collector stared out the window at the two Japanese men, then took in the second pair in the diner.

"Where do you find these people?" he asked.

"We attract them," said Louis. "Like moths to light," he added, appropriating the Collector's metaphor for himself.

"Is that what you are now? The force of light?"

"In the absence of another."

"Yes, I suspect yours is only reflected light," said the Collector. "You're looking for the ones who shot him. I can help you."

"How?"

"I can give you their names. I can tell you where to find them."

"And why would you do that?"

"To cut a deal. Eldritch is ill. He needs rest, and time to recuperate. The strain of the hunt is telling on him. As for me, it's interfering with my work. While I try to stay one step ahead of you, vicious men and women go unpunished. So I will give you the names, and as part of the bargain you will abandon the hunt. You must be tiring of it as much as I, and you know that your Mr. Garner did wrong. If I hadn't killed him, he would be spending the rest of his days in a cell. In a way, I did him a favor. He wouldn't have lasted long in prison. He wasn't as strong as we are."

Angel's grip tightened on his gun. For this creature to suggest that Jackie's murder was some kind of blessing was almost too much for him to bear.

"At least he'd have received a trial," said Angel.

"I tried him. He confessed. You're speaking of the trappings of legality, and nothing more."

Louis spoke. He said only one word, but it was both a warning and an imprecation.

"Angel."

After a second or two, Angel relaxed.

"You mentioned us backing off as 'part' of the bargain," said Louis. "What's the rest?"

"I know that your search for the ones who did the shooting has brought you into contact with all kinds of interesting individuals. I'm assuming one of those was Cambion."

"Why?"

"Because when you'd exhausted all other avenues, he would have been the only one left. I doubt that he gave you the answers you needed."

"We met him," confirmed Louis.

"And?"

"He told us that a couple, a man and a woman, carried out the attack. He promised more."

"Of course he did. What did he ask in return for the information?"

"The same thing that you just did—for us to call off the dogs. But it's like this: he may be a freak, but he's a freak who didn't kill one of our friends. If it comes down to it, I might be more inclined to take my chances with him."

"You'd be disappointed. He's going to feed you to the shooters, you and your boyfriend. They're potentially more valuable to him than you are. You'll never do his bidding, but they'll owe him a favor, and they're very, very good at what they do."

And Louis understood that the Collector was right. It simply confirmed what Louis had suspected: there would be more benefits to Cambion in siding with the shooters.

"Go on."

"Here is what I'm offering," said the Collector. "I give you the names. In return, I want a truce between us, and I want to know where Cambion is. He is long overdue a blade."

"And if we don't agree?" said Louis. "What if we just decide to kill you here?"

The gun in his hand moved so that it was aiming at the Collector beneath the table. The first shots would take him in the gut, the last in the back of the head as he fell forward and Louis delivered the coup de grâce from above.

The Collector gestured with his right hand toward the chair beside him. On it, unnoticed by Angel and Louis, until now, was a green cardboard folder.

"Open it," he said, as he restored his hands to the table.

Louis stood, never taking his eyes from the Collector as he went to retrieve the folder. The two Asian men in the diner moved too, their guns now visible. The Collector remained very still, his gaze fixed on the tabletop before him. He remained like that as Louis flipped through the file. It contained typewritten sheets, photographs, even transcripts of telephone conversations.

"It's your history," said the Collector. "The story of your life—every killing we could trace, every piece of evidence we could accumulate against you. By good fortune, it was one of a handful of records for which Eldritch retained secure copies. There's enough in there to have damned you, should I have chosen to take the knife to you. If I don't walk safely out of here today, Eldritch will ensure that a copy of it goes to the U.S. Attorney for the Southern District of New York, the New York County District Attorney, twelve different police departments throughout the nation, and the Criminal Investigative Division of the FBI. It should fill in any annoying gaps in their own research."

For the first time, the Collector relaxed. He sat back in his chair and closed his eyes.

"I told you, I'm tired of the hunt," he said. "It ends now. I could have used this material alone to force you to relent, but I feel that I have to make recompense for what happened to Mr. Garner. I want your promise that the chase is over. I want Cambion. In return, you get vengeance for what happened to the detective."

Louis and Angel looked at each other. Louis could see that Angel didn't want to make a deal with this man, but the file had tipped the scales, and Angel, Louis knew, would agree to whatever protected him. Bringing them closer to those who had carried out the attack on Parker would just have to be considered a bonus.

"Agreed," said Louis.

"If the detective survives, I'll take it that your word is a guarantee of his good behavior too," said the Collector. "Otherwise, our truce is void."

"Understood."

"The couple for whom you're looking are named William and Zilla Daund. They live in Asheville, North Carolina. They have two sons, Adrian and Kerr. The sons have no idea of their parents' sideline in killing."

"Who hired them?"

"You'll have to ask them."

"But you know."

"I believe the name Daund comes from the northeast

of England—Durham, or possibly Northumberland. I'll let them fill in any other details themselves. Now, I'd like you to fulfill the second part of our arrangement."

"Cambion is in Hunts Lane, over in Brooklyn," said Louis. "Assuming he hasn't already moved on. He's holed up in an old apothecary."

"Does he have anyone with him?"

"A big man named Edmund."

The Collector stood.

"Then we're done here," he said. "I wish you luck in your investigation."

He buttoned his coat and stepped around the table.

"And you can keep the file," he told Louis as he passed him. "We have more than one copy now."

They let him go, and he lost himself in the crowds on Lexington Avenue.

"I notice that you didn't mention the possibility of a third person at Hunts Lane with Cambion and his buddy," said Angel.

"No," said Louis. "I guess it must have slipped my mind."

L

I sat at the edge of a lake, on a wooden bench painted white. I was cold, even with a jacket on, and I kept my hands in my pockets to hold the worst of the chill at bay. To my left, at the top of a small hill, was the rehabilitation center, an old nineteenth-century sea captain's house surrounded by a series of more recently built single-story redbrick buildings. Evergreen trees bounded the lake, and most of the snow had been cleared from the grass. The grounds were quiet.

All was quiet.

A small black stone lay by my feet. It looked incredibly smooth. I wanted to hold it in my hand. I reached down to pick it up, and found that it was flawed beneath. A shard of it had fallen away, leaving the underside jagged and uneven. I stared out at the still expanse of the lake and threw the stone. It hit the water and the surface cracked like ice, even though it wasn't frozen. The cracks extended away from me and across the lake, then fractured the woods and mountains beyond, until finally the sky itself was shattered by black lightning.

I heard footsteps behind me, and a hand lit upon my shoulder. I saw the wedding ring that it wore. I remembered the ring. I recalled putting it on that finger before a priest. Now one of the nails was broken.

Susan.

"I knew that it wasn't real," I said.

"How?" said my dead wife.

I did not turn to look at her. I was afraid.

"Because I could not remember how I got here. Because there was no pain."

And I was speaking of the wounds left by the bullets, and the wounds left by loss.

"There doesn't have to be any more pain," she said.

"It's cold."

"It will be, for a time."

I turned now. I wanted to see her. She was as she had been before the Traveling Man took his knife to her. And yet she was not. She was both more and less than she once was.

She wore a summer dress, for she always wore a summer dress in this place. In every glimpse of her that I had caught since losing her, she had been wearing the same dress, although at those times I never saw her face. When I did, it was under other circumstances. The dress would be stained with blood, and her features a ruin of red. I had never been able to reconcile the two versions of her.

Now she was beautiful once again, but her eyes were distant, focused elsewhere, as though my presence here had called her from more pleasant business and she wished to return to it as quickly as possible.

"I'm sorry," I said.

"For what?"

"For leaving you. For not being there when he came for you."

"You would have died with us."

"I might have stopped him."

"No. You weren't as strong then, and he had so much rage. So much rage . . ."

Her nails dug into my shoulder, and I was transported with her, back to our home, and together we watched as the Traveling Man had his way with her and our daughter. As he worked, another version of my wife stood behind him, her face a scarlet blur as her head and body shook. This was the one whom I had seen before. This was the wife who walked through my world.

"Who is she?" I asked. "What is she?"

"She is what remains. She is my anger. She is all my hatred and my sorrow, my hurt and my pain. She is the thing that haunts you."

Her hand stroked my cheek. Her touch burned.

"I had a lot of anger," she said.

"So I see. And when I die?"

"Then she dies too."

The remains of our daughter were stretched across her mother's lap. Jennifer was already dead when he began cutting. It was, I supposed, a mercy.

"And Jennifer?"

I felt her hesitate.

"She is different."

"How?"

"She moves between worlds. She holds the other in check. She would not desert you, even in death."

"She whispers to me."

"Yes."

"She writes upon the dust of windowpanes."

"Yes."

"Where is she now?"

"Close."

I looked, but I could not find her.

"I saw her here, in this house, once before."

I had been stalked through these rooms years after their lives were ended, hunted through my former home by a pair of lovers. But my daughter had been waiting for them—my daughter, and the creature of rage she tried to control, but which on that occasion she was content to unleash.

"I'd like to see her."

"She'll come, when she's ready."

I watched the Traveling Man continue his cutting. There was no pain.

Not for me.

WE WERE BACK AT the lake. The cracks and fissures were repaired. The fragile world was undisturbed. I stood by the shore. The water did not lap. There were no waves.

"What should I do?" I asked.

"What do you want to do?" she asked.

"I think I want to die."

"Then die."

I could not see my reflection, but I could see Susan's. In this world, it was she who had substance and I who had none.

"What will happen?"

"The world will go on. Did you think that it revolved around you?"

"I didn't realize the afterlife had so much sarcasm in it."

"I haven't had cause to use it in a while. You haven't been around."

"I loved you, you know."

"I know. I loved you too."

She stumbled over the words, unfamiliar in her mouth, but I sensed that speaking them aloud caused something deep inside her to thaw. It was as though my proximity reminded her of what it had once been like to be human.

"If you stay here," she said, "events will play out without you. The world will be different. You will not be there for those whom you might have protected. Others may take your place, but who can say?"

"And if I go back?"

"Pain. Loss. Life. Another death."

"To what end?"

"Are you asking me your purpose?"

"Perhaps."

"You know what they seek. The One Who Waits Behind the Glass. The God of Wasps. The Buried God."

"Am I supposed to stop them?"

"I doubt that you can."

"So why should I go back?"

"There is no 'should.' If you go back, you do so because

you choose it, and you will protect those who might not otherwise be protected."

She moved closer to me. I felt the warmth of her breath against my face. It bore a trace of incense.

"You wonder why they come to you, why they're drawn to you, these fallen ones." She whispered the words, as though fearful of being overheard. "When you spend time close to a fire, you smell of smoke. These things seek not only their Buried God. They are looking for a fire that they wish to extinguish, but they cannot find it. You have been near it. You have been in its presence. You carry its smoke upon you, and so they come for you."

She stepped away from me. Her reflection receded, then disappeared. I was alone. I closed my eyes. When I opened them again, my daughter was beside me. She put her hand in mine.

"You're cold," said Jennifer.

"Yes." My voice broke on the word.

"Would you like to go for a walk, Daddy?" she asked.

"Yes," I said. "I'd like that very much."

LI

The Battery Park Book Exchange stood in the center of Asheville, North Carolina. It sold rare and used books, to which Louis had no objection, and wine and champagne, to which, if possible, he had even fewer objections.

The woman named Zilla Daund was taking part in a book club in the store. She and four other women were discussing Stacy Schiff's biography of Cleopatra over sparkling wine and the kind of single-mouthful treats that passed for food where thin, attractive women were concerned. Louis sat with a glass of Pinot Noir by his right hand and a copy of *Max Perkins: Editor of Genius*, by A. Scott Berg, on his lap. He had picked up the Berg book because Perkins had edited Thomas Wolfe, probably Asheville's most famous son, and Louis, who couldn't stand Wolfe's writings, was trying to understand why Perkins had bothered. As far as he could tell from reading the relevant sections in Berg's biography, the only reason that Wolfe's début, *Look Homeward, Angel*, was even marginally tolerable was that Perkins had forced Wolfe to remove more than sixty thousand words from it. At Louis's rough estimate, that still left *Look Homeward, Angel*—which, in the store's Scribner edition, ran to about 500 pages—at least 499 pages too long.

Zilla Daund looked like the kind of woman who took reading books very seriously without actually understanding how the act could be enjoyable as well. Her copy of *Cleopatra* was marked with narrow Post-it notes of different colors, and Louis felt certain that the interior was dotted with words such as "Interesting!" "Agree strongly!" and "VIP!" like a high schooler in freshman year working her way through *The Catcher in the Rye* for the first time. She was slim and blond, with the build of a long-distance runner. She might even have been considered good-looking had she not prematurely aged herself through a probable combination of excessive exposure to the elements and a steely determination that had left her brow permanently furrowed and her jaw set in a thin rictus, like a serpent about to strike.

Louis had been watching Daund for the past thirty-six hours, but this was as close as he had yet come to her. It was his way: begin at a distance, then slowly move in. So far, from his brief exposure to her routine, she seemed an ordinary suburban housewife living a moderately comfortable existence. She'd gone to her local gym that morning, training for an hour before returning home to shower and change, then leaving shortly after lunch to come to her book club. The day before, she'd eaten a late breakfast with some friends, shopped at the Asheville Mall, browsed the aisles at Mr. K's Used Books at River Ridge, and had dinner at home with her husband and their younger son—their older son, a sophomore at George Washington University, being currently absent. The younger son was just sixteen, but he wouldn't be coming home for dinner anytime soon. At that precise moment, he was in the back of a van being driven deep into the Pisgah National Forest by two men whose faces he had not even glimpsed before he was snatched. He was probably terrified, but the boy's terror didn't concern Louis. He wanted something to use against the Daunds if they proved unwilling to talk.

Meanwhile, Angel was staying close to William Daund, who was on the faculty of the Department of Literature and Language at the University of North Carolina at Asheville. Louis would have bet a dollar that William Daund had read *Look Homeward, Angel* so often he could recite passages of it by heart. He probably even liked the book. Louis was looking forward to killing him.

Zilla Daund finished giving her opinion on Cleopatra's ruthlessness, which apparently extended to slaughtering her own relatives when the situation required it. "She lived in an age of murder and betrayal," Daund told her friends. "I don't believe that she killed because she liked it. She killed because it was the most effective solution to the problems that she faced."

The other women laughed—that was their funny old Zilla, always following the shortest route between two points, no matter who or what happened to be in the way—and Louis watched as Daund laughed along with them. The group broke up. Louis returned his attention to Maxwell Perkins. In a letter dated November 17, 1936, Perkins was trying to come to terms with the fact that Wolfe was severing ties with him. "I know you would not ever do an insincere thing, or anything you did not think was right," wrote Perkins to Wolfe.

Louis had to admire Perkins's faith, even if he adjudged it ultimately to have been misplaced.

"He ruined Thomas Wolfe, you know."

Louis looked up. Zilla Daund was standing before him, her copy of *Cleopatra* cradled beneath her left arm, her right hidden in a pocket of her coat.

"He did good by Hemingway and Fitzgerald," said Louis. "Can't win 'em all."

He didn't allow his eyes to drift to her right hand. He held her gaze.

"No," she said. "Maybe you can't. Enjoy your wine—and your book."

She walked away, and Louis thought: She's made me, or thinks she has. It didn't matter. If she and her husband were as smart as Cambion and the Collector seemed to think, they must have learned quickly that the private detective they'd tried to kill was different, and that the perpetrators of the attack on him were being hunted not only by the police but by men who weren't unlike themselves. Perhaps they had simply not expected to be found so quickly, if they were found at all. Louis wondered if Cambion had already warned them.

He called Angel as he watched her walk across the street to the parking garage.

"Where is he?"

"In his office," said Angel. "He's been in tutorials since this morning, and he's about to give a class until four."

"If he cancels, call me."

"Why?"

"I think the woman is spooked. If I'm right, she'll contact him. You know where he's parked?"

"Yes."

"Watch the car."

"What about you?"

"I'll take the house. Stay with the husband. And, hey?"

"What?"

"You ever read *Look Homeward, Angel*?"

"Fuck, no. It must be a thousand pages long. Why would I want to do that?"

"I knew there was a reason why I liked you," said Louis.

"Yeah?" said Angel. "Well, if I think of one in return I'll let you know."

LOUIS WAS AHEAD OF the woman all the way. He had parked at a meter just outside the store, so as soon as she was out of sight he left cash for his wine and returned to his car. Angel had already taken care of the house alarm earlier in the day, once he was certain that William Daund was committed to his tutorials. It meant that when Zilla Daund entered the house Louis was waiting for her. She said only one word as she set her bag down, Louis's suppressed .22 inches from her head.

"Fuck."

"I prefer 'fucked,'" said Louis. "And, just for the record, you're wrong about Maxwell Perkins."

He closed the front door with his foot and took a step back from her.

"You know what this is about?" he asked.

"The hit in Maine."

"Someone told you to expect trouble?"

"We knew from the aftershock, but we got a call."

"Cambion?"

She didn't respond.

"Not that it's any consolation, but he told us about you as well," said Louis. "Not everything, but a start."

"Like you say, we got fucked."

"Yes, you did. Drop the bag."

A big purse hung from her left shoulder. He'd watched her as she drank her wine earlier, so he knew that she was right-handed, even before she'd spoken to him with that hand concealed, probably holding a weapon aimed at him. He figured she had at least one gun on her person, and maybe another in the purse.

"If you're armed, you better tell me now."

"In my purse."

"But not your right coat pocket?"

"Oops."

Louis stepped back and told her to let the coat fall from her body. It landed on the wood floor with a heavy thud.

"You got anything else?"

"You're welcome to frisk me."

"We're below the Mason-Dixon Line. Us colored folks got to be careful with the white women down here. I'd prefer it if you just told me."

"Left side, on the belt."

"You expecting war to break out?"

"We live in a dangerous world."

She was wearing a loose-fitting cardigan under a light suit jacket, the kind that would easily cover a gun.

"Use your left hand," Louis said. "Thumb and index finger only. Slowly."

Zilla Daund lowered her left hand, pushed aside her jacket with her forearm, and used the palm of her hand to raise the cardigan, exposing the gun. It looked like a little hammerless S&W 642 in a .38 Special.

"This is awkward," she said. "The holster's tight."

He saw her tense, and was a second ahead of her. She was fast, twisting her body at the same time that she raised her right hand to lash out at him, but by then Louis was already bringing the butt of his gun down on her right temple. He followed her to the floor, wrenching the .38 from its holster and tossing it aside. She was stunned but conscious. He kept the gun at the base of her neck while he pulled her jacket and cardigan to her elbows, trapping her arms, then patted her down. Her jeans were skintight, but he still checked them for a blade. He released her when he was done, and watched as she rearranged her clothing. He found her phone and handed it to her.

"Call your husband," he said.

"Why?"

She looked dazed, but he thought that she might have been exaggerating for his benefit. He allowed her to sit up with her back against the wall, although he insisted that she keep her legs outstretched and her hands away from her body. This would make it harder for her to raise herself up if she tried to attack him again. Louis was under no illusions about how dangerous this woman was.

"Because I know that you called your husband after you spoke to me at the bookstore. My guess is that he's expecting the all clear."

Angel had called Louis when he was within sight of the house to tell him that William Daund was on the move. "Let him come" had been Louis's instruction.

Louis waited while she went to her recent calls and found "Bill." He let the gun touch her left temple as her finger hovered above the call button.

"If I was aware that your husband was coming, then you understand I'm not working alone. Your husband is being followed. If you say anything to alert him, we'll know. This doesn't have to end badly for you."

She stared at him. Any aftereffects, real or feigned, of the blow to her head were now almost entirely gone.

"We both know that's not true," she said. "I've seen your face."

"Ma'am," said Louis, "right now you have no idea just how much worse this could get for you and your family."

It was the mention of her family that did it. This wasn't just about her and her husband.

"Fuck," she said again, softly.

"You were that concerned about the safety of your boys, maybe you should have picked another line of work," said Louis. "Make the call. Raise the volume, but don't put it on speaker."

She did as she was told. Louis listened.

"Zill?" said her husband.

"I'm home," she said. "But we still need to talk."

"I'm on my way. No more over the phone."

"Okay. Just be quick."

The call ended.

"Zill and Bill," said Louis. "Cute."

She didn't reply. He could see her calculating, trying to figure out what moves were open to her. Seconds later, Louis's phone buzzed.

"Angel."

"He's about five minutes from you."

"Stay as close as you can."

"Got it."

Louis continued to point the gun at Zilla Daund.

"Crawl into the kitchen on your belly," he said. "Do it."

"What?"

"If you try to get to your feet, I'll kill you."

"You're an animal."

"Now you're just being hurtful," said Louis. "Kitchen."

He stayed behind her as she crawled, keeping the gun on her all the way. The kitchen was mostly walnut, with a matching table and four chairs at the center. When Zilla Daund reached the table, Louis told her to get up slowly and take a seat facing the door. He removed a cup from a shelf and placed it in front of her. The kitchen extended the width of the house, with a connecting door leading to a big living room with a dining area at one end. Between the table and the connecting door was a refrigerator and a glass-fronted cabinet filled with canned goods. It was there that Louis took up position. He couldn't see the front door, but he could see the woman.

The sound of a car pulling up came from the front of the house. About a minute later, there was the rattle of a key in the door. This was the moment. This was when Zilla Daund would warn her husband.

The door opened. Three things happened almost simultaneously.

Zilla Daund screamed her husband's name and threw herself to the kitchen floor.

William Daund raised the gun that was already in his hand and prepared to fire.

And Angel appeared behind William Daund and killed him with a single suppressed shot to the back of the head. Angel then proceeded into the house and closed the door behind him. He didn't look at Daund's body as he stepped over it. It wasn't callousness. He just didn't want to see what he had done. He checked the street from the living-room window, but there was no indication that anyone had witnessed what had occurred. Then again, they wouldn't know for sure unless the cops arrived on the doorstep. This had to be quick.

When he joined Louis in the kitchen, Zilla Daund was standing by the utility room. She was under Louis's gun, but she had a big kitchen knife in her hand. On whom she intended to try to use it wasn't clear, but turning it on anyone in that room, including herself, wouldn't have a good result.

"You were only ever going to let one of us live," she said.

"No," said Louis. "Neither of you was ever going to live. The first one into the house was just going to live longer."

Zilla Daund turned the knife in her hand and placed the tip of it against her throat.

"You'll leave with nothing," she said.

"Before you do that," said Louis, "you ought to call your son."

He placed a cell phone on the kitchen table and slid it carefully to the end nearest Zilla. He lowered his gun. Angel did the same. Zilla Daund approached the table. She picked up the phone. There was one name on the display: Kerr, her younger boy.

She called his number. He answered.

"Kerr?" she said.

"Mom? *Mom?*"

"Kerr, are you okay?"

"I don't know where I am, Mom. I got jumped by some men, and they've been driving me around for hours. Mom, I'm scared. What's happening?"

"You're going to be fine, honey. It's a big mistake. Those men are about to let you go. I love you."

"Mom? What—"

Zilla Daund killed the connection. She placed the knife back in its block. She bit her lower lip and shook her head.

Her eyes were elsewhere. A tear trickled down one cheek, but whether it was for her son, her husband, or herself could not be known.

"Your word?" she said.

"He'll be released unharmed," said Angel.

He didn't like this. He didn't like it at all. Threatening kids wasn't in his nature. It was necessary, but that didn't make it right.

"How can I trust you?" said Zilla Daund.

"Without overstating the obvious," said Louis, "you don't have much choice. But I figure Cambion told you enough about us, and you've maybe learned a little more in the meantime."

"We made some calls," she admitted.

"And?"

"If we'd known about you, we'd have killed you before we went after the detective."

"Ambitious."

"And careful."

"No. If you were careful, you'd have done your homework first."

Zilla Daund conceded the point

"Who told you to kill the detective?" said Louis.

"Hayley Conyer."

"Who's Hayley Conyer?"

"The chief selectman of the town of Prosperous, Maine."

"Why?"

"I didn't ask, but everything Hayley does is for the good of the town."

"You kill for anyone else?"

"No, just her."

"For money?"

"She pays, but we'd have helped her for nothing if we had to. We're of the town from generations past."

"Who else knew?"

"Morland, the chief of police. Pastor Warraner. The rest of the board of selectmen."

"Did you kill a homeless man named Jude in Portland and make it look like suicide?"

"Yes."

"And his daughter?"

"No."

"What's so special about Prosperous?" asked Angel.

Zilla Daund's mouth settled into the odd grimace of determination that Louis had identified back at the bookstore, her teeth gritted, her lips slightly parted.

"That's all you get," she said.

"You sold out your town pretty easily," said Louis.

"I didn't sell it out at all," said Zilla Daund. "Prosperous will eat you alive."

Louis shot her twice. She shuddered on the kitchen floor for a time before she died. Louis walked to the front window of the house and looked out. It was already getting dark. The houses in this modern dormitory community all sat on large lots divided by hedges and trees. Lights burned in some of the homes, but there was nobody on the streets. Louis wondered how anyone could live in a development like this, with its near-identical dwellings on clearly delineated lots, the tiny differences in detail or aspect designed to give a false impression of individuality. Maybe killing people was the only way the Daunds could keep from going crazy.

Given more time, they would have searched the house, but Angel was uneasy and eager to be on the move. From his jacket pocket he produced two flasks of carbolic acid, or liquefied phenol. He and Louis retraced their steps through the house, spraying the carbolic acid as they went. Phenol was a useful contaminant of DNA samples. Once they were done, they left the house and returned to their cars. Each had a false adhesive number plate attached to the original. They took only seconds to remove, and melted in open flame. Louis made the call to Kerr Daund's captors, but they were instructed not to release him until the following morning, by which time Angel and Louis would be far from Asheville, North Carolina—but considerably closer to Prosperous, Maine.

LII

They did not immediately descend on Prosperous. Instead, Angel and Louis waited, and they planned.

An apartment on Eastern Promenade, in Portland, was rented in the name of one of Louis's shelf companies. At the Great Lost Bear, Dave Evans turned a blind eye as a succession of meetings took place in his office, until eventually he resigned himself to doing his paperwork in a booth by the bar. Prosperous was visited by a pair of Japanese businessmen and their wives, who endeared themselves to everyone they met with their courtesy and their enthusiasm. They took a lot of photographs, but then that was to be expected of tourists from the Far East. They even accepted it in good spirits when they were prevented from entering the cemetery that surrounded the old church. The ground was unsafe, they were told, but plans were being put in place to mark a route through the gravestones to the church itself. Perhaps next time, if they returned.

And one evening, shortly after Angel and Louis's arrival in Portland, Ronald Straydeer came to the Great Lost Bear. Ronald had rarely frequented the city's bars when he did drink, and now that he had given up he had no cause to visit them at all, but Angel and Louis preferred to conduct their business away from their apartment, for the fewer people who knew about it the better. The meeting with Ronald had been arranged through Rachel Wolfe, as Ronald did not know of any other way to contact the two men whom he sought. He had left a message for her at the hospital where the detective still lay in a coma. Ronald's short note requested simply that Rachel call him. Rachel had met Ronald on a couple of occasions while she was living in Scarborough, so she knew who he was, and was aware of the mutual respect that existed between him and her former lover. She asked no questions when he told her that he wanted to be put in touch with Angel and Louis, but simply passed the message on to them. When Angel eventually called, Ronald had said only this: "I saw something happen in Prosperous, something bad."

And Angel knew that they were about to be handed another piece of the puzzle.

Over coffee in the back office, Ronald told Angel and Louis what he had witnessed: a girl swallowed by the earth in the shadow of an old church, while a group of older men and a woman, accompanied by a pastor and a policeman, stood by and watched. If the two men were surprised by his tale, they didn't show it. If they were skeptical, Ronald could detect no trace.

"What do you think happened to her?" asked Louis.

"I think something pulled her underground," said Ronald.

"Something?" said Louis.

It seemed to Ronald to be the first expression of any doubt, but he was mistaken. It came to him that these men had seen and heard things stranger even than this.

"It's not enough," Louis continued. "We need more. We can't go in blind."

Ronald had thought on this too. He had ransacked his memories of tribal lore—the Cherokee worship of the cedar tree, based on the belief that the Creator had imbued it with the spirits of those who had perished during the times of eternal night; the Canotila, or tree dwellers, of the Lakota; the Abenakis' tale of the creation of man from the bark of ash trees; and the forest-dwelling Mikum-wasus of his own Penobscot people—but he could find no explanation for what he had seen. He had a vision of a great tree growing upside down, its leafless crown far below the ground, its trunk extending upward to roots that twitched and groped, breaking through the earth to the air above; and at its heart, surrounded by the husks of dead girls, was an entity that had come from far away, a spirit that had infused the stones of an old church, traveling with it as it crossed land and sea before retreating into the new ground in which the foundations of that church were laid, creating a form for itself from wood and sap. But the question that consumed him most was its nature, for he believed that men created gods as much, if not more, than gods created men. If this old god existed, it did so because there were men and women who permitted it to continue to exist through their beliefs. They fed it, and it, in turn, fed them.

Ronald took from his jacket a sheaf of photocopied pages and laid them before Angel and Louis. The images on them were undated, but they depicted the carved heads that could be seen both inside and outside the Blessed Chapel of the Congregation of Adam Before Eve & Eve Before Adam.

He had found the pictures buried in the archives of the Center for Maine History, and then, unbeknownst to him, had followed a research path similar to the one pursued by the detective, staring at images of the foliate heads to be found on the churches and cathedrals of Western Europe. The English had called it the Green Man, but it predated that name by more than a millennium, and its spirit was older still. When the first men came, it was waiting for them among the trees, and in their minds it formed itself in their image: a human face rendered in wood and leaf.

"It may be that it looks like this," said Ronald.

Angel picked up one of the pictures. It was the face of winter, the bleakest and most hostile of the visages from the Prosperous church. He thought of what Agent Ross had said to them back in Brooklyn. It didn't matter whether a thing existed or not. What mattered was the trouble caused by those who believed in its existence.

"You talked of roots," he said.

"Yes," said Ronald. "I think roots drew the girl down."

"Roots and branches," said Angel. "Wood."

"And what does wood do?" asked Louis.

Angel smiled as he replied.

"It burns."

THE KILLINGS IN ASHEVILLE hadn't gone unremarked in Boston, for Garrison Pryor's people had been following trails similar to those walked by Angel and Louis, albeit a little more discreetly. The deaths of William and Zilla Daund simply confirmed what Pryor had begun to suspect: that the attack on the detective had been ordered from the town of Prosperous. This indicated that the decision to leave the Believers' mark at the scene had also been taken there, which meant, finally, that all of Pryor's current troubles could be laid at the town's door.

Prosperous had rarely troubled Pryor until now. It was a community unto itself, and he saw no reason to interfere with it as long as it was discreet in its activities. Now the town's very insularity—its refusal to recognize its relationship to the larger world and the possible impact of its decisions upon those beyond its boundaries—and the commitment of its protectors to its preservation, at any cost, had disturbed this state of equilibrium.

Prosperous, by its actions, had made retribution inevitable.

THE CALL CAME THROUGH to Angel's cell phone, its ID hidden. Louis felt that he should have been more surprised when Angel handed him the phone and he heard the Collector's voice.

"Very impressive," said the Collector. "To be honest, I had wondered if Cambion might not have been right to bet everything on them, but clearly they weren't quite as accomplished as he believed them to be."

"I think killing homeless men had blunted their edge," said Louis.

"Oh, they've killed more than homeless men, but I won't disagree. They swam in a small pool."

"How did you know about them?"

"A process of elimination. I asked questions, and found out that Parker had been nosing around in Prosperous's business. It was possible that the town might not have been involved, but Cambion sealed it for me. He's long been interested in Prosperous's pet husband-and-wife killers."

"You could just have told us. You could just have given us the name of the town."

"But where would be the sport in that? And I know you, Louis, perhaps better than you know yourself. You're meticulous. You want to fill in the blanks. What did the Daunds give you? Prosperous, or more? Wait, names; they gave you names. You wouldn't have left without them. Am I correct?"

Louis put down his glass of orange juice. He'd just been settling into the business pages of the *New York Times*, but now he recognized that any interest he might have had in the newspaper or, indeed, the orange juice had largely dissipated.

"*A* name," he conceded. "The woman gave me a name."

"Hayley Conyer."

"Shit."

"Oh, she wouldn't like to hear you swear like that. She's a god-fearing woman. That's 'god' with a small 'g,' incidentally."

"You interested in her? Looking for a date?"

"She's very old."

"Begging your pardon, but I don't believe you can afford to be particular."

"Don't be facetious. She's an interesting woman, and Prosperous is a fascinating town. You'll like it."

"Is she on your list?"

"Oh, yes."

"So why haven't you taken her?"

"Because it's not just her but the whole town. And *generations* of it. To do the sins of Prosperous justice, I'd have to dig up centuries of bones and burn them on a pyre. The whole town would have to be put to the torch, and that's beyond my capabilities."

Louis understood.

"But not beyond ours."

"No."

"Why should we destroy an entire town?"

"Because it colluded in what happened to the detective, and if you don't wipe it from the earth it will continue its traditions into future generations, and those traditions are very, very nasty. Prosperous is a *hungry* town."

"So you want us to do your dirty work for you? Fuck you."

"Don't be like that," said the Collector. "You'll enjoy it, I guarantee it. Oh, and pay special attention to that church of theirs. Flames won't be enough. You'll have to dig much deeper, and tear it apart with something far stronger."

Louis sensed that the conversation was coming to a close.

"Hey, since we're being all civil and all, you find your friend Cambion?"

The Collector was standing in the premises of Blackthorn, Apothecary. He held a blade in his hands. Upon it was just a hint of blood.

"I'm afraid he seems to have made his excuses and left before we could become better acquainted."

"That's unfortunate," said Louis. And he meant it.

"Yes, it is," said the Collector, and he meant it too.

Seconds passed.

"You told me that he lived here with someone else," said the Collector.

"Yeah, big man. Dressed in yellow. Hard to miss."

"And no other?"

"Not that I was aware of."

"Hmmm."

The Collector stared at the tattered, partial wreckage of a human being that lay on a gurney before him. The man had no eyes, no ears, and no tongue. Most of his fingers and toes were also missing. Stitches marked the site of his emasculation. The Collector had killed him as an act of mercy.

"You know," he said, "I believe I may have discovered Mr. Cambion's missing physician. Be sure to send me a postcard from Prosperous."

The Collector hung up. Angel looked up at Louis from over the *Portland Press Herald*.

"Are you two, like, all buddies now?"

Louis sighed.

"You know," he said, "sometimes I wish I'd never heard the name Charlie Parker. . . ."

GARRISON PRYOR WAS SITTING in a quiet corner of the Isabella Stewart Gardner Museum in Boston. He could see into the next public room, so he knew that he was not being overheard or observed. Since the FBI's visit to his offices, Pryor had grown concerned about surveillance to the point of paranoia. He no longer made or received delicate calls outside or on the office phones, especially when he was dealing with the Principal Backer. The most important of the Backers now exchanged numbers for clean cell phones each day, but otherwise they had fallen back on a primitive but virtually untraceable means of communicating sensitive information like cell phone numbers, a simple code based on the print edition of the *Wall Street Journal*: page, column, paragraph, line. Many of the older Backers found the routine almost reassuring, and Pryor thought that some might advocate retaining it once the FBI had exhausted itself chasing after imagined breaches of financial regulations.

The bureau's attention was irritating and an inconvenience, but little more than that. His business, Pryor Investments, had learned from past mistakes, and was now entirely scrupulous in its dealings. Of course, the business was merely a front: a fully functioning and lucrative one, but a front nonetheless. The Backers' real machinery had been hidden so deeply, and for so long, in established companies—in banks and trusts, charities and religious organizations—as to be untraceable. Let the FBI and its allies expend their energy on Pryor Investments. Admittedly, it was unfortunate that the private detective in Maine had become interested in Pryor Investments to begin with. It was a piece of bad luck, and nothing more. But he had clearly spoken to others of his suspicions, which was why the FBI had ended up on Pryor's doorstep. But they would find nothing, and eventually their attention would turn elsewhere.

Now, in the quiet of the museum, he spoke on the phone with the Principal Backer.

"Who killed this couple in Asheville?"

"We don't know for sure," said Pryor, "but we believe it was Parker's pet assassins."

"They did well to find what we couldn't."

"We were close," said Pryor. "The Daunds' blood was still pooling on the floor of their house when I got their names."

"So they saved us the trouble of killing the Daunds ourselves."

"I suppose they did. What now?"

"Now? Nothing."

Pryor was surprised. "What about Prosperous?"

"We let Parker's friends finish what they started. Why should we involve ourselves when they'll do the job for us?" The Principal Backer laughed. "We won't even have to pay them."

"And then?"

"Business as usual. You have mines to acquire."

Yes, thought Pryor. Yes, I have.

LIII

Lucas Morland felt as though he had aged years within a matter of days, but for the first time he was starting to believe that Prosperous might be free and clear, at least as far as the law was concerned. The MSP hadn't been in touch with him in forty-eight hours, and its investigators were no longer troubling the town. A certain narrative was gaining traction: Harry Dixon, who had been depressed and suffering from financial problems, killed his wife, her half sister and her huband, and, it was presumed, their daughter, before turning his gun on himself. Extensive searches of the town and its environs had failed to uncover any trace of Kayley Madsen. The state police had even done some halfhearted exploring in the cemetery under Pastor Warraner's watchful eye. The only tense moment occurred when some disturbance to the earth near the church walls was discovered, but further digging exposed only the remains of what was believed to be an animal burrow of some kind—too narrow, it seemed, to allow for the burial of a young woman's body.

Then there was the matter of the detective. The hit on him had been botched, and, just as Morland had warned, the attack had brought with it a series of convulsive aftershocks, culminating in the killing of the Daunds. Morland didn't know how the couple had been tracked down. Neither did he know if they had kept silent as they died, or confessed all to their killers in an effort to save themselves or, more likely, their son, who had been held captive while his parents were shot dead in their own home. At best, those who were seeking to avenge the shooting of the detective were now only one step away from Prosperous. He had tried to get Hayley Conyer and the others to understand the danger they were in, but they refused to do so. They believed that they had acted to protect the town, and that the town, in turn, would protect them. Why wouldn't it? After all, they had given a girl to it.

Now he was back in Conyer's house, sitting at that same table in that same room, sipping tea from the same mugs. Sunlight flooded through the trees. It was the first truly warm day in months. The air was bright with the sound of snow and ice melting, like the dimly heard ticking of clocks.

"You've done well, Lucas," Conyer told him, as she sipped her tea. Morland had barely touched his. He had begun to resent every minute he was forced to spend in Conyer's presence. "Don't think the board doesn't appreciate all your efforts."

He was there only because that old bastard Kinley Nowell had finally given up the ghost. He had died that morning in his daughter's arms. It was a more peaceful passing than he deserved. As far as Morland was concerned, Kinley Nowell had been severely lacking in the milk of human kindness, even by the standards of a town that fed young women to a hole in the ground.

But Nowell's death had also provided him with what might be his final chance to talk some sense into Hayley Conyer. The board would need a replacement, but Conyer had vetoed the suggestion that the young lawyer Stacey Walker should be the one, despite the majority of her fellow board members being in favor. Instead, Conyer was holding firm on Daniel Cooper, who wasn't much younger than Nowell and was among the most stubborn and blinkered of the town's elders, as well as an admirer of Conyer's to the point of witlessness. Even after all that had occurred, Conyer was still attempting to consolidate her position.

"We just need to stand together for a little while longer," Conyer continued. "And then all this will pass."

She knew why he was here, but she wasn't about to be dissuaded from her course. She'd already informed Morland that she felt that Stacey Walker was too young, too inexperienced, to be brought onto the board. Hard times called for old heads, she told him. Morland couldn't tell whether she'd just made that up or it was an actual saying, but he rejected it totally in either case. It was old heads that had gotten them into all this trouble to begin with. The town needed a fresh start. He thought of Annie Broyer, and a question that had come to mind after he and Harry Dixon had spent a cold night burying her.

What would happen if we stopped feeding it?

Bad things, Hayley Conyer would have told him had she been there. She would have pointed to the misfortunes that had blighted Prosperous so recently—the deaths of those boys in Afghanistan, of Valerie Gillson, of Ben Pearson—and said, "There! See what happens when you fail in your duty to the town?"

But what if this was all a myth in which they had mistakenly chosen to believe? What if their old god was more dependent on them than they were on it? Their credence gave it power. If they deprived it of belief, what then?

Could a god die?

Let the town have its share of misfortunes. Let it take its chances with the rest of humanity, for good or ill. He was surprised by how much Kayley Madsen's fate had shaken him. He'd heard stories, of course. His own father had prepared him for it, so he thought he knew what to expect. He hadn't been ready for the reality, though. It was the speed of it that haunted him most—how quickly the girl had been swallowed by the earth, like a conjurer's vanishing trick.

If Morland had his way, they would feed this old god no longer.

But Hayley Conyer stood in his way: she and those like her.

"We have to put old disagreements behind us and look to the future," said Hayley. "Let all our difficulties be in the past."

"But they're not," he said. "What happened to the Daunds proves that."

"You're making assumptions that their deaths are linked to their recent efforts on our behalf."

"You told me yourself that they worked only for the town. There can be no other reason why they were targeted."

She dismissed what he said with a wave of her hand.

"They could have been tempted to take on other tasks without our knowledge. Even if they didn't, and they were somehow tracked down because of the detective, they wouldn't betray us."

"They might, to save their child."

But Hayley Conyer had no children, had apparently never shown any desire to be a mother, and to possess such feelings for a child was beyond her imaginative and emotional reach.

"Hayley," said Morland, with some force, "they will come here next. I'm certain of it."

And it's your fault, he wanted to tell her. I warned you. I told you not to take this course of action. I love this town as much as you. I've even killed for it. But you believe that whatever decision you take, whatever is right for you, is also right for Prosperous, and in that you are mistaken. You're like that French king who declared that he was the state, before the people ultimately proved him wrong by cutting off his descendant's head.

Morland wasn't the only one who felt this way. There were others too. The time of the current board of selectmen was drawing to a close.

"If they do come, we'll deal with them," said Conyer. "We'll . . ."

But Morland was no longer even listening. He drifted. He wasn't sleeping well, and when he did manage to doze off his dreams—he had begun to dream in earnest—were haunted by visions of wolves. He stood and removed a handkerchief from his pocket. Hayley Conyer was still talking, lecturing him on the town's history, his obligations to it, the wisdom of the board. It sounded to him like the cawings of an old crow. She mentioned something about his position, about how nobody was irreplaceable. She talked of the possibility of Morland's taking a period of extended leave.

Morland stood. It took a huge effort. His body felt impossibly heavy. He looked at the handkerchief. Why had he taken it from his pocket? Ah, he remembered now. He walked behind Hayley Conyer, clasped the handkerchief over her nose and mouth, and squeezed. He wrapped his left arm around her as he did so, holding her down in the chair, her sticklike arms pressed to her sides. She struggled against him, but he was a big man, and she was an elderly woman at the end of her days. Morland didn't look into her eyes as he killed her. Instead, he stared out the window at the trees in the yard. He could see the dark winter buds on the nearest maple. Soon they would give way to the red and yellow flowers of early spring.

Hayley Conyer jerked hard in her chair. He felt her spirit depart, and smelled the dying of her. He released his grip on her face and examined her nose and mouth. There were no obvious signs of injury: a little redness where he had held her nostrils closed, but no more than that. He let her fall forward on the table and made a call to Frank Robinson, who operated the town's only medical practice and who, like Morland, felt that the time for a change was fast approaching. Robinson would make a fine selectman.

"Frank," he said, once the receptionist put him through. "I've got some bad news. I came over to talk to Hayley Conyer and found her collapsed on her dining table. Yeah, she's gone. I guess her old heart gave out on her at last. Must have been the stress of all that's happened."

It was unlikely that the state's chief medical examiner would insist on an autopsy, and even if one was ordered, Doc Robinson had the designated authority to perform it. Meanwhile, Morland would take photographs of the scene to include in his report.

He listened as Robinson spoke.

"Yeah," said Morland. "It's the town's loss. But we go on."

Two down, thought Morland. Three, and he could take over the board. The one to watch would be Thomas Souleby, who had always wanted to be chief selectman. Warraner too might be a problem, but it was traditional that the pastor did not serve on the board, just as Morland himself, as chief of police, was prevented from serving by the rules of the town. But Warraner didn't have many friends in the town, while Morland did. And perhaps, if Morland were finally to put an end to this madness, he would have to take care of Warraner as well. Without a shepherd, there was no flock. Without a pastor, there was no church.

He stared down at his hands. He had never even fired his gun in anger until the evening he killed Erin Dixon and her relatives, and now he had more deaths on his conscience than he could count on one hand. He had even fired the bullet that killed Harry Dixon. Bryan Joblin had offered to do it, but Morland wasn't sure that Joblin could do something that was at once so simple, yet so dangerous, without botching it. He'd let Bryan watch, though. It was the least he could do.

He should have been more troubled than he was, but, Kayley Madsen's final moments apart, he felt comparatively free of any psychological burden, for he could justify each killing to himself. By fleeing, Harry Dixon had given Morland no choice but to move against him. Eventually, he would have told someone about Annie Broyer and how she had come to die in the town of Prosperous. The town's hold on its citizens grew looser the farther from it they moved. This was true of any belief system. It was sustained by the proximity of other believers.

A car pulled up outside, and he watched Frank Robinson emerge from it. Morland wished that he could get into his own car and drive away, but he had come too far now. A line from a play came to him, or the vaguest memory of it. It had to be from high school, because Morland hadn't been to a play in twenty years. Shakespeare, he guessed, something about how, if it were to be done, then it was best to do it quickly.

If Morland could get rid of Souleby, the board would be his.

The board, and the town.

THE NEWS OF HAYLEY Conyer's passing made the papers, as anything involving Prosperous now tended to do. The general consensus was that the old woman's heart had been broken by the troubles visited on her town, although this view was not shared by everyone.

"Jesus!" said Angel to Louis. "If it goes on like this there'll be nobody left for us to kill."

He remained surprised by Louis's patience. They were still in Portland, and no move had yet been made on Prosperous.

"You think it was natural causes, like they're saying?" said Angel.

"Death is always by natural causes, if you look hard enough."

"That's not what I meant."

"I'd be surprised if she didn't die kicking at something," said Louis. "Zilla Daund told us that the order to hit Parker came from the board of selectmen, and this Conyer woman in particular. Now she's dead. If I was on that board, I'd start locking my door at night. It's like that Sherlock Holmes thing. You know, once you eliminate the impossible, whatever is left, no matter how improbable it seems, is the truth."

"I don't get it," said Angel.

"Once everyone else in the room is dead, the person left standing, no matter how respectable, is the killer."

"Right. You have anyone in mind?"

Louis walked over to the dining room table. An array of photographs lay on it, including images of the town, its buildings, and a number of its citizens. Some of the pictures had been provided by the Japanese "tourists." Others had been copied from Web sites. Louis separated pictures of five men from the rest.

"Souleby, Joblin, Ayton, Warraner, and Morland," he said.

He pushed the photographs of Joblin and Ayton to one side.

"Not these," he said.

"Why?" said Angel.

"Just a feeling. Souleby might have it in him, I admit, but not the other two. One's too old; the second's not the type."

Louis then separated Warraner.

"Again, why?"

"Makes no sense. If this is all connected to something in their old church, then Conyer and the board acted to protect it. The church is Warraner's baby. He has no reason to hurt anyone who took measures for its benefit."

Louis touched his fingers to Souleby's picture. A file had been compiled on each of the selectmen, as well as on Warraner and Morland. Souleby was an interesting man— ruthless in business, with connections in Boston. But . . .

"Lot of killing for an old man," said Louis. "Too much." And he put Souleby's photograph with the rest.

"Which leaves Morland," said Angel.

Louis stared at Morland's photograph. It had been taken from the town's Web site. Morland was smiling.

"Yes," said Louis. "Which leaves Morland."

LIV

Thomas Souleby tried to pack a bag as his wife looked on. Constance was growing increasingly disturbed at the casual way in which her husband was tossing his clothing into the big leather duffel. He never could pack for shit, she thought. She didn't say this aloud, though. Even after forty years of marriage, her husband still professed to be shocked by what he termed her "salty tongue."

"Here, let me do that," said Constance. She gently elbowed Thomas aside, removed the shirts and pants, and began folding them again before restoring them to the bag. "You go and get your shaving kit."

Thomas did as he was told. He didn't opine that there might not be time for the proper folding and placement of his clothing. She was working faster and yet more efficiently than he could have done anyway—he was all haste without speed—and there was little point in arguing with his wife, not when it came to the organizational details of his life. Without her involvement, they would never have achieved the degree of financial security and comfort they now enjoyed. Thomas had never been a details man. He worked in concepts. His wife was the meticulous one.

When he returned to the bed, she had half filled the bag with shirts, a sweater, two pairs of pants, and a second pair of shoes with his socks and underwear neatly fitted inside. To these he added his shaving kit and a Colt 1911 pistol that had belonged to his father. The Colt was unlicensed. Long ago, his father had advised him of the importance of keeping certain things secret, especially in a place like Prosperous. As Souleby had watched the slow, steady ascent of Lucas Morland, he came to be grateful for the bequest. Thomas Souleby considered himself a good judge of character—he couldn't have succeeded in business if he weren't—and had never liked or trusted Lucas Morland. The man thought he knew better than his elders, and that wasn't the way Prosperous worked. Souleby had also noticed a change in Morland in recent weeks. He could almost smell it on him, an alteration in his secretions. Conyer had sensed it too. That was why, before her death, she had been planning to remove Morland from his post and replace him with one of his more malleable deputies. Souleby could still feel the old woman's hand on his arm, the strength of her grip, as she had spoken to him for the last time the day before.

"You listen, Thomas Souleby, and you listen good," she said. "I'm as healthy as any woman in this town. My mother lived to be ninety-eight, and I plan on exceeding that age with room to spare. But if anything happens to me you'll know. It'll be Morland's doing, and he won't stop with me. You're no friend to him, and he sure as hell doesn't care much for you. He doesn't understand the town the way we do. He doesn't care for it the way we care. He has no *faith*."

And then the call came from Calder Ayton: Calder, who was everyone's friend, but hadn't been the same since the death of Ben Pearson. Souleby figured that Calder had loved Ben, and had Ben not been resolutely heterosexual, and Calder not a product of a less enlightened, more cloistered time, the two of them could have lived together in domestic bliss, protected by the amused tolerance of the town. Instead, Calder had settled for a sexless relationship of a sort, aided by Ben's status as a widower and Calder's share in the store, the two of them clucking and fussing over each other, snipping and sniping and making up like the old married couple that they secretly were. Calder wouldn't last long now, thought Souleby. Morland wouldn't have to kill him, even if Calder had the backbone to stand up to him, which Souleby doubted. Calder had been widowed, and without Ben to keep him company he would fade away and die quickly enough.

It was Calder who got in touch to tell Souleby of Hayley Conyer's passing. That didn't surprise Souleby. They were two of the last three selectmen, and he had always been closer to Calder than to Luke Joblin, who was too flashy for Souleby's liking. What did surprise Souleby was Calder's tone. He knew. He *knew*.

"Who found her?" Souleby asked.

"Chief Morland," Calder told him, and it was there, in the way that he said "Chief." "He thinks she might have had a heart attack."

"And I'll bet Frank Robinson is signing off on it as we speak."

"That's what I hear." A pause. "Morland will be coming for you, Thomas."

The phone felt slick in Souleby's hand. His palms were sweating.

"I know," he said. "What about you?"

"He's not afraid of me."

"Maybe he's underestimated you."

Souleby heard Calder chuckle sadly.

"No, he knows me inside and out. This is my little act of defiance, my last one. I'll be resigning from the board."

"Nobody resigns from the board."

Only death brought an end to a selectman's tenure. The elections were just for show. Everyone knew that.

Calder was sitting in the back of Ben Pearson's store. In reality it was as much his as it had been Ben's, but Calder didn't regard it as anything other than Ben's store, even with Ben no longer around. He looked at the bottles of pills that he had been accumulating since Ben's death.

Soon, he thought. Soon.

"There are ways, Thomas," he said. "You step lively."

Now, with his bag packed, Thomas kissed his wife and prepared to leave.

"Where will you go?" asked Constance.

"I don't know. Not far, but far enough to be safe from him."

Calls had to be made. Souleby still had plenty of allies in the town, although he couldn't see many of them standing up to Morland. They weren't killers, but Morland was.

"What will I tell him when he comes?" asked Constance.

"Nothing, because you know nothing."

He kissed her on the mouth.

"I love you."

"I love you too."

She watched him drive away.

He had been gone less than an hour before Lucas Morland arrived at her door.

SOULEBY DROVE AS FAR as Portland and parked in the long-term garage at the Portland Jetport. He then took a bus to Boston, paying cash for the ticket. He didn't know how far Morland would go to track him, and he was no spy, but he hoped that, if Morland did somehow discover the whereabouts of the car, it would throw him a little. He asked his son-in-law to book a room for him under the name Ryan at a club off Massachusetts Avenue that advertised through Expedia. Souleby knew that the club didn't ask for ID, but simply held a key for the name listed on the reservation. He then walked over to Back Bay, sat in a coffee shop across from Pryor Investments, and waited. When Garrison Pryor eventually appeared, cell phone to his ear, Souleby left the coffee shop and followed him. Souleby caught up with Pryor when he stopped at a pedestrian signal.

"Hello, Garrison," he said.

Pryor turned.

"I'll call you back," he said, and hung up the phone. "What are you doing here, Thomas?"

"I need help."

The light changed. Pryor started walking, but Souleby easily kept up with him. He was considerably taller than Pryor, and fitter too, despite his age.

"I'm not in the helping business," said Pryor. "Not for you or your board."

"We've exchanged information in the past."

"That was before tridents began appearing in the woodwork of houses in Scarborough, Maine. Have you any idea
of the trouble you've caused me?"

"I counseled against that."

"Not hard enough."

"We're having difficulties in Prosperous. Serious
difficulties."

"I noticed."

"Our chief of police is out of control. He has to be . . .
retired before we can restore stability. Recompense can be
made to you and your colleagues."

"It's gone too far."

"Garrison." Souleby put a hand out to stop Pryor, forcing the shorter man to look up at him. "Morland is going
to kill me."

"I'm sorry to hear that, Thomas," said Pryor. "Truly, I
am. But we're not going to intervene. If it's any consolation
to you, whatever happens, Prosperous's days are drawing to
a close. In the end, it doesn't matter who's left standing—
you, Morland, the board. There are men coming to wipe
you from the map."

Souleby's hand dropped. "And you'll let this happen?"

Pryor took out his cell phone and redialed a number. He
watched it connect, raised the phone to his ear, and patted
Souleby on the shoulder in farewell.

"Thomas," said Pryor, as he walked away, "we're going to
watch you all burn."

MORLAND SAT IN HIS office. He was frustrated, but no more
than that. Souleby would have to return. His life was here.
In Souleby's absence, Luke Joblin and Calder Ayton had
agreed that elections to the board should be held just as
soon as Hayley Conyer was safely interred. Neither had

objected to Morland's list of nominees for the three vacant positions.

Morland had a fourth name ready too. He had a feeling that another vacancy would soon arise.

LV

C hief Morland next faced Thomas Souleby as they stood over Hayley Conyer's open grave. In recognition of her long and generous service to the town of Prosperous, she was buried in the old cemetery, in the shadow of the church whose legacy she had done so much to protect, and in which her body had reposed on the night before its burial. Only a handful of the most important citizens were permitted to enter the church for the funeral service, although a temporary sound system relayed the proceedings to the townsfolk who stood outside. God played a part, but so too did nature, and the metaphor that ran through Warraner's oratory was of the changing of the seasons, a life's journey from spring to winter, and thence to a new form of rebirth.

Once the coffin was lowered into the ground, it was left to the selectmen, assisted by Morland and Warraner, to fill in the grave. It was a sign of respect, but Morland was inevitably reminded of the last time he had wielded a spade in service of a body. The townsfolk started to leave. Tea and coffee were being served at the Town Office, where memories of Hayley Conyer would be exchanged, and talk would turn to the election of the new selectmen. In addition, nobody wanted to miss the chance to gossip a little under the flag of mourning: Thomas Souleby's absence until the morning of the funeral had not gone unremarked, and the tension between him and Chief Morland was common knowledge in the town, even if the catalyst for this particular bout of hostilities—Hayley Conyer's forced departure from this world—was not.

Morland caught up with Souleby halfway across the churchyard. He grabbed the older man's arm, steering him away from the gate.

"Walk with me awhile, Thomas," he said.

Souleby's wife was waiting for him outside the railings. Morland thought that she might spring over them to protect her husband when she saw the chief approach him, but Souleby raised a hand to let her know that he was okay. If Morland intended him harm, he would do so another day, and under other circumstances.

"We missed you," said Morland. "Your absence was unfortunate. The town was in mourning. It looked to the board for leadership, and the board, in its turn, looked to you as the senior selectman, but you weren't there."

Souleby wasn't about to accuse Lucas Morland of murder—not here, not anywhere. There remained a possibility that he could still survive this, and even turn the situation to his advantage. The three nominees to the board were comparatively young, and open to manipulation. They were not his creatures, but neither were they Morland's. He could not give Morland an excuse to act against him, although the flaw in this line of reasoning was easily apparent, for Morland might not even need a reason to act.

"I had business to conclude," said Souleby.

"You mind my asking what kind of business?"

"Private. Personal."

"You sure about that? Because if it had to do with the town I really ought to know about it. This is a delicate time. We all need to pull together."

Souleby stopped walking and faced Morland.

"What do you want, Chief Morland?"

"I want you to give up your place on the board."

"You know that's not possible. Under the rules—"

"The rules have changed. The board met while you were away."

"There *was* no board," said Souleby. "Two members isn't a quorum."

"Like I said, this is a delicate time. We didn't know what had happened to you, and your wife was of little help. Decisions had to be made. Calder Ayton and Luke Joblin consented to temporary measures pending the election of a new board and the permanent retention of those rules. Selectmen will no longer serve for life, and no selectman will be able to serve more than two terms in succession. I'd have informed you of the changes before now if I'd been able to find you."

Souleby understood what was happening. If he resigned from the board, any power that he had would disappear. He would have no protection.

And, eventually, Morland would come for him. He would do so because, alive, Souleby would always be a threat. Calder Ayton would soon be dead, while Luke Joblin was on Morland's side, and perhaps always had been. Only Souleby knew the details of what had been done in the board's name, and what Morland himself had done.

"And if I refuse to resign?"

Souleby noted movement among the trees, and saw that many members of the senior families hadn't left the environs of the cemetery. They were watching from the woods, and as he stared they began to turn their backs on him, one by one, until he could see their faces no longer. Then, and only then, did they begin to disperse.

"The will of the people will prevail, Thomas," said Morland, and Souleby knew that he was alone.

Morland smiled sadly and walked away. Only when Souleby had seen Morland's Crown Vic drive off, and was certain the chief was gone, did he join his wife outside the railings.

"What did he say to you?" said Constance.

"I want you to go and stay with Becky and Josh," he told her.

Becky was their eldest daughter. She lived down in Portsmouth. Her husband, Josh, was Calder Ayton's nephew. Souleby trusted him.

"No, I won't."

"You will," he said. "All this will pass, but for a time things will be difficult. I can't be worrying about you while I try to make this good."

"No," she said. "No, no . . ."

She started to cry. He held her.

"It'll be all right," he lied. "Everything will be all right."

CONSTANCE LEFT LATE THAT afternoon. Becky drove up to collect her. Becky tried to question her father, but he wouldn't answer her, and she knew the ways of Prosperous well enough to pursue the matter no further for now.

Souleby poured himself a glass of brandy. He watched the sun set. He felt drowsy, but he didn't sleep.

It was Luke Joblin who came for him, shortly after eight. His son Bryan waited in the backseat. Souleby saw him when the interior light came on as Luke opened the driver's door. He could have fought them, of course, but what would have been the point? Instead, the old Colt now lay under his wife's pillow. She would find it there, and she would know.

"Come along, Thomas," said Luke. He spoke gently but firmly, the way one might speak to an elderly relative who refused to do what was best for him. "It's time to go. . . ."

LVI

The call came through the following evening as Morland was preparing for bed. He was fresh out of the shower, and had changed into pajama pants and an old Red Sox T-shirt. He was quietly eating a late-night sandwich in the dark prior to hitting the sack and maybe spending some quality time with his wife. They hadn't made love in more than a week. Understandably, Morland hadn't been in the mood. His wife didn't like him eating late at night, but Morland took the view that what she didn't know, or couldn't prove, wouldn't hurt her. It was, he thought, true of so many things.

He had just returned from a visit to Souleby's bitch wife, Constance, at her daughter's house, accompanied by Luke Joblin and three representatives of the most senior families. They'd commented on Constance Souleby's lovely grand-children, and the fine house in which her daughter and son-in-law lived, for the best kind of threat was the one that didn't sound like a threat at all, the kind that planted bad pictures in the imagination. Becky, Constance's daughter, offered coffee, but nobody accepted.

"What have you done with Thomas?" Constance asked Morland, once the pleasantries were done with.

"Nothing," he said. "We just want him to stay out of the way until after the election. We don't need him interfering, and you know he'll interfere. He's safe."

The election was scheduled for Saturday. Elections to the board were always held on Saturdays, just to be sure that the maximum number of people could vote.

"Why hasn't he called me?"

"If you want him to call, we'll have him do that," said Luke Joblin, all reasonableness and reassurance. "We had to take away his cell phone. You understand why."

If Constance Souleby did understand, she wasn't giving any sign of it.

"You had no right," she said. "No right."

"The town is changing, Mrs. Souleby," said Morland. "We just barely survived the mess of the last couple of weeks. That can't happen again. There can be no more blood spilled in Prosperous. The old board, and all that it did, has to be consigned to history. We have to find a way to survive in the twenty-first century."

A shiver of unease ran through the three representatives of the senior families—two men, one woman, all as old as any in the town. Morland had convinced them of the necessity for change, but this didn't mean that they weren't frightened by it.

"Thomas can adapt," said Constance. She was trying not to plead, but it bled into her voice nonetheless.

"That's not the issue," said Morland. "The decision has been made."

There was nothing more to be said. Morland, Joblin,

and the three other visitors got to their feet. Someone mumbled an awkward goodbye, to no reply.

Morland was almost at his car when he heard Constance Souleby begin to wail. Luke Joblin heard it too. Morland could see him tense, even as he tried to ignore the old woman's cries.

"Why did you tell her that her husband would call her?" said Morland. Thomas Souleby wouldn't be calling anyone ever again. There would probably be no body. Once the elections were concluded, he would be reported missing.

"I was trying to keep her calm."

"You figure it worked?" said Morland, as the cries rose in intensity and then were smothered. Morland could almost see Constance Souleby's daughter holding her mother's head, kissing her, shushing her.

"No, not really," said Joblin. "You think she knows?"

"Oh, she knows."

"What will she do?"

"Nothing."

"You sound very certain of that."

"She won't turn on the town. It's not in her blood."

NOW, AS MORLAND LISTENED to the ringing of his cell phone, he wondered if he had been right to sound so confident. Great change was always traumatic, and with trauma came actions that were unanticipated, and out of character.

His wife appeared on the stairs, come to see where he was. She was wearing a sheer nightgown. Through it he could see the curves of her body. He tossed the remains of the sandwich into the sink before she noticed. He'd get rid of them in the morning. He was usually awake before her.

"Can't you ignore it?" she asked.

"Just let me see who it is."

He went to the hall and looked at the display.

Warraner.

He had yet to tackle the pastor. Rumors of what Morland was proposing had certainly already reached him. Warraner would have to be convinced of the necessity of acceding to the will of the town, but it wouldn't be easy. Still, he could continue to tend his church, and pray to his god behind the silence of its walls. Perhaps the pastor also hoped that, when bad times came, the town would turn once again to the church, and the old ways could resume. If that was the case, Morland thought that Warraner's prayers to his god would have to be powerful as all hell, because Morland would send Warraner the way of Hayley Conyer and Thomas Souleby before he let another girl end up kneeling by a hole in the cemetery.

Morland considered ignoring the call, but he remained the chief of police. If Warraner wanted to argue, Morland would put him off until morning, but if it was something more urgent . . .

He hit the green button.

"Pastor," he said. "I'm just about to go to bed."

"There's a homeless man on the church grounds," said Warraner. "He's shouting about a murder."

Shit.

"I'm on my way," said Morland.

He looked to his wife.

"I'm sorry," he said.

But she was already gone.

WARRANER HUNG UP THE phone. In a corner of the living room lay the body of Bryan Joblin. It was Joblin's misfortune to have been present at Warraner's house when the men arrived, and to have reached for his gun at the sight of them. Joblin had died instantly. He had recently fixed his eye on Warraner's eldest daughter, Ruth, a development about which Warraner had been deeply unhappy. That problem, at least, now appeared to have been solved.

Nearby, Warraner's wife and children were under a gun. One not dissimilar to it was only inches from the pastor's face. If he focused on the muzzle—and he *was* focusing, because it was very, very close to him—the masked face of the man holding the weapon became a blur. Warraner could only see one or the other properly, but not both: the instrument of killing, or the man who might let him live.

"You did good."

Warraner couldn't reply. It was all he had been able to do just to keep his voice steady as he spoke to Morland. He managed to generate some spittle in his mouth, and found his voice.

"What's going to happen to my family?"

"Nothing," replied the gunman. "Although I can't promise the same for you."

THE PROSPEROUS POLICE DEPARTMENT kept one officer on duty at night. In the event of an emergency, that officer could call the chief, or even the Maine State Police, but so far no nighttime incident had ever been sufficiently serious to require the assistance of the MSP. The officer on duty that night was Connie Dackson, and she was trying to rewire the plug on the coffee machine when two men entered the Town Office. One carried a shotgun, the other a pistol. Both wore black ski masks.

"Not a move," said the one holding the shotgun, which was now pointing at Dackson.

Nobody had ever pointed a gun at her before. She was so scared that she couldn't have moved even if she wanted to. She was forced facedown onto the floor, and her hands were secured with her own cuffs. A gag was placed over her mouth, and she was shown into the town's single holding cell. It was more than a hundred years old, just like the building that housed it. The bars were green, and Dackson had a clear view through them as the two men began disabling the department's entire communications system.

MORLAND COULDN'T RAISE Connie Dackson on her cell phone as he drove. He wasn't worried, though, not yet. She might have left it in her vehicle if she was patrolling, or simply be in the john. She might already even be with Warraner, trying to coax some bum out of the churchyard, a bum who was muttering about murder. That was when Morland knew that he was tired: Warraner wouldn't be dumb enough to call Dackson if there was a chance that she might hear something she shouldn't. This was up to him, and him alone.

The first thing that struck him as he reached the churchyard was the fact that the door of the church was open. The gate to the churchyard was unlocked, the chain lying on the ground. The chain had been cut, just like the one farther down the road.

The second was that he could find no trace of any bum.

He didn't call out Warraner's name. He didn't have to. He could now see the pastor kneeling in the doorway of the church. Beside him stood a tall man in a ski mask. He held a gun to the pastor's head.

"Chief Morland," said the man. "Glad you could make it."

Morland thought that he sounded like a black man. Prosperous didn't have any black residents. This wasn't unusual in such a white state. Maine was one of the few places where nobody could try to blame blacks for crime. The white folk had that one all sewn up.

Morland raised his own gun.

"Lower your weapon," he said.

"Look around you, Chief," said the man.

Morland risked a glance. Three other figures, also masked, materialized from the gloom of the cemetery. Two were armed, their weapons pointing in his direction. The third held a coil of wire, and the sight of it caused Morland to notice for the first time the cables that crossed the cemetery and hung over some of the gravestones. He moved slightly to the right, and saw one of the holes that had so interested the state police investigators when they'd come looking for Kayley Madsen. A length of wire led into its depths.

"What are you doing?" said Morland.

"Putting the finishing touches to thermite and Semtex devices," said the man. "We're about to destroy your town, starting here. Now put down your gun. I want to talk. The pastor has been telling me a lot about you."

But Morland wasn't about to talk to anyone.

Instead, he simply started shooting.

NOBODY LIVED ON PROSPEROUS'S Main Street. It was strictly businesses only. As midnight approached, the street and its surround stood empty.

Slowly, men began to emerge from the shadows, eight in all. Ronald Straydeer led them, his features, like those of the others with him, concealed.

"You sure you're okay to do this?" asked Ronald.

"I'm sure," said Shaky.

He held an incendiary device in his good hand. A cold wind was blowing from the east. That was good. It would fan the flames.

There came the sound of breaking glass.

Minutes later, Prosperous started to burn.

MORLAND WAS RUNNING FOR his life. Shots struck the old gravestones, or whistled past his ear to vanish into the forest beyond. He stayed low, using the monuments for cover—weaving, dodging, firing blindly, but never stopping. He was outnumbered, and these men could easily surround and kill him, but he knew the woods and they did not. Anyway, staying in the cemetery was not an option, for it was now one massive explosion waiting to occur.

He didn't head for the gate. That would be too obvious. Instead, he sprinted for the railings and scrambled over them. He took a shot to the upper arm but didn't pause. The woods were ahead of him, and he lost himself in their darkness. He risked only one look back, and saw that the church door was now closed. The shooting had stopped, and in the silence Morland heard Warraner's voice raised in song from behind the old stone walls. Somehow, in the confusion, he had managed to lock himself inside.

"*When men begin to weed,*" sang Warraner, "*the thistle from the seed . . .*"

The figures in the churchyard started to run. Morland reloaded his gun and drew a bead on the nearest man. Perhaps he could yet stop this. His finger tightened on the trigger.

But he didn't fire. Was this not what he wanted, what he sought? Let this be an end to it. He lowered his gun, and retreated deeper into the trees, faster now, putting as much distance between him and the church as he could. If he could get to his car and return to town, he and Dackson could hole up in the Town Office while they called for backup.

He reached the road and saw an orange glow rising from Prosperous. The town was already burning, but he barely had time to register that fact before a massive blast rent the night. The ground shook, and Morland was knocked off his feet by the force of it. Debris was hurled high into the air, and earth, stone, and wood rained down on him where he lay. He could feel the heat of the detonation, even from the road.

He covered his head with his hands, and prayed to every god and none.

LVII

Main Street was gone, reduced to brick shells and vacant, charred lots. At least one of the ruined buildings had dated back to the eighteenth century, and others were only marginally younger. Historians and architecture experts described it as a tragedy.

The Chapel of the Congregation of Adam Before Eve & Eve Before Adam was scattered over woods, roads, and what was left of the cemetery, which wasn't much at all. Charred human remains, most of them long interred, would be discovered for years after. Incredibly, the total number of fatalities amounted to just three: Pastor Michael Warraner, who had been inside his church when it was blown sky high; Bryan Joblin, killed in cold blood at Warraner's house; and Thomas Souleby, the senior selectman of the town, who was said to have accompanied Chief Morland to the cemetery when the original call was received about a homeless trespasser, and who had not been able to get clear of the cemetery before the explosion occurred.

Frank Robinson conducted the autopsy on Souleby, just so that there could be no confusion about the matter. Unlike Pastor Warraner, Souleby's body remained undamaged enough to allow for a proper burial. Morland had suffocated Souleby, just as he had done with Hayley Conyer. If nothing else, the chaos at the church had given him a way of avoiding another cold night of burying a body.

It was not much, but it was enough.

The newspapers and TV cameras were back. It would be a long time before they left. When asked about plans to rebuild, Morland told them that work would begin on Main Street almost immediately, but he was unsure about plans for the church. The damage caused by the high explosives used meant that rebuilding the original structure would be ruinously expensive if it was possible at all, which was doubtful. Perhaps a monument might be erected in its place, he suggested. Discussions on the issue would begin, said Morland, once the new board of selectmen was elected.

It remained unclear who might have been responsible for what was described, almost immediately and inevitably, as an "act of terrorism." Attention was focused variously on Muslims, fascists, secessionists, opponents of the federal government, radical socialists, and extreme religious organizations, but Morland knew that none of those avenues of inquiry would ever yield any results.

The truth was that they should never have gone after the detective.

The Town Office had suffered significant damage, mostly in a successful effort to destroy the engines in the fire department. Officer Connie Dackson had watched it burn. Her captors had removed her from her cell and left her tied up at a safe distance from the conflagration. She thought that they might have been Asian, judging by their accents and their unusual politeness, but she couldn't be certain. The Prosperous Police Department had immediately moved to temporary lodgings at the local Veterans of Foreign Wars meeting hall.

On the third day after the attack on his town—for that was what it now was, "his" town—Lucas Morland watched the thawing snow from his window in the local hall. Meltwater ran down what remained of Main Street, starting clear at the top and ending up black as oil by the time it reached the bottom. More snow might come, but it wouldn't last long. They were done with winter, and winter was done with them. They had survived—*he* had survived—and the town would be better and stronger for this purging. He felt a deep and abiding sense of admiration for its people. No sooner were the fires extinguished than the cleanup operation had begun. Buildings were being assessed for demolition or restoration, according to the damage they had sustained. Pledges of aid numbering into six figures had already been received. Calls had been made to the heads of the insurance companies involved, warning them that any weaseling out of their commitments would not be tolerated, those calls having significant impact, since they came from members of their own boards who had ties to Prosperous.

Morland was under no illusions that the town's troubles—or, more particularly, his troubles—were at an end. Those responsible for the partial destruction of his town might well decide to return. He recalled the words of the man at the cemetery: "The pastor has been telling me a lot about you." Even in his final moments, Warraner had found a way to screw him over. At least Bryan Joblin was dead too. He was one loose end about whom Morland no longer needed to worry.

Let them come, Morland thought. Let them come, and

I will face them down. Next time I'll be ready, and I will kill them where they stand.

Morland didn't hear the woman approach. He no longer had his own office. His desk was just one part of the jumble of town services in the old hall. People were constantly arriving and departing, and there was a steady hum of noise.

"Lucas."

He turned from the window. Constance Souleby was standing before him. She held a gun in her hand: an old Colt. It did not shake, for the woman holding it was a picture of calm.

"You could have spared him," she said.

He was aware of movement behind her, of someone approaching fast. He heard cries of shock. The gun had been noticed.

"I am—" Morland said.

The gun spoke in denial, and he ceased to be.

4

RETURNING

The forenoon is burn-faced and wandering
And I am the death of the moon.

Below my countenance the bell
of the night has broken
And I am the new divine wolf.

Adonis (Ali Ahmad Said Esber), "The Divine Wolf"

LVIII

Ronald Straydeer was standing in his yard when the car arrived. Winter was departing, and he was piling the snow behind the woodshed, where it could melt away and be damned without him having to see it.

He rested his hands on his shovel as the car drew to a halt, and felt a small ache of fear when the two men emerged from it. He hadn't seen or spoken to them since that night in Prosperous, but they weren't men who liked to leave loose ends. They had no cause for concern on his part, nor on the part of those whom he had brought with him to put Prosperous to the torch. Some had already left the state. Those who remained would keep silent.

The two men leaned on their car doors and regarded him.

"Beautiful day," said Angel.

"Yes, it is."

"Looks like winter may be ending."

"Yes."

Angel looked at Louis. Louis shrugged.

"We came to thank you," said Angel. "We're going to see Parker, then we're heading home. It's time for us to get back to civilization."

"I've called the hospital," said Ronald. "They tell me there's no change."

"There's always hope," said Angel.

"Yes," said Ronald. "I believe that's true."

"Anyway," said Angel, "we have a gift for you, I guess, if you want it."

He opened the rear door of the car and reached inside. When he emerged again, he held a female German shepherd puppy in his arms. He walked up to Ronald, placed the dog at his feet, and held out the leash. Ronald didn't take it. He looked at the dog. The dog sat for a moment, scratched itself, then stood and placed its front paws against Ronald's right leg.

"Parker talked about you," said Angel. "He used to tell us it was time you got another dog. He thought you might be starting to feel the same way too."

Ronald put the shovel aside. He leaned down and scratched the puppy's head. It wriggled with joy and continued trying to climb his leg.

Ronald took the leash from Angel and unclipped it from the dog's collar.

"You want to come with me?" he said to the dog.

He began walking toward his home. Without looking back at Angel, the dog followed, leaping to keep up with the long strides of its master.

"Thank you," said Ronald Straydeer.

Louis got back into the car. Angel joined him.

"Told you he'd keep the dog," said Louis.

"Yeah. I think you're getting soft in your old age."

"That may be."

He reversed out of Ronald's drive.

"How come we never got a dog?" said Angel.

"I don't need a dog," said Louis. "I got you."

"Right," said Angel.

He thought about it for a moment.

"Hey . . ."

LIX

I sat on the bench by the lake, my daughter by my side. We did not speak.

On an outcrop of land to the east stood a wolf. He watched us as we watched him.

A shadow fell across the bench, and I saw my dead wife reflected in the water. She touched my shoulder, and I felt the warmth of her.

"It's time," she said. "You must decide."

I heard the sound of a car approaching. I glanced over my shoulder. Parked on the road was a white 1960 Ford Falcon. I had seen pictures of it. It was the first car that my father and mother ever owned outright. A man sat in the driver's seat, a woman beside him. I could not see their faces, but I knew who they were. I wanted to talk to them. I wanted to tell them that I was sorry. I wanted to say what every child wishes to say to his parents when they're gone and it's too late to say anything at all: that I loved them, and had always loved them.

"Can I talk to them?" I asked.

"Only if you go with them," said my dead wife. "Only if you choose to take the Long Ride."

I saw the heads of the people in the car turn toward me. I still could not see their faces.

No more pain, I thought. No more pain.

From the hills beyond the lake arose a great howling. I saw the wolf raise his muzzle to the clear blue sky in response to the summoning, and the clamor from the hills grew louder and more joyous, but still the wolf did not move. His eyes were fixed on me.

No more pain. Let it end.

My daughter reached out and took my hand. She pressed something cold into it. I opened my fingers and saw a dark stone on my palm, smooth on one side, damaged on the other.

My daughter.

But I had another.

"If you take the Long Ride, I'll go with you," she said. "But if you stay, then I'll stay with you too."

I stared at the car, trying to see the faces behind the glass. I slowly shook my head. The heads turned from me, and the car pulled away. I watched it until it was gone. When I looked back at the lake, the wolf was still there. He gazed at me for a moment longer, then slipped into the trees, yipping and howling as he went, and the pack called out its welcome.

The stone felt heavy in my hand. It wanted to be thrown. When it was, this world would shatter, and another would take its place. Already I could feel a series of burnings as my wounds began to sing. My dead wife's hand remained on my shoulder, but its touch was growing colder. She whispered something in my ear—a name, a warning—but I was already struggling to remember it once the final word was spoken. Her reflection in the water began to dim as mine started to come into focus beside it. I tried to hold on tighter to my daughter's hand.

"Just a little while longer," I said. "Just—"

ACKNOWLEDGMENTS

First of all, the Family of Love did exist, and much of their history as recounted in this book is true. Whether they ever made it to the New World, I cannot say, but I am grateful to Joseph W. Martin's *Religious Radicals in Tudor England* (Hambledon Continuum, 1989) for increasing my small store of knowledge of them. The history of the foliate heads on churches is also true, and the following books proved highly illuminating, and slightly disturbing: *The Green Man in Britain,* by Fran and Geoff Doel (The History Press, 2010); *The Green Man,* by Kathleen Basford (D. S. Brewer, 1998); and *A Little Book of the Green Man,* by Mike Harding (Aurum Press, 1998).

The Oxford Street Shelter, the Portland Help Center, Skip Murphy's Sober House, and Amistad are all real agencies that provide critically important services to the homeless and the mentally ill in the Portland area. Thanks very much to Karen Murphy and Peter Driscoll of Amistad, Sonia Garcia of Spurwick, and Joe Riley of Skip Murphy's for permission to mention these organizations by name. If you would like to donate to any of these organizations, or get more information about their services, you may do so here:

Amistad Inc.
www.amistadinc.com
PO Box 992
Portland, ME 04101
207-773-1956

Oxford Street Shelter
203 Oxford Street
Portland, ME 04101
207-761-2072

The Portland Help Center (Spurwink Services)
www.spurwink.org
899 Riverside Street
Portland, ME 04013
888-889-3903

Skip Murphy's Sober Living
www.skipmurphys.com/soberhouse
P.O. Box 8117
Portland, ME 04104
774-269-4700

My thanks, as always, go to Sue Fletcher, Swati Gamble, Kerry Hood, Lucy Hale, Auriol Bishop, and all at Hodder & Stoughton; Breda Purdue, Jim Binchy, Ruth Shern, Siobhan Tierney, Frank Cronin, and all at Hachette Ireland; Emily Bestler, Judith Curr, Megan Reid, David Brown, Louise Burke, and the staff at Atria/Emily Bestler Books and Pocket Books; and my agent Darley Anderson and his wonderful team. Clair Lamb and Madeira James do sterling work, looking after Web sites and much, much more. Jennie Ridyard has now become my fellow author as well as my other half in life, but continues to show remarkable forbearance with me, as do our sons, Cameron and Alistair. To you, the reader, thank you for continuing to read these odd little books. Without you, there really wouldn't be much point to all this.

And hello to Jason Isaacs.

Read on for the next chilling installment
in the Charlie Parker series by
best-selling author John Connolly

A SONG OF

SHADOWS

Available online and wherever
books are sold in Fall 2015

The Hurricane Hatch stood at the end of a strip of land midway between Jacksonville and St. Augustine on the Florida coast, far enough away from the real tourist traps to ensure that it retained a degree of local custom while still attracting enough business of any stripe to sustain it. A man named Skettle owned ninety percent of the Hurricane Hatch, but he rarely frequented it, preferring to leave the running of the place to its chief bartender and ten percent shareholder, Lenny Tedesco. Skettle liked to keep quiet about the fact that he had a big piece of the Hurricane Hatch. His family, from what Lenny knew of them, contained a high percentage of Holy Rollers, the kind who visited the Holy Land Experience down in Orlando a couple of times a year, and regarded the Goliath Burger at the theme park's Oasis Palms Café as damn fine dining, although Lenny doubted if they would have used that precise term to describe it. Lenny Tedesco had never been to the Holy Land Experience, and had zero intention of ever visiting it. He reckoned that a Christian theme park wasn't really the place for a Jew, not even a nonobservant Jew like himself, and he didn't care if it did boast a recreation of a Jerusalem street market.

Then again, the Hurricane Hatch was about as authentic in Florida bar terms as the Holy Land Experience was as an accurate reflection of the spiritual makeup of Jerusalem in the first century AD. It looked like what a classic Florida beach bum's bar was supposed to look like—wood, stuffed fish, a picture of Hemingway—but had only been built at the start of the nineties, in anticipation of a housing development named Ocean Breeze Condos which never got further than a series of architect's plans, a hole in the ground, and a tax write-off. The Hurricane Hatch remained, though, and had somehow managed to prosper, in large part because of Lenny and his wife, Pegi, who was a good fry cook of the old school. She prepared fried oysters that could make a man weep, the secret ingredients being creole seasoning, fine yellow cornmeal, and Diamond Crystal—*kosher*—salt. Neither did Skettle evince too much concern about making a large profit, just as long as the Hatch didn't lose money. Lenny figured that Skettle, who didn't drink alcohol and appeared to subsist primarily on chicken tenders and chocolate milk, just enjoyed secretly giving the finger to his holier-than-thou, pew-polishing relatives by owning a bar. Lenny's wife, however, claimed that Skettle's sister Lesley, a Praise-Jesus type of the worst stripe, was not above polishing other things too, and could give a pretty accurate description of half the motel ceilings between Jacksonville and Miami, giving rise to her nickname of Screw Anything Skettle.

Lenny was alone in the bar. Entirely alone. This was one of Pegi's nights off, and Lenny had sent the replacement cook, Fran, home early, because he knew she'd have better luck selling fried oysters in an abandoned cemetery than in the Hurricane Hatch on this particular evening. Midweeks were always quiet, but lately they had been quieter than usual, and even weekend business was down from previous years. There just wasn't as much money around as before, but the Hatch was surviving.

Lenny glanced at his watch. It was nine thirty. He'd give it until ten, maybe ten thirty, then call it a night. Anyway, he was in no hurry to go home—not that he didn't love his wife, because he did, but sometimes he thought that he loved the Hatch more. He was at peace there, regardless of whether it was empty or full. In fact, on evenings like this, with the wind blowing gently outside, and the boards creaking and rattling, and the sound of the waves in the distance, visible as the faintest of phosphorescent glows, and the TV on, and a soda water and lime on the bar before him, he felt that he would be quite content just to stay this way forever. The only blot on his happiness—if "blot" was a sufficient word for it, which he doubted—was the subject of the TV news report currently playing in front of him. He watched the footage of the two old men being transported by United States Marshals into a holding facility somewhere in New York City: Engel and Fuhrmann, with almost two centuries of life clocked up between them, Engel barely able to walk unaided, Fuhrmann stronger, his gaze fixed somewhere in the distance, not even deigning to notice the men and women who surrounded him, the cameras and the lights, the protestors with their signs, as if all of this was a show being put on for another man, and the accusations leveled against him were somehow beneath his regard. The men disappeared from the screen, to be replaced by an attorney from the Human Rights and Special Prosecutions Section, the arm of the Justice Department entrusted with investigating assorted human rights violations and, particularly, Nazi war criminals. The attorney was a pretty young woman, and Lenny was surprised by the passion with which she spoke. She didn't have a Jewish name, or Demers didn't sound like one. Not that this was a requirement for justice under the circumstances. Perhaps she was just an idealist, and God knew the world needed as many of those as it could find.

Engel and Fuhrmann, she said, had been fighting the U.S. government's decision to rescind their citizenship, but that process had now been exhausted. The delivery of the arrest warrant for Fuhrmann from the Bavarian state public prosecutor's office in Munich a week earlier meant that his extradition could now proceed immediately, and Engel's deportation would follow shortly after for breaches of immigration law, regardless of whether or not charges were filed against him in his native land. Soon, she said, Engel and Fuhrmann would be banished from American soil forever.

Deportation didn't sound like much of a punishment to Lenny, whose family had lost an entire branch at Dachau. He hadn't understood why they couldn't be put on trial here in the United States until Bruno Perlman had explained to him that the U.S. Constitution precluded prosecution of criminal acts committed abroad before and during World War II, and the best that the United States could do was send war criminals back to countries that did have jurisdiction, in the hope that proceedings might be taken against them there. Not that Perlman was happy about the situation either. He would tell Lenny admiringly about the activities of the TTG, the Tilhas Tizig Gesheften, a secret group within the Jewish Brigade Group of the British Army who, after the German surrender, took it upon themselves to hunt down and assassinate *Wehrmacht* and SS officers believed to have committed atrocities against Jews; and of the Mossad killers who trapped the Latvian Nazi collaborator Herberts Cukurs, "the Butcher of Riga," in a house in Montevideo in 1965, beating him with a hammer before shooting him twice in the head and leaving his body to rot in a trunk until the Uruguayan police found him, drawn by the smell. The gleam in Perlman's eye as he spoke of such matters disturbed Lenny, but he supposed that the end met by such foul men was no more than they deserved. Lately, though, that light in Perlman's eyes had grown brighter, and his talk of vengeance had taken a personal turn. Lenny worried for him. Perlman had few friends. Obsessives rarely did.

"How do they even know it's really them?" said a voice. "Old men like that, they could be anyone."

A man was seated at the far end of the bar, close to the door. Lenny had not heard him enter. Neither had he heard a car pull into the lot. The visitor's face was turned slightly away from the television, as though he could not bear to watch it. He wore a straw fedora with a red band. The hat was too large for his head, so that it sat just above his eyes. His suit jacket was brown, worn over a yellow polo shirt. The shirt was missing two buttons, exposing a network of thin white scars across the man's chest, like a web spun by a spider upon his skin.

"Sorry, I didn't hear you come in," said Lenny, ignoring the question. "What can I get you?"

The man didn't respond. He seemed to be having trouble breathing. Lenny looked past him to the parking lot outside. He could see no vehicle.

"You got milk?" the man rasped.

"Sure."

"Brandy and milk." He rubbed his stomach. "I got a problem with my guts."

Lenny prepared the mix. The milk was cold enough to create beads of condensation on the glass, so he wrapped it in a napkin before placing it on the bar. The man exuded a sour, curdled odor, the rankness of untold brandy-and-milk combinations. He raised the glass and drank it half-empty.

"Hurts," he said. "Hurts like a motherfucker."

He lowered the glass, raised his left hand, and removed the hat from his head. Lenny tried not to stare before deciding that it was easier just to look away entirely, but the image of the man's visage remained branded on Lenny's vision like a sudden flare of bright, distorted light in the dimness of the bar.

His bare skull was misshapen, as pitted with concave indentations as the surface of the moon. His brow was massively overdeveloped, so that his eyes—tiny dark things, like drops of oil in snow—were lost in its shadow, and his profile was suggestive of one who had slammed his forehead into a horizontal girder as a child, with the soft skull retaining the impression of the blow as it hardened. His nose was very thin, his mouth the barest slash of color against the pallor of his skin. He breathed in and out through his lips with a faint, wet whistle.

"What's your name?" he asked.

"Lenny."

"Lenny what?"

"Lenny Tedesco."

"This your place?"

"I got a share in it. Skettle owns the rest."

"I don't know any Skettle. You're a bitch to find. You ought to put up a sign."

"There is a sign."

"I didn't see none."

"Which way did you come?"

The man waved a hand vaguely over his shoulder— north, south, east, west, what did any of it matter? The only issue of consequence was that he was here at last.

"Tedesco," he said. "That's a Sephardic name. Some might mistake it for Italian, but it's not. It means 'German,' but you most likely had Ashkenazi forbears. Am I right?"

Lenny wished that the bar had remained empty. He didn't want to engage in this discussion. He wanted this vile man with his pungent stink to be gone.

"I don't know," he said.

"Sure you do. I read once that the word 'Nazi' comes from 'Ashkenazi.' What do you think of that?"

Lenny worked on polishing a glass that didn't need a

cloth taken to it. He rubbed so hard that the glass cracked under the pressure. He tossed it in the trash and moved on to another.

"I've never heard that before," he replied, and hated himself for responding. "My understanding is that it refers to National Socialism."

"Ah, you're probably right. Anything else is just the frothings of ignorant men. Holocaust deniers. Fools. I don't give no credit to it. As though so much slaughter could be ascribed to Jew-on-Jew violence."

Lenny felt the muscles in his neck cramp. He clenched his teeth so hard that he felt something come loose at the back of his mouth. It was the way the man spoke the word "Jew."

On the television screen, the news report had moved on to a panel discussion about Engel and Fuhrmann, and the background to their cases. The volume was just low enough for the content to remain intelligible. Lenny moved to change the channel, but that same voice told him to leave it be. Lenny glanced at the glass of brandy and milk. A curl of red lay upon the surface of the remaining liquid. The man saw it at the same time as Lenny did. He dipped a finger and swirled the blood away, then drained the glass dry.

"Like I said, I got a problem with my guts. Got problems all over. I shit nails and piss broken glass."

"Sorry to hear that."

"Hasn't killed me yet. I just don't care to think about what my insides might look like."

Couldn't be any worse than what's outside, Lenny thought, and those dark eyes flicked toward him, as though that unspoken wisecrack had found form above Lenny's head.

"You got another of these?"

"I'm closing up."

"Won't take you much longer to make than it'll take me to drink."

"Nah, we're done."

The glass slid across the bar.

"Just the milk then. You wouldn't deny a man a glass of milk, would you?"

Oh, but Lenny wanted to. He wanted to so badly, yet still he poured three fingers of milk into the glass. He was grateful that there was no more left in the carton.

"Thank you."

Lenny said nothing, just tossed the empty container in the trash.

"I don't want you to get me wrong," said the man. "I got no problem with Jews. When I was a boy, I had a friend who was a Jew. Jesus, it's been a long time since I thought about him. I can hardly remember his name now."

He put the thumb and forefinger of his right hand to the bridge of his nose and squeezed hard, his eyes closed as he tried to pull the name from the pit of his memory.

"Asher," he said at last. "Asher Cherney. That was his name. Damn, that was hard. I called him Ash. I don't know what anyone else called him, because no one else palled around with him much. Anyway, I'd hang out with Ash when none of the other boys were there to see. You had to be careful. The people I grew up with, they didn't care much for Jews. Niggers neither. Fuck, we didn't even like Catholics. We stuck with our own, and it wasn't good to be seen making friends outside your own circle. And Ash, you see, he had a deformity, which made it worse for him. You listen to Kiss?"

Lenny, who had somehow been drawn into the tale despite himself, was puzzled. Following the man's thought processes was like trying to keep track of a ricochet in a steel room.

"What, the band?"

"Yeah, the band. They're shit, but you got to have heard of them."

"I know them," said Lenny.

"Right. Well, their singer has the same thing that Ash had. They call it microtia. It's a deformity of the ear. The cartilage doesn't grow right, so you have a kind of stump. Makes you deaf too. They say it usually occurs in the right ear, but Ash, he had it in his left, so he was strange even among other people like him. Now they can do all kinds of grafts or implants, but back then you just had to live with it. Ash would grow his hair long to try to hide it, but everybody knew. If his life didn't suck already, being a Jew in a town that didn't care much for anyone who wasn't in some white-bread church, he had to deal with the ignorance and bile of kids who spent their lives just looking for some physical defect to hone in on.

"So I felt sorry for Ash, though I couldn't show it, not in public. But if I was alone, and I saw Ash, and *he* was alone, then I'd talk to him, or walk with him, maybe skim stones by the river if the mood took us. He was okay, Ash. You never would have known he was a Jew, unless he told you his name. That microtia, you think it's a Jew thing?"

Lenny said that he didn't know. He felt as though he were watching some terrible accident unfold, a catastrophic collision of bodies that could only result in injury and death, yet was unable to tear his eyes away from it. He was hypnotized by this man's awfulness, the depth of his corruption only slowly revealing itself by word and intonation.

"Because," the man went on, "there are diseases that Jews are more likely to carry than other races. You, being Ashkenazi from way back, are more likely to get cystic fibrosis. I mean, there are others, but that's the one that sticks in my mind. Cystic fibrosis is a bitch. You don't want to get that. Anyhow, I don't know if this microtia thing is like it. Could be. Doesn't matter, I suppose. Unless you have it, and don't want to pass it on to your kids. You got kids?"

"No."

"Well, if you're thinking about having them, you ought to get checked out. You don't want to be transmitting shit to your kids. Where was I? Oh yeah: Ash. Ash and his fucked-up ear. So, me and Ash would do stuff together, and we'd talk, and I got to like him. Then, one day, this kid, a degenerate named Eddie Tyson, he saw us together, and next thing you know they were saying I was queer for Ash, that me and Ash were doing things under bridges and in his mom's car, and Eddie Tyson and a bunch of his buddies caught me alone on my way home and beat the living shit out of me, all on account of how Ash Cherney was my friend.

"So you know what I did?"

Lenny could barely speak, but he found the strength to say the word "no."

"I went around to Ash's house, and I asked if he wanted to go down to the river with me. I told him what had happened, because I looked like hell after what they'd done to me. So me and Ash went down to the river, and I got a stone, and I hit Ash with it. I hit him so hard in the face that I was sure I'd knocked his nose into his brain. I thought I'd killed him, but somehow he stayed conscious. Then I threw the stone away and used my fists and feet on him, and I left him by the river in a pool of his own blood, spitting teeth, and I never heard from him again, because he never came back to school, and his parents moved away not long after."

He sipped his milk.

"I guess me and Ash weren't such good friends after all, huh?"

The television was showing black-and-white footage of emaciated men and women standing behind wire fences, and holes filled with bones.

"You ever wonder what would make men do such things?"

He wasn't looking at the screen, so Lenny didn't know if he was still speaking of what he had done to Ash Cherney, or about the evidence of atrocities committed decades before. Lenny was cold. His fingertips and toes hurt. He figured that it didn't matter what the man was referring to. It was all part of one great mass of viciousness, a cesspit of black, human evil.

"No," said Lenny.

"Course you do. We all do. Wouldn't be human if we didn't. There are those who say that all crimes can be ascribed to one of two motives—love or money—but I don't believe that. In my experience, everything we do is predicated on one of two other things: greed or fear. Oh, sometimes they get mixed up, just like my brandy and milk, but mostly you can keep them separated. We feel greed for what we don't have, and fear because of what we might lose. A man desires a woman who isn't his wife, and takes her—that's greed. But, deep down, he doesn't want his own wife to find out because he wants to keep what he has with her, because it's different, and safe. That's fear. You play the markets?"

"No."

"You're wise. It's a racket. Buying and selling, they're just other names for greed and fear. I tell you, you understand that, and you understand all there is to know about human beings and the way the world works."

He sipped his milk.

"Except, of course, that isn't all. Look at those pictures from the camps. You can see fear, and not just in the faces of the dying and the dead. Take a look at the men in uniform, the ones they say were responsible for what happened, and you'll see fear there too. Not so much fear of what might happen if they didn't follow orders. I don't hold with that as an excuse, and from what I've read the Germans understood that killing naked Jews and queers and Gypsies wasn't for every man, and if you couldn't do it then they'd find someone who would, and send you off to shoot at someone who could shoot back.

"But there's still fear in those faces, no matter how well they try to hide it: fear of what will happen to them when the Russians or the Americans arrive and find out what they've done; fear of looking inside themselves to see what they've become; maybe even fear for their immortal souls. There will also be those who feel no fear of that at all, of course, because sometimes men and women do terrible things just because they gain pleasure from the act, but those ones are the exceptions, and exceptions make bad law. The rest, they just did what they did because they were told to do it and they couldn't see much reason not to, or because there was money in gold teeth and rendered human fat. I guess some of them did it out of ideology, but I don't have much time for ideologies either. They're just flags of convenience."

The man's voice was very soft, and slightly sibilant, and held a note of regret that most of the world could not see itself as clearly as he did, that this was his cross to bear.

"You hear that woman on the TV?" he continued. "She's talking about evil, but throwing around the word 'evil' like it means something don't help anyone. Evil is the avoidance of responsibility. It doesn't explain. You might even say that it excuses. To see the real terror, the real darkness, you have to look at the actions of men, however awful they may appear, and call them human. When you can do that, then you'll understand."

He coughed hard, spattering the milk with droplets of blood.

"You didn't answer my question from earlier," he said.

"What question was that?" said Lenny.

"I just can't figure out how they know that those two old men are the ones they were looking for. I seen the pictures of the ones they say did all those things, the photographs from way back, and then I see those two old farts and I couldn't swear that it's the same men sixty, seventy years later. Jesus, you could show me a picture of my own father as a young man, and I wouldn't know him from the scarecrow he was when he died."

"I think there was a paper trail of some kind," said Lenny. To be honest, he didn't know how Engel and Fuhrmann had been traced. He didn't much care either. They had been found at last, and that was all that mattered. He just wanted this conversation to reach its end, but that was in the hands of the man at the bar. There was a purpose to his presence here, and all Lenny could do was wait for it to be revealed to him, and hope that he survived the adumbration.

"I can't even say that I've heard of the camps that they're supposed to have done all that killing in," said the man. "I mean, I heard of Auschwitz, and Dachau, and Bergen-Belsen. I suppose I could name some others, if I put my mind to it, but what's the place that Fuhrmann was at, or the one they claim is Fuhrmann. Ball Sack? Is that even a place?"

"Belzec," said Lenny softly. "It's called Belzec."

"And the other?"

"Lubsko."

"Well, you have been paying attention, I'll give you that. You had people there?"

"No, not there."

"So, it's not personal, then."

Lenny had had enough. He killed the TV.

"I don't want you to mistake me," said the man, not even commenting upon the sudden absence of light and sound from the screen. "I got no problem with any race or creed: Jews, niggers, spics, white folks, they're all the same to me. I do believe, though, that each race and creed ought to keep to itself. I don't think any one is better than the other, but only trouble comes when they mix. The South Africans, they had it right with apartheid, except they didn't have the common sense, the basic human fucking decency, to give every man the same privileges, the same rights. They thought white was superior to black, and that's not the case. God made all of us, and he didn't put one above another, no matter what some might say. Even your own folk, you're no more chosen than anyone else."

Lenny made one final effort to save himself, to force this thing away. It was futile, but he had to try.

"I'd like you to leave now," he said. "I'm all done for the night. Have the drinks on me."

But the man did not move. All this was only the prelude. The worst was yet to come. Lenny felt it. This creature had brought with him a miasma of darkness, of horror. Maybe a small chance still remained, a chink in the wall that was closing in around him through which he might escape. He could not show weakness, though. The drama would play out, and each would accept the role that had been given to him.

"I haven't finished my milk yet."

"You can take it with you."

"Nah, I think I'll drink it here. Wouldn't want it to spill."

"I'm going to be closing up around you," said Lenny. "You'll have to excuse me."

He moved to take the drawer from the register. Usually he counted the takings before he left, but on this occasion he'd leave that until the morning. He didn't want to give this man any cause to linger.

"I'm no charity case," said the visitor. "I'll pay my own way, just as I always have."

He reached into his jacket pocket.

"Well, what do you think this is?"

Lenny couldn't help but look to see what had drawn the other's attention. He glimpsed something small and white, apparently drawn from the man's own pocket. "Jesus, it's a tooth." He pronounced it "toot." He held the item in question up to the light, like a jeweler appraising a gemstone. "Now where do you suppose that came from? It sure ain't one of mine."

As if to put the issue beyond doubt, he manipulated his upper row of teeth with his tongue, and his dentures popped out into his left palm. The action caused his mouth to collapse in upon itself, rendering his appearance stranger still. He smiled, nodded at Lenny, and replaced his appliance. He then laid the single tooth on the surface of the bar. A length of reddish flesh adhered to the root.

"That's certainly something, isn't it?" he said.

Lenny backed off. He wondered if he could get away for long enough to call the cops. There was no gun on the premises, but the back office had a strong door and a good lock. He could seal himself inside and wait for the police to come. Even if he could make it to a phone, what would he tell the operator—that a man had produced a tooth for his inspection? Last he heard, that wasn't a crime.

Except, except . . .

Like a conjuror, the customer reached into his pocket again and produced a second tooth, then a third. Finally, he seemed to tire of the whole business, rummaged for a final time, and scattered a full mouth's worth of teeth on the bar. Some were without roots. At least one appeared to have broken during extraction. A lot of them were still stained with blood, or trailed tails of tissue.

"Who are you?" asked Lenny. "What do you want from me?"

The gun appeared in the man's hand. Lenny didn't know from guns, but this one looked big and kind of old.

"You stay where you are now," said the man. "You hear me?"

Lenny nodded. He found his voice.

"We got next to nothing in the register," he said. "It's been quiet all day."

"I look like a thief to you?"

He sounded genuinely offended.

"I don't know what you look like," said Lenny, and he regretted the words as soon as they left his mouth.

"You got no manners," said the man. "You know that, you fucking kike?"

"I'm sorry," said Lenny. He had no pride now, only fear.

"I accept your apology. You know what this is?"

He gave the weapon a little jerk.

"No. I don't know much about guns."

"There's your first error. It's not a gun, it's a *pistol*: a Mauser C96 military pistol, made in long nine millimeter, which is rare. Some people call it a Broomhandle Mauser on account of the shape of the grip, or a Red 9 after the number carved into the grip. Consider that an education. Now move away from the door. You pay attention to me and what I say, and maybe this won't go as bad for you as it might."

Lenny knew that wasn't true—men who planned to let other men live didn't point guns at them without first concealing their faces—yet he found himself obeying. The man reached into his pocket again. This time his hand emerged holding a pair of cuffs. He tossed them to Lenny and instructed him to attach one to his right wrist, then to put his hands close together behind his back and place them on the bar. If he tried to run away, or pull a fast one, he was assured that he would be shot in the back. Once more, Lenny did as he was told. When he turned his back and put his hands on the bar, the second cuff was quickly cinched tight around his left wrist.

"All done," said the man. "Now come around here and sit on the floor."

Lenny moved from behind the bar. He thought about running for the door, but knew that he wouldn't get more than a few feet without being shot. He gazed out into the night, willing a car to appear, but none came. He walked to the spot indicated by the man, and sat down. The TV came on again, blazing into life at the gunman's touch on the remote. It continued to show images of the camps, of men and women climbing from trains, some of them still wearing ordinary clothing, others already dressed in the garb of prisoners. There were so many of them, and they outnumbered their captors. As a boy, Lenny would wonder why they didn't try to overcome the Germans, why they didn't fight to save themselves. Now he thought that he knew.

The man leaned against the bar, the pistol leveled at Lenny.

"You asked me who I am," he said. "You can call me Steiger. It doesn't matter much. It's just a name. Might as well have plucked it from the air. I can give you another, if you don't like that one."

And again Lenny felt a glimmer of hope warm the

coldness of his insides. Perhaps, just perhaps, this night might not end in his death. Could it be that, if he was withholding his true name, this freakish individual planned to return to the hole from which he had emerged and leave Lenny alive? Or was all this a ruse, just one more way to torment a doomed man before the inevitable bullet brought all to an end?

"You know where these teeth came from?"

"No."

"Your wife. They came from her mouth."

Steiger grabbed a handful of the teeth from the bar and threw them on the floor before Lenny. One landed in his lap.

For a moment Lenny was unable to move. His vomit reflex activated, and he tasted sourness in his throat. Then he was moving, trying to rise to his feet, but a bullet struck the floor inches from the soles of his shoes, and the noise as much as the sight of the splintered mark upon the floor stilled him.

"Don't do that again," said Steiger. "If you try, the next one will take out a kneecap, or maybe your balls."

Lenny froze. He stared at the tooth stuck to his jeans. He didn't want to believe that it had once been his wife's.

"I'll tell you something," said Stegner. "Working on your wife's teeth gave me a renewed admiration for the skill of dentists. I used to believe that they were just failed doctors, because, I mean, how difficult can it be to work on teeth, all the nerves and stuff apart. I hated going to the dentist as a kid. Still do.

"Anyway, I always thought extractions would be the easy part. You get a grip, and you yank. But it's harder to get a good grip on a tooth than you might think, and then you have to twist, and sometimes—if there's a weakness—the tooth just breaks. You'll see that some of your wife's teeth didn't emerge intact. I like to think that it was a learning experience for both of us.

"If you doubt me, and are trying to convince yourself that they're not your wife's teeth," said Steiger, "I can tell you that she was wearing jeans and a yellow blouse, with green—no, blue—flowers. It was hard to tell in the dark. She also has a mark here, on her left forearm, like a big freckle. That would bother me, I have to say. She's a nice-looking woman, but I'd always have been aware of that mark, like a reminder of all that's wrong inside, because we all have things wrong with us inside. That sound like your wife? Pegi, right? Spelled with an *i*. Short for Margaret. That's what she said, while she could still speak.

"No, no, don't go getting all upset now. You'll move, or you'll try to lash out, and this will all get a whole lot worse for you both. Yeah, that's right: she's still alive, I swear to you. And—listen to me, now, just listen—there are worse things than losing your teeth. They can do all kinds of miracles with implants now. She could have teeth that are better than her old ones. And if that's too expensive, or just doesn't work out because of the damage—because, to remind you, I'm no professional— then there's always dentures. My mother wore dentures, just like I do, and I thought that they made her look younger, because they were always clean and even. You ever see old people with their own teeth? They look like shit. Nothing you can do about old age. It's pitiless. It ravages us all."

He squatted before Lenny, still careful to remain just beyond his reach should Lenny's anger overcome his fear, but he needn't have worried. Lenny was weeping.

"Here's how it will go," said Steiger. "If you're straight with me, and answer my questions, I'll let her live. She's all dosed up on painkillers, so she's not feeling much of any-thing right now. Before I leave, I'll call an ambulance for her, and she'll be looked after. I promise you that.

"As for you, well, I can't promise anything other than, if you're honest, you won't be aware of your own dying, and you'll have saved your wife in the process. Are we clear?"

Lenny was now sobbing loudly. Steiger reached out and slapped him hard across the side of the head.

"I said, are we clear?"

"Yes," said Lenny. "We're clear."

"Good. I have only two questions for you. What did the Jew named Perlman tell you, and who else knows?"

When the questions were answered at last, and Lenny Tedesco was dead, Steiger removed from the dishwasher the glasses that he had used and placed them in a bag. He also emptied the register for appearances' sake. He had been careful to touch as few surfaces as possible, but he went over them once again with some bleach that he found behind the bar. Some traces of his presence would still remain, but they would be useless without a suspect, or a record against which to check them, and Steiger was a ghost. He traced the hard drive for the bar's security camera, and removed it. He turned off the lights in the Hurricane Hatch before he left, and closed the door behind him. Lenny's car was parked behind the bar, and would not be noticed unless someone came looking for it.

Steiger walked for five minutes to where his car was parked, out of sight of both the bar and the road, then drove to the Tedescos' small, neat home. He opened the door with Pegi Tedesco's key, and went upstairs to the main bedroom, where he had left her tied to the bed. Beside her were the tools with which he had removed all of her teeth, along with some others for which he had not yet found a use. The painkillers were wearing off, and Pegi was moaning softy against the gag.

Steiger sat down beside her on the bed, and brushed the hair from her face.

"Now," he said, "where were we?"

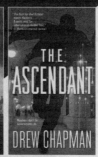

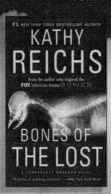
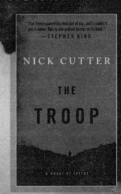
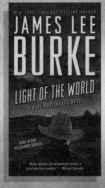